Cross-Cultural Management

T0384103

This book is where East meets West by understanding intercultural communication in the context of [the] globalized world!

Tran Nguyen Khang—Vietnam National University, Vietnam

[A] very refreshing, original and innovative way of presenting the subject. This book brings a breath of fresh air to the work of interculturalists. Absolutely essential and desirable reading for those who want to thrive in the current international business world.

Agata Szkiela—European Academy of Diplomacy and Translating Cultures, Poland

Cross-Cultural Management: With Insights from Brain Science explores a broad range of topics on the impact of culture in international business and vice versa, and the impact of businesses and individuals in shaping a culture. It provides critical and in-depth information on globalization, global/glocal leadership, cross-cultural marketing, and cross-cultural negotiation. It also discusses many other topics that are not typically found in the mainstream management textbooks, such as those on diversity management, bias management, cross-cultural motivation strategies, and change management.

While most literature in the field is dominated by the static paradigm, that is, culture is fixed, nation equates to culture, and values are binary, this book takes a different approach. It regards indexes of national values as a first-best-guess and balances them with an introduction of the dynamic paradigm. This school of thought posits that culture is not static, context is the software of the mind, opposing values coexist, change is constant, and individuals can develop a multicultural mind.

A unique feature of this book is the contribution of an interdisciplinary approach. It's the first textbook of cross-cultural management that incorporates latest findings from the emerging discipline of cultural neuroscience and evolutionary biology, thanks to the author's study in neuroscience. Such a holistic approach helps readers gain a deeper and broader understanding of the subjects.

Mai Nguyen-Phuong-Mai is Associate Professor at the Amsterdam School of International Business, the Netherlands. She also owns a training agency and freelances for diverse media channels. As a world citizen, she comes from the East, works in the West, and lives everywhere in between. She can be reached at CultureMove@CultureMove.com.

Routledge International Business Studies
Series Editor: Raj Aggarwal, University of Akron College of Business Administration

In an increasingly global business environment, even "domestic" business is hardly domestic anymore. Globalization has made proficiency in international business topics relevant for every business student. As more and more programs are launched in this area, there is a dearth of materials to accompany such classes.

Routledge International Business Studies is a series that offers a range of relatively short yet comprehensive books covering the core topics taught in international business programs. Each book serves as core reading in a dedicated class, while also useful as a secondary reading source in broader, related classes. With consistent production quality, pedagogical features and writing style, the series is a trustworthy source of educational resources in this important discipline.

Cross-Cultural Management: With Insights from Brain Science
Mai Nguyen-Phuong-Mai

For more information about this series, please visit: www.routledge.com/business/series/RIBS

Cross-Cultural Management
With Insights from Brain Science

Mai Nguyen-Phuong-Mai

Routledge
Taylor & Francis Group

NEW YORK AND LONDON

First published 2020
by Routledge
52 Vanderbilt Avenue, New York, NY 10017

and by Routledge
2 Park Square, Milton Park, Abingdon, Oxon, OX14 4RN

Routledge is an imprint of the Taylor & Francis Group, an informa business

© 2020 Taylor & Francis

Library of Congress Cataloging-in-Publication Data
A catalog record for this book has been requested

ISBN: 978-1-138-30465-9 (hbk)
ISBN: 978-1-138-30466-6 (pbk)
ISBN: 978-0-203-72991-5 (ebk)

Typeset in Galliard
by Newgen Publishing UK

Visit the eResources: www.routledge.com/9781138304666

To Mal
Because of you, this all began

Contents

Figures

Tables

Preface

Mai Nguyen-Phuong-Mai has set sail across recently discovered seas of neurological research, riding currents of cognitive science, to update and transport the best of contemporary intercultural know-how through its often-turbulent straits of contention to global ports of call. Fortunately, she has invited us to make this timely journey with her.

Despite the urgency we have long felt to address cultural conflict, diversity, inclusion, and bias, efforts to minister to these issues have made less progress than desired or expected. The recent surge in populism politics and the social unrest it is bringing to our communities and organizations came as a shock to many of us. It flew in the face of our conviction, perhaps complacency, that we were making significant progress in our intercultural and diversity interventions and policies. Yes, there has been progress, good work has been done. For this we are thankful, but we now realize the enormity of what remains to be done as we face threats aimed at its undoing.

In the following pages you will better understand both where and why both personal and corporate good intentions and energetic efforts in these domains may have fallen short. You will gain fresh insight into the nature of the challenges facing individuals and organizations. You will be given tools to enable you to map out and implement more effective strategies to meet them in the specific areas of responsibility that belong to leadership and management.

What stands out in Mai Nguyen-Phuong-Mai's work is not only her insight into and effective marshalling of the current scientific insights into human cognitive integrity, but the shift of perspective in how we see diversity and intercultural work. We do not need to avoid problems or challenges, but we desperately need to shift from methodologies and interventions focused on fear of loss due to cultural differences and conflict, to more positive reward-based insights that see human variety not only as problematic differences, but also as the resource and raw material for synergy and creativity. If, as we have long maintained, our cultures are strategies for survival and success in the singular environments we inhabit, we have a treasure trove of possibilities when their diverse wisdoms can be brought to bear in the various contexts in which we meet in everyday life and work.

Put bluntly, *we ourselves are culture*, but culture is not an entity. It is instead a powerful living part of our human constitution, a living process that we both inherit and create and with which we continually create and recreate ourselves individually and collectively. Our use of it may give shape to our genes as well as to the criteria by which we choose the jeans we wear. In short, it fuels and propels our endless choices of who to be when, what to do now, and how to do it. It affects who we are, who we think we are like, and whom we want to be with. This means that in a shifting and globalizing world we are challenged to reshape and create the cultures required by and populated by complex individuals such as ourselves and the groups of which we are part.

Cross-Cultural Management: With Insights from Brain Science is not a repudiation of past research and pedagogy in the intercultural field, but a refinement of the perspective of where and how and to what degree past models and frameworks are valid as well as where they fall short in the light of what current scholarship and professional methodologies demand and can offer.

The book makes much of narrative and metaphor, so, whatever image you choose to represent a profound or notable transformation. It is a game changer or a sea change, a watermark moment, destined to revitalize and leave its imprint on both our intercultural mentality and our diversity praxis. Thank you, Mai Nguyen-Phuong-Mai, for stretching out this helpful hand to bring us on board with you at a moment of perspiration and desperation.

George Simons, PhD

Introduction

I have never talked with anyone from customer service like Saymahn. He was helping me to change my Internet package. A 20-year-old Dutch with Liberian background, he sounded much more mature than his age. He also seemed to be genuinely interested in knowing about his customers. At one point, he asked: "Madam, what does your name mean?" I answered: "I was named after a flower that blossoms in the winter, when everything else is frozen," to which he replied: "Madam, now I understand why you have overcome so much in your life. Your name means *hope*." After what he said, honestly, I could have agreed to whatever price his company asked me to pay.

I often use this experience with Saymahn to tell my clients and students about the power of being genuinely curious about the cultural background of others. But more recently, I also used it to talk about the subconscious influence that our names have upon our life. In a self-fulfilling prophecy, we are under the spell of our names, we even look like our names.[1] If parents name their child Daisy, they have in their mind how a Daisy would look like (e.g., blond girl with flowery dress running next to a big dog on a field of flowers in spring). The child will internalize these stereotypes from the parents and the society, and will grow up with some subconscious influence on how she should behave. In a classic study,[2] the Ashanti in Africa believe that the day of the week on which a person was born determines her/his character throughout life. For instance, Monday will be mild mannered but Wednesday is aggressive. In Ashanti tradition, a person's name would include the day of the week (s)he was born. Based on the records of the local juvenile court, a researcher found out that the number of violent acts committed by boys born on Wednesdays was significantly higher than other days. In short, we do live up to our names.

Saymahn and I shared some stories of immigrants who struggled when settling in a new country. The talk with him and the search on literature afterward made me think there could be a possibility that my name has an impact on me as well. When I was two or three months old in my mother's womb, she bled black blood for weeks. Knowing that my father—a military officer—spent much of his life in areas of the country that were heavily exposed to and destroyed by toxic Agent Orange during the war, the doctor suggested that my parents consider an abortion. My mother, 40 years old at that time, refused to listen to that advice. She knew I would be the last child she could bear. Instead, she followed some traditional medicine, practiced yoga, and meditated. Because Agent Orange is known to cause birth abnormalities, when I was born, all she wanted to know was that I had the right amount of eyes, toes, and fingers. I did. And as Saymahn said, she named me after a flower that blossoms against all odds.

The blessing of my name has probably helped me through many of ups and downs as a young journalist living on her own across many foreign lands during many phases of her life. But it is also a double-edged sword because in those foreign lands, a foreign-sounding name subconsciously leads to biases and discrimination. Humans like to hear simple and familiar names, especially names that are similar to their own names. Cultural biases kick in, and names become a subconscious indicator of who we are, not according to the fact, but according to the media. Thus, white-sounding names like Emily received 50% more callbacks than black-sounding names such as Lakisha—an advantage equivalent to eight years of work experience.[3] Immigrants who changed their names made an average of 26% more than those who chose to keep their names.[4] Names that sound distinctively black become, over time, a more reliable indicator of socioeconomic status. It is not that a name has a destiny, but the signals and implication that a name sends.

Once, I asked my students if they thought I should change my name, also because hardly anybody could pronounce or write it correctly, and the first facial expression I get when people try to say my name is a mixture of pain, confusion, and guilt. Some of them said "yes," pointing to the fact that I could get 26% more salary if I whitewash my name. Some of them said "no," because we are not supposed to succumb to stereotypes and let them dictate our life.

It was a great point to talk about culture at large. Replace "name" with "culture" and we get the picture. *Just like names, culture is embedded with meanings.* Black, Caucasian, Latino, Jew, Muslim, millennial, men, women, banker, accountant, and so forth—these names are laden with expectations. Each label is not a vacuum but full of implications, assumptions, values, and stereotypes accumulated over time. *Just like the way we live up to our names, we expect others to live up to their cultural stereotypes as well.* And they do. I lost count of Asian IT experts who, after my training, told me they wanted to break free, show their rebellious side, talk about racism at work. But in the end, they kept silent because the cultural stereotype of hard-working and overpolite Asians is stronger, and it does them good. They have somehow morphed themselves to fit into the Minority Model. People live up to and down to our expectations. And to a certain extent, we have evolved our life the way societies stereotypically portray and expect from the labels of our cultures. As the saying goes, the difference between a girl and a lady is not how she behaves, but how she is treated. If you treat someone like an animal, they will start acting like one.

We got a name we did not choose. Similarly, we were born into a culture that already has terrains, currents, patterns, roads, traffic directions, and so forth—all imply what we should do and where we should go. We can change our name to make life easier. Similarly, we can adapt to our culture, so we could move from A to B as quick as possible. But the quickest way is not always the way we love most. We can choose to keep our name and all the baggage it has, and try to change the social perception about it. Similarly, we can choose to keep our cultural identity, but change the way people look at it.

This kind of thinking does not perfectly align with mainstream theories in the field. Cross-cultural management has long been dominated by the static paradigm that casts a spell of *cultural determinism* over our thinking. The static paradigm considers a cultural name almost as a book of destiny. Our literature is dominated by indexes that look like a fortune teller's note. Each country has a score, indicating how collectivistic or individualistic it is on the average. Based on these scores, we talk about culture as if it is an invisible master that dictates how we will act and behave, what our business partners will do, and how easy we are going to cooperate or compete with each other. If a culture has a low index of 20 on individualism, then think about building relationship because we should gain trust first; but with an index of 80, then think about getting down to business because these people don't waste time socializing. Culture is seen as a software, and we are the computer, running the first program that is installed. It's a scary and pessimistic analogy because it leaves open the question of who created the software and who is behind the keyboard.

As my students continued to discuss the similarities between "name" and "culture," they decided that names need not dictate how one's life will be, and culture needs not decide how we should behave. Each human is born with a capacity to *accept* what has been established, and to *create* new elements and reshape the existing way of life. Culture is not static with an index, we are not just the consequence of it, because we can change it. If culture is fixed with a number, then who created culture in the first place? If we are just a product of culture, then isn't it ironic to expect people to be the change they want to see?

At the end of the discussion, somehow, I got their approval and encouragement to keep my name. They wanted me to fight, face cultural biases, challenge the injustice, and *rewrite* any negative implication of my name. They promised to do the same with their names and their cultural identities.

Thus, the notion that *culture is dynamic, humans are both products and producers of culture* is the most critical point of this book. As businesspeople, corporates, leaders, employees, HR managers, and so forth we all have choices to make: Go with the flow or lead the change. As I was writing this, Nike's product orders rose 27% after it chose Colin Kaepernick as the face of their 30th anniversary campaign "Just Do It." The NFL footballer became a national figure when he chose to kneel rather than stand during the anthem to protest against racial injustice in the United States. With the Kaepernick campaign, Nike is embracing activism at a time when many other companies still try to be neutral by avoiding political, racial, and cultural clashes. This is a choice that Nike made, taking a side, even if it means losing Trump's supporters and facing boycott from many others. The tagline said it loud and clear: "Believe in something. Even if it means sacrificing everything." With this move, it's clear that Nike wants to lead a culture of activism and justice, for better or worse.

This authorship of culture is what I have repeatedly emphasized in this book, and incorporated in all topics of cross-cultural management. In Chapter 5, we will talk about the choice to look at cultural differences as potential for synergy and mutual benefit. In Chapter 6, we will discuss how to actively create a culture that supports business success and gives individuals the opportunities to influence. In Chapter 7, we will touch on one of the most critical topics of contemporary business: Change management. In Chapter 8, we not only learn about biases but also highlight the capacity to win over biases and make biases work for us. In Chapter 9, we will look at a wide range of diversity strategies that may help businesses to optimize the benefits of differences. In Chapter 10, we advocate a motivation/reward approach that is situational, contextual, and free from national stereotypes. In Chapter 11, we reframe global leadership as "glocal" and "diversity" leadership—one that not only adapts to local culture but also has the courage to challenge the existing norms and change the way things are done. In Chapters 12 and 13, we will explore how to actively use language, body movement, and the surrounding environment to purposely change the meaning of conversation, the outcomes of negotiation, and the behaviors of ourselves and our business partners. In the last chapter, a significant part of the text is dedicated to the role of advertisements as a producer of culture and the role of businesses as societal change agents. This thread of culture creation and change is the spirit I want to share. Because in all areas of international business, the choice we make can reflect who we are, or who we want to be. It also reflects what customers essentially think about purchases. They don't buy a product, they buy a progress, that is what helps them achieve the better version of themselves.

As you will see in the first four chapters of this book, I have made an effort to incorporate insight from *evolutionary biology*. My interest in this field began with a book written by a biologist: Mark Pagel and his publication *Wired for Culture*. As I delved into further reading and later on, followed a master study on neuroscience at King's College London, my view of culture changed dramatically. A cultural value such as collectivism is no longer something one simply acquires from young age as a blank slate. DNA, neurons, geography, and behaviors constantly and dynamically play a role in the interaction. Far from the assumption that the mainstream theories have embraced, *culture is not just socially learned, but also genetically inherited*. Risk-taking, for example, is a very important trait for entrepreneurship. Communities at the end of our migration route such as the Native Americans tend to have a higher rate of genes that are associated with risk-taking, but that doesn't mean they are blessed with a great career in business. Cultural background and socioeconomic environment regulate these genes in both positive and negative ways, so much so that these factors can turn this genetic susceptibility into opposite life directions: Addiction/gambling or entrepreneurship. It's nature *and* nurture.

Next to evolutionary biology, *cultural neuroscience* plays a critical role in this book. The mainstream literature of cultural neuroscience heavily focuses on how culture changes our brain's function. For example, if you embrace a collectivistic lifestyle, the same brain area is activated when you think about *both* yourself and your family. In your brain's language, the "self" and the close "other" are the same person. On the contrary, another line of research discusses gender in an out-of-context way, making the brain of men and women look like a body part from two different species. Being limited to these two approaches is not exactly helpful. We either fall in the same old trap of (1) cultural fatalism, that is culture determines your life, and essentialism, that is you have a collectivistic brain, or (2) sexism, that is men and women are born that way, culture does not matter. In short, culture is everything or nothing.

In this book, I chose to mention studies of both approaches, but added insight from a new line of research that emphasizes the incredible ability of the brain to reconstruct according to an immediate context. For example, just by priming individuals with plural pronouns such as "we" and "us," we can trigger the collectivistic patterns of thinking in our brain. The brain is not essentially collectivistic or individualistic. It can host *both* at the same time, and activate the appropriate value when the context is right. The goal of an international businessperson is, therefore, to cultivate a *multicultural mind*, so that (s)he can dynamically adapt or create the kind of cultural pattern that suits a context the best. Indeed, if we have to use the software metaphor, then it's not culture as Hofstede proposed, but *context is the software of the mind*. Particular situations and circumstances will influence the interactions, prompting environment, genes, culture, brain, and behaviors to develop, adapt, and change in a particular way. This is the reason why I consistently use the phrase "when a value prevails" to indicate that collectivism or individualism, for example, can emerge as a dominant driving force of behavior in a specific context, regardless of the culture we are working in, or the type of person with whom we are working.

The following table highlights the main arguments that this book has to offer by (1) taking into account the potential of the dynamic paradigm in cross-cultural management; and (2) employing an interdiscplinary approach that incorporates insight from other fields such as evolutionary biology and neuroscience.

In sum, this book provides initial reading for a wide range of topics in cross-cultural management, with an attempt to incorporate the dynamic paradigm of culture and the insight from other disciplines. It has been a daunting task, taking into account the infancy of cultural neuroscience and the underrepresentation of the dynamic paradigm in literature. It is my hope that this book will open up further discussion to widen the choices of tools and methods we have in the field, and hence, giving pluralism a chance.

To all those who helped me finish this book, I would like to express my thanks. As always, many of the examples I used come from people I met during the early days of my journalistic career and during corporate training in the last twenty years. I now understand their stories many fold better through the academic lens, and for that, I extend my thanks to them again. I am grateful to the anonymous reviewers and to many colleagues and students who commented on the manuscript and helped me look at the content in a much more constructive way. George Simons, I owe you my thanks for your inspiration and for being the living example of how our brain does not get a chance to age as long as we keep putting it at work. I would like to thank the Dean of AMSIB—John Sterk—for his visionary leadership. Thanks to his support, I was so intrinsically motivated that sometimes it felt I would probably still do the same thing even if I didn't get paid. Finally, I thank my research assistants Egidija Lasinskaite and Wantin Wei for their patience and hard work.

Table 0.1 A comparison between (1) the static paradigm and (2) the dynamic paradigm with insight from an interdisciplinary approach

Static Paradigm	Dynamic Paradigm + Interdisciplinary Approach
Difference is the starting point. Businesses need to learn about how they are different from others to avoid pitfalls.	*Similarity is the starting point.* Businesses first build trust with a foundation of sameness— which will act later as a springboard to explore the differences in a safe and constructive way.
Country equates to culture. Nationality is the primary unit of analysis. Businesses can rely on information at the national level to inform themselves about the culture in which they will operate.	*There are at least four units of collective cultures: Global, national, organizational, and group culture.* Their values can align or contradict each other in the same country.
Culture is fixed, and culture acts as a software of the mind. Businesses should learn about culture to predict what would happen in doing business internationally.	*Culture is dynamic, and context acts as the indicator of how a mind would respond.* Businesses should analyze context and learn how culture expresses itself in each particular context.
Values guide behaviors. Businesses should learn about cultural values so they can predict the behaviors of their business partners.	*Values guide behaviors, but repeated behaviors can change even deep-seated values.* Businesses should optimize the power of action to change and create an effective corporate culture.
Values are binary. A culture is collectivistic, individualistic, or somewhere in between. Businesses should know the score of this value for each country they work with, so they can understand why people behave that way.	*Values are dynamic.* Paradoxes and opposing values coexist in a culture. This is also applied to individuals, as a person can be both collectivistic and individualistic, depending on the context. Businesspeople should take specific context into account, and cultivate a multicultural mind.
Cultural relativism means all cultural practices should be understood from insiders' perspectives, and not judged by outsiders. Only insiders have the right to change their own culture. Businesses should respect local values and adapt to local practices.	*Culture is a process of communication and negotiation, both within and between insiders and outsiders.* The world has become so interconnected that we are all involved. Businesses should work with the locals to advocate for the values and practices that would benefit both sides, even if that means changing a (negative) local norm.
Individuals are not the focus. Cultural values do not apply at the individual level. Businesses should look outside mainstream cross-cultural theories for implications that can apply for individuals.	*Individuals are both products and producers of culture.* Individual level is where culture is made personally, dynamically, and contextually. We don't do business with a country, but often work (in)directly with a unique person. An individual can have multiple identities and accommodate a multicultural mind. An individual can both conform and contradict, follow and reshape a culture, even when (s)he was previously an outsider to this culture.
Think global—Act local	*Think global—Plan local—Act individual*

Notes

1 Zwebner, Yonat., Anne-Laure Sellier, Nir Rosenfeld, Jacob Goldenberg, and Ruth Mayo. 2017. "We Look Like Our Names: The Manifestation of Name Stereotypes in Facial Appearance." *Journal of Personality and Social Psychology* 112(4): 527–554. doi:10.1037/pspa0000076.

2 Jahoda, G. 1954. "A Note on Ashanti Names and Their Relationship to Personality." *British Journal of Psychology: General Section* 45(3): 192–195. doi:10.1111/j.2044–8295.1954.tb01244.x.

3 Bertrand, Marianne., and Sendhil Mullainathan. 2004. "Are Emily and Greg More Employable Than Lakisha and Jamal? A Field Experiment on Labor Market Discrimination." *American Economic Review* 94(4): 991–1013. doi:10.1257/0002828042002561.
4 Arai, Mahmood., and Peter Skogman Thoursie. 2006. "Giving Up Foreign Names: An Empirical Examination of Surname Change and Earnings." *Research Papers in Economics* 13, Stockholm University, Department of Economics.

1 Globalization
Evolutionary Roots and Contemporary Version

Globalization is an interesting word to use in connection with cross-cultural management. For many, globalization is a powerful force that either (1) *erases borders* and creates a homogeneous global culture or (2) *reveals borders* as a result of differences being juxtaposed and clashing with each other. The former implies that cross-cultural management will slowly become redundant, and the latter emphasizes the essential role of cross-cultural management. The truth is, of course, everywhere or somewhere in between.

In this chapter, we will look at globalization from its deepest roots, that is, the evolutionary reasons why we have been consistently crossing more and more borders, reaching out for nonrelated strangers, and making our community larger and larger over time. As a result of this historical process, how does our world look today? What makes globalization so exciting, yet, of so much concern in our era? Do we live in a small global village or in a dynamic and divided world? What is the power of local cultures in a globalized economy? Why do international managers need to give an attentive eye to them? These are the questions that we will address in this chapter. We will also welcome insight from *evolutionary biology*, which will help to shed more light on the matter from different perspectives. After all, cross-cultural management is an interdisciplinary study, and so, we must integrate.

1.1 The Traditional Force of Globalization

Globalization is not new. Despite numerous wars and disputes, our species has never stopped to connect and form larger and larger groups. In the history of mankind, small tribes have constantly transformed into chiefdoms, city states, nation-states, empires, and collections of nations such as the European Union. The global village or globalization is simply a logical step of this continuous process. So what has driven this ancient process historically? We will go all the way back to the evolutionary root of our species to find out what, despite periods of withdraws and setbacks, has motivated us to reach out for others to create a bigger and bigger community.

1.1.1 The Nature of Humans

1.1.1.1 Are Humans Naturally Selfish?

Globalization as a process of crossing boundaries has to start with the cooperation between individuals, and with altruism—a behavior of reaching out to others even at one's own personal cost. Biologists since Charles Darwin were puzzled because they could not properly explain how such behaviors could ever evolve in the world of natural selection. In the end, it is supposed to be a struggle for existence, a competitive battle that is gladiatorial in nature: Red in tooth and claw. Every individual is expected to look out for her/himself because your gain means my loss.

Darwin's theory leads to the question of whether human nature is good or bad—something that has long divided theorists. Earlier scholars advocated the selfishness of the human mind, illustrated by popular phrases such as "law of the jungle," "every man for himself," "dog eat dog," and "survival of the fittest."[1-2-3-4] Some philosophers such as Thomas Hobbes argued that cooperation is necessary, but because human's nature is selfish, the only way of attaining cooperation as a social contract is through a coercive authority, and that cooperation has to be a covenant *forced by the sword*. This is considered the original role of governments (i.e., authority orders people to cooperate) and, to a certain extent, of religion (e.g., be good, or else, hellfire).

1.1.1.2 Capitalism is Natural Law

In 1799, Thomas Malthus published his *Essay on the Principle of Population*.[5] The main argument is that population growth outstrips food production, and hence, population is naturally kept in check by poverty, famine, war, and low living standards. They are inevitable, and therefore, welfare programs such as helping the poor would only delay the catastrophe. At the time when the industrial revolution demanded more science and a new paradigm other than the Bible to guide research, Malthus's writing was considered the beginning of *Social Darwinism*—a school of thought widely accepted in Western universities.

Proponents of Social Darwinism applied the biological idea to social sciences. Herbert Spencer invented the term "survival of the fittest" in 1852 and argued that governments should not interfere in human competition, stay away from attempts to regulate the economy, and let the invisible hand control the market. Later on, when Social Darwinism got its wild support in the United States, William Sumner, for example, proclaimed that millionaires are the product of natural selection,[6] and Rockefeller said: "The growth of a large business is merely a survival of the fittest ... a law of nature and a law of God."[7]

In this context, laissez-faire policies were used to support for a competitive, ruthless, dog-eat-dog capitalism. Together with the Industrial Revolution, there emerged a large, underpaid, and exploited wage-earning class, and rich capitalists. In such a context, the concept of "struggle" and "survival of the fittest" was a useful justification for exploitation. Many continued to use the collapse of the Soviet Union and other socialist countries as a real-world confirmation of this core idea: Those who interfered with human selfishness would reap the whirlwind. A natural selection will weed out the weakest members, the less intelligent and less industrious of the society. Such thinking was later used to justify the eugenics movement, which has its most extreme manifestation in Nazi Germany and the selective breeding to improve the quality of the population.

1.1.1.3 Kin Selection Fosters Cooperation

However, recent studies have consistently proved that human nature is not naturally competitive.[8-9-10-11-12] We are also cooperative, and there is an evolutionary base for it.

Let's start with the most obvious: We are cooperative toward those who are genetically close to us—or the Hamilton's rule for evolutionary success of altruism.[13-14] In the following formula, c is the cost of the actor who performs the altruistic act, b is the benefit gained by the recipient of the altruistic act, and r is genetic relatedness between the two. The formula demonstrates the condition that an actor would assist another person, as long as the cumulative benefit to the recipient is greater than the cost to the actor. According to rumor, Haldane monumentalized this principle by declaring this in a pub: "I would lay down my life for two brothers or eight cousins." In evolutionary terms, it is a fair deal, because a sibling has the r factor = 50% and a cousin = 12.5%. Blood is thicker than water. From evolutionary point of view, kin selection makes a perfect incentive for cooperation. Actions that support my relatives benefit copies of my genes.

$c < r\,b$

1.1.1.4 Reciprocity Fosters Cooperation

We are not only cooperative toward those who share the same genes but also total strangers who share little to no genetic relatedness. Next to kin selection, the second strong force that binds all cooperative enterprise is fairness and reciprocity, that is, if you scratch my back, I will scratch yours. Resources are often limited, and naturally, we are cautious of who to share with, better be someone who is trustworthy and cooperative. Being considered trustworthy and cooperative is critical because it gives us an important currency called *reputation*. Good reputation grants us access to material and social rewards once trust has been won. This is so crucial that evolutionary biologist Mark Pagel concluded that humans *compete to cooperate*. In his words:

> We had no choice but to become altruism "show-offs," to compete with others for a slice of the cooperative pie. Our ultra-helpful nature is the altruism equivalent of a peacock's tail, except that the peacock uses his tail to attract a mate, we use our altruism to secure the spoils of cooperation.[15]

This social currency is so beneficial that we even go an extra mile to gain it, by showing that we are willing to sacrifice or even die for it. Pagel used the social bonding from Sebastia Junger's book *War* to illustrate this point. New soldiers who freshly joined the combat platoon were subjected to severe beating and humiliation, including officers. By enduring the beatings, new soldiers signaled that they are serious with the commitment, and the violent tests are a way to buy the fellows' trust.[16] If a soldier could not stand humiliation and violence at such a level, how can one expect her/him to sacrifice for others on the battlefield? Facing the enemy, the willingness to die for each other is the most effective strategy to keep each soldier alive. Evolutionary speaking, their bond was essentially not the love for the country or even the loyalty to their fellows. Rather, it is simply that they were individually more likely to survive when they were all prepared to die for each other. In essence, cooperation stemmed from reciprocal altruism is a selfish calculation for personal interests in the long run.

1.1.1.5 Cooperation is Instinctive

The third evolutionary basis for cooperation has a different argument: It's obvious that we are often cooperative *even when no one is watching*, even when we have nothing to gain. If we only care about reputation, we should rob, rape, free ride whenever we are sure that doing so is safe. We would not vote, or help a stranger anonymously because there is no reputation effect involved. This line of argument leads to an alternative theory of cooperation: Humans have evolved this behavior and developed a *cultural system that is extremely inhospitable to sociopaths*, who are nice only when others are looking. The end result is that humans have become a cooperative species by nature,[17] while sociopaths' population is kept as a small minority. This cooperative system is controlled by social values: We punish those who exploit, praise those who sacrifice, and evoke shame, guilt, elation, and pride to encourage cooperative behaviors.

If evolution favors self-interest, then we should *intuitively* maximize our personal gain. However, research has proved otherwise. In a series of public-goods game experiments, players can choose to either keep resources for themselves or contribute to a collective good.[18] One group was asked to reflectively think and write, that is using logic, before making decision. The other group was asked to make decision under time pressure, that is using intuition, without time to reflect and think. The result: The first group *contributed less* than the second group. In short, we are less cooperative when we are reflective and calculative, or better put, we are more cooperative by instinct.

Thus, it has been argued that we are born with cooperative tendency, which is what researchers observed among infants of 14–18 months old with *unrelated* adults.[19] They immediately helped these adults to fetch out-of-reach objects or to open cabinet doors when the adult's hands were full. They didn't help when the adult purposely threw objects on the floor, which showed that it was not just that they liked fetching stuff in general. Rewards also did not increase helping, and parent's verbal encouragement did not neither. These infants helped the same amount with or without it. With infants of 20 months old, rewards reduced their intrinsic willingness to help because it became extrinsic motivation.[20]

In their book *A Cooperative Species: Human Reciprocity and Its Evolution*, the economists Sam Bowles and Herbert Gintis argued that humans genuinely want to cooperate and sincerely care about the well-being of their own group.[21] This psychology helps to bond individuals in building a prosperous and united community for surviving and competing with other groups. In fact, humans are the only animals who can extend care beyond kinship to large numbers of unrelated individuals. We can cooperate with members of a different blood line, beating the family-bound sociality that is typical of the animal kingdom. We are the only species that can bring down the genetic fence and welcome strangers into our circle of trust. This psychology is so important that it has become our subconscious, intuitive response, or "first instinct."[22] Neuro-economic evidence has shown that this instinct makes us cooperative, even when we have nothing to gain and even at our own expense.[23] While being a hotly debated idea, *evolutionary processes at the group level* means that groups of highly cooperative individuals have higher chances of survival because they can work together to reach goals that are unattainable to less cooperative groups. In this case, the group's fitness outweighs the individual's fitness.

However, there's a twist: This cooperation often goes hand in hand with aggression toward outsiders. Groups that have a disproportionate number of selfish and warlike, or peaceful and altruistic people will die out. Interestingly, and also uncomfortably, Bowles and Gintis assert that war is a necessary tool for this cooperative trait to evolve in humans. However, wars and conflicts are not inevitable. According to the authors, humans are cultural animals, capable of making sure that our legacy need not to be our destiny.[24]

To conclude, thanks to the innate ability to cooperate beyond kinship, during the last 10,000 years, the tension between "cooperation within ingroup" and "aggression toward outgroups" has tended to *give more weight to cooperation* and softened group boundaries. Despite numerous wars, over a long period, reaching out to cooperate with strangers has steadily proved to be a successful strategy that returns better outcomes than endless conflicts and revenge. Evolution favors cooperative traits. The consequence of this process is that human beings have reshaped many levels of group boundaries. The history of mankind has witnessed a constant growth of the cooperation process that bonds communities previously separated by bloodlines, ethnicities, religions, genders, generations, and political ideologies, and so forth. *There has never been a boundary that humans fail to cross*—an achievement rooted in the evolutionary nature of cooperation.

1.1.1.6 Caring Economy

At this point, we should revisit the notion of Social Darwinism–based capitalism. Darwin's idea is clearly misapplied by proponents of laissez-faire capitalism. "Fittest" has nothing to do with being strong, and "survival" has little to do with a savage dog-eat-dog competition. Each species has a unique way to evolve, and for humans, "altruism" happens to be on the list of instruments we need to use.

With the cooperative nature of humans in mind, the mainstream neoclassical economic theory of *homo economicus* appears to be problematic. We don't act rationally to maximize our own utility, although this assumption of human nature underpins our current economic model, which allows Adam Smith's "invisible hand" to function freely for a better world.[25] We are not only motivated by power and wanting but also by care and systems of affiliation.[26] Cooperation isn't just a byproduct of kin selection, or something calculatedly done because both parties receive some benefit from the partnership. On the contrary, cooperation has evolved to be an essential trait of the society, enhanced by genes and social control, because it is an evolutionary strategic way to advance. This view of cooperation supports an emerging ideology featuring the *caring economy*.[27-28] It strives for an economic system characterized not only by competition but also cooperation for greater good. In this system, labor division empowers every individual, the less fortunate receive support and become productive, and most important of all, "wealth" and "growth" are not the sole marker of development. Pioneered by Scandinavian countries, this new paradigm reflects what it is to be human as we shift from the industrial to the postindustrial knowledge era in an attempt to build a more equitable and sustainable world.

1.1.2 The Economy of Scale

At this point, we understand that humans are capable to go beyond any boundaries for cooperation. But a few questions remain: Why does it lead to the forming of larger and larger groups? Can we cross boundaries to cooperate with others without making the group bigger? What is the incentive of a bigger community?

Our ancestors spent a long period living in small, close-knit communities. However, as we know, humans are not totally intimidated by this ingroup-outgroup boundary. When our ancestors realized that large groupings work better, they figured out ways to go beyond the tribal confine and cooperate with total strangers. Living in a larger community allows "economies of scale,"[29] with increased production of more or less the same costs. It is the reason why printing 1,000 copies costs less (per copy) than printing only a few. Similarly, infrastructure built for a big community brings more benefit than making many separate roads to isolated and remote houses. As a result, this cost-benefit incentive has been a powerful driver that merges more and more cultural boundaries and creates bigger and bigger societies since time immemorial.

It's important to note that, because it is based on resource management, boundary fusion has never been a smooth process. To make it simple, *globalization is a zigzag line*. Wars and resource competition make the line go backward, while periods of trust, peace, and cooperation make the line go forward. It is a constant negotiation of going back and forth, pull-and-push, convergence and divergence, inclusion, exclusion, and fusion of local cultures.[30] Regardless of the patterns in details, from a bird's-eye view, on the whole, the zigzag line of globalization has a moving-forward direction.

1.2 Globalization in Our Modern Era

While globalization is not completely new, its contemporary version brings about issues that our ancestors did not have to deal with. In this section, we will highlight the new elements and patterns of globalization in our modern era.

1.2.1 New Elements of Modern Globalization

1.2.1.1 Technology and Information Systems

Advances in technology are one of the main reasons why globalization has escalated in our time. For example, transport technology has moved us faster than ever with roads, rails, sea routes, and air travels. Legend has it that Moses spent 40 years leading the Israelites from Egypt through the desert to find the Promised Land in Canaan—a journey that may cost us a few hours by plane. It is not only the change but the *speed of change* that is so mind-blowing, leading to the term "future shock," a psychological state of having to cope with too much change in too short a period.[31]

Nowadays, information technology (IT) is reshaping the economies around the world with its revolution. On the one hand, it promotes prosperity in many aspects of the society. Communication technology such as the Internet connects people at the fingertips. Media spreads news faster than light, galvanizing revolutions and social upheavals such as the Arab Spring. New industries and workforces emerge. Education and healthcare revolutionize. For example, doctors in remote regions of Uganda can rapidly transmit their findings during the outbreak of Ebola to experts around the world. On the other hand, IT has created concerns in terms of weapon development, cyberattacks, privacy, and the disintegration of human connection in a virtual environment devoid of meaningful context.

1.2.1.2 Demographic Change

Humans have been migrating since time immemorial, but the increase in redistribution of the world's demographics we witness today is unprecedented. Around 360,000 new babies are born each day, 133 million each year. In 2015, more than 244,000 million people lived outside the country of their birth,[32] and that is not counting long-term immigrants' descendants and massive global diasporas. If we consider those who *want* to leave their countries, the figure is mind-blowing. According to a Gallup survey,[33] one in every four people in the world wishes to migrate permanently, including 35% of all Chilies and 27% of all Britons, South Koreans, and Germans. Interestingly, only 1% of Saudis want to leave their country. Further, it's not just the numbers, but the *kinds* of international migrants that are so dynamic. For example, Australia controls the labor market by a point system, changing the kind of skilled workers it needs on the year-to-year basis.

From the profit's point of view, blocking international migration costs the world roughly half of its potential economic product. The reason is that a worker's economic productivity depends much more on *location* than skill. For example, a Nigerian moderately educated person who moves to North America will increase her/his wages by several hundred percent.[34] According to an Organisation for Economic Co-operation and Development (OECD) report,[35] immigration is basically good for the economy as it increases workforce (70% in Europe), addresses labor market imbalance, and provides ready-to-use skills and abilities. They contribute more in taxes than they receive in individual benefits. For example, migrants in Switzerland and Luxembourg provide a net benefit of approximately 2% of gross domestic product (GDP) to the public purse. However, demographic change is not a trouble-free gift. Flows of refugees and nationalism, to name a few, are recent and controversial issues that many countries have to deal with now.

1.2.1.3 Global Economy

Historically, international trade took place along the Silk Road, the Spice Route, the Incense Route, the Amber Road, and so forth. But the modern process of globalization distinguishes itself significantly from its predecessors. From a corporation's perspective, four critical elements stand out: (1) a globalized capital base, for example, money is transferred across the globe in a matter of seconds; (2) a global corporate mindset, for example, cultural diversity is viewed as a source of opportunities to exploit; (3) a global market presence, for example, targeting customers in all major markets throughout the world; and (4) a global supply chain, for example, accessing the most optimal locations for the performance of various activities in its supply chain.[36] These factors promote free trade, reduce the price, and demand cooperation. At the same time, they can widen the income gap, create trade deficit (more import than export), give political power to multination corporations, exploit labor in impoverished countries, and exert undue burden on the planet's resources.

In short, the inexorable integration of technology, demographics, labor forces, markets, capital, nation-states, and so forth are the new elements of modern globalization. They allow individuals, groups, corporations, and countries to reach around the world further, faster, deeper, and cheaper than ever before.[37] As a consequence, we have become so interconnected that nobody is untouchable, creating both opportunity for the "economy of scale" to flourish, but also challenges such as intergroup conflicts, privacy infringement, inequality, or the "domino effect" in financial crisis where the collapse of one critical pillar can bring the entire global system crashing down.

1.2.2 New Patterns of Modern Globalization

1.2.2.1 Flat World

In 1492, Christopher Columbus set sail for India by traveling in the western direction to reach the eastern continent. Scholars in his time believed that the earth was round and large, while Columbus believed that the earth was pear-shaped and small. With his wrong calculation, as history unfurled, he met the natives of America. He thought they were Asian, and hence, called these people "Indian." He reported to his queen that the earth was indeed "round." More than five hundred years later, author Thomas Freidman set off for India. He went east, came home, and reported only to his wife, and only in a whisper: "The world is flat."[38]

Freidman's main argument in his seminal book *The World is Flat* is that due to forces such as in/outsourcing, off-shoring, and open source, the world has flattened due to globalization. The playing field has been leveled, to the point that if you are lost and need to find the way to your destination in Europe, you dial the help line and the person who guides you home will probably be a Filipino answering your call from the other side of the planet. More interestingly, that person could very well be a transgender Filipino.[39] In the world's capital of call centers, this workplace has become more popular for gender-nonconforming people.[40] A transgender employee needs not to justify her/himself and can avoid the wall of social stigma because the client (s)he serves only communicates using the telephone line—a benefit that the flat world offers.

1.2.2.2 Spiky World

The idea that the world is flat and tiny has drawn many critics, one of them is Pankaj Ghemawat, who argued that the flatness is more of an illusion, or better put, a small fraction, than a reality. According to Ghemawat, two key indicators for the rise of globalization: (1) foreign direct investment data, which accounts for only 10%, and (2) trade-to-GDP ratio, which is roughly 20%, show that the vast majority of investment is local.[41] In other words, we are wired and connected, but not necessarily connecting. Backing up the argument of Ghemawat, an analysis using the DHL Global Connectedness Index 2014[42] pointed out that there is, in fact, a decrease in overall breadth of how countries are interacting with each other. For example, in the Bahamas, while the tourist trade is booming and scoring "high for *depth*, it doesn't have much *breadth* because more than 80% of the tourists come from one single country, the U.S., that is less than 200 miles away."[43]

Not globalization, but the big shift in economic activities and *regionalization* have prompted Richard Florida to claim that the world is not flat but spiky.[44] Half of the human population now lives in urban areas, up from about 3% two hundred years ago. In industrialized countries, this percentage is around 75%. According to Florida, leading cities and megaregions (e.g., Tokyo, New York, London, Singapore, Hong Kong, Amsterdam—Antwerp—Brussels) drive the global economy, dominating the landscape of international business. At the same time, it also means that the valleys mostly languish, as spiky globalization also wreaks havoc on poorer places, deepening inequality and the gap between the "have" and the "have not." Such a Hobbesian vision of global economy is far from sustainable because it can accelerate to reach a tipping point if peaks continue to grow and valleys continue to be left sinking.

1.3 Going Global and Going Local

The term *globalization* implies conducting business according to both local and global considerations. Mainstream literature has rich discussion on how global companies need to localize their products. However, "global goes local" is not the only manifestation of the interaction between globalization and local cultures. Two other directions of interaction that this book reveals to you are "local goes global" and "local transforms local." These interactions help us to understand the dynamics of local cultures when *borders have become both fluid and persistent*.

1.3.1 Global Goes Local

In *The Communist Manifesto*, Karl Marx famously warned that small local businesses will inevitably be wiped out by large multinational companies in a form of imperialist capitalism. The loss of local businesses will eventually lead to the loss of local culture and the rise of a corporate state culture dominating the business landscape. On the surface it is hard to argue, as global brands are ubiquitous and identical all over the world. But at a closer look, they are highly localized to accommodate local tastes.

Glocalization has its roots in the Japanese business term *dochakuka*, which refers to the adaption of farming techniques to local conditions. It's the strategy that prompted Nokia to offer a dust-resistant keypad to those in rural India, and explained why Thai food served in Sydney tastes different from Thai food in Bangkok. Even when people seem to buy the same products, they may use it for different reasons. Billions of people use Facebook, but this social media channel is a private friend-and-family zone in some cultures, while it is fully interwoven with business in others. In Shanghai, IKEA managers had to ban old people from turning its café into a dating club.[45] These lonely, divorced, or widowed elderly people could not find their peers in KFC or McDonald's, and so, IKEA became an ideal place to hang around. These examples show that a global brand and its facilities may look the same everywhere, but they sell localized products and carry different status and meanings in different contexts.

In short, becoming a global company is an achievement of successfully combining two major factors: (1) a universal, fundamental, and consistent part of the product; and (2) a localized, customized, and flexible part that is compatible with the new market. Deciding what to keep and what to change, finding a delicate balancing of having both global features and a local identity are essentially the art of international business.

1.3.2 Local Goes Global

Flat-world advocates tend to hold an assumption that cultural barriers will be brought down or a dominant culture will triumph. However, the fact that my cucumber was grown 20,000km away from my salad bowl also means that this cucumber stands a chance to become popular outside the border of its faraway little farmland. With distance being reduced, local cultures, events, and ideas can spread virally across the world and become globally branded products. For instance, the idea of "Restaurant Day" from Helsinki, which invites everyone to set up a pop-up food stand has spread around since 2011 and become the world's largest food carnival.[46] Similarly, *Pecha Kucha* from Tokyo is now being seen in nearly 1,000 cities worldwide as a presentation night for young talented people.[47] Numerous other signature cultures have gone global such as Valentine's Day from England, Halloween from ancient Celtic culture, K-pop from Korea, and Bollywood from India. Mindfulness, for example, has gone from a practice in Hindu and Buddhist tradition to a $1.1 billion business, prompting the *Financial Times* to call the trend "the madness of mindfulness"[48] and *Inc.* to name it one of the best industries for starting business in 2017.[49] Food industry has no shortage of examples, from pizza to curry and kebab. In short, "local goes global" is essentially the case of local cultures being embraced at the global scale while *retaining some of their local identities*.

1.3.3 Local Transforms Local

Opponents of globalization often point to the negative effects on local businesses, especially the case of big companies with sprawling resources willing to sacrifice margins to take out local competitors. While such scenario does occur, it is not always the case. A recent study showed that powerful local companies are winning out against multinational competitors.[50] Unilever CEO Paul Polman pointed out that his stiffest competition comes from fast-growing local companies.[51] According to a report, 73% of executives at large multinational companies considered that local economies are more effective competitors than other multinationals in emerging markets.[52]

As a consequence of having to compete with big companies, local businesses have evolved effective strategies that are *rooted in local knowledge*. They identify new local segments of customers, explore local habits that others do not recognize, partner with local suppliers, create new local products, accentuate local values, engage deeply with customers, and foster the development of the local talent pool. These "local dynamos" thrive by catering to local conditions, operating at warp speed, and adapting to uncertainty[53]—skills that big companies often lack. They are also capable of forging alliances with other competitors to fight against multinationals. At the same time, they learn skills commonly found in multinationals and localize to apply. Riding the wave of globalization, they are dynamic, transformative, and able to combine the best of both worlds.

At the governmental level, policy makers now pay more attention to small firms for their innovative and entrepreneurial capabilities because of their critical roles in the economic growth.[54-55] In Australia for example, the vast majority (more than nine in ten) of businesses are small businesses. They account for 33% of Australia's GDP, employ more than 40% of Australia's workforce, and pay around 12% of total company tax revenue.[56] They maintain their viability and vitality as the market becomes volatile and consumer sentiment unpredictably evolves. In short, local small businesses are making a comeback, exerting their role as the backbone of any economies because they are the essential source of stability, innovation, and job creation.

1.4 The Power of Local Identity

The previous two sections have shown us that our contemporary version of globalization is complex. It has new elements (technology, demographics, and global economy), volatile patterns (both flat and spiky), and dynamic interactions (global goes local, local goes global, and local transforms local). At this point, it should be clear to us that cultural boundaries will not simply disappear and local cultures will not simply fuse into a melting pot of a newly emergent global culture. So why are local boundaries so persistent, despite the powerful force of globalization?

1.4.1 *Extra Wealth Revives Cultural Identities*

At the surface, it is easy to have the impression that everyone wants the same products. However, it has been pointed out that we tend to converge until societies reach a tipping point, and from this point we start to diverge according to our norms and values. For example, most poor countries share a preference for low-priced, high-quality products rather than high-priced, added-value brands. However, as such countries become richer and more educated, consumers start to pick products that fit more with their own cultural preferences and tradition.[57] Take the case of India. After reaching the tipping point, the spread of satellite TV in India increased the popularity of regional channels and, consequently, led to local cultural awareness.[58] When people possess a sufficiency of everything, they will spend their discretionary income on what most *fits their value patterns.*

1.4.2 *Value Clashes Enhance Cultural Identities*

When different values come into direct contact, they can either merge or clash with each other. In many cases, the latter would lead to a reinforcement of their own distinct traits. It is when there is a perceived imbalance of power, and when people regard this cultural contact as a *threat* to the stability and order of society. They may choose to react conservatively in response to the unfair trading of cultural knowledge. The world has witnessed many communities with a tendency to shield and protect their traditions by distancing themselves from modernity.

In most cases, reaction to globalization is a combination of both openness and protection. Here is an account of how France, while being a full member of the global economy, furiously defends its cultural heritage such as food and language.[59] A report[60] gives countless examples, for instance, how many French talked about coming to fast food chains for the first and last time, as if they were coming out of an X-rated movie. Facing this climate of distrust, McDonald's had to run a large-scale ad campaign with the slogan: "Born in the US. Made in France." When it comes to language—the soul of the people and the genetic code of a country, cultural protectionism in France involves legal enforcement. Jacques Toubon—a former justice minister—called the spread of English "a new form of colonization." In 1975, the Bas-Lauriol law made French mandatory in all written and spoken advertising, instructions on packages, and official documents. Thousands of linguistic inspections, warnings, court cases, and fines have occurred, including a fine for The Body Shop because it used English in its products. The law also banned the use of foreign words when French alternatives are available. In March 2000, the Ministry of Finance banned many common English business words such as "start-up," "e-mail," "hashtag," "deadline," "business," "cash," "digital," "asap," "news," "live," "dealer," and "label."[61]

In a spiky world, valleys may be forgotten or sunken so deeply they eventually disappear. But this fate is neither a rule nor an exception. Islamism, to a certain extent, was born in an era of the Middle East's stark decline, as a reaction against Western influences in politics, economy, and social values. One of its main visions is that the Golden Age could come back if Muslims returned faithfully to the religion and let it guide their social, political, and personal life. As the consequence, the Islamic revival has led to significant shifts at the global scale, from the widespread network of politico-religious movements such as Muslim Brotherhood to Islam-inspired economies. By 2021, Islamic finance is expected to reach $3.5 trillion, Halal food industry $1.9 trillion, Halal travel $243 billion, modest fashion $368 billion, Halal pharmaceuticals and cosmetics $213 billion, and Halal media and recreation $262 billion.[62]

The example of Islamic revival reminds us that globalization can be the very reason for the revival of local culture identities (i.e., local goes global), for they are vital and can act as a trigger to turn the table around, raising valleys and creating spikes. With culture as a source of inspiration and unity, impoverished regions can avoid falling deeper into a spiral pattern while giving ways to ultra-developed centers of global commerce.

1.4.3 Cultural Identities as Foundation for Business

Tourism is an obvious example of industries in which local cultures have to thrive for the business to exist. Arguing for a sustainable relationship between South Pacific culture and tourism, author Levani Tuinabua wrote:

> A stretch of white sandy beach edged by swaying palm trees is no unique attribute. It looks the same whether it is in the Caribbean, Mauritius or in the South Pacific … [But] where else in the world can one experience the captivating sways of a Tahitian tamure or the serenity and grace of a Tongan taualunga? Where else in the world can one experience the myriad of colors and costumes of traditional Papua New Guinean outfits? Where else in the world can one experience the raw challenge of a Pentecost dive or the pomp and precision of a Fijian yaqona ceremony?[63]

Not only can culture be the unique selling point, but it also acts as a moral anchor to establish business. Here is a case of young entrepreneurs in the United Arab Emirates (UAE):

> As a barren desert, the UAE has never been a major stage of civilization. In 1971, seven autonomous sheikhdoms, consisting of several tribes from all around the peninsula, were challenged with the task of establishing a national identity based on a thin desert history. Islam was seen as the primary binding force to the newly formed nation, lending moral and legal substance to the fragile national culture. The author of this book witnessed a start-up in Dubai whose founder actively donned a *hijab* because she wanted to convince customers that she was an ambitious *Emirati* woman. When the search for an Emirati identity ended up pretty swiftly on Islamic ground, she took a dramatic turn and completely changed her way of life. Her entire wardrobe was thrown out and replaced with a new one, all previous pictures on Facebook were erased. The young entrepreneur set out on a greater mission to show people how a true Emirati woman can also be progressive, liberal, honest and advanced: "If I appeared like I used to be, nobody would take me serious. They would immediately regard me as a non-Emirati. If I want to influence, I need to be seen as an Emirati. And being an Emirati means being a Muslim." As we can see, religion does not just replace the UAE's national history; it defines it and is a source for the people to dwell on in their search for identity.[64]

1.4.4 Resource Management

Last but not least, the reason why local boundaries are constantly reinforced despite the powerful impact of globalization has to do with our own survival. Our ancestors spent millions of year in close-knit communities, where the group was their source of help, comfort, and survival, protecting them against human and nonhuman enemies. By contrast, outgroup members can mean "threat." For this reason, the ability to make a distinction between ingroup and outgroup at the right moment could mean "life or death." As a result, *cultural and linguistic diversity evolved as a crucial mechanism for us to recognize ingroup and outgroup.* Someone who dresses up similar to me and has the same values as mine is more likely to be my friend, who I don't have to run away from, who I can trust, and with whom I can safely do business. If this person and I speak a unique language and practice a unique cultural ritual, we then stand a better chance that our ideas and knowledge are less likely to be stolen by other outgroup.[65] In fact, cultural diversity was actively pursued in Papua New Guinea. The anthropologist Don Kulick gave one example of the Buian tribe, which purposely fostered linguistic diversity by switching all its masculine and feminine gender agreements, so that their language would be *different* from their neighbors' dialects.[66] Thus, evolutionary speaking, different languages and cultures are formed so that cultural and trade secrets, such a successful recipe or construction of an effective weapon, are protected from those who want to obtain it unfairly.

But it doesn't mean these cultural boundaries will never be crossed. Don't forget we are a cooperative species. Once a business prospect has shown her/his intentions to be good and fair, we will somehow overcome the cultural and language barrier to cooperate. Trading across the globe has operated in more or less this way, with linguistic and cultural diversity as an inherent *regulator*, used by one group to safeguard and negotiate cultural resources with another. It's hard to overemphasize that cultural boundaries are there to be *maintained* and to be *crossed* at the same time, depending on the predicted result of interaction.

As we have concluded earlier, globalization has never been a smooth and straightforward process, but a constant negotiation of going back and forth, pull and push, convergence and divergence, inclusion, exclusion, and fusion of local cultures.[67] At any given moment, there are many pull-and-push drivers, thus creating uncertainty and paradoxes. One of the most prominent examples is the seemingly contrasting tendency between economic integration and the forming of new nations. In other words, we are witnessing the increase of *both globalization and nationalism*. We saw a burst of 16 new countries after the fall of the Soviet Union and Yugoslavia. We have to acknowledge the inherent possibility of splitting in many multicultural societies such as the Hmong in Laos, the Kurdish in Turkey, or the Catalans in Spain. We can't deny the anti-immigration in Europe. The fact that people want to be part of a greater network, yet, at the same time, seek to draw a clearer and smaller boundary that distinguishes who they are and where they live tells us that the globalization is anything but a linear and simple process.

Reviewing the history of mankind, while the merging of cultures seems to be winning the race over a *long* period, diversity persists. Local cultures interact with the force of globalization in a very dynamic and complex way, a tug of war, *a negotiation rather than a straightforward process*. That is why, despite the overwhelming power of globalization, we still need to pay attention to collective cultures and the role of individuals.

To conclude, it can be far-fetched to assume that globalization is nullifying cultural boundaries. International business is not going to be homogenized in a global village, or to be precise, *not yet*. In our contemporary time, we cannot talk about global business without making it *local* business. *International business is not universal business*. As Kevin Roberts, CEO of Saatchi & Saatchi said: "Anyone who wants to go global has to understand the local. People live in the local. I've never met a global consumer. I never expect to. We define ourselves by our differences. It's called identity."[68]

Summary

1. Evolutionary speaking, globalization is made possible because humans are capable of crossing boundaries and reaching out to cooperate with others, both relatives and strangers. Here are three explanations for this trait:
   - Kin selection: We tend to cooperate with genetic-related people because it benefits the reproduction of our genes.
   - Reciprocity: Reputation gained through doing good to others will return benefit in the long run.

- Group selection: Cooperation has evolved as an innate trait to aid the advance of human species in the process of reaching out to others because it proves to be more beneficial than noncooperative traits.
- Thanks to these features, there has never been a boundary that humans fail to cross. It enables us to take advantage of the "economy of scale."

2. Globalization is not new, but in the modern era, this process is driven by different factors: (1) speed of technology and information development; (2) rapid changes in global demography; and (3) the emergence of a global economy.

3. The patterns of modern globalization are dynamic, leading to a complex tapestry of not only a "flat world" but also a "spiky world."

4. Three major interactions of globalization and local cultures are:
   - Global goes local: Multinationals localize their products to accommodate local tastes while not losing the universal features.
   - Local goes global: Products of local cultures are embraced at the global scale while retaining some local identities.
   - Local transforms local: Taking the advantages of both (1) globalization and (2) local knowledge. Local businesses have evolved to be dynamic and transformative, creating a mini-globalization process at the local economic scale.

5. Despite the force of globalization, local cultures persist because:
   - Extra wealth can revive cultural identities: After reaching the tipping point, people tend to spend extra income on what most fits their value patterns.
   - Values clashes can enhance cultural identities: Contrasts that threaten stability and deep-rooted values tend to provoke withdrawal or revival.
   - Cultural identities act as foundation for business: In many economic sectors, culture is the unique selling point or the basis of business identities.
   - Cultural identities act as regulator in resource management: Cultural similarities and differences are evolutionary mechanisms to recognize who we can trust. Cultural boundaries are to be both maintained and crossed, depending on the predicted result.

6. Globalization is not a straightforward linear process but a constant negotiation with local cultures. In our lifetime, *international business is not universal business.* Local cultures still play a vital role. The world is not a global village. Not yet.

Notes

Don't forget to go to the end of the book for case studies.

1 Huxley, Thomas Henry. 1888. "Huxley's Collected Essays Volume IX." http://aleph0.clarku.edu/huxley/CE9/Str.html.
2 Hippo, Saint Augustine of. 2011. *The Confessions of St. Augustine.* Greensboro, NC: Empire Books.
3 Hobbes, Thomas. 2016. "Of the Natural Condition of Mankind as Concerning Their Felicity and Misery." *Leviathan.* The University of Adelaide. https://ebooks.adelaide.edu.au/h/hobbes/thomas/h68l/chapter13.html.
4 Lorenz, Konrad. 1974. *On Aggression.* San Diego, CA: Harvest Books.
5 Malthus, Thomas. 1798. *An Essay on the Principle of Population.* London: J. Johnson in St Paul's Church-yard. https://archive.org/details/essayonprincipl00malt.
6 Kennedy, David M., Lizabeth Cohen, and Mel Piehl. 2017. *The Brief American Pageant: A History of the Republic.* 9th ed. Boston: Cengage Learning.
7 Hofstadter, Richard. 1955. *Social Darwinism in American Thought.* Boston: The Beacon Press.
8 Burkart, Judith M., O. Allon, Federica Amici, Claudia Fichtel, Christa Finkenwirth, A. Heschl, J. Huber et al. 2014. "The Evolutionary Origin of Human Hyper-Cooperation." *Nature Communications* 5 (4747). doi:10.1038/ncomms5747.

9   Sussman, Robert W., and Robert C. Cloninger. 2011. *Origins of Altruism and Cooperation.* New York: Springer-Verlag.

10 Boehm, Christopher. 2012. *Moral Origins: The Evolution of Virtue, Altruism, and Shame.* New York: Basic Books.

11 Tomasello, Michael. 2009. *Why We Cooperate.* Boston: MIT Press, Boston Review Books.

12 Fehrl, Ernst., and Urs Fischbacherl. 2003. "The Nature of Human Altruism." *Nature* 425 (October): 785–791. doi:10.1038/nature02043.

13 Hamilton, W. D. 1964. "The genetical evolution of social behaviour. I." *Journal of Theoretical Biology* 7(1): 1–16. doi:10.1016/0022-5193(64)90038-4.

14 Hamilton, W. D. 1964. "The genetical evolution of social behaviour. II." *Journal of Theoretical Biology* 7(1): 17–52. doi:10.1016/0022-5193(64)90039-6.

15 Pagel, Mark. 2012. "Adapted to Culture." *Nature* 482 (February): 297–298.

16 Pagel, Mark. 2012. *Wired for Culture: Origins of the Human Social Mind.* New York: W. W. Norton & Co.

17 Sussman, Robert W., and Robert C. Cloninger. 2011. *Origins of Altruism and Cooperation.* Vol. 36. New York: Springer-Verlag.

18 Rand, David G., Joshua D. Greene, and Martin A. Nowak. 2012. "Spontaneous Giving and Calculated Greed." *Nature* 489 (September): 427–430. doi:10.1038/nature11467.

19 Warneken, Felix., and Michael Tomasello. 2006. "Altruistic Helping in Human Infants and Young Chimpanzees." *Science* 311 (5765): 1301–1303. doi:10.1126/science.1121448.

20 Tomasello, Michael. 2008. "Origins of Human Cooperation." *The Tanner Lectures on Human Values.* October 29: 77–80, https://tannerlectures.utah.edu/_documents/a-to-z/t/Tomasello_08.pdf.

21 Bowles, Samuel., and Herbert Gintis. 2011. *A Cooperative Species: Human Reciprocity and Its Evolution.* Princeton, NJ: Princeton University Press.

22 Rand, David G., Joshua D. Greene, and Martin A. Nowak. 2012. "Spontaneous Giving and Calculated Greed." *Nature* 489 (September): 427–429. doi:10.1038/nature11467.

23 Fehr, Ernst., Serge-Christophe Kolm, and Jean Mercier Ythier. 2006. "The Economics of Fairness, Reciprocity and Altruism: Experimental Evidence and New Theories." In *Handbook of the Economics of Giving, Altruism and Reciprocity,* 615–691. Amsterdam, the Netherlands: Elsevier.

24 Santa Fe Institute. 2011. "How the Human Species Came to Be Both Nasty and Nice." *Update.* http://samoa.santafe.edu/media/update_pdf/SFI_Update_Sept_Oct2011_FNL.pdf.

25 Singer, Tania. 2017. "How to Build a Caring Economy." *World Economic Forum.* www.weforum.org/agenda/2015/01/how-to-build-a-caring-economy/.

26 Insel, Thomas R., and Larry J. Young. 2011. "The Neurobiology of Attachment." *Nature Reviews Neuroscience* 2 (2): 129–136. doi:10.1038/35053579.

27 Eisler, Riane. 2013. "Building a Caring Economy and Society." *Cadmus* 1 (6): 49–65. http://rianeeisler.com/building-a-caring-economy-and-society/.

28 Singer, Tania. 2015. *Caring Economics: Conversations on Altruism and Compassion, between Scientists, Economists, and the Dalai Lama.* New York: Picador.

29 Silberston, Aubrey. 1972. "Economies of Scale in Theory and Practice." *The Economic Journal* 82 (325): 369–391. doi:10.2307/2229943.

30 Steers, Richard, Carlos Sanchez-Runde, and Luciara Nardon. 2010. *Management across Culture: Challenges and Strategies.* Cambridge: Cambridge University Press.

31 Toffler, Alvin. 1984. *The Future Shock.* New York: Bantam.

32 Connor, Phillip. 2016. "International Migration: Key Findings from the U.S., Europe and the World." *Pew Research Center.* December 15. www.pewresearch.org/fact-tank/2016/12/15/international-migration-key-findings-from-the-u-s-europe-and-the-world/.

33 Gallup, Inc. 2008. "One-Quarter of World's Population May Wish to Migrate." June 24. http://news.gallup.com/poll/108325/OneQuarter-Worlds-Population-May-Wish-Migrate.aspx.

34 Clemens, Michael, Claudio Montenegro, and Lant Pritchett. 2009. "The Place Premium: Wage Differences for Identical Workers across the US Border." *HKS Faculty Research Working Paper Series RWP09-004.* https://dash.harvard.edu/bitstream/handle/1/4412631/Clemens%20Place%20Premium.pdf?sequence=1.

35 OECD. 2014. *Is Migration Good for the Economy?* Migration Policy Debates. www.oecd.org/migration/OECD%20Migration%20Policy%20Debates%20Numero%202.pdf.
36 Gupta, Anil K., and Vijay Govindarajan. 2007. *Global Strategy and Organization.* New York: John Wiley.
37 Freidman, Thomas. 2000. *The Lexus and the Olive Tree.* New York: Anchor Books.
38 Freidman, Thomas. 2005. "It's a Flat World, after All." *The New York Times Magazines.* April 3.
39 David, Emmanuel. 2014. "Purple-Collar Labor." *Gender and Society* 29 (2): 169–194. doi:10.1177/0891243214558868.
40 Talusan, Meredith. 2017. "Why Call Centers Might Be the Most Radical Workplaces in the Philippines." *BuzzFeed.* www.buzzfeed.com/meredithtalusan/the-philippines-call-center-revolution? utm_term=.ynj9ee1k5#.ubNKOOoVe.
41 Ghemawat, Pankaj. 2017. "Why the World Isn't Flat." *Foreign Policy.* January 17. http://foreignpolicy.com/2009/10/14/why-the-world-isnt-flat/.
42 Ghemawat, Pankaj., and Steven A. Altman. 2017. "DHL Global Connectedness Index 2014." *DHL.* NYU Stern School of Business and IESE Business School. www.dhl.com/content/dam/Campaigns/gci2014/downloads/dhl_gci_2014_study_high.pdf.
43 Fox, Justin. 2015. "The World Is Still Not Flat." *Harvard Business Review.* May 20. Emphasis added. https://hbr.org/2014/11/the-world-is-still-not-flat/.
44 Florida, Richard. 2005. "The World Is Spiky." *The Atlantic Monthly.* October. http://creativeclass.com/rfcgdb/articles/other-2005-The%20World%20is%20Spiky.pdf.
45 Embury-Dennis, Tom. 2016. "Ikea Bans 'Illegal' Blind-Dating Group from Store Cafeteria in Shanghai." *The Independent.* October 13. www.independent.co.uk/news/world/asia/ikea-bans-illegal-blind-dating-group-store-cafeteria-in-shanghai-china-a7359271.html.
46 Restaurant Day. 2017. "More about Restaurant Day." www.restaurantday.org/en/info/about/.
47 PechaKucha 20 × 20. 2017. "The Art of Concise Presentations." www.pechakucha.org/.
48 Garlick, Hattie. 2017. "The Madness of Mindfulness." *Financial Times.* February 3. www.ft.com/content/9b8c0c6e-e805-11e6-967b-c88452263daf.
49 Scott, Bartie. 2017. "Why Meditation and Mindfulness Training Is One of the Best Industries for Starting a Business in 2017." www.inc.com/bartie-scott/best-industries-2017-meditation-and-mindfulness-training.html.
50 Santos, Jose., and Peter Williamson. 2015. "The New Mission for Multinationals." *MIT Sloan Management Review* 56: 45–54. www.researchgate.net/publication/283883202_The_New_Mission_for_Multinationals.
51 Daneshkhu, Scheherazade. 2014. "Stiffest Competition from Local Business, Says Unilever Chief." *Financial Times.* July 30. www.ft.com/content/38ec7140-17d6-11e4-b842-00144feabdc0?mhq5j=e5.
52 BCG. 2014. "How Companies in Emerging Markets Are Winning at Home." *2014 BCG Local Dynamos.* July. www.iberglobal.com/files/How_Companies_in_Emerging_Markets_are_Winning_at_Home_Jul_2014.pdf.
53 Ibid.
54 Deo, Sukh. 2013. "The Impact of Globalisation on Small Business Enterprises (SBEs)." In *26th Annual SEAANZ Conference Proceedings.* Sydney. www.seaanz.org/sites/seaanz/documents/2013SEAANZConference/SEAANZ-2013-Deo.pdf.
55 Eurostat. 2015. "Dependent and Independent SMEs and Large Enterprises." *Statistics on Small and Medium-Sized Enterprises: Statistics Explained.* September. http://ec.europa.eu/eurostat/statistics-explained/index.php/Statistics_on_small_and_medium-sized_enterprises#Main_statistical_findings.
56 Australian Small Business and Family Enterprise. 2016. "Small Business Counts." *Australian Government.* www.asbfeo.gov.au/sites/default/files/Small_Business_Statistical_Report-Final.pdf .
57 Mooij, Marieke de. 2010. *Consumer Behavior and Culture: Consequences for Global Marketing and Advertising.* Thousand Oaks, CA: SAGE.
58 Rani, Padma. 2013. "Privatisation, Convergence and Broadcasting Regulations: A Case Study of the Indian Television Industry." *The Asian Conference on Media and Mass Communication*: 387–396.

Nagoya, Japan: IAFOR. http://papers.iafor.org/wp-content/uploads/conference-proceedings/MediAsia/MediAsia2013_proceedings.pdf.

59 Gordon, Philip H., and Sophie Meunier. 2001. "Globalization and French Cultural Identity." *French Politics, Culture and Society* 19 (1): 22–41. www.brookings.edu/wp-content/uploads/2016/06/globalfrance.pdf.

60 McQueen, Paul. 2017. "20 English Words Rejected by the Académie Française." *Culture Trip*. February 10. https://theculturetrip.com/europe/france/articles/20-english-words-rejected-by-the-academie-francaise.

61 Ibid.

62 Thomson Reuters., and Dinar Standard. 2016. "State of the Global Islamic Economy Report." CEIF. https://ceif.iba.edu.pk/pdf/ThomsonReuters-stateoftheGlobalIslamicEconomyReport201617.pdf.

63 Tuinabua, Levani V. 2005. "Tourism and Culture: A Sustainable Partnership." Culture and Sustainable Development in the Pacific (187–189). http://press-files.anu.edu.au/downloads/press/p99101/pdf/ch1412.pdf.

64 Nguyen-Phuong-Mai, Mai. 2017. *Intercultural Communication – An Interdisciplinary Approach: When Neurons, Genes, and Evolution Joined the Discourse*. Amsterdam, the Netherlands: Amsterdam University Press.

65 Pagel, Mark. 2012. *Wired for Culture: Origins of the Human Social Mind*. New York: W. W. Norton & Company.

66 Kulick, Don. 1992. *Language Shift and Cultural Reproduction: Socialization, Self, and Syncretism in a Papua New Guinean Village*. Cambridge: Cambridge University Press.

67 Steers, Richard., Carlos Sanchez-Runde, and Luciara Nardon. 2010. *Management across Culture: Challenges and Strategies*. Cambridge: Cambridge University Press.

68 Roberts, Kevin. 2002. "Running on Empty." *Media and Marketing in Europe*. January. www.saatchikevin.com/wp-content/uploads/2014/06/1017_scan_MM-Europe-Jan02-Run-on-Empty.pdf.

2   The Driving Forces of Diversity

Chapter 1 has helped us to understand that the impact of culture is immense, either *despite* or *because* of the force of globalization. One of the main reasons why we have formed so many local cultures is because we need diversity to recognize our own ingroup and, thus, who we can trust. That's the "why" question. In this chapter, we will deal with the "what" questions: What is culture? And what are the factors that make us so similar, yet so different from one another?

With regard to the first question, ask yourself why culture is something unique among humans and not any other species in the animal kingdom. Understanding the evolutionary basis of culture will help us understand why culture is crucial to human beings, and in what way culture is a survival strategy that helps our species advance. With regard to the second question, we will look to the level of genes and neurons to understand the driving forces that make us so similar, yet so different. We will tackle these questions with an interdisciplinary approach, incorporating insight from evolutionary biology and cultural neuroscience, for this allows us to gain deeper understanding of the subject.

2.1   Survival of the Fittest?

For many, the quote of Herbert Spencer has become a principle of life: "The survival of the fittest."[1] It implies the natural selection of evolution, which favors organisms that are *best adapted to their environments* and, thus, having the most reproductive success at the cost of others' extinction. This theory of evolution is so simple and plausible in biology that it is tempting to see it as a universal phenomenon, including human's society—an idea that led to Social Darwinism, that is applying Darwin's biology principle in social interactions of humans. Quite understandably, it is often used to illustrate the brutal reality of competitive market. In Chapter 1, we discussed the disadvantages of this analogy, for example, the way it justifies ruthless exploitation, inequality, and lack of support for the marginalized. In this section, we will gain more understanding on this matter, and draw our conclusion of what culture really is from an interdisciplinary point of view.

2.1.1   Tarzan and the Giant Tortoises

Many of us grew up with the exciting stories of Tarzan—a baby boy adopted by an ape tribe in the African jungle. Despite being born as human, Tarzan naturally developed an ape's way of life. He would swing the trees and sleep up high. His favorite food was raw meat, killed by himself, and buried for a week so that the decaying process would make it tender to eat. In essence, Tarzan lived and behaved like those apes that adopted him, becoming a full member of the culture in which he was raised. In real life, cases like Tarzan do exist, and they are called "feral children." They were raised by wolves, primates, dogs, or pumas. They generally lacked social skills for communicating with humans, walked on all fours, and often ate raw food.

What about the giant tortoises?

In his trip around the world, Darwin observed the genetic adaptation of the giant tortoises on different islands of the Galapagos. Those who lived on the well-watered islands have evolved to gently curve the front edge of their shell due to the abundance of the short-cropped vegetation. Those who lived on more arid islands have evolved to develop long necks that enabled them to stretch their heads almost vertically, also causing a high peak to the front edge of their shells. This sort of observation formed the foundation of Darwin's evolution theory, which, in essence, posits that *genetic adaptation is a survival strategy* for organisms.

Let's compare these two stories. For the giant tortoises, Darwin's theory holds true. They slowly change their genetic design to adapt to the environment. This survival strategy is "coded" in their genes. They don't have to go to school and do a great deal of thinking on how to catch a prey or run away from a predator. Animals are born with a set of genes that tell them how to do so. Their survival is largely dependent on genetic improvements after many generations such as better wings, feathers, shells, claws, and poisons.

For humans, while our physical features have diversified to a certain extent due to the environment we live in (e.g., skin color), genetic improvement is *not* exactly our survival strategy. Tarzan didn't rely on his genes to survive in the jungle. Instead, he had to listen to his mother ape, and learned to swing the tree fast enough to catch up with his tribe. Many generations of giant tortoises must have died until their descendants evolved the right genetic design that enabled them to reach high vegetation. Tarzan didn't die but fit right in. Unlike animals, humans don't change genetic makeup, don't wait for many years to evolve the right physical features. Instead, we change our attitudes, values, and behaviors. Our survival strategy relies on the ability to learn from others, to adopt the host culture, no matter where this culture is situated, be it in a hot desert, cold climate, chaotic city, isolated island, or deep in the jungle with nonhuman groups. In short, Darwin's theory of *genetic* adaption as survival strategy does not apply to humans. This is the point where many scholars interpret his theory from a broader view: If not genetic, then is *cultural* adaption a survival strategy for humans?

2.1.2 Culture as Survival Strategy

We are often amazed at how our species is able to live in all kinds of environments without changing our genes, as it is the case in animals. We settle deep in the jungles without the genetic ability to swing the trees, we explore the deep water without evolving fishlike gills, we survive extreme cold without having to make our skin furry, we conquer the desert and our backs don't grow humps like camels, and we fly beyond the moon despite having no wings. Clearly, genetic adaptation is not our survival strategy. Biologists such as Mark Pagel[2] argue that the force behind what has made our species a spectacular ecological success is "culture."

Around 200,000 years ago, humans started to develop the *ability to learn from others*. In the form of simple art and adornment, we slowly began to communicate ideas to others through the meanings attached to each object or symbol. Of course, animals can observe and imitate others as well, but humans differ in the way that we can be *conscious* of what we copy and why we copy. We do not just mindlessly imitate others, but we understand why, as we pick the best bits and teach them to someone else, making it *cumulative* across generations—something that animals fail to do. Slowly, culture—in terms of traditions passed from one generation to the next—has mostly replaced genes to provide us the survival information we need. While animals can just rely on their genes and know how to survive without learning (e.g., put an abandoned fox in the jungle, it will be led by its genes and start to live like a fox), newborn humans are clueless how to survive without *learning a culture*, in fact, *any* cultures. Put an abandoned baby in the jungle, it will forget that it is a human. It will adopt the culture of whoever saves its life, be it a gorilla or a wolf. Why? Because that is the only way a human can survive.

In sum, if we trace the purpose of culture down to its biological root, the definition of culture should contain the recurring theme of survival strategies through social learning. For that reason, culture is defined as "a set of evolving man-made elements that have increased the probability of survival, and thus become shared among those who could communicate with each other."[3] An example of cultural as survival strategy can be found in the worship of cows in India. The important role of cows in agriculture and transportation led to the development of a belief that cows were sacred and should not be eaten.[4] This belief was a good cultural strategy to ensure that people did not kill the animals that were crucial to their survival.

2.1.3 *The Survival of the Most Cultured*

The survival game for humans is essentially different in comparison with animals in the sense that we do not need to evolve sharper teeth or bigger wings. Instead of waiting for our genes to evolve—which may take forever—we put the best *ideas* together, creating weapons and aircrafts, destroying enemies a million times more effectively than the sharpest teeth, and flying a million times further than any birds ever existed on earth. Unlike genes, cultural elements (e.g., ideas, languages, music, art, innovation) can jump directly from one mind to another, allowing us to acquire knowledge in a split second, without having to wait many generations to see some "good" genes become dominant in a population.

While genes are largely fixed at birth, each culture is an immense and active archive of what is best to do to survive. It is a vast store of continuous and rich information that humans can (1) choose, and (2) play a role of improving and broadening it. Regarding point (1), our culture will give us a hint about the right course of action. For example, we may want to embrace a certain value, dress in a certain way, go to a certain school, or make a certain career choice, depending on the demands and expectations of the specific culture that hosts us at that moment. The most likely survivors are those who can best attune to a culture, or the most cultured, as Pagel argued.

Up to this point, our story sounds like the *fittest* part in the phrase we are discussing. However, culture as a strategy of human species is not static, or in other words, not a fixed entity that exists for humans to fit in. Through a dynamic interaction, we don't just adapt to our own culture but actively *change* it, which is point (2). We don't just follow the values and practices of the culture that hosts us but purposefully or subconsciously reshape them at the same time. In a cause and effect circle of actions and reactions, culture has become a powerful strategy for humans to advance. Note that the term "strategy" implies both passive and active roles that humans play in the relationship with culture. We are under the influence of a strategy, but we can also change it. From this perspective, the "survival of the fittest" in the plant and animal kingdom should be replaced with the "survival of the most cultured" in the human's world. "The most cultured" are those who not only know how to adapt to a culture but also know how to change or create a new culture.

In business, going international means strategically using culture to navigate a new market. A product or a businessperson should maintain a fine balance between adapting and reshaping the local culture. In many cases, this process creates hybrids or a new culture that significantly revolves around a specific lifestyle that a brand develops. Think about products and services that have immensely changed our way of living, or have become so attached that they even represent our identities. Legend has it that the owner of giant footwear company Bata once fired a salesman who returned from Africa and reported that there was no market for shoes because everyone walked around barefoot.[5] In a feat of classic business expansion, Mr. Bata—a man from Czech Republic—and his company conquered the market of Africa with their affordable shoes by changing the way local people walk. Successful business strategies don't always mean trying to meet the need of the customers, but also making cultures and forming new habits that customers want to follow. Because culture is dynamic, the survival of the most cultured means a great balance between "fitting-in" and "creating new."

2.2 The Diversity Pathways

The diversity around us is both challenging and beneficial. Similarities and differences can dynamically pull and push the interaction, acting as anything from opportunities to obstacles, relentlessly shaping and reshaping business activities. This raises a question regarding where this diversity comes from. Why are we so different from each other, yet, so similar? And how can we adapt, and actively reshape the situation in this dynamic interaction of so many elements? In this section, the Diagram of Diversity Pathways (Figure 2.1) will be introduced and help us to gain a holistic understanding of the complexity businesses may face. It consists of interdisciplinary elements, in line with the emerging view that diversity of life comprises both living forms and human's cultures.[6] For the ease of our mind, we will morph this diagram into a simple acronym: GCEB-Be (pronounce as "Gi-Ce-Bi") with each letter standing for Gene, Culture, Environment, Brain, and Behavior.

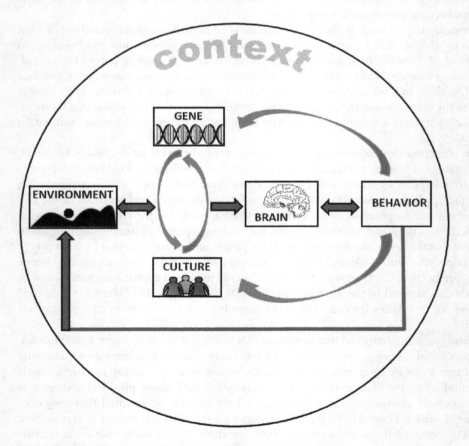

Figure 2.1 The Diagram of Diversity Pathways (GCEB-Be)

2.2.1 Pathway Environment—Culture

2.2.1.1 The Impact of Environment

Natural environment has long been used to explain economic growth and business culture of various regions in the world. For example, Jared Diamond, a follower of neo-environmental determinism, argued that the reasons why Eurasia (Europe and Asia) has been historically more developed than other parts of the world are: (1) The plant species native to Eurasia, such as wheat and barley were excellent for agriculture. In contrast, the natives of North and South America had only maize, which is much less nutritious and a very difficult to plant, while most of the African continent lacked water; (2) Eurasia had 13 species of large domesticable animals to plow the fields while North and South America had just one: The llamas; (3) Eurasia stretches from east to west, while Africa and the Americas stretch from north to south. Because climate varies depending on longitude, this means knowledge, migration, and businesses can flow easier along the latitude, that is, the axis east-west than north-south. The combination of better plants, domesticable animals, and favorable flow of climate enabled ancient inhabitants of Eurasia to have more food surplus, allowing the formation of food trading and other division of labor.[7]

To this day, landlocked countries and tropical regions with higher disease burdens are believed to hinder international trade and economic growth.[8] The "North-South divide" in development exists at the global scale,[9] the regional scale,[10] and within geographically long countries, such as Italy.[11] A 2012 study reported that wide countries with an east-west axis are more linguistically homogeneous than long countries with a north-south one.[12] This finding can be interpreted that businesses may need to deal with more cultural diversity in markets that stretch along the longitudes. The size of a country is critical for international trade because it affects the size of a market.[13] Befitting a large, geographically isolated country means a rich and self-sufficient consumer culture, while dense, small, and landlocked countries have to sell across the borders if they want to thrive.[14]

Geographical environment has been linked to some specific national psyches. The "island mentality," for example, has been used to explain the introvert way of business communication in the United Kingdom, to the extent that the country is dubbed "the Asian in the middle of Europe." By perceiving themselves as either exceptional or superior to the rest of the world, this island mentality was also accounted for shaping the United Kingdom's view of Europe and Brexit.[15] It also influences Japan's pride in a pure, self-perceived superiority of their origin.[16] To a certain extent, geographical environment can help to understand the United States' pragmatism and idealism as it is geographically far away from Europe, thus it is pretty free from the heavy burden of ideology. However, this environmental feature also fuels its arrogance and ambivalence because the country is quite safe from external attacks.[17]

2.2.1.2 Economic Geography

With environment as the core framework, the field of *economic geography* covers a great varieties of other aspects, such as how the distribution of natural resources, long distances, terrain, and climates affect the economy and business culture. For example, business cycles may follow the rhythm of seasons, so the peak sale for real estate is more likely during summer because few people want to uproot their family in the middle of the school year.[18] The old adage about critical factors in retail success (location, location, location) can be applied to many other aspects of business as well. Despite the interconnectedness of globalization, geography and borders do not simply disappear. Issues such as where to set up the headquarters and where to build facilities are critical to any businesses. Such decisions can also influence the mental consequences of those involved. Michael Cannon-Brookes—Vice President of IBM—is believed to have said: "You get a very different thinking if you sit in Shanghai or Sao Paulo or Dubai than if you sit in New York."[19]

2.2.1.3 Sustainability

Environment undoubtedly influences human societies. Likewise, humans have dramatically changed the environment as well. We have flattened forests, dried up rivers, reclaimed land from the ocean, and, for the first time since the dinosaur disappeared, humans are driving animals and plants to extinction faster than new species can evolve.[20] Technically, there is no more such thing as "wilderness."[21] Most landscapes today have been (in)directly shaped by human activities, including the poles and the depths of the oceans. This is because climate change has touched the deepest and furthest point on Earth, and carbon dioxide levels already hit the "point of no return" in 2016.

The current situation of our environment has created increasing awareness among the public. Buyers now demand corporate responsibility. As a result, sustainability has been integrated in virtually all international business agendas. Even without pressure from customers, companies have come to understand that climate change can disrupt business operation,[22] affecting many multinationals such as Toyota, General Mills, and Amazon.[23] For example, Iceland enjoys constant flows of tourists flocking to the country using airways thanks to its beautiful natural landscapes. While this is good for the economy, the increase in traffic can cause significant threats. Melting glaciers due to rising temperatures could cause erupted volcanoes as much as one in seven years, and could, in turn, drive tourists away. Facing these challenges, Icelandair took a proactive approach to mitigate their carbon footprint by developing greener aircrafts and using renewable energy instead of fossil fuel.[24] The carbon consciousness is the core of Icelandair's business culture and is so well published, to the point that when the Eyjafjallajökull volcano erupted in 2010, it gave the country a PR boost. Instead of being seen as a gloomy warning of climate change, the volcanic eruption was not viewed negatively by the media as it was linked to nature's beauty and adventurous travel. The world was quick to forgive the massive disruption of air travel, and travelers were drawn to Iceland once they learned more about Icelandair's pioneer policies in eco-responsibility. In short, by proactively pursuing a progressive sustainability agenda, Icelandair not only prepares for environmental consequences but can also turn an otherwise disastrous event into its advantages.

To conclude, in the Diversity Pathways GCEB-Be, the bi-directional interaction between C-culture and E-environment creates diversity in terms of (1) how geography influences the economy and psychology of the inhabitants, and (2) how cultural ways of living have dramatically reshaped the environment, making sustainability a top concern for business nowadays.

2.2.2 Pathway Environment—Culture—Gene

"Leaders are made or born?" "Personality is genetic or developed?" And so forth. These questions are directly linked to the debate of "nature or nurture." The common view is *both*. This applies not only to human traits but also to human's culture.

In the previous section, we learned that cultural adaption and creation are human's survival strategies, not genetic change. To be precise, genes do change, albeit with a different purpose. They change to make the cultural adaption and creation easier. The culture-gene coevolution theory (or dual inheritance theory) posits that *genes change so humans can acquire the necessary culture, and useful cultural values are turned into genetic traits for the next generation*. We are going to look at how a gene can contribute to this process. While there is still much to know, the following example may act as a symbolic case with some oversimplification, giving us a hint of how the culture-gene co-evolution theory is at work.

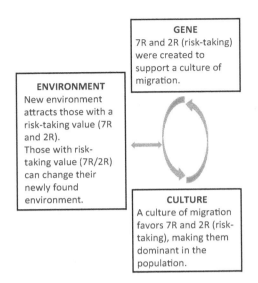

Figure 2.2 The interaction among environment, risk-taking genes, and a culture of migration

The gene that encodes dopamine receptor D4 (DRD4) in our brain exists in several alleles (or versions). The 7-repeat- and 2-repeat alleles (7R and 2R) have been linked to impulsive and exploratory behavior, risk-taking, and novelty seeking.[25-26-27] Both alleles are less sensitive to dopamine than the common ancestral 4R, and thus, both seek more stimulation to generate a "normal" level of dopaminergic activity to feel good. When researchers looked at the frequency of 7R and 2R in 18 indigenous populations spreading along the routes of human migration from Africa, it turned out that the further on the move away from Africa, the more likely people were to have either of these two alleles.[28] The interesting thing is that the 7R arose as a rare mutation about 40,000 to 50,000 years ago, after our ancestors left Africa.[29] Because there is no link between the 7R and recent migration, a conclusion from these pioneer studies is that people with the 7R and 2R are not prone to migrate, but they may experience higher fitness in response to many generations of migration, thus dealing more effectively with ecological and social stressors that migration presents.

To conclude, the diversity we see in the world today is the result of how the environment exerts demands on culture and genes to co-adapt. A particular cultural value (e.g., risk-taking) can help humans to cope with the environment. This value favors a set of genes (e.g., 2R/7R), and in turn, these genes become dominant and reinforce that value in future generation. Culture is not just socially learned as the mainstream theories have always assumed. Cultural is also *genetically inherited.* Figure 2.2 illustrates this example in the framework of the Diversity Pathways GCEB-Be.

2.2.3 Pathway Behavior—Gene

2.2.3.1 Epigenetics

For a long time, we held tight to the idea that DNA is nature's blueprint. But scientists have figured out that the proteins (or epigenomes) that sit atop of the DNA sequence are still a mystery. It turns out that these epigenomes are the boss of the DNA. Think of our DNA as a lamp. While the *DNA code is fixed, epigenomes act as switches* (Figure 2.3). Methyl groups act as an on-off switch, activating a gene or making it stay dormant, modifying a gene's interaction.[30]

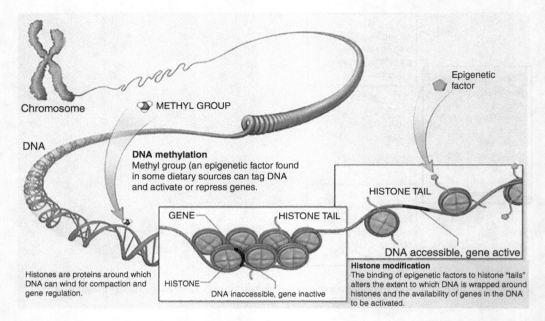

Figure 2.3 Epigenomes can regulate the expression of DNA (adapted from the National Institutes of Health)

Histones, however, act as a volume control or a dimmer, regulating gene activity up or down by controlling how tightly the DNA is spooled around its central thread.[31]

There are millions of those switches, controlling approximately 25,000 genes in human DNA. A great amount of epigenomes can be affected by our behaviors, our lifestyles, such as the thoughts we have, what we eat, how we work, who we have relationship with, and an act of kindness or hatred. Behavioral changes in three months could turn on or off 500 genes,[32] and just a single week of insufficient sleep altered the activities of 711 genes.[33] Only 5% of diseases-related gene mutations are fully deterministic, while 95% can be influenced by behaviors and environmental conditions because a positive lifestyle can alter 4,000 to 5,000 different genes.[34]

Epigenetics can happen at the collective and trans/intergenerational level as well. To further reinforce the link between culture and biology, in a study, researcher reported that among Latino children living in two cultures, Puerto Rico and Mexico, the differences in cultural practices account for 25% of the differences in their genetic expressions.[35] This kind of alteration may endure in four subsequent generations without changing the DNA coding.[36] For example, both children and grandchildren of women who survived the Dutch famine in 1944–1945 were found to be more prone to diseases such as obesity[37] with a 10% increase in mortality after 68 years.[38] In another study, descendants of Holocaust survivors have different stress hormone profiles, which may predispose them to anxiety disorders; even 70 years have passed and they do not experience the trauma at all.[39] It means the choice we make in our lifetime can lead to changes in the epigenomes and will be passed on to our offspring in a hundred years. We inherit from our parents not just their DNA but also how they work.

Based on the hypothesis that the DNA can't quickly change to help humans adapt through genetic mutations, epigenetics is argued to be an evolutionary solution—a "medium-term" mechanism[40] that helps us to rapidly adapt to a new environment. Pembrey[41] even argued that that cultural inheritance is also epigenetically mediated rather than just learnt. In other words, cultural transmission is more than social learning and imitation because it is also biologically embedded. As much as people can inherit trauma from distant ancestors, members of a collective can inherit numerous cultural values and practices through transgenerational epigenetic inheritance.

2.2.3.2 Genes and Business

Genes are among many factors that can give a good indication of behaviors, for example self-employment.[42] In his book *Born Entrepreneurs, Born Leaders*, Scott Shane argued that 45% of the variation in annual income is the result of genetics, and so is 60% in occupational status, 55% in the willingness to take risk, 61% in being persistent, 19% in liking sales, and 36% in liking finance. Because all these traits support a strong likelihood of shaping a good leader and entrepreneur, the author concluded that 37–48% of the tendency to be an entrepreneur is genetic.[43]

Connecting Shane's argument with epigenetics, one may argue that such a gene-centric perspective can be misleading. Epigenetics indicates that within the same population with similar genes, people with supportive behaviors can activate good genes and deactivate bad genes, while destructive behaviors will do the opposite. The same genes can manifest in *both* desirable and undesirable outcomes. In this study,[44] people with the 7R variant of the gene that encodes dopamine receptor D4 who come from higher family socioeconomic status tend to change jobs voluntarily by moving upward to better positions, while people with the 7R who come from neighborhoods with poverty tend to change jobs involuntarily because they are fired. Thus, the gene-culture interaction model posits that cultural influences can shape how these predispositions manifest in the final behavioral outcomes. In other words, cultural elements can "activate" the same gene in exactly opposite ways.

The common mistake people often make when interpreting genetic heritability is that they drop elements of culture and environment out of the picture. Saying "IQ is 70% heritable" does not mean that parents have "70% chance of passing" it onto their children, or "70% of your intelligence is genetic, and 30% is upbringing." Think about height, and the fact that it is 80% heritable. It makes no sense to say that if you are 160cm tall, and thus 80% of your height (i.e., 128cm) is genetic, and the rest is because of the food you eat and the sport you do.[45] Heritability tells us if *this variation* in *this specific population* occurs because (1) people have different genes, or (2) people live in different environment and culture. Tim Spector—a scientist who has studied identical twins since early 1990s—put the example of IQ heritability in words:

> If you go to the US, around Harvard, it's above 90%. Why? Because people selected to go there tend to come from middle-class families who have offered their children excellent educational opportunities. Having all been given very similar upbringings, almost all the remaining variation is down to genes. In contrast, if you go to the Detroit suburbs, where deprivation and drug addiction are common, the IQ heritability is *close to 0%*, because the environment is having such a strong effect.... *Any change in environment has a much greater effect on IQ than genes*, as it does on almost every human characteristic. That's why if you want to predict whether someone believes in God, it's more useful to know that they live in Texas than what their genes are.[46]

In line with this explanation, a study on gene transcription[47] reported that among those who grew up in low social class contexts, genes associated with proinflammatory actions were up-regulated, while genes responsive to glucocorticoid receptor-mediated signaling were down-regulated. This is a defensive solution because the *body wants to react to threatening environments*. In a short term, this solution is good because it heightens the immune activation and cortisol. But in the long term, it is destructive, very much similar to how accumulated stress will eventually lead to a burnout. In short, the culture where one grows up can overpower the effect of gene.

At a larger scale, the gene-centric approach has even managed to explain the root of global economic development. A study proposed that too much genetic diversity encourages innovation but reduces cooperation, while too few differences in genetic makeup support cooperation but fail to kick development into high gear.[48] Taking into account the migration routes of humans, the genetic gene pool in Africa is the richest, while it is the lowest in America where the human migration finished. According to the authors, both the excessive and inadequate diversity in the gene pool are responsible for the slower rate of development in these regions. Hitting the economic jackpot are Asia and Europe, somewhere midway of the migration, at least 3,000 miles from East Africa. Such finding is interesting, but controversial at best. For example, it does not take into account the long period of economic setback in Europe before constant wars triggered its innovation; the many glorious and advanced civilizations in Africa and America that existed in the past; the impacts of other factors such as environment, culture, and willful behaviors of people. Such a simplistic way of viewing the world not only risks oversight but may also fall into the realm of eugenics, fatalism and determinism, that is it's fixed, and there is not much we can do.

2.2.4 Pathway Behavior—Brain

A critical body organ that enables the dynamic process of nature-nurture is our brain. It consists of approximately 100 billion neurons and 100 billion supporting glia cells.[49] Each neuron typically has an axon (sender) and can form about 1,000 connections with other neurons through many of its dendrites (receivers). A 2015 study[50] revealed that memory capacity of our brain is ten times greater than previously thought. It can contain 4.7 billion books or the whole World Wide Web.[51]

When two neurons communicate, they do not really touch each other, but send neurotransmitters through a small space called a *synapse* with the help of receptors. If we repeat a

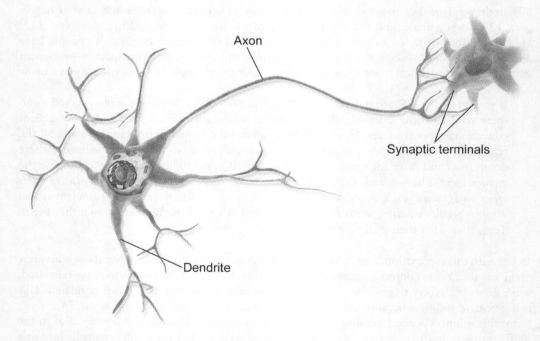

Figure 2.4 Anatomy of a multipolar neuron (Bruce Blaus)

certain thought, action, or ritual frequently enough, the dendrite will grow bigger and there will be more neurotransmitters and receptors. Eventually, the neuron will grow a new branch, and the sending-receiving of neurotransmitters become super quick and effortless. This happens with routines (e.g., brush your teeth) or jobs (e.g., chair a meeting) that you can do so easily because your brain has physically rewired itself to form networks or cell assemblies of neurons that fire together, helping you to do a repeated and familiar work without thinking too much about it. Imagine you have to go from Dublin to Amsterdam, first by swimming to the United Kingdom, then you walk through the United Kingdom and swim again across the English channel to Amsterdam. That is a bit tiring. But if you keep doing it over and over again, the footpaths will widen to become highways, different waterways and flying routes will be established, and millions of people will work together to help you move even faster. At one point, you will get from Dublin to Amsterdam effortlessly, without even thinking about it. In essence, the geography has physically changed to assist you in a task of moving from A to B effectively. Similarly, the brain anatomy will physically change to make a repeated thought and behavior happen as quickly and easily as possible (Figure 2.5).

Research has well demonstrated the plasticity of our brain. It's often said that kids' minds are like sponge. That's thanks to their brain plasticity that allows the brain to rewire itself. The brain in adults is less flexible, but the principle of plasticity remains. For example, if you spend years of training to memorize 25,000 streets in London as a taxi driver, you will grow bigger volume of gray matter in the posterior and reduce the volume in the anterior hippocampus[52] and become a wizard of direction. Even at older age, the brain does not easily fail us, as long as we keep forcing those neurons to wire together, so they can fire together. Here are two stories that prove the point: A 97-year-old Vietnamese grandma managed to master the Internet,[53] and another 81-year-old Singaporean grandma rocked the stage away with her music skill that she only started learning at her old age.[54] Thus, the ancient wisdom makes sense: *Practice makes perfect.*

The culturally patterned brain enables us to voluntarily take actions that are appropriate in a specific culture.[55] This explains why some professionals can do their job effortlessly and others can't. They were not necessarily born that way, but probably have *become* that way. Newly arrived or visiting people, whose brains are not (yet) equipped with the necessary neural basis, may find it challenging to conform to the behavioral scripts and social rules in the new social environment. That is why meeting people from a different culture, moving to work in a new country, or starting work at a company can be challenging because our brain has not yet physically changed to respond effectively. A recent study[56] gives us some hope as it reported that scientists

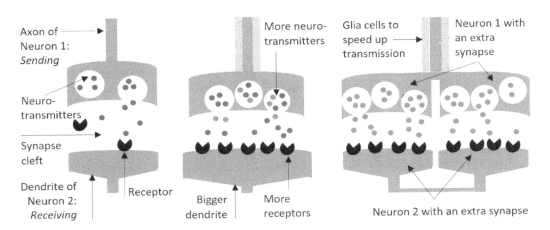

Figure 2.5 Long-term potentiation

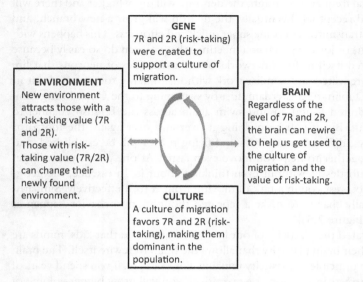

Figure 2.6 The interaction among environment, risk-taking genes, a culture of migration, and the brain

can return a mice's brain to the sponge level of plasticity by tweaking a single gene. If that also happens in humans, we can boost our brain plasticity, fight aging, and adapt quicker to a new culture of demand.

To illustrate this point in a clearer manner, we can continue to use our example in the previous section and put it in the framework of the Diversity Pathways GCEB-Be with Figure 2.6.

2.2.5 Pathway Behavior—Culture

Just as we are not completely at the mercy of our genetic makeup at birth, we are not stuck with our cultural values either. While culture has mostly replaced genes in giving guidance to our behaviors, this interaction is also a two-way street. Social learning allows behavior to be a dynamic force that both reflects and reshapes cultural values at the same time. For example, the strict state-mandated one-child policy in China has decidedly transformed the entrenched cultural value of gender equality, filial piety, and patrilineality. Traditionally, boys are preferred because they carry the family name and take care of senile parents. One-child policy and its consequential behaviors have created a significant value shift because daughters, as the only offspring, are expected to be breadwinners and to have just as many responsibilities as sons do.[57] Once a much-criticized policy, even when lifted, the norm has sunken so deep that when combining with other economic factors, few women want to have a second child.[58]

The one-child-policy case is interesting because it shows us that repeated behaviors can make us embrace the value that we initially *disliked*. Let's get back to the study of how London taxi drivers can easily navigate the massive labyrinth of this metropolitan city in an almost automatic process. This effortless conduct can only happen if we have zero or little conflict between our thought and action. If we value one thing and have to act the opposite, we face a state called *cognitive dissonance*.[59] This conflict will reduce productivity. Taxi drivers can't do their job perfectly if they consciously hate every minute of their drive.

But if we have to do it anyway and still dislike it, evolutionary has a solution for us. To avoid this conflict, we will slowly *change our value* to make it consistent with our behavior so that there is no conflict between the reason to do it and the action of doing it.[60] Brain studies weigh in, demonstrating a causal role for the posterior medial frontal cortex (pMFC), which plays an active role in detecting and resolving inconsistency between attitude and behavior.[61]

Many studies have demonstrated the change of attitude as a result of behaviors. In an experiment, students were paid to tell the lie. Half of them were offered $20 whereas the other half were offered only $1. In the evaluation afterward, students who had been paid $20 said the task was boring (which is the truth). In contrast, those who were paid only $1 changed their attitude toward the task and rated it as significantly more interesting.[62] They simply changed their feeling to justify the reality. In the same vein, customers raised their rating of the product's value after they had chosen it. The product became worthier as a result of a behavior: They chose it.[63] In another experiment, people drank an unpleasant-tasting beverage, and then were asked to write down a lie on a small slip of paper that they liked it. They then immediately crumpled it up and threw away. Even though the lie could not possibly harm anyone, the act of lying nevertheless made the participants express more positive attitudes toward the drink.[64] In short, when we lie, we can start to believe our own lie.

We see an abundance of this phenomenon in everyday life. Routines that we hated when we were young such as practicing piano or praying slowly became part of our life and value system. Many people during the Nazi era did not believe in its agenda, but the frequent practice muted their conscience to be in sync with the behavior. It is a principle of brainwashing, based on the fact that our brain can become habitual to unfavorable conditions. Similarly, soldiers may not initially believe their enemies are evils, but frequent demonization of enemies will make them eventually believe that they are fighting evil ones. As a self-defense mechanism, we are able to paint others black to reduce internal conflict and justify our action. In the famous blue-eyes/brown-eyes experiment by Jane Elliott,[65] children were told that brown-eyed classmates were less intelligent and, hence, discrimination such as less recess time and sitting at the back of the room could be justified. As the consequence, the victims struggled on class assignments as the privileged blue-eyed viciously put them down. The role then reversed the next day with blue-eyed children now became the marginalized. This well-known experiment confirms a principle of brain's functioning: Once given a role, we soon act that role and gradually *become* that role.

The "foot-in-the-door" tactic is a good example that can be seen across all aspects of business and everyday life. Once people agree to go with the first step, they would feel an inner need to go all the way through, making their attitude consistent with their behavior. For example, in fund raising: "Can you sign this petition?" then "Can you make a donation?"; in sale: "Would you buy this product for a discount price?" then "Would you buy this part to make the product complete?"; in salary negotiation: "Would you prefer a flexible work hour?" then "Would you accept this salary?"; in diplomacy: "Would you accept an aid program from us?" then "Will you open the market for our products?"[66]

In the same principle, organizational change can start with action and reinforcement of the target action, even without having to spend time in convincing a complete change in thinking. A case in point is how a multimillion company has successfully changed their culture by focusing on desired behaviors.[67] Here is another example. A teacher often has students who are subtly or explicitly anti-Muslim in her class. Instead of trying to challenge their view firsthand, what she does is bring the whole group to a mosque, then let them walk around and talk to mosquegoers. Most of the time, she can see a change in their attitudes, evidenced by their reflection essays. Behavioral change can start with a change in the mind, but it is not a unidirectional process. Thought can be the child of action as well. And thus, an action can be a trigger to lead the mind. This is a strategy we will touch back in the chapter on change management (Chapter 7).

We tend to interpret most theories on cross-cultural management, such as those from Hall, Hofstede, and Trompenaars, and so forth, that culture and its values are quite stable. Because values are stable, they act as anchors, so we can predict behaviors. If you want to work effectively

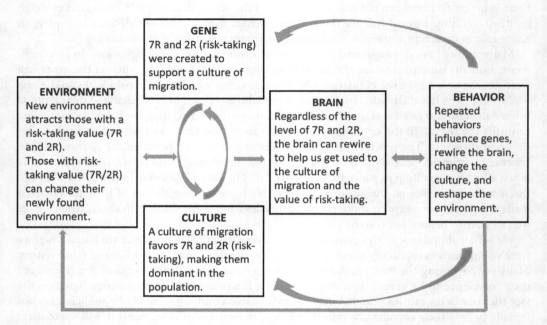

Figure 2.7 The interaction among environment, risk-taking genes, a culture of migration, the brain, and behaviors

with people from a different culture, you should learn their values. It is very reassuring because it reduces ambiguity. However, from the perspectives of evolutionary biology and neurosciences culture—as an evolving survival strategy—can't be static. Neural plasticity tells us that the brain physically rewires itself so we can forge new pathways, create new habits, and adapt to different cultures. In a sort of chicken and egg, so to speak, repeated thought and behaviors will create strong neural pathways, and in turn, these neural pathways will guide our behaviors and change even deep-rooted values, as we see in the example of China's one-child policy.

To conclude, behaviors interact with genes, brain, and culture in bi-directional ways. Genes give a template for behaviors, but repeated behaviors decide the content. The brain directs behaviors, but repeated behaviors reshape the very structure of the brain as well. Culture influences how we behave, but repeated behaviors can change even deep-seated values of culture. Behaviors are not only the result but also a driving force in the potential change of genes, culture, and environment. Thus, *culture is geographically influenced, socially learned, genetically inherited, neurally enabled, and constantly created.* Following our symbolic example of the 7R/2R alleles, we can add another of diversity's driving forces to our picture (Figure 2.7).

2.2.6 *Context as Indicator*

Context is represented by a circle that envelops all varieties of interaction. From the viewpoint of culture as a survival strategy that responds dynamically to internal and external factors, context becomes the ultimate power in terms of predicting the "change" within and between cultures. It implies that particular situations and circumstances will influence the interactions, prompting environment, genes, culture, brain, and behaviors to develop, adapt, and change in a particular way. The role of context is so crucial in understanding changes that Osland and Bird[68] suggested "indexing" context instead of indexing countries, while Oyserman and colleagues put forward the concept of "culture-as-situated cognition"[69] because everything we do is context dependent. Context helps us to understand complex aspects of change such as paradoxes and the dynamic speed of change across various time frames. From this point of view, understanding culture and its diversity becomes a quest of learning not only what culture "is" but also how culture "responds" and what kinds of circumstances and situations drive these responses. This is the reason why globalization and the change it induces can be so complex, depending on each specific local situation. The force of globalization can be so different in two neighboring villages, let alone two industries or two countries. As contexts differ, so does the nature of each scenario, so do the speed and result of the change. These dynamics can be traced down to the minuscule level of neural pathways within each individual. Subtle environmental cues, such as single and plural forms of a word, can act as powerful priming frameworks, activating relevant cultural mindsets and their associative networks in our brain. In line with this argument, the author of this book questioned the Hofstede's book's title and proposed that not culture, but particular context is the "software of the mind."[70]

In sum, the Diagram of Diversity Pathways demonstrates five factors (GCEB-Be) that underline the immense diversity we see in culture-related development of the human species, down to the level of gene and neuron. All factors dynamically and simultaneously relate to each other. Each factor is both a driving force and is under the impact of other factors at the same time. None of these factors is static. Cultural, neural, and genetic plasticity lead to an incredible behavioral ability to adapt to novel input and environment pressures across multiple levels of analysis.[71] Due to this complexity, any cultural analysis should take into account a particular context in which an event occurs because the force of environment, genes, brain, culture, and behaviors varies in each circumstance. We will use GCEB-Be as a framework to explore other topics in this book, knowing that such an interdisciplinary approach has the potential to provide us with new angles, encourage critical thinking, and even challenge conventional knowledge in the field.

To conclude, we have incorporated in this chapter insight from evolutionary biology and cultural neuroscience to gain a deep understanding of (1) the role of culture and (2) the driving forces of diversity. This interdisciplinary approach revealed a dynamic web of interaction. While this certainly poses challenges in doing business across cultures and contexts, the good news is, as a result of *exposure to different cultures* and purposely *changing our behaviors*, our brain can culturally attune to the target culture. It can forge new neural pathways, build new cells, and so forth. This enables us to adapt to any culture on demand. We take guidance from culture to fit in or change the very culture that hosts us. We do not just passively adapt to a way of living but we can also actively construct new customs, slowly change the values, influence our genes, reshape the surrounding environment, and rewire our brain structure. It is hence safe to say that, regardless of the complexity in the constant dividing and merging of local cultures in the process of globalization, a *capacity for cultural adaption and creation* can and will enable us to advance.

Summary

1. In animals, *genetic adaption* is the survival strategy. In humans, *culture adaption and creation* is the survival strategy. Instead of waiting for genes to evolve so we can fly, we pull ideas (culture) together and build airplanes. Instead of waiting for a gene that makes us dislike eating useful animals such as cows, we create a belief (culture) that makes cows sacred.
2. While genes are rather fixed, culture is dynamic. Humans can (1) fit in a culture and (2) actively reshape that culture.
3. International business involves using culture to navigate a market. Successful companies can (1) adapt to the local cultures and (2) actively reshape or create new cultures.

4. The Diversity Pathways GCEB-Be illustrates five driving forces that dynamically interact with each other to create the immense diversity we see in the world today:

    - C-E: The bi-directional interaction between C-culture and E-environment creates diversity in terms of (1) how geography influences the economy and psychology of the inhabitants, and (2) how cultural ways of living have dramatically reshaped the environment, making sustainability a top concern for business nowadays.
    - G-C-E: Environment exerts demands on culture and genes to adapt. A particular cultural value (e.g., risk-taking) can help humans to cope with the environment. This value favors a set of genes (e.g., 2R/7R), and in turn, these genes become dominant and reinforce that value in future generation.
    - GCEB-Be: Behaviors are not only the result but also the driving force to change genes, the brain, and culture: (1) Repeated behaviors can switch a gene on/off, regulate a gene up or down; (2) repeated behaviors can rewire the brain to help us fit in a new culture; and (3) repeated behaviors can change deeply seated values, even if we disliked that value initially.
    - Culture is geographically influenced, socially learned, genetically inherited, neurally enabled, and constantly created.

5. Context is a circle that envelops all varieties of interactions. It implies that particular situations and circumstances will influence the interactions, prompting environment, genes, culture, brain, and behaviors to develop, adapt, and change in a particular way. Not culture, but *context is the software of the mind*.

Notes

Don't forget to go to the end of the book for case studies.

1 Spencer, Herbert. 1864. *The Principles of Biology*, 444. Vol. 1. London: Williams and Norgate.
2 Pagel, Mark. 2012. *Wired for Culture: Origins of the Human Social Mind*. New York: W. W. Norton & Company.
3 Nguyen-Phuong-Mai, Mai. 2017. *Intercultural Communication—An Interdisciplinary Approach: When Neurons, Genes, and Evolution Joined the Discourse*. Vol. 18. Amsterdam, the Netherlands: Amsterdam University Press.
4 Sturgis, R. C. 2015. *The Mammals That Moved Mankind: A History of Beasts of Burden*. Bloomington, IN: Author House.
5 Simon, Bernard. 2008. "Humility Laced with Toughness," 18. *Financial Times*. September 3.
6 Maffi, Luisa., and Ellen Woodley. 2001. *On Biocultural Diversity*. Washington, DC: Smithsonian Institution Press.
7 Diamond, Jared. 1977. *Guns, Germs and Steel*. New York: W. W. Norton.
8 Office of Emerging Markets., John Luke Gallup, Jeffrey D. Sachs, and Andrew D. Mellinger. 1999. *Geography and Economic Development*. Center for International Development. http://pdf.usaid.gov/pdf_docs/Pnace757.pdf.
9 Karlsson, Sylvia. 2002. "The North-South Knowledge Divide: Consequences for Global Environmental Governance." In *Global Environmental Governance: Options and Opportunities*, ed. Daniel C. Esty and Maria H. Ivanova, 1–24. New Haven, CT: Yale Center for Environmental Law and Policy.
10 Koukakis, Nasos. 2016. "A Widening North-South Country Divide Threatens EU Solidarity." *CNBC*. September 9. www.cnbc.com/2016/09/09/eus-struggling-economies-meet-as-north-south-divide-widens.html.
11 Romei, Valentina. 2017. "North v South: Italy's Foreign Investment Gulf." *Financial Times*. June 29.
12 Laitin, David D., Joachim Moortgat, and Amanda Lea Robinson. 2012. "Geographic Axes and the Persistence of Cultural Diversity." *PNAS* 109(26): 10263–10268. doi:10.1073/pnas.1205338109.

13 Alesina, Alberto. 2003. "The Size of Countries: Does It Matter?" *Journal of the European Economic Association* 1(2–3): 301–316. doi:10.1162/154247603322390946.

14 Thompson, Derek. 2011. "How Geography Explains Economics for Germany and the U.S." *The Atlantic*. June 9. www.theatlantic.com/business/archive/2011/06/how-geography-explains-economics-for-germany-and-the-us/240222/.

15 Jacques, Jessica. 2016. "Island Mentality Shapes UK View of Europe." *The Irish Times*. June 9. www.irishtimes.com/student-hub/island-mentality-shapes-uk-view-of-europe-1.2676655.

16 Morgan, James. 1991. *Cracking the Japanese Market: Strategies for Success in the New Global Economy*. New York: Simon and Schuster.

17 Miller, Aaron David. 2013. "How Geography Explains the United States." *Foreign Policy*. April 16. http://foreignpolicy.com/2013/04/16/how-geography-explains-the-united-states/.

18 Boykin, Ryan. 2017. "Seasons Impact Real Estate More Than You Think." *Investopedia*. July 10. www.investopedia.com/articles/investing/010717/seasons-impact-real-estate-more-you-think.asp.

19 Cannon-Brookes, Michael. 2008. "The Empire Strikes Back," 12. *The Economist*. September 20.

20 Jowit, Juliette. 2010. "Humans Driving Extinction Faster Than Species Can Evolve, Say Experts." *The Guardian*. March 7. www.theguardian.com/environment/2010/mar/07/extinction-species-evolve.

21 Callicott, Baird J., and Michael Nelson, eds. 1998. *The Great New Wilderness Debate*. Athens, GA: University of Georgia Press.

22 Henderson, Rebecca M., A. Reinert Sophus, Polina Dekhtyar, and Amram Migdal. 2016. "Climate Change in 2017: Implications for Business." *Harvard Business School Background Note 317-032*. October. www.hbs.edu/faculty/Pages/item.aspx?num=51755.

23 Harvard Business School. 2016. "Climate Change Challenge." *Technology and Operations Management*. https://rctom.hbs.org/assignment/climate-change-challenge/.

24 Scharfstein, Rebecca. 2016. "Traveling to Iceland? Perhaps Think Twice." *Technology and Operations Management*. November 4. https://rctom.hbs.org/submission/traveling-to-iceland-perhaps-think-twice/.

25 Ebstein, Richard P., Olga Novick, Roberto Umansky, Beatrice Priel, Yamima Osher, Darren Blaine, Estelle R. Bennett, Lubov Nemanov, Miri Katz, and Robert H. Belmaker. 1996. "Dopamine D4 Receptor (D4DR) Exon III Polymorphism Associated with the Human Personality Trait of Novelty Seeking." *Nature Genetics* 12(1): 78–80.

26 Dreber, Anna., David G. Rand, Nils Wernerfelt, Justin R. Garcia, Miguel G. Vilar, J. Koji Lum, and Richard Zeckhauser. 2011. "Dopamine and Risk Choices in Different Domains: Findings among Serious Tournament Bridge Players." *Journal of Risk and Uncertainty* 43(1): 19–38.

27 Reist, Christopher., Vural Ozdemir, Eric Wang, Mehrtash Hashemzadeh, Steven Mee, and Robert Moyzis. 2007. "Novelty Seeking and the Dopamine D4 Receptor Gene (DRD4) Revisited in Asians: Haplotype Characterization and Relevance of the 2-Repeat Allele." *American Journal of Medical Genetics Part B: Neuropsychiatric Genetics* 144(4): 453–457.

28 Matthews, Luke J., and Paul M. Butler. 2011. "Novelty-Seeking DRD4 Polymorphisms Are Associated with Human Migration Distance Out-of-Africa after Controlling for Neutral Population Gene Structure." *American Journal of Physical Anthropology* 145(3): 382–389. doi:10.1002/ajpa.21507.

29 Wang, Eric. 2004. "The Genetic Architecture of Selection at the Human Dopamine Receptor D4 (DRD4) Gene Locus." *American Journal of Human Genetics* 74(5): 931–944. doi:10.1086/420854.

30 Jin, Bilian., Yajun Li, and Keith D. Robertson. 2011. "DNA Methylation: Superior or Subordinate in the Epigenetic Hierarchy?" *Genes and Cancer* 2(6): 607–617.

31 Bannister, Andrew J., and Tony Kouzarides. 2011. "Regulation of Chromatin by Histone Modifications." *Cell Research* 21(3): 381–395.

32 Ornish, Dean., Mark J. M. Magbanua, Gerdi Weidner, Vivian Weinberg, Colleen Kemp, Christopher Green, Michael D. Mattie et al. 2008. "Changes in Prostate Gene Expression in Men Undergoing an Intensive Nutrition and Lifestyle Intervention." *Proceedings of the National Academy of Sciences* 105(24): 8369–8374. doi:10.1073/pnas.0803080105.

33 Möller-Levet, Carla S., Simon N. Archer, Giselda Bucca, Emma E. Laing, Ana Slak, Renata Kabilijo, and June C. Y. Lo. 2013. "Effects of Insufficient Sleep on Circadian Rhythmicity and Expression Amplitude of the Human Blood Transcriptome." *PNAS* 110(12): E1132–E1141. www.pnas.org/content/110/12/E1132.abstract.

34 Chopra, Deepak., and Rudolph E. Tanzi. 2017. *Super Genes: Unlock the Astonishing Power of Your DNA for Optimum Health and Well-Being*. Vol. 1. New York: Harmony.

35 Galanter, Joshua M., Christopher R. Gignoux, Sam S. Oh, Dara Torgerson Maria Pino-Yanes, Neeta Thakur, Celeste Eng et al. 2017. "Differential Methylation between Ethnic Sub-Groups Reflects the Effect of Genetic Ancestry and Environmental Exposures." *ELife* 6. doi:10.7554/elife.20532.

36 Weinhold, Bob. 2006. "Epigenetics: The Science of Change." *Environmental Health Perspectives* 114(3): 160–167. www.ncbi.nlm.nih.gov/pmc/articles/PMC1392256/.

37 Tobi, Elmar W., Jelle J. Goeman, Ramin Monajemi, Hongcang Gu, Hein Putter, Yanju Zhang, Roderick C. Slieker et al. 2014. "DNA Methylation Signatures Link Prenatal Famine Exposure to Growth and Metabolism." *Nature Communications* 5: 5592.

38 Ekamper, Peter., F. van Poppel, A. D. Stein, and L. H. Lumey. 2014. "Independent and Additive Association of Prenatal Famine Exposure and Intermediary Life Conditions with Adult Mortality between Age 18–63 Years." *Social Science and Medicine* 119: 232–239.

39 Yehuda, Rachel., Nikolaos P. Daskalakis, Linda M. Bierer, Heather N. Bader, Torsten Klengel, Florian Holsboer, and Elisabeth B. Binder. 2016. "Holocaust Exposure Induced Intergenerational Effects on FKBP5 Methylation." *Biological Psychiatry* 80(5): 372–380.

40 Osborne, Alexander. 2017. "The Role of Epigenetics in Human Evolution." *Bioscience Horizons: The International Journal of Student Research* 10: n.a.

41 Pembrey, Marcus E. 2018. "Does Cross-Generational Epigenetic Inheritance Contribute to Cultural Continuity? " *Environmental Epigenetics* 4(2): dvy004.

42 Nicolaou, Nicos., Scott Shane, Lynn Cherkas, Janice Hunkin, and Tim Spector. 2008. "Is the Tendency to Engage in Entrepreneurship Genetic?" *Management Science* (January): 167–179. doi:10.1287/mnsc.1070.0761.

43 Shane, Scott. 2010. *Born Entrepreneurs, Born Leaders: How Your Genes Affect Your Work Like*. Oxford: Oxford University Press.

44 Chi, Wei., Wen-Dong Li, Nan Wang, and Zhaoli Song. 2016. "Can Genes Play a Role in Explaining Frequent Job Changes? An Examination of Gene-Environment Interaction from Human Capital Theory." *Journal of Applied Psychology* 101(7): 1030–1044.

45 Lynch, Kate. 2018. "Explainer: What Is Heritability?" *The Conversation*. January 1. http://theconversation.com/explainer-what-is-heritability-21334.

46 Baggini, Julian. 2015. "Do Your Genes Determine Your Entire Life? | Julian Baggini." *The Guardian*. March 19. www.theguardian.com/science/2015/mar/19/do-your-genes-determine-your-entire-life.

47 Miller, Gregory E., Edith Chen, Alexandra K. Fok , Hope Walker, Alvin Lim, Erin F. Nicholls, Steve Cole, and Michael S. Kobor. 2009. "Low Early-Life Social Class Eaves a Biological Residue Manifested by Decreased Glucocorticoid and Increased Proinflammatory Signaling." *Proceedings of the National Academy of Science* 106(34): 14716–14721. doi:10.1073/pnas.0902971106.

48 Ashraf, Quamrul., and Oded Galor. 2013. "The 'Out of Africa' Hypothesis, Human Genetic Diversity, and Comparative Economic Development." *American Economic Review* 103(1): 1–46. www.aeaweb.org/articles?id=10.1257/aer.103.1.1.

49 Azevedo, Frederico A. C., Ludmila R. B. Carvalho, Lea T. Grinberg, José Marcelo Farfel, Renata E. L. Ferretti, Roberto Lent, and Suzana Herculano-Houzel. 2009. "Equal Numbers of Neuronal and Nonneuronal Cells Make the Human Brain an Isometrically Scaled-Up Primate Brain." *The Journal of Comparative Neurology* 513(5): 532–541. doi:10.1002/cne.21974.

50 Bartol, Thomas M., Cailey Bromer, Justin Kinney, Michael A. Chirillo, Jennifer N. Bourne, Kristen M. Harris, and Terrence J. Sejnowski. 2015. "Nanoconnectomic Upper Bound on the Variability of Synaptic Plasticity." *e Life* 4: e10778. doi:10.7554/eLife.10778.

51 Telegraph Reporter. 2016. "Human Brain Can Store 4.7 Billion Books: Ten Times More Than Originally Thought." *The Telegraph*. January 21. www.telegraph.co.uk/news/science/science-news/12114150/Human-brain-can-store-4.7-billion-books-ten-times-more-than-originally-thought.html.

52   Maguire, Eleanor A. 2000. "Navigation-Related Structural Change in the Hippocampi of Taxi Drivers." *Proceedings of the National Academy of Science USA* 97(8): 4398–4403. doi:10.1073/pnas.070039597.

53   Yeh, Ray. 2017. "At 97, This Vietnamese Grandma Has Mastered the Internet." *Channel NewsAsia.* May 27. www.channelnewsasia.com/news/cnainsider/at-97-this-vietnamese-grandma-has-mastered-the-internet-8888460.

54   Pusparani, Indah Gilang. 2017. "Meet 81-Year-Old Rock Star Granny from Singapore." *Good News from Southeast Asia.* https://seasia.co/2017/08/09/meet-81-year-old-rock-star-granny-from-singapore.

55   Freeman, Jonathan B., Nicholas O. Rule, Reginald B. Adams Jr, and Nalini Ambady. 2009. "Culture Shapes a Mesolimbic Response to Signals of Dominance and Subordination that Associates with Behaviour." *NeuroImage* 47(1): 353–359. doi:10.1016/j.neuroimage.2009.04.038.

56   Jenks, Kyle., Taekeun Kim, Elissa Pastuzyn, Hiroyuki Okuno, Andrew Taibi, Haruhiko Bito, Mark Bear, and Jason Shepherd. 2017. "Arc Restores Juvenile Plasticity in Adult Mouse Visual Cortex." *PNAS* 114(34): 9182–9187. doi:10.1073/pnas.1700866114.

57   Sudbeck, Kristine. 2012. "The Effects of China's One-Child Policy: The Significance for Chinese Women." *Nebraska Anthropologist*, Paper 179.

58   Levin, Dan. 2014. "Many in China Can Now Have a Second Child, but Say No." *The New York Times.* February 25. www.nytimes.com/2014/02/26/world/asia/many-couples-in-china-will-pass-on-a-new-chance-for-a-second-child.html?mcubz=1.

59   Aronson, Elliot. 1992. "The Return of the Repressed: Dissonance Theory Makes a Comeback." *Psychological Inquiry* 3(4): 303–311. doi:10.1207/s15327965pli0304_1.

60   Bem, Daryl J. 1970. *Beliefs, Attitudes, and Human Affairs.* Belmont, CA: Brooks/Cole.

61   Izuma, Keise., Shyam Akula, Kou Murayama, Daw-An Wu, Marco Iacoboni, and Ralph Adolphs. 2015. "A Causal Role for Posterior Medial Frontal Cortex in Choice-Induced Preference Change." *The Journal of Neuroscience* 35(8): 3598–3606. doi:10.1523/JNEUROSCI.4591-14.2015.

62   Festinger, Leon., and James M. Carlsmith. 1959. "Cognitive Consequences of Forced Compliance." M. Brewster Smith, ed., *Journal of Abnormal and Social Psychology* 58(2): 203–210. doi:10.1037/h0041593.

63   Brehm, Jack W. 1956. "Postdecision Changes in the Desirability of Alternatives." M. Brewster Smith, ed., *Journal of Abnormal and Social Psychology* 52(3): 384–389. doi:10.1037/h0041006.

64   Harmon-Jones, Eddie., Jack W. Brehm, Jeff Greenberg, Linda Simon, and David E. Nelson. 1996. "Evidence That the Production of Aversive Consequences Is Not Necessary to Create Cognitive Dissonance." Arie W. Kruglanski, ed., *Journal of Personality and Social Psychology* 70(1): 5–16. doi:10.1037/0022-3514.70.1.5.

65   Peters, William. 1987. *A Class Divided: Then and Now.* New Haven, CT: Yale University Press.

66   Mar, Anna. 2013. "Foot in the Door Sales Strategy." *Simplicable.* http://business.simplicable.com/business/new/foot-in-the-door-sales-strategy.

67   Power, Brad. 2014. "If You're Going to Change Your Culture, Do It Quickly." *Harvard Business Review.* August 7. https://hbr.org/2013/11/if-youre-going-to-change-your-culture-do-it-quickly.

68   Osland, Joyce S., and Allan Bird. 2000. "Beyond Sophisticated Stereotyping: Cultural Sensemaking in Context." *Academy of Management Executive* 14(1): 65–79.

69   Oyserman, Daphna., Sheida Novin, Nic Flinkenflogel, and Lydia Krabbendam. 2014. "Integrating Culture-as-Situated-Cognition and Neuroscience Prediction Models." *Culture Brain* 2(1): 1–26. doi:10.1007/s40167-014-0016-6.

70   Nguyen-Phuong-Mai, Mai. 2017. "Intercultural Communication—An Interdisciplinary Approach: Context Is Software of the Mind." Keynote roundtable ELLTA Conference, July 24–28, Bangkok.

71   Chiao, Joan Y., and Ying-Yi Hong. n.d. "Cultural Neuroscience: Understanding Human Diversity." In *Advances in Culture Psychology*, ed. Michele J. Gelfand and Chie-yue Chiu, 1–77. Oxford: Oxford University Press.

3 The Tree of Culture
Evolutionary and Practical

In Chapter 2, we have used biology to understand the role of culture as the survival strategy for human species. In the evolutionary sense, if culture is the strategy to survive, then it could be said that *there is only one culture*—a dynamic human function that we create and which in turn creates us. But its product is an incredible tapestry of diversity in all aspects: Cognitive, physical, material, spiritual, conscious, and subconscious. A simple comparison between any two cultures will attest this observation. Let's also not forget that we (sub)consciously create many local cultures and ingroups to recognize whom we can trust. Human's capacity for culture (in the evolutionary sense) has produced a myriad of particular sets of values and behaviors (in the practical sense). In short, *culture produces cultures*.[1] The former is an evolutionary mechanism, the latter is the reality we witness every day. The former has been discussed in the previous chapter. It will now be combined with the latter to be the focus in this chapter.

3.1 The Metaphorical Tree of Culture

As an "archive" of survival strategies, a culture consists of myriad elements that constantly evolve to serve the purpose of helping humans to advance. In this book, we will use the metaphor of a *tree* to help us understand this complexity. A typical tree has three layers: Its trunk and roots, branches, and a massive canopy of twigs and leaves. So does our culture.

3.1.1 Fundamental Concerns

The roots and the trunk of the tree represent fundamental concerns, or the building blocks of our culture. They are generic with fundamental elements such as politics, arts, religions, and languages—components that help us to be less dependent on genes and move ahead of other species in the animal kingdom. None of them can produce a product that directly affects our reproduction and survival, but they are *cultural enhancers*, evolved to increase our performance.[2]

Here is an example. Music has been evolved to be a cultural instrument that is sharper than any weapon, more powerful than any army, and more effective than any leader. Evolutionarily speaking, any human group that failed to acquire music as a cultural strategy could find themselves in competition with those who had. When our ancestors fought their battles, warriors were energized by the patriotic rhythm of battle cries. Heroes were immortalized in folksongs. In the modern era, "sonic weapon" is a case in point. During the Cold War, the United States deployed a secret instrument in its fight against communism: Jazz.[3] US musicians traveled to all parts of the world as ambassadors of the value that the United States wanted its friends and foes to see: Black artists embraced the freedom of enjoying, cooperating, and creating their own magical, deep, soft, and enlightened world of music. It challenged the stereotypes and propaganda that projected the United States as being racially divided, aggressive, and culturally hollow. Globalization has given music extra power, as we see with the case of K-pop. In 2015, the United Kingdom led the world in soft power ranking,[4] thanks to a great contribution from its music industry as UK artists sold a third of Top 40 best-selling albums worldwide.[5] Thus, music in itself does not directly create any food or shelter, but as a cultural enhancer, it is evolutionarily and fundamentally a basic concern that all human societies have to care about, unless they want to be left behind.

Similarly, what we often term "values," such as "loyalty" and "freedom," are the building blocks of culture as well. Regardless of structure, size, or time of existence, all human societies have to embrace them to survive. Take "loyalty" as an example. For animals, they follow their gene's instruction to express their loyalty and attachment to their own kind. Their DNA tells them to live as solitary or herd animals. Depending on the size of the prey and the amount of food needed to consume per day, animals evolve to live alone or with others. For instance, a single kill of a zebra can feed several females at once, so lions live in a pride. But a single kill of a mouse can only feed one cat, and that's why cats tend to be on their own. This survival strategy has been coded in their genetic structure, and animals can't deliberately change it. If any change happens, it has to be evolved over many generations.

Humans are fundamentally herd animals, as we live with others and obtain from them the culture needed to survive. However, the level of loyalty and attachment we have toward our ingroup is not as well-defined by genes as it is among animals. In essence, it is the products of (1) cultural upbringing; (2) reinforced by genes; (3) in interaction with environmental circumstances; (4) shaped by repeated behaviors; and (5) the plasticity of the brain (see the Diversity Pathways GCEB-Be in Chapter 2). We are capable of being extremely attached to an ingroup, or living a relatively solitary life. We can be *loyal to different groups at different times*: A family, a school, a company, a religion, a country, a favorite restaurant, a leader, or an ideology. We can also switch loyalty, using it as a survival mechanism to fit in new situations, build a new culture, or influence others. No group understands this better than the one million Druze in the Middle East. As their homeland spreads across three countries with conflicts: Israel, Lebanon, and Syria, the strategy to survive in this hostile situation is to have *strategic loyalty*. They maintain loyalty to the country in which they live, but carefully protect their religion so to avoid total assimilation. Loyalty is not a trait out of the blue, for the Druze it is a survival strategy.

In the business world, a quick look at the many varieties of corporate loyalty programs will tell us how this trait has been a vital strategy in management. "Reward loyalty" helps to build a customer base, and "employee loyalty" helps to motivate workers. However, if the organizations do not meet the expectation, customers' and employees' loyalty will fade away. They will seek attachment to a new company or a new brand. In essence, group loyalty among humans is a versatile instrument, a fundamental and basic mechanism for us to both (1) adapt to a culture and (2) influence and create a culture.

Thus, from this evolutionarily point of view, what we often label as values such as hierarchy, loyalty, or freedom belong to the category of "fundamental concerns." Name any value you can think of, and mostly, it will turn out to be essential in any human society. Evolutionarily speaking, they are not values, but are critical cultural strategies. "Hierarchy" helps us to organize resources effectively, while "equality" safeguards fairness; "empathy" connects us emotionally while "competition" motivates us to strive forward; "discipline" ensures orderliness while "freedom" allows creativity, and so forth. In the evolutionary sense, we don't speak of bad or negative cultural strategies. If they exist, there must be a reason for it, be it "competitiveness," "discrimination," or "dominance." Regardless of the salience they represent in a society, these cultural strategies

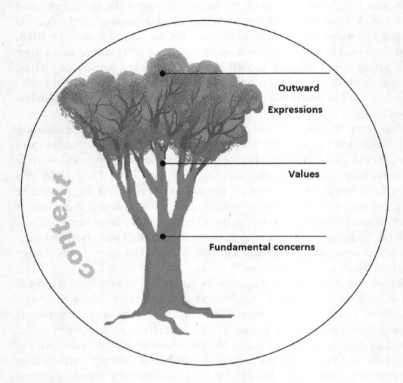

Figure 3.1 The metaphorical tree of culture

are shared by all and understood by all. They are the commonality and sameness among us as human beings, without which we will be disadvantaged in the survival game. This is the "culture" in the evolutionary sense. There is only one, and we all share it. The metaphorical tree of culture is illustrated in Figure 3.1.

3.1.2 Value

Values are defined as the *degree of importance* we place on a certain concern, and they are represented by the branches of the metaphorical tree. The "degree of importance" starts at the *baseline* level. Above the baseline level, the differing degrees of importance we place on these concerns create the tapestry of diverse culture in reality. This is the "culture" the in practical sense. And there are many.

To continue with "loyalty," above the baseline level, the degree of how important loyalty is can be very different for a particular person, a specific group, or a unique context: *High, low, and everywhere in between.* The length of a branch (read "loyalty") can be very short, close to the baseline or very long, strong, and dominant. For example, in Japan, the term "corporate samurai" refers to ultraloyal employees, who normally have lifetime employment and would rather die than betray the company. We can say that corporate loyalty has a *high* value in traditional Japanese companies. However, making this generalization is risky because this high value does not necessarily count for all companies and contexts. In the aftermath of multiple recessions, freelancing has become a trend in this country. Historically, it has been a norm in Japan that one starts and ends her/his career with a single company. As the situation changes, freelancers now account for 17% of the nation's working population, and the number is rising.[6] Outside Japan, the flux of young and ambitious workforce also creates changes. According to SAP's Workforce 2020 survey, just 27% of executives in the Asia-Pacific region considered long-term loyalty and retention as a critical component in their talent strategy,[7] a significant shift of human resources (HR) strategy in the region. What we learn from this loyalty example is that for culture in the practical sense, the tree branches are dynamic. They can grow and they can shrink, changing their size in response to the environment. So do the values. They can be at the baseline and change between high, low, and average.

In short, to indicate values, we can simply ask "Above the baseline level, how important is XYZ for this person, in this society, organization, or situation?" This counts for almost every cultural notion we can think of, such as integrity, competition, altruism, freedom, democracy, bravery, wealth, and power. These are fundamental concerns (i.e., culture in the evolutionary sense, there is only one for the whole humankind), and values are the *degree of importance above the baseline level* that each group, individual, or context places on them (i.e., cultures in practical sense, there are many among the humankind).

3.1.3 *Outward Expressions*

Represented by the leaves and the canopy of the metaphorical tree, outward expressions are visible, tangible *objects*, *symbols*, and *behaviors*—manifestations of concerns and values. It is the myriad of things such as specific kinds of tools, specific styles of houses and technology, specific words and documents, specific policies, and specific actions and practices. This diversity and complexity are what we witness in culture every day.

In our example of work loyalty, the outward expressions of this fundamental concern manifest themselves in an intricate web of specific behaviors, policies, incidents, and communication. For example, a "high value" in work loyalty can be seen in outward expressions such as long-term employment, seniority-based pay system, or the way managers and staff agree to cut their salary to help the company through a difficult time instead of downsizing. When an employee chooses to prioritize company over private life, (s)he is elevating the value of work loyalty. In an extreme case, a Japanese government civil worker was too busy meeting an important deadline that he failed to be at his wife's deathbed—a behavior (outward expression) that is less frequent today but is respected and understood by older workers.[8]

On the contrary, a "low value" in work loyalty manifests itself in outward expressions such as high turnover, job switching, low commitment, having multiple jobs, working for competitors, and so forth. We may see employees being punished for staying too long in a job. It sounds absurd at first, but we should factor in (1) the average inflation rate of 2%; (2) the average annual raise of 3%; and (3) the average raise an employee receives for leaving, usually between 10 and 20%.[9] This means employees get only 1% raise each year for being loyal, and have the possibility to double their incomes by switching jobs several times. This policy regarding salary raise is an outward expression that reflects a low value some companies place on work loyalty.

To conclude, in our "tree of culture," the roots/trunk of the tree represent shared fundamental concerns of all societies, regardless of backgrounds. They are the building blocks and cultural enhancers that help humankind advance. The branches of the tree represent values. At the baseline level, values are evolutionary, that is the minimum degree of importance all human societies place on a certain concern to survive. Beyond the baseline level is value in the practical culture, with various degrees of importance (high, low, average) for each specific group, individual, or context. The canopy represents visible outward expressions. Humans everywhere universally share a certain number of objects, symbols, and behaviors. But beyond this is culture in the practical sense. It refers to the immense diversity of culture we see with our own eyes in the world around us.

3.2 A Framework of Fundamental Concerns

With the metaphorical tree of culture, we now understand why, from the evolutionary point of view, fundamental concerns such as loyalty and hierarchy at the baseline level are the building blocks of any human group. Those who failed to acquire them and dynamically use them contextually would risk losing out to those who had.

To gain a better understanding of these concerns, we face a challenge: They are virtually endless. There is a need to simplify this exhaustive list, despite the fact that such simplification risks oversight. This is a task that many theorists struggled with. Kluckhohn and Strodtbeck[10] were among the first to come up with five universal concerns: (1) The relationship between an individual and others; (2) the aspect of time that is our primary focus; (3) the relationship between humans and nature; (4) the prime motivation for behavior; and (5) the moral nature of human beings.

Kluckhohn and Strodtbeck's framework has inspired many theorists to work on different taxonomies, such as Hall, Hofstede, and Trompenaars. In this section, we will take a look at some of the most cited concerns: Group attachment, hierarchy acceptance, gender association, uncertainty avoidance, and time orientation. We will briefly explore how these concerns play a crucial role in our strategies for survival (i.e., culture in the evolutionary sense), and the ways in which different cultures, individuals, and contexts call for different values and outward expressions (i.e., culture in the practical sense).

3.2.1 Group Attachment

3.2.1.1 Group Attachment as Universal and Fundamental Concern

In the metaphorical tree of culture, group attachment is represented by the trunk and the roots of the tree. The main reason why group attachment is a fundamental concern is because we are a cultural species who uses culture instead of gene to survive. We are born with a very perceptive mind, ready to join and attach to the first cultural group we see after birth. Hence, it is natural that we have evolved to love our own culture and ingroup. Our ancestors spent thousands of years on the savannah, living in close-knit communities, where the ingroup was their source of survival, identity, advancement, and protection. On the contrary, outgroup can mean "threat." A quick decision on who is a friend or foe could mean a difference between life and death.

According to the Diversity Pathways GCEB-Be, because ingroup culture is our survival strategy, genes have evolved to create a biological mechanism that allows us to quickly recognize our ingroup or those we can trust (Gene—Culture pathway). In general, we can read the emotions of those who come from the same culture with us much easier.[11] As uncomfortable as it may sound, ingroup bias is rooted in our evolution and we have evolved to love our culture and, together with this love, to have an inherent suspicion and dislike toward other groups.[12-13] In our brain, the amygdala—a subcortical structure in the anterior-temporal lobe that regulates emotion and acts as a danger detector or warning system[14-15]—becomes more active when we see someone who looks different from us, indicating an outgroup member, and thus a potential threat (Gene—Culture—Brain pathway).[16-17] Neural studies show that we also feel less empathy toward outsiders and more empathy toward our own ingroup.[18-19-20-21] When observing Korean people suffering from pain, Korean participants exhibited strong activation of the left temporoparietal junction (TPJ)—a brain region associated with perspective taking. The empathy signal was weaker when those who suffered from pain came from the United States—an outgroup.[22]

In sum, genes have coevolved with culture and prepared us by giving us the biological ability to effectively fit into *any group* at birth, and to be on alert against any outgroup members. In the same vein, the brain's plasticity has also prepared us by giving us the incredible capacity to adjust to *new groups* during the course of our life. As a value, *group attachment is defined as the extent to which one gives her/his ingroup priority over oneself.*

3.2.1.2 The Diversity in Group Attachment

While a minimum amount of group attachment is needed for all human societies, beyond the baseline level, the degree of importance varies across national cultures, organizational cultures, group cultures, individuals, and particular contexts. The value of group attachment can be at any level higher than the baseline: Weak, strong, and everywhere in between. Some people prepare to die for their own ingroup, some are happy to loosely connect. The common stereotypes are that Western cultures are more individualistic (i.e., weak attachment) and Eastern cultures are more collectivistic (i.e., strong attachment). This differing level of value is represented by the branches of the metaphorical tree.

In terms of outward expressions, or the canopy of the tree, beyond the universal components, group attachment manifests itself in specific and tangible way people use to maintain group harmony, keep face, build trust, and rely on support they can get from each other. When weak group attachment prevails (i.e., individualistic), these outward expressions are less important than when strong group attachment prevails (i.e., collectivistic).

Here are some examples of the outward expressions produced by weak versus strong group attachment. Following pathway Culture—Brain, self-construal studies have proved that the brain is culturally formed according to the level of group attachment one experiences in the culture of her/his group. For example, Chinese participants in a study tended to have a neural overlap when they thought about themselves and their mother.[23] It seems culture has constructed their brain so that "myself" and "my mother" are more or less the same person. The tendency to diffuse the "self" and "related others" also suggests why compared to British subjects, Chinese subjects showed weaker advantage for recognizing their own face over familiar faces.[24]

The weak versus strong emphasis on the "self" leads to differences on how people evaluate their own achievement and ability. For example, compared to European Americans, East Asians demonstrate lower levels of unrealistic optimism of their own outcomes, show less self-serving bias, and have less biased memories for their own success, with weaker evidence of self-enhancement or even negative view of the self.[25] This is supported by a neural study in which the US participants with European backgrounds showed stronger evidence of self-enhancement whereas the Chinese participants showed stronger evidence for other-enhancing bias.[26]

With regard to motivation, strong group attachment influences how people make choices. A number of neural studies suggest that for those who embrace collectivistic values, a reward for themselves is similar to a reward for their close others such as their mothers or friends.[27-28] In a study with Latino participants, the brain's signal of reward for others was even stronger than that for themselves, prompting the researchers to conclude that for these participants, they were "gaining while giving."[29] We will look deeper into the neuroscience of motivation across cultures in Chapter 10.

It's tempting to think of strong group attachment (collectivism) and weak group attachment (individualism) as one spectrum along which a culture can be measured. However, this static view is problematic. For example, a 2015 study found that values are dynamic: Both individualism and collectivism coexist in Canada, and individualism characterizes Morocco even more than Canada.[30] Another study comparing this value in Vietnam, China, and the United States shows that North Vietnam scores high for both individualism and collectivism.[31] In countries with a rich history of immigration, multiculturalism, or a fast pace of development, paradoxes and changes are the norm and not the exception. Further, cultural borders among different groups overlap each other. In the Middle East for example, tribal loyalty is much more influential than religious affinity or even national pride. In a study, 62% of Middle Eastern people expected their governments to do what is good for either Muslims or Arabs generally, while only 31% thought that national policies should benefit their own country.[32] In sum, different identities and affinities with different collective cultures, such as clans, tribes, religious sects, ethnicities, companies, and nationalities, make it problematic to rely solely on a static country index. Rather, to know the level of group attachment, the appropriate question should be: "Which group?"

In our metaphorical tree of culture, while group attachment is a fundamental concern (the trunk and the roots), collectivism and individualism can be presented as *two separate branches* of the tree or two values. The suggestion to see them as two or more separate values is supported by a number of studies. The GLOBE study[33] identified two types of collectivism: Institutional collectivism (which maximizes the interests of the collective) and ingroup collectivism (loyalty, pride, and cohesiveness within a group). Triandis and colleagues[34] distinguished four separate dimensions: Vertical individualism (individuals want to be distinct and desire special status); horizontal individualism (individuals want to be distinct *without* desiring special status); vertical collectivism (individuals want interdependence and competition with outgroups), and horizontal collectivism (individuals want interdependence but do not submit easily to authority). We will look further at the dynamics of culture in Chapter 4.

3.2.1.3 Where Does This Diversity Come From?

The reason why there are differing levels of group attachment among human societies is probably rooted in our survival need. Here is a hypothesis: In the ancient time, our ancestors migrated from Africa to many different regions of the world. In the new environment, pathogens—infectious agents, such as bacteria and fungus—are a risk factor because they cause diseases. To cope with the constant risk of infection, our ancestors didn't just wait for genes to evolve an immune system to battle diseases, as is the case in animals. Instead, they slowly developed a cultural strategy to deal with high pathogen loads: A group-oriented mindset that conforms to collective rules regarding sanitation, food preparation, and so forth. Over a period, those who followed the cultural rules of group conformity had a higher chance of survival. These conformers also tend to have a high rate of s5-HTTLPR—the shorter variant of a gene that encodes serotonin transporters. This short version makes people *more sensitive* to emotions, causing their amygdala to have increased activation compared to those who carry the long allele.[35] This sensitivity is critical because it helps people to read others' mood quickly and precisely, making it easier to understand the importance of the group's rules and the significance of following those rules, avoid actions that can cause negative emotional states in others, and be cautious in expressing individual opinions that may damage social harmony.[36] Because social sensitivity and heightened selective attention were crucial and rewarded,[37] in areas with high loads of pathogens, those with s5-HTTLPR were more successful in reproduction, and s5-HTTLPR slowly became dominant. Pathogens are historically high in warm and moist climates such as East Asia, which may explain why humans who migrated there developed a *higher* need for social sensitivity, and the population of East Asia also has twice the rate of s5-HTTLPR in comparison with the Western population.[38] Thus, group mindset became a strategic cultural value to cope with pathogens, and genes coevolved to reinforce the desirable value (Environment—Culture—Gene pathway).[39-40] *Culture is not only socially learned but culture is also genetically inherited.*

On a side note, being more sensitive to emotions also means s5-HTTLPR is connected with depression (however, note that this serotonin hypothesis has been challenged).[41] Because a group mindset favors s5-HTTLPR, it also means East Asian people also have a higher rate of depression genes. Interestingly, this doesn't make them more vulnerable to depression. The opposite happens. Despite having more depression gene, East Asian people are much less depressed than other populations.[42] There are several hypotheses for this paradox, for example, East Asians avoid acknowledging depression for fear of losing face or being perceived as having a weak personality.[43] Another plausible hypothesis that aligns with the gene-culture coevolution is that values of social harmony and support act as buffers to reduce stress and resultant affective disorders among genetically susceptible populations. Nations with greater historical and con-temporary prevalence of disease-causing pathogens (e.g., malaria, typhus, and leprosy) are more likely to embrace collectivism due to its anti-pathogen defense function. Nature has made a brilliant trade-off. As long as a person with s5-HTTLPR can *attach* strongly to her/his ingroup, (s)he will be happy, despite having the "depression gene". Social support in such a society can "mute" the destructive effect of the gene and prevent them from causing damage (GCEB-Be: Behavior—Gene pathway). In a study,[44] abused children with the short variant of 5-HTTLPR in both copies of the gene suffered at almost twice the rate as did maltreated children with the long/long or the short/long variant. However, social support can regulate this effect. Even a modest form of social support such as monthly contact with trusted mentor figures can eliminate about 80% of the combined risk of gene and environmental risk. In fact, short allele carriers are at no higher risk for depression provided that they have good social support.[45] This is another example of how DNA is fixed, but through repeated behaviors, the epigenomes on top of DNA can regulate the expression of genes (see Chapter 2).

While an ancient environment with high loads of pathogens might have influenced the original root of strong group attachment, contexts have driven the diversity of this value beyond a simple pattern connected with environment. For example, economic development can dynamically increase *or* decrease group attachment.[46] A study suggested that that those of lower socioeconomic status are more helpful and generous.[47] Poor people learn to solve problems by turning to others, relying on others to watch for their back. Such a way of living increases empathy and strengthens social bonds. Another factor that influences the level of group attachment is external threat. When there is a perceived threat from outside, a common goal can be reinforced, bringing individuals together. The rise of populism and nationalism in the United States and Europe since 2010 illustrates clearly how far-right leaders can unite a large number of voters under the banner of protecting national identity and stability. In short, the level of group attachment in different cultures should be seen in a specific context because environment, gene, brain, and collective behaviors can dynamically interact and result in a very particular pattern of collectivism and individualism.

3.2.2 Hierarchy Acceptance

3.2.2.1 Hierarchy Acceptance as a Universal and Fundamental Concern

Hierarchy was born out of evolutionary pressure. This is true at all levels of organization, be it a biological system or a manmade system such as a machine. In essence, the main reason for hierarchy is the *cost of connection*.[48] Connections are expensive because they have to be designed, built, and maintained. Imagine you want to a keep good relationship with 20 people on an individual basis. That sounds just fine, especially in a small hunter-gatherer group, but your life in the modern era can't run smoothly if you only know 20 people because everything from shopping, traveling, cooking, and so forth needs thousands, if not hundreds of thousands or millions of people involved to produce an end product. Hierarchy came into existence to reduce the number of connections you need to make and maintain, in the same way as you organize files into different levels of folders on the computer. In human societies, this is also the starting point of labor division, which allows for better extraction of resources.[49] Now, you only need to know the shop's owner to get the groceries, and it is *her/his* responsibility to make other connections and ensure a smooth chain of supply. Everyone does not need to know everyone else. For this reason, hierarchy has evolved to become an element of culture—the survival strategy for human beings. In our tree of culture, hierarchy acceptance is represented by the trunk and the roots of the tree.

Universally, hierarchy is a fundamental concern because it is needed for the advancement of the whole community. Human groups everywhere are organized into a hierarchy, and hierarchical groups ultimately outlived egalitarian groups.[50] All of us accept, to a baseline degree, that we are not equal. No matter where you come from, you will always acknowledge that your tribal leader, your managers, your parents, your teachers, and even those who are older than you have a degree or two more prestige, status, and resources than you do. Put any two persons in a room, in the end we will have a senior and a junior. Hence, *hierarchy acceptance indicates the extent to which subordinates accept a hierarchical (unequal) distribution of prestige, status, influential power, and resources between them and their superiors.* It was named "relation to authority" by Inkeles and Levinson,[51] "lineal" versus "collateral" by Kluckhohn and Strodtbeck,[52] "power distance" by Hofstede,[53] and "achievement" versus "ascription" by Trompenaars and Hampden-Turner.[54]

3.2.2.2 The Diversity in Hierarchy Acceptance

In terms of value, the level of hierarchy acceptance varies from a baseline level, to weak and strong, and everywhere in between. This variation depends on national cultures, organizational cultures, group cultures, individuals, and particular context. The common stereotypes are that Western cultures are less likely to accept hierarchy, while Eastern cultures are more likely to accept hierarchy. This differing level of value is represented by the branches of the metaphorical tree.

In term of outward expressions, that is the tree's canopy, the relationship between superiors and subordinates is two-way, manifesting itself in how people specifically give respect and care, express loyalty and protection, and show obedience and guidance. Some employees show absolute respect, loyalty, and obedience to the authority, while others challenge or makes joke about their bosses and jump jobs. Some managers care deeply for their employees, giving them full attention and detailed instruction, while others expect their staff to exercise autonomy and self-decision making.

Neuroscience offers some interesting insight. While human adults typically respond faster to their own face than to the faces of others, the "boss effect" suggests that those who embrace strong hierarchy acceptance respond faster to their supervisor's face than to their own (pathway Culture—Brain).[55]

Of course, this does not mean that people were born with this mindset. Culture is learned, and the brain's plasticity means one's cultural values can change. Various factors interact and create an intricate web of paradoxes and complexity. For example, stereotypically seen as a culture with strong hierarchy acceptance, Brazil also gives us Semco—an exemplar of flat hierarchy in the corporate world. Here, your question of "who is charge?" will be answered with: "No one."[56]

3.2.2.3 Where Does This Diversity Come From?

The differing level of importance that various human groups place on hierarchy acceptance can be traced back in time using GCEB-Be. Here is a hypothesis: Similar to the case of group attachment, during the early human migration, in some parts of the world, the prevalence of pathogens in the environment posed a risk for our ancestors. To cope with the situation, they developed a culture of group mindset *and* hierarchical dominance. This is especially true in environments with a high level of territorial and resource threats[57]—situations in which hierarchical groups can respond faster and more efficiently than egalitarian groups.[58] Those who followed the cultural rules of group conformity and hierarchical order had a higher chance of survival. These individuals also tend to carry a higher rate of the shorter variant of serotonin transporter gene (s5-HTTLPR). This biological trait is beneficial when facing environmental threats because short allele carriers are more likely to be vigilant in detecting stressors and avoid them.[59] At the same time, this version of the gene also makes people more prone to negative experiences, *unless* the group evolved a strong hierarchy to organize effectively the social life, increasing predictability and reducing stress in social interaction.[60] Thus, societies with more short-allele carriers are more likely to foster social order, strict judgment of behaviors, and a preference for norm enforcement because such a norm would help to coordinate activities and enhance safety within a population that is genetically at risk for anxiety (Environment—Gene—Culture pathway).

However, this is only a hypothesis of the biological root of hierarchy acceptance, and the connection between the short allele and depression has been challenged. Besides, the pattern has become much more complex across different cultures in the world. Throughout history, the dynamic context of culture, genes, behaviors, and the brain's plasticity constantly shape how we accept hierarchical distribution of status, power, and wealth. Take Korea for example. As a consequence of World War II and the Cold War, it was divided into two countries in 1945. The Korean culture in the North and South has evolved differently as the two countries pursue diametrically opposed political, economic, and social systems. North Korea has supreme leaders who are revered. In extreme cases, people have lost their lives and loved ones to save portraits of Kim Jong-il during natural disasters.[61] Many leaders in the South, on the contrary, were overturned by protests, as its citizens believed they could challenge the government and choose their own leaders.[62] To conclude, the level of hierarchy acceptance in different cultures should be seen in a specific context because environment, gene, brain, and collective behaviors can dynamically interact and result in a very particular pattern of egalitarian or authoritative outward expressions.

3.2.3 *Gender Association*

3.2.3.1 *Gender Association as Universal and Fundamental Concern*

Sex is fundamentally different from *gender*. While sex (male/female) refers to the biological makeup such as chromosomes, reproductive organs, and hormones, gender (masculinity/femininity) refers to two sets of behaviors: (1) Traits that are associated with femininity, such as modesty and caring; and (2) traits that are associated with masculinity, such as competitive and assertive. Originating from gender's role, these traits have become a fundamental concern for all societies, as they not only express what is expected of men and women but also the way members of a cultural group should behave in general. Gender association is represented by the trunk and the roots of the metaphorical tree.

In this book, *gender association is defined as the extent to which people are associated with either masculine or feminine traits*. Femininity emphasizes care, modesty, and sustainability. Masculinity emphasizes competition, assertiveness, and performance. Looking at this list, we can quickly recognize that everyone needs both to survive and advance, at least at the *baseline level*. No human being or societies can survive with only one set of concerns and one level of value salience.

3.2.3.2 *The Diversity in Gender Association*

In terms of value, masculinity and femininity are two separate constructs, and their levels of importance vary from a baseline, to weak and strong, and everywhere in between. It depends on national cultures, organizational cultures, group cultures, individuals, and particular context. The common stereotype is that Scandinavian cultures are more feminine with their model of caring economy (high tax and progressive social welfare). In contrast, the United States is masculinity with a spirit of "from rags to riches." Southern European and African cultures may come across as masculine with a passionate, sometimes assertive style of communication. In Asia, people can be masculine in thought (competitive) but feminine in behavior (modest). This differing level of value is represented by the branches of the metaphorical tree.

When it comes to gender role, the stereotype has been quite often that men are masculine and women are feminine. However, because gender is a social construct, what we associate with masculinity and femininity today can be very different in comparison with the past. In some traditional societies, the lists of masculine and feminine traits were almost reversed. As anthropologist Margaret Mead described in her classic study of tribes in Papua New Guinea, both men and women of the Arapesh displayed feminine temperaments, but among the Mundugamor, both men and women were masculine. Among the Tchambuli, men were feminine and women were masculine. Among the Mosuo, for example, women are in charge, children don't normally know who their father is, and men are feminine.[63] The change in gender roles and the dynamics of traits associated with them throughout history pose a critical question: How will our current perceptions of masculinity and femininity change in the future? For the sake of argument, will "tolerance" become a masculine trait?

The terms pose another issue. While both men and women have to be both masculine and feminine to fulfill their responsibilities in life, women may feel pressured to act feminine and men to be masculine. The traits are *unisex*, but the names signal otherwise. If a trait can interchangeably and simultaneously exist in both men and women, it is neither masculine, nor feminine, but a sexless, androgynous trait. This branding problem has not yet been solved because no terms have been created to address the traits properly.

3.2.3.3 Where Does this Diversity Come From?

Tracing down the evolutionary roots of masculinity and femininity is a complex task. There are too many factors that influence the way, for example, some cultures tend to favor a "dog eat dog" competitive market while others strive for a caring economy. Further, these terms cover a wide range of meanings. Masculinity implies "competitive," "assertive," "achievement-oriented," "materialistic," and so forth, while femininity implies "modest," "well-being," "caring," "work-life balance," "consensus," and so forth.

However, we can still scratch the surface with some hypotheses on the origin of gender role. Let's start with the impact of *resources*, that is "environment" in the Diversity Pathways. Particular division of labor evolved in response to environment. Between two forms of soil cultivation, the *shifting* type that uses handheld devices favors women, and the *ploughing* type that requires upper-body strength favors men.[64] The result is that men dominated the field in plough cultivation, pushing women back home. Masculine traits became associated with market employment, political participation, success, and competition, while feminine traits became associated with homebound activities such as caring. Modern societies with traditional plough agriculture have lower rates of female employment and higher gender inequality (Environment—Culture—Behavior pathway).[65]

Resource also influences family structure and gender role, giving rise to masculine and/or feminine values. Polyandry (one women—many men) was a common system in early history[66] because when the resource is limited, polyandry enables Tibetan families to hold agricultural estates together. The marriage of all brothers in a family to the same wife helps to keep the land intact and undivided. Among the Inuit, the husband can arrange for his brother to marry his wife, so his interest is protected when he is away, and if there are children, they will be from the one he approved. With the Bari in Venezuela, a child may have two legitimate fathers because it is believed that (s)he would be more likely to survive with some extra support. We can hypothesize that this may partly contribute to the evolutionary root of femininity in which both men and women are expected to be nurturing and caring.

Polyandry usually occurs in landowning cultures, but it is not always the solution. It emerged mostly with egalitarian societies in which there were no massive governmental bureaucracies and class systems. In other landowning cultures, a surplus of men was not solved by marrying them off to one woman. Instead, they were sent to the priesthood, wars, and expeditions in new territories. Whether this did foster masculine values such as risk-taking, competitive, assertiveness, and so forth remains an open question.

Another solution to deal with the issue of resource is polygamy (one man—many women). This system is likely to occur (1) during/after war times when there was a *scarcity of males*, (2) in *disease-prone countries* where women pick physically attractive men because they are more likely to survive, and (3) when rich men can monopolize *wealth* to provide better for women. While without consensus,[67] the common assumption is that the trade-offs that women make in polygamy could contribute to a clear-cut division between a prevalence of masculine values for men and feminine values for women.

Then comes monogamy (one man—one woman). It's speculated that monogamy works because men stay with women to ensure *child safety*, that is their young were not killed by other men.[68] It also increases the surplus *resources available to be invested in children*, and *reduces conflicts* caused by unmarried men who are unable to get partners. As humans evolve to live in big societies, the *risk of sexually transmitted diseases* can be destructive.[69] This puts social pressure on humans to stay monogamous.[70] As a consequence of monogamy, men can afford to be less competitive, more caring, and more focused on child investment and cooperation with their female partners. This might well have been a factor for feminine values to become more prevalent than in the past.

In sum, "natural resources," "scarcity of partners," "child safety," "diseases," and "wealth" can be the factors that dynamically influence how inhabitants of a culture embrace masculine and feminine values. We have not seen *genes* in this picture. The reason is because there are very limited findings to consider. However, one particular aspect of gender association does attract a great deal of research attention: Aggression and violence, often associated with masculine traits.

In our brain, MAOA (monoamine oxidase A) is an enzyme that breaks down neurotransmitters such as serotonin, norepinephrine, and dopamine in the anterior cingulate cortex—a brain region that helps us deal with the distress of social rejection. The gene coding for MAOA generally has two variants. The high-activity variant (MAOA-4R) speeds up the metabolism of serotonin, norepinephrine, and dopamine. The low-activity variants (MAOA-2R and 3R) are less effective, producing less MAOA enzyme, breaking down the neurotransmitters at a slower speed. As a consequence, the high level of serotonin, norepinephrine, and dopamine left in the brain can hinder how people deal with social rejection. It is linked with heightened response from the amygdala and decreased activity in the prefrontal regions of the brain that protect against anxiety.[71] The result is a tendency in aggressive behaviors and violence.[72] For this reason, it's also called the "warrior gene." Abused children with this variant of the gene grew up with a likelihood of having more antisocial problems later in life, however, note that this candidate gene has been challenged.[73-74] The interesting gender twist with MAOA is that, while it causes problems in men, it contributes to increased happiness in women, probably because they don't suffer from the counterproductive effect of testosterone on MAOA like men.[75]

In 2007, the controversy started when a study reported that the low-activity variant (MAOA-3R) was more common among the Maori of New Zealand (56%) in comparison with the white population (34%).[76] It seems to suggest that genetic makeup could explain why the Maori—famous for their war dance Haka and a history of intertribal conflicts—was lagging behind the white in achievement and social outcomes. However, this gene-centric explanation is problematic because the same variant is found in black men (59%), Chinese men (54%),[77] and Taiwanese men (61%).[78] Upbringing culture and behavior can moderate the low-activity variant and regulate the expression of the "warrior gene" (epigenetics). Accordingly, a study shows that there is *no* correlation between the MAOA brain level and MAOA gene variants.[79] It means the amount of MAOA enzyme in the brain is partially regulated by nongenetic factors such as parental style or practices of self-control (pathway Behavior—Gene).

At this point, we have discussed how environment, genes, behaviors, and culture can influence the way people embrace differing levels of masculine and feminine values. Let's complete the picture with the role of the *brain*. Both academic and popular literature is replete with accounts of how the brain of men and women are distinctively different, as if they are two separate species. While it is true that they work slightly differently, researchers have also argued that this difference is not as distinct as many want to believe,[80] and may be due to a difference in *size* rather than a difference in *gender*.[81-82] High levels of connectivity can be found between two hemispheres in women's brains, and within each hemisphere in men's brains.[83] However, when the researchers suggested that this could account for behavioral differences in men and women, it became a statement that is not only beyond the scope of an imaging study but also misleading.[84] Unlike genitalia, brains do not come in male or female forms.[85-86] Up to 53% of brains cover both male-end and female-end features.[87] This means one can be highly masculine when undertaking one task, but highly feminine undertaking another. We can seriously challenge the assumption of "left brain for men" and "right brain for women" by pointing out that removing even half of the brain will *not* significantly affect how one mentally develops.[88] At the very least, men and women are no different than two men with unique emotional styles.[89]

If neural differences between men and women exist, regardless of the degree, they should always be seen in specific cultural contexts.[90-91] A woman's brain may show high levels of connectivity between two hemispheres, which allows her to be better at multitasking and cooperation. But she was not necessarily born that way. Her brain is structured that way probably because her culture expects that of her, so she uses that part of her brain more often. The same is true for other stereotypical beliefs, that is that men are "hard-wired" to do better at jobs related to math, cars, and engineering. An array of brain studies has been criticized for *neurosexism* and failing to recognize the plasticity of gender differences[92] and thus contributing to inaccurate misunderstanding about the sexes,[93-94] leading to misguided practices in HR, leadership, and recruitment while perpetuating harmful gender biases[95] (Behavior—Brain pathway).

To conclude, there is a wide range of factors that influence the way people embrace masculine and feminine values. Biological makeup, brain plasticity, and external factors such as natural and social resources dynamically interact with each other, enabling masculine and/or feminine values to emerge as *strategies for us to survive and advance*. We should look no further than Scandinavian countries for a case of consideration. The Viking culture has gone from a (stereotypically) bloodthirsty reputation of pillages and raids to become a poster child of progressive government with the world's top living standards. Did they replace a masculine mindset by a feminine worldview to race ahead of everyone? We still need to prove this hypothesis, but such a speculation is not entirely baseless, taking into account the principle that cultural values evolve as strategies to cope with external problems.

3.2.4 Uncertainty Avoidance

3.2.4.1 Uncertainty Avoidance as Universal and Fundamental Concern

Trying to predict and avoid the unknown is universal and a basic human instinct. Fear is the result of both strongly innate feelings and social learning. In general, we have several inborn fears, for example the fear of falling and the fear caused by loud noises. These fears are genetically coded in our body and are healthy emotions that keep us from harm. Most other types of fear are learned from the culture of our life, what is good and what is bad, what is safe and what is dangerous. Our fear may have an object (fear of the dark) or no specific object (what will happen to us in the future, when we take a new job, or after we die?). The latter is called *uncertainty*. As a value, *uncertainty avoidance is the extent to which members of collectives seek orderliness, consistency, structure, formalized procedures, and laws to cover situations in their daily lives.*[96] It is represented by the trunk and the roots of the metaphorical tree.

The origin of our tendency to avoid the unknown is rooted in our nature as social animals. We need each other in the form of an ingroup for protection, and the culture of this ingroup will provide us with what we need to survive. Rules emerged from the need to keep this ingroup culture effective, maintain trust among members, safeguard cultural ideas from outsiders, and gauge between the choice of cooperating or fighting with other groups over resources. The three universal forms of cultural strategy in dealing with uncertainty are religion, law, and technology.

With regard to religion, this cultural enhancer has historically given humans more assurance of an otherwise unpredictable future. It is the hope that justice will be served, our enemy will be defeated, rain will come, travel will be safe, or our eternity will be in heaven. Religion as a cultural strategy can *reduce our worries and anxieties*, giving us the motivation to stride ahead—something that genes simply can't. For this reason, according to Pagel,[97] regardless of our subjective opinion of religions, whether they are true, frivolous, or hedonistic, human groups have adopted them.

Religion is also among the earliest forms of law. With codes of morality and conduct, it has given us some certainty and direction in this arbitrary, capricious, and unpredictable world. Traditional religions and beliefs still influence many modern law systems.[98] The prehistoric notion of religion was connected with science. For our ancestors, religion was a form of science, signaling an attempt to understand the world and to answer questions such as "why is the harvest bad this year?" or "why do earthquakes happen?" Religion provided a framework for understanding the universe, the nature, and the logic of life.

In the modern era, science and technology seem to have become divorced from religion, but their original purpose is quite similar: To predict the future, give the unknown a structure, and reduce uncertainty. To a certain extent, when strong uncertainty avoidance prevails, we tend to rely more on religion, law, control, rigid rules of conduct, procedure and morality, and, in some cases, technology.[99]

3.2.4.2 The Diversity in Uncertainty Avoidance

While all societies want to avoid the negative impact of the unknown, cultures and individuals differ from the universal *baseline value* in the degree of avoidance, based on the particular context. This differing level of value is represented by the branches of the metaphorical tree. When uncertainty avoidance is strong, religion, law, and, to a certain extent, technology tend take a more central role to prevent the unknown, and vice versa.

However, the picture is more complex when we distinguish between *institutional* and *social* rules. The former focuses on regulations, written laws, structured guidelines, and formal organized procedures ("How rigid is the legal system?"); the latter is informally agreed-upon codes of conducts and social values ("How much respect one is expected to give to one's teacher?"). To be strong on social rules means values and codes of conducts are expected to be followed strictly (e.g., one is expected to show great respect to one's teacher, and not doing so will be frowned upon). To be weak on social rules means values and codes of conducts are more relaxed (e.g., one can show both high and low hierarchy acceptance toward one's teacher and expect little consequences).

Some cultures, such as those in Scandinavia, tend to be strong on institutional rules but weak on social rules. Others, such as Vietnam, Laos, Cambodia, and Myanmar, exercise strong social rules but are not so strict in terms of institutional rules. This categorization of "rules" versus "values" can help us to guess why, in the index provided by Hofstede,[100] these countries/regions score so similarly: Between Germany (65) and Thailand (64); between Bangladesh (60) and Quebec (60); or between Canada (48) and Indonesia (48). It also highlights the biggest paradox of the index: The champion of dealing with ambiguity—Singapore (8)—should be a country of flexibility and spontaneity according to its score, but is in fact a country that exercises one of the world's strictest systems of laws and punishment. It bans chewing gum and littering can invoke a fine of up to $1,000.[101] As a society made up of three Asian ethnicities, which strongly embrace certain values and codes of conduct (Chinese, Indian, and Malay), Singapore is both strong on institutional rules (laws) and social rules, somewhat the opposite of its score. To conclude, national indexes can only give the first-best-guess because reality and the number on the index may contradict each other.

3.2.4.3 Where Does this Diversity Come From?

In Chapter 2, we mentioned the 7-repeat (7R) and 2-repeat (2R) versions of the dopamine receptor D4. Both the 7R and the 2R versions have been linked to impulsive and exploratory behavior, risk-taking, and novelty-seeking.[102-103-104] Among 18 indigenous populations spreading along the routes of human migration from Africa, the farther on the move away from Africa, the more likely people were to have either of the 7R and 2R. Those that carry the 7R and 2R may experience higher fitness in response to many generations of migration, thus, dealing more effectively with ecological and social stressors that migration presents.[105] Novelty-seeking traits are adaptive in regions unsuitable for sedentary lifestyles, exposing human genes to strong selective pressure and enhancing the reproductive success of those exhibiting these traits.[106] While the 7R has been linked with some mental health issues,[107] when it comes to attention-deficit hyperactivity disorder (ADHD), some studies[108-109-110] suggest that ADHD symptoms could be evolutionarily advantageous. Taken together, migration histories may have favored individuals with some particular gene variants associated personality traits such as novelty seeking, perseverance, unpredicted behaviors, hyperactivity, rapidly shifting focus, and quick movements because they might have been an evolutionary advantage to the unfamiliar and frequently changing environments.

Because the behaviors associated with the 7R and the 2R can be argued to share some characteristics with weak uncertainty avoidance, this may provide us some basis to hypothesize that South American and nomadic cultures have a genetic support to be weak uncertainty avoiding. Future research could investigate if there is a correlation between variants of this gene and levels of novelty-seeking across different cultural groups. We still don't know why the 7R is replaced by the 2R in Southeast Asia. It is possible that the two alleles may not be "functionally" equivalent[111] and novelty seeking/uncertainty accepting may have very different characteristics in Asia compared to other parts of the world. Taken together, the curious case of 2R with both similarities and differences with the 7R may hold the answer for the origin of variation in novelty seeking or uncertainty avoidance/acceptance across different cultures.

While the gene-culture coevolution theory is plausible, it may lead to false interpretation if genes are seen as having a simple and fixed working mechanism. Next to the gene-culture coevolution, the gene-culture interaction model, for instance, posits that cultural influences can shape how these predispositions manifest in the final behavioral outcomes. The evidence has started to emerge, showing how genes interact with culture, creating a great level of complexity and dynamics. In a study, participants were primed with religious words by playing a game in which they had made a sentence out of a string (e.g., "felt she eradiate spirit the" needs to be "she felt the spirit"). The researchers reported that only those with the 7R and 2R alleles showed an increase on prosocial behaviors.[112] In another study, individuals with the 7R and 2R alleles tended to report a more *independent* social orientation in the United States, but a more *interdependent* social orientation in Japan.[113] Thus, the cultural difference was more pronounced for carriers of the 7R or 2R alleles.[114]

The indication from the previously mentioned studies is critical. In essence, they suggest that the *same gene may support totally opposite values.* Those with the 7R and 2R are probably endowed with a greater predisposition to fit in a new culture, to conform to the values of that culture, behaving in a collectivistic or individualistic way if they need to. In short, they may have a genetic asset to be adaptive to the new environment. Note that the 7R and 2R are also associated with risk-taking. This means those with the 7R and 2R may quickly fit in a new culture, but probably also quickly get bored and leave for novelty. We must wait for further research to provide us with more insight and test these hypotheses.

A gene-centric approach is never complete. Here is an example. Before the mid-nineteenth century, the frontier of Japan was a remote territory with stormy sea, rugged volcanic landscape, and savage wildlife. Fearing Russian invasion, the Japanese government decided to reclaim the land, recruiting people to settle in Hokkaido. It now has a population of six million. While Hofstede's index places Japan as a strong uncertainty avoiding country, the inhabitants of Hokkaido (Japan) showed a conquer spirit of somewhat weak uncertainty avoidance. They attest to the Frontier Thesis,[115] which posits that the process of conquering new land, venturing into the unknown, and striving for survival tends to cultivate a strong sense of personal achievement, adventurousness, and independence. The mindset of conquering the unknown lives on, making Hokkaido a unique cultural profile, which is different from people living in Honshu just 54km away.[116] This example reminds us that gene is just one of many driving forces in the creation of cultural diversity.

In the volatile context of contemporary globalization, regardless of the presence of the DRD4-7R and 2R, communities can withdraw in fear of uncertainty. Environmental and social threats can force a group to form a cautious view of the world and outsiders, hence, doubling on social rules and institutional rules as an attempt to safeguard identities and cultures. For example, the Hasidic Ultra-Orthodox Jews have a major cultural principle: "Change Nothing." A culture can also choose to open up and face the uncertainty of the modern time, rapidly changing rules to adapt. Saudi Arabia is one of the most conservative countries in the world. Yet, since 2015, to response to economic pressure, the country is making significant shifts in its cultural practices and values. To conclude, many factors interact to create an evolving culture.

3.2.5 *Time Orientation*

3.2.5.1 *Time Orientation as Universal and Fundamental Concern*

Time perspective is a universal construct that refers to thoughts and attitudes toward the past, present, and future.[117] We measure days and nights, calculate the cycles of seasons and stars, predict the coming and going of natural phenomenon, and organize our life activities in a way that ensures our survival in the most effective way.

Evolutionarily speaking, animals gained a sense of future when, 350 million years ago, species evolved out of the water and made way onto land. In the sea water, aquatic animals can't see faraway because 63% of the light is blocked. Most fish don't see farther than the point to which they can swim. Every event happens suddenly, which makes the nervous system highly activate and stressful. Because light travels much farther in air than in seawater, land animals can scan a much bigger area than they can physically cover. As they no longer are restricted to reacting to immediate stimuli, they can deliberately observe before moving. This is the beginning point of an ability to *plan ahead*, and as evolutionists argue, the first sign of *consciousness*.[118] Thus, species that have sensory volume bigger than motor volume gained an evolutionary advantage, allowing them to control the environment rather than lurching from crisis to crisis. Not surprisingly, of all the species, humans seem to be the one that can think furthest in the future. We even think about time far beyond what we can possibly prove to be fact, for instance a time machine, life after death, or what the universe looked like at the beginning of time. In short, time orientation with the ability to think about the past, present, and future is a fundamental concern for human species. It is represented by the trunk and the roots of the metaphorical tree.

3.2.5.2 The Diversity in Time Orientation

Time orientation is defined as the extent to which one emphasizes the past, present, or future. These values are represented by the branches in the metaphorical tree of culture. When the past prevails, the importance of tradition, family, religion, and heritage tends to increase. It gives us a sense of stability and pride. When the present prevails, short-term benefit, quick reward, immediate result, spending, and enjoyment of life tend to be the focus. It helps us to embrace spontaneity, novelty, and a full experience of being in the moment. When the future prevails, long-term goals shape our actions and planning, as we are willing to sacrifice, work hard, save every penny, and persistently keep our eye on the prize. Such a mindset enables us to seek challenge and strive for possibilities of change and new selves.

Stereotypically, conservative and traditional societies tend to embrace the past orientation with a strong emphasis on rituals, customs, history, and time-honored practices. Cultures with young history of immigration may look more at the future where their dreams of change may come true. However, this is an oversimplified generalization. The reality is often much more complex. For example, Eastern Asian cultures value tradition, family, religion, and heritage (past orientation), yet, at the same time, they emphasize thrift, saving, stability, education, secured investment, hard work, stable relationships, and planning (future orientation). The United States with its young history is stereotypically present and future oriented, but at the same time, it is much more conservative and religious than its European counterparts. Scandinavian countries, Ireland, and Canada are not typically seen as future-oriented cultures, yet, they have a reputation of making long-term policies trademarks of their national values, putting forward progressive visions and practices with regard to the environment, social welfare, animal rights, diversity, and multiculturalism, all of which are outward expressions (i.e., the canopy of the tree) that are future oriented.

The reason why we seem to find it challenging in understanding the paradoxes mentioned is partly because we have been so used to the notion that time is linier. This narrow way of thinking prevents us from seeing two *seemingly opposing values prevailing simultaneously*. Brain studies have proved to us that time can't be compartmentalized. While with different intensity, the same regions of the brain lit up in the fMRI scan when people were asked to think about the past and about the future.[119] This means memories are not a property of the past, but also material to construct the future. Again, this reminds us that learning about specific context is the most reliable method to understand when the past, present, and future orientation prevails in a certain community at a particular period and circumstance.

3.2.5.3 Where Does this Diversity Come From?

With regard to the brain, language does play a significant role in changing the neural structure and a sense of time and space. For example, in Swedish, the word for future is *framtid*, which literally means "front time." This enables speakers to visualize the future as in the front. But for speakers of Aymara in Peru, the word for future, *qhipuru*, means "behind time." Their logic is that one can only see what has happened, so we face the past in front of us. The future is what we can't see, so it should be behind out back. Does this linguistic structure make the Swedish more future oriented and the speakers of Aymara more past oriented? Such is a major quest in the discipline of linguistic studies. There is a rich line of research on how language reshapes the way we perceive the world. This concept is beautifully depicted in *Arrival*—a movie in which a linguistic professor can see the future by learning a new language because it helps her to flip her point of view. We will have a much deeper discussion on this matter in Chapter 12.

Historically, the diversity in time perception among different groups is strongly influenced by how a society is structured. Bands and tribes lived a primarily first-person existence in the present, with a lack of vocabulary that implies the passage of time. They hunted animals and gathered fruits without worrying much about the future. For them, the past was also not important, because it had gone. Some tribes in the Amazon have a language that can only count to ten. The sense of past and future probably developed with the formation of chiefdoms and agricultural states, when humans drew on sophisticated observation of the nature to calculate the best time for crops and harvests. Tradition played a crucial role because it was the knowledge accumulated throughout generations. This explains the pan-orientation (across the past, present, and future) of many Asian and Middle Eastern cultures—fittingly, as they were also the world's cradles of agricultures. To compare, the emphasis on the present and future without a strong regard for the past may stem from the previously mentioned frontier theory. In a new territory, where humans were unable to rely on existing knowledge and tradition, the can-do spirit, if-then reasoning, and long-term planning were essential.

In the modern era, various cultural and environmental factors can influence time orientation. For example, the urge to achieve economic growth has forced many countries to turn a blind eye to permanent destruction of natural resources and ecological balance. Globalization goes hand in hand with perceived external threats against cultural identities and economic stability—a reason for some communities to roll back and take refuge in the past's glory or heritage. To conclude, many factors can contribute to the value, that is the high, low, or average level of importance we place on the time orientation toward the past, present, and future.

In this chapter, we have touched on the five most widely cited concerns and their associated values. We have looked at how different societies and contexts place differing levels of importance on the universal/fundamental concerns, for example Eastern cultures strongly emphasize group attachment and Western culture tend to do it less. However, it is critical to go beyond this kind of stereotypes. They are handy as *first best guesses*, but can be harmful because they make us look for cases and examples that confirm our worldview, to disregard paradoxes as nontypical incidents, and to be selective of what we want to see. Change is dynamic, paradoxes are a natural part of culture, and we are not only the products but also the producers of our cultures.

In this chapter, we also attempted to trace the evolutionary paths that lead to the way we value our universal concerns in differing levels, that is, *why* Eastern cultures tend to be seen as collectivistic and Western cultures tend to be seen as individualistic. Here is the conclusion: There is no solid evidence that a certain gene or fixed brain structure can hold a monopoly power in influencing the way people embrace different values. Instead, the diversity we see today is the result of a dynamic interaction between genes, brain, and many other factors from the surrounding environment, the culture we live in, and the activities we do every day. Culture is dynamic, and thus, the original driving forces of a cultural value are also interactive and complex.

In the modern era, factors such as feminism, human rights, overpopulation, international trade, postcolonialization, terrorism, hyperconnectedness, environmental problems, globalization, and so forth constantly reshape these values. At a glance, these factors seem to suggest a hypothesis that we need to embrace a *weak* hierarchy acceptance, *strong* group attachment, *femininity*, and *future*-orientation values as strategies. Just like our ancestors who evolved the group mindset or risk-taking value to cope with the environmental pressure of the ancient time, humans of the modern era have realized that cultural strategies such as democracy, teamwork, cooperation, consensus, work-life balance, tolerance, inclusiveness, empathy, sustainability, and so forth will be the tools to solve world problems. We have epigenetics and the brain on our side, as they have evolved to be "plastic," changing and adapting to help us survive and advance.

Summary

1. Culture in the evolutionary sense is a strategy for humankind to survive and advance. There is only one evolutionary culture, and we all share it.
2. Humans embody and create one evolutionary culture and produce many practical cultures, leading to the immense diversity in the world today.
3. The metaphorical tree of culture has three layers: The trunk/roots, branches, and canopy.
4. The trunk/roots of the tree represent *fundamental concerns*. They are building blocks that help humans survive and advance such as language, music, hierarchy, loyalty, and so forth.
5. The branches of the tree represent *values*, that is the degree of importance we place on a fundamental concern.
   - Beyond the baseline level, values range from low, to high, and everywhere in between.
   - This differing level of values creates the diversity of culture in the practical sense.
6. The canopy represents *outward expressions*, which are symbols, objects, and behaviors. It is an intricate web of *specific* behaviors, policies, incidents, and communication that we see every day. This immense mosaic of outward expression is the diversity of culture in the practical sense that we can see with our own eyes.
7. Because the list of fundamental concerns can be endless, there is a need for a simplified framework. The following five concerns are among the most popular. They are the building blocks of our culture in the evolutionary sense:
   - *Group attachment* is the extent to which one gives her/his ingroup priority over oneself. Other concerns that belong to this category include interdependence, independence, trust, freedom, autonomy, conformity, loyalty, harmony, and so forth.
   - *Hierarchy acceptance* is the extent to which subordinates accept a hierarchical (unequal) distribution of prestige, status, influential power, and resources between them and their superiors. Other concerns that belong to this category include respect, obedience, loyalty, protection, leading, guidance, and so forth.
   - *Gender association* is the extent to which people are associated with either masculine or feminine traits. Other concerns that belong to this category include competition, assertiveness, confidence, modesty, well-being, nurturing, empathy, confrontation, tolerance, dominance, and so forth.
   - *Uncertainty avoidance* is the extent to which members of collectives seek orderliness, consistency, structure, formalized procedures, and laws to cover situations in their daily lives. Other concerns that belong to this category include religion, law, technology, morality, stability, integrity, control, risk-taking, spontaneity, curiosity, diversity, and so forth.
   - *Time orientation* is the extent to which one emphasizes the past, present, or future. Other concerns that belong to this category include education, tradition, thrift, stability, persistence, saving, planning, enjoyment, and so forth.
8. Culture in practical sense is diverse, due to:
   - The differences of fundamental concerns each group, organization, and individual places have in a particular context. Diversity in fundamental concern creates cultural diversity.

- The differing degrees of importance each group, organization, and individual places on fundamental concerns. Diversity in values creates cultural diversity.
- The differences of outward expressions in objects, words, and behaviors. Diversity in outward expressions creates cultural diversity.

9. The variance of cultural diversity depends on particular context in which all five factors of GCEB-Be dynamically interact with each other. Genes coevolve with culture to create ultimate strategies that help humans survive and advance. The brain plasticity helps humans adapt to a host culture. Behaviors can be both the consequence of a culture and the driver in creating a new culture. Again, culture is not only socially learned but also geographically influenced, genetically inherited, neurally enabled, and constantly created.

Notes

Don't forget to go to the end of the book for case studies.

1 Foley, Robert A., and Mirazón M. Lahr. 2011. "The Evolution of the Diversity of Cultures." *Philosophical Transactions of the Royal Society B: Biological Sciences* 366(1567): 1080–1089. www.ncbi.nlm.nih.gov/pmc/articles/PMC3049104.
2 Pagel, Mark D. 2013. *Wired for Culture: Origins of the Human Social Mind*. New York: W. W. Norton & Company.
3 Fosler-Lussier, Danielle. 2015. *Music in America's Cold War Diplomacy*, 183. Oakland: University of California Press.
4 Soft Power 30. 2017. "Ranking 2017." https://softpower30.com/.
5 Ward, Victoria. 2016. "UK Artists Sell a Third of Top 40 Best-Selling Albums Worldwide." *The Telegraph*. February 7. www.telegraph.co.uk/news/celebritynews/12145349/UK-artists-sell-a-third-of-top-40-best-selling-albums-worldwide.html.
6 Murai, Shusuke. 2017. "Can Japan, Land of Lifetime Employment, Handle the Rise of Freelancers?" *The Japan Times*. May 14. www.japantimes.co.jp/news/2017/05/14/national/can-japan-land-of-lifetime-employment-handle-the-rise-of-freelancers/#.WZuX_1N97IU.
7 SAP. 2014. "Workforce 2020 Insights." *Success Factors*. www.successfactors.com/en_us/lp/workforce-2020-insights.html.
8 Alston, Jon P., and Isao Takei. 2005. *Japanese Business Culture and Practices: A Guide to Twenty-First Century*, 2. Lincoln, NE: iUniverse. https://books.google.nl/books?id=6lJTqe_IwdsC&pg=PA2&lpg=PA2&dq=extreme example of word loyalty&source=bl&ots=l9daHChJ6Q&sig=AB00vmtWpvF0KwnfSUTHOHLqTZE&hl=en&sa=X&ved=0ahUKEwic8aWAkNvWAhUSM8AKHffuDtk4ChDoAQg4MAQ#v=onepage&q=extreme example of word loyalty&f=false.
9 Keng, Cameron. 2018. "Employees Who Stay in Companies Longer Than Two Years Get Paid 50% Less." *Forbes*. January 2. www.forbes.com/sites/cameronkeng/2014/06/22/employees-that-stay-in-companies-longer-than-2-years-get-paid-50-less/#47962f1ae07f.
10 Kluckhohn, Florence Rockwood., and Fred L. Strodtbeck. 1961. *Variations in Value Orientations*. Evanston, IL: Row, Peterson.
11 Chiao, Joan Y., Tetsuya Iidaka, Heather L. Gordon, Junpei Nogawa, Moshe Bar. Elissa Aminoff, Norihiro Sadato, and Nalini Ambady. 2008. "Cultural Specificity in Amygdala Response to Fear Faces." *Journal of Cognitive Neuroscience* 20(12): 2167–2174. doi:10.1162/jocn.2008.20151.
12 Masuda, Naoki., and Feng Fu. 2015. "Evolutionary Models of In-group Favoritism." *F1000Prime Reports* 7(27). doi:10.12703/p.7–27.
13 Blair, Irene V., Charles M. Judd, Melody S. Sadler, and Christopher Jenkins. 2002. "The Role of Afrocentric Features in Person Perception: Judging by Features and Categories." *Journal of Personality and Social Psychology* 83(1): 5–25. doi:10.1037/0022-3514.83.1.5.
14 Phelps, Elizabeth A., and Joseph E. LeDoux. 2005. "Contributions of the Amygdala to Emotion Processing: From Animal Models to Human Behavior." *Neuron* 48(2): 175–187. doi:10.1016/j.neuron.2005.09.025.
15 Olsson, Andreas., Katherine I. Nearing, and Elizabeth A. Phelps. 2007. "Learning Fears by Observing Others: The Neural Systems of Social Fear Transmission." *Social Cognitive Affective Neuroscience* 2(1): 3–11. doi:10.1093/scan/nsm005.

16 Kubota, Jennifer T., Mahzarin R. Banaji, and Elizabeth A. Phelps. 2012. "The Neuroscience of Race." *Nature Neuroscience* 15(7): 940–948. doi:10.1038/nn.3136.

17 Hart, Allen J., Paul J. Whalen, Lisa M. Shin, Sean C. McInerney, Håkan Fischer, and Scott L. Rauch. 2000. "Differential Response in the Human Amygdala to Racial Outgroup vs. Ingroup Face Stimuli." *Neuroreport* 11(11): 2351–2355. doi:10.1097/00001756-200008030-00004.

18 Meyer, Meghan L. 2012. "Empathy for the Social Suffering of Friends and Strangers Recruits Distinct Patterns of Brain Activation." *Social Cognitive and Affective Neuroscience* 8(4): 1–9. doi:10.1093/scan/nss019.

19 Hein, Grit., Giorgia Silani, Kerstin Preuschoff, C. Daniel Batson, and Tania Singer. 2010. "Neural Responses to Ingroup and Outgroup Members Suffering Predict Individual Differences in Costly Helping." *Neuron* 68(1): 149–160. doi:10.1016/j.neuron.2010.09.003.

20 Xu, Xiaojing., Xiangyu Zuo, Xiaoying Wang, and Shihui Han. 2009. "Do You Feel My Pain? Racial Group Membership Modulates Empathic Neural Responses." *Journal of Neuroscience* 29(26): 8525–8529. doi:10.1523/jneurosci.2418-09.2009.

21 Adams, Reginald B., Nicholas O. Rule, Robert G. Franklin, Elsie Wang, Michael T. Stevenson, Sakiko Yoshikawa, and Mitsue Nomura et al. 2012. "Cross-Cultural Reading the Mind in the Eyes: An FMRI Investigation." *Journal of Cognitive Neuroscience* 22(1): 97–108. doi:10.1162/jocn.2009.21187.

22 Cheon, Bobby K., Dong-Mi Im, Tokiko Harada, Ji-Sook Kim, Vani A. Mathur, Jason M. Scimeca, and Todd B. Parrish et al. 2011. "Cultural Influences on Neural Basis of Intergroup Empathy." *NeuroImage* 57(2): 642–650. doi:10.1016/j.neuroimage.2011.04.031.

23 Zhu, Ying., Li Zhang, Jin Fan, and Shihui Han. 2007. "Neural Basis of Cultural Influence on Self-Representation." *NeuroImage* 34(3): 1310–1316. doi:10.1016/j.neuroimage.2006.08.047.

24 Sui, Jie., Chang Hong Liu, and Shihui Han. 2009. "Cultural Difference in Neural Mechanisms of Self-recognition." *Social Neuroscience* 4(5): 402–411. doi:10.1080/17470910802674825.

25 Heine, Steven J., and Takeshi Hamamura. 2007. "In Search of East Asian Self-Enhancement." *Personality and Social Psychology Review* 11(1): 4–27. doi:10.1177/1088868306294587.

26 Hampton, Ryan S., and Michael E. W. Varnum. 2017. "Do Cultures Vary in Self-Enhancement? ERP, Behavioral, and Self-Report Evidence." *Social Neuroscience* 13(5): 566–578. doi:10.1080/17470919.2017.1361471.

27 Kitayama, Shinobu., and Jiyoung Park. 2014. "Error-Related Brain Activity Reveals Self-Centric Motivation: Culture Matters." *Journal of Experimental Psychology: General* 143(1): 62–70. doi:10.1037/a0031696.

28 Zhu, Xiangru., Yan Zhang, Suyong Yang, Haiyan Wu, Lili Wang, and Ruolei Gu. 2015. "The Motivational Hierarchy between Self and Mother: Evidence from the Feedback-Related Negativity." *Acta Psychologica Sinica* 47(6): 807. doi:10.3724/sp.j.1041.2015.00807.

29 Telzer, Eva H., Carrie L. Masten, Elliot T. Berkman, Matthew D. Lieberman, and Andrew J. Fuligni. 2010. "Gaining While Giving: An fMRI Study of the Rewards of Family Assistance among White and Latino Youth." *Social Neuroscience* 5(5–6): 508–518. doi:10.1080/17470911003687913.

30 Riadh Ladhari, Nizar Souiden., and Yong-Hoon Choi. 2015. "Culture Change and Globalization: The Unresolved Debate between Cross-National and Cross-Cultural Classifications," *Australian Marketing Journal* 23(3): 235–245. doi:10.1016/j.ausmj.2015.06.003.

31 David A. Ralston., Nguyen Van Thang, and Nancy K. Napier. 1999. "A Comparative Study of the Work Values of North and South Vietnamese Managers." *Journal of International Business Studies* 30(4): 655–672. doi:10.1057/palgrave.jibs.8490889.

32 Shibley Telhami. 2013. *The World through Arab Eyes*. New York: Basic Books.

33 House, Robert J., Paul J. Hanges, Mansour Javidan, Peter W. Dorfman, and Vipin Gupta. *Culture, Leadership, and Organizations: The GLOBE Study of 62 Societies*. Thousand Oaks, CA: Sage Publications, 2004.

34 Singelis, Theodore M., Harry C. Triandis, Dharm P. S. Bhawuk, and Michele J. Gelfand. 1995. "Horizontal and Vertical Dimensions of Individualism and Collectivism: A Theoretical and Measurement Refinement." *Cross-Cultural Research* 29(3): 240–275. doi:10.1177/106939719502900302.

35 Kobiella, A., M. Reimold, D. E. Ulshöfer, V. N. Ikonomidou, C. Vollmert, S. Vollstädt-Klein, and M. Rietschel. 2011. "How the Serotonin Transporter 5-HTTLPR Polymorphism Influences Amygdala Function: The Roles of in Vivo Serotonin Transporter Expression and Amygdala Structure." *Translational Psychiatry* 1(8): e37. doi:10.1038/tp.2011.29.

36 Chiao, Joan Y., and Katherine D. Blizinsky. 2009. "Culture-Gene Coevolution of Individualism-Collectivism and the Serotonin Transporter Gene." *Proceedings of the Royal Society B: Biological Sciences* 277(1681): 529–537. doi:10.1098/rspb.2009.1650.

37 Mrazek, Alissa J., Joan Y. Chiao, Katherine D. Blizinsky, Janetta Lun, and Michele J. Gelfand. 2013. "The Role of Culture–Gene Coevolution in Morality Judgment: Examining the Interplay between Tightness–Looseness and Allelic Variation of the Serotonin Transporter Gene." *Culture and Brain* 1(2–4): 100–117.

38 Gelernter, Joel., Henry Kranzler, and Joseph F. Cubells. 1997. "Serotonin Transporter Protein (SLC6A4) Allele and Haplotype Frequencies and Linkage Disequilibria in African- and European-American and Japanese Populations and in Alcohol-Dependent Subjects." *Human Genetics* 101(2): 243–246.

39 Way, Baldwin M., and Matthew D. Lieberman. 2010. "Is There a Genetic Contribution to Cultural Differences? Collectivism, Individualism and Genetic Markers of Social Sensitivity." *Social Cognitive and Affective Neuroscience* 5(2–3): 203–211.

40 Fincher, Corey L., Randy Thornhill, Damian R. Murray, and Mark Schaller. 2008. "Pathogen Prevalence Predicts Human Cross-Cultural Variability in Individualism/Collectivism." *Proceedings of the Royal Society B: Biological Sciences* 275(1640): 1279–1285.

41 Caspi, Avshalom., Karen Sugden, Terrie E. Moffitt, Alan Taylor, Ian W. Craig, HonaLee Harrington, Joseph McClay et al. 2003. "Influence of Life Stress on Depression: Moderation by a Polymorphism in the 5-HTT Gene." *Science* 301(5631): 386–389. doi:10.1126/science.1083968.

42 Goldman, Noreen., Dana A. Glei, Yu-Hsuan Lin, and Maxine Weinstein. 2010. "The Serotonin Transporter Polymorphism (5-HTTLPR): Allelic Variation and Links with Depressive Symptoms." *Depression and Anxiety* 27(3): 260–269.

43 Griffiths, Kathleen M., Yoshibumi Nakane, Helen Christensen, Kumiko Yoshioka, Anthony F. Jorm, and Hideyuki Nakane. 2006. "Stigma in Response to Mental Disorders: A Comparison of Australia and Japan." *BMC Psychiatry* 6(1): 21–33.

44 Kaufman, Joan., Bao-Zhu Yang, Heather Douglas-Palumberi, Shadi Houshyar, Deborah Lipschitz, John H. Krystal, and Joel Gelernter. 2004. "Social Supports and Serotonin Transporter Gene Moderate Depression in Maltreated Children." *Proceedings of the National Academy of Sciences* 101(49): 17316–17321.

45 Kilpatrick, Dean G., Karestan C. Koenen, Kenneth J. Ruggiero, Ron Acierno, Sandro Galea, Heidi S. Resnick, John Roitzsch, John Boyle, and Joel Gelernter. 2007. "The Serotonin Transporter Genotype and Social Support and Moderation of Posttraumatic Stress Disorder and Depression in Hurricane-Exposed Adults." *American Journal of Psychiatry* 164(11): 1693–1699.

46 Ball, Richard. 2001. "Individualism, Collectivism, and Economic Development." *Sage Publications* 573(1): 57–84. www.jstor.org/stable/pdf/1049015.pdf.

47 Piff, Paul K., Michael W. Kraus, Stéphane Côté, Bonnie Hayden Cheng, and Dacher Keltner. 2010. "Having Less, Giving More: The Influence of Social Class on Prosocial Behavior." *Journal of Personality and Social Psychology* 99(5): 771–784. doi:10.1037/a0020092.

48 Mengistu, Henok., Joost Huizinga, Jean-Baptiste Mouret, and Jeff Clune. 2016. "The Evolutionary Origins of Hierarchy." *PLOS Computational Biology* 12(6): e1004829. doi:10.1371/journal.pcbi.1004829.

49 Pratto, Felicia., Jim Sidanius, and Shana Levin. 2006. "Social Dominance Theory and the Dynamics of Intergroup Relations: Taking Stock and Looking Forward." *European Review of Social Psychology* 17(1): 271–320. doi:10.1080/10463280601055772.

50 Sosis, Richard. 2000. "Religion and Intragroup Cooperation: Preliminary Results of a Comparative Analysis of Utopian Communities." *Cross-Cultural Research* 34(1): 70–87. doi:10.1177/106939710003400105.

51 Inkeles, Alex., and Daniel J. Levinson. 1969. "National Characters: The Study of Modal Personality and Sociocultural Systems." In *The Handbook of Social Psychology*. 2nd ed., Vol. 4, ed. G. Lindzey and E. Aronson, 418–506. Reading, MA: Addison-Wesley.

52 Kluckhohn, Florence., and Fred Strodtbeck. 1961. *Variations in Value Orientations*. Evanston, IL: Row, Peterson.

53 Hofstede, Geert., Gert-Jan Hofstede, and Michael Minkov. 2005. *Cultures and Organizations: Software of the Mind*. New York: McGraw-Hill.

54 Trompenaars, Fons., and Charles Hampden-Turner. 1997. *Riding the Waves of Culture: Understanding Diversity in Global Business*. 3rd ed. London: Nicholas Brealey.

55 Liew, Sook-Lei., Yina Ma, Shihui Han, and Lisa Aziz-Zadeh. 2011. "Who's Afraid of the Boss: Cultural Differences in Social Hierarchies Modulate Self-Face Recognition in Chinese and Americans." *PLoS ONE* 6(2): e16901. doi:10.1371/journal.pone.0016901.

56 "Semco—Insanity That Works." *Freibergs*. www.freibergs.com/resources/articles/leadership/semco-insanity-that-works/.

57 Fischer, Ronald. 2013. "Gene-Environment Interactions Are Associated with Endorsement of Social Hierarchy Values and Beliefs across Cultures." *Journal of Cross-Cultural Psychology* 44(7): 1107–1121. doi:10.1177/0022022112471896.

58 Sidanius, Jim., and Felicia Pratto. 1999. *Social Dominance: An Intergroup Theory of Social Hierarchy and Oppression*. New York: Cambridge University Press.

59 Mrazek, Alissa J., Joan Y. Chiao, Katherine D. Blizinsky, Janetta Lun, and Michele J. Gelfand. 2013. "The Role of Culture–Gene Coevolution in Morality Judgment: Examining the Interplay between Tightness–Looseness and Allelic Variation of the Serotonin Transporter Gene." *Culture and Brain* 1(2–4): 100–117.

60 Ibid.

61 Reuters in Seoul. 2004. "Asia Koreans Die 'Saving Kim Portraits.'" *The Guardian*. April 29. www.theguardian.com/world/2004/apr/29/northkorea.

62 Premack, Rachel. 2016. "Koreans Have Mastered the Art of the Protest." *Foreign Policy*. December 7. http://foreignpolicy.com/2016/12/02/koreans-have-mastered-the-art-of-the-protest.

63 Booth, Hannah. 2017. "The Kingdom of Women: The Society Where a Man Is Never the Boss." *The Guardian*. April 1. www.theguardian.com/lifeandstyle/2017/apr/01/the-kingdom-of-women-the-tibetan-tribe-where-a-man-is-never-the-boss.

64 Zeidenstein, Sondra A. 1970. "Review: Woman's Role in Economic Development." Review of *Women's Role in Economic Development*, by Ester Boserup. *The Bangladesh Economic Review* 2(1): 507–510. www.jstor.org/stable/40795751.

65 Alesina, Alberto., Paola Giuliano, and Nathan Nunn. 2013. "On the Origins of Gender Roles: Women and the Plough." *The Quarterly Journal of Economics* 128(2): 469–530. doi:10.3386/w17098.

66 Starkweather, Katherine E., and Raymond Hames. 2012. "A Survey of Non-Classical Polyandry." *Human Nature* 23(2): 149–172. doi:10.1007/s12110-012-9144-x.

67 Barber, Nigel. 2008. "Explaining Cross-National Differences in Polygyny Intensity." *Cross-Cultural Research* 42(2): 103–117. doi:10.1177/1069397108314587.

68 Opie, Christopher., Quentin D. Atkinson, Robin I. M. Dunbar, and Susanne Shultz. 2013. "Male Infanticide Leads to Social Monogamy in Primates." *Proceedings of the National Academy of Sciences* 110(33): 13328–13332. doi:10.1073/pnas.1307903110.

69 Macedo, Stephen. 2017. *Just Married: Same-Sex Couples, Monogamy and the Future of Marriage*. Princeton, NJ: Princeton University Press.

70 Bauch, Chris T., and Richard Mcelreath. 2016. "Disease Dynamics and Costly Punishment Can Foster Socially Imposed Monogamy." *Nature Communications* 7: 11219. doi:10.1038/ncomms11219.

71 Zhong, Songfa., Salomon Israel, Hong Xue, Richard P. Ebstein, and Soo Hong Chew. 2009. "Monoamine Oxidase A Gene (MAOA) Associated with Attitude towards Longshot Risks." *PLoS ONE* 4(12): e8516. doi:10.1371/journal.pone.0008516.

72 Beaver, Kevin M., Matt Delisi, Michael G. Vaughn, and J. C. Barnes. 2010. "Monoamine Oxidase A Genotype Is Associated with Gang Membership and Weapon Use." *Comprehensive Psychiatry* 51(2): 130–134. doi:10.1016/j.comppsych.2009.03.010.

73 Caspi, Avshalom., Joseph Mcclay, Terrie E. Moffitt, Jonathan Mill, Judy Martin, Ian W. Craig, Alan Taylor, and Richie Poulton. 2002. "Role of Genotype in the Cycle of Violence in Maltreated Children." *Science* 297(5582): 851–854. doi:10.1126/science.1072290.

74 Choe, Daniel Ewon., Daniel S. Shaw, Luke W. Hyde, and Erika E. Forbes. 2014. "Interactions between Monoamine Oxidase A and Punitive Discipline in African American and Caucasian Men's Antisocial Behavior." *Clinical Psychological Science* 2(5): 591–601. doi:10.1177/2167702613518046.

75 Chen, Henian., Daniel S. Pine, Monique Ernst, Elena Gorodetsky, Stephanie Kasen, Kathy Gordon, David Goldman, and Patricia Cohen. 2013. "The MAOA Gene Predicts Happiness in Women." *Progress in Neuro-Psychopharmacology and Biological Psychiatry* 40: 122–125. doi:10.1016/j.pnpbp.2012.07.018.

76 Lea, Rod., and Geoffrey Chambers. 2007. "Monoamine Oxidase, Addiction, and the 'Warrior' Gene Hypothesis." *The New Zealand Medical Journal* 120(1250): u2441. www.researchgate.net/publication/6466626/download.

77 Lung, For-Wey., Dong-Sheng Tzeng, Mei-Feng Huang, and Ming-Been Lee. 2011. "Association of the MAOA Promoter UVNTR Polymorphism with Suicide Attempts in Patients with Major Depressive Disorder." *BMC Medical Genetics* 12(1): 74. doi:10.1186/1471-2350-12-74.

78 Lu, Ru-Band., Jia-Fu Lee, Huei-Chen Ko, Wei-Wen Lin, Kevin Chen, and Jean Chen Shih. 2002. "No Association of the MAOA Gene with Alcoholism among Han Chinese Males in Taiwan." *Progress in Neuro-Psychopharmacology and Biological Psychiatry* 26(3): 457–461. doi:10.1016/s0278-5846(01)00288-3.

79 Shumay, Elena., Jean Logan, Nora D. Volkow, and Joanna S. Fowler. 2012. "Evidence That the Methylation State of the Monoamine Oxidase A (MAOA) Gene Predicts Brain Activity of MAO A Enzyme in Healthy Men." *Epigenetics* 7(10): 1151–1160. doi:10.4161/epi.21976.

80 Gur, Ruben C., Jan Richard, Monica E. Calkins, Rosetta Chiavacci, John A. Hansen, Warren B. Bilker, James Loughead et al. 2012. "Age Group and Sex Differences in Performance on a Computerized Neurocognitive Battery in Children Age 8–21." *Neuropsychology* 26(2): 251–265. doi:10.1037/a0026712.

81 Leonard, Christiana M., Stephen Towler, Suzanne Welcome, Laura K. Halderman, Ron Otto, Mark A. Eckert, and Christine Chiarello. 2008. "Size Matters: Cerebral Volume Influences Sex Differences in Neuroanatomy." *Cerebral Cortex* 18(12): 2920–2931. doi:10.1093/cercor/bhn052.

82 Im, Kiho., Jong-Min Lee, Oliver Lyttelton, Sun Hyung Kim, Alan C. Evans, and Sun I. Kim. 2008. "Brain Size and Cortical Structure in the Adult Human Brain." *Cerebral Cortex* 18(9): 2181–2191. doi:10.1093/cercor/bhm244.

83 Ingalhalikar, Madhura., Alex Smith, Drew Parker, Theodore D. Satterthwaite, Mark A. Elliott, Kosha Ruparel, Hakon Hakonarson, Raquel E. Gur, Ruben C. Gur, and Ragini Verma. 2013. "Sex Differences in the Structural Connectome of the Human Brain." *Proceedings of the National Academy of Sciences* 111(2): 823–828. doi:10.1073/pnas.1316909110.

84 Joel, Daphna., and Ricardo Tarrasch. 2014. "On the mis-presentation and misinterpretation of gender-related data: the case of Ingalhalikar's human connectome study." *Proceedings of the National Academy of Sciences* 111(6): E637–E637.

85 Eliot, Lise. 2010. *Pink Brain, Blue Brain: How Small Differences Grow into Troublesome Gaps—And What We Can Do About It.* New York: Mariner Books.

86 Fine, Cordelia. 2011. *Delusions of Gender: How Our Minds, Society, and Neurosexism Create Difference.* New York: W. W. Norton & Company.

87 Joel, Daphna., Zohar Berman, Ido Tavor, and Nadav Wexler, Olga Gaber, Yaniv Stein, Nisan Shefi et al. 2015. "Sex beyond the Genitalia: The Human Brain Mosaic." *Proceedings of the National Academy of Sciences* 112(50): 15468–15473. doi:10.1073/pnas.1509654112.

88 Choi, Charles. 2007. "Strange but True: When Half a Brain Is Better Than a Whole One." *Scientific American.* May 24. www.scientificamerican.com/article/strange-but-true-when-half-brain-better-than-whole.

89 Jain, Naveen. 2012. "If Men Are from Mars, Then Women Are Too." *Inc.* August 14. www.inc.com/naveen-jain/study-men-and-women-do-think-the-same.html.

90 Jordan-Young, Rebecca., and Raffaella I. Rumiati. 2012. "Hardwired for Sexism? Approaches to Sex/Gender in Neuroscience." *Neuroethics* 5(3): 305–315. doi:10.1007/s12152-011-9134-4.

91 Kaiser, Anelis. 2012. "Re-Conceptualizing 'Sex' and 'Gender' in the Human Brain." *Zeitschrift für Psychologie* 220(2): 130–136. http://dx.doi.org/10.1027/2151-2604/a000104.

92 Fine, Cordelia. 2013. "Is There Neurosexism in Functional Neuroimaging Investigations of Sex Differences?" *Neuroethics* 6(2): 369–409. doi:10.1007/s12152-012-9169-1.

93 Fine, Cordelia. 2011. "Explaining, or Sustaining, the Status Quo? The Potentially Self-Fulfilling Effects of 'Hardwired' Accounts of Sex Differences." *Neuroethics* 5(3): 285–294. doi:10.1007/s12152-011-9118-4.

94 Fine, Cordelia., Rebecca Jordan-Young, Anelis Kaiser, and Gina Rippon. 2013. "Plasticity, Plasticity, Plasticity and the Rigid Problem of Sex." *Trends in Cognitive Sciences* 17(11): 550–555. doi:10.1016/j.tics.2013.08.010.

95 O'Connor, Cliodhna., and Helene Joffe. 2014. "Social Representations of Brain Research: Exploring Public (Dis) Engagement with Contemporary Neuroscience." *Science Communication* 36(5): 617–645.

96 De Luque, Marry Sully., and Mansour Javidan. 2004. "Uncertainty Avoidance." In *Culture, Leadership, and Organizations: The GLOBE Study of 62 Societies*, ed. Robert J. House et al., 603–653. Thousand Oaks, CA: SAGE Publication.

97 Pagel, Mark. 2012. *Wired for Culture: Origins of the Human Social Mind*, 83. New York: W. W. Norton & Company.

98 Evan, Carolyn. 2005. "The Double-Edged Sword: Religious Influences on International Humanitarian Law." *Melbourne Journal of International Law* 6(1): 1–32. http://law.unimelb.edu.au/__data/assets/pdf_file/0003/1681140/Evans.pdf.

99 De Luque, Marry Sully., and Mansour Javidan. 2004. "Uncertainty Avoidance." In *Culture, Leadership, and Organizations: The GLOBE Study of 62 Societies*, ed. Robert J. House et al., 602–653. Thousand Oaks, CA: SAGE Publication.

100 Hofstede, Geert., Gert-Jan Hofstede, and Michael Minkov. 2005. *Cultures and Organizations: Software of the Mind*, 168–169. New York: McGraw-Hill.

101 Plaue, Noah. 2012. "If You Think the Soda Ban Is Bad, Check Out All The Things That Are Illegal in Singapore." *Business Insider*. June 19. www.businessinsider.com.au/absurd-laws-of-singapore-2012-6.

102 Ebstein, Richard P., Olga Novick, Roberto Umansky, Beatrice Priel, Yamima Osher, Darren Blaine, Estelle R. Bennett, Lubov Nemanov, Miri Katz, and Robert H. Belmaker. 1996. "Dopamine D4 Receptor (D4DR) Exon III Polymorphism Associated with the Human Personality Trait of Novelty Seeking." *Nature Genetics* 12(1): 78–80.

103 Dreber, Anna., David G. Rand, Nils Wernerfelt, Justin R. Garcia, Miguel G. Vilar, J. Koji Lum, and Richard Zeckhauser. 2011. "Dopamine and Risk Choices in Different Domains: Findings among Serious Tournament Bridge Players." *Journal of Risk and Uncertainty* 43(1): 19–38.

104 Reist, Christopher., Vural Ozdemir, Eric Wang, Mehrtash Hashemzadeh, Steven Mee, and Robert Moyzis. 2007. "Novelty Seeking and the Dopamine D4 Receptor Gene (DRD4) Revisited in Asians: Haplotype Characterization and Relevance of the 2-Repeat Allele." *American Journal of Medical Genetics Part B: Neuropsychiatric Genetics* 144(4): 453–457.

105 Matthews, Luke J., and Paul M. Butler. 2011. "Novelty-Seeking DRD4 Polymorphisms Are Associated with Human Migration Distance Out-of-Africa after Controlling for Neutral Population Gene Structure." *American Journal of Physical Anthropology* 145(3): 382–389. doi:10.1002/ajpa.21507.

106 Gören, Erkan. 2016. "The Biogeographic Origins of Novelty-Seeking Traits." *Evolution and Human Behavior* 37(6): 456–469.

107 Ptacek, Radek., Hana Kuzelova, and George B. Stefano. 2011. "Dopamine D4 Receptor Gene DRD4 and Its Association with Psychiatric Disorders." *Medical Science Monitor* 17(9): RA215–A220. doi:10.12659/msm.881925.

108 Williams, Jonathan., and Eric Taylor. 2005. "The Evolution of Hyperactivity, Impulsivity and Cognitive Diversity." *Journal of the Royal Society Interface* 3(8): 399–413.

109 Ding, Yuan-Chun., Han-Chang Chi, Deborah L. Grady, Atsuyuki Morishima, Judith R. Kidd, Kenneth K. Kidd, Pamela Flodman et al. 2002. "Evidence of Positive Selection Acting at the Human Dopamine Receptor D4 Gene Locus." *Proceedings of the National Academy of Sciences* 99(1): 309–314.

110 Shelley-Tremblay, John F., and Lee A. Rosen. 1996. "Attention Deficit Hyperactivity Disorder: An Evolutionary Perspective." *The Journal of Genetic Psychology* 157(4): 443–453.

111 Wang, Eric. 2004. "The Genetic Architecture of Selection at the Human Dopamine Receptor D4 (DRD4) Gene Locus." *American Journal of Human Genetics* 74(5): 931–944. doi:10.1086/420854.

112 Sasaki, Joni Y., Heejung S. Kim, Taraneh Mojaverian, Lauren D. S. Kelley, In Young Park, and Skirmantas Janušonis. 2011. "Religion Priming Differentially Increases Prosocial Behavior among Variants of the Dopamine D4 Receptor (DRD4) Gene." *Social Cognitive and Affective Neuroscience* 8(2): 209–215. doi:10.1093/scan/nsr089.

113 Kitayama, Shinobu., Anthony King, Carolyn Yoon, Steve Tompson, Sarah Huff, and Israel Liberzon. 2014. "The Dopamine D4 Receptor Gene (DRD4) Moderates Cultural Difference in Independent Versus Interdependent Social Orientation." *Psychological Science* 25(6): 1169–1177. doi:10.1177/0956797614528338.

114 Kitayama, Shinobu., and Sarah Huff. 2015. "Cultural Neuroscience: Connecting Culture, Brain, and Genes." In *Emerging Trends in the Social and Behavioral Sciences: An Interdisciplinary, Searchable, and Linkable Resource for the 21st Century*, ed. Robert Scott, Stephen Kosslyn, and Marlis Buchmann, 1–16. Hoboken, NJ: John Wiley & Sons.

115 Kidd, Michael W. 1997. "The Frontier in American History." *University of Virginia*. September 30. http://xroads.virginia.edu/~HYPER/TURNER/.

116 Robson, David. 2017. "Future—How East and West Think in Profoundly Different Ways." *BBC*. January 19. www.bbc.com/future/story/20170118-how-east-and-west-think-in-profoundly-different-ways.

117 Mello, Zena R., and Frank C. Worrell. 2015. "The Past, the Present, and the Future: A Conceptual Model of Time Perspective in Adolescence." In *Time Perspective: Theory, Research and Application: Essays in Honor of Philip G. Zimbardo*, ed. Maciej Stolarski, 115–129. Cham, Switzerland: Springer.

118 MacIver, Malcolm. 2011. "Why Did Consciousness Evolve, and How Can We Modify It?" *Discover—Science for the Curious*. March 14. http://blogs.discovermagazine.com/sciencenotfiction/2011/03/14/why-did-consciousness-evolve-and-how-can-we-modify-it/.

119 Szpunar, Karl K., Jason M. Watson, and Kathleen B. Mcdermott. 2007. "Neural Substrates of Envisioning the Future." *Proceedings of the National Academy of Sciences* 104(2): 642–647. doi:10.1073/pnas.0610082104.

4 The Dynamics of Culture

In the previous chapter, we learned that there is only one culture in the evolutionary sense, and it is a strategy for humankind to survive and advance. This evolutionary culture consists of universal fundamental concerns, values at the baseline level, and certain outward expressions that all human societies share. However, culture in the practical sense is immensely diverse. It is the result of many concerns that are unique to each culture, the differing degrees of importance we place on them, and the way we express these concerns and values using a myriad of symbols, objects, and behaviors.

This diversity of the practical culture is the outcome of an interactive play among five factors in the Diversity Pathway GCEB-Be. That sounds plausible, but also challenging because GCEB-Be interactions are complex, unpredictable, and situational. Researchers have suggested "indexing" context,[1] but the method is still far from an easy application. While we can't possibly morph all interactions of GCEB-Be into a fixed framework, we can still discuss some patterns of its dynamics. For example, with all five driving forces of GCEB-Be, how fast does a culture change? How diverse is a culture? Can opposing values coexist in a culture and in an individual? These are the questions we will address in this chapter.

4.1 Changing Culture

Technically, no scholars have ever stated that culture does not change. What divides them, however, is the speed and nature of the change. In this section, we will review these schools of thought and gain insight from their debate.

4.1.1 Static versus Dynamic

Theories of intercultural communication split into two main paradigms: Static culture and dynamic culture. The former school of thought is more dominant with the classic work of Hofstede.[2] He proposed an index in which he put each country on a binary ranking, measuring their average level of, for example, individualism and masculinity. Giving the culture of each country a fixed number makes sense for the static paradigm because it posits that culture is very stable, values are difficult to change, and national cultures are "as hard as a country's geographic position."[3] "Differences between national cultures at the end of the last century were already recognizable in the years 1900, 1800, and 1700, if not earlier. There is no reason they should not remain recognizable until at least 2100."[4] "While change sweeps the surface, the deeper layers remain stable, and the [national] culture rises from its ashes like the phoenix."[5] If changes in values do happen somehow, they occur at a very slow rate, and because *the whole world changes together* at more or less the *same speed*, the gaps between national cultures remain more or less the same.[6] Based on this assumption, supporters of the static paradigm argue that the ranking of countries is valid because cultures tend to change together in unison. Speaking of individual

values, Hofstede argued that by the age of ten, most of the child's basic values have been pro-
grammed into his or her mind: "We assume that each person carries a certain amount of mental
programming which is stable over time."[7]

The advantage of seeing culture as stable is that it gives us the idea that behaviors can be
predicted,[8-9] hence, reducing ambiguity and variability[10] when businesses decide to go international. Culture is "a set of control mechanisms—plans, recipes, rules, instructions—for
governing behavior."[11] By calculating a score of each country, Hofstede stated that his index on
five value systems can "affect human thinking, feeling, and acting, as well as organizations and
institutions, in predictable ways."[12] For example, Australia scores 90 on the fundamental concern of individualism.[13] This means the value they place on this concern of independence is high
(90) and this value is very stable. Assuming that Australian customers consistently have this individualistic characteristic, we can prepare a business approach that taps into that value, and stand
more chance to succeed. The view of culture as static led Kogut and Singh to develop a simple,
standardized quantitative measurement for international business.[14] Their following equation is
based on Hofstede's index where KSij is the cultural distance between countries; idx is the index
of a country x in the dimension d; Vd is the variance of the index for the dimension d; and n is
the number of cultural dimensions.

The assumption behind this equation has received a great amount of criticism. First, defining
culture only as a persistent heritage of values rejects the *authorship of people*. It assumes that "at
some time in the past, the inhabitants of a supposedly culturally uniform location are defined
as active in creating a culture, but for multiple generations, the inhabitants have [somehow]
ceased to be creative, and instead, have [become] passive inheritors."[15] In other words, people
first created culture, then, at some point during the history, they stopped and let culture shape
them. From then on, they have become "cultural dopes" who collectively relay under the complete dictatorship of predetermined values, unable to exercise any influences or revolutionary
impact.

Second, the static paradigm discourages organizations to look at change, evolution, and
learning. If national culture is coherent and stable, change rarely happens. If it does, "the transformation is country-wide (not in particular locations—region, sectors, industries, or whatever); and because absolute within-country cultural complementarily is posited, the source of
change cannot be internal to a country, it must necessarily come from beyond its border."[16] In
other words, rare changes can only be created through an exogenous (i.e., external) shock. This
conflicts with many empirical studies[17] because endogenous (internal) change does happen,[18]
even within isolated "primitive" societies.[19-20]

Third, in the business context, the equation of Kogut and Singh has become so entrenched in
management research that it forms a basis for many derivatives, such as "knowledge distance,"[21]
"technology distance,"[22] and "institutional distance."[23] Critics[24-25-26] argued that the equation
put a final touch in reducing culture to a set of discrete variables "that can be documented and
manipulated in an instrumental way."[27] Using a study on the inherent transaction disabilities in
joint ventures,[28] the equation was criticized as it provides a perfect proxy to deal with environmental uncertainty, to cope with the firms' inability to specify transaction contingencies due to
the fear that whatever they might gain in terms of knowledge would apparently be lost because
of the potential exploitation by the local partner.[29] Because culture is treated as an information

$$KS_{ij} = \frac{1}{n} \sum_{d=1}^{n} \frac{\left(I_i^d - I_j^d \right)}{V^d}$$

Figure 4.1 Kogut and Singh's formula of cultural distance

cost,[30] its static nature discourages organizations to look at change, evolution, and learning. The extremely simple and user-friendly measure of the equation is so attractive that it *gained* popularity after receiving hash critique from scholars.[31]

By contrast, the dynamic paradigm argues that culture is not stable, but rather dynamic in the process of responding to the external environment.[32-33-34-35-36] In essence, "[C]ultures are fusions, remixes and recombinants. They are made and remade through exchange, imitation, intersection, incorporation, reshuffling; through travels, trade, subordination."[37] It is anything but a time-free "fossil."[38] Depending on particular context, that is the unique synergy of GCEB-Be at a given time, culture can adapt to meet eco-socio-politico demands.[39] Thus, culture evolves in response to the impacts of influential individuals, historical events, environmental changes, innovation development, and so forth. According to this paradigm, static indexes can be helpful, but should be regarded as *the first best guess.* Obviously, no businesses can be successful based on a guess. Market analysis, partnership building, product development, and so forth are developed with solid and in-depth data. Hence, the dynamic paradigm advocates a holistic and thorough view of culture instead of using regression equation to deal with complex features of cross-cultural interaction.

4.1.2 General Speed of Change

While the static paradigm posits that cultures are stable and if they change, all countries change in unison, the dynamic paradigm does not advocate a fixed pattern of change. From evolutionary point of view, to fulfill the role of survival strategies, a practical culture can't be static. Its changes, however, depend on the interaction with other factors (GCEB-Be) and can't be forced into a fixed framework or index. What we can generally predict is the speed of change in different parts of the metaphorical tree. As a general rule, the leaves change regularly and quickly (outward expressions), the twigs and branches change more slowly (values), and the trunk and roots change slowest of all (fundamental concerns).

Like a tree, culture is a constant process. However, not all parts of culture change at a similar rate. Our fundamental concerns are subjected to the least amount of change because they are the building blocks of culture as a survival strategy, the very foundation of our secret to advancing as a species (education, religion, music, freedom, hierarchy, etc.). Culture in the evolutionary sense is the same for every society and is very stable. By contrast, culture in the practical sense is extremely diverse. Values indicate how important we perceive a concern ought to be, that is low, average, or high. These positions change with a speed that depends on particular contexts as we see with case of Japanese employees' work loyalty mentioned in Chapter 3. Being extremely loyal to one's company was the norm because it meant a lifetime employment and absolute support. However, when markets change, corporate loyalty became less of a requirement. Finally, outward expressions change the fastest of all. We constantly experience new things, create new policies, do different things on different days, and behave and communicate differently to various people and situations.

4.1.3 Using Context to Predict and Understand Change

A culture would generally follow a pattern of change as described in the previous section, that is concerns are stable, values change according to contexts, and outward expressions change the fastest of all. What we can't emphasize strongly enough is the role of context. By giving us the holistic picture of GCEB-Be interactions in a particular situation, context helps us to predict and understand the change, its nature, and its speed.

Here is an example: In Australia, due to many historical changes, the Liberal party is currently conservative, and the Labor party is now more progressive than their rival. Their names (read: outward expressions) do not quite reflect their values, if not the opposite. Only by understanding the context of the political history in Australia can one grasp the seeming contradiction and follow the course of political change in this country.

Context can drive change dramatically, transforming even deep-rooted values and entrenched habits. Take Singapore for an example. Business integrity is universally a fundamental concern, quite likely that it belongs to the concern category of uncertainty avoidance. Singapore is undoubtedly a champion in this aspect, ranking seventh on the Corruption Perceptions Index.[40] However, *high* level of integrity is *not* a traditional value of the Singaporean culture. Instead, it was deliberately decided, enforced, nurtured, and maintained over a pretty short period. As a key entrepôt in the drug trade between India and China, the island was beset by crime and corruption. In his book, CapitaLand's CEO recalled that to make sure one's posts would be duly delivered, it was not unusual to pay a small bribe.[41] With a "zero-tolerance" approach to corruption, the founding Prime Minister Lee Kuan Yew and his government turned Singapore into one of the most transparent countries in the world within just a few decades. Although collectivist people such as Indians and Chinese (two major ethnicities of Singapore) can be more prone toward accepting bribes,[42] Lee Kuan Yew proved that this value is not static, and it can change with strong will, comprehensive laws, and recognition of desired behaviors. A symbolic outward expression that is well remembered from his government is when they wore white shirts and trousers to be sworn into office, signaling the purity of their intentions.[43] This example shows us that we can push the speed of cultural changes with different strategies (i.e., outward expression) that help to shift how a fundamental concern is perceived (i.e., value). It illustrates the pathway Behavior—Culture in GCEB-Be and shows us that not only culture guides behaviors, but also repeated behaviors can quickly change even deeply rooted values and institutionalized outward expressions of a culture.

Globalization and the interconnectedness of multicultural societies also act as powerful drivers for cultural change, such as the case of Canada, Japan, and Morocco, where collectivistic values have been changing over time.[44] As survival strategies, cultures around the world are more dynamic processes than entities fixated with a number. In short, changes in values and expressions can be quite dynamic. Hence, what matters to businesses is not only understanding how fast or slow their markets change but also the context of the change: What kinds of circumstances and situations that drive the change? *As contexts differ, so do the speed and nature of the change.*

In fact, the word "culture" can't be understood in a static way. It is derived from the Latin word *"colere"*—to "till" the soil for farming. It is a *verb*, not a noun.[45] The concept signals growth and development rather than stability. Interestingly, the Chinese word for culture *"wen-hua"* is the combination of two components: "Literature" and "change." Again, it can be erroneous to assume stability in a concept that is inherently dynamic.

4.2 Diverse Culture

In the previous section, we learned that the static paradigm gained its popularity through the premise of stable culture, unchanging values, calculated as a set of fixed scores on a binary spectrum. Benefit not withstanding, in this section, we will critically look at this assumption and recognize the risks behind such a view of culture. We will discuss the notion that culture is not only changing but also internally diverse.

4.2.1 Culture Is Not Homogeneous

The static paradigm has given rise to many frameworks that position each country on a scale for comparison. For example, as we mentioned in the previous section, Australia scores 90 and thus, is a very individualistic country. However, is this average useful?

For the "first best guess," yes. And for a country that is very homogeneous, yes. The problem is, not a single country in the world is considered homogeneous in a cultural sense,[46] if we understand culture in terms of language, religion, generation, ethnicity, profession, gender, and so forth. It is fine knowing that, on the average, Australia is the second most individualistic country in the world because it is a good start. But at the same time, it is utterly naïve to believe that this index gives a correct picture of how group-oriented or self-oriented Australian people are. The index is meant to reflect the average of Australian culture, but 100% of the time we don't do business with an average person. In fact, there is no such thing as an average Australian because no single person has a profile that scores average on every single aspect of her/his culture. When we factor in the immense diversity of this country, the index brings more questions than answers. Out of a population of 24 million, nearly 30% of all Australians were born overseas,[47] and 20% of them do not speak English at home. The index makes no sense when applied for the Indigenous, Lebanese, Vietnamese, Italian, Greek, or Chinese communities. For example, cultural-savvy businesses know they need to ditch the individualistic index and adopt a *collectivistic* sale approach if they want to align with a massive segment of Australian customers whose consuming habits are determined by group mentality. For this segment, their buying patterns should reflect status and reputation—elements highly valued by peers. As a result, sale approaches should follow a collectivistic strategy that highlights prestige stores and expensive cars.[48] Along this line of reasoning, the average index of Australia risks painting in too broad of a stroke over the extremely rich and versatile landscape of ethnic economy in this continent.[49] Hence, it would be wise to go beyond the static index and take a particular context into account, starting by simple questions such as: Who is your company's partner? Where do the owners come from? How (non)Australian are they? Will they behave stereotypically Australian in this situation? Will they change along the way, and if so, what will possibly be the motives?

The human species is a young one. As a result, we are not genetically diverse, and we are biologically a single race. Interestingly, the tiny difference in our genetic makeup occurs among those who live next to each other rather than far away from each other. Approximately 85% of our genetic variation is observed *within* rather than *between* populations.[50-51] In other words, if you care about genetic difference at all, then it is possible that you are genetically more similar to a foreigner than to your friend who was born and raised in the same street.

While we are genetically similar as a single species, we are culturally diverse. As we know, this is because culture, not genes, is the archive of our survival strategies. However, despite the immensity of differences in cultural values and outward expressions, we observe the same situation as with our genes. Culturally, diversity *within* a society is often greater than *between* societies. According to a 2016 study that covers 32 countries around the world, 80% of the differences in values were found within countries, and less than 20% of the differences were found between countries.[52] In other words, you are likely to find more similarities with a business partner working in the same profession from the other side of the planet than with your friend who shares the same homeland.

The case of Australia questions the notion of static culture with an index indicating the average value of a diverse society. And such a case is virtually everywhere. The studies of genetic and cultural diversity confirm that morphing the complexity of a country into a single number is not only problematic but also statistically challenged.

4.2.2 Institutional Plasticity

Beyond the debate of static and dynamic, there is an increasing evidence of converging divergences, or within-country diversity, especially in work employment. To keep up with the changes in external environment and remain competitive, institutional evolution in business is essential.[53] In general, there are three approaches to change: (1) Incremental change, (2) disruptive change, and (3) institutional plasticity. Incremental change evolves around the concept of *path dependence*, which means contingent events in the past influence a later sequence of events, by which actors are liable to reach a certain outcome.[54] Once a path has been taken and decided, actors adjust their strategies to accommodate the prevailing pattern, which can lead to a "locked-in" situation.[55] Path dependence explains why it is so difficult to change because people are placed in a historic sequence of *preexisting commitments* accumulated over a long period. In short, it is "the way things have been done around here." By contrast, disruptive change advocates *radical reforms*. Disruptive events can sharply end what has become locked in by institutional inertia,[56] "throwing entire industries into the throes of quantum change."[57]

Not conforming to either of these extremes, *institutional plasticity* draws from the "plasticity" concept of natural sciences, and posits that change is about *how* actors create new development trajectories within the overarching institutional system. It is not about slow or quick change, but the flexibility born through endless interpretation and actions of change agents. In a study of German IT industry,[58] it was argued that despite the unfavorable institutional environment, a subsector—customized business software—has been able to position itself internationally in the world market by adopting institutional plasticity, such as diversifying its workforce and exploiting numerous opportunities hidden in a rigid system. The flexibility embedded in this approach creates a significant shift in the internal makeup of organizations and the nationwide workforce, resulting in an increased level of national diversity.[59] Institutional plasticity is the driver for neoliberalism, deregulation policies, firm internationalization, and *uneven* pace of change in organization—that is factors that contribute to greater level of *diversity from within*.[60] For this reason, it has been argued that "national forms of capitalism [have become] more institutionally fragmented, internally diverse and display greater plasticity."[61] To conclude, there are three forms of cultural change in general: slow, radical, and uneven. Institutional plasticity or uneven change can be a significant driver for organizations.

4.3 "Misleading" Culture

In the previous sections, it was proposed that culture is *changing* and culture is *diverse*. Too make it more dynamic, culture can be *confusing* as well. Looking at the tree metaphor, which group of elements do we observe most in our everyday life? Clearly, it is the top one. We do not see a "value" such as the "high degree of uncertainty avoidance," but we can point out its outward expressions: Excessive amount of laws and regulations, a long list of cultural taboos, serious consequences when social rules are violated, disciplined workplace, meticulous planning, rigid bureaucracy, critical roles of religion, and so forth. Can what we see deceive us? Yes, unfortunately most of the time, because what we see is just the outward expression of the whole system. When looking at this tree from a bird's-eye view, flying over it, we assume "Yes, I've seen the (whole) tree!" even though, in fact, we have only seen the leaves.

The underlying message is: What we see is just a very small part of the whole. Fundamental life concerns and values are deep under the forest canopy. We cannot rush above it and expect a thorough understanding. You need to be "down to earth," on your feet, standing next to the tree to observe it. More importantly, this warns us that the superficial embracing of food, music, clothes, or even working procedures does not mean people have changed their cultural values. Of course, repetition of behaviors can eventually change a deep-seated value (Behavior—Culture pathway), but we are never sure if the value change is *complete* just by looking at the outward expressions. Vice versa, values may have completely changed, but outward expressions do not show it. Let's explore this complexity of the somewhat "misleading" culture we are living in.

4.3.1 One Outward Expression, Many Values

It is easy to have an illusion of change based on outward expressions because they are all that we can see. Global marketers often make a mistake of assuming that similarity in practices equals similarity in perception. More often than not, it fails to be true. For example, *Dallas* was watched all over the world, but different audiences gained different meanings from the TV show: The Dutch learned a lesson that money does not guarantee happiness, Israeli Arabs confirmed that women abused by their husbands should return to their fathers, and Ghanaian women were reminded that where sex is at issue, men are not to be trusted.[62] *One outward expression, many different values.*

The same counts for a myriad of other objects, words, symbols, and behaviors. For example, depending on cultures and contexts, the "swastika" symbolizes both well-being and racism; "democratic" label is used by both dictators and liberals alike; "telling the truth" signals both virtue and bad manner; giving a "bribe" can be both expectation and a crime; and making someone "the employee of the month" works as a strong work incentive, but also can be a way to destroy team cohesiveness, and so forth. This explains why globalization may show convergence and sameness at the surface, but local cultures and particular contexts follow their own transformative and dynamic patterns.

4.3.2 One Value, Many Outward Expressions

In reverse, *one value can have many different outward expressions.* Take "religious freedom" as an example—a fundamental concern that may well fall within the category of uncertainty avoidance. Depending on cultures, individuals, and contexts, a high value of religious freedom manifests itself in many opposing outward expressions: The right to keep many parallel religious courts alongside a secular legal system, but also the right to ban religious courts and keep religion a spiritual matter; the right to integrate religious teaching at school, but also the right to ban religious teaching at school and to let people decide when they have matured, and so forth. The same situation counts for many other values. The lesson here is, outward expressions and values do *not* always match. Both "it shows what it is" and "it is what it shows" can be incorrect. Values and behaviors do not always reflect on each other the way we think they should.

4.3.3 Value and Outward Expression Contradiction

Not only values and behaviors don't always match, they may even *contradict* each other, as a study of 17,000 managers worldwide—GLOBE project—found out.[63] What people do (culture as it is) can be the *opposite* of what they believe (culture as it should be). Among Chinese employees for example, many feel the urge to behave according to the traditional value of showing *high* respect to seniority. However, they do not necessarily agree with it and may expect the value to become less rigid.[64] This sort of tension has become normality in corporate environments where millennials—those born between 1980 and 2000—are quickly changing the labor demographic and influencing business strategies. Thus, behaviors contradict values. However, we can solve this puzzle by applying a principle of microeconomics: The law of diminishing marginal utility. Put it simple, an individual who lives in a society where hierarchy acceptance is extremely high (think dictatorship) would have a stronger marginal preference for autonomy than someone who has experienced chaos as a consequence of anarchy. Thus, culture as it should be is not value, but marginal preference.[65] Despite this shortcoming, GLOBE still gives us a valid point of attention: The contradiction between behavior and temporary preference.

In Chapter 2, we discussed the contradiction between belief and behavior (cognitive dissonance). We learned that such contradiction is not beneficial for productivity. Efficiency requires a coordinated flow of doing only what one believes in. Because culture is dynamically used as a strategy for us to adapt and actively change, we can assume that this sort of tension signals a *transitional period* of cultural (re)shaping. Back to the example of Chinese millennials at the workplace, depending on the context of each organization, these millennials have two major options: (1) Slowly *change their value* to be in accordance with their behavior of respecting authority, despite the fact that this behavior is initially disrupting to them; or (2) slowly *change their behaviors* to be more in accordance with their value, showing more egalitarian patterns of communication, lobbying for new policies that attach less to the seniority system, establishing new work structure such as a buddy support in which young and old employees can help each other, and so forth. While the first choice is changing one's own value to fit in an existing culture (humans as a product of culture), the second choice is changing an existing culture by strategic use of repeated behaviors (humans as a producer of culture, following the Culture—Behavior pathway). We will discuss more about change management in Chapter 7.

To conclude, because of the immense dynamics between values and outward expressions, we should constantly be mindful of different layers of meaning in everything we see. Not only do we mean different things when we say the same word, but even when we share the same value, we may express it in totally different ways. You can challenge your cross-cultural knowledge by doing this simple exercise. Start with a value (e.g., high importance level placed on "family"—a concern that belongs to group attachment), and list as many opposing outward expressions of this value as possible, depending on different cultures, individual circumstances, and contexts. Then start with an outward expression (e.g., low income tax), and list as many opposing values behind it as you can, depending on particular cultures, individual circumstances, and contexts. The scale of contrasting values and outward expressions revealed from this simple brainstorm activity will act as a reality check for the complex world in which we are living. And for this reason, in doing business across cultures, we should learn to resist the automatic reaction, and practice a mindful technique of stop-and-think: "What does this mean?"

4.4 Contradicting Culture

Culture is not only *changing, diverse, misleading* (in terms of what it is and what it looks like) but also *contradicting* with many opposing values coexisting. The static paradigm measures culture along a binary spectrum. For example, a culture is collectivistic, individualistic, or somewhere in between. This paradigm does not tolerate a culture in which both values of weak and strong group attachment coexist.

However, paradox seems to be more often the norm than an exception. Observing a culture, we will see that it intrinsically embraces seemingly opposing values and behaviors. If global managers choose to disregard paradoxes, they will be frustrated by cultural contradictions that do not accord with the famous cross-cultural manual,[66] that Japanese negotiators don't "act Japanese,"[67] or Chinese negotiators are both very deceptive and very sincere.[68] While abundant in generally homogeneous cultures, paradoxes are a *normality* in multicultural societies such as Israel, Malaysia, and South Africa, where opposing values and outward expressions coexist.

The tendency to categorize things according to a binary pattern is completely normal because it has a great deal of benefit. However, it also discourages us to gain plural thinking when dealing with complexity. We often try to understand even complicated issues along a binary spectrum: Men-women, day-night, and so forth. We also manage to transform the reality into a line, simplifying complexity for the sake of our lazy mind, for example, analyzing of the world as east-west, despite the fact that our planet is round. In this section, we will critically look at this tendency and recognize the potential of plural thinking when it comes to culture.

4.4.1 The Digital Brain

The inherent dualistic thinking pattern has much to do with how neurons work. When a neuron is not sending a signal, it is *at resting state*, –70mV. This means the inside is 70mV less than the outside. When we have a thought/stimulus, information is sent down the axon, creating an explosion of electrical activity, opening the sodium channel, letting Na+ into the neuron, causing depolarization, moving the resting state from –70mV toward the *threshold*, usually at –55mV. If a threshold is crossed, we have an *action potential*, meaning a neuron is fired (Figure 4.2). The size of all action potentials is the same. For any given neuron, there are no weak or strong action potentials. Neurons work on an "all-or-nothing" principle. A neuron fires or does not fire. There is no in-between. In this sense, the brain is computing using binary signals. Instead of 1s and 0s, "on" or "off," it uses "spike" or "no spike."

The second ground for neural binary can be found in the "preparedness theory."[69] Most of sensory information entering our central nervous system would go through a "filter" called reticular activating system, or RAS (we will discuss this in Chapter 7), to the thalamus—our brain's "switchboard." If we oversimplify this process, we can imagine that, from this information center, data is immediately relayed in two directions: (1) *System 1* or the "autopilot" takes only 12–80 milliseconds to reach the amygdala—our emotional detective device; and (2) *System 2* or the "conscious pilot" takes the information toward the *cerebral cortex*—our thinking brain and consciousness (Figure 4.3). Even when being activated simultaneously, System 1 has priorities. The amygdala can respond quickly, instantly *deciding whether the stimuli is good or bad*. It takes longer for the information to be processed through System 2 by our thinking brain, about 200–400 milliseconds longer than the autopilot System 1. Thus, *before* the cortex has even managed to figure out what the object is (consciousness), the amygdala already decided if the object is safe or dangerous. By showing images of untrustworthy faces for only 33 milliseconds, researchers

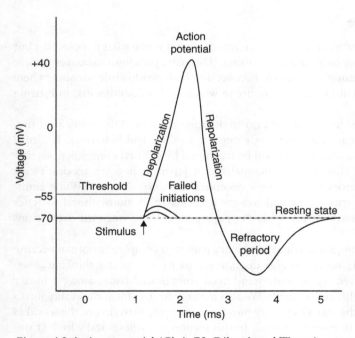

Figure 4.2 Action potential (Chris 73, Diberri, and Tizom)

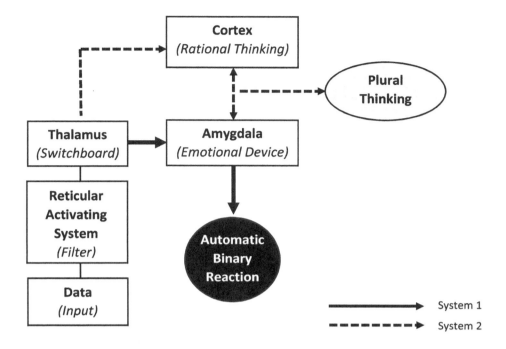

Figure 4.3 System 1 versus System 2: An oversimplified illustration of two major thinking patterns in the brain

found out that participants could not process the faces, but their amygdala did.[70] Hence, the good-bad judgement made before the awareness kicks in is called *subconscious*. This quick and binary assessment is essential for survival because we can save time and escape danger without too much thinking, using fight-or-flight automatic response. However, it also means that we have the tendency to disregard complexity by categorizing them into a simple binary, "either-or" system.[71] A knee-jerk judgment tends to be binary: A person is either good or bad, not both; a company is either ethical or immoral, not both; a relationship is either love or hate, not both.

4.4.2 The Analog Brain

However, it is erroneous to conclude that the brain is entirely digital and humans are destined to be trapped with a binary thinking system. While the action potentials that occur within each single neuron are binary, all-or-nothing, the communication between neurons is analog, or *graded potential*. As we learned from Chapter 2 on brain's plasticity, most synapses work by neurotransmitters, and this is a chemically mediated graded response. Let's say neuron 1 fires and sends a signal to neuron 2 by releasing neurotransmitters, causing a change in the membrane of neuron 2. This change can be small, below the threshold of –55mV, and by the time it reaches the trigger zone (at the beginning of neuron 2's axon) it decays and will not cause an action potential in neuron 2. However, if neuron 1 keeps on "poking" neuron 2 with more signals (temporal summation) or if other neurons also help along (spatial summation), these graded potentials will accumulate, eventually cross the threshold and create an action potential in neuron 2 at the trigger zone. Clearly, neurons do not communicate with each other in a binary system. It's almost as if neurons have to work hard, or cooperate with others to *convince*

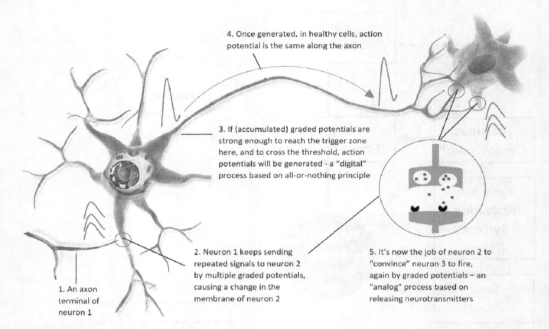

4. Once generated, in healthy cells, action potential is the same along the axon

3. If (accumulated) graded potentials are strong enough to reach the trigger zone here, and to cross the threshold, action potentials will be generated - a "digital" process based on all-or-nothing principle

2. Neuron 1 keeps sending repeated signals to neuron 2 by multiple graded potentials, causing a change in the membrane of neuron 2

1. An axon terminal of neuron 1

5. It's now the job of neuron 2 to "convince" neuron 3 to fire, again by graded potentials – an "analog" process based on releasing neurotransmitters

Figure 4.4 Graded potential and action potential: How neurons communicate (Original image of the neuron by Bruce Blaus, modified by Mai Nguyen-Phuong-Mai)

a specific neuron to fire. Put it this way: A neuron is analog with "persuasion," but digital with "decision making." The persuasion includes "please," "come on," "let me explain to you one more time," and "look, other neurons agree with me." The decision-making results in either a "yes" or a "no." Once the persuasion crosses the threshold, a neuron will act decisively, sending a nerve impulse (i.e., action potential) with exactly the same power along the axon terminal. Now it is the "analog job" of neuron 2 to "convince" another neuron in the network to fire. This is what happens in our brain day in, day out. If a network of neurons fire with each other quickly without too much persuasion, so to speak, it means you have learned something thoroughly, a certain thought has become regular, or a habit has formed (Figure 4.4).

Now that we know neurons communicate both with graded and action potentials, let's have a closer look at the System 1 versus System 2 of our emotional reaction. In a similar fashion, System 1 is digital, but System 2 is analog, or better put, *System 1 represents binary thinking*, but *System 2 represents plural thinking*. The fact that System 1 reacts on the basis of polarity such as yes-no, right-wrong, and good-bad does not mean we can't comprehend complexity. However, it takes time for information to be processed using System 2, reaching consciousness, being processed, and communicating *back and forth* with different brain regions (Figure 4.2). It takes time and effort to understand nuances. To use an analogy, logical and clear thinking can be achieved when the amygdala does not guide our behaviors on its own, but it has time to "discuss" thoroughly with the cerebral cortex, exchanging data, and eventually reaching a final conclusion. In short, good decisions happen at the crossing point between the two systems. A knee-jerk reaction is binary, but complex thinking is plural.

To conclude, the brain's mechanism cannot be reduced to a binary or graded system. A combination of both can be found between neurons and different regions of the brain. This is the foundation for us to explore how we, as individuals, can execute both strategies of viewing the world: Digital *and* analog, binary *and* plural, simple *and* complex.

4.4.3 *Plural Thinking with Opposing Values in Individuals*

Thanks to the incredible ability to accommodate complex thinking, both behavioral[72-73] and neuroscience studies[74-75-76] have proposed that we are able to have a *multicultural mind*. We don't even need intensive training to see how malleable the brain is because every thought, action, and simulation can slightly change its neural patterns.[77] Simple cues such as a symbol or the difference in using plural pronouns (e.g., "we" and "our") and singular pronouns (e.g., "I" and "me") can activate relevant cultural mindsets and their associate networks. For example, people primed with individualistic values showed enhanced evaluation of *general* self (e.g., I'm honest), whereas those primed with collectivistic values showed enhanced processing of *contextual* self (e.g., *When talking to my mother*, I am honest).[78] Our brain is so flexible that we are capable of representing *multiple cultures*[79] in our mind, switching between values simultaneously, and communicating very complex information, to the point that we can be both collectivistic and individualistic, as long as a specific context activates that element in us.

Most of us practice this kind of value switching daily with basic communication tasks. For example, we know pretty well when to be polite and tell a little lie, and when to be honest and tell the truth. When it comes to more complex tasks, value switching takes more practice and energy. But it can be done. Don't forget that with repeated behaviors, the brain physically changes itself to help us advance in response to a new culture. For example, you can be competitive in a cutthroat sale project, but shift yourself to be more cooperative with a partner with whom you want to establish a long-term relationship. At the same time, you can carefully combine both strategies in another ongoing negotiation project. In *The Postmodern Brain*, the author argued that the brain is a nonlinear framework, responding dynamically to changing demands.[80] You are not necessarily *either* collectivistic *or* individualistic because you can be both. It may take System 2 a long time to work this complexity out, but as the old saying goes, "practice makes perfect," even a challenging task such as value switching can become automatic and eventually become autopilot using System 1 (Behavior—Brain pathway).

Value switching aside, it is also crucial in seeing beyond opposing values and binary systems. In many cases, we don't have the luxury of choosing to act "either-or," but have to come up with a complex solution. In an answer on *Quora*, the author Charles Duhigg offered an excellent way of looking at it. Good decision making is almost never "this" or "that," but involves thinking through various contradictory possibilities, and then trying to figure out which ones are more or less likely, and why. In his words:

> Say, for instance, that you are trying to decide whether your group of rebels should attack the Death Star. Seems like an easy decision, right?... You'll think about this decision in binary terms ("The Empire = bad. The rebels = good. What can go wrong?").
>
> But, if you are practiced at decision-making, you'll probably do something a bit differently; you'll sit down with Adm. Ackbar, and you'll try to envision the dozens of different outcomes that are possible (i.e. going through endless "what if …?").... [By] forcing yourself to think through all the possibilities and then simply trying to assign odds will be really helpful in revealing what you do and don't know.... Now you know which parts of your plan are weakest.
>
> Our brains, left to their own devices, prefer to think about choices in binary terms. (And, from an evolutionary standpoint, this is really efficient.) But to make better decisions, we have to force ourselves to think probabilistically—and then we need to get comfortable with the fact that probabilistic thinking tends to reveal how much we don't know. It is scary to confront uncertainty. It can make you crazy and anxious. That's why it is so much easier to look at choices as binary options ("I'll either succeed or fail") or deterministic outcomes ("I ended up married to her because she was my soulmate.") But if you

genuinely want to make better decisions, you have to fight that instinct, and make yourself think about multiple possibilities—both the good and the bad—and be really honest with yourself about what you do and don't know (and what is knowable and unknowable.). And then you have to take a leap, and make a decision, and see it as an experiment that gives you data, rather than a success or failure that you should congratulate yourself on/ beat yourself up about.

Because, unfortunately, the force doesn't really exist. But probabilities do.[81]

4.4.4 Complex Culture with Opposing Values

If we can find opposing values coexisting within our own mind as individuals, it is easy to understand that opposing values coexist in any other social institutions such as a culture. We are reminded here that the diversity *within* is greater than *between* a population, both genetically and culturally. If we are able to view culture as dynamic instead of a stable, fixed, and static set of unchanged values, then opposites and paradoxes should be understood as an inherent part of culture. This means we are able to see complexity (System 2) and avoid the neural tendency to simplify reality for the sake of quick and easy understanding (System 1).

Like the yin-yang philosophy, opposites coexist and can reverse their positions at a given point in history, depending on the context. A 2015 study[82] suggested that collectivistic pattern exists in Canadian society—a culture stereotypically known for individualism. The same study found that in comparison with Canada, vertical individualism is more prevalent in Morocco—a culture stereotypically known for collectivism. The author concluded that a culture not only dynamically changes but it can also be both collectivistic *and* individualistic.

In multicultural societies such as Lebanon and Israel, opposing values and outward expressions are a *normality* with both collectivistic *and* individualistic way of living. We need not to look further than the increasingly political polarization around us for a good example. In Colombia and Mexico, an overwhelming number of 30–36% of the population consider itself either extreme right or extreme left.[83] The United States is historically polarized and becoming more so.[84] Recently, circumstances have turned Europe into a political hotspot, where far-right and far-left parties equally battle for power.

More often than not, opposing values shape how a business practice is conducted, for example, "decision making." In France, managers expect and demand their right in authority (high hierarchy acceptance), but at the same time, there is support for a strong union system and debate culture where workers can voice their opinions and question authorities' orders (low hierarchy acceptance). This probably explains why there are so many protests in France. In Japan, decision making is very much about reaching consensus at each level of the organization, but this consensus has to climb one step at a time, slowly up along a steep hierarchy to the top. In the United States, flat management is popular, but decision making is often reserved for a few at the top only, and so forth. In short, opposing values and outward expressions are inherent in many business activities.

Such paradoxes can be found in a much deeper level of national psyches. For example, Scandinavian businesspeople are sometimes misjudged because of their humble and subtle way of communication. However, their successful economies have much to thank to the Viking[85] and "*sisu*" working spirit. The former is rooted in the history of their ferocious sailor-warrior ancestors; the latter is a national Finnish pride that emphasizes courage, grit, and bravery against all odds.[86] The result is that Finish culture contains both contrasting values: A high level of importance placed on humbleness and subtlety (femininity), but also a strong emphasis attached to inner assertiveness and combatant spirit (masculinity).

Thus, no matter how strong the dominant or stereotypical values are, we can always find paradoxes in a country, a community, an organization, a family, or even within an individual.

Carl Jung—the Swiss founder of analytical psychology—thought that being fully human means being forever tossed between conflicting forces.[87] However, this dilemma does not always have to end up with being caught in the middle, between the alternatives of "this" *or* "that." The dialectical method posits that a thesis is followed by an anti-thesis, resulting in four possible outcomes: (1) Either thesis or antithesis wins; (2) both thesis and antithesis cease to have a contrasting relationship; (3) the contrasting relationship remains, both thesis and antithesis coexist; and (4) synthesis, that is a new pattern emerged from a combination of both thesis and antithesis. If we choose to view the world with only outcome number 1, a binary system "either-or" can exert an archaic hold on us beyond its usefulness, forcing us to choose one or another. Three other possibilities are feasible, and each of them allows us to wrench free out of the archaic process of binary functioning. Attempts to deconstruct a binary system have a rich record in literature, from postmodernism to poststructuralism, both favoring deconstruction theory to dissemble binary assumptions and knowledge systems that cloud human understanding of buried realities.[88]

In our metaphorical tree of culture, values are represented by branches of the tree and they are not binary. Each value such as masculinity or femininity can be a *separate* branch of the tree, either the same size or a different size. Depending on a particular context, a value will prevail. Over time, circumstances constantly influence these values and drive them toward responsive changes, very much as a tree changes according to its environment.

To conclude, we recognize the evolutionary root in our knee-jerk tendency to operate with the autopilot System 1 and categorize things according to a simple "either-or" structure. However, culture and the ability to learn from others with complex thinking in System 2 enable us to comprehend the world with a "both-and" mentality. For the advances of humans as a species, this capacity to take a plural and dynamic view is essential in all units of life, from a society at large, down to the microlevel of neurons. It is not a given, but as long as there is a context in which the coexistence of opposites and the ability to live with it can support humans in the game of survival, slowly and surely, such reality and perception will definitely evolve as part of our everyday life. If you have doubt, look at third-culture kids, global citizens, multi-/ bicultural people, or international managers who have developed an acute second nature or multiple natures of effectively working in various contexts. In essence, becoming successful in cross-cultural business largely relies on the ability to cultivate such a multicultural mind.

Summary

1. Theories of cross-cultural communication and management split into two main paradigms: Static and dynamic.
    *   The static paradigm posits that culture is stable, values are difficult to change. If change happens, it is due to external shocks. All national cultures change in unison, and so, the gap between them remains the same. This assumption justifies the use of cultural index in which each country's value is calculated with an averaged fixed score.
    *   The static paradigm allows the first-best-guess, a prediction of behaviors based on a predetermined set of values. However, it ignores the active role of people in creating cultures, undermines the force of change, and discourages businesses to gain a holistic and plural view of international cooperation.
    *   The dynamic paradigm posits that culture is a flux, a series of dynamic responses to internal and external factors. It reflects the reality more accurately, but it requires extra effort to understand the complexity of culture.
2. A culture is constantly changing. While the fundamental concerns are quite stable, values change according to particular contexts, and outward expressions change the fastest of all.

3. A culture is often diverse. Genetically and culturally, differences within a population are greater than differences between populations. Institutional plasticity has significantly contributed to the increased diversity within a culture. It refers to *uneven* pace of change in an organizations.

4. A culture can look misleading because outward expressions do not always match values. A change of outward expressions does not readily reflect a genuine change of value, and vice versa.

5. A culture can be contradictory because of paradoxes. An individual as well as a culture can "host" opposing values at the same time.

   • The brain's mechanism consists of both binary and plural working patterns. This parallel can be found within/between neurons (action vs. graded potential) and different working mechanisms of the brain (System 1 vs. System 2).

   • Individuals have the capacity of multicultural mind, accommodating both seemingly opposing values, switching them when the context demands, and working to reach a fine, plural, and complex thinking pattern that goes beyond a binary system.

   • Similarly, a culture can be so dynamic that seemingly opposing values coexist with complex interactions through time and space.

Notes

Don't forget to go to the end of the book for case studies.

1 Osland, Joyce S., and Allan Bird. 2000. "Beyond Sophisticated Stereotyping: Cultural Sensemaking in Context." *Academy of Management Executive* 14(1): 65–79.

2 Hofstede, Geert., Gert-Jan Hofstede, and Michael Minkov. 2005. *Cultures and Organizations: Software of the Mind*. 3rd ed. New York: McGraw-Hill.

3 Hofstede, Geert., and Gert-Jan Hofstede. 2005. *Cultures and Organizations: Software of the Mind*, 13. 2nd ed. New York: McGraw-Hill.

4 Hofstede, Geert. 2001. *Cultural Consequences: Comparing Values, Behaviors, Institutions and Organizations across Nations*, 36. 2nd ed. Thousand Oaks, CA: Sage.

5 Hofstede, Geert., and Gert-Jan Hofstede. 2005. *Culture and Organization: Software of the Mind*, 36. 2nd ed. New York: McGraw-Hill.

6 Hofstede, Geert. 2001. *Cultural Consequences: Comparing Values, Behaviors, Institutions and Organizations across Nations*, 36. 2nd ed. Thousand Oaks, CA: Sage.

7 Hofstede, Geert. 1980. *Culture's Consequences: International Differences in Work Related Values*, 14. Beverly Hills, CA: Sage.

8 Weick, Karl E., and Robert E. Quinn. 1999. "Organizational Change and Development." *Annual Review of Psychology* 50(1): 361–386. doi:10.1146/annurev.psych.50.1.361.

9 Leana, Carrie R., and Bruce Barry. 2000. "Stability and Change as Simultaneous Experiences in Organizational Life." *Academy of Management Review* 25(4): 753–759. www.jstor.org/stable/259203.

10 Erez, Miriam., and P. Christopher Earley. 1993. *Culture, Self-Identity, and Work*. Oxford: Oxford University Press.

11 Geertz, Clifford. 1973. *The Interpretation of Cultures*, 44. New York: Harper Collins.

12 Hofstede, Geert. 2001. *Cultural Consequences: Comparing Values, Behaviors, Institutions and Organizations across Nations*, xix. 2nd ed. Thousand Oaks, CA: Sage.

13 Hofstede, Geert., and Jan Gert. Hofstede. 2005. *Cultures and Organizations: Software of the Mind*, 78–79. New York: McGraw-Hill.

14 Kogut, Bruce., and Singh, Harbir 1988. "The Effect of National Culture on the Choice of Entry Mode." *Journal of International Business Studies* 19(3): 411–432. doi:10.1057/palgrave.jibs.8490394.

15 McSweeney, Brendan. 2012. "Constitutive Context: The Myth of Common Cultural Values." In *Handbook of International Approaches to International Business*, ed. Geoffrey Wood and Mehmet Demirbag, 142–172. Cheltenham, UK: Edward Elgar Publishing Limited.

16 Ibid.

17 Chris, Smith., Brendan McSweeney, and Robert Fitzgerald. 2008. *Remaking Management: Between Local and Global*. Cambridge: Cambridge University Press.

18 Archer, Margaret S. 1988. *Culture and Agency: The Place of Culture in Social Theory*, 6. Cambridge: Cambridge University Press.

19 Brightman, Robert. 1995. "Forget Culture: Replacement, Transcendence, Reflexification." *Cultural Anthropology* 10(4), 509–546. doi:10.1525/can.1995.10.4.02a00030.

20 Boas, Franz. 1982 [1940]. *Race, Language and Culture*. London: Routledge.

21 Farjoun, Moshe. 1998."The Independent and Joint Effects of the Skill and Physical Bases of Relatedness in Diversification." *Strategic Management Journal* 19(7): 611–630. doi:10.1002/(SICI)1097-0266(199807)19:7<611::AID-SMJ962>3.0.CO;2-E.

22 Vassolo, Roberto S., Jaideep Anand, and Timothy B. Folta. 2004. "Non-Additivity in Portfolios of Exploration Activities: A Real Options-Based Analysis of Equity Alliances in Biotechnology." *Strategic Management Journal* 25(11): 1045–1061. doi:10.1002/smj.414.

23 Kostova, Tatiana. 1997. "Country Institutional Profiles: Concept and Measurement." *Academy of Management Best Papers Proceedings*, 180–184. doi:10.5465/ambpp.1997.4981338.

24 Berry, Heather., Mauro F. Guillén, and Nan Zhou. 2010. "An Institutional Approach to Cross-National Distance." *Journal of International Business Studies* 41(9): 1460–1480. doi:10.1057/jibs.2010.28.

25 Tung, Rosalie L., and Alain Verbeke. 2010. "Beyond Hofstede and GLOBE: Improving the Quality of Cross-Cultural Research." *Journal of International Business Studies* 41(8): 1259–1274. doi:10.1057/jibs.2010.41.

26 Håkanson, Lars., and Björn Ambos. 2010. "The Antecedents of Psychic Distance." *Journal of International Management* 16(3): 195–210. doi:10.1016/j.intman.2010.06.001.

27 Morgan, Gareth. 2006. *Images of Organization*. London: Sage Publications.

28 Beamish, Paul W., and John C. Banks. 1987. "Equity Joint Ventures and the Theory of the Multinational Enterprise." *Journal of International Business Studies* 18(2): 1–16. doi:10.1057/palgrave.jibs.8490403.

29 Shenkar, Oded., Yadong Luo, and Orly Yeheskel. 2008. "From 'Distance' to 'Friction': Substituting Metaphors and Redirecting Intercultural Research." *Academy of Management Review* 33(4): 905–923. doi:10.5465/amr.2008.34421999.

30 Caves, Richard E. 1996. *Multinational Enterprise and Economic Analysis*. Cambridge: Cambridge University Press.

31 Zaheer, Srilata., Margaret Spring Schomaker, and Lilach Nachum. 2012. "Distance without Direction: Restoring Credibility to a Much-Loved Construct." *Journal of International Business Studies* 43(1): 18–27. doi:10.1057/jibs.2011.43.

32 Hanges, Paul., Robert Lord, and Marcus Dickson. 2000. "An Information Processing Perspective on Leadership and Culture: A Case for Connectionist Architecture." *Applied Psychology: An International Review* 49(1): 133–161. doi:10.1111/1464-0597.00008.

33 Hong, Ying-Yi., Michael W. Morris, Chie-Yue Chiu, and Veronica Benet-Martinez. 2000. "Multicultural Minds: A Dynamic Constructivist Approach to Culture and Cognition." *American Psychologist* 55(7): 709–720. doi:10.1037//0003-066X.55.7.709.

34 Peng, Kaiping., and Eric D. Knowles. 2003. "Culture, Education, and the Attribution of Physical Causality." *Personality and Social Psychology Bulletin* 29(10): 1272–1284. doi:10.1177/0146167203254601.

35 Tinsley, Catherine H., and Susan E. Brodt. 2004. "Conflict Management in Asia: A Dynamic Framework and Future Directions." In *Handbook of Asian Management*, ed. Kwon Leung and Steven White, 439–458. New York: Kluwer.

36 Kitayama, Shinobu. 2002. "Cultural Psychology of the Self: A Renewed Look at Independence and Interdependence." In *Psychology at the Turn of the Millennium, Vol. 2: Social, Developmental, and Clinical Perspectives*, ed. Claes von Hofsten and Lars Backman, 305–322. New York: Taylor & Francis/Routledge.

37 McSweeney, Brendan. 2012. "Constitutive Context: The Myth of Common Cultural Values." In *Handbook of International Approaches to International Business*, ed. Geoffrey Wood and Mehmet Demirbag, 142–172. Cheltenham, UK: Edward Elgar Publishing Limited.

38 Fang, Tony. 2005–2006. "From 'Onion' to 'Ocean': Paradox and Change in National Cultures." *International Studies of Management and Organization* 35(4): 71–90. doi:10.1080/00208825.2005.11043743.

39 Berry, John W., John Widdup Berry, Ype H. Poortinga, Marshall H. Segall, and Pierre R. Dasen. 2002. *Cross-Cultural Psychology: Research and Application*, 2nd ed. New York: Cambridge University Press.

40 Transparency International. 2017. "Corruption Perceptions Index 2016." January 25. www.transparency.org/news/feature/corruption_perceptions_index_2016.

41 Liew, Mun Leong. 2017. *Building People: Sunday Emails from a CEO*. Singapore: John Wiley & Sons.

42 Mazar, Nina., and Pankaj Aggarwal. 2011. "Greasing the Palm: Can Collectivism Promote Bribery?" *Psychological Science* 22(7): 843. doi:10.1177/0956797611412389.

43 Civil Service College. 2015. "Upholding Integrity in the Public Service." *OCSC*. www.ocsc.go.th/sites/default/files/attachment/article/upholding_integrity_in_the_public_service.pdf.

44 Ladhari, Riadh., Nizar Souiden, and Yong-Hoon Choi. 2015 "Culture Change and Globalization: The Unresolved Debate between Cross-National and Cross-Cultural Classifications." *Australian Marketing Journal* 23(3): 235–245. doi:10.1016/j.ausmj.2015.06.003.

45 Jones, Rodney H. 2013. "The Paradox of Culture in a Globalized World." *Language and Intercultural Communication* 13(2): 237–244. doi:10.1080/14708477.2013.770869.

46 Fearon, James D. 2003. "Ethnic and Cultural Diversity by Country." *Journal of Economic Growth* 8(2): 195–222. doi:10.1023/A:1024419522867.

47 Australian Bureau of Statistics. 2016. "2016 Census of Population and Housing. General Community Profile." www.censusdata.abs.gov.au/CensusOutput/copsub2016.NSF/All docs by catNo/2016~Community Profile~036/$File/GCP_036.zip?OpenElement.

48 Cleaver, Megan., Myung-Soo Jo, and Thomas E. Muller. 2015. "Individualist vs. Collectivist Cultures: Shopping for Prestige in Australia." In *Proceedings of the 1998 Multicultural Marketing Conference Developments in Marketing Science: Proceedings of the Academy of Marketing Science*, ed. Jean-Charles Chebat and A. Ben Oumlil, 530–534. Cham: Springer. doi:10.1007/978-3-319-17383-2_108.

49 Kaplan, David H., and Wei Li. 2006. *Landscapes of the Ethnic Economy*. Lanham, MD: Rowman & Littlefield.

50 Lewontin, R. C. 1972. "The Apportionment of Human Diversity." *Evolutionary Biology* 6: 381–398.

51 Witherspoon, D. J., S. Wooding, A. R. Rogers, E. E. Merchani, W. S. Watkins, M. A. Batzer, and L. B. Jorde. 2007. "Genetic Similarities within and between Human Populations." *Genetics* 176(1): 351–359. www.ncbi.nlm.nih.gov/pmc/articles/PMC1893020/.

52 Taras, Vas., Piers Steel, and Bradley L. Kirkman. 2016. "Does Country Equate with Culture? Beyond Geography in the Search for Cultural Boundaries." *Management International Review* 56(4): 455–487. doi:10.1007/s11575-016-0283-x.

53 North, Douglass C. 1990. *Institutions, Institutional Change and Economic Performance*. Cambridge: Cambridge University Press.

54 Kickert, Walter J. M., and Frans-Bauke van der Meer. 2011. "Small, Slow, and Gradual Reform: What Can Historical Institutionalism Teach Us?" *International Journal of Public Administration* 34(8): 475–485. doi:10.1080/01900692.2011.583768.

55 Vergne, Jean-Philippe., and Rodolphe Durand. 2010. "The Missing Link between the Theory and Empirics of Path Dependence: Conceptual Clarification, Testability Issue, and Methodological Implications." *Journal of Management Studies* 47(4): 736–759. doi:10.1111/j.1467-6486.2009.00913.x.

56 White, Harrison C. 1992. *Identity and Control: A Structural Theory of Social Interaction*. Princeton, NJ: Princeton University Press.

57 Hoffman, Andrew J. 1999. "Institutional Evolution and Change: Environmentalism and the U.S. Chemical Industry." *Academy of Management Journal* 42(4): 351–371. doi:10.5465/257008.

58 Strambach, Simone. 2008. "Path Dependency and Path Plasticity: The Co-Evolution of Institutions and Innovation—the German Customized Business Software Industry." *Working Papers on*

Innovation and Space. www.uni-marburg.de/fb19/fachgebiete/wirtschaftsgeographie/wps_ag/archiv_workingpapers/wpis_2008/wp02_08.pdf.

59 Katz, Harry., and Wailes Nick. 2014. "Convergence and Divergence in Employment Relations." In *The Oxford Handbook of Employment Relations: Comparative Employment Systems*, ed. Adrian Wilkinson, Geoffrey Wood, and Richard Deeg, 42–61. Oxford: Oxford University Press.

60 Lane, Christel., and Geoffrey Wood. 2009. "Capitalist Diversity and Diversity within Capitalism." *Economy and Society* 38(4): 531–551. doi:10.1080/03085140903190300.

61 Deeg, Richard., and Gregory Jackson. 2007. "Towards a More Dynamic Theory of Capitalist Variety." *Socio-Economic Review* 5(1): 149–179. doi:10.1093/ser/mwl021.

62 Appiah, Kwame Anthony. 2006. "The Case for Contamination." *The New York Times*. January 1. www.nytimes.com/2006/01/01/magazine/the-case-for-contamination.html?mcubz=1.

63 Venaik, Sunil., and Paul Brewer. 2010. "Avoiding Uncertainty in Hofstede and GLOBE." *Journal of International Business Studies* 41(8): 1294–1315. doi:10.1057/jibs.2009.96.

64 Haworth. 2015. "A Shifting Landscape: Chinese Millennials in the Workplace," 16. http://media.haworth.com/asset/82857/a-shifting-landscape_chinese-millennials-in-the-workplace.pdf.

65 Maseland, Robbert., and André van Hoorn. 2008. "Explaining the Negative Correlation between Values and Practices: A Note on the Hofstede–GLOBE Debate." *Journal of International Business Studies* 40(3): 527–532. doi:10.1057/jibs.2008.68.

66 Osland, Joyce S., Allan Bird, June Delano, and Mathew Jacob. 2000. "Beyond Sophisticated Stereotyping: Cultural Sensemaking in Context." *Academy of Management Executive* 14(1): 65–79. www.jstor.org/stable/4165609.

67 Bird, Allan., and Michael J. Stevens. 2003. "Toward an Emergent Global Culture and the Effects of Globalization on Obsolescing National Cultures." *Journal of International Management* 9(4): 395–407. doi:10.1016/j.intman.2003.08.003.

68 Fang, Tony. 1999. *Chinese Business Negotiating Style*. Thousand Oaks, CA: Sage.

69 LeDoux, Joseph. 1996. *The Emotional Brain: The Mysterious Underpinnings of Emotional Life*. New York: Touchstone Books.

70 Freeman, Jonathan B., Ryan M. Stolier, Zachary A. Ingbretsen, and Eric A. Hehman. 2014. "Amygdala Responsivity to High-Level Social Information from Unseen Faces." *The Journal of Neuroscience* 34(32): 10573–10581. https://psych.nyu.edu/freemanlab/pubs/2014Freeman_JNeuro.pdf.

71 Wood, Jack D., and Gianpiero Petriglieri. 2005. "Transcending Polarization: Beyond Binary Thinking." *Transactional Analysis Journal* 35(1): 31–39. doi:10.1177/036215370503500105.

72 Sui, Jie., and Shihui Han. 2007. "Self-Construal Priming Modulates Neural Substrates of Self-Awareness." *Psychological Science* 18(10): 861–866. doi:10.1111/j.1467-9280.2007.01992.x.

73 Oyserman, Daphna., Sheida Novin, Nic Flinkenflögel, and Lydia Krabbendam. 2014. "Integrating Culture-as-Situated-Cognition and Neuroscience Prediction Models." *Culture and Brain* 2(1): 1–26. doi:10.1007/s40167-014-0016-6.

74 Chiao, Joan Y., Tokiko Harada, Hidetsugu Komeda, Zhang Li, Yoko Mano, Daisuke Saito, Todd B. Parrish, Norihiro Sadato, and Tetsuya Iidaka. 2010. "Dynamic Cultural Influences on Neural Representations of the Self." *Journal of Cognitive Neuroscience* 22(1): 1–11. doi:10.1162/jocn.2009.21192.

75 Sui, Jie., Ying-Yi Hong, Chang Hong Liu, Glyn W. Humphreys, and Shihui Han. 2012. "Dynamic Cultural Modulation of Neural Responses to One's Own and Friends Faces." *Social Cognitive and Affective Neuroscience* 8(3): 326–332. doi:10.1093/scan/nss001.

76 Wang, Chenbo., Daphna Oyserman, Qiang Liu, Hong Li, and Shihui Han. 2013. "Accessible Cultural Mind-Set Modulates Default Mode Activity: Evidence for the Culturally Situated Brain." *Social Neuroscience* 8(3): 203–216. doi:10.1080/17470919.2013.775966.

77 Han, Shihui., and Glyn Humphreys. 2016. "Self-Construal: A Cultural Framework for Brain Function." *Current Opinion in Psychology* 8: 10–14. doi:10.1016/j.copsyc.2015.09.013.

78 Chiao, Joan Y., Tokiko Harada, Hidetsugu Komeda, Zhang Li, and Yoko Mano. 2009. "Neural Basis of Individualistic and Collectivistic Views of Self." *Human Brain Mapping* 30(9): 2813–2820. doi:10.1002/hbm.20707.

79 Hong, Ying-Yi., Michael W. Morris, Chi-Yue Chiu, and Verónica Benet-Martínez. 2000. "Multicultural Minds: A Dynamic Constructivist Approach to Culture and Cognition." *American Psychologist* 55(7): 709–720. doi:10.1037//0003-066x.55.7.709.

80 Globus, Gordon G. 1995. *The Postmodern Brain*. Amsterdam, the Netherlands: John Benjamins Publishing Company.

81 Klipp, Paul. 2016. "What Are Some Tools to Use for Effective Decision Making?" Quora. June 16. www.quora.com/What-are-some-tools-to-use-for-effective-decision-making.

82 Ladhari, Riadh., Nizar Souiden, and Yong-Hoon Choi. 2015. "Culture Change and Globalization: The Unresolved Debate between Cross-National and Cross-Cultural Classifications." *Australian Marketing Journal* 23(3): 235–245. doi:10.1016/j.ausmj.2015.06.003.

83 Cárdenas, Mauricio. 2016. "Political Polarization in Latin America." *Brookings*. July 29. www.brookings.edu/blog/up-front/2009/11/06/political-polarization-in-latin-america/.

84 Gentzkow, Matthew. 2016. "Polarization in 2016." Thesis. Stanford University, Stanford, CA. https://web.stanford.edu/~gentzkow/research/PolarizationIn2016.pdf.

85 Fang, Tony. 2012. "Yin Yang: A New Perspective on Culture." *Management and Organization Review* 8(1): 25–50. doi:10.1111/j.1740-8784.2011.00221.x.

86 "Northern Theatre: Sisu" 1940. *Time*. January 8. http://content.time.com/time/magazine/article/0,9171,763161,00.html.

87 Jung, Carl G., and Aniela Jaffe. 1983. *Memories, Dreams, Reflections*. London: Flamingo.

88 Long, Lo Yew. 2013. "Postmodernism, Neuroscience and the Brain." *Proceedings of Singapore Healthcare* 22(3): 158–162. doi:10.1177/201010581302200301.

5   Fear-Free Cross-Cultural Management

Culture and the forces that drive the diversity around us are dynamic. First, we have the Diversity Pathways GCEB-Be with the complex and interactive interplay of five factors, from the macrolevel of environment to the microlevel of gene and neuron (Chapter 2). Second, our culture is not static but rather a "changing" culture, a "diverse" culture, a seemingly "misleading" culture because of the contrast between values and behaviors, and a "contradicting" culture due to paradoxes and the coexistence of opposing values (Chapter 4). Third, the contemporary version of globalization makes the process of reshaping borders even more complicated than in the past (Chapter 1) with new elements (technology, demography, global economy), complex patterns (both flat world and spiky world), and dynamic interaction with local cultures (global goes local, local goes global, and local transforms local).

It's normal to be both excited and anxious about this dynamic (re)shaping of elements within and between borders. The optimistic voice in our mind admits that a world without borders makes perfect economic sense. The pessimistic voice reminds us of differences, distrust, unfairness, inequality, and terrorism. Regardless of the view, globalization is an economic tsunami that is sweeping the planet. From the cross-cultural perspective, we can't stop it, but we can adopt the right attitude toward it. Facing a world in which complexity and uncertainty reign supreme, should we employ a suspicious and careful approach or should we embrace the incredible dynamics of this force?

For some historical reasons, mainstream theories in cross-cultural management tend to follow the cautious pathway, regarding cultural differences as potential *threats* for business rather than opportunities for synergy and mutual benefit. In this chapter, we will critically reevaluate this cautious approach that dominates the mainstream theories. We will understand why priming our mind with the negativity of cultural differences can do harm for international business endeavors. Finally, we will consider an alternative approach that may prepare us better for the unpredictability and complexity of a globalized world.

5.1 Fear-Embedded, Difference-Oriented, Problem-Focused

Have you noticed that many of the books, lectures, or training programs on cross-cultural management often start with a blunder, or a business failure due to cultural misunderstanding? It works because it captures your attention immediately. It works because it is based on *fear*.

So why are differences and defeat, instead of similarities and synergy, considered the starting point, not only among practitioners but also among the most prominent scholars of the field? The answer can be found in history.

5.1.1 *From the Cradle of Fear*

The history of intercultural communication study began at the US Foreign Service Institute in the 1950s during the Cold War. It was a time of fierce competition between opposing ideologies,

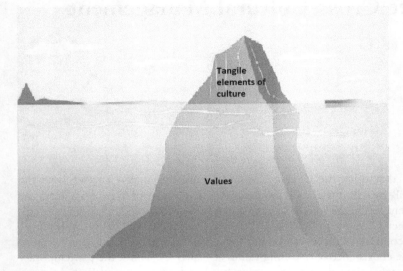

Values

Tangile
elements of
culture

Figure 5.1 The iceberg metaphor of culture

led by the Soviet Union and the United States. International diplomacy was characterized by distrust, tension, and readiness for reprisal. On the diplomatic front, it was clear that the US diplomats had shortcomings compared to the Russians. While 90% of all Russian diplomatic staff, including secretaries and chauffeurs, spoke the local language where they were posted, the US diplomatic corps seldom learned the culture of the country to which they were assigned.[1] A founder of cross-cultural study—Edward Hall—was employed to educate the US diplomats about how and why cultural differences could contribute to the failure of their missions.

Given this context, it is understandable why Hall emphasized cultural differences as the focus of intercultural communication. He opened his landmark book *Beyond Culture* with alarming crises, conflicts, and potential turmoil. The relationship between the different sides was so hostile that he even described the emergence of China, Japan, and Latin America and their demand to be recognized in their own right" as a "crisis."[2] Fittingly, Hall's metaphor for culture is a floating *iceberg*, which implies that we are misled by what we see, and catastrophes can happen when we collide with the mass deep underwater (Figure 5.1). By emphasizing the "dark side" of culture and the adverse consequences of differences, this metaphor prepares for a defensive and reactionary state of mind typical of the Cold War era.

5.1.2 A Bias toward Differences and Problems

The legacy of this context is that theories and development of cross-cultural management have unwittingly been influenced by the hostile environment and cautious mentality of this period.[3] Consequently, there is a strong bias toward emphasizing differences and a prevalent view that foreignness equates to liability.[4] The *static paradigm* of culture strengthens this perception by providing theoretical frameworks supporting the notion that cultural borders are fixed, values are hard to change, and each country can be represented with a score (see Chapter 4). Culture is important, but according to Hofstede—an influential theorist of the static paradigm—it is "a source of conflict than of synergy" and "cultural differences are a nuisance at best and often a disaster."[5]

Under the influence of this view, research in international business has long assumed that companies face costs arising from cultural differences and foreignness when crossing borders.

Diversity is generally viewed negatively as a barrier, a source of costs, risks, and potential failures. A wide range of terminologies have been generated to demonstrate this assumption such as "cultural distance,"[6] "psychic distance,"[7] "institutional distance,"[8] "liability of foreigners,"[9] "cultural consequences,"[10] or cultural "collide."[11] International alliances must overcome border-crossing problems such as destructive conflicts,[12] impeding knowledge exchange,[13] decreasing alliance longevity,[14] acquisition cultural risk,[15] disruptive cultural clashes,[16] and merger disaster.[17] Culture is treated as an "information cost"[18] with aspects of conflicts being highlighted to signal the price we have to pay when we fail to invest sufficiently in knowing how we are different from others. The more cultural differences there are, the more problems arise.[19]

The bias toward difficulties, obstacles, and conflicts caused by cultural differences results in little effort to develop theories that capitalize on the benefit of diversity. Consequently, there is a 17:1 imbalance of negative over positive theoretical research assumptions on the role of culture in international business contexts.[20] In a review of team diversity literature,[21] the authors reported that, except for one, all the dominant theoretical perspectives on cultural diversity are consistent with the problem-focused view of diversity. Negative phenomena dominate in business press and organizational studies literature by a factor of four.[22] Out of 500 published articles on organizational change between 1990 and 2007, 40% addressed negative change whereas only 4% addressed positive change.[23] Five out of the six most-cited articles in two prominent business journals focused on problems in organization,[24] and the presence of negatively biased words increased fourfold in the business press.[25] Many books on cross-cultural management are illustrated *entirely* using mishaps and blunders in which cultural differences are the culprit. The lucrative business of cross-cultural training has been mainly about helping clients to navigate around dangerous icebergs. Businesses don't seem to have enough of it, and desperately want more. In sum, it is largely the fear of failure that underlines incentives of learning about culture and training on cross-cultural management, to the extent that "a fear of uncertainty and the unknown dominates cross-cultural communication strategies."[26] The major reason behind this state of mind is because fear is the most powerful motivating force in our working culture today.

5.2 The Neuroscience of Fear

We are born with only two innate fears: The fear of falling and the fear of loud noise. Most fear is learned: Snakes, darkness, failure, devil, God(s), different values, and so forth. In this section, we will explore the neuroscience of fear: How we learn what to fear, and why fear is so critical in the survival of human species. This will help us understand why negativity has played such a prominent role in the mainstream theory of cross-cultural management.

5.2.1 How We Learn to Fear

Because most fear is culturally conditioned, contexts are crucial for humans to learn what should be feared. The hippocampus—the seat of our memory[27]—provides context for the data we receive, putting problems into perspective. There is a complex dialogue between the amygdala (emotional memory) and the hippocampus (factual memory) in the formation of fear.[28-29] Together, they hold all the fear memories in relation to contextual information about the stimulus.[30] If we have a cultural encounter, for example, meeting a business partner from Iran, who is an artist, is Jewish, and dresses up in his traditional attire. The amygdala and hippocampus play a crucial role in giving this encounter a big picture with all relevant information from past memory, preparing us for making good guesses and acting properly. If our memory is influenced by positive data, it will trigger reward pathways (e.g., I went to college with a Jewish artist and she was extremely smart). However, with negative data from the memory, it will trigger anxiety (e.g., The media tells me that Iran is such a different and conservative culture.

A Jew living in Iran sounds unusual as well. And I heard conservative people don't really excel in art.). In this sense, we are strongly shaped by what we remember. Memories make data meaningful, especially in conditioning fear where stimuli match a signal previously associated with threat response. *We are shaped by what we remember.* The contextual power of memory explains why a negative bias toward cultural exchange can prime our brain and condition it to provide a biased framework. Many negative stereotypes we have are also based in the same principle. The more we hear about a certain thing, the easier it is stored in our brain, and the quicker it is released as a context to understand new data.

5.2.2 How We Respond to Fear

The best summary that describes how mammals respond to fear is *freeze, fight, or flight.* When a danger approaches, freezing starts because it is the best way to stop the movement that attracts the predator, be instantly invisible, see the predator before the predator see them, and prepare for action: Fight or flight.

Just like mammals, when we face stressors, our body prepares us to get moving. The short-hand sequence goes like this: The amygdala signals the *hypothalamus*—the part of the brain that is responsible for metabolic processes and automatic nervous system. The hypothalamus then signals the *pituitary gland*, which controls some critical hormones of the body. The pituitary gland sends a message to the *adrenal glands* near the kidneys, telling them to secrete adrenaline (another name of epinephrine) to deal with the stress. Our heart rate increases to send

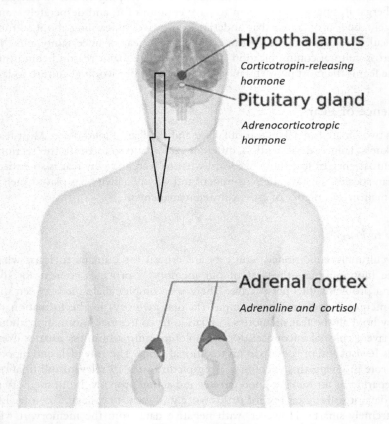

Figure 5.2 The neuroscience of fear response (anatomography)

more oxygen to the muscles, the blood vessels constrict to minimize bleeding, and the digestive system shuts down to conserve energy. This chain of interaction is called the hypothalamus-pituitary-adrenal (HPA) axis.

If the stress is beyond a quick response, then the adrenal glands will also release cortisol—a hormone that can keep us charged up longer than adrenaline. On a short-term basis, cortisol facilitates dopamine—a hormone that keeps us focused. But too much of a good thing is not good. Excessive and prolonged cortisol makes the level of dopamine depleted, which leads to depression.

5.2.3 *The Evolutionary Root of Fear*

Universally, all humans share six types of emotions that can be recognized through facial expressions regardless of our cultural backgrounds: Fear, sadness, anger, disgust, surprise, and joy.[31] The first four represent *avoidance*, which can be linked with the fight-or-flight instinct that evolved to keep us safe. "Fear" helps us to recognize danger. "Sadness" and "anger" motivate and guide us in fighting for what is important. And finally, "disgust" signals poison and bad practices to avoid. The middle emotion point—"surprise"—prepares us to go either into the direction of avoidance or the last emotion of "joy."

Clearly, evolution is biased in using emotions as survival strategies (four vs. one), and for good reasons. Escape and avoidance are essential to our survival, much more than joy and happiness. Ignoring the positive may produce regret, but ignoring the negative can result in life-altering effects. Similarly, one single positive thing or person cannot make the whole system thrive, but a single negative thing or person (the weakest link) can cause a system to fail. Because fear is the most powerful negative emotion, it is easier to run on fear than anything else. It triggers the shortest route to reaction.

The fact that fear is the most basic and profound emotion is evidenced in how our brain has evolved over millions of years. Using MacLean's *triune brain model* (Figure 5.3), we can oversimplify the human brain as three parts: (1) The most ancient part, *reptilian* complex, originated from our reptilian past in the evolution process about 500 million years ago, ensuring survival and bodily functions such as breathing, heartbeat, digestion, and balance; (2) the *limbic* system evolved about 300 million years ago from our mammalian past, governing emotion and memory; and (3) the *cerebral cortex* (neomammalian) evolved approximately 200 million years ago, acting as the thinking brain, the seat of consciousness. Most animals have this kind of cortex, but it is relatively small with no folds—indicating complexity and development. A mouse without cortex can live in a fairly normal way, but a human without cortex is a vegetable.[32]

Contrary to what we often hear, fear is *not* rooted in the reptilian complex.[33] Reptiles do not have fear, they rely purely on habit and instinct. Fear emanates from the limbic system, which exists only in mammals. It started with the olfactory bulb[34] with cells that could analyze smell, hence, knowing what food is safe and poisonous, which can be linked to the saying "smell the fear."[35-36] To this day, while most sensory pathways (image, sound, taste, touch) project to *reticular activating system* (RAS) and the thalamus (see Figure 4.3 in Chapter 4), smell does not. Olfactory pathways from the nose go through the olfactory bulb straight to the olfactory cortex, instantly evoking a flood of memories and emotions.

According to the preparedness theory,[37] data can quickly reach the amygdala. This is the autopilot System 1.[38] The thinking brain (cerebral cortex) that enables us to make logical and rational decisions was developed much *later*, hence, takes longer to be accessible. As we know from Chapter 4, the amygdala in the limbic system is much quicker than the cerebral cortex in assessing information. Note that the amygdala detects all emotions, but reacts in hierarchy, and fear is always the priority. It picks up fear even when we are not aware of it, our eyes do not

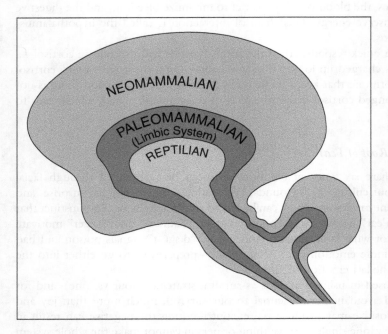

Figure 5.3 The triune brain (Bill Benzon)

see it, for example, images of untrustworthy faces that last only 33 milliseconds.[39] This is called subconscious fear—a fear that we don't know we have, yet, being under its spell. An experiment with cortically blind people (those with brain damage in the visual cortex despite functional eyes) shows that even when we can't consciously see fearful faces, our brain still picks up the visual signal of fear.[40] The amygdala response to eye contact does not require an intact primary visual cortex[41] because it acts like an internal eye. More interestingly, subconscious fear remains robust even when people consciously perceive happy facial expression or emotional voice.[42] In other words, subconscious fear is registered *despite* conscious happiness. To conclude, the brain prioritizes fear above all other emotions and registers fear before consciousness, even in the absence of consciousness and visual contact.

The neural pathway of fear explains why we tend to pay more attention, and to a certain extent, want to know more about bad news, negative stories, destructive behaviors, and unpleasant relationships. This also explains why the media is prone to be sensational. For evolutionary reasons, "bad" trumps "good,"[43] or better put, a bad event has a stronger impact than a comparable good event. In initial hiring decisions, 3.8 unfavorable bits of information were required to shift a decision to rejection, whereas 8.8 favorable pieces of information were necessary to shift a negative decision toward acceptance.[44] Bad information signals malfunction and a need to change. Organisms that were better attuned to bad things are more likely to survive threats and, consequently, are able to increase probability of passing along their genes.

The neurobiology of fear explains reasons why negative factors win the focus and capture more attention in scholarly analysis and theory development.[45-46] Businesses tend to emphasize negative phenomena because they imply threats to survival. We can hypothesize that intercultural communication that evolves around the danger of differences may tap directly on this fear, activating the most natural and the quickest way for the brain to switch on its alert mode, ready to fight with a potential enemy, or ready to run away from problems.

5.3 The Downside of Fear

Emotions are protective mechanisms for humans, stopping us from being a thinking machine. And it's not for no reason that fear is the "crown" of all emotions we have. While holding the ultimate important role in our course of survival, this crown is not all glowing and shiny. It sits on our head as an absolute necessity, but it also gives us terrible headaches.

5.3.1 False Alarm

Evolutionary advantages notwithstanding, the bias we have toward fear poses challenges in the modern era. Historically, the subconscious fight-or-flight reaction using the autopilot System 1 helped our ancestors survive for millions of years on the savannah. A quick decision without thinking meant a difference between life and death. However, in today's world, there are not so many lions and vicious enemies, but plenty of demanding bosses, unreasonable colleagues, impossible deadlines, and of course, shocking cultural differences. These issues may sound troublesome, but unlike problems in the savannah where dangers and safety are clearly defined in black and white (a lion is definitely a threat), problems in the modern world go hand in hand with benefits. Demanding bosses can be both an irritation and an asset. Similarly, cultural differences can be both a source of threats and synergy.

While the good news is that we have developed the cerebral cortex (thinking brain/System 2), the bad news is we still employ the ancient fight-or-flight response for all those modern sources of threats. System 1 can't distinguish between a "real danger" (e.g., lion) and a "perceived danger" (e.g., my business partner doesn't speak the language I can understand), so our amygdala reacts with lightning *speed* and *intensity* as if we are being attacked by a lion and we might die. Fact is, we are just overwhelmed. It takes System 2 to develop a plural thinking ability that comprehends this as both potential problems and positive synergy.

Unwittingly, cross-cultural management can capitalize on this illusive fear. By portraying differences as threats, it is possible that diversity is blown out of proportion. Cultural differences are seen not as some *overwhelming issues* that can be both advantageous and disadvantageous, but decidedly a *source of business failure*. We have false alarm and we can overact. This is where cross-cultural experts come in to explain that the fear is legit, differences are disastrous, but can be understood and overcome.

However, if we constantly have false alarms, a destructive process will slowly occur. As we know, stressors trigger the release of cortisol so we can stay awake and focused. But when cortisol production is excessive or prolonged, the hippocampus and the amygdala have two opposite ways of reaction. In long-lasting anxiety, cortisol receptors in the hippocampus *shut down*. The hippocampus begins to atrophy, which means our memory fades away. The reverse happens for the amygdala. When anxiety endures, instead of atrophy, it becomes *hypersensitized* by an increase in cortisol, which is logical from evolution's point of view. If we are in danger, we should be hyperalert and not think about anything else. The end result is a hypersensitive amygdala takes over the hippocampus. Context and nuance go through the window. Any stimuli that trigger fear response will activate the amygdala faster and faster: Different language, different skin tone, different working approach, different body language, and so forth. In short, anxiety leads to hyperanxiety in an upward spiral.

Linking this insight with the disproportionate ratio of negativity over positivity (17:1) in cross-cultural management and the remark that "a fear of uncertainty and the unknown dominates cross-cultural communication strategies," there seems to be a need to consider whether this imbalance has created a hypervigilant culture toward diversity. By seeing culture as "a source of conflict than of synergy" and "cultural differences … often [as] a disaster," have we tipped the scale by seeing cultural diversity largely as a source of business and communication failure instead of some overwhelming and complex issues that can be both advantageous and disadvantageous? And if these hypotheses hold true, then to what extent does fear play a role in the formation, development, and existence of our discipline? Have we, unintentionally, used fear to capture attention and prove the significance of cross-cultural work?

5.3.2 *Wasting Energy*

According to Selye—the father of modern stress theories, there are two kinds of stress: Eustress and distress.[47] Both release cortisol that helps us wake up and stay alert, mobilizing our body for action. Eustress is often linked with a tangible goal, and *cortisol returns to normal* upon completion of the task. Distress, however, is a free-floating anxiety that doesn't provide an outlet for the cortisol, and thus can backfire. As much as a constant alarm will drive you crazy, being drawn toward the negative constantly over a long period will take its toll. When we stew on a problem or constantly have a (sub)conscious problem at the back of our mind, (sub)conscious fear continuously triggers cortisol, which, in turn, triggers stem cells to malfunction.[48] Worry—the brain's response to fear slows thinking down.[49] A study showed that for worried people, the time to transfer negative emotional information from the left to the right hemisphere is increased.[50] When fear is triggered, survival strategies take precedence over logics and creativity.

Another downside of cortisol is that when the stress is long-lasting, cortisol takes over the role of adrenaline to manufacture energy (glucose). For our ancestors, stress was often caused by predators or enemies, so the solution was a *physical* boost of energy to fight or flight. In the modern era, stressors don't require vigorous physical response, but our body keeps the *same* system of reaction, that is maintaining a high level of glucose. But because modern stress is not cured by physical response of fight or flight, glucose levels remain high over a long period. This triggers insulin—the storage hormone that helps the body to stock energy. The result is cortisol increases insulin and stress is associated with obesity.[51] Problems remain unsolved in the brain, energy is produced and stored, but not for the right purpose.

Understanding both positive and negative sides of stress, it's logical that we should evaluate the impact of the traditional communication approach, one that emphasizes problems and differences. To what extent has this approach produced eustress, optimizing energy and driving dedication? And to what extent has this approach stripped us from motivation with the destructive power of distress?

Studies have shown that when we are in pain and focusing on pain, the feeling and thinking are the same, thus the *anterior cingulate cortex* (ACC)—part of the thinking brain that helps us detect errors[52]—sees no conflict, and we feel *more* pain because we pay attention to it. But when we are in pain and do *not* focus on it, the ACC detects a conflict and gets activated. We get in the mode of reasoning with distraction, and we feel less pain.[53-54] Taking indication from these studies, focusing on the negativity of communication is like putting a magnifying glass on the downturns. This requires us to consider the impact of half a century in which theories and practices of the field are constant reminders that cultural difference is "often a disaster" or "a source of conflict," that "cultural misfit" and "liability of foreignness" can lead to "collide." By taxing our subconscious and conscious mind with fear of the "others," we may have used valuable brain resources that could otherwise be used to focus on win-win business.

5.3.3 *Counterproductive Effect*

The *ironic process theory* states that under a situation of stress, we will do exactly what we want to avoid.[55] A trainer made a mistake when coaching an executive on how *not* to behave while negotiating with a potential partner in the Middle East (DON'T say you are an atheist). To their horror, this was exactly what happened. The executive was so worried about cultural differences that by trying to suppress doing the wrong thing, his brain failed to have enough energy to do so, and letting unwanted behavior come flooding out. The fear of doing the wrong thing can override the will of doing the right thing.

Studies have suggested that our brain does not distinguish negation such as "don't" in the way we expect.[56-57-58] If we are told "not" to imagine a disaster, we *will* imagine a disaster. This kind of ironic process is partly due to the fact that our reaction to fear is *faster* than conscious action, which again, serves as a survival skill.

The counterproductive effect of negation can be seen in cross-cultural training programs that exist to "tick the box," satisfy an agenda, or act as preemptive strategies. Far from reaping reward, trainings that emphasize the threat of failures or stem from the purpose of avoiding lawsuits have a negative effect because they create stress and fear.[59] To reassert their autonomy, unwilling and stressful training participants may psychologically challenge the whole system by doing exactly the opposite, hence perpetuating the bias and stereotypes rather than confronting them. It can be tiring, stressful, and furious when people are constantly told to attend training after training (are we *that* incompetent?), adapt to foreigners (they choose to be here, why don't they change?), adapt themselves (why not the other way around?), respect the "others" (where is the limit?), understand foreign cultures (why not use common sense?), accept alien practices (who said it works for us?), and so forth. All these demands are quite challenging if people perceive them as threats to comfort, values, and stability. A great number of corporate trainings fail because they are based on this stressful and reactionary mentality, one that elicits rebellion, secret sabotage, and (sub)conscious punishment for revenge.[60]

Fear creates the appearance that we are working harder, longer, faster on the solution, but only at the surface because we are just protecting ourselves and avoiding failures. Using fear as a motivation is counterproductive. In an experiment, teachers highlighted the consequence of bad grades, and this strategy backfired, leading to *lower* exam performance.[61]

5.3.4 Fear Trumps Reward

In principle, our brain constantly calculates to minimize risk and maximize reward. Anticipation of rewards such as food, money, promotion, stability, and so forth are crucial for survival because humans need to be motivated to be able to start doing something, in fact, anything. However, there is a *negative* correlation between performance and anxiety. In other words, rewarding anxious people will not help them to achieve better results. This is because fear and anxiety disrupt attention and memory consolidation, increase amygdala activation, and decrease the ACC.[62] Telling an anxious executive that her/his leadership can benefit from training in how to communicate better across cultural borders is unlikely to bring the benefit it should. Fear and anxiety have to be dealt with first, and only after that can people benefit from the anticipated reward.

5.3.5 Confirmation Bias and Self-Fulfilling Prophecy

Confirmation bias is the tendency to search for what confirms one's view, and self-fulfilling prophecy is "you see what you seek, you get what you expect"[63]—which is the principle by which placebo works.[64] There is a hypothesis that the neural basis of this phenomenon is in the RAS—a bundle of nerves at the top of our brainstem that acts as a door keeper, filtering unnecessary information so the important stuff gets through to the thalamus (see Figure 4.3 in Chapter 4). Without RAS, we would be overloaded with data and go crazy. The role of RAS is so critical that scholars have suggested that the midbrain reticular system is responsible for consciousness[65] because patients with total absence of the cerebral cortex still could recognize familiar faces and had some level of social interaction.[66-67]

While much is still unknown, based on RAS's functions in attention and consciousness, we can speculate the way RAS decides whether a bit of information is crucial or just noise. It is sorted by the values we believe in, the thought we have often, what we love, fear, and keep telling ourselves from time to time. It is *not the volume, but the value* of the data that puts RAS at work.[68] For example, if we decide that smiling is crucial in communicating with customers, we will start to see the abundance (or the lack) of it in the staff—a reality that has been there, but that we did not notice because our RAS filtered it out. In essence, RAS will collect information that fits and confirms a certain thought, which is the neural basis of how confirmation bias works. That's why by conditioning one's self to an imagined situation, this person will tend to behave accordingly, and may end up creating the matching reality.

Neuroscience has joined many behavioral studies to provide further evidence to this phenomenon. For example, the information-processing parts of the brain were more active with positive messages from ingroup leaders and negative messages from outgroup leaders.[69] In case of contradictory statements given by leaders, followers would subconsciously pick messages that reflect their own standpoints.[70] The brain even distorts facts to fit our beliefs. For instance, female faces are perceived as "happy" and black male faces as "angry," even when the opposite is the case.[71] This is the result of a society where women are expected to smile and black men are associated with aggression. The impact of confirmation bias on behaviors has been shown with a plethora of evidence from behavioral studies. For example, in a classic study,[72] the Ashanti in Africa believe that the day of the week on which a person was born determines her/his character throughout life. Monday will be mild mannered but Wednesday is aggressive. In Ashanti tradition, a person's name would include the day of the week (s)he was born. Based on the records of the local juvenile court, a researcher found out that the number of violent acts committed by boys born on Wednesdays was significantly higher than other days. In short, we do live up (or down) to our names, we even look like our names.[73] Other evidence can be found in the rich line of research on stereotype threats.[74-75] In essence, performance is significantly influenced based on the belief people have about themselves.

Following the same principle of self-fulfilling prophecy, the way we describe cultural differences as problems may lead to the way we subconsciously create exactly the kind of culture that sees "others" as potentially problematic.[76] If we connect failure in business with cultural differences, our RAS will work tirelessly so we can pick up the evidence everywhere, direct attention to mismatches, give them more energy, and perceive the whole situation based on this belief. At the same time, RAS *filters out* opportunities of mutual benefit and win-win situations. When the business partner says: "We've been around South East Asia for a while but still struggling to get to Myanmar because the country was isolated from the world for 60 years." Our RAS will filter the potential win of "first-mover advantage" when a company is the first to develop and market a product. Instead, it navigates our thought to the alarming words of "struggling" and "isolated." By conditioning ourselves to an imagined situation of cultural clash, we then start behaving accordingly, and may end up navigating toward that end. Where attention flows, energy and action go. We move in the direction of our dominant thought.

Because cross-cultural management has so heavily focused on the disadvantages of cultural differences, naturally, organizations will do their best to learn about the dark side of border crossing instead of the benefit it may bring. However, priming our thought in the negative may do our brain and organizations a disservice. Wrapped up in solving problem and deficiencies, we risk generating a self-fulfilling prophecy and building organizations that reflect this dismal state of mind.[77] According to GCEB-Be, this approach can even rewire our brain physically (Behavior—Brain pathway). It's proven that liberal thinkers (flexible, data-reliant, analytic reasoning, open-minded) tend to have bigger ACC, while conservative thinkers (emotional and stability driven) tend to have bigger amygdala.[78-79] They were probably born that way, but nevertheless, an equally plausible hypothesis is that by following a political agenda, they have changed their brain structure.

For the sake of argument, have we, by any chance, evolved bigger amygdala and smaller ACC as a result of half a century regarding cultural differences as a source of failure and disasters? To what extent can our failure in doing business across cultures be blamed on the way we (have learned to) perceive others as potentially different, and the exchange with others to be potentially problematic? Operating on fear is probably one of the reasons why despite the fact that intercultural communication is a long-standing discipline, the practical achievement is far from terrific. We still have up to 40% of expatriates returning home before the completion of their foreign assignments due to failure in coping with cultural differences,[80] and up to 90% of mergers and acquisition fail miserably due to cultural shock.[81]

5.4 Fear-Free Metaphors

In cross-cultural management, the metaphor of "culture distance" is influential. Because it is rooted in the bias toward negative phenomena, this metaphor has unwittingly guided the development of theories and practices toward a problem-focused approach.[82-83-84] Can a metaphor exert such a strong impact? Why is a seemingly simple metaphorical comparison so powerful? And what can we do to reap benefits from this instrument of brain functioning, while eliminating consequences of its suggestive power?

In this section, we will discuss the significance of cultural metaphors in guiding theory and practice development. Subsequently, we will discuss the way metaphors such as the icebergs and the distance play a critical role in steering cross-cultural research toward such a difference-oriented, problem-focused, and fear-embedded approach. Finally, we will consider some alternative cultural metaphors that have the potential to produce more positive neural pathways, and thus, having a different suggestive power in guiding expectation and behavior in cross-cultural management.

5.4.1 *Metaphors Connect Mind and Body*

Western thought has been strongly influenced by Descartes's dualism, which claims that the mind and the body are distinct and separable.[85] This philosophy was strengthened in the early twentieth century when computer science and artificial intelligence began to develop, spreading the idea that the mind functions as a program, completely separated from the body, which is regarded as a general-purpose hardware.

The notion that the body does not influence cognition puzzled Lakoff, prompting him and a colleague to bring forward the idea of *embodied cognition*.[86] For example, we say "warm affection" because of our experience with physical care in early childhood, connecting "hugs" and "heat" together.[87] Embodied cognition means the mind influences the body, but the body influences the mind as well. In a study, participants holding *warm* cups of coffee judged a confederate as more trustworthy in comparison to those who held *cold* cups of coffee.[88] In reverse, after recalling a memory of being warmly and socially accepted, people felt the room to be 5 degrees warmer in comparison to those who had recalled being coldly snubbed.[89]

5.4.2 *Metaphors Guide Theories and Behaviors*

These previously mentioned experiments show us that metaphors are more than mere language and literary devices. They serve as a vehicle for contemplating concept at higher levels of abstraction, an explicatory tool to facilitate the creation and interpretation of social reality,[90] a powerful catalyst for eliciting new insight, encouraging us to think and act in novel ways.[91] For this reason, metaphors play a quintessential role in theory development. When theorists design, they conduct and interpret mental experiments where they rely upon metaphors to provide them with vocabularies and images to understand, express, map, and construct complex and abstract phenomena.[92] Imagination takes place through a simulated image, and theorists can *actively select* theoretical representations and retain them for the target subject under consideration. In other words, once a metaphor has been chosen (e.g., an iceberg), we are more likely to develop theories that associate with that image (e.g., because of hidden values, cultural exchange can be risky). Thus, the heuristic power of metaphors in schematizing new theoretical perspectives can open up new research directions and lay out the groundwork for investigation.[93-94] Because metaphors act as one of the primary ways by which theorists frame and analyze phenomena, they have become a staple of social science.[95]

Metaphors not only guide theory development but they are also powerful in guiding action. The employment of metaphors results in behaviors that correspond with the metaphor because we subconsciously want coherent experience.[96-97-98] Neural circuits asymmetrically link two brain regions of source and target, triggering consequential actions. For example, two metaphors "crime is a virus" and "crime is a beast" primed participants to propose very different solutions. They wanted to investigate the root causes, education, and eradicating poverty when "crime" was framed as "virus," arguably because the source implies an illness that needs care and treatments. However, when "beast" was the source, participants proposed to catch the criminals, jail them, and enact harsher enforcement laws.[99]

In organizational studies, certain metaphors are used to promote morale and cohesion,[100] and managers are advised to purposely change them to influence how individuals perceive and function within an organization.[101] In his classic book *Images of Organizations*,[102] Morgan critically analyzed eight metaphors that represent organizations, each has particular impact in policies and decision making. For an example, let's look at the metaphor "sustainability as a journey." While "journey" embraces change and continuous improvement, it also has negative influences in guiding organizational policies: (1) It has the effect of *deferring* sustainability, forestalling radical change that is necessary for achievement; (2) it *deflects* dissenting voices and, at the same time, enables businesses to avoid the stigma of being seen as doing nothing while in fact, it is business as usual; and (3) it reflects *process* and not *outcome*, offering a rhetoric of presentation, the same as does the saying "Rome was not built in a day."[103] In another study,[104] the authors argued that the comparing organization with "organism" or "machine" could result in the *objectification* and *dehumanization* of humans as functional components. Such images prime our brain and direct our behaviors, resulting in HR policies that remove humans from a place of stewardship or responsibility,

In a similar fashion, the iceberg metaphor has contributed to a strong bias toward negative phenomena and a cautious view of cultural diversity.[105] It immediately leads to an intuitive association with primitive concepts of "cold," "unfriendly," and, to a certain extent, "disaster" and "Titanic." Before we even manage to evaluate the image, the metaphor has already alarmed our subconscious system. How likely is it that the embodied cognition may prompt us to be reactive rather than proactive, defensive rather than cooperative, viewing differences as problems rather than opportunities? How likely is it that the iceberg metaphor has guided our collective experience with reification and self-fulfilling prophecy?[106]

In management, the "distance" metaphor connotes barriers that need to be surmounted. The notion of cultural distance posits that firms should expand first to markets that are culturally similar before venturing into those that are culturally distant. Based on a study on the inherent transaction disabilities in joint ventures,[107] researchers reported that this metaphor provides a perfect proxy to deal with environmental uncertainty, to cope with the firms' inability to specify transaction contingencies[108] due to the fear that whatever they might gain in terms of knowledge would apparently be lost because of the potential exploitation by the local partner. The metaphor and its consequential theories thus discourage organizations to look at border crossing, change, and learning, while emphasizing deficiencies and obstacles. Facing a business counterpart from a different culture, this "distance" metaphor subconsciously guides managers to look for *problems* because "they are so different" rather than *opportunities* because "they are so different."

5.4.3 Dynamic Metaphors

Scholars of the dynamic paradigm have proposed a number of cultural metaphors that help to (1) *eliminate the inherent fear* in border crossing and (2) *encourage the proactive role* of businesspeople as the authors of culture. For example, in the "dialogical self," culture and individuals are in constant dialogue and negotiating positions.[109] In the "ocean" metaphor, depending on the context, a particular value may rise to the surface. Another metaphor of "card game" implies that players respond by choosing specific cards (i.e., value/outward expression) that seem most appropriate in a given situation.[110] A manager can tell her/himself: "This partner is so tough. I will be masculine and match her." In the same vein, with the cultural "toolkit," cultures and values are socially contested and the best "toolkit" wins.[111] For example, two brands can use two different approaches, one promotes status to sell products (e.g., "Buying this will make you powerful"), and the other promotes responsibility (e.g., "Buying this will save the planet"). The market is not destined to be perceptive with only one value. Depending on the context, one of these values (tools) can win the customers.

In this book, we utilize the metaphor of culture as a "tree" because it is a neutral entity. It is not entirely a soulless tool as "card game" in which humans have absolute power to control a culture. A tree is a living organism, left on its own, it will survive and humans can be just a product of a culture. However, a tree can grow and change dramatically if we nurture and care about it. It implies that humans can be an active producer of a culture as well.

A convergent point of these dynamic metaphors (dialogical self, ocean, toolkit, card game, and tree) is that they embrace a "strategy of action"[112] with a pragmatic emphasis on people as active and creative problem solvers rather than a passive "cultural dope."[113] Unlike the iceberg and the distance, these theorists "restore human agency to social theory,"[114] allowing the dynamics of context to reign as a driving factor to predict change and communication behaviors instead of predetermined values.

Thus, as a hegemonic tool to influence perception and interpretation through brain's functions, the metaphor of choice indirectly creates the very culture we live in, through both theory development and behaviors. That is to say, the tree metaphor adopted in this book (Chapter 3) is subject to be replaced by other alternatives, depending on particular purposes. Knowing the critical suggestive power of metaphors and how they catalyze our thinking and behaviors, the metaphor of choice should be taken seriously with regard to specific context because it allows us to approach a phenomenon in a novel way.

5.5 Shifting Left to the Positive

While the bias toward *negativity helps us to survive, positivity helps us to thrive*. Fear does motivate people to work harder on the spot, but passion and optimism result in sustainability and long-term engagement. For this reasons, scholars and practitioners are calling for a more balanced approach in cross-cultural management. Here is a good illustration. A person of mixed race is often called "half blood," but in Iran, such as person is called "doubled vein." Moving from "half" to "double" is a shift of mindset, seeing differences not as "less" but "more."

In this section, we will explore this idea, and recognize the benefits of shifting paradigm to the left. The metaphorical language of "left-shifting" comes from a controversial and hotly debated hypothesis in neuroscience, that the left hemisphere processes more "positive emotions" than the right hemisphere (emotional lateralization).[115-116]

5.5.1 The Benefits of Positivity

For both individuals and organizations, there is evidence that a dominance of positivity leads to creativity,[117] productivity,[118] customer loyalty, and employee retention.[119] Superior performance among top management teams was characterized by a ratio of five positive statements for each negative statement during their work communication, whereas the lowest performing teams had a ratio of three negative statements for every positive statement.[120] We associate happy people with more positive outcomes,[121] they are viewed as more dominant,[122] their positive mood affects brain activity in a manner that leads to better insight,[123] and a more "global scope of attention."[124] The preference toward the positive seems to be a natural human attribute as well. A study found that infants as early as age three months overwhelmingly preferred positive traits, a bias detected in more than 90% of the subjects.[125]

Focusing on the positive such as rewards supports the brain to learn easier thanks to the release of dopamine—a neurotransmitter that modulates the brain's ability to perceive reward reinforcement, that is, making us want to repeat the experience again. This neural basis has led to a strategy of breaking a long-term mission down to small achievable tasks, thus cultivating many small, short-term wins that can propel us to bigger success. It is the idea that the power of progress[126] is what makes success beget success. We will look deeper into this "small wins" strategy in Chapter 7.

5.5.2 The Benefits of Differences

Trompenaars is a well-known theorist who proposed a framework of cultural values that belongs to the same static paradigm as that of Hofstede. It consists of seven value dimensions, and each country has an average score. However, an important part of the work conducted by Trompenaars and his colleague Hampden-Turner is often sidelined. They proposed a *dilemma reconciliation* process[127] that may bring benefit from combining, for example, collectivism and individualism. While this notion is plausible, the label still signals an inherent negativity by seeing differences as problematic, that's why we need to mend and "reconcile." Further, this model suggests that values can't change, only outward expressions do. Put it simple, two business partners may try to reconcile their differences by making creative solutions to achieve a shared goal. But when business is over, they automatically go back to their default cultures. Their worldviews, values, and perceptions don't change as a result of this meaningful cooperation. Because if they do, an accumulation of change in individual interaction and global business can lead to a change in wider culture—which contradicts the very ranking system that Trompenaars and Hampden-Turner proposed.

Despite this shortcoming, the spirit of the reconciliation model aligns with what we discuss here. In a timely and important call, intercultural scholars strongly advocated for an alternative way of seeing foreignness as asset instead of the traditional view of seeing foreignness as liabilities.[128-129-130-131-132] When diversity evokes no fear and the time is right, differences can be critical resources. There is strong evidence in the benefit of different thinking styles,[133] multicultural team,[134-135-136] gender diversity,[137-138-139], racial diversity,[140] and ability diversity.[141-142] We will focus on this in Chapter 8. As long as differences don't trigger continuous fear responses that push the energy consumption pass the *tipping point* of eustress, diversity can be a competitive edge. This is the reason why a corporate culture historically characterized by ingroupness like Japan is responding swiftly to the new governance code that requires at least two outsiders as independent directors.[143] In fact, adding an outsider versus an insider doubles the chances of arriving at the correct solution, from 29 to 60%.[144]

Differences are the essential elements to create powerful synergy and hybridity. For example, in Japan, being foreign could be advantageous because it allowed nonlocal banks to implement innovation strategies that domestic rivals found challenging in dealing with fundamental local norms, deeply institutionalized practices, and communication patterns.[145] Similarly, by emphasizing their foreignness, multinational enterprises (MNEs) can achieve a viable edge over local competitors.[146] In less developed countries, good employees prefer to work for companies coming from more developed backgrounds, and many MNEs deliberately accentuate their "otherness" in brand strategies.[147] By highlighting different values and outward expressions such as a merit-driven system or life-time employment, MNEs can promote themselves as employer of choice in markets where these values and practices are desirable but uncommon. In emerging markets where local standards are not advisable such as when managers abuse their power, being foreign signals investors, customers, and other stakeholders that they are trustworthy partners in the absence of governmental control.[148] Further, the presence of obvious differences helps those involved to increase awareness, be better prepared, and pay attention to less tangible but more critical issues that are often overlooked in cooperation between companies from the same country.[149]

Facing differences, hybrid management emerges. A key to the success of Hyundai is how the company promotes an employee backpack travel program around the globe focusing on what they hope to learn from different cultures and then share with colleagues at home.[150] Even when headquarters impose a dominant working culture on subsidiaries, hybridity occurs because people do not passively adopt and transmit cultures. In Thailand and Israel for example, local managers reviewed and selectively created an in-progress form of hybrid management style that (1) brings out the best of the Swedish long-term planning and the Israelis championship in improvisation and (2) strikes the right note between the European fast-execution process and the need to maintain harmonious communication style in Thailand.[151] When hybridity is practiced effectively at all levels of organization, the result is often a thriving working environment. Here is a case in point: Sugar Bowl Bakery is $45 million business built by a Vietnamese refugee family in the United States. It integrates different elements of many cultures. Contrary to the Asian tradition, the CEO of the company is not the oldest son, also the oldest people in the family do not make the final decision. There is a flat structure to speed up communication, innovation, and response time to customers. However, consensus reigns supreme; each new project has to receive the unanimous support of all family members. Job titles do exist, but in reality, there are no fixed assigned jobs, rather, they split everything up so things were being done 24/7.[152] In sum, there is a hybridity of high, low, and average values in several fundamental concerns: Hierarchy acceptance, group attachment, and uncertainty avoidance.

In short, if we see culture as a resource, then cross-cultural management is no longer about the minimization or overcoming of differences, but a form of *knowledge management*. Looking at culture with a mindset of willingness to use it as a resource will shift the way we do business.

5.5.3 *Positive Organizational Scholarship*

During his term as the president of the American Psychological Association, Martin Seligman officially placed on the agenda Positive Organizational Scholarship (POS)—a paradigm of research defined as "the study of conditions and processes that contribute to the flourishing of optimal functioning of people, groups, and institution."[153] In essence, POS is the response to the strong bias toward negative phenomenon, dysfunction, and illness that are so prevalent in psychology. The underlying argument is that we have learned a great deal about how to bring people from a negative state to normalcy, but relatively little about how to enable human functioning beyond normalcy to extraordinary states.[154] POS has triggered a paradigm shift across many disciplines, including international business and cross-cultural management. POS paved the way for Positive Organizational Behavior (POB)—a research line with emphasis on strengths that can be developed, cultural values, and practices that foster authenticity and continuous self-improvement.[155] Similarly, the concept of *positive business* refers to high-performing organizations that also promote the well-being of their employees by bringing out the best in the employees, not burning them out but helping them grow.[156]

It is critical to point out the risk of *oversight* and collective *negligence of problems* that POS is frequently criticized for.[157] The call for a positive approach is essentially a reminder that too much emphasis is being placed on the negative. For this reason, fixating exclusively on either the positive or the negative is not fruitful, but being strategic with what to focus on (positive or negative) and when to do so. POS's ultimate goal is to expand focus and to employ a more balanced methodology instead of fixating primarily on deficiencies. By advocating a more complete and balanced approach, POS can provide a rich interdisciplinary platform for businesses to expand perspectives, enrich the possibilities, and consider alternative frameworks and theories. In essence, POS is not the ultimate solution but simply a different tool in our toolkit.[158] The traditional problem-focused approach is also a tool. However, it shouldn't be the only tool we have. Because, if all we have is a hammer, everything looks like a nail.[159]

Summary

1. The discipline of cross-cultural study was born out of a fearful and hostile environment during the Cold War. We inherit theories and practices that focus on differences and potential problems as a legacy of this history.
2. Most fear is culturally conditioned, learned by a dialogue between the amygdala (emotional memory) and the hippocampus (factual memory). *We are shaped by what we remember.*
3. To survive, we have evolved more negative emotions (4) than positive ones (1) because being able to recognize danger is more important for survival than being happy. The amygdala reacts to all emotions, but reacts the quickest to fear, even when we can't see it (i.e., subconsciously). Hence, fear triggers the shortest route to reaction.
4. The problem-focused mindset of cross-cultural management triggers our brain to operate on fear, which results in many disadvantages:
    •   The modern workplace is not the ancient savannah, but our fear response activates with the same speed and intensity. By regarding cultural differences as a source of failure, we treat an overwhelming issue that can be both positive and negative with a neural solution for a real danger.
    •   When stress is prolonged, the amygdala becomes hypersensitive and responds more frequently to false alarms.
    •   Reacting on fear costs a great deal of energy, which can otherwise be spent on win-win business.
    •   Fear can be a motivation to learn, but it is not sustainable. Fear can backfire (i.e., we do exactly what we should not) and elicit (sub)conscious motivation to rebel and do the opposite.
    •   Fear trumps the benefit of reward.
5. Metaphors are powerful in directing theories and guiding behaviors.

- Under the influence of the fear-embedded, problem-focused approach, metaphors in cross-cultural managements may prompt us to formulate further bias in theories and practices (e.g., "iceberg" and "distance").
- Adopting and creating alternative metaphors can help to (1) eliminate inherent fear in working across borders and being out of the comfort zone and (2) encourage a proactive role of businesspeople also as actors rather than mere products of cultures. Examples of these metaphors are ocean, toolkit, card game, and tree.

6. By conditioning ourselves to see cross-cultural interaction with potential problems, RAS focuses our attention to mismatches, filtering out opportunities, moving us in the direction of our dominant thought. We may end up creating the exact matching reality, which merely started as an imagination.

7. The benefits of positivity and differences are:
- While a bias toward negativity helps us to survive, positivity helps us to thrive.
- When differences evoke no fear and threat, they can be asset instead of liability.
- Because too much emphasis is being placed on the negative, POS can be a new tool for business to explore the potential.
- Fixating exclusively on the negative or positive impacts of differences is not fruitful, but being strategic with what to focus on (positive or negative), and when to do so.

Notes

Don't forget to go to the end of the book for case studies.

1 Leeds-Hurwitz, Wendy. 1990 "Notes in the History of Intercultural Communication: The Foreign Service Institute and the Mandate for Intercultural Training." *Quarterly Journal of Speech* 76(3): 262–281. doi:10.1080/00335639009383919.
2 Hall, E. T. 1976. *Beyond Culture*. New York: Doubleday.
3 Fang, Tony. 2005–2006. "From 'Onion' to 'Ocean': Paradox and Change in National Cultures." *International Studies of Management and Organization* 35(4): 71–90. doi:10.1080/00208825.2005.11043743.
4 Stahl, Günter K., and Rosalie L. Tung. 2015. "Towards a More Balanced Treatment of Culture in International Business Studies: The Need for Positive Cross-Cultural Scholarship." *Journal of International Business Studies* 46(4): 391–414. doi:10.1057/jibs.2014.68.
5 Hofstede, Geert. 2001. *Culture's Consequences: Comparing Values, Behaviours, Institutions and Organizations across Nations*. 2nd ed. Thousand Oaks, CA: Sage.
6 Kogut, Bruce., and Harbir Singh. 1988. "The Effect of National Culture on the Choice of Entry Mode." *Journal of International Business Studies* 19(3): 411–432. doi:10.1057/palgrave.jibs.8490394.
7 Johanson, Jan., and Jan-Erik Vahlne. 1977. "The Internationalization Process of the Firm: A Model of Knowledge Development and Increasing Foreign Market Commitments." *Journal of International Business Studies* 8(1): 23–32. doi:10.1057/palgrave.jibs.8490676.
8 Kostova, Tatiana. 1996. "Success of the Transnational Transfer of Organizational Practices within Multinational Companies." Unpublished doctoral dissertation. Minneapolis: University of Minnesota.
9 Zaheer, Srilata. 1995. "Overcoming the Liability of Foreignness." *Academy of Management Journal* 38(2): 341–363. doi:10.2307/256683.
10 Hofstede, Geert., Gert-Jan Hofstede, and Michael Minkov. 2005. *Cultures and Organizations: Software of the Mind*. New York: McGraw-Hill
11 Lewis, Richard D. 2000. *When Cultures Collide: Managing Successfully across Cultures*. 2nd ed. London: Nicholas Brealey.
12 Lyles, Marjorie A., and Jane E. Salk. 1996. "Knowledge Acquisition from Foreign Parents in International Joint Ventures: An Empirical Examination in the Hungarian Context." *Journal of International Business Studies* 27(5): 877–903. doi:10.1057/palgrave.jibs.8490155.

13 Wijk, Raymond Van., Justin J. P. Jansen, and Marjorie A. Lyles. 2008. "Inter- and Intra-Organizational Knowledge Transfer: A Meta-Analytic Review and Assessment of Its Antecedents and Consequences." *Journal of Management Studies* 45(4): 830–853. doi:10.1111/j.1467-6486.2008.00771.x.

14 Barkema, Harry G., and Freek Vermeulen. 1997. "What Differences in the Cultural Backgrounds of Partners Are Detrimental for International Joint Ventures?" *Journal of International Business Studies* 28(4): 845–864. doi:10.1057/palgrave.jibs.8490122.

15 David, Kenneth., and Harbir Singh. 1994. "Sources of Acquisition Cultural Risk." In *The Management of Corporate Acquisitions*, ed. G. Krogh and A. Sinatra, 251–292. London: Macmillan.

16 Marks, Mitchell Lee., and Philip H. Mirvis. 2010. *Joining Forces: Making One Plus One Equal Three in Mergers, Acquisitions, and Alliances*. 2nd ed. San Francisco: Jossey-Bass.

17 Black, J. Stewart., and Mark Mendenhall. 1991. "The U-Curve Adjustment Hypothesis Revisited: A Review and Theoretical Framework." *Journal of International Business Studies* 22(2): 225–247. doi:10.1057/palgrave.jibs.8490301.

18 Caves, Richard E. 1996. *Multinational Enterprise and Economic Analysis*. Cambridge: Cambridge University Press.

19 Blomstermo, Anders., and Deo D. Sharma. 2003. *Learning in the Internationalisation Process of Firms*. Northampton, MA: Edward Elgar.

20 Stahl, Günter K., and Rosalie L. Tung. 2015. "Towards a More Balanced Treatment of Culture in International Business Studies: The Need for Positive Cross-Cultural Scholarship." *Journal of International Business Studies* 46(4): 391–414. doi:10.1057/jibs.2014.68.

21 Stahl, Günter K., Kristiina Mäkelä, Lena Zander, and Martha L. Maznevski. 2010. "A Look at the Bright Side of Multicultural Team Diversity." *Scandinavian Journal of Management* 26(4): 439–447. doi:10.1016/j.scaman.2010.09.009.

22 Margolis, Joshua D., and James P. Walsh. 2003. "Misery Loves Companies: Rethinking Social Initiatives by Business." *Administrative Science Quarterly* 48(2): 268–305. doi:10.2307/3556659.

23 Cameron, Kim S. 2008. "Paradox in Positive Organizational Change." *The Journal of Applied Behavioral Science* 44(1): 7–24. doi:10.1177/0021886308314703.

24 Caza, Brianna Barker., and Arran Caza. 2005. *Positive Organizational Scholarship: A Critical Theory Perspective*. Working paper. University of Michigan, Ann Arbor.

25 Walsh, J. P. 1999. Business Must Talk About Its Social Role. *Financial Times* (Mastering Strategy Series). November 8, 14–15.

26 Cameron, Kim. 2017. "Cross-Cultural Research and Positive Organizational Scholarship." *Cross Cultural and Strategic Management* 24(1): 13–32. doi:10.1108/ccsm-02-2016-0021.

27 Riedel, Gernot., and Jacques Micheau. 2001. "Function of the Hippocampus in Memory Formation: Desperately Seeking Resolution." *Progress in Neuro-Psychopharmacology and Biological Psychiatry* 25(4): 835–853. doi:10.1016/s0278-5846(01)00153-1.

28 Isaacs, Sofie. 2015. "The Roles of the Amygdala and the Hippocampus in Fear Conditioning." Bachelor Degree Project. Skovde: University of Skovde. www.diva-portal.org/smash/get/diva2:839668/FULLTEXT01.pdf.

29 Desmedt, Aline. 2017. "The Key Amygdala-Hippocampal Dialogue for Adaptive Fear Memory." In *The Amygdala: Where Emotions Shape Perception, Learning and Memories*, ed. Barbara Ferry, 285–304. Rijeka: InTech. doi:10.5772/67582.

30 Izquierdo, Ivan., Cristiane R. G. Furini, and Jociane C. Myskiw. 2016. "Fear Memory." *Physiological Reviews* 96(2): 695–750. doi:10.1152/physrev.00018.2015.

31 Ekman, Paul., Richard E. Sorenson, and Wallace V. Friesen. 1969. "Pan-Cultural Elements in Facial Displays of Emotion." *Science* 164(3875): 86–88. doi:10.1126/science.164.3875.86.

32 MacLean, P. D. (1990). *The Triune Brain in Evolution: Role in Paleocerebral Functions*. Berlin: Springer & Business Media.

33 Kaas, Jon H. 2013. "The Evolution of Brains from Early Mammals to Humans." *Wiley Interdisciplinary Reviews: Cognitive Science* 4(1): 33–45. doi:10.1002/wcs.1206.

34 Ibid.

35 Groot, Jasper H. B. De., Gün R. Semin, and Monique A. M. Smeets. 2014. "I Can See, Hear, and Smell Your Fear: Comparing Olfactory and Audiovisual Media in Fear Communication." *Journal of Experimental Psychology: General* 143(2): 825–834. doi:10.1037/a0033731.

36 Kondoh, Kunio., Zhonghua Lu, Xiaolan Ye, David P. Olson, Bradford B. Lowell, and Linda B. Buck. 2016. "A Specific Area of Olfactory Cortex Involved in Stress Hormone Responses to Predator Odours." *Nature* 532(7597): 103–106. doi:10.1038/nature17156.

37 LeDoux, Joseph. 1996. *The Emotional Brain: The Mysterious Underpinnings of Emotional Life*. New York: Touchstone Books.

38 Kahneman, Daniel. 2013. *Thinking, Fast and Slow*. New York: Farrar, Straus and Giroux.

39 Freeman, Jonathan B., Ryan M. Stolier, Zachary A. Ingbretsen, and Eric A. Hehman. 2014. "Amygdala Responsivity to High-Level Social Information from Unseen Faces." *Journal of Neuroscience* 34(32): 10573–10581. doi:10.1523/jneurosci.5063-13.2014.

40 Morris, J. S., B. Degelder, L. Weiskrantz, and J. R. Dolan. 2001. "Differential Extrageniculostriate and Amygdala Responses to Presentation of Emotional Faces in a Cortically Blind Field." *A Journal of Neurology* 124(6): 1241–1252. doi:10.1093/brain/124.6.1241.

41 Burra, Nicolas., Alexis Hervais-Adelman, Dirk Kerzel, Marco Tamietto, Beatrice De Gelder, and Alan Pegna J. 2013. "Amygdala Activation for Eye Contact Despite Complete Cortical Blindness." *Journal of Neuroscience* 33(25): 10483–10489. doi:10.1523/JNEUROSCI.3994-12.2013.

42 Gelder, B. De., J. S. Morris, and R. J. Dolan. 2005. "Unconscious Fear Influences Emotional Awareness of Faces and Voices." *Proceedings of the National Academy of Sciences* 102(51): 18682–18687. doi:10.1073/pnas.0509179102.

43 Baumeister, Roy F., Ellen Bratslavsky, Catrin Finkenauer, and Kathleen D. Vohs. 2001. "Bad Is Stronger Than Good." *Review of General Psychology* 5(4): 323–370. doi:10.1037/1089-2680.5.4.323.

44 Bolster, B. I., and B. M. Springbett. 1961. "The Reaction of Interviewers to Favorable and Unfavorable Information." *Journal of Applied Psychology* 45(2): 97–103. doi:10.1037/h0048316.

45 Seligman, M. E. P. 1999. "The President's Address." *American Psychologist* 54(8): 559–562.

46 Czapinski, J. 1985. "Negativity Bias in Psychology: An Evaluation of Polish Publications." *Polish Psychological Bulletin* 16(5): 27–44.

47 Selye, Hans. 1974. *Stress without Distress*. Philadelphia: J. B. Lippincott Co.

48 Chetty, S., A. R. Friedman, K. Taravosh-Lahn, E. D. Kirby, F. Guo, C. Mirescu, Fuzheng Guo, Danna Krupik et al. 2014. "Stress and Glucocorticoids Promote Oligodendrogenesis in the Adult Hippocampus." *Molecular Psychiatry* 19: 1275–1283. doi:10.1038/mp.2013.190.

49 Mohlman, Jan., Rebecca B. Price, Dana A. Eldreth, Daniel Chazin, Dorie M. Glover, and Wendy R. Kates. 2009. "The Relation of Worry to Prefrontal Cortex Volume in Older Adults with and without Generalized Anxiety Disorder." *Psychiatry Research: Neuroimaging* 173(2): 121–127. doi:10.1016/j.pscychresns.2008.09.010.

50 Compton, Rebecca J., Joshua Carp, Laura Chaddock, Stephanie L. Fineman, Lorna C. Quandt, and Jeffrey B. Ratliff. 2008. "Trouble Crossing the Bridge: Altered Interhemispheric Communication of Emotional Images in Anxiety." *Emotion* 8(5): 684–692. doi:10.1037/a0012910.

51 Jackson, Sarah E., Clemens Kirschbaum, and Andrew Steptoe. 2017. "Hair Cortisol and Adiposity in a Population-Based Sample of 2,527 Men and Women Aged 54 to 87 Years." *Obesity* 25(3): 539–544. doi:10.1002/oby.21733.

52 Van Veen, Vincent., and Cameron S. Carter. 2006. "Conflict and Cognitive Control in the Brain." *Current Directions in Psychological Science* 15(5): 237–240. doi:10.1111/j.1467-8721.2006.00443.x.

53 Dowman, Robert. 2004. "Distraction Produces an Increase in Pain-Evoked Anterior Cingulate Activity." *Psychophysiology* 41(4): 613–624. doi:10.1111/1469-8986.00186.x.

54 Sprenger, Christian., Falk Eippert, Jürgen Finsterbusch, Ulrike Bingel, Michael Rose, and Christian Büchel. 2012. "Attention Modulates Spinal Cord Responses to Pain." *Current Biology* 22(11): 1019–1022. doi:10.1016/j.cub.2012.04.006.

55 Wegner, Daniel M. 2009. "How to Think, Say, or Do Precisely the Worst Thing for Any Occasion." *Science* 325(5936): 48–50. doi:10.1126/science.1167346.

56 Wason, P. C. 1961. "Response to Affirmative and Negative Binary Statements." *British Journal of Psychology* 52(2): 133–142. doi:10.1111/j.2044–8295.1961.tb00775.x.

57 Hasson, Uri., and Sam Glucksberg. 2006. "Does Understanding Negation Entail Affirmation?" *Journal of Pragmatics* 38(7): 1015–1032. doi:10.1016/j.pragma.2005.12.005.

58 Kaup, Barbara., Jana Lüdtke, Richard H. Yaxley, Carol J. Madden, Rolf A. Zwaan, and Jana Lüdtke. 2007. "The Experiential View of Language Comprehension: How Is Negated Text Information Represented?" In *Higher Level Language Processes in the Brain: Inference and Comprehension Processes*, ed. F. Schmalhofer and C. A. Perfetti, 255–288. Mahwah, NJ: Erlbaum.

59 Dobbin, Frank., Alexandra Kalev, and Erin Kelly. 2007. "Diversity Management in Corporate America." *Contexts* 6(4): 21–27. doi:10.1525/ctx.2007.6.4.21.

60 Kalev, Alexandra., and Frank Dobbin. 2016. "Try and Make Me: Why Corporate Training Fails." *Harvard Business Review.* July–August. https://hbr.org/2016/07/why-diversity-programs-fail.

61 Putwain, David., and Richard Remedios. 2014. "The Scare Tactic: Do Fear Appeals Predict Motivation and Exam Scores?" *School Psychology Quarterly* 29(4): 503–516. doi:10.1037/spq0000048.

62 Callan, Daniel E., and Nicolas Schweighofer. 2008. "Positive and Negative Modulation of Word Learning by Reward Anticipation." *Human Brain Mapping* 29(2): 237–249. doi:10.1002/hbm.20383.

63 Sternberg, Esther., Simon Critchley, Shaun Gallagher, and V. V. Raman. 2011. "A Self-Fulfilling Prophecy: Linking Belief to Behavior." *Annals of the New York Academy of Sciences* 1234(1): 83–97. doi:10.1111/j.1749-6632.2011.06190.x.

64 Bingel, Ulrike., Vishvarani Wanigasekera, Katja Wiech, Roisin Ni Mhuircheartaigh, Michael C. Lee, Markus Ploner, and Irene Tracey. 2011. "The Effect of Treatment Expectation on Drug Efficacy: Imaging the Analgesic Benefit of the Opioid Remifentanil." *Science Translational Medicine* 3(70): 70–114. doi:10.1126/scitranslmed.3001244.

65 Merker, Bjorn. 2007. "Consciousness without a Cerebral Cortex: A Challenge for Neuroscience and Medicine." *Behavioral and Brain Sciences* 30(1): 63–81. doi:10.1017/s0140525x07000891.

66 Beshkar, Majid. 2008. "The presence of consciousness in the absence of the cerebral cortex." *Synapse* 62(7): 553–556. doi:10.1002/syn.20524.

67 Greco, Filippo., Maria Finocchiaro, Piero Pavone, Rosario R. Trifiletti, and Enrico Parano et al. 2001. "Hemihydranencephaly: Case Report and Literature Review." *Journal of Child Neurology* 16(3): 218–221. doi:10.1177/088307380101600311.

68 Crawford, John Robert. 2010. *The Incredible Power of Choice*, 72. Summerville: Holy Fire Publishing.

69 Molenberghs, Pascal., Guy Prochilo, Niklas K. Steffens, Hannes Zacher, and S. Alexander Haslam. 2017. "The Neuroscience of Inspirational Leadership: The Importance of Collective-Oriented Language and Shared Group Membership." *Journal of Management* 43(7): 2168–2194.

70 Westen, Drew., Pavel S. Blagov, Keith Harenski, Clint Kilts, and Stephan Hamann. 2006. "Neural Bases of Motivated Reasoning: An fMRI Study of Emotional Constraints on Partisan Political Judgment in the 2004 US Presidential Election." *Journal of Cognitive Neuroscience* 18(11): 1947–1958.

71 Stolier, Ryan M., and Jonathan B. Freeman. 2016. "Neural Pattern Similarity Reveals the Inherent Intersection of Social Categories." *Nature Neuroscience* 19(6): 795–797.

72 Jahoda, Gustav. 1954 "A Note on Ashanti Names and Their Relationship to Personality." *British Journal of Psychology* 45(3): 192–195.

73 Zwebner, Yonat., Anne-Laure Sellier, Nir Rosenfeld, Jacob Goldenberg, and Ruth Mayo. 2017. "We Look Like Our Names: The Manifestation of Name Stereotypes in Facial Appearance." *Journal of Personality and Social Psychology* 112(4): 527–554.

74 Steele, Claude M., and Joshua Aronson. 1995. "Stereotype Threat and the Intellectual Test Performance of African Americans." *Journal of Personality and Social Psychology* 69(5): 797–811.

75 Gonzales, Patricia M., Hart Blanton, and Kevin J. Williams. 2002. "The Effects of Stereotype Threat and Double-Minority Status on the Test Performance of Latino Women." *Personality and Social Psychology Bulletin* 28(5): 659–670.

76　Bennett, Milton J. 2013. *The Ravages of Reification: Considering the Iceberg and Cultural Intelligence, Towards De-Reifying Intercultural Competence.* Lecture presented at FILE IV, Colle Val d'Elsa in Intercultural Development Research Institute. September 28. www.idrinstitute.org/allegati/IDRI_t_Pubblicazioni/77/FILE_Documento_Intercultura_Reification.pdf.

77　Ghoshal, Sumantra. 2005. "Bad Management Theories Are Destroying Good Management Practices." *Academy of Management Learning and Education* 4(1): 75–91. doi:10.1109/emr.2005.26768.

78　Amodio, David M., John T. Jost, Sarah L. Master, and Cindy M. Yee. 2007. "Neurocognitive Correlates of Liberalism and Conservatism." *Nature Neuroscience* 10(10): 1246–1247. doi:10.1038/nn1979.

79　Kanai, Ryota., Tom Feilden, Colin Firth, and Geraint Rees. 2011. "Political Orientations Are Correlated with Brain Structure in Young Adults." *Current Biology* 21(8): 1–4. doi:10.1016/j.cub.2011.03.017.

80　Ko, Hsiu-Ching., and Mu-Li Yang. 2011. "The Effects of Cross-Cultural Training on Expatriate Assignments." *Intercultural Communication Studies* 20(1): 158–174.

81　HayGroup. 2007. *Dangerous Liaisons. Mergers and Acquisitions: The Integration Game.* Brochure. www.haygroup.com/downloads/de/misc/dangerous_liaisons_lo_res_r.pdf.

82　Shenkar, Oded., Yadong Luo, and Orly Yeheskel. 2008. "From 'Distance' to 'Friction': Substituting Metaphors and Redirecting Intercultural Research." *Academy of Management Review* 33(4): 905–923. doi:10.5465/amr.2008.34421999.

83　Shenkar, Oded. 2012. "Cultural Distance Revisited: Towards a More Rigorous Conceptualization and Measurement of Cultural Differences." *Journal of International Business Studies* 43(1): 1–11. doi:10.1057/jibs.2011.40.

84　Stahl, Günter K., Rosalie L. Tung, Tatiana Kostova, and Mary Zellmer-Bruhn. 2016. "Widening the Lens: Rethinking Distance, Diversity, and Foreignness in International Business Research through Positive Organizational Scholarship." *Journal of International Business Studies* 47(6): 621–630. doi:10.1057/jibs.2016.28.

85　Hart, W. D. 1996. "Dualism." In *A Companion to the Philosophy of Mind*, ed. S. Guttenplan, 265–267. Oxford: Blackwell.

86　Lakoff, George., and Mark Johnson. 1980. *Metaphors We Live By.* Chicago: University of Chicago Press.

87　Kövecses, Zoltán. 2005. *Metaphor in Culture: Universality and Variation.* Cambridge: Cambridge University Press.

88　Williams, Lawrence E., and John A. Bargh. 2008. "Experiencing Physical Warmth Promotes Interpersonal Warmth." *Science* 322(5901): 606–607. doi:10.1126/science.1162548.

89　Zhong, Chen-Bo., and Geoffrey J. Leonardelli. 2008. "Cold and Lonely Does Social Exclusion Literally Feel Cold?" *Psychological Science* 19(9): 838–842. doi:10.1111/j.1467-9280.2008.02165.x.

90　Putnam, L. L., N. Phillips, and P. Chapman. 1996. "Metaphors of Communication and Organization." In *Handbook of Organization Studies*, ed. S. R. Clegg, C. Hardy, and W. R. Nord, 375–408. London: Sage.

91　Inns, Dawn. 2002. "Metaphor in the Literature of Organizational Analysis: A Preliminary Taxonomy and a Glimpse at a Humanities-Based Perspective." *Organization* (9)2: 305–330. doi:10.1177/1350508402009002908.

92　Weick, Karl E. 1989. "Theory Construction as Disciplined Imagination." *The Academy of Management Review* 14(4): 516–531. doi:10.2307/258556.

93　Cornelissen, Joep P. 2005. "Beyond Compare: Metaphor in Organization Theory." *Academy of Management Review* 30(4): 751–764. doi:10.5465/amr.2005.18378876.

94　Oswick, Cliff., Tom Keenoy, and David Grant. 2002. "Metaphor and Analogical Reasoning in Organization Theory: Beyond Orthodoxy." *The Academy of Management Review* 27(2): 294–303. doi:10.2307/4134356.

95　Kaplan, A. 1964. *The Logic of Inquiry.* New York: Chandler.

96　Burr, Vivien. 2003. *Social Constructionism.* London: Routledge.

97 Ford, Jeffrey D., and Laurie W. Ford. 1995. "The Role of Conversations in Producing Intentional Change in Organizations." *The Academy of Management Review* 20(3): 541–570. doi:10.2307/258787.

98 Tsoukas, Haridimos. 1993. "Analogical Reasoning and Knowledge Generation in Organization Theory." *Organization Studies* 14(3): 323–346. doi:10.1177/017084069301400301.

99 Thibodeau, Paul H., and Lera Boroditsky. 2013. "Natural Language Metaphors Covertly Influence Reasoning." *PLoS ONE* 8(1): e52961. doi:10.1371/journal.pone.0052961.

100 Akin, Gib., and Emily Schultheiss. 1990. "Jazz Bands and Missionaries: OD through Stories and Metaphor." *Journal of Managerial Psychology* 5(4): 12–18. doi:10.1108/02683949010142731.

101 Marshak, Robert J. 1993. "Managing the Metaphors of Change." *Organizational Dynamics* 22(1): 44–56. doi:10.1016/0090-2616(93)90081-B.

102 Morgan, Gareth. 1998. *Images of Organization*. Thousand Oaks, CA: Sage Publications.

103 Milne, Markus J., Kate Kearins, and Sara Walton. 2006. "Creating Adventures in Wonderland: The Journey Metaphor and Environmental Sustainability Organization." *The Critical Journal of Organization, Theory and Society* 13(6): 801–840. doi:10.1177/1350508406068506.

104 Barter, Nick., and Sally Russell. 2013. "Organisational Metaphors and Sustainable Development: Enabling or Inhibiting?" *Sustainability Accounting, Management and Policy Journal* 4(2): 145–162. doi:10.1108/sampj-jan-2012-0002.

105 Nguyen-Phuong-Mai, Mai. 2017. "A Critical Analysis of Cultural Metaphors and Static Cultural Frameworks with Insight from Cultural Neuroscience and Evolutionary Biology." *Cross Cultural and Strategic Management* 24(4): 530–553. doi:10.1108/ccsm-07-2016-0144.

106 Bennett, Milton J. 2013. "The Ravages of Reification: Considering the Iceberg and Cultural Intelligence, towards De-Reifying Intercultural Competence." https://www.idrinstitute.org/resources/the-ravages-of-reification/

107 Beamish, Paul W., and John C. Banks. 1987. "Equity Joint Ventures and the Theory of the Multinational Enterprise." *Journal of International Business Studies* 18(2): 1–16. doi:10.1057/palgrave.jibs.8490403.

108 Shenkar, Oded., Yadong Luo, and Orly Yeheskel. 2008. "From 'Distance' to 'Friction': Substituting Metaphors and Redirecting Intercultural Research." *Academy of Management Review* 33(4): 905–923. doi:10.5465/amr.2008.34421999.

109 Hermans, Hubert J. M. 2001. "The Dialogical Self: Toward a Theory of Personal and Cultural Positioning." *Cultural Psychology* 7(3): 243–281. doi:10.1177/1354067X0173001.

110 Osland, Joyce S., and Allan Bird. 2000. "Beyond Sophisticated Stereotyping: Cultural Sensemaking in Context." *Academy of Management Executive* 14(1): 65–79.

111 Swidler, Ann. 1986. "Culture in Action: Symbols and Strategies." *American Sociological Review* 51(2): 273–286. doi:10.2307/2095521.

112 Ibid.

113 Crane, D. 1994. "Introduction: The Challenge of the Sociology of Culture to Sociology as a Discipline." In *The Sociology of Culture: Emerging Theoretical Perspectives*, ed. D. Crane, 1–19. Oxford: Blackwell.

114 Forte, James A. 1999. "Culture: The Tool-Kit Metaphor and Multicultural Social Work." *Families in Society: The Journal of Contemporary Social Services* 80(1): 51–62. doi:10.1606/1044-3894.639.

115 Alfano, Keith M., and Cynthia R. Cimino. 2008. "Alteration of Expected Hemispheric Asymmetries: Valence and Arousal Effects in Neuropsychological Models of Emotion." *Brain and Cognition* 66(3): 213–220. doi:10.1016/j.bandc.2007.08.002

116 Ahern, Geoffrey L., and Gary E. Schwartz. 1985. "Differential Lateralization for Positive and Negative Emotion in the Human Brain: EEG Spectral Analysis." *Neuropsychologia* 23(6): 745–755. doi:10.1016/0028-3932(85)90081-8.

117 Amabile, Teresa M., Sigal G. Barsade, Jennifer S. Mueller, and Barry M. Staw. 2005. "Affect and Creativity at Work." *Administrative Science Quarterly* 50(3): 367–403. doi:doi.org/10.2189/asqu.2005.50.3.367.

118 Bolino, Mark C., and William H. Turnley. 2002. "Citizenship Behavior and the Creation of Social Capital in Organizations." *Academy of Management Review* 27(4): 505–522. doi:10.5465/amr.2002.7566023.

119 Cameron, Kim., Carlos Mora, Trevor Leutscher, and Margaret Calarco. 2011. "Effects of Positive Practices on Organizational Effectiveness." *Journal of Applied Behavioral Science* 47(3): 266–308. doi:10.1177/0021886310395514.

120 Losada, Marcial., and Emily Heaphy. 2004. "The Role of Positivity and Connectivity in the Performance of Business Teams—A Nonlinear Dynamics Model." *American Behavioral Scientist* 47(6): 740–765. doi:10.1177/0002764203260208.

121 Averbeck, Bruno B., and Brad Phelps Duchaine. 2009. "Integration of Social and Utilitarian Factors in Decision Making." *Emotion* 9(5): 599–608. doi:10.1037/a0016509.

122 Hareli, Shlomo., Noga Shomrat, and Ursula Phelps Hess. 2009. "Emotional versus Neutral Expressions and Perceptions of Social Dominance and Submissiveness." *Emotion* 9(3): 378–384. doi:10.1037/a0015958.

123 Subramaniam, Karuna., John Kounios, Todd B. Parrish, and Mark Jung-Beeman. 2009. "A Brain Mechanism for Facilitation of Insight by Positive Affect." *Journal of Cognitive Neuroscience* 21(3): 415–432. doi:10.1162/jocn.2009.21057.

124 Hirt, Edward R., Erin E. Devers, and Sean M. McCrea. 2008. "I Want to Be Creative: Exploring the Role of Hedonic Contingency Theory in the Positive Mood-Cognitive Flexibility Link." *Journal of Personality and Social Psychology* 94(2): 214–230. doi:10.1037/0022-3514.94.2.94.2.214.

125 Hamlin, J. Kiley. 2013. "Moral Judgment and Action in Preverbal Infants and Toddlers: Evidence for an Innate Moral Core." *Current Directions in Psychological Science* 22(3): 186–193. doi:10.1177/0963721412470687.

126 Kramer, Teresa., and Steven J. Amabile. 2016. "The Power of Small Wins." *Harvard Business Review*. June 8. https://hbr.org/2011/05/the-power-of-small-wins.

127 Hampden-Turner, Charles., and Fons Trompenaars. 2000. *Building Cross-Cultural Competence: How to Create Wealth from Conflicting Values*. New Haven, CT: Yale University Press.

128 Stahl, Günter K., Christof Miska, Hyun-Jung Lee, and Mary Sully De Luque. 2017. "The Upside of Cultural Differences: Towards a More Balanced Treatment of Culture in Cross-Cultural Management Research." *Cross Cultural and Strategic Management* 24(1): 2–12. doi:doi.org/10.1108/ CCSM-11-2016-0191.

129 Ikegami, Jusuke J. J., Martha Maznevski, and Masataka Ota. 2017. "Creating the Asset of Foreignness: Schrödinger's Cat and Lessons from the Nissan Revival." *Cross Cultural and Strategic Management* 24(1): 55–77. doi:doi.org/10.1108/CCSM-12-2015-0194.

130 Pesch, Robin., and Ricarda B. Bouncken. 2017. "The Double-Edged Sword of Cultural Distance in International Alliances: How Perceived Cultural Distance Influences Trust and Task Discourse to Drive New Product Development Performance." *Cross Cultural and Strategic Management* 24(1): 33–54. doi:doi.org/10.1108/CCSM-03-2016-0065.

131 Dietz, Joerg., Stacey Fitzsimmons R., Zeynep Aycan, Anne Marie Francesco, Karsten Jonsen, Joyce Osland, Sonja A. Sackmann, Hyun-Jung Lee, and Nakiye A. Boyacigiller. 2017. "Cross-Cultural Management Education Rebooted: Creating Positive Value through Scientific Mindfulness." *Cross Cultural and Strategic Management* 24(1): 125–151. doi:doi.org/10.1108/ CCSM-01-2016-0010.

132 Stahl, Günter K., Rosalie L. Tung, Tatiana Kostova, and Mary Zellmer-Bruhn. 2016. "Widening the Lens: Rethinking Distance, Diversity, and Foreignness in International Business Research through Positive Organizational Scholarship." *Journal of International Business Studies* 47(6): 621–630. doi:10.1057/jibs.2016.28.

133 Diaz-Uda, Anesa., Carmen Medina, and Beth Schill. 2013. *Diversity's New Frontier: Diversity of Thought and the Future of the Workforce*. Toronto: Deloitte University Press.

134 Gao, Huasheng., and Wei Zhang. 2014. "Does Workforce Diversity Pay Evidence from Corporate Innovation." *SSRN Electronic Journal*. http://images.transcontinentalmedia.com/LAF/lacom/workforce_diversity.pdf.

135 Page, Scott. 2007. *The Difference: How the Power of Diversity Creates Better Groups, Firms, Schools and Societies.* Princeton, NJ: Princeton University Press.

136 Antonio, Anthony Lising., Mitchell J. Chang, Kenji Hakuta, David A. Kenny, Shana Levin, and Jeffrey F. Milem. 2004. "Effects of Racial Diversity on Complex Thinking in College Students." *Psychological Science* 15(8): 507–510. doi:10.1111/j.0956-7976.2004.00710.x.

137 Credit Suisse. 2012. *Gender Diversity and Corporate Performance.* August. www. calstrs.com/ sites/main/files/file-attachments/csri_gender_diversity_and_corporate_performance.pdf

138 Dezsö, Cristian L., and David Gaddis Ross. 2012. "Does Female Representation in Top Management Improve Firm Performance? A Panel Data Investigation." *Strategic Management Journal* 33(9): 1072–1089. doi:10.2307/23261318.

139 Hunt, Vivian., Dennis Layton, and Sara Prince. 2015. Diversity Matters. *McKinsey & Company.* January. www.mckinsey.com/business-functions/organization/our-insights/why-diversity-matters.

140 Nielsen, Bo Bernhard., and Sabina Nielsen. 2013. "Top Management Team Nationality Diversity and Firm Performance: A Multilevel Study." *Strategic Management Journal* 34(3): 373–382. doi:10.1002/smj.2021.

141 Smith, Zack. 2018. "Half of Silicon Valley Has Something You'd Call Asperger's: Interview with Temple Grandin." *Indy Week.* April 11. www.indyweek.com/artery/archives/2011/02/21/half-of-silicon-valley-has-something-youd-call-aspergers-interview-with-temple-grandin.

142 DCEO. 2007. "Exploring the Bottom Line: A Study of the Costs and Benefits of Workers with Disabilities." *De Paul University* and *Illinois Department of Commerce and Economic Opportunity.* October. http://bbi.syr.edu/_assets/staff_bio_publications/McDonald_ Exploring_the_Bottom_Line_2007.pdf.

143 Hiura, Toshihiko., and Junya Ishikawa. 2016. "Corporate Governance in Japan. Board Membership and Beyond." *Brain & Company.* www.bain.com/offices/tokyo/en_us/Images/ BAIN_REPORT_Corporate_Governance_in_Japan.pdf.

144 Grey, David R. 2016. "Diverse Teams Feel Less Comfortable – and That's Why They Perform Better." *Harvard Business Review.* September 22. https://hbr.org/2016/09/diverse-teams-feel-less-comfortable-and-thats-why-they-perform-better?utm_content=bufferc285e&utm_ medium=social&utm_source=facebook.com&utm_campaign=buffer.

145 Edman, Jesper. 2009. *The Paradox of Foreignness.* Stockholm: Stockholm School of Economics.

146 Brannen, Mary Yoko. 2004. "When Mickey Loses Face: Recontextualization, Semantic Fit, and the Semiotics of Foreignness." *Academy of Management Review* 29 (4): 593–616. doi:10.2307/ 20159073.

147 Stahl, Gunter K., Ingmar Björkman, Elaine Farndale, Shad S. Morris, Jaap Paauwe, Philip Stiles, Jonathan Trevor, and Patrick Wright. 2012. "Leveraging Your Talent: Six Principles of Effective Global Talent Management." *Sloan Management Review* 53(2): 25–42.

148 Doh, Jonathan P., Benjamin Littell, and Narda R. Quigley. 2015. "CSR and Sustainability in Emerging Markets: Societal, Institutional, and Organizational Influences." *Organizational Dynamics* 44(2): 112–120. doi:10.1016/j.orgdyn.2015.02.005.

149 Pucik, V., and P. Evans. 2004. "The Human Factor in Mergers and Acquisitions." In *Managing Complex Mergers,* ed. P. Morosini and U. Steger, 161–187. London: Financial Times Prentice Hall.

150 Matthews, Lowell C., and Bharat Thakkar. 2012. "The Impact of Globalization on Cross-Cultural Communication." In *Globalization—Education and Management Agendas,* ed. Hector Cuadra-Montiel. New York: IntechOpen. doi:10.5772/45816.

151 Shimoni, Baruch. 2011. "The Representation of Cultures in International and Cross Cultural Management: Hybridizations of Management Cultures in Thailand and Israel." *Journal of International Management* 17(1): 30–41. doi:10.1016/j.intman.2010.12.001.

152 Barmeyer, Christoph I., and Peter Franklin. 2016. *Intercultural Management: A Case-Based Approach to Achieving Complementarity and Synergy,* 229–232. Basingstoke, UK: Palgrave Macmillan.

153 Gable, Shelly L., and Jonathan Haidt. 2005. "What (and Why) Is Positive Psychology?" *Review of General Psychology* 9(2): 103–110.

154 Roberts, Laura Morgan. 2006. "Shifting the Lens on Organizational Life: The Added Value of Positive Scholarship." *Academy of Management Review* 31(2): 292–305. doi:10.5465/amr.2006.20208681.

155 Avolio, Bruce., and Fred Luthans. 2006. *The High Impact Leader*. New York: McGraw-Hill.

156 Spreitzer, Gretchen., and Kim Cameron. 2012. "Applying a POS Lens to Bring Out the Best in Organizations." *Organizational Dynamics* 41(2): 85–88. doi:10.1016/j.orgdyn.2012.01.001.

157 Fineman, Stephen. 2006. "On Being Positive: Concerns and Counter-Points." *Academy of Management Review* 31(2): 270–291. doi:10.5465/amr.2006.20208680.

158 Caza, Brianna Barker., and Arran Caza. 2005. *Positive Organizational Scholarship: A Critical Theory Perspective*. Working paper. University of Michigan, Ann Arbor.

159 Maslow, Abraham. 1962. *Toward a Psychology of Being*, 15. Princeton, NJ: Van Nostrand.

6 Think Global, Plan Local, Act Individual

In the previous chapter, we learned that historical context has unwittingly conditioned theories and practices of cross-cultural management toward negative phenomena. This, in turn, triggers fear of failure as a motivation to learn, which, benefit notwithstanding, can also be harmful. As a powerful instrument in perceiving the world and guiding behaviors, mainstream metaphors, such as the iceberg and the distance, might have influenced and worsened this bias, resulting in the dominance of a difference-oriented, problem-focused, and fear-embedded communication approach

In light of recent research that drew attention to the positive role of cultural differences in doing international business, a more balanced way of analyzing intercultural communication can help to bring nuances. In this chapter, we will incorporate insight from various models, studies, and disciplines to construct a framework called the *Inverted Pyramid Model*. It is argued that such a framework has the potential to reduce the shortcomings of the problem-focused approach and trigger a more dynamic, holistic, and balanced way of analyzing cultural diversity in business communication.

6.1 The Universal Level—Where Trust Begins

Doing business in our modern world is dealing with the immense dynamics of globalization. It is an environment where cultural borders are not only disappearing but also merging, growing, and intensifying. More than any time in the past, diversity and differences have become accentuated and complex. However, similarities and sameness have never been so easy to be found. The power of comparison allows us to see both. Evolutionary aside, it is our choice to turn head toward what *divides* us or what *unites* us.

6.1.1 Differences Alarm

As discussed in Chapter 1, an important reason why local boundaries are constantly reinforced despite the powerful impact of globalization has to do with our own survival. During several millions of years living on the savannah in small tribal groups, cultural similarities and differences became a mechanism for our ancestors to recognize ingroup and outgroup members, thus who are potentially enemies and whom they can trust. While our ancestors would eventually cross these boundaries, it is hard to deny the fact that from evolutionary point of view, differences signal cautiousness and distrust. To this day, the amygdala is still more active when we see faces of different racial characteristics.[1] Fear evolves to focus our attention on the negative consequences of encounters with outsiders (see Chapter 5). By and large, the bias toward negativity in cross-cultural management is partly a product of evolution. From this point of view, *humans inherently discriminate anyone who looks, thinks, and behaves differently.*

In the modern era, similarities don't necessarily mean ingroup, and differences don't necessarily imply threats. In fact, both similarities and differences can bring about benefit, danger, and everything in between. In Chapter 5, we briefly discussed the advantages when different corporate cultures combine and create synergy. The problem is, despite the benefit of differences, we still retain the ancient part of the brain with the subconscious tendency to guard against differences. Can we override this knee-jerk response to keep up with the demand of the modern era? The answer is a firm "yes." Chapter 4 explained to us that while the autopilot System 1 tends to quickly categorize things in black and white, good or bad, the conscious System 2 helps us to reach a fine, plural, and complex thinking pattern. Differences do send off an alarm, but as long as we can involve the cortex to join the force of judgement, System 2 will operate.

Note that System 2 can only optimize when (1) there is *no threat* and (2) there is *time*. Fear shuts down System 2 and a good dialogue between rationality and emotions. Urgency takes priority. The questions left for us are: How can we approach differences and minimize threat? And how can we "buy us some time" so the amygdala and the cortex can have a thorough "conversation" with each other?

The answer is, fortunately, simple enough. Instead of taking differences as the starting point as the mainstream literature and practices in cross-cultural management have long suggested, we should do the opposite. We should first *focus on similarities*.

6.1.2 Similarities Attract

As much as differences informed our ancestors who were potentially untrustworthy, similarities gave them signals of ingroup, signals of safety, and signals that cultural resources will be shared fairly. Think about the moment you meet a stranger. It is a very natural inclination that you and this person will talk about something you are both interested in, or something that you are both more likely to agree on. It is not for nothing that people tend to break the ice with comments about the weather. From that moment, the more shared points of contact one can establish, the more likely a relationship is to start forming.[2]

Because culture is our survival strategy, ingroup bias is rooted in our evolution and we have evolved to love our culture[3,4] and those who look,[5] think,[6] and behave[7] in a similar way, or have similar personalities[8]—a phenomenon called *implicit egotism*.[9] We are not only more attracted to those who have similar names or initial letters (so Maya may subconsciously prefer to work with Michael), we even *perform* better if the evaluation system has a similar element with our name. When students are awarded letter-based grades, with A as a high grade and D as a lower score, researchers found that students whose names began with C or D underperformed whilst students whose names began with A and B scored higher.[10] Back in 1979, a researcher in Japan conducted an experiment by dressing as a jogger and greeted everyone he passed. While only 42% of the non-joggers greeted him with *ohayo gozaimasu* (often reserved for ingroup members), 95% of the joggers used the phrase.[11] He became an ingroup member just because they were doing the same activity. Nearly 40 years later, our psychology still works the same way in the digital era. A 2017 study of eight million volunteers and their digital footprints on Facebook concluded that most of our interactions are with those who are a great deal like us.[12] Another study looks at photos of couples when they first got married and 25 years later.[13] Interestingly, as years passed, spouses looked more and more alike as they tended to mimic each other's facial expressions and behaviors—a process that has nothing to do with genetics. Similar others are more likely to have opinions and worldviews that *validate* our own, thus, interaction with similar others is an important source of social reinforcement and self-affirmation. The "just like me" bias[14] in hiring is a good example, which shows how employers (sub)consciously search for cultural and personal similarities in job candidates and favor those who share similar traits and backgrounds.

This tendency happens early. Two-day-old infants prefer their mother's face to that of a female stranger.[15] They prefer those who speak their native language, and among older infants, variations in accent are sufficient to evoke social preferences.[16] Neuroscience has given us quite a great deal of evidence. Brain-imaging studies show that we favor our own people to the extent that we feel their pain more intensely,[17] and we even want to share that pain at the expense of our own safety.[18] When we see people with similar values and attitudes winning, our brain excites and we feel rewarded as well.[19]

It is important to note that the amygdala does not see race, gender, or religion. It only sees ingroup and outgroup. Who belongs to ingroup or outgroup is a socially constructed process. Divide people into two groups with the flip of a coin or based on any trivial flimsy differences such as a choice of clothes, and each side will automatically develop ingroup favoritism with a shared interest. They also favor their mates even when groups only last for a short period. A computer-stimulated study reported that cultural groups automatically emerged as a result of matching trivial symbols (triangle vs. circles) and expected behaviors.[20] The implication of such a study is powerful because it means we can form ingroup with anyone as long as there is some common ground and shared interest that we can work on.

Based on this insight, cross-cultural management should start with the bottom layer (i.e. the universal level) of the Inverted Pyramid Model (Figure 6.1). This is culture in the evolutionary sense, the culture that is meant to unite us as human beings. The universal layer of culture indicates fundamental concerns, baseline values, and outward expressions that we all share as human beings, regardless of our background. *It weeds out fear.* It signals similarities as the starting point, springboard, and foundation for communication.

Here is an example from Alberto Gaiani—an Italian executive who had to find his way to work with a team of young software engineers based in Mumbai, India without sufficient travel budget. He explained how he solved it:

> I am forty-six years old with four children. My life is homework and diapers and weekend trips to grandma's house. But one thing I do love is music. I listen to music in the car, in the shower, while I'm working. Classical, rock, you name it. So then it occurred to me, why not use Indian pop music to make a connection?
>
> I Googled "Indian pop music what's hot." Then I spent two hours listening to the top songs that came up on YouTube and getting a feel for the rhythms and beats. For the song I liked the best, I sent my Indian staff a link. "Do you know this song?" I asked them. "Do you love it like I do?" They responded with a resounding "NO, we don't like that song—are you kidding?" "This is my twelve-year-old sister's favorite song! You can do better than that!" one of them told me. And then they sent me links to the songs they liked. I created a great dialogue with them over something that was very interesting to all of us personally.[21]

The story of Alberto Gaiani shows us how he started a good business relationship at the point of similarity. He chose a universal fundamental concern (music), a universal value (everyone loves and needs music at the base line level), and a universal outward expression (we listen to our favorite music). From this starting point, he got the attention and interest of the team, establishing a good base for cooperation and synergy. Now imagine what would happen if he had approached the Indian team who lived half the globe away with a proposal to have performance reviews, or an action plan to change what he perceived to be ineffective in the working process. Benefit notwithstanding, such an approach would initially trigger uncertainty rather than a willingness to listen and cooperate.

Shared interests and passions can act as a powerful instrument to combat the alarming level of low engagement among employees. Some CEOs are well aware of the fact that despite living in

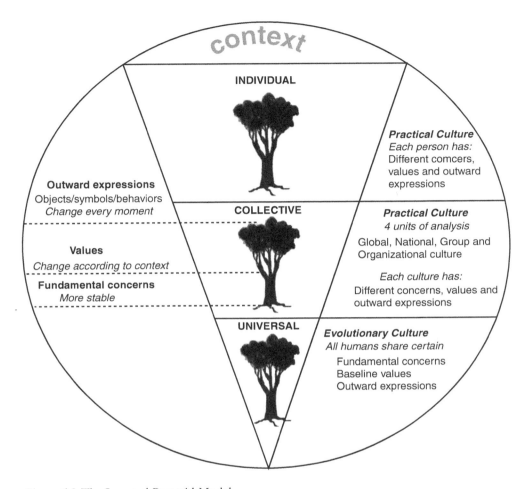

Figure 6.1 The Inverted Pyramid Model

an ultramodern era, deep down, we are still rooted in a tribal attachment, and thus, allow tribes to form and act on a shared purpose. Here are two examples:

Dana is the women's division of the Abu Dhabi Islamic Bank in the United Arab Emirates. Its female employees shared a purpose—wanting to help other Muslim women. They became aware of a specific need among their clients, and it brought them together to build a product that could be used for their community—Banun. These women employees realized the need of their divorced clients to open accounts in the name of their children without the signature of their husbands as required by the law. Once the need was detected, the managers consulted with the Sharia division that also asked for advice to Sharia Board, and after some discussions, they agreed to create the Banun account. Rooted in a shared interest, Dana has become a successful division that caters special lifestyles, privileges, and needs.

Another example is the Madrid-based multinational consulting firm Everis who actively uses employee's shared interest and passion as a constant fuel for company innovation. "Everis Initiatives" lets employees come together to develop business ideas without having to leave the organization. If the idea is approved, the group behind it will be granted the necessary time, coaching sessions, and the capital needed to launch the project and sustain its financial needs for a period of five years. Eight of these ideas have become stand-alone companies.[22]

In sum, "opposites attract" is possible only after a certain sameness has drawn people close together. It is not differences, but similarities that can initially trigger cooperation and a potential relationship. Consequently, identifying mutual objectives, backgrounds, practices, and interests should be an essential skill when doing business internationally. The emphasis on knowing cultural differences should be balanced with the need to establish a foundation of fellowship, sameness, like-mindedness, and connection. It is a springboard from which to approach differences more effectively, with the fundamental understanding that *we are not different in kind, only in level.*

6.2 The Collective Level—Where Synergy Evolves

The second layer of the Inverted Pyramid Model is *collective*. At this level, we have culture in the practical sense, one that generates the immense diversity we see in each society, country, or group. We start to differ from the universal fundamental concerns, universal value baseline, and universal outward expressions. The tree of culture at this level reflects typical and general characteristics of a collective. For example, in the culture of Egyptian fashion designers, what would be their common concerns, shared values, and symbolic outward expressions? How would a tree of their culture look like?

Let's go back to the example of Alberto Gaiani and the team. They have had a great starting point at the universal level, that is everyone loves music in some way and searches for a favorite rhythm at some point. Moving to the collective level, Alberto and the team began to differ from this baseline according to their own collective cultures. Alberto presented to the team Indian pop songs—outward expressions that may correspond with the culture of Indian youngsters. The team seemed to disagree, and suggested something else because they were probably influenced by a *different* youth culture. The Indian employees didn't seem to enjoy the same music that many other Indians rated at the top chart.

We know from Chapter 4 that culture is not homogeneous. A major contribution of the Inverted Pyramid Model is that it gives us a distinction of different collective cultures, so to avoid painting a brushstroke over a culture by equating it with a *country*. While our mind is pleased with simplicity, it is not wise to associate a culture with a nation. International business is not simply conducting business through a network of different nations. We have to broaden this view and take a more sophisticated approach to culture.

Imagine at this level of the Inverted Pyramid Model there are at least four trees of the collective *coculture*: Global, national, group, and organizational culture. This categorization comes from a model proposed by Erez and Gati.[23] Let's discuss these cocultures and their unique features.

6.2.1 Global Culture

6.2.1.1 Increased Number of Global Citizens

As the world becomes more and more interconnected, the notion of nationality and citizenship has evolved dynamically. In fact, global citizenship has become a marketable commodity, passport shopping is considered a big business, and citizenship for sale has been embraced by governments[24] and individuals[25] alike.

But global citizens aren't necessarily those with multiple passports or extensive living experience abroad. Exposure to global cultures affords many individuals opportunities to develop global identities[26-27] within their local homelands. Since philosopher Diogenes—born in 412 BC, modern-day Turkey—branded himself the first "citizen of the world," we are witnessing a great number of millennials (born between 1980 and 2000) and generation Z (born after 2000) who identify themselves as global rather than national citizens. According to a BBC World Service poll[28] in 2016 with 20,000 people in 18 countries, more than half of those asked (56%) in emerging economies saw themselves first and foremost as global rather than national citizens (Nigeria: 73%; China: 71%; Peru: 70%; and India: 67%). Note that while people from emerging economies see themselves as outward looking and internationally minded, the trend in some industrialized nations seems to head in the opposite direction, arguably as a result of the financial crash's serious hit in 2008 and the refugee crisis in 2015. For example, in Germany, only 30% of the respondents see themselves as global citizens.

6.2.1.2 The Tree of Global Culture

Imagine a tree for this "global culture" at the collective level of the Inverted Pyramid Model. What are the concerns that hold a critical place in their worldview? What do they care about? We can guess that, on this list, there would probably be diversity tolerance, education, social justice, sustainability, global awareness (which belongs to gender association), democracy, freedom (hierarchy acceptance), pragmatism, and flexibility (uncertainty avoidance).

In terms of values, the members of global culture may place a *high* degree of importance on the previously mentioned concerns.[29-30-31] The branches that represent their values are long and big, so to speak. Global citizens intrinsically care about the well-being and survival of the world.[32] They are aware that many of its ills have been caused by companies in the quest for wealth and want them to make amends.[33]

In term of outward expressions (leaves of the tree), global citizens demonstrate specific behaviors that we can observe. A 2015 study shows that 84% of global consumers are more likely to seek out responsible brands that reflect their global identities and ethics.[34] At the same time, 90% would boycott brands that conduct irresponsible practices. Global consumers are willing to make personal sacrifices for the greater good: Four in five are willing to consume fewer products to preserve natural resources or buy a product from an unknown brand if it has strong social commitments. According to a survey across 30 countries,[35] 77% of millennials are involved in a charity or good cause, 76% believe that business should be a positive force for social impact, and 88% believe business is a force for social change. With regard to emerging markets, not only do more global citizens come from these countries but they are also more likely to feel the impact of the company's efforts, and more likely to switch brands to one that supports a cause (China: 97%; Brazil: 96%; India: 95%). In short, global citizens have a number of concerns that are of great importance for them (i.e., values) and they show specific behaviors to outwardly express their views and demands.

6.2.1.3 Impact for Business

Back in 1989, Kenichi Ohmae—a Japanese management strategist—wrote that people have "become global citizens, and so must the companies that want to sell."[36] Many people wrongly understand this as they assume that brands need to develop *universal personalities* to completely *transcend the myriad of cultures*, and hence, big brands have better chance to do so. The fact is, none can do it. What Ohmae meant is that brands have to reflect the personalities of global citizens as a unique collective group, not a personality that represents *all* citizens in this globe. Big brands don't have the absolute power to create this personality. Global citizens buy and boycott big and small brands alike, depending on a match or mismatch in ideologies, values, and behaviors. That is why celebrities such as Emma Watson choose to wear a dress made of plastic bottle designed by Calvin Klein,[37] and many other items from less known brands, such as Edun and People Tree to promote sustainable fashion. Another example is from Uber. A great segment of Uber's customers are global citizens. In their opinion, CEO Travis Kalanick did his company a disservice to support Trump's executive order in 2017 to temporarily bar people from seven Muslim-majority countries. That's why he was forced to step down from President Trump's economic advisory council because customers believed that "there would be no Uber without immigrants."[38]

In response to the demands of global citizens, companies have acknowledged that they need to *become* global citizens, embracing concerns, values, and outward expression of this segment. They should even go a step further by *leading* the movement and *making* new trends, creating new markets instead of just responding to the market (i.e., becoming a *producer* of culture, Behavior—Culture pathway of GCEB-Be). According to a Costa Rican customer, "[L]ocal brands show what we are, global brands show what we want to be."[39] The idea that branded products are used as passport to show global citizenship[40] creates incredible opportunities for businesses to influence and profit in an alignment with a good cause. More and more companies are releasing their annual Global Corporate Citizenship report—a conviction that companies are stakeholders alongside governments and civil society, fully committing to sustainable development and addressing paramount global challenges.[41] Business schools now focus on educating global citizens,[42] simply because companies need managers and employees who are global citizens to understand this segment of collective culture and to become truly global brands.

It's important to remember that global citizens do not abandon their other identities such as being a member of a country, an ethnicity, an organization, or a social group. These identities continue to give meaning to their lives and define who they are. That is why, at the collective level of the Inverted Pyramid Model, we have more than just one unit of analysis.

6.2.2 National Culture

Cross-cultural management has been strongly associated with national borderlines because most available literature is organized around the concept of the "nation-state." At the collective level of the Inverted Pyramid Model, we can imagine that there are more than 200 trees, each representing a country on this planet. Each tree has a number of unique concerns with its own degree of importance placed on them (i.e., values) and a vast array of outward expressions through specific language, art, policies, cuisine, communication styles, and so forth.

While country is the most common unit of analysis, we need to bear in mind that it is also a new concept that only dates from the nineteenth century. Before that, much of the world was dominated by multiethnic societies such as the British, the Mongol, and the Ottoman empires, and so forth with a population belonging to many ethnic groups and speaking many languages.[43] The current borderlines are more man-made than culturally defined. Writing about the determination of national boundaries at the Versailles Peace Conference in 1919, Arthur Balfour— the United Kingdom's foreign secretary—angrily observed the spectacle of "all powerful, all ignorant men sitting there and partitioning continents."[44] Balfour's comment attests to the fact that a majority of current national boundaries have been formed as a consequence of arbitrary political interplay.

The practice of using the nation-state as a proxy independent variable has been criticized,[45-46-47] because it underestimates variations *within* a culture.[48] *Country is a bad container of culture* because it is so heterogeneous. "Country" only explains 20% of the differences, leaving 80% of the variation for individual diversity, other group cultures, and particular contexts.[49] This is exactly the reason why indexes that shrink a value held by a population to a simple average in number (i.e., the Nigerians are among the world's champions in short-term thinking, scoring 13 on Hofstede's index) can be misleading. Businesses that follow this indication at face value underestimate the complexity of many cocultures that exist within a national population such as those Nigerian who identify as global citizens (73% in the BBC poll—see previous section), or those who belong to different *group culture*, such as the Muslim-dominated north and the Christian-dominated south. Here is an example: When the Central Bank of Nigeria introduced Islamic banking—a practice seen as long-term thinking, ethical, and sustainable by Muslims—it angered many non-Muslims who saw that as a misuse of national resources to favor a particular religion.[50] However, the bank didn't back down, hoping that with time, perception will change and habits will follow (Behavior—Culture pathway). This example shows that business policies should be based on a thorough analysis of a particular context, taking into account all elements of the Diversity Pathway GCEB-Be while regarding general indexes as "the first best guess."

6.2.3 Group Culture

The third unit of analysis—*group culture*—is a wide range of different communities to which each of us belong. It can be based on categories such as religion, ethnicity, gender, age, or life-style. The Islamic banking example from the previous section is a case in point, demonstrating how group culture may hold opposing values and outward expressions despite living in the same country. Another good example can be found among brands that realize the power of youth culture. While four in ten respondents aged 16–34 complain that brands don't take young people seriously enough,[51] many others know how to tap on the generation of doers, making them superheroes of their stories. In this case, *active involvement* fueled by youthful energy is a magic match that aligns with various group cultures to which a young person identifies.

Let's come back to the study of "country versus culture" mentioned in the previous section. Based on a meta-analysis of 558 studies featuring 32 countries, the study concluded that the worst indicators of cultural homogeneity are gender, age, and country. The best indicators are profession, socioeconomic classes, and the freedom level of a society. In other words, any two secretaries in the world may share more similarities than two colleagues growing up in the same national culture, working in the same company, but having different job functions.

It is vital for businesses to identify the group culture they want to target. Because there are many group cultures, there is also a great deal of overlap among them. The boundaries are not static but often fluid. Here is an example. In 2017, John Lewis got rid of "boys" and "girls" labels in children's clothing. The UK retailer wanted to attract liberal parents (read that: group culture of progressive consumers) to lead the trend on gender equality and fight against stereotypes.[52] They wanted to promote high value of femininity. However, while the move was widely praised, John Lewis also divided its customers and lost some of the conservative buyers (read that: group culture of traditional consumers). Group cultures overlap on some values and clash head-on with other values. This means companies have to carefully calculate trade-offs when they decide to align corporate concerns, values, and outward expressions with one group at the expense of the other. This also means influential brands constantly face a challenge of balancing between two objectives: (1) *Reflecting* the target culture and (2) *creating* the evolution of a culture. Choosing when/what/how to *follow* and *lead* is an incredibly challenging task that requires brands to have a thorough understanding of their customers and the dynamics of the many groups to which they belong. This topic of being either a product or a producer of a culture will come back in Chapter 14.

6.2.4 Organizational Culture

6.2.4.1 Corporate Culture and Survival

The last analysis unit at the collective level of the Inverted Pyramid Model is organizational culture. There are millions of organizational trees because each organization has its own culture.

In essence, corporate culture refers to the way a *unique business environment* is created by how managers and employees express their fundamental concerns (power, motivation, money, status, etc.) through differing values and different outward expressions. We are reminded here of the notion of culture as a survival strategy for humankind (Chapter 2). To develop a good career, employees take hints from their corporate culture to modify their values and outward expressions. To be productive, managers and staff strive to build a suitable collective culture that makes people automatically behave in a productive way without having to impose rules and regulations. To tackle challenges, such as entering a new market, businesspeople don't rely on those employees with risk-taking genes (although they have been argued to exist), but pull heads together, change the culture, shape new values, switch the behaviors, practice new habits, and so forth. Culture is not static, and this notion is the most obvious when applied to the organizational level of analysis.

6.2.4.2 *Corporate Culture as Business Strategy*

People work for money, but they also work for what they truly believe in.[53] How one feels is often more important than how much one earns. For example, a congruence between the values/practices of the organization and that of the employees (Person-Organization Fit) results in a source of pride, motivation, work effectiveness,[54] and creativity.[55] Thus, a study of Indian IT workers shows that they are more loyal to the company because it values their heritage and uniqueness.[56] This example illustrates how a corporate culture can be strategic in motivating workers and, consequently, in boosting performance.

Many studies have proved that a strong organizational culture is a good business strategy.[57-58-59-60-61] There is a direct link between corporate culture and success. By observing 200 companies over a period of 11 years, one of the best-known studies on this issue reported that those with good corporate cultures vastly outperformed their competitors.[62] To be precise, companies that had good cultures increased a revenue average of 682%, compared to 166% among companies that did not. They expanded the workforce by 282% (vs. 36%), enjoyed a stock price growth by 901% (vs. 74%), and achieved a net income growth of 756% (vs. 1%). However, this link between culture and performance is not bidirectional. A study of 95 auto dealerships reported that while a positive corporate culture helps a company's bottom line, the reverse isn't true.[63] Good performance doesn't create a good culture, and *in the long run, without a good culture, performance will decline.*

A good corporate culture creates a powerhouse for driving performance, bringing every employee together, and creating a "weapon" for competing with other companies. Consider FPT, a Vietnamese multinational with branches in 20 countries whose corporate culture is seen as the power of the company.[64] Its top executive cited an example when FPT was disqualified from an important business deal. Instead of giving up, the CEO invited the contractor to join one of the company's communal gathering. Witnessing how managers and staff were closely bonded as they sang cheerfully with each other, the contractor changed his mind: "This wonderful spirit will overcome any shortcomings. I want to reopen the deal with you."[65]

However, you may be surprised to know that the corporate culture that FPT sees as a weapon for growth and development is very different from the national culture where FPT comes from: Vietnam. The company is famous for having an extremely casual and satirical way of communication. Employees confront managers directly and openly in staff meetings. They also make fun of managers in a series of parody songs and stunts. Satire reigns during the regular company parties, flying in the face of social taboos. In a famous incident, employees congratulated a bride—also an executive—with a parody toast, adopting a funereal tone and satirical wishes.[66] While many outsiders consider this culture disrespectful and inappropriate, FPT employees and managers seem to regard it as a sign of intimacy and an effective tool for building camaraderie.

Similar examples can be found in many other corporate cultures that hold contradicting values with their national culture.

6.2.4.3 Building Corporate Culture

What constitutes a good corporate culture? The case of FPT tells us the answer: *It depends*. Each particular context calls for a particular culture that can effectively respond to the market and benefit the business. There is no magic formula or set standard. This is fundamentally the main idea behind cross-cultural management. What makes a company successful in Doha does not necessarily tick in Cape Town. Similarly, what connects people in a tech start-up with young founders can't be readily applied to a medium-sized family business specialized in food produces. FPT has a corporate culture that is almost the opposite of the stereotypical national culture where it was originally born. And it works. For this reason, it is wise to take available archetypes of corporate cultures in the mainstream literature with some healthy skepticism. This especially counts for those models that specify corporate cultures on a spectrum from negative to positive, for example, the framework proposed by Jerome Want, who rates corporate cultures on a hierarchy: Predatory, frozen, chaotic, political, bureaucratic, service, and New Age.[67] This framework is clear, but it may undermine the impact of particular contexts and cocultures such as profession, social class, educational level, nationalities, or age diversity.

Because culture is seen as a tool to achieve business goals, corporate culture can be very dynamic. Strategic management policies often aim at promoting adjustment to respond to constantly changing environment.[68] For example, with the majority of the modern workforce comprised of millennials, organizations should foster fundamental concerns that this segment finds important: Flexibility, creativity, and social responsibility. In many cases, mergers, acquisitions, new markets, disruptive technologies, social and political changes, and so forth demand companies to be versatile and adaptive, making change management a critical component of international business, to the extent that business strategists see the situation as "change or die."[69] In short, culture is not static, change is expected, and differences can be ingredients of success.

The process of culture building is the most effective at the formative stage of a company. However, this is also the stage where new companies often get caught up in the make-and-sell cycle. Leaders are distracted and let their corporate culture freely evolve, taking care of itself. Employees are hired on the basis of "work capacity" instead of desired values and compatibility. As a result, each of the new hires brings in her/his own mindset, and the corporate culture gradually forms a life of its own like a sprawling suburb without planning. Leaders who undermine the role of corporate culture often don't know how to describe their own culture, don't care, or see that as an HR's domain. However, even leaders who can grasp the significance of corporate culture often don't know how to execute the change their companies need. The topic of reshaping a corporate culture will be the focus of Chapter 7.

6.3 The Individual Level—Where Culture Is Made

The third layer of the Inverted Pyramid Model is *individual*. We have almost eight billion trees on this level because each human being is unique.

While most cultural model ignore individuals, Erez and Gati's work distinguishes itself by adding the individual to the framework of cultural analysis. They argued that a dynamic approach of culture should reflect both top-down and bottom-up processes "through which adaptive behaviors at the individual level, when shared by all members of a social unit, emerge into a macro-level culture that reflects adaptation to the cultural change."[70] The acknowledgment of individual impact in this model is significant because it recognizes the impact of individuals in the shaping of a culture. It is the opposite of the static notion that individuals are "run" by a "cultural software," and thus, people are product of culture, devoid of any authorship and influential impact.

Nevertheless, no matter which view one holds, one thing is hard to deny: Culture is essentially *made* by individuals together. The making of culture never starts with a cohesive, united, orderly, identical, and uniform pattern across a population. It is done personally, uniquely, specifically, and contextually.

In this section, we will look deeper into the dynamics of culture at this level and discuss the interplay of individuals with their many collective cultures.

6.3.1 People Are More Than Their Culture

Most of the static cultural theories focus on the nation-state unit and do not deal with the individual level of analysis. According to Hofstede, the country index only explains 2 to 4% of the variance at the individual level.[71-72] Country explains only 1.2% of the variance in individual-level individualism score,[73] while "power distance" (i.e., hierarchy acceptance) and "individualism—collectivism" (i.e., group attachment) have near-zero intercorrelations.[74-75] Despite the warning that Hofstede's index is not meant to explain individual behaviors, the use of individual incidents in his own books and the enthusiast application among researchers and practitioners all point to the risk of ecological fallacy. This conflation of levels, that is inappropriately generalizing downward to the individuals, is rampant in cross-cultural communication and management.[76]

However, a key task of theory in the social sciences is to explain individual and collective human action. This shortcoming does not go unnoticed by neuroscientists whose work is intensively based on the examination of every single participant's neural images. Despite being a new discipline, some researchers in cultural neuroscience have begun to pay attention to the remarkable degree of within-culture variation and individual differences.[77] The call for a "dynamic constructivist approach"[78] strongly echoes with the essence of the dynamic paradigm, which sees individuals, even virtual figures, as potential units of cultural analysis.[79] After all, the end contact of intercultural communication is always a specific person. We don't do business with a country, but work (in)directly with a customer, partner, or colleague, and so forth. Assuming that this person is her/his culture is an outright stereotype. Taking such an essentialist approach not only risks "neo-racism"[80] but also denies the autonomy of the individuals and forces them to correspond to a conceptual essence. It is hard to overemphasize that *people are more than their cultures*. No matter how dominant and pervasive a value is within a society, you will always see individuals whose values and outward expressions completely contradict what the majority in that culture appear to adhere to. In the same vein, these indexes have been labeled as "sophisticated stereotypes"[81] because they immediately signal differences and problems at both personal and cultural levels, priming the mind toward a state of cautiousness rather than a healthy attitude of curiosity and synergy.

6.3.2 Multiple Identities

A person can be a member of multiple collective cultures, can have *multiple identities*, and is able to self-develop in a culturally selective way. For example, a person can be a global citizen with French nationality, while holding dear the values and outward expressions of other group cultures such as being a Muslim (religion), an Arab (ethnicity), a gay person (sexual orientation), an imam (profession), a feminist (life ideology), and an AIDS-awareness activist (health and capacity). If you wonder whether such a combination is possible, search for the name Dr. Ludovic-Mohamed Zahed. Born in Algeria, openly gay, he is the founding imam of Europe's first inclusive mosque in Paris. Being HIV positive, he also works hard to raise awareness and support those who suffer from social stigma and discrimination.

The complexity and hybrid structure of an individual's cultural profile poses both challenges and opportunities for businesses. On the one hand, companies need to be careful with the message they send out to customers because it can clash with their multiple identities. On the other hand, a good message can touch different identities in a single person, shifting her/his priorities to be in sync with the call.

6.3.3 Multicultural Mind

An individual not only has different identities but also multiple mindsets. In Chapter 4, we touched on the topic of multicultural mind. At the neural level, brain's plasticity enables us to actively take part in the process of change, and repeated behaviors can physically rewire the brain, helping us to adapt to multiple systems of values simultaneously. Our brain is so flexible that we are capable of representing "multiple cultures," switching between values, communicating very complex information, to the point that we can be both collectivistic and individualistic, as long as a specific context activates that element in us. The dynamics of an individual is a strong reminder that people are not a miniature representative of their collective culture, that people change, and that people can even hold opposing mindsets simultaneously.

6.3.4 The Impact of Individuals

We don't just change our individual values and outward expressions but also change our collective cultures. We "actively control the dynamics of construct accessibility rather than being just passively affected by them."[82] This view of individuals challenges the mainstream assumption in the static paradigm, which posits that individuals are merely the consequences of culture. On the contrary, the dynamic paradigm advocates a view that sees people not only as *products* but also *producers* of culture (GCEB-Be, Behavior—Culture pathway). We can recall here some metaphors of culture from the dynamic paradigm in Chapter 5 (e.g., "toolkit" and "card game"), which "restore human agency"[83] by a strategy of action, a pragmatic emphasis on people as active and creative problem solvers rather than a passive "cultural dope."[84]

Throughout history, ordinary and exceptional individuals have gradually or dramatically shaped the course of a culture, more often than not in unexpected directions. The leadership of Carlos Ghosn provides an excellent case study that highlights the synergy and hybridity a leader can achieve for her/himself and the organization. In 2000, a 45-year-old Brazilian-born Lebanese, French-educated executive came to Tokyo as the head of new Nissan after its merger with Renault. Ghosn's strategies and communication style broke every single norm of the traditional Japanese corporate culture. For example, his communication style was clear, simple, direct, and open. He also formed cross-functional teams consisting of young middle managers—a violation of the established hierarchy and seniority system in Japan. Ghosn redirected the traditional inward-looking Japanese corporate culture by refocusing managers' attention and their efforts on overall corporate objectives, instead of protecting their own departments. The pay-for-performance compensation system replaced the deeply entrenched seniority system in the Japanese work culture. The official company's language also changed from Japanese to English.[85]

Much of Ghosn's success is embedded in the asset of his foreignness,[86] being an outsider and being different in many ways. However, the foundation of Ghosn's extraordinary achievement is also grounded in how he focused on similarity. For example, he actively used numerical simplifications as the lingual franca of the organization, making numbers a rallying point that transcends language and cultural barriers.[87] At the same time, Ghosn studied Japanese language to better understand the local customs and to show employees his commitment to the firm and the Japanese culture. He frequently lauded the benefits of *monozukuri* in public—a Japanese notion of excellent craftsmanship and improvement in manufacturing. To avoid the fear of losing identity among the Japanese, he created a collective identity while valuing the local identity. With the alliance, many expected Renault to take a colonial and coercive approach toward Nissan because the Renault invested in 36.8% share in Nissan, while Nissan only took 15% share of Renault. However, Ghosn prioritized Nissan over Renault, including himself in the collective culture of Nissan, avoiding threatening the loss of local culture at all cost. In his words:

> National identity, national pride, flags are especially strong in the automotive industry. Renault will always be French, Nissan will always be Japanese. No matter where a company sources its parts or sells its cars, the customer sees national identity as an important part of the brand, and so do the employees. Our job was not to take away the Japanese identity from Nissan, it was to help Nissan become a great Japanese company again. Nissan must be proudly Japanese.[88]

The case of Ghosn and Nissan opens up many opportunities to explore the dynamics within an individual and between the individual and her/his collective cultures. We recognize in this case the crucial role of trust building based on similarities, psychological safety, and collective group formation ("we are in this together!"). We also see the incredible capacity of change, both within each individual and a culture. Above all, the case attests the influential impact an individual can exert on her/his collective culture, even when (s)he was previously an outsider. In fact, it is argued that Ghosn achieved such a success because he could bypass many traditional rules as an outsider—a case of diversity brings benefit. The success of Ghosn is rooted in an excellent combination of "creating similarities" and "optimizing differences," in his capacity of simultaneously having the potential to "conform" but also "contradict," to "follow" but also "reshape" his newly adopted culture.

It's wrong to assume that culture can change only if a massive amount of individuals decides to change. We are reminded of what Margaret Mead, a legendary researcher, once said: "Never doubt what a small group of thoughtful, committed citizens can change the world; indeed, it's the only thing that ever has."

6.4 The Role of Context

Researchers from the dynamic paradigm have strongly emphasized the impact of context as a causal factor, which differs invariably in any two situations.[89] Human diversity is viewed as a set of collective and individual adaptations to contextual factors, such as ecological and socio-political system. For example, the eco-cultural and eco-social model[90] conceptualizes how contextual factors influence communication and behaviors. Georgas and colleagues went one step further by specifying six principle contextual dimensions: Ecology, economy, education, mass media, population, and religion.[91] In this book, we took an interdisciplinary approach and defined *context* as particular circumstances that encompass the interactions of five driving forces: Environment, genes, culture, brain, and behaviors (GCEB-Be).

From the viewpoint of culture as a survival strategy that responds dynamically to internal and external factors, context becomes the ultimate power to shape the communicative patterns within and between cultures. The role of context is so crucial that Osland and Bird suggested "indexing" context instead of indexing countries.[92] In the same vein, "culture-as-situated cognition" is put forward because everything we do is context dependent (p. 8).[93] Context helps us to understand complex phenomenon such as paradoxes and the dynamic speed of change across various time frames. As contexts differ, so do the nature and result of each communication scenario. This dynamics is traced down to the minuscule level of neural pathways within each individual. Subtle environmental cues, such as single (I, me, mine) and plural forms of a word (we, us, they) can act as powerful priming frameworks, activating relevant cultural mindsets and their associative networks in our brain, prompting us to think in either collectivistic or individualistic ways (see Chapter 4). In line with this argument, we can question Hofstede's book title and propose that not culture but particular context is the "software of the mind."[94]

6.5 Think Global—Plan Local—Act Individual

The Inverted Pyramid Model offers an analysis framework that has the potential to minimize the shortcomings of the problem-focused approach and takes into account advantages of the dynamic paradigm of culture. Any attempt to understand cross-cultural issues should take into account a holistic view of all three layers because they provide us with a big picture and, at the same time, keep track of important details.

At the universal level, savvy businesspeople know that it's easier for their product to win if it taps into a human motivation or interest that is universally shared across cultures. This notion of "think global" resonates with our Inverted Pyramid Model and the tree metaphor in the sense that it regards the similarities of fundamental concerns, values, and outward expressions as the starting point of communication. Indications from both behavioral and neural studies help to confirm that the foundation of our sameness as human beings can positively support ingroup formulation and trust building. While differences can initially trigger fear and cautiousness, similarities create bonds and act as a springboard to explore diversity in a psychologically safe way.

Beyond the universal level of concerns, values, and outward expressions, each collective culture has its own set of concerns, with differing degrees of importance and different manifestations. This is where "plan local" needs to consider cultural identity and local engagement. To win people's hearts, you must engage them on their own terms and in their own languages. "Think global" and "plan local" go hand in hand on the road to success. Companies that move too far in the direction of global consistency may be disadvantaged when competing with local brands and, vice versa, companies that rely heavily on culturally specific identities and connections will be ill-equipped to expand their market beyond borders.

It is important to bear in mind that "plan local" doesn't mean "follow" the local. There can be parts of local standards that are not always the most suited, aspects of local customs that can or should be changed, and patterns of local identities that are ready to merge or reshape. Culture is a survival strategy, and businesses should see as such: They can follow a strategy, or actively change it.

Finally, business does not stop at the "local." The end contact is always a specific person: A customer, a partner, a colleague, and so forth. A competent businessperson will build a solid archive of knowledge of a certain culture, but the moment (s)he communicates with an *individual*, such as greeting a colleague, discussing with the team, convincing a customer, e-mailing a partner, and so forth, (s)he is open to anything that either fits or denies that cultural profile. Why? Because each individual is very different, capable of internalizing opposing values and practices; acting dynamically, even contradictorily; or actively creating and shaping new cultural elements, depending on particular contexts. This is the lesson that Sulzer Corporation—a Swiss heavy engineering company—formulated when it acquired some big European companies. To develop a new pan-European teamwork concept, it promoted the motto "One Winning Team." The goal was to *downplay national stereotypes* and encourage people to socialize and network outside the formal environment, *then* work together.[95] In other words, employees were encouraged to know each other first as unique individuals before cultural stereotypes could jump in and jeopardize the working relationship.

In short, competent businesspeople will skillfully develop themselves through the process of cultural sensitivity and interact mindfully with the social context in which they operate. They know it is natural to feel anxious at the complexity of culture, but they are willing to go above and beyond obvious outward expressions and sophisticated stereotypes of values. They understand the neuroscience of uncertainty and fear, and thus, they do not easily fall victim for the dark side of cultural clashes. They navigate the evolutionary root of fear by striving for shared interests, similarities, and synergy because they know small similarities can be used to overcome big differences. While using similarities as a springboard to explore all the opportunities that diversity may bring, they are well aware that small differences should not be overlooked by big similarities. In the end, diversity by itself does not indicate good or bad, but how we operate with it. Like almost everything else, it's situational.

Summary

1. As a legacy of the tribal, group-oriented life on the savannah, our brain codes similarities and differences as signals of ingroup and outgroup.
2. Two factors, among others, that help us to achieve plural, complex, and dynamic thinking are *safety* and *time*.
3. An effective strategy to create safety and time is initially focusing on similarities (concerns, values, and outward expressions). It acts as a springboard to approach differences later in a synergetic way.
4. At the universal level of the Inverted Pyramid Model, the tree metaphor indicates culture in the evolutionary sense: Universal concerns, a baseline of values, and outward expressions that we all share and agree upon, regardless of where we come from.
5. At the collective level of the Inverted Pyramid Model, the tree metaphor indicates culture in the practical sense. Each culture produces an immense level of diversity in terms of unique concerns, differing values, and different outward expressions.
6. There are at least four unit of analysis at the collective level: Global culture, national culture, group culture, and organizational culture.
    *   Global culture emerges as the latest collective culture. Their members are global citizens who have high values for fundamental concerns such as equality and social responsibility. Businesses should become global citizen themselves to (1) become a product of this culture by reflecting the identity of this cohort and (2) become a producer of new cultural elements by leading the evolution of this culture.
    *   National culture is the most available and the easiest unit of analysis due to the availability of data. However, it is also one of the worst containers of homogenous culture due to within-country diversity.
    *   Group culture is based on many categories such as profession, economic status, social status, freedom level, lifestyle, ethnicity, and so forth. They often overlap, interacting dynamically across fluid borders because a person is naturally a member of different group cultures. "Profession," "social class," and "levels of freedom" are three most reliable indicators of homogeneous group culture. Nevertheless, businesses should take a holistic view of group culture in approaching customers.
    *   Organizational culture is a unique business environment created to (1) help employees automatically behave in a productive way without explicit rules and regulations and (2) act as business strategy to improve performance.
7. At the individual level, each person is a tree of culture with her/his unique concerns, values and outward expressions.
    *   Individual level is where culture is made personally, dynamically, and contextually.
    *   The end contact of intercultural communication is always a specific person. We don't do business with a country, but work (in)directly with a unique person. Assuming that this person is his/her culture can be an unhelpful stereotype.

- An individual can have multiple identities and accommodate a multicultural mind.
- An individual can both conform and contradict, follow and reshape a culture, even when (s)he was previously an outsider to this culture.

8. Facing the immense dynamics of cultures and borders, businesses can apply the strategy of "Think global—Plan local—Act individual."
    - Think global: Tap on universal human motivation; build trust and weed out fear by using similarities as the starting point.
    - Plan local: Align with local culture; reshape local culture; create and lead a new local culture.
    - Act individual: Resist stereotypes; think and do contextually; expect surprises, changes, and contradictory values/ behaviors in a person.

Notes

Don't forget to go to the end of the book for case studies.

1 Eberhardt, Jennifer L. 2005. "Imaging Race." *The American Psychologist* 60(2): 181–190. doi:10.1037/0003-066X.60.2.181.
2 Griffin, Emory A. 1994. *A First Look at Communication Theory*, 173. 2nd ed. New York: McGraw-Hill.
3 Masuda, Naoki., and Feng Fu. 2015. "Evolutionary Models of In-Group Favoritism." *F1000Prime Reports* 7(27). doi:10.12703/P7-27.
4 Blair, Irene V., Charles M. Judd, Melody S. Sadler, and Christopher Jenkins. 2002. "The Role of Afrocentric Features in Person Perception: Judging by Features and Categories." *Journal of Personality and Social Psychology* 83(1): 5–25. doi:10.1037/0022-3514.83.1.5.
5 Laeng, Bruno., Oddrun Vermeer, and Unni Sulutvedt. 2013. "Is Beauty in the Face of the Beholder?" *Plos One* 8(7). doi:10.1371/journal.pone.0068395.
6 Bahns, Angela J., Christian S. Crandall, Omri Gillath, and Kristopher J. Preacher. 2016. "Similarity in Relationships as Niche Construction: Choice, Stability, and Influence within Dyads in a Free Choice Environment." *Journal of Personality and Social Psychology* 112(2): 329–355. doi:10.1037/pspp0000088.
7 Efferson, Charles., Rafael Lalive, and Ernst Fehr. 2008. "The Coevolution of Cultural Groups and Ingroup Favoritism." *Science* 321(5897): 1844–1849. doi:10.1126/science.1155805.
8 Klohnen, Eva C., and Shanhong Luo. 2003. "Interpersonal Attraction and Personality: What Is Attractive—Self Similarity, Ideal Similarity, Complementarity, or Attachment Security?" *Journal of Personality and Social Psychology* 85(4): 709–722. doi:10.1037/0022-3514.85.4.709.
9 Pelham, Brett W., Mauricio Carvallo, and John T. Jones. 2005. "Implicit Egotism." *Current Directions in Psychological Science* 14(2): 106–110. doi:10.1111/j.0963-7214.2005.00344.x.
10 Nelson, Leif D., and Joseph P. Simmons. 2007. "Moniker Maladies: When Names Sabotage Success." *Psychological Science* 18(12): 1106–1112. doi:10.1111/j.1467-9280.2007.02032.x.
11 Mizutani, Osamu. 1994. *Japanese: The Spoken Language in Japanese Life*. Translated by Janet Ashby. Tokyo: Japan Times.
12 Wu, Youyou., David Stillwell, Andrew H. Schwartz, and Michal Kosinski. 2017. "Birds of a Feather Do Flock Together." *Psychological Science* 28(3): 276–284. doi:10.1177/0956797616678187.
13 Zajonc, R. B., Pamela K. Adelmann, Sheila T. Murphy, and Paula M. Niedenthal. 1987. "Convergence in the Physical Appearance of Spouses." *Motivation and Emotion* 11(4): 335–346. doi:10.1007/bf00992848.
14 Rivera, Lauren A. 2012. "Hiring as Cultural Matching: The Case of Elite Professional Service Firms." *American Sociological Review* 77(6): 999–1022. doi:10.1177/0003122412463213.
15 Walton, Gail E., N. J. Bower, and T. G. Bower. 1992. "Recognition of Familiar Faces by Newborns." *Infant Behavior and Development* 15(2): 265–269. doi:10.1016/0163-6383(92)80027-R.
16 Kinzler, Katherine D., Emmanuel Dupoux, and Elizabeth S. Spelke. 2007. "The Native Language of Social Cognition." *Proceedings of the National Academy of Sciences of the United States of America* 104(30): 12577–12580. doi:10.1073/pnas.0705345104.

17 Meyer, Meghan L., Carrie L. Masten, Yina Ma, Chenbo Wang, Zhenhao Shi, Naomi I. Eisenberger, and Shihui Han. 2012. "Empathy for the Social Suffering of Friends and Strangers Recruits Distinct Patterns of Brain Activation." *Social Cognitive and Affective Neuroscience* 8(4): 446–454. doi:10.1093/scan/nss019.

18 Hein, Girt., Giorgia Silani, Kerstin Preuschoff, Daniel C. Batson, and Tania Singer. 2010. "Neural Responses to Ingroup and Outgroup Members' Suffering Predict Individual Differences in Costly Helping." *Neuron* 68(1): 149–160. doi:10.1016/j.neuron.2010.09.003.

19 Mobbs, Dean., Rongjun Yu, Marcel Meyer, Luca Passamonti, Ben Seymour, Andrew Calder, Susanne Schweizer, Chris D. Frith, and Tim Dalgleish. 2009. "A Key Role for Similarity in Vicarious Reward." *Science* 324(5929): 900. doi:10.1126/science.1170539.

20 Efferson, Charles., Rafael Lalive, and Ernst Fehr. 2008. "The Coevolution of Cultural Groups and Ingroup Favoritism." *Science* 321(5897): 1844–1849. doi:10.1126/science.1155805.

21 Meyer, Erin. 2014. *The Culture Map*. New York: Public Affair.

22 Anca, Celia de., and Salvador Aragón. 2014. "Let Your Employees Bring Their Interests to Work." *Harvard Business Review*. August 29. https://hbr.org/2014/08/let-your-employees-bring-their-interests-to-work.

23 Erez, Miriam., and Efrat Gati. 2004. "A Dynamic, Multi-Level Model of Culture: From the Micro Level of the Individual to the Macro Level of a Global Culture." *Applied Psychology: An International Review* 53(4): 583–598. doi:10.1111/j.1464-0597.2004.00190.x.

24 Newwork. 2015. "Comoros: Citizenship for Sale." *New African Magazine*. April 3. http://newafricanmagazine.com/comoros-citizenship-sale.

25 Abrahamian, Atossa A. 2015. *The Cosmopolites: The Coming of the Global Citizen*. New York: Columbia Global Reports.

26 Norris, Pippa. 2000. "Global Governance and Cosmopolitan Citizens." In *Governance in a Globalizing World*, ed. Joseph S. Nye and John D. Donahue, 155–177. Washington, DC: Brookings Institution Press.

27 Oxley, Laura., and Paul Morris. 2013. "Global Citizenship: A Typology for Distinguishing Its Multiple Conceptions." *British Journal of Educational Studies* 61(3): 301–325. doi:10.1080/00071005.2013.798393.

28 Grimley, Naomi. 2016. "Identity 2016: 'Global Citizenship' Rising, Poll Suggests." *BBC News*. April 28. www.bbc.com/news/world-36139904.

29 Bird, Allan., and Michael J. Stevens. 2003. "Toward an Emergent Global Culture and the Effects of Globalization on Obsolescing National Cultures." *Journal of International Management* 9(4): 395–407. doi:10.1016/j.intman.2003.08.003.

30 Gupta, Anil K., and Vijay Govindarajan. 2000. "Knowledge Flows within Multinational Corporations." *Strategic Management Journal* 21(4): 473–496. doi:10.1002/(sici)1097-0266(200004)21:43.0.co;2-i.

31 Reysen, Stephen., and Iva Katzarska-Miller. 2013. "A Model of Global Citizenship: Antecedents and Outcomes." *International Journal of Psychology* 48(5): 858–870. doi:10.1080/00207594.2012.701749.

32 Bhargava, Vinay K., ed. 2006. *Global Issues for Global Citizens: An Introduction to Key Development Challenges*. Washington, DC: World Bank Publication.

33 Kumar, Arun., and N. Meenakshi. 2011. *Marketing Management*, 838. 2nd ed. New Delhi: Vikas Publishing House.

34 CONE Inc. 2015. "2015 Cone Communications/Ebiquity Global CSR Study." www.conecomm.com/research-blog/2015-cone-communications-ebiquity-global-csr-study.

35 Deloitte. 2017. "The Deloitte Millennial Survey 2017." www2.deloitte.com/global/en/pages/about-deloitte/articles/millennialsurvey.html#.

36 Ohmae, Kenichi. 2014. "Managing in a Borderless World." *Harvard Business Review*. August 1. https://hbr.org/1989/05/managing-in-a-borderless-world.

37 Spedding, Emma. 2016. "Met Gala 2016: Emma Watson Wears a Calvin Klein Dress Made from Recycled Plastic Bottles." *The Telegraph*. May 3. www.telegraph.co.uk/fashion/events/met-gala-2016-emma-watson-wears-a-calvin-klein-dress-made-from-r/.

38 Isaac, Mike. 2017. "Uber C.E.O. to Leave Trump Advisory Council after Criticism." *The New York Times.* February 2. www.nytimes.com/2017/02/02/technology/uber-ceo-travis-kalanick-trump-advisory-council.html.

39 Wreden, Nick. 2004. "The Next Generation of Global Branding?" *MarketingProfs.* October 19. www.marketingprofs.com/4/wreden10.asp.

40 Strizhakova, Yuliya., Robin A. Coulter, and Linda L. Price. 2008. "Branded Products as a Passport to Global Citizenship: Perspectives from Developed and Developing Countries." *Journal of International Marketing* 16(4): 57–85. doi:10.1509/jimk.16.4.57.

41 Schwab, Klaus. 2009. "Global Corporate Citizenship." *Foreign Affairs.* January 29. www.foreignaffairs.com/articles/2008-01-01/global-corporate-citizenship.

42 Lilley, Kathleen., Michelle Barker, and Neil Harris. 2014. "Educating Global Citizens in Business Schools." *Journal of International Education in Business* 7(1): 72–84. doi:10.1108/jieb-06-2012-0010.

43 White, Philip L. 2006. "Globalization and the Mythology of the Nation State." In *Global History: Interactions between the Universal and the Local*, ed. Antony Gerald Hopkins, 257–284. Basingstoke, UK: Palgrave Macmillan.

44 McSweeney, Brendan. 2012. "Constitutive Context: The Myth of Common Cultural Values." In *Handbook of International Approaches to International Business*, ed. Geoffrey Wood and Mehmet Demirbag, 142–172. Cheltenham, UK: Edward Elgar Publishing Limited.

45 McSweeney, Brendan. 2009. "Dynamic Diversity: Variety and Variation within Countries." *Organization Studies* 30(9): 933–957. doi:10.1177/0170840609338983.

46 Gerhart, Barry., and Meiyu Fang. 2005. "National Culture and Human Resource Management: Assumptions and Evidence." *The International Journal of Human Resource Management* 16(6): 971–986. doi:10.1080/09585190500120772.

47 McSweeney, Brendan. 2013. "Fashion Founded on a Flaw: The Ecological Mono-Deterministic Fallacy of Hofstede, GLOBE, and Followers." *International Marketing Review* 30(5): 483–504. doi:10.1108/IMR-04-2013-0082.

48 Hong, Ying-yi., and Chi-yue Chiu. 2001. "Toward a Paradigm Shift: From Cross-cultural Differences in Social Cognition to Social-Cognitive Mediation of Cultural Differences." *Social Cognition* 19(3): 181–196. doi:10.1521/soco.19.3.181.21471.

49 Taras, Vas., Piers Steel, and Bradley L. Kirkman. 2016. "Does Country Equate with Culture? Beyond Geography in the Search for Cultural Boundaries." *Management International Review* 56(4): 455–487. doi:10.1007/s11575-016-0283-x.

50 Mawoli, Mohammed Abubakar., and Dauda Abdulsalam. 2012. "Effective Market Segmentation and Viability of Islamic Banking in Nigeria." www.semanticscholar.org/paper/Effective-Market-Segmentation-and-Viability-of-Isl-Mawoli-Abdulsalam/a0a6691873e1d710faa929a1d355c3cd9b11eda2.

51 HAVAS Worldwide. 2014. *Hashtagnation: Marketing to the Selfie Generation.* www.havasworldwide.hu/userfiles/insights/6/file/f724c7e101b875b29195bb50792e1d47.pdf.

52 Hosie, Rachel. 2018. "John Lewis Gets Rid of 'Boys' and 'Girls' Labels in Children's Clothing." *The Independent.* April 11. www.independent.co.uk/life-style/john-lewis-boys-girls-clothing-labels-gender-neutral-unisex-children-a7925336.html.

53 Geldenhuys, Madelyn., Karolina Łaba, and Cornelia M. Venter. 2014. "Meaningful Work, Work Engagement and Organisational Commitment." *SA Journal of Industrial Psychology* 40(1):1–10. doi:10.4102/sajip.v40i1.1098.

54 Yu, Kang Yang Trevor. 2014. "Organizational Behavior and Human Decision Processes." *Person-Organization Fit Effects on Organizational Attraction: A Test of an Expectations-Based Model* 124(1): 75–94.

55 Sarac, Mehlika., Ismail Efil, and Mehmet Eryilmaz. 2014. "A Study of the Relationship between Person-Organization Fit and Employee Creativity." *Management Research Review* 37(5): 479–501. doi:10.1108/MRR-01-2013-0025.

56 Jauhari, Hemang., and Shailendra Singh. 2013. "Perceived Diversity Climate and Employees' Organizational Loyalty." *Equality, Diversity and Inclusion: An International Journal* 32(3): 262–276. doi:10.1108/EDI-12-2012-0119.

57 Kotter, John P., and James L. Heskett. 1992. *Corporate Culture and Performance.* New York: Free Press.

58 Boyce, Anthony S., Levi R. G. Nieminem, Michael A. Gillespie, Ann Marie Ryan, and Daniel R. Denison. 2015. "Which Comes First, Organizational Culture or Performance? A Longitudinal Study of Causal Priority with Automobile Dealerships." *Journal of Organizational Behavior* 36(3): 339–359. doi:10.1002/job.1985.

59 Yu, Kang Yang Trevor. 2014. "Person-Organization Fit Effects on Organizational Attraction: A Test of an Expectations-Based Model." *Organizational Behavior and Human Decision Processes* 124(1): 75–94. doi:10.1016/j.obhdp.2013.12.005.

60 Jauhari, Hemang., Shailendra Singh. 2013. "Perceived Diversity Climate and Employees' Organizational Loyalty." *Equality, Diversity and Inclusion: An International Journal* 32(3): 262–276. doi:10.1108/EDI-12-2012-0119.

61 Zheng, Wei., Baiyin Yang, and Gary N. McLean. 2010. "Linking Organizational Culture, Structure, Strategy, and Organizational Effectiveness: Mediating Role of Knowledge Management." *Journal of Business Research* 63(7): 763–771. doi:10.1016/j.jbusres.2009.06.005.

62 Kotter, John P., and James L. Heskett. 1992. *Corporate Culture and Performance.* New York: Free Press.

63 Boyce, Anthony S., Levi R. G. Nieminem, Michael A. Gillespie, Ann Marie Ryan, and Daniel R. Denison. 2015. "Which Comes First, Organizational Culture or Performance? A Longitudinal Study of Causal Priority with Automobile Dealerships." *Journal of Organizational Behavior* 36(3): 339–359. doi:10.1002/job.1985.

64 FPT. 2017. "FPT Culture: Respect Individual—Innovative Spirit—Team Spirit." *Công Ty Cổ Phần FPT.* https://fpt.com.vn/en/about-us/culture.

65 Nguyen, Vy. 2015. "FPT Và Vũ Khí Mang Tên Văn Hóa Doanh Nghiệp." *SAGE – Applied Marketing Academy.* August 10. http://sage.edu.vn/blog/fpt-va-vu-khi-mang-ten-van-hoa-doanh-nghiep.

66 "Văn Hóa độc Lạ đến Kỳ Quái Của FPT—VTC News." 2015. Báo VTC. June 9. www.vtc.vn/van-hoa-doc-la-den-ky-quai-cua-fpt-d209597.html.

67 Want, Jerome. 2006. *Corporate Culture: Illuminating the Black Hole.* New York: St. Martin's Press.

68 Chatman, Jennifer A., and Sandra Eunyoung Cha. 2003. "Leading by Leveraging Culture." *California Management Review* 45(4): 20–34. doi:10.2307/41166186.

69 Deutschman, Alan. 2017. *Change or Die: Three Keys to Change at Work and in Life.* New York: HarperCollins.

70 Erez, Miriam., and Efrat Gati. 2004. "A Dynamic, Multi-Level Model of Culture: From the Micro Level of the Individual to the Macro Level of a Global Culture." *Applied Psychology* 53(4): 583–598. doi:10.1111/j.1464-0597.2004.00190.x.

71 Hofstede, Geert. 2001. *Culture's Consequences: Comparing Values, Behaviors, Institutions and Organizations across Nations,* 50. Thousand Oaks, CA: Sage.

72 Gerhart, Barry., and Meiyu Fang. 2005. "National Culture and Human Resource Management: Assumptions and Evidence." *International Journal of Human Resource Management* 16(6): 971–986. doi:10.1080/09585190500120772.

73 Oysernam, Daphna., Heather M. Coon, and Markus Kemmelmeier. 2002. "Rethinking Individualism and Collectivism: Evaluation of Theoretical Assumptions and Meta-Analyses." *Psychological Bulletin* 128(1): 3–72. doi:10.1037/0033-2909.128.1.3.

74 Bond, Harris. 2002. "Reclaiming the Individual from Hofstede's Ecological Analysis—A 20-Year Odyssey: Comment on Oyserman et al." *Psychological Bulletin* 128(1): 73–77. doi:10.1037/0033-2909.128.1.73.

75 Schwartz, Shalom H., and Wolfgang Bilsky. 1994. "Are There Universal Aspects in the Content and Structure of Values?" *Journal of Social Issues* 50(4): 19–45. doi:10.1111/j.1540-4560.1994.tb01196.x.

76 Gefland, Michele J., Miriam Erez, and Zeynep Aycan. 2007. "Cross-Cultural Organizational Behavior." *Annual Review of Psychology* 58: 479–514. doi:doi.org/10.1146/annurev.psych.58.110405.085559.

77 Chiao, Joan Y., Tokiko Harada, Hidetsugu Komeda, Zhang Li, Yoko Mano, Daisuke Saito, Todd B. Parrish, Norihiro Sadato, and Tetsuya Iidaka. 2010. "Dynamic Cultural Influences on Neural

Representations of the Self." *Journal of Cognitive Neuroscience* 22(1): 1–11. doi:10.1162/jocn.2009.21192.

78 Hong, Ying-Yi., Michael W. Morris, Chi-Yue Chiu, and Verónica Benet-Martínez. 2000. "Multicultural Minds: A Dynamic Constructivist Approach to Culture and Cognition." *American Psychologist* 55(7): 709–720. doi:10.1037//0003-066x.55.7.709.

79 Fang, Tony. 2005–2006. "From 'Onion' to 'Ocean': Paradox and Change in National Cultures." *International Studies of Management and Organization* 35(4): 71–90. doi:10.1080/00208825.2005.11043743.

80 Mateo, Marina Emartinez., Maurice Ecabanis, Julian Stenmanns, and Sören Krach. 2013. "Essentializing the Binary Self: Individualism and Collectivism in Cultural Neuroscience." *Frontiers in Human Neuroscience* 7:1–4. doi:10.3389/fnhum.2013.00289.

81 Osland, Joyce S., and Allan Bird. 2000. "Beyond Sophisticated Stereotyping: Cultural Sensemaking in Context." *Academy of Management Executive* 14(1): 65–77. doi:10.5465/ame.2000.2909840.

82 Hong, Ying-Yi., Michael W. Morris, Chie-Yue Chiu, and Veronica Benet-Martinez. 2000. "Multicultural Minds: A Dynamic Constructivist Approach to Culture and Cognition." *American Psychologist* 55(7): 709–720. doi:10.1037//0003-066X.55.7.70.

83 Forte, James A. 1999. "Culture: The Tool-Kit Metaphor and Multicultural Social Work." *Families in Society: The Journal of Contemporary Social Services* 80(1): 51–62. doi:10.1606/1044-3894.639.

84 Crane, D. 1994. "Introduction: The Challenge of the Sociology of Culture to Sociology as a Discipline." In *The Sociology of Culture: Emerging Theoretical Perspectives*, ed. D. Crane, 1–19. Oxford: Blackwell.

85 Steers, Richard M., Carlos J. Sanchez-Runde, and Luciara Nardon. 2010. *Management across Cultures: Challenges and Strategies*, 242–245. Cambridge: Cambridge University Press.

86 Kotaka, K. 2005. "The Strategic Role of 'Outsider' in Nissan's Management Revolution." *Nara Women's University Social Science Journal* 12: 233–252.

87 Ikegami, Jusuke J. J., Martha Maznevski, and Masataka Ota. 2017. "Creating the Asset of Foreignness: Schrödinger's Cat and Lessons from the Nissan Revival." *Cross Cultural and Strategic Management* 24(1): 55–77. doi:10.1108/CCSM-12-2015-0194.

88 Ibid.

89 Douglas, Susan P., and C. Samuel Craig. 2009. "Impact of Context on Cross-Cultural Research." In *Beyond Hofstede: Culture Frameworks for Global Marketing and Management*, ed. C. Nakata, 125–145. Basingstoke, UK: Palgrave Macmillan.

90 Berry, J. W. 2001. "Contextual Studies of Cognitive Adaptation." In *Intelligence and Personality: Bridging the Gap in Theory and Measurement*, ed. J. M. Collis and S. Messick, 319–333. Mahwah, NJ: Lawrence Erlbaum Associates.

91 Georgas, James., Fons J. R. van de Vijver, and John W. Berry. 2004. "The Ecological Framework, Ecosocial Indices, and Psychological Variables in Cross-Cultural Research." *Journal of Cross-cultural Psychology* 35(1): 74–96. doi:10.1177/0022022103260459.

92 Osland, Joyce S., and Allan Bird. 2000. "Beyond Sophisticated Stereotyping: Cultural Sensemaking in Context." *Academy of Management Executive* 14(1): 65–79.

93 Oyserman, Daphna., Sheida Novin, Nic Flinkenflogel, and Lydia Krabbendam. 2014. "Integrating Culture-as-Situated-Cognition and Neuroscience Prediction Models." *Culture Brain* 2(1): 1–26. doi:10.1007/s40167-014-0016-6.

94 Nguyen-Phuong-Mai, Mai. 2017. "Intercultural Communication—An Interdisciplinary Approach: Context Is Software of the Mind." Keynote roundtable ELLTA Conference, Bangkok. July 24–28.

95 Holden, Nigel J. 2002. *Cross-Cultural Management: A Knowledge Management Perspective*. Essex, UK: Pearson Education Limited.

7 Change Management
Creating Culture and Evolving Yourself

In Chapters 2 and 3, we learned that evolutionarily speaking, culture has mostly replaced genes to guide humans in the survival game. Each culture is an immense archive of ideas—what it is best to do to survive. For every decision we make, we rely on ideas from our immediate culture to give us a hint about the right course of action, for example embracing a certain value, dressing in a certain way, or making a certain career choice, depending on the demands and expectations of the specific culture that hosts us at that moment. Note that genes do not stand idly by, but actively evolve and adapt to support our process of adjustment, so that we can acquire the necessary culture (GCEB-Be).

In our modern era, that process of attuning is sped up by globalization because cultural borders are not only much more visible but also dynamically shifting, merging, and deepening at the same time (Chapter 1). The need to change and cross those borders has also become *a new survival skill* that humans of our time must acquire. A capacity for cultural adaption as well as cultural creation has never been so vital. Being both a product and a producer of culture, we need to find a fine balance between (1) taking culture as a resource and (2) shaping culture for better development. This process of changing ourselves and changing others applies to all units of human societies, covering all three levels of the Inverted Pyramid Model: (1) Individuals, (2) nation, organizations, groups, or (3) the whole mankind.

Knowing the critical role of corporate culture as business strategies (Chapter 6), in this chapter, we will touch on a number of ideas and possible routes that can help organizations face the challenges of cultural adaptation and creation, reaping benefit from being in sync with the dynamics of culture.

7.1 The Neuroscience of Change

Corporate adaptability and change are critical, but we can't turn away from a gloomy fact that change has a low rate of success. According to a Towers Watson study, which involved 276 organizations worldwide,[1] only 25% of change initiatives are successful over the long term. Old habits die hard. In this section, we will explore the three main reasons why: (1) The brain is lazy; (2) the brain is a "control freak"; and (3) the brain likes to imitate.

7.1.1 The Brain Is Lazy

7.1.1.1 Ritual and Cognitive Habit

A habit is something we can do effortlessly. In our brain, habits are mediated by the *basal ganglia*[2] and the *infralimbic cortex*.[3] Tasks that require complex thinking are undertaken by the *working memory*, which is mainly the prefrontal cortex. The basal ganglia uses very little energy, making habits effortless, freeing up the processing power for the prefrontal cortex. This is because the brain can't store fuel. It pays as it goes. Imagine if you see a predator and still have to think about how to pull the weapon and how to use it properly. Using the weapon should become an automatic routine if you want to stay alive. In the modern time, it's critical that we don't have to think about how to brush our teeth every morning, so energy can be spent on critical tasks such as how to write an important report. This is how the brain economizes energy with routines (less fuel). The brain is lazy in the sense that it tries to convert *as many activities as possible* into a habit to save energy. The end result is, much of our lives consist of routines, from driving to work, organizing meetings, communicating, or even managing people.

Habits are strong, persistent, and hard to change. If you have doubts, to start understanding the stubbornness of old habits, just look at the fact that 90% of "New Year resolutions" fail.[4] A case in point is the story of Angie Bachman. She sued a casino for exploiting her gambling habit, while clearly knowing she had lost her control.[5] Her attorney argued that once she walked into the casino, her habits took over and it was impossible for her to control her behavior. And so, she should bear no responsibility for the outcomes. The court didn't buy it. But her lawsuit became a prominent test case to explain the subconscious neurobiology of (gambling) habit.

Habits not only affect procedures and rituals but also cognitive perspectives and problem-solving methods. We often see managers applying their habitual business strategies from one company to another, from one culture to another, with both success and failure. For example, Merck's CEO Richard Clark was decisive about cutting 12% of its workforce to fix the company's serious revenue shortfall, largely because operational changes, such as downsizing, were what he knew best while running Merck's manufacturing unit. Commenting on this, author Jerome Want wrote that Merck's execs should have made an effort to improve the company's culture and restore it to its former reputation instead of relying on a habitual method of operational fix-its.[6] At the collective level, many brands such as Nokia and Kodak also collapsed because they fell prey to sleepwalking in the success.

7.1.1.2 Strong Neural Pattern

Habits are persistent because they can become a strong neural pattern. Repeated behaviors, thought, and feelings wire the brain, creating a strong neural pathway that fires instantly and easily without too much thinking. In Chapter 4, Figure 4.4 shows us how neurons communicate. They "convince" each other to fire by action potentials, sending electrical impulses that trigger the release of neurotransmitters to reach other neurons and bring the messages. If a network fires strongly together, this process of sending signals will be extremely fast. A habit always involves such a support. If some neurons can fire with ease, we can do a certain thing with ease. Brain's plasticity enables us to perfect a certain skill to the extent that we can execute it with minimum effort, even subconsciously.

For this reason, ironically, executives and experts are among the most difficult people to change, simply because of the cumulative weight of experience, and they, including us, all enjoy a sense of mastery, that is doing things easily with great result. That explains why chief innovators should be *less* experienced because they are less constrained by what usually works. Author Paul Zak offered an example from the self-driving car technology, which went through a stagnant progress for five years until a competitive prize was announced. Engineering students from Stanford University won the challenge and $2 million.[7]

7.1.1.3 Trigger Returns Habit

The neural pattern of a habit is often so strong that even when the habit ceases, as long as the cue that triggers the habit comes back, so does the pattern.[8] For example, you have stopped the habit of wanting to micro-manage your staff by poking your head in their office every 15 minutes. But just the sight of someone taking a private call can reset your burning urge to assert control, kicking off the habit again. Failure to identify the *cue that triggers* our latent neural pathway of habit is a main reason that makes change so challenging. The brain is lazy, once it sees a familiar signpost, it reverts back to the old way because it is much easier to follow an old route.

7.1.1.4 The Habit of Negativity

The brain has evolved to keep us away from danger, but even if danger = habit, we can still unwittingly cling to it. When heart disease patients were told to adjust their lifestyle unless they want to die, only 9% modified their behavior.[9] Those who live in warzone, or poisoning corporate culture for that matter, slowly consider it a normal terrain of work and life. The current situation is bad, but change is scary because it means venturing into the unknown—a phenomenon termed "learned helplessness" by psychologist Martin Seligman.[10] In his experiment, dogs were put in boxes with no escape route and given a small electrical shock. Initially, they would jump and try to break free. But after failed attempts, they would just lie down and take the pain, even when an escape route was *open*. A terrible situation has become a normality. We will look more into the reason why uncertainty is an obstacle to change in the section on "the brain is a control freak."

7.1.1.5 Change Means Loss

In the brain's language, change involves the loss of all investment in the past. *Loss aversion* is rooted in evolution. For our ancestors, losing one month of food stock could result in starvation, while the reward of gaining one month of extra food stock would only be some more rest. This psychology explains why until this day, the impact of losing is twice as powerful as the impact of gaining.[11] It's better to not lose $5 than to find $5. Our brain hates loss because it is lazy and does not want to spend energy in an unnecessary way. As a result, we have a hard time letting go of a project we know deep down will fail, just because we can't let go of the emotional and financial sunk cost. We also struggle to end a bad relationship because we can't come to term with the idea that the whole thing was for naught. Our brain automatically chooses to avoid loss because loss avoidance means the least perceived change, even when another choice is essentially identical, just with different framing.[12]

7.1.1.6 Change Means Effort

To win over loss aversion, the brain has to make an incredible effort to override the tendency to hold on to the past. Change is challenging because *it takes energy*. The brain is just 2% of our body but uses a huge 20% of our energy, burning about ten times the rate of other muscles. Consider this famous job interview question: "A bat and a ball cost $1.10. The bat costs $1 more than the ball. What is the price of the ball?" If your answer is 10 cents, then your autopilot System 1 is at work. We discussed these two modes of thinking in Chapter 4: System 1 (fast, implicit, and binary) and System 2 (slow, explicit, and plural). In this case, your brain operated with System 1, saving your energy, but also giving you a wrong answer (the right answer is 5 cents). A correct solution needs to involve System 2, which will cost you more effort. While good decisions are made with input from *both* systems, as soon as a behavior becomes automatic, the cortex starts working less and less, pushing easy, habitual routines to the basal ganglia and lets System 1 take over, allowing mental resources for something else.

7.1.1.7 Switch Cost Is Costly

When switching from one task to another, time and energy are involved, and this phenomenon is called *switch cost*. Even when you are a skilled worker, switching takes a toll on productivity, which is why multitasking is not effective,[13] and shifting between tasks can cost as much as 40% of your productive time.[14] If simply task switching can be so costly, we should now understand why a change of behaviors, or fundamental changes that involve values and emotional attachment can be a daunting task. This means neurons have to fire new pathways, building up different connections, "convincing" new neurons to join the network.[15] Switch cost is often connected with *backward inhibition*—the notion that a task has to be suppressed to allow new task to be completed. It means we have to put in extra effort to win over the old neural pathways, it means roadblocks, and it means pain. No pain no change, no pain no gain.

Frequently, *small unpredictable changes* are what cost the most amount of energy. Successful changes are more likely when the change is major, at points where old routines stop, such as during a holiday, when a baby is born, or during merges and organizational restructures. However, without *a sense of urgency*, people may be motivated with the bright future that changes will bring, but they can (sub)consciously cling to this blissful phase of inspiration because it feels good and no action (i.e., cost) is required. In fact, it takes an average of 66 days to change a simple habit.[16]

So to conclude, change is challenging because the brain is lazy. Strong neural patterns enable us to execute ritual and cognitive habits effortlessly. A trigger can activate the pattern even when a habit has ceased. Even when habit means danger, strong neural patterns can still keep us in the loop of self-harm. Change costs energy, and it means not only a loss in what has been invested in the past but also an immense task in overriding old habits and building new neural pathways.

7.1.2 The Brain Is a "Control Freak"

7.1.2.1 No News Is Worse Than Bad News

Our brains are prediction and sense-making machines. The ability to make a decision based on prediction quickly, even subconsciously, has helped our ancestors through millions of years on the savannah. For this reason, the brain constantly tries to detect errors or gaps between expectation and reality. Unexpected signals in the environment produce intense bursts of neural firing, drawing energy to the event and *away* from the prefrontal cortex. This also means information and certainty are vital. Ambiguity is a brain killer because it triggers the amygdala with fear. We experience *more* stress when we don't know than when we know for sure that bad things are coming.[17] Those who knew their positive medical test's result for Huntington's disease—a serious brain damage—suffered less from depression than those who lived with the uncertainty.[18] Similarly, it is more stressful wondering whether you'll get sacked as a result of organizational change than knowing for sure you will need to prepare for another job.

When consequences are unpredictable, which is essentially a feature of change, the brain constantly sends out the signal that something is wrong. Dopamine—a neurotransmitter that plays a critical role in attention—floods the *striatum*—the brain's action center. Logically, you're going to spend the *most energy* when the outcome is the *least predictable*, in the same way as spending the most time with the most difficult problem. Because the brain can't store fuel, such an investment of energy is costly and can't be sustained long, so the brain naturally tries to come back to normal—a state called *homeostasis*, defined as the natural movement of any organism toward equilibrium and away from change.[19] The brain naturally resists change because change means uncertainty, stress, and discomfort.

7.1.2.2 Uncertainty + Prediction = Worst Scenario

In the short term, stress is good (e.g., eustress, as opposed to distress). Eustress swings us to action effectively. However, long-term uncertainty will distort our views and can eventually lead to burnout, which is often the case of organizational change. You are left speculating why your name is not included in a certain e-mail, why you don't get invited for a certain meeting, why the manager suddenly seems to avoid eye contact with you, and so forth. When fear is triggered, we see threats where they don't even exist. When we speculate with fear, we speculate *the worst,* which makes uncertainty even more stressful.

It is important to emphasize that there are many changes we embrace, such as meeting new people, having a dream job, or winning a work assignment in a great country. The kind of change we find challenging has to do with uncertainty. This is the reason why we feel safer in a car than an airplane because we erroneously think we have more control if we can put our own hands on the steering wheel.

7.1.3 *The Brain Likes to Imitate*

The mirror neuron was discovered accidently when an Italian scientist raised his hand to eat an ice cream in the lab, and noticed that the brain cells of a monkey activated. It was strange because the monkey didn't move, but its motor neurons caught the signal and "lit up." The monkey's mirror neurons fired at *seeing* the movement, despite the fact that the monkey didn't move at all.[20] The discovery is: Mirror neurons fire in both situations: when we act and when we see someone else acting.

While their role is still debated,[21] some scientists argue that mirror neurons in human subconsciously pick up *movement, emotion,* and even *intention.* When communicating with others, our brains mirror their body language, feeling, and thought. This is the basis of empathy, a fundamental requirement to connect humans, enabling us to understand others' pain and happiness. Being on the same wavelength has biological basis because our thoughts can sync without us uttering a word. From an evolutionary point of view, mirror neurons help us to learn from each other by imitating, to bond with each other by reading the mind, and to evolve culture—an evolutionary strategy to advance among humans as social animals. For this reason, the mirror neuron has been considered the neuron that "shapes civilization."[22]

The nature of mirror neurons means that cultural change has to win over the tendency of mirroring old habits. During a change process, there will be polarized actions, feelings, and thoughts. People tend to absorb and move toward the most powerful ones, not entirely because these behaviors, emotions, and patterns of thinking are right, but because they have, among other reasons, the support of mirror neurons. Different outward expressions and values will compete at conscious and subconscious levels, negotiating the direction of change. This explains why cultural building has to be executed at the grass roots, headed by influential people, and modeled by the leaders.

To conclude, change is challenging because the brain wants routines (lazy), certainty ("control freak"), and imitation. In the next sections, we introduce a framework of change management called STREAP-Be. It covers the most fundamental aspects of a change process, taking into account the reasons that make change so challenging. STREAP-Be stands for: Safety, Trigger, Reward, Emotion, Alignment, People, and Behavior.

7.2 The "S" of STREAP-Be: Safety

Change can trigger both interest and fear. If we expect something positive, reward pathways will be activated and we are motivated to change. However, when change signals uncertainty, loss, and fear, we see the unknown future as threat and consequently want to avoid it. This is the reason why Chapter 4 emphasized the downside of a bias toward negativity in cross-cultural management. When we assume that cultural differences and diversity bring about problems and business cost, we tend to resist efforts to change the situation and bridge the perceived gap.

To understand the unpredictable but potential benefit of change, the brain has to operate with System 2, which enables us to obtain a fine, plural, and complex thinking pattern. Similar to differences, change does send off an alarm (System 1), but as long as we can involve the cortex to join the force of judgment, System 2 will activate. This process can only occur when there is *no threat*, and there is *time*. Fear of change shuts System 2, letting loss aversion, knee-jerk reactions, and habits take priority. To deal with fear caused by differences, we seek similarities (see Chapter 6). To deal with fear caused by change and uncertainty, we create *safety*—the "S" in STREAP-Be.

7.2.1 Identify Safety Issues

The first step in changing an old, or building a new, culture is to eliminate threat when people talk about the future and the changes ahead. Simply asking: "What can't you talk about in here?" and then "Why can't you talk about it?" can reveal a great deal of fear issues. Studies have shown that when we label negative feeling or fear, the ventrolateral prefrontal cortex activates and reduces the amygdala's activity.[23] In other words, consciously recognizing fear can *decrease* its impact.

In general, there are five primary concerns that tap into the brain's emotional system: (1) *Status*, that is position in a hierarchy; (2) *certainty*, that is ability to predict future; (3) *autonomy*, that is sense of control; (4) *relatedness*, that is sense of attachment with other; and (5) *fairness*, that is perception of fair exchange.[24] According to this SCARF model, a psychological safety should be in place that enables people to think, talk, share, and make decisions without being held back by fear. For instance, performance-driven culture is full of fear for status and fairness reduction because managers use a rating system and punishment as ways to assure productivity. An example can be found among top GE executives who ranked employees by performance and let the bottom 10% go. Mirror neurons pick up fear, and it can be detrimental around the time of performance appraisal, layoff, or organizational change. It shouldn't be a surprise that employees who knew they were ranked were less productive than those who didn't.[25]

Here is another example of how a lack of safety can stop even the most powerful element in change process: *Openness*. When there is no safety net, the freedom of expressing one's idea can turn into constant criticism, *disguised* as openness. A culture of honesty without mutual understanding, sympathy, and trust will end up with a hostile battlefield. Some will be hurt, many will become vulnerable, while others can act arrogant, and anyone can be opportunistic with the shared information made available through the so-called openness.

The scandal with Google helps us to understand the paradox of openness and fear. In August 2017, a Google engineer released a ten-page antidiversity manifesto in which he claimed that women just aren't cut out to work in tech like men are, and that the company's policy is politically correct. As the memo leaked, circulated, and caused frenzies, he was promptly fired. This subsequently led to a heated debate in which some critics accused Google of shaming dissenters into silence.[26] In the end, his claims about gender are easy to confront, and firing him created threats among those with conservative views. When certain values are hidden, fear can create pockets of underground resentment, while giving leaders the *illusion* of change at the surface.

7.2.2 Clarity

Concrete information, even negative information, is vital to calm the amygdala down. Because the brain likes to control, a black hole is worse than a known disaster. While too much information disclosure can be harmful, communication in the process of building culture should be transparent and crystal clear. This includes informing stakeholders about the process, expectation, and consequences. A 2015 study of 2.5 million manager-led teams in 195 countries found that workforce engagement improved when supervisors engaged in daily communication with direct reports.[27] Because change is unpredictable, backup plans should be available, outlining what will happen if things fall apart. A good example is how the new CEO of ABB managed to save the company from bankruptcy and consistently sent 150,000 employees an e-mail every week to communicate clearly and honestly about the situation and the solutions. There was also a feedback system, which allowed the CEO to incorporate responses in the next weekly e-mail.

7.2.3 Choice

The ability to make choice is connected with autonomy, a sense of control, and, hence, safety. We love to make our own decisions, or at least, we love to think that we can do it. In fact, the presence of extra choices, especially when they are very costly, makes the target choice more acceptable. We see this tactic in pricing plans, which offer three choices instead of two because customers tend to pick the middle one.[28] However, too many choices can be harmful because it also triggers uncertainty.

7.2.4 Control

The opportunity to be in charge of ourself is critical in reducing fear, and thus, it is a big motivator. A 2014 survey found that nearly half of employees would give up a 20% raise for greater control over how they work.[29]

7.2.5 Reevaluate Competition

Performance-driven companies that prioritize stakeholder's values above all else often encourage fierce internal competition. Benefit not withstanding, internal competition can cause fear if eustress turns to distress. Employees who feel pitted against one another can devote valuable time and energy trying to figure out how to outshine their peers, or worrying about lagging behind, instead of trying to figure out how to best contribute to projects.

7.2.6 Trust

Mistrust activates the amygdala. In an fMRI study, untrustworthy faces (higher inner eyebrows and pronounced cheekbones) were shown for only milliseconds—enough for the amygdala to react, but not enough for the participants to consciously make a decision. Their brains subconsciously picked up mistrust signals without them knowing it.[30] This is worrying if we link it with the fact that consciously, 50% of managers don't trust their own leaders.[31] In other words, half of the corporate world is working with suboptimal brains and conscious fear, let alone the amount of subconscious anxiety.

Trust is a strong predictor of national wealth because people are more likely to undertake long-term investments—which largely rely on mutual trust that both sides will fulfill their obligation.[32] Compared with people at low-trust companies, people at high-trust companies reported 74% less stress, 106% more energy at work, 50% higher productivity, 13% fewer sick days, 76% more engagement, 29% more satisfaction with their lives, and 40% less burnout, and each employee earned an additional $6,450 per year.[33] In a PwC's survey of 1,409 CEOs from 83 countries worldwide, 55% of them think that a lack of trust is a threat to business growth.[34] This number is high, but still baffling, if we assume that almost half of the CEOs don't share the same view.

In most cases, voluntary changes are only possible with trust. It is the moment people shift their outward expressions and values because they believe they are safer or better off with the proposed change. A critical prerequisite for trust is fairness. When a change is perceived as unfair, people are ready to *lose* rather than accept the gain from unfairness. We should recall here the ultimatum game, in which the first player is given an amount of money and told to give some to the second player. The second player can accept or refuse the split. But there's a hitch: If the second player refuses the offer, both leave empty-handed. A rational mind would prompt the second player to accept whatever given to her/him because refusing it would mean a "lose-lose situation," both end up with none. Interestingly, to punish the greedy partner, most people choose to refuse when they are given unfair splits (less than 30%).

The indication of this game is: When treated unfairly, people can sabotage to punish, even if that means their own loss. It is worrying if we link this with the amount of unfairness in the corporate world, for example, the gap between employees and executives in terms of salaries and privileges. During the process of culture change, such as mergers, many CEOs are rewarded with bonuses even when it means employees lose their jobs.

To conclude, safety is the first and foremost condition to support a sustainable change in culture. Safety issues are status, certainty, autonomy, relatedness, and fairness. Strategies to create safety include identifying safety issues, being on the same page (clarity), enabling self decision making (choice), fostering autonomy (control), keeping check of internal competition, and building trust.

7.3 The "T" of STREAP-Be: Trigger

A trigger is powerful because it activates the urge to fall back into the old patterns even when the habit has ceased. In this section, we will identify the habit loop and briefly learn a method to change a habit by learning a new routine.

7.3.1 *The Habit Loop*

In his book *The Power of Habit*, business reporter Charles Duhigg wrote that a simple neurological loop at the core of every habit was identified by MIT researchers: *A trigger*, *a routine*, and *a reward*. To make a change, we need to identify these components.[35] For example, whenever I turn on my laptop (trigger), I check my Facebook newsfeed (routine) because it feels great (reward) to keep updated with what is going on.

To change my habit, I first need to identify the trigger, bearing in mind that they can (re) activate habits uncontrollably. The second step is to react to that trigger by experimenting with different rewards. For example, whenever I turn on my laptop (trigger), I will work on a challenging task when my mind is still fresh such as learning five new foreign words, or whenever I feel the need to check social media, I will make a cup of my favorite tea. This process is to *test* different hypotheses to determine which craving can replace my old reward of "feeling so great" when scrolling down my Facebook newsfeed. By knowing the trigger and rewards, I can try to change my routine to reach the same reward, or to have very different rewards that are no less satisfying. According to Duhigg, to rid of a habit we need to acquire new ones: "You have to keep the same triggers and rewards as before, and feed the craving by inserting a new routine."

7.3.2 *Cultural Habits*

The method of Duhigg doesn't quite apply to cultural habits. Identifying triggers and rewards is often challenging, especially at the collective level. For example, some people tend to have a habit of thinking that "foreigners are less productive at work," despite being shown strong evidence against it. It takes time, usually with the help of scientific research, to know the triggers that prompt such a habituated thought. The reason is because a trigger in this case can be both conscious and subconscious. Is it their skin color, accent, conscious bias, or subconscious experience that triggers the prejudice? In the same vein, rewards of such thinking habit can be diverse, ranging from self-assurance (e.g., "I feel good because I know I'm right") to simplicity (e.g., "The reason is simple, 'race' it is. So I don't have to do difficult thinking on trying to figure out why foreigners are not good workers.")

Note that triggers are often embedded in the memories that shape our current thinking. Every thought we have at this moment is the consequence of many in the past, be it short-term or long-term memories. When we truly want to change, we must open it up, and it can be both wonderful recalls and a terrible can of worms. A person with prejudices against foreigners may be triggered by various cues from constant stream of media that casts immigrants in a negative light. By investigating the long-term memories, this person may figure out that her/his bias comes from a bad experience with a foreign teacher during childhood, or from a movie in which foreigners are portrayed negatively. In many cases, triggers are formed *accidently* and *subconsciously*. For example, a person got sacked when (s)he was in a big glass office. This feature secretly became a trigger that makes her/him nervous whenever (s)he enters a glass structure, without understanding why.

Here is another example: An employee grew up with disciplined parents and teachers who often told him exactly what to do. Later in his life, he responds more to a hierarchy, commands, and clear instructions, as these are the triggers for him to work best, which is a reward. If, out of nowhere, he is given autonomy and asked for contribution, the chance is great that he would stumble over this unexpected freedom and responsibility, his mind would search for familiar triggers so that he could employ the familiar routine. In such a case, to change these entrenched values and behaviors, it is much better to focus on the reward. If the employee could see that different triggers are to ensure that he would have the same reward (get things done effectively), he would be more likely to change.

To identify a trigger, it is important to look at the *past* with critical eyes. Knowing that certain memories are (sub)consciously holding us back can help to facilitate the change of routine. However, calling out a trigger hidden within memories should be balanced with a focus on reward, which is the discussion in our next section.

7.4 The "R" of STREAP-Be: Reward

Seeking pleasure and avoiding pain is important for survival, and that is what the brain constantly does: Maximize reward and minimize punishment. Sometimes, these two emotions compete for preference. A simple case would be when we have to accept a small pain to get closer to a large reward. From "eating a hot curry" to various doctrines of religions or organizational culture change, people always seek to balance the reward and the pain, short term and long term. This is also the principle behind the old adage: No pain no gain.[36]

7.4.1 Eyes on Prize

As mentioned in Chapter 5, the ACC is part of the brain that helps us detect errors and conflict.[37] Studies have shown that when we are in pain and do *not* focus on it, the ACC detects a conflict (in this case, a distraction) and gets activated. We get in the mode of reasoning. The beautiful consequence is: We think more, and we feel *less pain.*[38-39]

Taking indication from those studies, focusing on the negativity of cultural change and differences is like putting a magnifying glass on the downturns. On the contrary, focusing on the positive side can bring benefits, as this mentality reduces the psychological burden of problems and helps us cognitively. In a change process, problems should be seen as side posts on the road that leads us one step closer to the reward. IBM's former CEO Thomas Watson once said: "The fastest way to success is to double your failure rate." Helping the brain to focus on reward will make it *recode* the meaning of failure. Furthermore, people don't want to show their ignorance when asked to change and learn something new. That is why change should be recoded as an opportunity to master new skills.

It is essential to remind people who are in the process of change to *imagine* the end result. When we are stuck with an endless analytic mode of pros and cons, it also helps to tackle the problem starting with the positivity. Author Srinivasan Pillay offers a solution: "Okay, let's accept that you are stuck. Now, let go of that. Please imagine how things would look like if both sides got your way in a manner that served the company's goals. How does that look like? Now, work backward from this optimistic point where problems have been solved."[40]

Mental training has incredible self-fulfilling prophecy power, especially among professional athletes. They would act as if they had already won the competition, using their dominant body language. Our muscles will get stronger just by imagining exercise (i.e., sitting still for 11 minutes, 5 days a week, for 4 weeks, as conducted in neurophysiology research).[41-42] Because imagining an action stimulates the same brain region involved in the actual conduct of that action, imagining future success can enhance people's motivation to achieve it.[43]

The takeaway is, leaders should encourage people to imagine, visualize, talk about, and discuss the end and desirable result of the change. It's good to imagine possible roadblocks too, and how to overcome them. Mental rehearsal is also a technique used to train special navy forces. By continuously running an activity in your mind, when the real situation occurs, you are better prepared for it. In short, *imagery acts as a precursor to action*.

7.4.2 Create Small Achievable Goals

Another strategy to trigger the advantages of reward is to break goals up into *smaller tasks*, create *micro-deadlines*, or write an *achievement list* (NOT a to-do list), so that there are more reasons to celebrate and feel rewarded when a task is done. Cultural building is a long process and the end result is often abstract and far away. Note that the brain likes short-term rewards, such as eating sweets. This kind of reward can be so strong that it distorts long-term rewards, such as maintaining a healthy body. Each time we feel rewarded, repeated release of dopamine makes us want to have that experience again. And because the brain wants to have that experience again, it is easier to learn a little bit more. This neural basis has led to a strategy of breaking a long-term mission down to small achievable tasks, thus cultivating many small, *short-term wins* that can propel us to bigger success. It's essentially the idea that the power of progress[44] is what make success beget success. So, focus on progress, not perfection. A case in point is how the Rocky Flats project—the largest nuclear cleanup in the world history—was completed 60 years ahead of schedule, $30 billion under budget, with cleanup levels exceeding federal guidelines by a factor of 13.[45] The leadership at Rocky Flats steadily created "small wins" that helped motivate steadily positive changes in the underlying culture.

Neuroscience gives us some insight. Interestingly, we learn more from success than from failure. The brain cells *increase* their selectivity for the association to be learned, and *decrease* it after an incorrect trial.[46] In an experiment,[47] students won money for right answers and lost money with incorrect answers. For those who lost, there was an activation of the anterior insula. This feeling of regret leads to "avoidance learning," that is we focus on avoiding the mistake in the future. This is fine, but because the focus is on "avoiding mistake," what we did well does not deserve the right attention, and we don't learn much from what has done right. In the next round of experiment, students were allowed to look back at their answers and understood where they had gotten it wrong. During this process, their brains activated the reward circuit in the ventral striatum. Interestingly, this process looked similar to how their brain reacted when they won from correct answers. Thus, making a mistake is only rewarding when people have a chance to review the mistakes and learn from them in a safe environment because the brain sees this learning opportunity as a reward.

7.4.3 Time of Reward

Most companies tend to think that salary is the main reward. The problem is, salary is paid at a fixed period, and it becomes a habit (fixed ratio and fixed variable). Many other rewards also transform into entitlements to be expected, and that is the problem. What makes social media, shopping, and Pokémon Go so addictive is that reward is set at *variable ratio* and *variable interval*. You don't know what and how much (i.e., ratio) of the reward you will receive, and you don't know when (i.e., interval) you will receive it. So you continue to act, just in case. Let's recall here that dopamine—an arousal hormone and neurotransmitter that gets us ready for action—spikes because we *anticipate* rewards, and the nucleus accumbens that involves motor functions becomes *inactive* when people receive money.[48] This means chasing rewards is a reward in itself, and it can be more exciting than getting the reward. The principle of variable ratio and interval should be applied for reward in a cultural change process as well. Surprising employees with a dinner, prize, bonus, or compliment will reinforce the desired behavior effectively.

7.4.4 Type of Reward

Companies can spend up to 2% of payroll on reward and recognition programs, but this cash-focused approach is not always effective. Rewards should be *tangible*, *unexpected*, *personal*, and *public*. At Zappos for example, employees are given $50 to nominate a co-worker who embraces the company's core values to the fullest.[49] The "hero of the month" was surprised with a song performed by her/his colleagues, receives a covered parking spot, a $150 Zappo's gift card, and a cape to proudly wear. However, specific cultural values should be taken into account because team reward can be more appropriate in certain contexts.

To conclude, reward strategies for cultural change include focusing on the positive, imagining the end result, imagining how to solve a potential problem, recoding failures as necessary side posts, reframing challenges as opportunities to gain, creating small achievable goals, and making reward unexpected, tangible, personal, and public.

7.5 The "E" of STREAP-Be: Emotion

The rise of science during the Renaissance put consciousness and cognitive process at the center of "being human." As a result, emotion became a distraction and a sign of vulnerability. Only recently, with the seminal work of Daniel Goleman on Emotional Intelligence (EQ),[50] we started to view emotion as the driver of decision making and behavioral change.[51] The Latin root of emotion is *movere*, meaning "to move." In essence, emotion is the base of motivation and the very reason why we want to change.

7.5.1 The Role of Emotion in the Decision-Making Process

Three hundred years ago, the father of modern philosophy, René Descartes, said: "I think, therefore I am," which we have equated with "I am *rational*, therefore I am." However, neuroscience has proved that separating emotional and rational elements is impossible. System 1 operates with fast decisions, based on binary gut feelings, emotions, and ingrained habits, while System 2 operates with slow decisions, plurality, complexity, and consciousness. System 2 needs input from System 1 to reach the final destination. That input is emotion. Without emotion, one can't make a good decision. Evolutionary speaking, the limbic system was developed millions of years *before* the cerebral cortex, so the latter relies heavily on the former to act effectively. The regular story of cold, rational thinking in our pop cultures, sciences, and criticism is misleading, because no so-called rational thinking can be made *without* input from emotional feeling. Humans possess an incredible capacity of integrating thinking and feeling. We can feel that we are thinking, and think about feelings.

In *Descartes' Error*,[52] Anthony Damasio described the case of patient Elliot, who had a lesion in his orbitofrontal cortex—part of the brain that balances emotional input in decision making. One would think that without emotional/irrational "burden," Elliot would find it much easier to think purely based on facts. It was the contrary. His business acumen went haywire, as he eventually lost his career and family. He would spend too much time analyzing the pros and cons of a simple matter such as buying product A or B, lacking that final nudge of emotion as a prompt to make decision. Reflecting on Descartes's famous saying, for Elliot, he (only) *thinks*, and therefore, he is *lost*.

Thus, emotions drive decisions and movements. In one of the previous sections, we mentioned the ultimatum game, in which most people choose to be empty-handed when given an unfair share of the profit. Fairness is the driving emotion here, with the purpose of punishing the greedy partner. In fact, emotional branding[53] in marketing relies mostly on emotion to sell because people never just purely employ logic.

Emotions help to make *moral* decision. Without an emotional guidance of right and wrong, businesspeople risk becoming cold-blood psychopaths. In fact, one in five corporate executives are psychopaths, roughly the same rate as among prisoners.[54] Characterized with a profound lack of remorse, emotion, and empathy (feeling for others), nevertheless, these "snakes in suits"[55] mask themselves well and are considered ambitious and successful.[56] The rise of high-flyer psychopaths has recently been addressed as an effort to understand what caused the 2008 financial crisis. The lack of emotion is what makes executives opt for a wrong decision during major cultural change and restructuring programs. For example, they may favor a cost-benefit analysis approach without considering people's emotions. By doing so, they would lose talent and harness a socially irresponsible and inhuman business culture. Business schools play a crucial role in choosing to either cultivate or modify this cold-blooded calculative reasoning mentality.[57]

7.5.2 Storytelling

Because emotions are used to enhance memories and influence behaviors, business storytelling has emerged as a critical strategy to drive cultural change. Data can persuade people, but it doesn't inspire them to act.[58] When we look at a Power Point slide full of data, the brain regions for language are activated, turning words to meaning. But when listening to a well-told story, the whole brain lights up because all senses are awake with details of the story. For example, the olfactory cortex activates when people see the words "perfume" and "coffee."[59] The *same* region of brain also activates when people *enjoy* perfume and coffee. This means hearing and imagination have the same neural effect as actual experience. For survival purposes, humans have evolved to remember experiences better than unrelated facts. Storytelling is powerful because it influences us the way our actual life experience does. Hence, change should be in the form of stories.

7.5.3 Empathy Versus Perspective Taking

Empathy is made possible by mirror neurons,[60] which enable us to *feel what others feel*. It is a powerful mechanism that connects humans together. In fact, watching 40 seconds of videotaped compassion can reduce anxiety.[61] Empathy is a critical stage to deal with hostage situations by FBI. Their technique goes: (1) Active listening; (2) Empathy—feel what others feel; (3) Rapport: they feel it back; (4) Influence; and (5) Change. We can apply this model in a business setting with various active listening strategies that lead to empathy. For example, in fear-free meetings, employees voice their opinions or concerns while managers only listen with absolutely no interference.

However, too much empathy can make you confuse others' feelings with your own feelings, and thus, may distort clear thinking.[62] To compare, perspective taking, or *cognitive* empathy, is the ability to *think about what others feel*, and often occurs after emotional empathy.[63] These two processes activate different brain regions and prompt differences in behaviors.[64] During a cultural change, it is more vital to understand others, imagine what you would do if you were in the situation, and find common ground and consensus rather than simply being overwhelmed with similar feelings.

7.5.4 *Dealing with Undesired Emotions*

Emotions are not helpful when we show wrong emotions in the wrong time, or with the wrong intensity. This is the reason why mindfulness has become a booming practice in corporate's everyday life. Just 15 minutes of mindfulness a day enables people to make better business decisions.[65]

There are many techniques to manage emotion. Here is a technique developed by the author after a long time of practicing mindfulness, summarized in three letters: OAK.

"O" means *observe*. When unwanted emotions rise up, take several deep breaths. Long exhales mimic the process of relaxation. Long inhales provide oxygen to the brain for better cognition processes. Now try to "look" at your feeling as if you are another person, and describe it. Notice your physical state at that moment: The heartbeat, the sensation on the skin, the feeling in the stomach, and so forth. Look straight into your emotion and separate it from who you are. Talk with yourself and others about your emotion. This is important because suppressing emotion backfires, affecting memories and creating a threat response in others.[66] Instead of holding back, name the emotion. Labeling emotion calms the amygdala down and activates the right ventro-lateral prefrontal cortex—the brain's breaking and self-control system.[67] For example, say "there is anger," instead of associating yourself with the emotion as in "I'm angry." Observe your thought. Consider thoughts as actors on a stage and you are the audience, watching how they appear and disappear, *without* following them.

"A" means *analyze*. "Step back and ask why" is a powerful approach to deal with unwanted emotions. It allows us to distance ourselves from the event and think about the reasons behind it rather than fixating on the consequential emotion. "A" can also mean *anicca*—a Pali word for impermanence. This is an essential doctrine of Buddhism, which asserts that all things are transient and temporary. Understanding *anicca* helps us to decide if we should react on an emotion right here right now, or wait a little longer to see it from different perspectives. If many of the worries we had in the past seem ordinary today, then the same can apply to some of the worries we have today because they may mean a great deal less after a while. In other words, *if it's not urgent, analyze and wait*.

"K" means *kindness*. After you have calmly observed the emotion and tried to come up with all possible explanations, if you still have to act, do it with kindness, for the sake of both yourself and others. By choosing not to *react* to the knee-jerk emotion, you have allowed emotion to be a critical input and not a destructive power. By acting with kindness, you have stopped the vicious spiral of tit-for-tat between battling amygdalae. It's important to remember that emotional attack is not always the best strategy. Wanting to attack means it's you who is under emotional attack.

Mindfulness is a great tool to practice concentration. A moment of distraction, doubt, or anxiety can shatter a wining possibility, as seen in the famous Mindball game.[68] In this experiment, there is a large metal ball on the table with a magnetic field under it. Players wear a headband that picks up their electrical signals from the brain, and use them to control the position of the ball. Their goal is to push the ball, purely by their thought, to roll toward the opponent and fall in their lap. What happens very often is that players tend to *lose* when they almost *win*, that is when the ball is closer to the table edge of the opponent's side. The anxiety of winning interferes with control, and stops them from staying "in the zone." The ability to focus at critical moments is common among top sport players, successful business leaders, and other high-achievers.

7.5.5 *Create a Happy Workplace*

We often see success as a goal, and happiness is the consequence: "Success creates happiness." However, this means every time we reach success, happiness is there for a moment and gone because another goal (success) means happiness is again at the end of the striving road—a road that we need to travel without joy because joy is yet to be rewarded. The end result is that our working life consists of roads separated by happiness "markers," but never *full* of happiness.

But that's not how the brain works. When we are in positive moods, energy is not wasted in dealing with fear and stress. The brain's error detector ACC increases its activity with positive mood, hence, facilitates problem solving.[69] Statistically, happiness leads to a spike of 12% in productivity.[70] The fact that only 13% of employees worldwide are engaged at work[71] explains why 87% of employees support a position called Chief Happiness Officer[72]—a title created by the founder of Woohoo Inc. Thus, the formula needs to change. Instead of seeing success as a goal, we'd better see happiness as a *goal*, and expect success to follow as a *consequence*.[73]

Happiness is partly in our genes. Genetic variation explains about 33% of differences among individuals.[74] But let's recall GCEB-Be, with the fact that (1) behaviors can turn on or off a certain genes; (2) the brain is plastic; and (3) the impact of culture and environment is immense. Mirror neurons are there to pick up happiness and make us feel the same way, even subconsciously, because emotion is contagious. That's the benefit of an optimistic leader because her/his emotions prompt followers to mirror the same neural circuits.

However, it is impossible to avoid unwanted emotions. In fact, the best formula to thrive is a combination of both, as long as positive emotions outnumber negative ones. This is to *balance out* the evolutionary bias humans have toward negativity (i.e., bad things attract our attention more for survival purposes). Good can only triumph by force of numbers or perceptual *reframing* of the situation. The latter is a crucial strategy during change process, as it allows us to have more than one way to view an event.

Taking one step further, the simplistic good-bad, positive-negative dimension is outdated because emotions interact dynamically with complex results. In a study, people who experienced both happiness and sadness ended up better off than those who experienced one emotion only,[75] probably because they are in the optimal zone of eustress. When sadness or anger is caused by injustice, it is not useful to stuff it up, but allow it to drive behavior to be the change you want to see. "Full engagement" at work is a good example of combining all sort of emotions into a powerful synergy of forces: The thrill of hunt, the pleasure of feast, the eagerness to revenge, the warmth of trust, and to a certain extent, the fear of disappointment. Advocating this holistic view, some researchers have compared "wholeness is to psychology" with what "enlightenment is to spirituality."[76]

To conclude, no good decision is made without input from emotion. Emotion is what drives people to change. Emotion strategies for cultural change include storytelling, balancing empathy and perspective taking, controlling negative emotion, acting with kindness (OAK), and creating a happy workplace with eustress.

7.6 The "A" of STREAP-Be: Alignment

In Chapter 1 and 6, we have discussed the crucial role of similarity in recognizing our ingroup, that is who we can trust. For this evolutionary reason, we have evolved to quickly recognize and exercise favorable bias toward those who look, act, think, and hold the same values as we do.

During a change process, managers and outsiders often want to distinguish themselves immediately in an attempt to prove their quality. They may ignore the screaming amygdalae of the staff, who haven't got sufficient time to understand the new strategy, give a voice, build trust, and see their own benefit in the change. Knowing how the brain works, it is much more sensible and effective to be "on the same page" and acknowledge what "works well here" before convincing people to change.

Alignment or similarity can be recognized at all levels of social connections: Backgrounds, work benefits, hobbies, interests, emotions, values, and so forth. Author Andy Habermacher even suggested a common enemy or a common threat to put people in the same boat, to fight together.[77] At the Alliance of CEOs in 2006, Jeff Rodek, Chairman and CEO of Hyperion Solutions, said: "Every business needs one company to beat. Pick an enemy!" He recounted his FedEx days where everyone in the company was told, "Every time you see a brown truck (UPS), they're taking food from your children."[78] While this may involve a question of ethics, from evolution's perspective, it makes sense. When a harm is inflicted by an outsider on an ingroup's member, there is increased coupling between left orbitofrontal cortex (emotional control), the amygdala (emotional detector), and the *insula* (emotional context for physical experience).[79] The brain is highly sensitive to outgroup attacks on ingroup members because it poses an existential threat to the whole collective.

7.7 The "P" of STREAP-Be: People

Everyone in the company should be a change agent, that is identifying problems, finding solutions, and carrying the change. However, change leaders are those who orchestrate the whole process. Many companies make a classic mistake of appointing HR manager for the task, seeing culture building as just another HR project. This approach often recruits the wrong change leaders and risks the lack of both top sponsorship and bottom-up involvement.

7.7.1 Change Leaders

Change leaders should be influential people, simply because their attitudes, emotions, and behaviors will be picked up by others with the help of mirror neurons. Other candidates are up-and-coming managers who see changes as opportunities to reach their ambition and career development.

With the mirror neurons in mind, change leaders are those who demonstrate desired behaviors and lead the change by examples. The mirror neurons in the brain of the followers will be subconsciously activated, prompting the same behavior. In short, the old adage "walk the talk" has a solid neural basis.

7.7.2 Top Sponsor and Bottom Involvement

A change process should have support from both people in the boardroom and those by the rank and file. Without commitment from the executives, there will be no sense of urgency, no guiding vision, no alignment with the company's goals, and no watchful eyes for chaos. Similarly, if laypeople don't own the change process, corporate culture will only exist on paper. In his book, author Jerome Want described several cases in which change was facilitated ineffectively.[80] With

Verizon, it was a half-hearted attempt to change *without* the involvement of the top 20 officers. However, these senior managers had behaviors that were in complete opposition to the cultural change efforts taking place in the management ranks just below them. On the other extreme, at Time Warner, to change the company's slow-moving bureaucracy, CEO Jerry Levin made a 45-minute video starring himself, outlining his thought, and had it distributed to everyone. Both cases ended up with failure because either the top or the bottom was not involved.

7.8 The "Be" of STREAP-Be: Behavior

In Chapter 2, we discussed how repeated behaviors, regardless of being voluntarily or forced, can slowly change the structure of our genes, brain, environment, and culture. The "foot-in-the-door" tactic tells us that once people agree to go with the first step, they would feel an inner need to go all the way through, making their attitude consistent with their behavior.[81] In other words, we change our values to fit our past and current behaviors. The implication is, we can reshape a culture by changing behaviors (GCEB-Be, Behavior—Culture pathway).

Because changes don't just start from within, for those who are tasked with building a business culture, this is good news. We don't have to wait until we are 100% sure about the change because acting can compensate that doubt. It's noteworthy to mention here that Jewish tradition typically focuses more on religious *practice* than religious belief.[82] This is rooted in the idea that repeated behaviors will eventually lead to a change in attitude. One may not believe in God initially, but the rituals that (s)he follows day in and day out will bring her/him to God. The mind leads the action, but action can change the mind as well. We are what we repeatedly do (Aristotle).

7.8.1 Break the Pattern with "As If"

More often than not, what we often describe ourselves is only a *snapshot* of who we are at a particular time and place in life,[83] for example, "hot tempered but honest," "good at art, bad at science," "easily get provoked," and so forth. We are then told to embrace this true self, lovingly accept this genuine version of our authenticity, and let it define us forever. The fact is that when snapshots become *labels*, they will drive our behavior and guide our decisions, creating our life's patterns, slowly transforming incidents into habits, changing temporary emotional dispositions into more permanent characteristic, and constructing the so-called personality. In other words, the "true" self is nothing other than the result of self-fulfilling prophecy, and of patterns that have been built up over time. You have *become* an "easily provoked" person because that is how you have behaved and who you believe you are, but it is not who you are, or all that you can be.

A contemporary view of the self emphasizes impulse, process, and change.[84] You are not a single, unified being but complex, multifaceted, and changing constantly. The brain's plasticity enables us to represent multiple cultures in our mind and switch between values simultaneously. This makes change possible, as long as the new pattern wins over the old habitual reactions.

In their book *The Path*, Puett and Gross-Loh advised people to intentionally break the pattern, even if that goes against the emotion at that moment.[85] For example, you are in a long-simmering resentment with your colleague. The first step is to acknowledge that the problem is *not* because you two are incompatible, but that your communication has fallen into a pattern. Both you and he have responded to the genuine emotion of anger, irritation, and apathy. To break this pattern, you need to see him as a complex, multifaceted person with a pleasant side. And so do you. There is a more tolerant side in you that would not mind talking to the pleasant side of him at all. Ask yourself "Can I act *as if* this side of me is talking to that positive side of him?" If the answer is "yes," you are off to a good start. You may begin with a friendly greeting, even though that would be the last word you want to utter. You may want to force a deliberate moment of silence the next time you want to snarl. The chance is big that your colleague will react differently to that "as if" behavior, and that means both of you stand a chance to break away from the dangerous pattern. Puett argues that by actively working to shift ourselves "as if" we were different people in that moment, we may open up infinite possibilities that we didn't know existed. Thus, fake it until you *become* it.

7.8.2 Identify and Reward Desirable Behaviors

To change by behaviors, desirable behaviors need to be identified. For example, if the desirable behavior is "people should talk directly to each other," it would be formally labeled "Direct with Respect." In combination with trainings, leaders would consciously mentor employees and demonstrate their "Direct with Respect." They would reward employees with a "thank you" when the targeted behavior was shown. This strategy was employed for six months in an $8 billion company, and a cultural pulse survey revealed a significant reduction in the number of employees leaving the company (from 12 to 6%). Customers clearly noticed a change in service and the company's market share on certain products grew by two points without the addition of new features.[86]

Here is another example. Violence is a daily routine in high-security prisons. But when the warden in a Californian prison approved an 11-day trial of the Compassion Game, the culture started to change. Gang leaders identified themselves as "compassion ambassadors" and inmates as "compassionistas." They earned points by logging in compassion acts such as sharing food and helping to clean up each other's cell. The 11-day trial observed 4,600 acts of compassion and zero violence.[87] The game changed people significantly, for example, a women known as "evil" changed her name to "Tinker Bell"—a sweet, sassy, and tiny fairy who always has her friends' back.

7.8.3 A Good Enough Decision Is Good Enough

It's not wise to be stuck in the analysis stage because it means you are just rearranging the problem in different ways. From neuroscience's point of view, making a decision helps to bring about control. There is no need to make a perfect decision, but *good enough* ones. It calms the limbic system and engages the prefrontal cortex.[88] Trying to make the absolute best decision can have the opposite effect because being a perfectionist can be stressful. Again, focus on progress, not perfection.

7.8.4 Use Action Orientation

Making a decision to change does not always mean people will automatically act accordingly. More often than not, a decision is hard, and we are left with a state of cognitive dissonance—conflicting between attitude and action. We may have decided to create a culture of transparency, but the extra effort and problems that will occur in the process of doing so don't just disappear because of this decision. This is when psychological processing assists us to start viewing the choice we made more favorably, helping us to follow through the decision easier (see Chapter 2). Research has shown that after making a decision, an action-oriented approach with clear course of what to do will increase our preference for the choice we made.[89] It increases the left frontal cortical activity and decision commitment.[90] In other words, we will evaluate a choice with action plan much more favorable and commit to it much stronger than the one without.

To conclude, in this chapter, we have discussed the neurobiology of change and the challenges we face in change management. Following the STREAP-Be model, organizations can touch on the most fundamental aspects of change and selected strategies. A collective such as a company is not different from humans as a species or individual persons in the sense that its culture is both persistent and evolving. We may find it difficult to change, but we are *built to adapt*, and we are the only the species that can do so *deliberately*.

Summary

1. Change is challenging because:
    *   The brain is lazy. Strong neural patterns enable us to execute ritual and cognitive habits effortlessly. A trigger can activate the pattern even when a habit has ceased. Even when habit means danger, strong neural patterns can still keep us in the loop of self-harm. Change costs energy. It means a loss in what has been invested in the past, and an immense task in overriding old habits and building new neural pathways.
    *   The brain is a "control freak." It constantly detects errors to avoid danger, and then tries to come back to status quo. Change tends to bring uncertainty and the brain resists it.
    *   The brain likes to imitate. Mirror neurons reinforce habits because we tend to (sub) consciously pick up cues and imitate each other.
2. The STREAP-Be framework of cultural change covers the most fundamental aspects of a change process, taking into account the reasons that make change so challenging.
3. The "S" of STREAP-Be means "safety." It is the first and foremost condition to support a sustainable change in culture.
    *   Safety issues are status, certainty, autonomy, relatedness, and fairness.
    *   Strategies to create safety include identifying safety issues, being on the same page (clarity), enabling self decision making (choice), fostering autonomy (control), keeping check of internal competition, and building trust.
4. The "T" of STREAP-Be means "trigger."
    *   It is part of a habit loop that consists of (1) trigger, (2) routine, and (3) reward.
    *   To change a habit, different routines have to be replaced to achieve the same or a better reward.
    *   To identify the trigger in complex cultural habits, we need to look into our memories and expect that triggers and routines can associate subconsciously.
5. The "R" of STREAP-Be means "reward."
    *   Complex neural pathways allow us to choose a reward even when it means a bit of pain.
    *   Reward strategies for cultural change include focusing on the positive, imagining the end result, imagining how to solve a potential problem, recoding failures as necessary side posts, reframing challenges as opportunities to gain, creating small achievable goals, and making reward unexpected, tangible, personal and public.
6. The "E" of STREAP-Be means "emotion."
    *   No good decision is made without input from emotion. Emotion is what drives people to change.
    *   Emotion strategies for cultural change include storytelling, balancing empathy and perspective taking, controlling negative emotion, acting with kindness (OAK), and creating a happy workplace with eustress.
7. The "A" of STREAP-Be means "alignment."
    *   It creates similarities and ingroups.
    *   Alignment strategies for cultural change can be based on all aspects of life such as common enemy, background, interest, values, vision, and so forth.

8. The "P" of STREAP-Be means "people."
   - Change agents should be influential people, top management with the involvement of the rank and file.
   - Change agents' attitudes, emotions, and behaviors will be picked up by others with the help of mirror neurons.
9. The "B" of STREAP-Be means "behavior."
   - Our thoughts and feelings can change as a result of our behaviors. Hence, cultural values can change as a result of collective behaviors.
   - Behavioral strategies for cultural change include seeing one's self as evolving, faking it until one becomes it, identifying and rewarding desirable behaviors, making good-enough decisions, and using action plan to motivate behavior.

Notes

Don't forget to go to the end of the book for case studies.

1 Emerman, Ed. 2013. "Quarter of Employees Gain from Change Management Initiatives." *Willis Towers Watson.* August 29. www.towerswatson.com/en/Press/2013/08/Only-One-Quarter-of-Employers-Are-Sustaining-Gains-From-Change-Management.

2 Vicente, Ana M., Pedro Galvão-Ferreira, Fatuel Tecuapetla, and Rui M. Costa. 2016. "Direct and Indirect Dorsolateral Striatum Pathways Reinforce Different Action Strategies." *Current Biology* 26(7): 267–269. doi:10.1016/j.cub.2016.02.03.

3 Smith, Kyle S., and Ann M. Graybiel. 2013. "A Dual Operator View of Habitual Behavior Reflecting Cortical and Striatal Dynamics." *Neuron* 79(2): 361–374. doi:10.1016/j.neuron.2013.05.038.

4 Statistic Brain. 2017. "New Year's Resolution Statistics." *Statistic Brain.* January 4. www.statisticbrain.com/new-years-resolution-statistics/.

5 Sturges, Fiona. 2013. "The Week in Radio: It's Worth Taking a Gamble on This American Life." *The Independent.* July 10. www.independent.co.uk/arts-entertainment/tv/features/the-week-in-radio-its-worth-taking-a-gamble-on-this-american-life-8701295.html.

6 Want, Jerome H. 2006. *Corporate Culture: Illuminating the Black Hole*, 179. New York: St. Martin's Press..

7 Zak, Paul J. 2017. "The Neuroscience of Trust." *Harvard Business Review.* January 1. https://hbr.org/2017/01/the-neuroscience-of-trust.

8 Barnes, Terra D., Yasuo Kubota, Dan Hu, Dezhe Z. Jin, and Ann M. Graybiel. 2005. "Activity of Striatal Neurons Reflects Dynamic Encoding and Recoding of Procedural Memories." *Nature* 437(October): 1158–1161. doi:10.1038/nature04053.

9 Deutschman, Alan. 2005. "Change or Die." *The Fast Company.* May. www.fastcompany.com/52717/change-or-die.

10 Seligman, Martin E. P. 1972. "Learned Helplessness." *Annual Review of Medicine* 23(1): 407–412. doi:10.1146/annurev.me.23.020172.002203.

11 Kahneman, Daniel., and Amos Tversky. 1992. "Advances in Prospect Theory: Cumulative Representation of Uncertainty." *Journal of Risk and Uncertainty* 5(4): 297–323. doi:10.1007/BF00122574.

12 Tversky, Amos., and Daniel Kahneman. 1981. "The Framing of Decisions and the Psychology of Choice." *Science*, New Series 211(4481): 453–458. https://psych.hanover.edu/classes/cognition/papers/tversky81.pdf.

13 Rubinstein, Joshua S., David E. Meyer, and Jeffrey E. Evans. 2001. "Executive Control of Cognitive Processes in Task Switching." *Journal of Experimental Psychology: Human Perception and Performance* 27(4): 763–797. doi:10.1037/0096-1523.27.4.763.

14 American Psychological Association. 2006. "Multitasking: Switching Costs." March 20. www.apa.org/research/action/multitask.aspx.

15 Loose, Lasse S., David Wisniewski, Marco Rusconi, Thoma Goschke, and John- Dylan Haynes. 2017. "Switch-Independent Task Representations in Frontal and Parietal Cortex." *The Journal of Neuroscience* 37(33): 8033–8042. doi:10.1523/JNEUROSCI.3656-16.2017.

16 Lally, Phillippa., Cornelia H. M. van Jaarsveld, Henry W. W. Potts, and Jane Wardle. 2010. "How Are Habits Formed: Modelling Habit Formation in the Real World." *European Journal of Social Psychology* 40(6): 998–1009. doi:10.1002/ejsp.674.

17 De Berker, Archy O., Robb B. Rutledge, Christoph Mathys, Louise Marshall, Gemma F. Cross, Raymond J. Dolan, and Sven Bestmann. 2016. "Computations of Uncertainty Mediate Acute Stress Responses in Humans." *Nature Communications* 10996(7). doi:10.1038/ncomms10996.

18 Wiggins, Sandi., Patti Whyte, Marlene Huggins, Shelin Adam, Jane Theilmann, Maurice Bloch, Samuel B. Sheps, Martin T. Schechter, and Michael R. Hayden. 1992. "The Psychological Consequences of Predictive Testing for Huntington's Disease." *The New England Journal of Medicine* 327(20): 1401–1405. doi:10.1056/NEJM199211123272001.

19 Recordati, G., and T. G. Bellini. 2003. "A Definition of Internal Constancy and Homeostasis in the Context of Non-Equilibrium Thermodynamics." *The Psychological Society* 89(1): 27–38. doi:10.1113/expphysiol.2003.002633.

20 Pellegrino, G. Di, L. Fadiga, L. Fogassi, V. Gallese, and G. Rizzolatti. 1992. "Understanding Motor Events: A Neurophysiological Study." *Experimental Brain Research* 91(1): 176–180. doi:10.1007/bf00230027.

21 Kilner, J. M., and R. N. Lemon. 2013. "What We Know Currently about Mirror Neurons." *Current Biology* 23(23): 1057–1062. doi:10.1016/j.cub.2013.10.051.

22 Ramachandran, Vilayanur S. 2012. *The Tell-Tale Brain: A Neuroscientist's Quest for What Makes Us Human*. New York: W. W. Norton & Company.

23 Lieberman, Matthew D., Naomi I. Eisenberger, Molly J. Crockett, Sabrina M. Tom, Jennifer H. Pfeifer, and Baldwin M. Way. 2007. "Putting Feelings into Words." *Psychological Science* 18(5): 421–428. doi:10.1111/j.1467-9280.2007.01916.x.

24 Rock, David. 2008. "SCARF: A Brain-Based Model for Collaborating with and Influencing Others." *Neuro Leadership Journal* 1. www.epa.gov/sites/production/files/2015-09/documents/thurs_georgia_9_10_915_covello.pdf.

25 Barankay, Iwan. 2014. "Rank Incentives Evidence from a Randomized Workplace Experiment." *Research Gate*. November. www.researchgate.net/publication/260345423_Rank_Incentives_Evidence_from_a_Randomized_Workplace_Experiment.

26 Nicas, Jack. 2017. "Google Cancels Staff Meeting on Diversity." *The Australian*. August 11. www.theaustralian.com.au/business/media/google-cancels-staff-meeting-on-diversity-citing-safety-fears/news-story/53ef5d375a6ddbd1f9b93478bcac5fab.

27 Gallup. 2015. "State of the American Manager: Analytics and Advice for Leaders Report." www.gallup.com/services/182138/state-american-manager.aspx.

28 Rodway, Paul., Astrid Schepman, and Jordana Lambert. 2012. "Preferring the One in the Middle: Further Evidence for the Centre-Stage Effect." *Applied Cognitive Psychology* 23(2): 215–222. doi:10.1002/acp.1812.

29 Feintzeig, Rachel. 2014. "Flexibility at Work: Worth Skipping a Raise?" *The Wall Street Journal*. October 31. https://blogs.wsj.com/atwork/2014/10/31/flexibility-at-work-worth-skipping-a-raise/.

30 Freeman, Jonathan B., Ryan M. Stolier, Zachary A. Ingbretsen, and Eric A. Hehman. 2014. "Amygdala Responsivity to High-Level Social Information from Unseen Faces." *Journal of Neuroscience* 34(32): 10573–10581. doi:10.1523/JNEUROSCI.5063-13.2014.

31 Hurley, Robert F. 2006. "The Decision to Trust." *Harvard Business Review*. September. www.researchgate.net/publication/6822603_The_Decision_to_Trust.

32 Zak, Paul J. 2008. "The Neurobiology of Trust." *Scientific American* 298(6): 88–95. www.scientificamerican.com/article/the-neurobiology-of-trust/.

33 Zak, Paul J. 2017. "The Neuroscience of Trust." *Harvard Business Review*: 84–90. https://hbr.org/2017/01/the-neuroscience-of-trust.

34 PwC. 2016. "Redefining Business Success in a Changing World. CEO Survey." CEO Survey. www.pwc.com/gx/en/ceo-survey/2016/landing-page/pwc-19th-annual-global-ceo-survey.pdf.

35 Duhigg, Charles. 2014. *The Power of Habit*. New York: Random House Trade.

36 Leknes, Siri., and Irene Tracey. 2008. "A Common Neurobiology for Pain and Pleasure." *Nature Reviews Neuroscience* 9 (April): 314–320. doi:10.1038/nrn2333.

37 Veen, Vincent Van., and Cameron S. Carter. 2006. "Conflict and Cognitive Control in the Brain." *Current Directions in Psychological Science* 15(5): 237–240. doi:10.1111/j.1467-8721.2006.00443.x.

38 Dowman, Robert. 2004. "Distraction Produces an Increase in Pain-Evoked Anterior Cingulate Activity." *Psychophysiology* 41(4): 613–624. doi:10.1111/1469–8986.00186.x.

39 Sprenger, Christian., Falk Eippert, Jürgen Finsterbusch, Ulrike Bingel, Michael Rose, and Christian Büchel. 2012. "Attention Modulates Spinal Cord Responses to Pain." *Current Biology* 22(11): 1019–1022. doi:10.1016/j.cub.2012.04.006.

40 Srinivasan, Pillay S. 2011. *Your Brain and Business.* Upper Saddle River, NJ: Pearson Education.

41 Clark, Brian C. 2014. "The Power of the Mind: The Cortex as a Critical Determinant of Muscle Strength/Weakness." *Journal of Neurophysiology* 112(12): 3219–3226. doi:10.1152/jn.00386.2014.

42 Ranganathan, Vinoth K. 2004. "From Mental Power to Muscle Power—Gaining Strength by Using the Mind." *Neuropsychologia* 42(7): 944–956. doi:10.1016/j.neuropsychologia.2003.11.018.

43 Vasquez, Noelia A., and Roger Buehler. 2007. "Seeing Future Success: Does Imagery Perspective Influence Achievement Motivation?" *Personality and Social Psychology Bulletin* 33(10): 1392–1405. doi:10.1177/0146167207304541.

44 Amabile, Teresa., and Steven J. Kramer. 2017. "The Power of Small Wins." *Harvard Business Review.* https://hbr.org/2011/05/the-power-of-small-wins.

45 Lavine, Marc., and Kim Cameron. 2012. "From Weapons to Wildlife: Positive Organizing in Practice." *Organizational Dynamics* 41(2): 135–145. doi:10.1016/j.orgdyn.2012.01.007.

46 Histed, Mark H., Anitha Pasupathy, and Earl K. Miller. 2009. "Learning Substrates in the Primate Prefrontal Cortex and Striatum: Sustained Activity Related to Successful Actions." *Neuron* 63(2): 244–253. doi:10.1016/j.neuron.2009.06.019.

47 Palminteri, Stefano., Mehdi Khamassi, Mateus Joffily, and Giorgio Coricelli. 2015. "Contextual Modulation of Value Signals in Reward and Punishment Learning." *Nature Communications* 6(1): 1–14. doi:10.1038/ncomms9096.

48 Kumar, Arun., and N. Meenakshi. 2009. *Organizational Behavior: A Modern Approach*, 186. New Delhi: Vikas Publishing House.

49 Zappos. 2012. "Four Peer-to-Peer Ways Zappos Employees Reward Each Other." *Zappos Insights.* October 9. www.zapposinsights.com/blog/item/four-peertopeer-ways-zappos-employees-reward-each-other.

50 Goleman, Daniel. 2005. *Emotional Intelligence: Why It Can Matter More Than IQ.* 10th anniversary ed. New York: Bantam Books.

51 Lerner, Jennifer S., Ye Li, Piercarlo Valdesolo, and Karim Kassam. 2014. "Emotion and Decision Making." *Annual Review of Psychology* (June): 1–45. https://scholar.harvard.edu/files/jenniferlerner/files/annual_review_manuscript_june_16_final.final_.pdf.

52 Damasio, Anthony. 2005. *Descartes' Error: Emotion, Reason, and the Human Brain.* Reprint Edition. New York: Penguin Books.

53 Gobe, Marc. 2010. *Emotional Branding: The New Paradigm for Connecting Brands to People.* Updated and Revised Edition. New York: Allworth Press.

54 Brooks, Nathan. 2016. "Understanding the Manifestation of Psychopathic Personality Characteristics across Populations." PhD dissertation. Bond University, Robina, Australia. http://epublications.bond.edu.au/cgi/viewcontent.cgi?article=1215&context=theses.

55 Babiak, Paul., and Robert D. Hare. 2016. *Snakes in Suits: When Psychopaths Go to Work.* New York: Harper Collins.

56 Reynolds, Megan. 2017. "Apparently Psychopaths Make Good CEOs—Especially in Silicon Valley." CNBC. March 21. www.cnbc.com/2017/03/21/apparently-psychopaths-make-good-ceos.html.

57 Gudmundsson, Amanda., and Gregory Southey. 2011. "Leadership and the Rise of the Corporate Psychopath: What Can Business Schools Do about the 'Snakes Inside'?" *e-Journal of Social and Behavioural Research in Business* 2(2): 18–27. http://citeseerx.ist.psu.edu/viewdoc/download?doi=10.1.1.696.9506&rep=rep1&type=pdf.

58 Monarth, Harrison. 2014. "The Irresistible Power of Storytelling as a Strategic Business Tool." *Harvard Business Review.* March 11. https://hbr.org/2014/03/the-irresistible-power-of-storytelling-as-a-strategic-business-tool.

59 Gonzalez, Julio., Alfonso Barros-Loscertales, Friedemann Pulvermuller, Vanessa Meseguer, Ana Sanjuan, Vicente Belloch, and César Avila. 2006. "Reading Cinnamon Activates Olfactory Brain Regions." *Neuroimage* 32(2): 906–912. doi:10.1016/j.neuroimage.2006.03.037.

60 Ferrari, Pier Francesco., and Giacomo Rizzolatti. 2014. "Mirror Neuron Research: The Past and the Future." *Philosophical Transactions of Royal Society of London* 369(1644). doi:10.1098/rstb.2013.0169.

61 Fogarty, L. A., B. A. Curbow, J. R. Wingard, K. McDonnell, and M. R. Somerfield. 1999. "Can 40 Seconds of Compassion Reduce Patient Anxiety?" *Journal of Clinical Oncology* 17(1): 371–379. doi:10.1200/JCO.1999.17.1.371.

62 Galinsky, Adam D., William W. Maddux, Debra Gilin, and Judith B. White. 2008. "Why It Pays to Get Inside the Head of Your Opponent: The Differential Effects of Perspective Taking and Empathy in Negotiations." *Psychological Science* 19(4): 378–384. doi:10.1111/j.1467-9280.2008.02096.x.

63 Li, Wei., and Shihui Han. 2010. "Perspective Taking Modulates Event-Related Potentials to Perceived Pain." *Neuroscience Letters* 469(3): 328–332. doi:10.1016/j.neulet.2009.12.021.

64 Tusche, Anita., Anne Bockler, Philipp Kanske, Fynn-Mathis Trautwein, and Tania Singer. 2016. "Decoding the Charitable Brain: Empathy, Perspective Taking, and Attention Shifts Differentially Predict Altruistic Giving." *The Journal of Neuroscience* 36(17): 4719–4732. doi:10.1523/JNEUROSCI.3392-15.2016.

65 Hafenbrack, Andrew C., Zoe Kinias, and Sigal G. Barsade. 2014. "Debiasing the Mind through Meditation: Mindfulness and the Sunk-Cost Bias." *Psychological Science* 25(2): 369–376. doi:10.1177/0956797613503853.

66 Gross, James J., and Oliver P. John. 2003. "Individual Differences in Two Emotion Regulation Processes: Implications for Affect, Relationships, and Well-Being." *Journal of Personality and Social Psychology* 85(2): 348–362. doi:10.1037/0022-3514.85.2.348.

67 Iyer, Lakshminarayan M., A. Maxwell Burroughs, Swadha Anand, Robson F. De Souza, and L. Aravind. 2017. "Polyvalent Proteins, a Pervasive Theme in the Intergenomic Biological Conflicts of Bacteriophages and Conjugative Elements." *Journal of Bacteriology* 199(15): e00245-17. doi:10.1128/jb.00245-17.

68 Slingerland, Edward G. 2014. *Trying Not to Try: The Art and Science of Spontaneity.* New York: Crown.

69 Subramaniam, Karuna., John Kounios, Todd B. Parrish, and Mark Jung-Beeman. 2009. "A Brain Mechanism for Facilitation of Insight by Positive Affect." *Journal of Cognitive Neuroscience* 21(3): 415–432. doi:10.1162/jocn.2009.21057.

70 Oswald, Andrew J., Eugenio Proto, and Daniel Sgroi. 2014. "Happiness and Productivity." University of Warwick, Coventry, UK. February 10. www2.warwick.ac.uk/fac/soc/economics/staff/eproto/workingpapers/happinessproductivity.pdf.

71 Gallup, Inc. 2013. "Worldwide, 13% of Employees Are Engaged at Work." October 8. http://news.gallup.com/poll/165269/worldwide-employees-engaged-work.aspx.

72 JLL. 2016. "Workplace." JLL Human Experience. http://humanexperience.jll/wp-content/uploads/2017/07/7686-JLL-HUMAN-EXPERIENCE_GLOBAL-REPORT_SPS_A4_V4.pdf.

73 Achor, Shawn. 2015. "Why a Happy Brain Performs Better." *Harvard Business Review.* March 30. https://hbr.org/2010/11/why-a-happy-brain-performs-bet.

74 De Neve, Jan-Emmanuel., Nicholas A. Christakis, James H. Fowler, and Bruno S. Frey. 2012. "Genes, Economics, and Happiness." *Journal of Neuroscience, Psychology, and Economics* 5(4): 193–211. doi:10.1037/a0030292.

75 Adler, Jonathan M., and Hal E. Hershfield. 2012. "Mixed Emotional Experience Is Associated with and Precedes Improvements in Psychological Well-Being." *PLoS ONE* 7(4): e35633. doi:10.1371/journal.pone.0035633.

76 Kashdan, Todd B., and Robert Biswas-Diener. 2015. *The Power of Negative Emotion: How Anger, Guilt and Self Doubt Are Essential to Success and Fulfillment.* Richmond, UK: Oneworld.

77 Habermacher, Andy. 2011. *Leading 100 Billion Neurons.* Smashwords. www.smashwords.com/books/view/99670.

78 Sher, Robert. 2006. "Case: Every Business Needs a Common Enemy." *Alliance of Chief Executives, LLC.* February 28. www.allianceofceos.com/exp_cases/detail/every-business-needs-a-common-enemy.

79 Molenberghs, Pascal., Joshua Gapp, Bei Wang, Winnifred R. Louis, and Jean Decety. 2014. "Increased Moral Sensitivity for Outgroup Perpetrators Harming Ingroup Members." *Cerebral Cortex* 26(1): 225–233. www.researchgate.net/publication/265298420_Increased_Moral_Sensitivity_for_Outgroup_Perpetrators_Harming_Ingroup_Members.

80 Want, Jerome H. 2006. *Corporate Culture: Illuminating the Black Hole.* New York: St. Martin's Press.

81 Harmon-Jones, Eddie., and Judson Mills. 1999. *Cognitive Dissonance: Progress on a Pivotal Theory in Social Psychology.* Washington, DC: American Psychological Association.

82 Cohen, Adam B., Joel I. Siegel, and Paul Rozin. 2003. "Faith versus Practice: Different Bases for Religiosity Judgments by Jews and Protestants." *European Journal of Social Psychology* 33(2): 287–295. doi:10.1002/ejsp.148.

83 Harmon-Jones, Eddie., and Judson Mills. 1999. *Cognitive Dissonance: Progress on a Pivotal Theory in Social Psychology.* Washington, DC: American Psychological Association.

84 Howard, Judith A., and Peter L. Callero. 2006. *The Self-Society Dynamic: Cognition, Emotion, and Action.* Cambridge: Cambridge University Press.

85 Puett, Michael J., and Christine Gross-Loh. 2016. *The Path: What Chinese Philosophers Can Teach Us about the Good Life.* New York: Simon & Schuster.

86 Power, Brad. 2014. "If You're Going to Change Your Culture, Do It Quickly." *Harvard Business Review.* August 7. https://hbr.org/2013/11/if-youre-going-to-change-your-culture-do-it-quickly.

87 Compassion Games. 2017. "Compassion Games Creates 'Climate Change.'" www.youtube.com/watch?v=zZLGHZ1lSjU

88 Korb, Alex. 2015. *The Upward Spiral: Using Neuroscience to Reverse the Course of Depression, One Small Change at a Time.* Oakland, CA: New Harbinger Publications.

89 Harmon-Jones, Eddie., and Cindy Harmon-Jones. 2002. "Testing the Action-Based Model of Cognitive Dissonance: The Effect of Action-Orientation on Post-Decisional Attitudes." *Personality and Social Psychology Bulletin* 28(6): 711–723. doi:10.1177/0146167202289001.

90 Harmon-Jones, Eddie., Cindy Harmon-Jones, Meghan Fearn, Jonathan D. Sigelman, and Peter Judd Johnson. 2008. "Left Frontal Cortical Activation and Spreading of Alternatives: Tests of the Action-Based Model of Dissonance." *Journal of Personality and Social Psychology* 94(1): 1–15. doi:10.1037/0022-3514.94.1.1.

8   Bias Management

In Chapters 6 and 7, we learned that in the era of globalization and cooperation, we still carry some part of the psychological and biological baggage of our hunter-gatherer predecessors. We prefer similarities, and changes can be challenging. Benefit notwithstanding, this results in hundreds of biases that can seriously skew our decision making, leading to unfairly treatments. That's why bias training has become one of the most critical topics in corporate agenda. In this chapter, we will discuss the nature of biases, look at some of the most common biases in the workplace, and get to know strategies in dealing with them.

8.1 The Neuroscience of Bias

In diversity terms, a stereotype is a fixed, oversimplified, overgeneralized, and possibly inaccurate belief about a particular social category or collective culture, for example Asians are good at maths, white men can't dance to rap music, women are masters of communication, and homosexuals excel in art. When stereotypes turn into a tendency, preference, or behavior, they become biases. Assuming that Asians are good at maths is stereotyping, but using this assumption or letting this assumption influence a hiring process means you are behaving in a biased way. Stereotypes almost always lead to biased behaviors.

8.1.1 The Evolutionary Root of Bias

Let's go back to Chapter 4 and the simplified system of System 1 and System 2. Biases are fundamentally products of the autopilot System 1, which is automatic, binary, and instinctive. Our ancestors were constantly coping with situations that required them to react quickly and avoid danger. A rattle in the bush could signal a poisonous snake or a dangerous predator, and it would be much wiser to run away, rather than stay and investigate what the curious noise is. Better safe than sorry. If they had wondered too long, we wouldn't have been here right now. Such a knee-jerk reaction is probably the *wrong response* 99.9 % of the time (there is, usually, no snake), but it only takes a single occasion for the guess to be correct to save a life.

Thus, biases are formed by connecting bits of *loose information* to reach a significant *whole*—something that gives us a meaning to act quickly. Our ancestors applied this rule to people too. Those who look and think alike automatically signaled patterns of ingroup and those who were different signaled patterns of potential outgroup. "Judging a book by its cover" was an effective survival skill back in the time on the savannah. This mental shortcut helps humans to retain knowledge using minimal thinking effort and provides us with a sense of structure to deal with an otherwise chaotic universe.[1] Thus, stereotyping and social biasing are negative outcomes, but the result is also crucial for survival functions. Some call it a "necessary evil," and that's a pretty good way to describe it.

8.1.2 The Modern Manifestation of Bias

In today's world, our problems are not predators, our decisions don't always involve matters of life and death, and those who look alike or different can be both friends and foes. However, we still receive the same automatic response using System 1. Subconsciously, we still judge people by the way they look, the language they speak, and the cultural background from which they come. Fitting people in boxes is such an instinctive response, to the extent that a minimal exposure of as little as 100 milliseconds is sufficient to draw a judgment about a stranger's face.[2] In the first few seconds of contact, we will have already answered four fundamental questions: (1) Do I like you? (2) Can I trust you? (3) Am I safe with you? (4) Who do you remind me of?[3] In short, we size up people literally from the first glance. We use their nonverbal cues, such as body language, clothes, skin color, gender, and makeup, to match with stereotypes and our own personal experiences. Employers often trust their first impressions more than objective tests.[4] An article in *Harvard Business Review* stated that when assessing individuals, 85 to 97% of professionals rely to some degree on intuition or a mental synthesis of information.[5] In an interesting study, two groups of students rated their teachers, one group after an entire semester of class interaction, and the other group only by watching several two-second video clips, without sound, of teachers who they had never met. The rating results of these two groups were very similar. This means first impressions are decisive, taking into account that the second group based their evaluation *solely on body language*, without hearing the voice or attending the lessons.[6]

In short, cultural biases are formed based on our previous experiences. We judge people with our own measurement of what is personally good or bad. We focus on what fits our patterns the most, and ignore other data. A rich line of research illustrates this notion. For example, back in 1957, researchers created a series of stereograms that made the viewers to have one eye exposed to a bullfight and the other eye to a baseball game. They found that the Mexican children tended to see the bullfight and the US children tended to see the baseball game even though they were simultaneously exposed to both scenes. In other words, they only saw what was more familiar to them and their culture.[7] This effect applies to other categories of culture as well. People see different things when looking at one object in different historical eras,[8] and women and men notice different aspects of a scene.[9] Here is a simple test you can try right now: How many letter Fs do you see in this sentence "Finished files are the result of years of scientific study combined with the experiences of years"? If you see only two or three, you are probably native or fluent English users. Your brain has skipped quite a few Fs (there are six) because you have been used to skipping Fs when they are not in important words. This is where your RAS is at work. It filters out unnecessary data before they are sent in for process (Chapter 5).

8.1.3 The Power of Bias

Stereotypes and biases are strong, to the extent that it is impossible *not* to have them. With the classic scenario of "lawyer-engineer,"[10] imagine you are in a room with 995 lawyers and five engineers. You are introduced to Jack, who is 45 years old with four children. He has little interest in politics or social issues, and is generically conservative. He likes sailing and mathematical puzzles. Is Jack a lawyer or an engineer?

Logically, 99.5 % of the chance, Jack is a lawyer. But, he fits the stereotype of an engineer. Researchers watched the volunteers' brains as they tried to decide whether Jack is a lawyer or an engineer, and they found that the ACC (error detector) lit up in *both* situations: Those who rationally conclude that Jack is a lawyer, and those who give in to biases and stereotypes, and think Jack is an engineer. Apparently, *we all detect the conflict* and recognize that it is completely out of sync with reality. But the comfort of the stereotype is so tempting that many of us choose to listen to it anyway. This experiment shows that even when our brain points out the bias, we still tend to go the easy way. We conduct a major part of our life with assumptions, going through the autopilot System 1 because it saves energy by using familiar neural patterns.

8.2 The Consequences of Biases

Biases shape the world around us, filtering data, distorting the reality, and bypassing logics. In a vicious circle, we use this perception to create new reality, data, and logics that perpetuate the original biases. The benefits of this tendency probably outweighed disadvantages in the early history of humans, but in the modern era, consequences are immense.

8.2.1 Biases Constrain Life Choice

Stereotypes put people in boxes (Latinos know how to have fun), and biases use the labels on these boxes to judge (Latinos are not serious with work). The main problem is, boxes don't mix and change, but human's life is dynamic. Every single one of us, sooner or later, will face a few options: Being forced into a box, being left out of the picture, or struggling to fit in a box that is not "meant" for us.

A good case in point is the numerous gender stereotypes with which we struggle. The overwhelming stereotype is that women are homemakers, that is generally, women want to be, should be, or have to be a caregiver. This social expectation hampers women, and they have to struggle much harder than their male counterparts to advance in some workplaces. Popular profiles present girls and women as young, thin, beautiful, passive, dependent, and often incompetent. At the same time, boys and men are portrayed as active, adventurous, powerful, sexually aggressive, and largely uninvolved in human relationships.[11] It perpetuates the false idea that a woman's purpose in life is to get married and make a home, and a man's mission is to escape any serious commitment. The consequence of such a biased thinking is tremendous. In a computer simulation, men and women start equally at the bottom of a hierarchy for promotion across eight levels. The men's performance was rated with only 1% higher than women. This tiny bit of bias quickly accumulated and resulted in a whopping 65% of men being promoted at the top level.[12] This study shows that a small bias of just 1% can lead to serious consequences (Table 8.1).

Likewise, men suffer from gender stereotypes as well. They are expected to defend and support their families; sacrifice their lives if necessary in the military; choose dangerous and exhausting occupations; work longer hours; and have less time for children and hence, less significant bond with them. These role stereotypes have become something that few of us bother to argue against. Societies trapped in these stereotypes fail to pay due respect and give equal opportunities to either half of the workforce. Businesses that don't recognize these biases fail to

Table 8.1 A tiny bias of 1% at the rank and file leads to an advantage of 30% at the management level (Martell, Lane, and Emrich [1996])

Level	Incumbent's Mean Score	Number of Positions	Percentage of Women
8	74.08	10	35
7	67.14	40	39
6	62.16	75	43
5	59.15	100	46
4	56.03	150	48
3	53.64	200	48
2	49.77	350	50
1	144.02	500	53

promote women who pursue serious careers, strive to be executives, desire to lead, and make an impact. At the same time, they also fail to see the immense stress and pressure of overworked men. This is the case of Ali (not his real name) from Pakistan. He grew up knowing he would have to work hard to take care of the whole family. He left his dream of becoming a cook and studied banking. He had no choice, but worked 12 hours a day for a job that was giving him serious mental and physical health problems.

It's well documented that there is a great gender and ethnicity pay gap, and those who deny this often argue that this is due to women's and minority's choices to enter low-paid jobs instead of discrimination. However, choice and discrimination are not mutually exclusive. Writer Joan Williams explained it excellently by a simple example: A black man, let's call him Jim Crow, walks up to two water fountains, one marked "Colored" and the other marked "Whites Only." He chooses to drink from the former. For sure he made a choice. But that *choice was made in the context of discrimination.* His choice probably reflected not that he preferred the fountain he drank from (a voluntary choice), but that he preferred not to get lynched (a choice within constraint).[13]

Researchers proved this in a study.[14] In an experiment, two groups of participants acted as hiring managers. Before the decision, one group read an essay about choices as voluntary options (e.g., women *choose* to become mothers, people *choose* to become obese by following a certain lifestyle). The other group read an essay about choices within constraints (e.g., women are *socially expected* to give birth and care for children, losing weight may be not be entirely under control for people with obesity due to factors such as biology). After reading, they had to decide on hiring a mother and child-free woman, a gay man and a straight man, a person of normal weight and a person with obesity—all pairs have the same work competence. Here is the result: The "choice" crowd recommended $6,429 less in salary for the mother, $4,667 less for the obese person, and $2,342 less for the gay candidate. They also rated these three candidates as less competent. In short, this study proves that mothers, gay men, and people with obesity are punished at work because they *choose* to be a mother, gay, and obese. It goes on to show that when marginalized groups choose certain jobs, that choice is made in the context of biases and never entirely a free will.

8.2.2 Poorer Performance

For those who are biased against, the situation can be more detrimental. *Stereotype threat* is a situation in which your performance is influenced by negative assumptions that others have about your collective culture, and hence, indirectly about you.[15] For example, women would perform mental rotation tasks *worse* if they were told men do better, and vice versa, men would perform *worse* if they were told women are superior.[16-17] Latinos and Latinas perform more poorly than do whites when a task is described as a diagnostic of intelligence because they suffer from the stereotype that their group is less educated.[18] Even privileged groups such as white men can't escape stereotype threats. If you told white men that, generally, they have *lower* athletic ability than black men, consequently, they would perform *worse* than those white men who were *not* made aware of this stereotype.[19] White men perform more poorly on math tests when they are told their result will be compared with that of Asian men.[20]

Thus, instead of putting more effort into solving a problem, we start to question our own ability and attribute this temporary failure to our age, race, gender, nationality, skin color, and so forth: "Why can't I do it? Is it because what people say is correct? Maybe the stereotype is correct! Oh dear! It *is* indeed correct!" In a self-fulfilling prophecy, this belief begins to guide our behaviors and, eventually, we internalize the idea, creating the reality that originally was just an idea, an idea that was not even correct.

This phenomenon also works in our interaction with others, for example, in job interviews. If you stereotype a candidate as intelligent, you will subconsciously act in a way that encourages an intellectual response. If you expect them to be dull, your behavior is likely to elicit this trait. For those who are free of stereotype threat, their brain's energy focused on problem solving.[21-22] On the contrary, for those who had been reminded of their inferiority, they are constantly under three neural disruptions that tax the working memory:[23] (1) A physiological stress response that directly impairs prefrontal performance; (2) a block against automated routines; and (3) efforts to suppress negative thoughts.[24-25] Thus valuable cognitive resources are spent on emotional regulation *rather than on the task at hand*. This, in turn, results in poorer performance.

8.2.3 Lack of Confidence

But poorer performance is only the detrimental consequence of biases on the surface. Confidence is the root cause. As a remnant of the evolutionary past, we tend to listen to those who display confident behavior, and not necessarily those with the most knowledge. Let's use gender bias as a case in point because it is a well-researched area.

Biases start early in childhood, shaped by children's literature.[26] For example, scientist men outnumber women three to one in textbooks,[27] 80 % of characters in Iran's textbooks are male,[28] and in Chinese social studies text, *all* scientists are male.[29] In a Turkish textbook for example, a girl is pictured dreaming of her wedding day while a boy imagines becoming a doctor.

At schools, the different kinds of feedback boys and girls receive shape their attitude at work later in their life. In a study that has now become classic in the field;[30] most of the mistake feedback boys received had nothing to do with intellectual aspects, so they learn to discount criticism from very young age and believe they are intellectually excellent (e.g., "The teacher tells me to dress neater. But she doesn't know I can read well"). On the contrary, most of the negative feedback girls received was about their competence, and less so due to a lack of effort, so they learned to take them seriously. Taking it all together, boys learn to *ignore criticisms* and *build confidence for their ability*. On the contrary, girls learn to *take criticism seriously*, associate mistakes with a *lack of ability*, and see *good behavior as a must* for quality. Facing a challenging task, boys think: "It's harder than I thought," while girls are prompted to think: "I'm not good enough."

Life at school and at home develops very different attitudes for girls and boys. Being a "good" girl is fervently rewarded (study hard, obedient, neat, thoughtful, attentive, great social adeptness, and a willingness to please). However, being a "good girl" transforms into an employee who is knowledgeable, resourceful, respectful, cautious, prudent, and nice—not a stereotypical leader in the competitive business world. On the contrary, boys get more chance to be rough and tumble in sports, verbal language, and social activities. They call out teacher attention eight times more often than girls, and they receive it because teachers think boys by nature are unruly and they need more attention.[31-32-33-34] The problem is that between the classroom and the office, *the rules change*. While that kind of attitude gives them more troubles at school, the very same approach to life serves them well in the male-dominated corporate world.

The result of this systematic bias is that girls leave school with much less confidence than boys. In a vicious circle, girls lose confidence, so they quit competing, thereby letting go of the very best way to regain it. In the United Kingdom for example, 50% of the female managers reported self-doubt, compared with 31% of male managers.[35] This self-doubt is the legacy of a biased upbringing. In an experiment,[36] test 1 showed equal ability between men and women who both scored 80%. In test 2, the researcher asked participants to report their confidence in their answer, and the performance changed instantly. The women's scores dipped to 75%, while the men's jumped to 93%. Thus, simply mentioning confidence destroys women's performance and reminds them of the stereotypes, while the very same little nudge reminds men that they're terrific and boosts their capacity.

With a lack of confidence, women have learned to make a decision only when they are totally sure of the result, to answer a question only when they know the best answer, to submit a report only when they have edited it carefully, and to apply for a promotion only when they are over-qualified. Where they should see failures as a lack of effort or luck, women have learned to see mistakes as a lack of capacity. They are less likely to criticize because women are supposed to be nice. These consequences accumulate, building up a cautious attitude that stops women from advancing ahead, holding back even overqualified and overprepared women.

It is important to note that accepted and culturally pervasive gender biases can be detrimental to men as well as to women. Men are more likely to experience burnout as a result of striving to be ideal defenders and providers. They frequently suffer from a lack of emotional support because they are discouraged from sharing a fuller range of emotions. They have a higher suicide rate and are more prone to drugs and unintentional accidents because they often lack emotional support. Most men die earlier than women due to an accumulation of these constraints along with being hired for more risky and dangerous occupations than women. In the Manhood diversophy game developed by George Simons and colleagues[37] to raise awareness on these issues, one author said: "Guns magnify the degree to which a boy who feels devoid of power and purpose, because he has not had his testosterone and intelligence constructively channeled by the love and discipline of his dad as a role model, can fantasize a moment of power to compensate for his black hole of *powerlessness*." Thus, though both women and men almost equally initiate domestic violence,[38] men have become almost exclusively the perpetrators of mass shootings. They constitute the vast majority of prison inmates, where they normally receive much stiffer sentences than women who may have committed the same crimes.[39]

Unlike women, when men have fragile self-esteem it is because they have been conditioned by cultural biases to measure their status through success in certain narrow aspects of life such as honor, money, and sexual prowess—factors often related to each other. Unfortunately, money and sex are among the most ambiguous, unpredictable, and least objective measures of life. Like women, men measure themselves according to the popular but mostly unrealistic images perpetrated by the media.[40] Not matching up to these is a major factor in depleting their confidence. A survey[41] of 2,000 British men aged 16 to 65 reported that men felt insecure at work (50%), around friends (40%), and during sex (25%). More than half of those questioned wished their "self-image" was more masculine. Three in four men admitted their lack of assurance as they got older and they were haunted by the conviction that other men are more confident than they are. A surprising one in five had lucky charms, with a third admitting they own "lucky" jewelry, one in four wearing auspicious socks, and one in five putting their faith in lucky pants.

The lack of confidence in men is not easy to detect, and thus, harder to deal with. When they doubt their confidence, they may drag others down—a behavior that is often mistaken for aggression. As men are not taught to express a full range of emotions and seek support, they put on a front and fake confidence, aggravating their problems. They "man up" and fail to access to appropriate solutions.

In this section, we have used the confidence gap in gender bias as a case study. However, the same issue happens in other types of bias as well such as assumptions about ethnicity and disability. Racism and ableism in early education[42] gradually result in detrimental consequences later in the workplace. People of color, those with immigrant backgrounds, followers of nonmainstream religions, and so forth are conditioned to think *less* of themselves due to cultural biases (e.g., blacks don't do well in academics; Latinos don't take work serious; Muslims can't control their anger; Asians don't excel in politics; whites are racist). This "soft bigotry of lower expectation" results in a lack of confidence when they enter the fields, causing a glass ceiling effect—you can see the goal but it is impossible to touch it. Likewise, so-called positive stereotypes (e.g., blacks are good at sports; Asians are good at math) may raise unfulfillable expectations of oneself that diminish confidence.

To conclude, confidence matters just as much as competence, if not more. The reason is that confidence leads to better performance, and vice versa. A person does a good job not entirely because (s)he is good at it, but because (s)he believes (s)he can do it. In turn, "doing" is the best way to improve competence. Lack of confidence discourages people to give it a try, and hence, takes away the only way to become good at it. The axiom, "fake it until you make it," may be negatively interpreted as putting up a front, but it is valid if it is understood as an encouragement "keep on trying," a confidence that success can be had.

8.3 Common Biases at Workplace

There are hundreds of bias categories. For example, *anchoring bias* causes us to use the first experience to judge the next (e.g., "I previously hired a Bulgarian and it turned out badly"). *Availability bias* prompts us to grab readily available data and make decisions rather than use relevant and insightful data, which will take longer to analyze (e.g., "My ex-boss told my current boss that her working style didn't quite match with mine. The new boss took it as fact and never gives me a chance"). *Status quo bias* keeps us from changes[43] (e.g., 95% of CEOs are men, so they are more likely to keep hiring men—an option that is less risky and preserves their authority). Because we can't possible list all biases here, in this section, we will look at the most common biases in the workplace that are the most detrimental for diversity.

8.3.1 Ingroup Bias

Naturally, ingroup or affinity bias is the most common one because, evolutionarily speaking, it signals who we can trust. We favor those who share similarities in ethnicity, gender, educational background, experience, hobbies, religion, or behavior.[44] While similarities initially act as a springboard to gain empathy and cooperation (Chapter 6), there are certainly disadvantages when it comes to objective decision making. In a 2016 study, 32% of participants reported using the applicant's religion as a source of evaluation, and Christians were rated more suitable for the job than Muslims and atheists.[45] Ingroup bias is the single biggest roadblock to diversity, simply because it *overuses* similarity and falls on the side of disadvantages.

Ingroup bias is what creates invisible bubbles such as men's club, women's group, or geeks' network. In these closed circles, members recruit similar people in new positions, sharing essential information with those who have the same identities, supporting each other while (sub) consciously discriminating others. One of the most obvious examples is all-male panels (or "*manel*") in management boards, hiring teams, decision-making processes, and conferences. In 2017, for example, an all-male White House passed a bill on women's health sparking outrage.[46] Similarly, we can see all-white/native panels dealing with multicultural audience, all-women panels deciding education of boys and men, all-elite panels solving problem of the poor, or all-Christian panels working on secular funding policies, and so forth. To take it one step further, this is not only the consequence of ingroup bias but also the result of a (sub)conscious belief that a certain cultural or biological trait exclusively decides work quality. We will look at this bias in the very next section.

8.3.2 Gender Bias

Strictly, gender bias is a combination of many forms of biases such as negativity bias and implicit associations. Gender bias based on the stereotypical belief of what men and women can do is one of the most pervasive biases in the workplace. Businesses (sub)consciously use genders as an indicator to search for qualities that fit their belief. As a result, men are discriminated against in stereotypically female jobs,[47] such as education and communication, especially if they had a part-time job in recent employment history.[48]

Vice versa, women are treated unfairly in jobs predominantly occupied by men. With the *same* CV sent to 1,029 hiring managers, those with the male name Simon were more likely to be called for an interview than those with the female name Susan. Analyzing 1.4 million users of an open-source program-sharing service, researchers found that code written by women has a higher approval rating than code written by men, but only if their gender is not identifiable.[49] Female lawyers with more masculine names, such as Barney, Dale, Leslie, and Rudell have better chances of winning judgeships. All else being equal, changing a candidate's name from Sue to Cameron tripled a candidate's likelihood of becoming a judge; a change from Sue to Bruce quintupled it.[50] It is worrying that big companies are *more* biased than small ones, and experienced recruiters are *more* biased than less experienced recruiters.[51]

Women are also more likely to be judged by their looks and how they dress than are their male counterparts. They are not only discriminated against for being "provocative" but also are discriminated against for being not pretty enough, too old, or, in some positions (especially sales and public relations), for not being sexy enough. In South Korea, *oemo jisang juui* (looks are supreme) is standard practice in hiring. Applicants are often asked to attach a photo in their resume. A study of 3,500 recruitment posts found that each included four discriminatory questions such as age, appearance, gender, birth region, marital status, and pregnancy. Some advertisements went so far as to ask for "pretty eyes," "high noses," or a bra cup size "C."[52] Facing intense competition for jobs with benefits, many applicants feel compelled to resort to dermatology or plastic surgery. It's not unusual that South Korean parents give their children surgery as graduation gifts.

Another gender issue, the "maternal bias," leads us to value those who *might* become pregnant and those with children as less capable and suitable for hiring.[53] With identical resume, compared to nonmothers, mothers are 79% less likely to be recommended for hire, half as likely to be recommended for promotion. They are offered an average of 7.4% less in salary.[54]

While women are held back by gender biases, men struggle too, as we already discussed in the previous section on the issue of "confidence gap." The social pressure on them to be provider and career-oriented makes it extremely challenging for men to change, even if they want. For example, fathers are often (sub)consciously forced to cut short their parental leave[55] because they are worried others may see it as a weakness, a sign of noncommitment, an unmanly thing to do, and a chance to be replaced by someone else who is more available.[56] There is a great deal of discussion on Sweden's daddy quota: Fathers get parental time off, and they lose it if they don't take it. This law also helps hiring managers to bypass their gender bias because male and female candidates will take the same parental leave when they have children.

The increased focus on women's right has also recently led to a controversial concern about men's exclusion. For example, in 2018, a women's organization was sued because it refused to accept men in a women-only camp on empowerment.[57] Some argue that a "men-only event" is out of question, but the same does not count for women. This is a complex issue that involves the understanding of *catching up with a historical power unbalance*. One can choose to see it as discrimination, but another way is to regard such move as a compensation act to create an equal playing field.

8.3.3 Competence-Likability Tradeoff

The competence-likability tradeoff forces people to choose between showing competence and gaining likability. Research on this bias has been abundant with regard to gender. For example, women are stereotypically perceived to be communal, nice, caring, and warm.[58] This presses them to take on office housework such as taking notes or organizing meetings.[59] If they refuse, they won't be seen as friendly colleagues or team players. When men performed such a task, they were rated 14 % more favorably than their female counterpart. When both declined, a woman was rated 12 % lower than a man.[60] Giving identical help, a man was more likely to be recommended for promotions, important projects, raises, and bonuses. A woman had to help just to get the same rating as a man who didn't help. Consequently, women often sacrifice themselves for the quest of helping others,[61] resulting in more burnout at work.[62]

The double standard applied for women and men plays a significant role at holding back women from advances in their career. An assertive woman is bossy but an assertive man shows leadership; an ambitious women is selfish but an ambitious man knows what he wants; a man is persuasive but a woman is pushy; a man is hard but a women is a bitch, and so forth. Thus, women are held back in leadership because they are viewed negatively in this role.[63-64] Having to produce results *and* be liked makes it harder for women to get hired, promoted, negotiated, lead, and avoid office housework. There is the fairy narrow space to fit in and they have to walk a tightrope between risking to be seen as either a doormat or a monster. It is a classic catch-22 for women in the professional world as a result of not being able to escape contradictory rules: How to be feminine and not soft, how to be masculine and not aggressive. If they don't speak up, they lag behind. If they act the same way as men, they are disliked.

Unsurprisingly, such a catch-22 can be found in other group categories as well. Minorities such as people of immigrant backgrounds, for example, often struggle between two kinds of expectations. On the one hand, they are conditioned to think *less* of themselves due to cultural biases (e.g., blacks don't excel in academics, Asians don't excel in politics). On the other hand, they are expected be successful, fulfilling the unofficial ambassador role of their ethnicity. Natives can behave badly and they are just idiots. Immigrants behave badly and the whole race could be blamed. But here is the twist. Minorities should do well, but *not too well* because it may threaten those who are still in power. As a Japanese Australian writer put it: "Be good, quiet, and assimilated."[65] It's a double catch-22. Do it well, people think it is normal. Do it badly, it's a sin you bring upon the whole group. Live down to the lower expectation, you just prove that minority is truly a lesser race. Live beyond the expectation and suddenly you are a threat. An essay in *The Atlantic* in 2015 illustrates this fine line pretty well with the title: "Being Black—but Not Too Back—in the Workplace."[66]

8.3.4 Minority Pool Bias

Minority pool bias causes us to negatively evaluate applicants from marginalized or nonmainstream demographics. It starts with trivial data such as a name. Because similarities and simplicity please our mind, being able to pronounce someone's name is directly related to how close you feel to that person. Our brains tend to believe that if something is difficult to understand, it must be risky.[67] In the United Kingdom for example, people with foreign-sounding names are a third less likely to be shortlisted for jobs than people with white-, British-sounding names.[68] Emily and Greg get callbacks almost 50 % more often than Lakisha and Jamal, even when they have exactly the same curriculum vitae.[69] Having a white-sounding name is worth about eight years of work experience. In fact, many Jewish Hollywood actors changed their names to sound more Christian such as Allen Konigsberg (Woody Allen) and Larry Zeiger (Larry King).

Biases against marginalized groups have serious consequences. In the United States, black men *without* criminal records receive similar call-back rates for interviews as white men just released from prison.[70] In India, the bias against Muslims has compelled some to pose as Hindus to get jobs.[71] Recruiters with biases can (sub)consciously twist merit to justify job discrimination by *redefining* criteria for success and use these new requirements as an excuse for rejecting the applicants they don't like.[72]

8.3.5 *Performance Attribution Bias*

Performance attribution bias occurs when we try to find a reason to justify certain outcomes or behaviors. In combination with stereotypes, this often leads to unjust evaluation of performance. For example, we may judge one group based on *capacity* (e.g., they did it well because they are brilliant) and other group on *external factors* (e.g., they did it well because they are lucky, have great mentors, and just work hard). We also judge one group on their *potential* (e.g., he has no experience, but he has what it takes) and another group on their *accomplishment* (e.g., he scores well, but he has little experience). Further, we judge the marginalized group harsher, so their mistakes will be remembered longer. This is evidenced in a study conducted with female scientists in which 77% of black women and 66% of other women said they had to "prove themselves over and over again."[73]

8.3.6 *Confirmation Bias*

When our ancestors lived in small bands of hunter-gatherers, analyzing what was right and what was wrong didn't add too many advantages. In contrast, winning arguments helped to bolster their social status. Hence, humans embraced the tendency to accept facts and opinions, which *reaffirm* our view, and reject those which challenge it, especially when we do not have the resources to counter such information.[74] Confirmation bias, hence, is the tendency to search for what confirms one's view, not what is factually correct. We do not see things as they are, we see thing as *we* are (Talmud Bavli).

The neural basis of confirmation bias is the same as self-fulfilling prophecy, as we discussed in Chapter 5. Acting as a filter of information, RAS is biased toward information that fits and confirms our thought. The brain even *distorts* facts to fit our beliefs.[75] For instance, female faces are perceived as "happy" and black male faces as "angry," even when the opposite is the case. This is the result of a society where women are constantly told to smile and black men are associated with masculine aggression.

Among similar candidates, those with nonverbal behaviors that *match the expectation* of recruiters stand out (the salience hypothesis).[76] HR executives may make their decision at the beginning of the job interview and spend the rest of the talk *reinforcing* their first impression (the reinforcement theory).[77] In a vicious circle, the recruiter's behaviors will cause the applicant to interact in a manner that *confirms* the recruiter's impression.[78] This means a candidate will show competence if s(he) is treated as a competent applicant with approval cues (smiling, nodding, eye contact, hand gestures, etc.), and vice versa.

In many cases, confirmation bias is implicit and a belief is subconscious. For example, support for Obama would have been 6% higher if he were white. In fact, he lost votes from those well-educated whites, who genuinely believe in racial equality, but unconsciously have no intention of voting for a black president. They may have criticized him for lack of experience, but this would not have been an issue if he were white.[79]

In other cases, when confirmation bias is explicit, facts and evidence only make their (wrong) belief *stronger*.[80-81-82] This "backfire effect" happens when facts threaten a worldview or self-concept. If someone strongly believes that males are bad at communication, Italian people are chaotic, Jews are calculative, millennials are ungrateful, or executives are exploitive and greedy then information and transparency that prove otherwise may even reinforce that belief. Confirmation bias is stronger than fact. Their brain only hears and sees what it wants to hear and see. This is the reason why a bias toward the negative in cross-cultural management can be harmful because if we believe that crossing a cultural border is problematic and differences mainly cause troubles, we set ourselves to select only evidences that fit our mindset (Chapter 5).

The brain helps along to filter out whatever contradicts that belief, and we can mine data selectively to continue that belief. Neuroscience proves this. In a study, the brain areas involved in processing information were more active when people observed positive messages from *ingroup* leaders, and negative messages from *outgroup* leaders.[83] Even when leaders gave contradictory statements, the brains of their followers would subconsciously pick messages that reflect their own belief.[84]

8.3.7 Halo Effect

The halo effect happens when positive feelings in one area influence opinion in another. For example, *heightism* leads us to favor tall people—a remnant of our evolutionary bias toward physically strong leaders who can protect us from danger. Tall men are perceived to be more dominant and of higher status,[85] leaders are expected to be 12% taller than their average citizen,[86] and an inch (2.5cm) is worth 1.8 % increase in wages.[87] Different features of primate's masculine prowess such as a wide mouth are also correlated with leadership selection.[88] The halo effect associated with physical suitability for combat is especially detrimental for women, people with disabilities, and those whose physical appearance does not match the stereotypes for leaders. A case in point is the US former president Franklin Roosevelt who had to use a wheelchair but decided to keep it a secret from the public.

Similarly, asymmetry in physical features evolutionarily signals health and fertility. To this day, this association lingers. Attractiveness affects perception tied to success, trustworthiness, friendliness,[89] humor, intelligence,[90] competence,[91] and leadership.[92] When having their essays evaluated, attractive writers received higher rating than unattractive ones. The gap is much bigger with essays of poor quality, suggesting that readers are more willing to give attractive people the benefit of the doubt when performance is below standard.[93] In the West, blond women earn an average of 7% more than women with other hair colors. This is because the association of blond hair with beauty outweighs the association of blond hair with lack of intelligence.[94]

In cultures where slim body is the norm, people with curvy figures suffer from the *devil* (or horn) effect, and are increasingly discriminated against (body/fat shaming). They are perceived as incompetent,[95] lazy, lacking willpower,[96] and less likely to get job.[97] They also receive lower salary,[98] especially women[99] who bear the brunt of both sexism and weight discrimination. However, black and Hispanic women tend to maintain strong self-esteem no matter what size they are, regardless of their income and education levels.[100]

Colorism is another example of the halo effect. A society full of sexism may connect "good" with "whiteness," resulting in the detrimental bias that lighter skin is seen to be more intelligent;[101] employers rated light-skin black men with bachelor degrees higher than dark-skin black men with MBAs;[102] educated black men become *lighter* in the observers' memory;[103] and women with lighter skin received less severe prison sentences than their darker peers.[104]

8.3.8 Intersectionality

"Intersectionality" is not a bias, but the effect of all biases combined in one individual. It reflects the relationship between identity and power, or the lack thereof. A gay person has to deal with homophobia, a person of color has to deal with racism, and a woman or man has to deal with sexism. But a nonwhite lesbian or gay has to deal with all these forms of discrimination *at the same time*. Adding ableism, ageism, or Islamophobia to that list, one can start to imagine why categories unfairly simplify the complexity of a human being: "Being a person with an intersectional identity is like standing in the middle of the road being hit by cars from many sides."[105]

8.4 Dealing with Biases

While it is impossible to rid of biases, with the capacity for culture, we are not prisoners of these tendencies. Let's go back to the "lawyer-engineer" experiment. The bad news is that we tend to follow easy stereotypes even though our brain did signal the mistake. The good news is that the ACC lights up regardless of the result, and we *do* see the biases. By the means of social learning, we have overcome the worst aspects of our nature. We may not be born ready to assess facts and arguments carefully, but we are capable of learning from mistakes, choosing from the best ideas, and reducing the impact of impulsive reactions. It's impossible to overemphasize that we are able to reshape the culture by adopting strategic behaviors (GCEB-Be: Behavior—Culture pathway).

In this section, we will use STREAP-Be—a model for change management discussed in Chapter 7—and explore many ways we can change a culture of negative biases into a culture of inclusiveness and understanding.

8.4.1 The "S" of STREAP-Be: Safety

8.4.1.1 Acknowledge Biases

Nobody likes to be called sexist or racist. This label attacks a person's dignity. Yet, nobody can escape it entirely. Therefore, the first step is to make people feel safe by acknowledging that, despite awareness and good intention, we all have biases. A good start is the popular and free Implicit Association Test (IAT), which basically gives us a statistical result of how racist, sexist, homophobic, and so forth we are. IAT is developed by Mahzarin Banaji—a Harvard professor who experienced firsthand how her light skin made her more marriageable in her South Indian community (the halo effect). IAT is excellent in detecting subconscious biases that we think we could never have. For example, Melissa (not her real name) is an expert who has developed some expertise in Islamic culture, lived and traveled extensively in the Middle East, written articles and books about Muslims, worked closely with colleagues from Indonesia to Morocco, vocally protested against any forms of Islamophobia, and so forth. Yet, she was shocked to find out she had a light subconscious bias *against* Muslims. This means despite personal experience, the result of IAT can be opposite because we are constantly bombarded by data that tells us otherwise. IAT and bias training help us to unveil this hidden conflict.

8.4.1.2 Unconscious Bias Training

Implicit biases are not visible. We don't know we have them. We even deny we have them. We get extremely offended when accused of having them because we oppose such an idea. This is exactly the reason why implicit bias is more harmful and widespread, as we hurt others unknowingly. Unconscious bias training reveals this uncomfortable truth in a safe way, and hence, has become the cornerstone in corporate diversity programs and the biggest corporate training trend lately. In a show of goodwill, both Google and Facebook have made their training available for public.[106-107] It is also important to create a safe forum for people to talk about their biases in a *nonconfronting and understanding atmosphere*.

8.4.2 The "T" of STREAP-Be: Trigger

8.4.2.1 Expose to Counterstereotypes

A great deal of our biases is *socially constructed*, based on the available social cues around us that will act as triggers to evoke biases (e.g., young black men with hoodies trigger the bias that they can be aggressive). While we can't eliminate this impulsive reaction, what we can do is consciously regulate those "available social cues and triggers." In essence, we can fight the subconscious mechanism of bias by consciously reminding ourselves of the opposite, purposely reaching out to the stories that tell otherwise. By doing so, we are actively *alternating* the "available triggers" around us, creating a new direct culture. The influence of counterstereotypical examples is so powerful that even a picture of "This is Rebecca. She is a bricklayer." or "This is Christopher. He is a makeup artist." can help to overcome spontaneous gender bias.[108] More interestingly, this can also be done just by *imagining* a counterstereotype. In a series of experiments, participants were asked to imagine a "strong woman." Their subsequent bias test showed that this simple mental exercise *lowered* their level of implicit sexism.[109]

The implication of this study is promising, as there are many ways organizations can do to regulate the social triggers and gear them toward supporting a target culture. For example, if a business is fighting a bias against workers with foreign backgrounds, ideas of counterstereotypes are endless: Calculate their contribution in concrete number; highlight their stellar performance; narrate their life achievements and struggles; invite external keynote speakers of the same background; put posters of counter-stereotype image in the hallway, and so forth. These tactics not only alternate available social cues and triggers but also boost the confidence, which in turn will increase the performance.

8.4.2.2 Call Out Biases

If the destructive power of biases is that they are implicit and subconscious, then we need to *purposely make it conscious*. One way to do this is to create an environment where biases can be exposed, people have to justify their decisions, and everyone is constructively vigilant against any signals or triggers of biases. We need to show *explicit* conscious efforts to challenge such *subconscious* impulses. We can reduce these automatic mechanisms by purposely looking twice. The more we are aware of it, the better we can overcome it. And the best way to be aware is to have more eyes watching. Biases can be overcome collectively. There is evidence that when we are told "Hey, you are biased" we can self-correct.[110] This kind of trigger will make us think harder about what we want to say, holding us accountable for what we say and do. Such culture has shown impact at Google where a panel of all men was reminded of the potential bias when they were evaluating female employees.[111]

However, it is important to differentiate between such an open culture with one that is *threatening*. Psychologically, it takes incredible courage to admit that we are wrong. "Backfire" happens when people feel they are being cornered. The more threatened they feel, the less likely they are to listen to dissenting opinions, and the more easily controlled they will be. It's hard to overemphasize that psychological safety is the condition for any effort in diversity to show effect. The last thing we want is to create threatening triggers by calling outs biases in a way that make people feel intimidated and terrorized.

8.4.3 The "R" of STREAP-Be: Reward

8.4.3.1 Recognize Effort to Overcome Biases

Victories over biases are often measured by how diverse a corporate culture has become, the percentage of employees from ethnic backgrounds, women/men, sexual orientations and disability. This helps to change the trigger. The process can be sped up if we add reward to the recipe, for example, by recognizing managers and teams who have achieved the diversity goals and beyond, who have the courage to open up and start the dialogue, who come with an inclusive solution, who foster a supportive and understanding working environment, and so forth.

8.4.3.2 *Highlight the Capacity to Override Biases*

Bias training often gives the impression that we are hopeless with biases. Neuroscientists have long suggested and demonstrated that we don't quite have absolute free will.[112-113] Based on our memory and experience, the brain commits to certain decisions *before* we become aware of those thoughts. When we decide to do something, our brain already initiated that process 0.3 second before our conscious mind recognized the intention to act. In other words, unconscious brain activities lead up to conscious decisions. We feel we choose, but we don't. Human agency is not composed of conscious choices. What we often think of as intentional, deliberate, purposeful action is very well the result of training unconscious habits after a long period. Playing piano is intentional, but each key press could be initiated unconsciously based on previous practice. Making a decision on who to hire is intentional, but every tiny bit of thought that led to that decision could be the result of many habitual subconscious neural patterns accumulated over time.

As a result, a dangerous phenomenon has been recently revealed by researchers: It turns out that educating people about the deleterious effects of biases can be counterproductive. Being exposed to the prevalence of stereotypes, people learn to *normalize* these unfair treatments, making biases a norm, in effect encouraging rather than discouraging the promulgation of biases.[114] If a person knows that everyone (s)he is communicating with has biases, (s)he would be less likely to change her/his own biases for fear of being taken advantage of. Men who are (now) aware of their stereotypical negotiation manner (competitive) can purposefully act even more assertive because they know it simply works for their own benefit. The downside of awareness is that people can abuse it. Further, if we all have biases, and it is almost impossible to escape this tendency, what's the point of fighting it?

The advice from researchers is that to reduce biases, organizations have to highlight the incredible ability and willingness of people to win over biases rather than merely informing them about their prevalence.

However, it doesn't mean we are trapped with the unconscious. The brain is evolutionarily conditioned to stereotyping and prejudice, but it also has the power to recognize and override those biases, as long as we can focus and train the brain.

In Figure 8.1, from the moment we are aware of the desire to act, it then takes us 0.2 second to reach the moment we execute the action. This 0.2 second is the window that we have conscious control over our voluntary action, the *veto power*. In the words of David Rock—a neuro-coach: "[W]hile we don't seem to have the ability to control our thoughts, we do have a say over which thoughts we act on. It seems we may not have much 'free will,' but we do have 'free won't'—the ability to not follow our urges."[115]

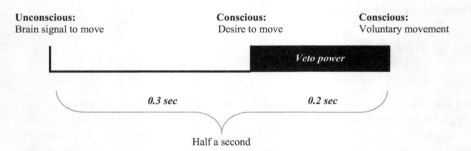

Figure 8.1 Veto power: Unconscious brain signals lead to conscious thoughts and behaviors (adapted from David Rock)

In short, combating biases is a fight we can win. But it requires more than just good intentions. We need to be focused to take advantage of the veto power. We cannot control biased thought but we have a *choice not to act on it.* More importantly, we need to actively change the surrounding environment and our habits, actively train the brain, thus, slowly reshape the unconscious brain signals that drive our decisions. We should remember that although we can't control our thoughts instantly, we can indirectly and gradually *control the environment that gives rise to those thoughts.*

8.4.4 The "E" of STREAP-Be: Emotion

8.4.4.1 Celebrate Success

In her book *What Works for Women at Work,* professor Joan Williams interviewed 127 female executives for insight into gender biases.[116] She suggested creating a "posse," which is a group of both men and women that regularly celebrates each other's successes. According to the author, this combats two significant biases marginalized groups face: Having their mistakes highlighted more than their successes (performance attribution bias) and receiving backlash for being decisive, masculine, and asserting themselves (attribution bias).

8.4.4.2 Boost Confidence

Confidence is a belief in one's ability to succeed, and it can get us far in life. In an experiment, students were asked to check historical names and events that they knew, among them also some fakes. Instead of leaving those fakes blank, there were students who did check them, meaning they simply lied or genuinely believed they knew more than they did. At the end of the semester, those very students were evaluated the most favorably among their peers for competence. It can be argued that overconfidence has helped those students to impress others and has stimulated them to give better performances. *Confidence and competence increase each other in a bidirectional way.* This is confirmed by another experiment[117] in which researchers randomly complemented some participants that they did well. In the next test, these were the people whose scores increased dramatically, and the impact of sex difference evaporated. Thus, confidence matters just as much as ability and it can be self-perpetuating.

There are many ways to boost confidence such as praises, rewards, public recognition, acknowledgment, feedback, constructive review, and so forth. It is beyond the scope of this book to discuss them. However, the indication that confidence overpowers gender difference is a strong guideline to deal with biases and others stereotype threats.

8.4.5 The "A" of STREAP-Be: Alignment

8.4.5.1 Be on the Same Side

If ingroup love is the origin of prejudices against others, it can also be the tactic to fight against it. A neural experiment shows that simply putting people in a mixed group reduces biases.[118] Another fMRI study shows that a group learning task that lasts 15 minutes can make white and Asian people become attached to each other that they would feel the pain of each other as if they were from the same racial background.[119] People form ingroup favoritism very easily, at the flip of a coin. We should remember that the amygdala doesn't see race, gender, or religion. *It only sees ingroup and outgroup.* The implication of such a study is powerful because it means we can form *new* ingroups to "cheat" the amygdala. It means we can deal with biases by the idea of *unity.* Organization can come up with a variety of teamwork, group projects, games, competitions, and so forth. This way we can benefit from the brain's capacity of super-quick group attachment, not on the basis of race, gender, religion, and professional background, but on the basis of whatever we want the new group to be.

8.4.6 The "P" of STREAP-Be: People

8.4.6.1 Role Model

Seeing is believing. Studies tell us that female students who see female science professors and experts are more interested and self-confident in STEM (science, technology, engineering, and math).[120-121] In India, gender gap in teen educational goal *disappeared* in areas with long-serving governmental female leaders.[122] In a very important study, researchers reported that the brain of white participants activated stronger when they interacted and imitated Africans, in comparison with Asians—a pattern that reflects differences in racial assumption among the white participants.[123] This means our brain is more alert, the learning process can be more effective, and we can fight biases better when we work with or receive training from those who are the victims of the bias.

8.4.7 The "Be" of STREAP-Be: Behavior

8.4.7.1 Collect Data

Collecting data is essential[124] because it is hard to improve what we can't measure. In the absence of information, we have a tendency to use stereotypes to fill the empty space. For example, when women and men are evaluated separately, women score equally (7.57) in comparison with men (7.33). But when they are collectively evaluated, women's work is evaluated with less quality (5.33) than that of men (6.50). This means that the less information we have, the more likely we are to rely on stereotypes.[125] Organizations that want to combat biases should build a database with not only the usual demographics but also continuous surveys and work records, which are useful indicators for areas that need improvement. By doing this, the available triggers that are the *material of biases* will be replaced by available triggers that help to *confront* them.

Collecting data is a good tactic for individuals as well, especially for those who suffer from the pressure of "prove-it-again" when they are evaluated based on achievement and not potential. Here are a few strategies suggested by researchers: (1) Keep a logbook of what you have accomplished, and present them in a timely fashion to the management as a reminder of your worth; (2) delegate office housework or rotate the responsibilities, for example instead of voluntarily taking notes, give it to an intern; (3) turn a request for help into a negotiation, for example mentoring a new colleague will be seen as a factor for promotion or a return of favor in the future; and (4) calculate your value, for example adding up all the hours you have spent on office housework or other unpaid tasks and transfer them into cost. Use that figure to negotiate for more resources.[126]

8.4.7.2 Ask "What If?"

Biases are fundamentally double standards that we use for different collective cultures and individuals. An effective way to check our biases is to swap the roles and ask ourselves: "*What if* that is applied to women/men/lesbians/ black/Asians/Latinas/old people/millennials, Jews, and so forth?" Consider this situation—one that triggers much annoyance among working mothers. A finance executive, let's call her Aisha, just comes back from her maternity leave. Everyone is excited, some sympathize to the extent that their remarks sound patronizing or subconsciously signal lower expectation: "You must be tired all the time. How can you do your job properly?"

"Do you need to share some responsibilities?" If we apply the "What if…" strategy, we would ask ourselves: "What if this is applied to a male executive? Would we ask him the same questions?" The answer is very likely no, which reveals our subconscious bias of seeing women as primary caregivers.

The same tactic can be applied to specific persons. Here is another example from real life. A project team consisted of three female coordinators from three different nationalities, working in the Netherlands: Dutch, Vietnamese, and Moroccan. When the team evaluated customers' feedback with the management, there were some complaints toward the Dutch coordinator, while there was a praise toward the Vietnamese coordinator. The Dutch coordinator explained herself and blamed external factors. Nobody objected to the Dutch coordinator, and nobody mentioned the praise for the Vietnamese coordinator either. Later on, the Moroccan coordinator reflected on this meeting: "What if the Dutch had got the praise and the Vietnamese had received complaints? Would the meeting have gone that way? Because I know for sure that if customers complained about me, I would be in big trouble. The management would never let me walk away with such a lame excuse. And if the Dutch had been complimented, the management would never have ignored it as if nothing happened."

8.4.7.3 Act

In a self-fulfilling prophecy, the belief in one's self stimulates action, and in turn, action bolsters the belief in one's ability to succeed. To test the hypothesis that "action" and "confidence" drive each other, researchers conducted a performance test of 3D images among men and women.[127] In test 1, women did worse than men because they had given up halfway and had not tried to solve all the puzzles. The researchers then ran the test again, this time telling everyone that they had to attempt every puzzle. The result: Women did just as well as men. Conclusion: Stereotype threats lead to low confidence, low confidence leads to inaction, and inaction leads to bad results. When people act, even if it's because they are forced to, their performance increases.

Thus, what dooms minorities and marginalized demographics is not their actual ability to do well, but the constant reminders from the surrounding culture that they are not that good. This stops them from trying—the only way to win back confidence. The strategy to deal with lack of confidence and stereotype threat is similar to the strategy to deal with fear: Action. Brain's plasticity means the more we do anything, the more our brains physically change to make that happen easily. Fear becomes worse by avoidance because it turns a thought or a brain signal into a perpetual and deeply connected neural pathway, or a habit. The best way to deal with fear is to look straight at fear in its face. If you fear public speaking, speak more. If you fear a senior manager because (s)he appears too standoffish, try every way to connect. Action calms the amygdala and engages the cortex. Repeated actions change the perception and values. If you keep at it, you can make your "brain more confidence-prone. What the neuroscientists call plasticity, we call hope."[128]

8.4.7.4 Reshape the Culture

The strategy of exposing ourselves to counterstereotypes means that we can't control our subconscious mind, but we can control the environment that gives rise to it. This also indicates we need to make a strategic choice. Facing an issue, for example, a bias that men are not as good in training roles as women, we can support the status quo (e.g., "Oh that's right, my manager can't mentor new hires. He just doesn't have enough patience."), or we can actively change the social cues that trigger that bias (e.g., "My manager is not [yet] a good mentor, but I will show him some role models which can encourage him to work on it.").

Here is another case from real life. We have learned that women are trapped in a catch-22 of competence-likability tradeoff. If they act as socially expected, they lag behind. If they act like men, they are disliked. We have the choice to maintain the status quo of the current corporate culture and tell women: "Speak up, even if that means people don't like you. You have only yourselves to blame, because that's how things work." In fact, this is basically the advice women hear most. An alternative choice is to gradually reshape the existing culture to make it inclusive, where both men and women feel safe and confident to optimize their performance.

The second choice takes time and effort, but it is obviously the way that our business world is heading. Corporate culture is dynamic, built, shaped, and reshaped to meet business goals. This reminds us of our role as authors of our own culture. At any moment that consciousness allows, we can either choose to be the product or producer of this culture. To make this choice is to decide if we want to be the "prisoner" or the "cocreator" of our experience. Because, very often, it's not our ability that defines us, but the choice we make.

Summary

1. Biases helped our ancestors with snap judgment on the savannah, but they can be unhelpful in the modern era.
2. Biases are strong because they are based on *survival instinct* and the brain's tendency to *save energy*.
3. The negative consequences of biases lead to unfair treatments, the pay gap, and the glass-ceiling effect for minorities and marginalized groups:
   - Negative biases shape social expectation, *constrain us* within limited life choices, discourage us to go beyond borders, and deny us opportunities to explore and develop.
   - Biases create stereotype threat, which decreases performance because energy is spent on *emotion regulation* instead of *tasks at hand*.
   - Biases create confidence gap, which decrease performance for some at the expense of others.
4. Here are some common negative biases at work:
   - *Ingroup bias* causes us to favor those who are like us, perpetuating the status quo.
   - *Gender bias* is based on what men and women can do and what they are socially expected to do.
   - *Competence-likability tradeoff* forces minorities to choose between (1) acting according to social norms but letting their career suffer, and (2) acting like those who are in power but letting their likability suffer.
   - *Minority pool bias* leads us to negatively evaluate those from marginalized demographics.
   - *Performance attribution bias* involves different standards for different groups. For example, one is judged on potential, the other is judged on accomplishment, forcing the latter to have to prove themselves over and over again.
   - *Confirmation bias* causes us to look for evidence that fits our (false) belief, prompting us to create a reality that fits that belief.
   - *Halo effect* causes us to link irrelevant physical traits with competence.
5. Bias management according to the STREAP-Be framework of cultural change:
   - *S for Safety.* Acknowledge that everyone has biases. Holding (sub)conscious biases doesn't mean we are bad people. Despite positive experiences, one can still have unconscious negative biases because data from surrounding culture tells us otherwise. Taking IATs and bias training are two safe methods to talk about biases in a nonthreatening environment.
   - *T for Trigger.* Expose yourself to counterstereotypes, prime the brain with alternative social cues that give rise to unconscious biased thought. Make new triggers by creating a vigilant culture where biases can be *safely* called out and discussed without fear.

- *R for Reward*: Highlight the capacity to win over biases. We cannot control biased thought but we have a choice not to act on it. Reward achievement in combating biases. Celebrate success.
- *E for Emotion*: Confidence leads to ability and ability leads to confidence. This vicious circle counteracts bias. Boost confidence with praises, recognition, review, feedback, and acknowledgment.
- *A for Alignment*: The amygdala doesn't see race, gender, or religion. It only sees ingroup and outgroup. We can create new ingroups to make the amygdala work for our purpose.
- *P for People*: Seeing is believing. Role models are one of the most critical factors to combat biases.
- *B for Behavior*: Collect data to measure impact of biases; to reveal double standards, practice role-switching by asking "What if...?" Take an action-oriented approach because repeated actions change self-perceptions and boost confidence. Take an active role to reshape culture, not reflect culture.

Notes

Don't forget to go to the end of the book for case studies.

1 Martin, Douglas., Jacqui Hutchison, Gillian Slessor, James Urquhart, Sheila J. Cunningham, and Kenny Smith. 2014. "The Spontaneous Formation of Stereotypes via Cumulative Cultural Evolution." *Psychological Science* 25(9): 1777–1786. doi:10.1177/0956797614541129.

2 Willis, Janine., and Alexander Todorov. 2006. "First Impressions: Making Up Your Mind after a 100-Ms Exposure to a Face." *Psychological Science* 17(7): 592–598. doi:10.1111/j.1467-9280.2006.01750.x.

3 Harris, Peter. 2015. "Four Things Employers Decide About You in Four Seconds." *Workopolis*. October 16. http://careers.workopolis.com/advice/first-impressions-four-things-employers-decide-about-you-in-four-seconds/

4 Dipboye, Robert L. 1994. "Structured and Unstructured Selection Interviews: Beyond the Job-Fit Model." *Research in Personnel and Human Resources Management* 12(79): 79–123.

5 Kuncel, Nathan R., Deniz S. Ones, and David M. Klieger. 2014. "In Hiring, Algorithms Beat Instinct." *Harvard Business Review*. May 1. https://hbr.org/2014/05/in-hiring-algorithms-beat-instinct.

6 Ambady, Nalini., and Robert Rosenthal. 1993. "Half a Minute: Predicting Teacher Evaluations from Thin Slices of Nonverbal Behavior and Physical Attractiveness." *Journal of Personality and Social Psychology* 64(3): 431–444. doi:10.1037/0022-3514.64.3.431.

7 Bagby, James W. 1957. "A Cross-Cultural Study of Perceptual Predominance in Binocular Rivalry." *The Journal of Abnormal and Social Psychology* 54(3): 331–334. doi:10.1037/h0046310.

8 Laqueur, Thomas W. 1990. *Making Sex: Body and Gender from the Greeks to Freud*. Cambridge, MA: Harvard University Press.

9 Powers, Peter A., Joyce L. Andriks., and Elizabeth F. Loftus. 1979. "Eyewitness Accounts of Females and Males." *Journal of Applied Psychology* 64(3): 339–347. doi:10.1037/0021-9010.64.3.339.

10 Neys, Wim De., Oshin Vartanian, and Vinod Goel. 2008. "Smarter Than We Think When Our Brains Detect That We Are Biased." *Psychological Science* 19(5): 484–489. doi:10.1111/j.1467-9280.2008.02113.x.

11 Adler, Nancy J. 1991. *International Dimensions of Organizational Behavior*, 74. 2nd ed. Boston: PWS-KENT.

12 Martell, Richard F., David M. Lane, and Cynthia Emrich. 1996. "Male-Female Differences: A Computer Simulation." *American Psychologist* (February): 157–158. www.ruf.rice.edu/~lane/papers/male_female.pdf.

13 Williams, Joan. 2013. "Pay Gap Deniers." *The Huffington Post*. August 6. www.huffingtonpost.com/joan-williams/pay-gap-deniers_b_3391524.html.

14 Kricheli-Katz, Tamar. 2013. "Choice-Based Discrimination: Labor-Force-Type Discrimination against Gay Men, the Obese, and Mothers." *Journal of Empirical Legal Studies* 10(4): 670–695. doi:10.1111/jels.12023.

15 Steele, Claude M., and Joshua Aronson. 1995. "Stereotype Threat and the Intellectual Test Performance of African Americans." *Journal of Personality and Social Psychology* 69(5): 797–811. doi:10.1037/0022-3514.69.5.797.

16 Moè, Angelica., and Francesca Pazzaglia. 2006. "Following the Instructions! Effects of Gender Beliefs in Mental Rotation." *Learning and Individual Differences* 16(4): 369–377. doi:10.1016/j.lindif.2007.01.002.

17 Spencer, Steven J., Claude M. Steele, and Diane M. Quinn. 1999. "Stereotype Threat and Women's Math Performance." *Journal of Experimental Social Psychology* 35(1): 4–28. doi:dx.doi.org/10.1006/jesp.1998.1373.

18 Gonzales, Patricia M., Hart Blanton, and Kevin J. Williams. 2002. "The Effects of Stereotype Threat and Double-Minority Status on the Test Performance of Latino Women." *Personality and Social Psychology Bulletin* 28(5): 659–670. doi:10.1177/0146167202288010.

19 Stone, Jeff., Christian I. Lynch, Mike Sjomeling, and John M. Darley. 1999. "Stereotype Threat Effects on Black and White Athletic Performance." *Journal of Personality and Social Psychology* 77(6): 1213–1227. doi:10.1037/0022-3514.77.6.1213.

20 Aronson, Joshua., Michael J. Lustina, Catherine Good, Kelli Keough, Claude M. Steele, and Joseph Brown. 1999. "When White Men Can't Do Math: Necessary and Sufficient Factors in Stereotype Threat." *Journal of Experimental Social Psychology* 35(1): 29–46. doi:10.1006/jesp.1998.1371.

21 Delazer, Margarete., Frank Domahs, Lisa Bartha, Christian Brenneis, Aliette Lochy, Thomas Trieb, and Thomas Benke. 2003. "Learning Complex Arithmetic—An fMRI Study." *Cognitive Brain Research* 18 (1): 76–88. doi:10.1016/j.neuroimage.2004.12.009.

22 Dehaene, S., E. Spelke, P. Pinel, R. Stanescu, and S. Tsivkin. 1999. "Sources of Mathematical Thinking: Behavioral and Brain-Imaging Evidence." *Science* 284(5416): 970–974. doi:10.1126/science.284.5416.970.

23 Schmader, Toni., Michael Johns, and Chad Forbes. 2008. "An Integrated Process Model of Stereotype Threat Effects on Performance." *Psychology Review* 115(2): 336–356. doi:10.1037/0033-295X.115.2.336.

24 Moran, Joe M., C. Neil Macrae, Todd F. Heatherton, Carrie L. Wyland, and William M. Kelley. 2006. "Neuroanatomical Evidence for Distinct Cognitive and Affective Components of Self." *Journal of Cognitive Neuroscience* 18(9): 1586–1594. doi:10.1162/jocn.2006.18.9.1586.

25 Somerville, Leah H., Todd F. Heatherton, and William M. Kelley. 2006. "Anterior Cingulate Cortex Responds Differentially to Expectancy Violation and Social Rejection." *Nature Neuroscience* 9(8): 1007–1008. doi:10.1038/nn1728.

26 Peterson, Janet.. 1996. "Gender Bias and Stereotyping in Young Adult Literature." *Children's Book and Media Review* 17(3). Article 2. https://scholarsarchive.byu.edu/cgi/viewcontent.cgi?referer=https://www.google.com.au/&httpsredir=1&article=1661&context=cbmr.

27 Kerkhoven, Anne H., Pedro Russo, Anne M. Land-Zandstra, Aayush Saxena, and Frans J. Rodenburg. 2016. "Gender Stereotypes in Science Education Resources: A Visual Content Analysis." *PLoS ONE* 11(11). doi:10.1371/journal.pone.0165037.

28 Amini, Mohadeseh., and Parviz Birjandi. 2012. "Gender Bias in the Iranian High School EFL Textbooks." *English Language Teaching* 5(2): 134–147. https://files.eric.ed.gov/fulltext/EJ1078900.pdf.

29 Blumberg, Rae Lesser. 2007. "Gender Bias in Textbooks: A Hidden Obstacle on the Road to Gender Equality in Education." Background paper. http://unesdoc.unesco.org/images/0015/001555/155509e.pdf.

30 Dweck, Carol S., William Davidson, Sharon Nelson, and Enna Bradley. 1978. "Sex Differences in Learned Helplessness: II. The Contingencies of Evaluative Feedback in the Classroom and III. An Experimental Analysis." *Developmental Psychology* 14(3): 268–276. http://psycnet.apa.org/record/1979-27278-001.

31 Sadker, Myra., and David Sadker. 1995. *Failing At Fairness: How Our Schools Cheat Girls*. New York: Scribner.

32 Sadker, Myra P., David Miller Sadker, and Karen Zittleman. 2009. *Still Failing at Fairness: How Gender Bias Cheats Girls and Boys in School and What We Can Do About It*. Rev. and updated ed. New York: Scribner.

33 Stevens, Kaily. 2015. "Gender Bias in Teacher Interactions with Students." Master of Education Program Theses. Paper 90. Dordt College, Sioux Center, IA. https://digitalcollections.dordt. edu/cgi/viewcontent.cgi?referer=https://www.google.com.au/&httpsredir=1&article=1089& context=med_theses

34 Rothchild, Jennifer. 2006. *Gender Trouble Makers: Education and Empowerment in Nepal*. New York: Routledge.

35 ILM. 2014. *Ambition and Gender at Work*. https://30percentclub.org/wp-content/uploads/ 2014/08/ILM_Ambition_and_Gender_report_0211-pdf.pdf.

36 Estes, Zachary., and Sydney Felker. 2012. "Confidence Mediates the Sex Difference in Mental Rotation Performance." *Archives of Sexual Behavior* 41(3): 557–570. doi:10.1007/ s10508-011-9875-5.

37 Diversophy. 2019. https://diversophy.com/.

38 Whitaker, Daniel J., Tadesse Haileyesus, Monica Swahn, and Linda S. Saltzman. 2007. "Differences in Frequency of Violence and Reported Injury between Relationships with Reciprocal and Nonreciprocal Intimate Partner Violence." *American Journal of Public Health* 97(5): 941–947. doi:10.2105/ajph.2005.079020.

39 Starr, Sonja B. 2012. "Estimating Gender Disparities in Federal Criminal Cases," 1–32. Research paper. University of Michigan Law School.

40 Thomas, Sam. 2014. "21st Century Britain: Are Men More Body Anxious Than Women?" *HuffPost UK*. August 5. www.huffingtonpost.co.uk/sam-thomas/male-body-image-b_ 5456186.html?utm_hp_ref=uk-health.

41 Hill, Amelia. 2008. "Men Lack Confidence in Boardroom and Bedroom." *The Guardian*. December 7. www.theguardian.com/world/2008/dec/07/men-low-esteem-work-bedroom.

42 CRDC. 2014. *School Discipline, Restraint, and Seclusion Highlights*. US Department of Education Office for Civil Rights. https://ocrdata.ed.gov/downloads/crdc-school-discipline-snapshot.pdf

43 Samuelson, William., and Richard Zeckhauser. 1988. "Status Quo Bias in Decision Making." *Journal of Risk and Uncertainty* 1(1): 7–59. doi:10.1007/BF00055564.

44 Eagleson, Geoff., Robert Waldersee, and Ro Simmons. 2000. "Leadership Behaviour Similarity as a Basis of Selection into a Management Team." *Social Psychology* 39 (2): 301–308. doi:doi.org/ 10.1348/014466600164480.

45 Camp, Debbie Van., Lloyd R. Sloan, and Amanda Elbassiouny. 2016. "People Notice and Use an Applicants Religion in Job Suitability Evaluations." *The Social Science Journal* 53(4): 459–466. doi:10.1016/j.soscij.2016.02.006.

46 BBC. 2017. "All-Male White House Health Bill Photo Sparks Anger." *BBC News*. March 24. www.bbc.com/news/world-us-canada-39375228.

47 Riach, Peter A., and Judith Rich. 2006. "An Experimental Investigation of Sexual Discrimination in Hiring in the English Labor Market." *Advances in Economic Analysis and Policy* 5(2): 169– 185. doi:10.2202/1538-0637.1416.

48 Pedulla, David S. 2016. "Penalized or Protected? Gender and the Consequences of Nonstandard and Mismatched Employment Histories." *American Sociological Review* 81(2): 262–289. doi:10.1177/0003122416630982.

49 Terrell, Josh., Andrew Kofink, Justin Middleton, Clarissa Rainear, Emerson Murphy-Hill, Chris Parnin, and Jon Stallings. 2017. "Gender Differences and Bias in Open Source: Pull Request Acceptance of Women Versus Men." *PeerJ Computer Science* 3: e111. doi:10.7717/peerj-cs.111.

50 Coffey, Bentley., and Patrick McLaughlin. 2009. "From Lawyer to Judge: Advancement, Sex, and Name-Calling." Working paper. www.abajournal.com/files/NamesNLaw.pdf.

51 HAYS and InsyncSurveys. 2014. "Gender Diversity Why Aren't We Getting It Right: Research and Insights That Impact Your World of Work. " www.insyncsurveys.com.au/media/128377/ 2014-10-1_hays_insync_gender_diversity_white_paper_web__1_.pdf.

52 Stiles, Matt. 2017. "In South Korea's Hypercompetitive Job Market, It Helps to Be Attractive." *Los Angeles Times*. June 13. http://beta.latimes.com/world/asia/la-fg-south-korea-image- 2017-story.html.

53 Correll, Shelley J., Stephen Benard, and In Paik. 2007. "Getting a Job: Is There a Motherhood Penalty?" *American Journal of Sociology* 112(5): 1297–1339. http://gender.stanford.edu/sites/ default/files/motherhoodpenalty.pdf.

54 Ibid.

55 Hall, Jason. 2013. "Why Men Don't Take Paternity Leave." *Forbes*. June 14. www.forbes.com/ sites/learnvest/2013/06/14/why-men-dont-take-paternity-leave/#4c470eed1bd7.

56 Werber, Cassie. 2016. "A Year after the UK Created Near-Equal Parental Leave, Women Still Do Almost All the Parenting." *Quartz*. April 21. https://qz.com/659022/a-year-after-the-uk-created-near-equal-parental-leave-women-still-do-almost-all-the-parenting/.

57 Holman, Jordyn. 2018. "Men Cry Discrimination in Legal Attack on Women's Organizations." May 11. www.bloomberg.com/news/articles/2018-05-11/men-cry-discrimination-in-legal-attack-on-women-s-organizations.

58 Koenig, Anne M., Alice H. Eagly, Abigail A. Mitchell, and Tiina Ristikari. 2011. "Are Leader Stereotypes Masculine? A Meta-Analysis of Three Research Paradigms." *Psychological Bulletin* 137(4): 616–642. doi:10.1037/a0023557.

59 Kanter, Rosabeth Moss. 1993. *Men and Women of the Corporation: New Edition*. 2nd ed. New York: Basic Books.

60 Heilman, Madeline E., and Julie J. Chen. 2005. "Same Behavior, Different Consequences: Reactions to Men's and Women's Altruistic Citizenship Behavior." *Journal of Applied Psychology* 90(3): 431–441. doi:10.1037/0021-9010.90.3.431.

61 Helgeson, Vicki S., and Heidi L. Fritz. 1998. "A Theory of Unmitigated Communion." *Personality and Social Psychology Review* 2(3): 173–183. doi:10.1207/s15327957pspr0203_2.

62 Purvanova, Radostina K., and John P. Muros. 2010. "Gender Differences in Burnout: A Meta-Analysis." *Journal of Vocational Behavior* 77(2): 168–185. doi:10.1016/ j.jvb.2010.04.006.

63 McGinn, Kathleen L., and Nicole Tempest. 2010. "Heidi Roizen." Harvard Business School Case 800-228, Revised. January. www.hbs.edu/faculty/Pages/item.aspx?num=26880.

64 Brescoll, Victoria L. 2011. "Who Takes the Floor and Why." *Administrative Science Quarterly* 56(4): 622–641. doi:10.1177/0001839212439994.

65 Fukui, Masako. 2018. "Being a Good, Quiet and Assimilated 'Model Minority' Is Making Me Angry." *The Guardian*. July 28. www.theguardian.com/world/2018/jul/28/ being-a-good-quiet-and-assimilated-model-minority-is-making-me-angry.

66 Wingfield, Adia Harvey. 2015. "Being Black—but Not Too Black—in the Workplace." *The Atlantic*. October 14. www.theatlantic.com/business/archive/2015/10/being-black-work/ 409990/.

67 Song, Hyunjin., and Norbert Schwarz. 2009. "If It's Difficult to Pronounce, It Must Be Risky: Fluency, Familiarity, and Risk Perception." *Psychological Science* 20(2): 135–138. doi:10.1111/j.1467-9280.2009.02267.x.

68 ENAR. 2014. "Shadow Report on Racism and Discrimination in Employment: No Equal Opportunities in Jobs for Ethnic and Religious Minorities in Europe." March 17. www.enar-eu.org/ENAR-Shadow-Report-on-racism.

69 Bertrand, Marianne., and Sendhil Mullainathan. 2004. "Are Emily and Greg More Employable Than Lakisha and Jamal? A Field Experiment on Labor Market Discrimination." *American Economic Review* 94(4): 991–1013. doi:10.1257/0002828042002561.

70 Pager, Devah. 2003. "The Mark of a Criminal Record." *American Journal of Sociology* 108(5): 937–975. doi:10.1086/374403.

71 Rahman, Shaikh Azizur. 2012. "Indian Muslims Pose as Hindus to Get Jobs." *ABC News*. October 31. www.abc.net.au/news/2012-10-31/an-indian-muslims-dress-as-hindus-to-avoid-discrimination/4343462.

72 Uhlmann, Eric Luis., and Geoffrey L. Cohen. 2005. "Constructed Criteria Redefining Merit to Justify Discrimination." *American Psychological Science* 16(6): 474–480. doi:10.1111/ j.0956-7976.2005.01559.x.

73 Williams, Joan C., Katherine W. Phillips, and Erika V. Hall. 2015. "Double Jeopardy? Gender Bias against Women of Color in Science." *UC Hastings College of the Law*. www.uchastings.edu/ news/articles/2015/01/double-jeopardy-report.pdf.

74 Sherman, Jeffrey W., Frederica R. Conrey, and Carla J. Groom. 2004. "Encoding Flexibility Revisited: Evidence for Enhanced Encoding of Stereotype-Inconsistent Information under Cognitive Load." *Social Cognition* 22(2): 214–232. doi:10.1521/soco.22.2.214.35464.

75 Stolier, Ryan M., and Jonathan B. Freeman. 2016. "Neural Pattern Similarity Reveals the Inherent Intersection of Social Categories." *Nature Neuroscience* 19(6): 795–797. doi:10.1038/nn.4296.

76 Forbes, Ray J., and Paul R. Jackson. 1980. "Non-Verbal Behaviour and the Outcome of Selection Interviews." *Journal of Occupational Psychology* 53(1): 65–72. doi:10.1111/j.2044–8325.1980. tb00007.x.

77 Webster, Edward C., and Clifford Wilfred Anderson. 1964. *Decision Making in the Employment Interview*. Montreal: Industrial Relations Centre, McGill University.

78 Darley, John M., and Russel H. Fazio. 1980. "Expectancy Confirmation Processes Arising in the Social Interaction Sequence." *American Psychologist* 35(10): 867–881. doi:10.1037/ 0003-066X.35.10.867.

79 Kristof, Nicholas D. 2008. "Racism without Racists." *The New York Times*. October 5. www. nytimes.com/2008/10/05/opinion/05kristof.html.

80 Tavris, Carol, and Elliot Aronson. 2007. *Mistakes Were Made (but Not by Me): Why We Justify Foolish Beliefs, Bad Decisions, and Hurtful Acts*. New York: Houghton Mifflin Harcourt.

81 Ecker, Ullrich., Stephan Lewandowsky, Briony Swire, and Darren Chang. 2011. "Correcting False Information in Memory: Manipulating the Strength of Misinformation Encoding and Its Retraction." *PubMed* 18(3): 570–578. doi:10.3758/s13423-011-0065-1.

82 Nyhan, Brendan., and Jason Reifler. 2010. "When Corrections Fail: The Persistence of Political Misperceptions." *Political Behavior* 32(2): 303–333. doi:10.1007/s11109-010-9112-2.

83 Molenberghs, Pascal., Guy Prochilo, Niklas K. Steffens, Hannes Zacher, and S. Alexander Haslam. 2015. "The Neuroscience of Inspirational Leadership: The Importance of Collective-Oriented Language and Shared Group Membership." *Journal of Management* 43(7): 1–27. doi:10.1177/ 0149206314565242.

84 Westen, Drew., Pavel S. Blagov, Keith Harenski, Clint Kilts, and Stephan Hamann. 2006. "Neural Bases of Motivated Reasoning: An fMRI Study of Emotional Constraints on Partisan Political Judgment in the 2004 US Presidential Election." *Journal of Cognitive Neuroscience* 18(11): 1947–1958. doi:10.1162/jocn.2006.18.11.1947.

85 Brewer, Gayle., and Charlene Riley. 2009. "Height, Relationship Satisfaction, Jealousy, and Mate Retention." *Evolutionary Psychology* 7(3): 477–489. doi:10.1177/147470490900700310.

86 Murray, Gregg., and David Schmitz. 2011. "Caveman Politics: Evolutionary Leadership Preferences and Physical Stature." *Social Science Quarterly* 92(5): 1215–1235. doi:10.1111/ j.1540-6237.2011.00815.x.

87 Persico, Nicola., Andrew Postlewaite, and Dan Silverman. 2004. "The Effect of Adolescent Experience on Labor Market Outcomes: The Case of Height." *Journal of Political Economy* 112(5): 1019–1053. doi:10.1086/422566.

88 Re, Daniel E., and Nicholas O. Rule. 2016. "The Big Man Has a Big Mouth: Mouth Width Correlates with Perceived Leadership Ability and Actual Leadership Performance." *Journal of Experimental Social Psychology* 63: 86–93. doi:10.1016/j.jesp.2015.12.005.

89 Wade, T. Joel., and Cristina DiMaria. 2003. "Weight Halo Effects: Individual Differences in Perceived Life Success as a Function of Women's Race and Weight." *Sex Roles* 48(9/10): 461–465. doi:10.1023/A:1023582629538.

90 Moore, F. R., D. Filippou, and D. Perrett. 2011. "Intelligence and Attractiveness in the Face: Beyond the Attractiveness Halo Effect." *Journal of Evolutionary Psychology* 9(3): 205–217. doi:10.1556/JEP.9.2011.3.2.

91 Palmer, Carl L., and Rolfe D. Peterson. 2012. "Beauty and the Pollster: The Impact of Halo Effects on Perceptions of Political Knowledge and Sophistication." Paper presented at the Annual Meeting of the Midwest Political Science Association. http://web.archive.org/web/ 20140309023825/http://cas.illinoisstate.edu/clpalme/research/documents/Beauty_and_ the_Pollster_revision.pdf.

92 Verhulst, Brad., Milton Lodge, and Howard Lavine. 2010. "The Attractiveness Halo: Why Some Candidates Are Perceived More Favorably Than Others." *Journal of Nonverbal Behavior* 34(2): 111–117. doi:10.1007/s10919-009-0084-z.

93 Landy, David., and Harold Lanzetta Sigall. 1974. "Task Evaluation as a Function of the Performers' Physical Attractiveness." *Journal of Personality and Social Psychology* 29(3): 299–304. doi:10.1037/h0036018.

94 Johnston, David W. 2010. "Physical Appearance and Wages: Do Blondes Have More Fun?" *Economics Letters* 108(1): 10–12. doi:10.1016/j.econlet.2010.03.015.

95 Levine, Emma E., and Maurice E. Schweitzer. 2015. "The Affective and Interpersonal Consequences of Obesity." *Organization Behavior and Human Decision Process* 127: 66–84. doi:10.1016/j.obhdp.2015.01.002.

96 Perelman School of Medicine at the University of Pennsylvania. 2017. "Fat Shaming Linked to Greater Health Risks." *ScienceDaily*. January 26. www.sciencedaily.com/releases/2017/01/170126082024.htm.

97 Flint, Stuart W., Martin Čadek, Sonia C. Codreanu, Vanja Ivić, Colene Zomer, and Amalia Gomoiu. 2016. "Obesity Discrimination in the Recruitment Process: 'You're Not Hired!'" *Frontiers in Psychology* 7(647). doi:10.3389/fpsyg.2016.00647.

98 Schulte, Paul A., Gregory R. Wagner, Aleck Ostry, Laura A. Blanciforti, Robert G. Cutlip, Kristine M. Krajnak, Michael Luster et al. 2007. "Work, Obesity, and Occupational Safety and Health." *American Journal of Public Health* 97(3): 428–436.

99 Shinall, Jennifer Bennett. 2015. "Occupational Characteristics and the Obesity Wage Penalty." Vanderbilt Law and Economics Research Paper No. 16-12; Vanderbilt Public Law Research Paper No. 16–23. doi:10.2139/ssrn.2379575.

100 Angier, Natalie. 2000. "Who Is Fat? It Depends on Culture." *The New York Times*. November 7. www.nytimes.com/2000/11/07/science/who-is-fat-it-depends-on-culture.html.

101 Hannon, Lance. 2015. "White Colorism." *Social Currents* 2(1): 13–21. doi:10.1177/2329496514558628.

102 Harrison, Matthew S., and Kecia M. Thomas. 2009. "The Hidden Prejudice in Selection: A Research Investigation on Skin Color Bias." *Journal of Applied Social Psychology* 39(1): 134–168. doi:10.1111/j.1559-1816.2008.00433.x.

103 Ben-Zeev, Avi., Tara C. Dennehy, and Robin I. Goodrich. 2014. "When an 'Educated' Black Man Becomes Lighter in the Mind's Eye Evidence for a Skin Tone Memory Bias." *SAGE Open* 4(1): 1–9. doi:10.1177/2158244013516770.

104 Viglione, Jill., Lance Hannon, and Robert DeFina. 2011. "The Impact of Light Skin on Prison Time for Black Female Offenders." *The Social Science Journal* 48(1): 250–258. doi:10.1016/j.soscij.2010.08.003.

105 "How to Be Better: On Intersectionality, Privilege and Silencing." 2012. *Stavvers*. October 22. https://stavvers.wordpress.com/2012/10/22/how-to-be-better-on-intersectionality-privilege-and-silencing/.

106 GoogleVentures. 2014. YouTube. September 25. https://www.youtube.com/watch?v=nLjFTHTgEVU.

107 Facebook. 2018. "Managing Unconscious Bias." *Managing Bias Facebook*. https://managingbias.fb.com/.

108 Finnegan, Eimear., Jane Oakhill, and Alan Garnham. 2015. "Counter-Stereotypical Pictures as a Strategy for Overcoming Spontaneous Gender Stereotypes." *Frontiers in Psychology* 6(1291). doi:10.3389/fpsyg.2015.01291.

109 Blair, Irene V., Jennifer E. Ma, and Alison P. Lenton. 2001. "Imagining Stereotypes Away: The Moderation of Implicit Stereotypes through Mental Imagery." *Journal of Personality and Social Psychology* 81(5): 828–841. doi:I0.1037//0022-3514.81.5.828.

110 Monteith, Margo J., Aimee Y. Mark, and Leslie Ashburn-Nardo. 2010. "The Self-Regulation of Prejudice: Toward Understanding Its Lived Character." *Group Processes and Intergroup Relations* 13: 183–200. doi:10.1177/1368430209353633.

111 Manjoo, Farhad. 2014. "Exposing Hidden Bias at Google." *The New York Times*. September 24. www.nytimes.com/2014/09/25/technology/exposing-hidden-biases-at-google-to-improve-diversity.html.

112 Libet, Benjamin., Curtis A. Gleason, Elwood W. Wright, and Dennis K. Pearl. 1983. "Time of Conscious Intention to Act in Relation to Onset of Cerebral Activity (Readiness-Potential)." *Brain* 106(3): 623–642. doi:10.1093/brain/106.3.623.

113 Haggard, Patrick. 2011. "Decision Time for Free Will." *Neuron* 69(3): 404–406. doi:10.1016/j.neuron.2011.01.028.

114 Duguid, Michelle M., and Melissa C. Thomas-Hunt. 2015. "Condoning Stereotyping? How Awareness of Stereotyping Prevalence Impacts Expression of Stereotypes." *The Journal of Applied Psychology* 100(2): 343–359. doi:10.1037/a0037908.

115 Rock, David. 2006. "A Brain-Based Approach to Coaching." *International Journal of Coaching in Organizations* 4(2): 32–43. www.crowe-associates.co.uk/wp-content/uploads/2013/10/Coaching-The-Brain-Article1.pdf.

116 Williams, Joan C., Rachel Dempsey, Anne-Marie Slaughter, and Nan McNamara. 2016. *What Works for Women at Work: Four Patterns Working Women Need to Know.* New York: New York University Press.

117 Estes, Zachary., and Sydney Felker. 2012. "Confidence Mediates the Sex Difference in Mental Rotation Performance." *Archives of Sexual Behavior* 41(3): 557–570. doi:10.1007/s10508-011-9875-5.

118 Bavel, Jay J., Dominic J. Packer, and William A. Cunningham. 2008. "The Neural Substrates of In-Group Bias." *Psychological Science* 19(11): 1131–1139. doi:10.1111/j.1467-9280.2008.02214.x.

119 Shen, Fengtao., Yang Hu, Mingxia Fan, Huimin Wang, and Zhaoxin Wang. 2018. "Racial Bias in Neural Response for Pain Is Modulated by Minimal Group." *Frontiers in Human Neuroscience* 11. doi:10.3389/fnhum.2017.00661.

120 Stout, Jane G., Nilanjana Dasgupta, Matthew Hunsinger, and Melissa A. McManus. 2011. "STEMing the Tide: Using Ingroup Experts to Inoculate Women's Self-Concept in Science, Technology, Engineering, and Mathematics (STEM)." *Journal of Personality and Social Psychology* 100(2): 255–270. doi:10.1037/a0021385.

121 Dasguptaa, Nilanjana., Melissa McManus Scircle, and Matthew Hunsinger. 2015. "Female Peers in Small Work Groups Enhance Women's Motivation, Verbal Participation, and Career Aspirations in Engineering." *Psychological and Cognitive Sciences* 112(16): 4988–4993. doi:10.1073/pnas.1422822112.

122 "Female Politicians Inspire Women in India to Pursue More Education, MIT Study Finds." 2012. *The Huffington Post.* January 18. www.huffingtonpost.com/2012/01/18/mit-study-india-female-leaders-politicians-aspirations_n_1213998.html

123 Losin, Elizabeth A. Reynolds., Marco Iacoboni, Alia Martin, Katy A. Cross, and Mirella Dapretto. 2012. "Race Modulates Neural Activity during Imitation." *NeuroImage* 59(4): 3594–3603. doi:10.1016/j.neuroimage.2011.10.074.

124 Welle, Brian. "Watch Unconscious Bias @ Work." *Google People Analytics.* https://rework.withgoogle.com/guides/unbiasing-raise-awareness/steps/watch-unconscious-bias-at-work/.

125 Heilman, Madeline E., and Michelle C. Haynes. 2005. "No Credit Where Credit Is Due: Attributional Rationalization of Women's Success in Male-Female Teams." *Journal of Applied Psychology* 90(5): 905–916. doi:10.1037/0021-9010.90.5.905.

126 Kolb, Deborah M., and Jessica L. Porter. 2015. "'Office Housework' Gets in Women's Way." *Harvard Business Review.* April 16. https://hbr.org/2015/04/office-housework-gets-in-womens-way.

127 Estes, Zachary., and Sydney Felker. 2012. "Confidence Mediates the Sex Difference in Mental Rotation Performance." *Archives of Sexual Behavior* 41(3): 557–570. doi:10.1007/s10508-011-9875-5.

128 Kay, Katty., and Claire Shipman. 2015. "The Confidence Gap." *The Atlantic.* August 26. www.theatlantic.com/magazine/archive/2014/05/the-confidence-gap/359815.

9 Diversity Management

In Chapter 5, we discussed how the difference-oriented, problem-focused, fear-embedded view of culture has guided much of the theory development in the literature of intercultural communication. Under the influence of the Cold War, the underlying assumption of mainstream theories is that differences are a source of problem, cost, risk, danger, and difficulties. Hofstede—an influential theorist—stated that cultural gaps are "a source of conflict than of synergy, a nuisance at best and often a disaster."[1] This approach is not always helpful. It undermines the bright side of diversity. Focusing on the potential mismatches when cultures collide may do our brain a disservice by preparing us to be reactive rather than proactive, defensive rather than cooperative, viewing differences as problems rather than opportunities.

Rather than looking at culture from such a problem-focused approach, in this chapter, we will discuss both sides of cultural diversity: The benefits *and* the challenges of differences in fostering a diverse workforce. Because biases are the major roadblocks of diversity, we will look at a range of recruitment and management strategies on how to eliminate the negative influences of bias while optimizing the positive impact of diversity.

9.1 The Benefits of a Diverse Workforce

Diversity is primarily challenged by our biological tendency to prefer similar attributes, such as the "similar to me" bias in hiring.[2] It creates the perception of easiness and comfort when we work with think-alike look-alike people. Hence, when we cross borders to communicate with those who still regard us as outgroup members, when trust is yet to be built and when mutual interests are still not clearly clarified, evidence from neuroscience and evolutionary biology tends to support similarity as the starting point (Chapter 6). By contrast, diversity and differences *initially* activate the amygdala. Differences can overwhelm the cerebral cortex—part the brain that mediates cognitive logical processing—and hence, prevent us from a sophisticated exploration of the environment.

However, when differences don't trigger continuous fear responses that push the energy consumption past the tipping point of eustress, diversity can be an asset. In contemporary management, diversity is no longer something "nice" to have, but a *strategy* aimed at achieving organizational outcomes. It is not diversity for the sake of diversity but an acknowledgment that it should be seen as a performance driver. In essence, the art of diversity management is to create a balance of similarities and differences to support business imperatives. Similarities should help to create a bond, not a bubble of close-mindedness. Employees should feel excited with differences and not threatened. A right balance creates a synergy that helps businesses thrive.

9.1.1 Creativity and Productivity

The dynamics within each individual and between employees fosters an environment of creativity and increase performance. Innovation is boosted with an increase of 26% in the number of patents and 31% in the number of patent citations just with a one-standard deviation in diversity.[3] Neuroscience tells us that it is not the IQ of the individual members, but the *average social intelligence* of the team that can help them mitigate many biases by offering completely different perspectives.[4] Differences wake up the brain, and that's why we tend to pay attention to the same argument presented by an *outsider*,[5] especially when those differences don't signal threats.

While similarities within a group can boost performance at the beginning, over a long period similarities can backfire. In a homogeneous group, people feel more comfortable and *assume* they understand one another; hence they can have group think, overlook problems, and do *less* preparation. Diversity tells the brain that things are no longer familiar. That psychological state prompts us to work harder[6] because we assume more effort is needed to convince outsiders. In a study, self-identified Republican and Democratic Party participants in the United States were told to write a persuasive essay to convince a partner who disagreed. The result showed that people prepared better for their discussions when their partners were from the other party. They were less prepared when they knew they were going to argue with people from the same party.[7] Adding an outsider versus an insider doubles the chances of arriving at a correct solution, from 29% to 60%.[8] Even if the members of the homogeneous teams are more capable, diverse teams still perform better; in other words: "Diversity trumps ability."[9] None of us is as smart as all of us.

Under the premise of diversity, we should rethink the concept of disability and its negative connotation. For example, according to a noted doctor, half the innovators in Silicon Valley may have Asperger's syndrome, reflected in their ability to program for long hours.[10] In fact, German software firm SAP actively recruits people with autism diagnoses because they can perform complex tasks that require a high level of concentration and exhibit potent ability in relation to finding patterns and making connections.[11] Their "Autism at Work" program aims to have 1% of its total workforce (approx. 650 people) fall on the spectrum by 2020—an initiative that Microsoft has since adopted.[12]

Taking into account the productivity that employees with disabilities bring to work, we should reframe the description as "mismatched human interaction," that is the person is not disable but the environment is disable in supporting the person. This is the basis of *neurodiversity*—a notion that neurological differences can be recognized as any human variation. These differences include dyslexia, attention deficit hyperactivity disorder (ADHD), autism, dyspraxia, and so forth. As such, neurodiversity questions the idea that these are diseases, and should be cured because they are variations of human neural wiring and can bring their own advantages to the society at large.

9.1.2 Financial Gain

A diverse workforce can lead to immense financial benefits.[13] In terms of gender, a report examining 2,360 companies across the world demonstrates that companies with one or more women on the board delivered higher average returns on equity and better average growth.[14] A move from no female leaders to 30% representation is associated with a 15% increase in the net revenue margin.[15] Similar results are found in 800 companies in Malaysia[16] and the top 30 firms on the Bombay Stock Exchange in India.[17] In Vietnam, companies led by women gained twice as much as others over five years.[18] In the United Kingdom, for every 10% increase in gender diversity, EBIT (Earnings Before Interests and Taxes) rose by 3.5%.[19]

In terms of ethnic diversity, nationality diversity of top management teams resulted in 35% more likelihood of having financial returns above their respective national industry medians.[20] Combined with gender diversity, ethnic diversity accounts for 16.5% of the variance in sales revenue.[21] In terms of ability diversity, 90% of people with disabilities did as well or better at their jobs than nondisabled co-workers; 86% rated average or better in attendance; and staff retention was 72% higher among persons with disabilities.[22] Employees with disabilities are also loyal, reliable, and hardworking.[23]

9.1.3 *Marketing Competitive Edge*

Organizations with a diverse workforce are more likely to understand different market segments better. Let's take the words of Brad Jakeman—President of Global Beverages at PepsiCo—as a hint: "I am sick and tired as a client of sitting in agency meetings with a whole bunch of white, straight males talking to me about how we are going to sell our brands that are bought 85% by women."[24]

Customer service can greatly benefit from having a staff that reflects the communities they serve. Similarities please the brain, and smooth out the communication. When one member of a team shares a client's trait such as ethnicity or gender, the *entire* team is 152% more likely to understand that user better than another team.[25] A good example is Westpac Australia's financial service, which over a period of ten years successfully changed its workforce from predominantly under 35 years old to an age diversity of between 18 and 70 because it wants to truly *reflect its customer base*.[26]

Another case in point is the way businesses market to women. The booming of *she-economy* is a strong reminder that companies should become "women literate" to understand their customers. While women drive an estimated 70–80% of consumer spending[27] and, by 2024, the average woman will out-earn the average man in some developed Western countries,[28] marketers still need to capture the power of this considerable purchasing force. Nearly half of the women surveyed say that marketers don't understand them[29] and 90% say that advertisers don't advertise to them.[30] In short, to tap into the power of the she-economy, companies should reconsider their workforce structure, tailor their marketing,[31] and change the gender balance of product development teams.[32]

In the same vein, the term "handicapitalism" has been used to describe an increasingly powerful cohort of customers with disability, who have approximately $8 trillion in annual disposable income globally.[33] They are more brand loyal than other consumers[34] and are well aware of organizations that promote their voice, employ positive advertising messages,[35] and include staff with a disability in the marketing team. Ninety-two percent of people with disabilities favor companies that employ individuals with disabilities, and 87% would do business with them.[36] It is a simple rule: Customers will purchase products that *reflect and support their personal identities and causes*. The very same principle can be applied for LGBTQ (Lesbian-Gay-Bisexual-Queer or Questioning) customers who form an enormous segment of $3.7 trillion.[37] Many multinationals have openly supported LGBTQ and promote their representation in the workforce. It's better to be known as an inclusive employer *before* trying to market to the larger community.[38]

Making diversity a market-based policy helps organizations gain access to new international customer bases with more success.[39] A good example is Australia where one in four jobs is Asia related and the future of the country's business will be on this continent. The government has been actively shaping an "Australia in the Asian century" with a "National Taskforce for an Asia-Capable Australia."[40] Efforts to be more "Asia literate" and "Asia capable" begin with early education, such as teaching Asian languages at primary school.[41] Organizations actively recruit staff who understand Asia's cultures because this has become a must for doing business with this continent.[42] In short, as the head of HR at Royal Bank of Canada—a Tanzanian immigrant herself—said: "To win the market, one needs to *hire* the market."[43]

Taking one step further, businesses not only want to hire the market because they need to reflect a specific customer segment. Nowadays, businesses are also expected to be socially responsible by playing a role in *shaping* the societies. They can choose to be a product of culture, mirroring the status quo, for example, building a workforce with 5% Muslims because that is the reality in the population. However, they can also drive the social change by actively hiring more Muslims, advocating a positive image of Muslim talents, and counteracting the backlash that the Muslim community is suffering from collective biases and marginalization. Creating positive cultures, changing the societies, and reshaping social landscapes are challenging tasks that contemporary businesses have to tackle because that's how they stand out, not as followers, but as influencers and creators of a culture. Humans are not just products but also producers of culture, as we can actively take an authorship's position to build our culture. This reflects the Behavior—Culture pathway of GCEB-Be (Chapter 2) and the role of "Be-behavior" in the STREAP-Be model for change management (Chapter 7).

In short, the benefits of diversity are manifold. It can boost creativity, productivity, and reduce group-think. It can lead to financial gain and access to new markets. Diversity done right has a significant impact in driving the positive change in the society.

9.2 Diversity Policies

Since it was coined by a McKinsey study in 1997, the "War for Talent" has become even more competitive due to a dramatic demographic shift that is seeing more women, millennials, foreigners, and other minorities joining the workforce. Together with this shifting demographic, employees are now more frequently *free agents*. They have greater choices, their bargaining power has increased, and the job market is highly transparent, all of which make attracting top-skilled employees fiercely competitive. Talent retention is an important issue for business, second only to the challenge of building global leadership.[44] Employees jump jobs more frequently; two-thirds believe they could find a better job in less than 60 days.[45] Obviously, hiring from the narrow, conventional pool means losing the war for talent. HR now finds new recruits in what have hitherto been minority groups in the workforce. However, these potential employees must be convinced that organizations are genuinely interested in diversity and the hiring process is bias free.

But hiring managers, who typically get between 85 and 124 resumes for any given entry-level job opening, often rely on their experience (read: bias) or find it hard to combat biases. Neuroscientists suggest that they should focus on the *goal* of the activity. Without a goal, biases reign, but when eyes are on the prize, rationality has a greater chance. In a study,[46] participants had to categorize faces according to their race. Because we often stereotype black people, researchers observed greater amygdala activity when participants saw black faces on the screen. However, when participants had a specific goal, in which race was not relevant, for example trying to guess what type of vegetable the person preferred, the amygdala response to black faces was *equal* to that for the white ones.

How does this play in real life? In this section, we will look at a number of strategies that can help to eliminate the detrimental impact of biases in diversity recruitment while creating an inclusive and positive environment for diversity to work. We will continue to use the STREAP-Be framework (Chapter 7) to systematically assist us in covering all necessary aspects of a cultural change process.

9.2.1 The "S" of STREAP-Be: Safety

9.2.1.1 Fear of Losing Autonomy

Diversity means a mental shift. Obviously, it can evoke a wide range of fear, especially with diversity policies that tell people how they should behave without a proper forum for open discussion. In a study, two groups of people read two essays: One contained voluntarily statements such as "You are *free* to choose to value non-prejudice" and the other contained demanding statements, such as "We *should* all refrain from negative stereotyping." Bias tests showed that readers of the second essay became *more* prejudiced than they had before.[47] An autonomy of opinion and choice is extremely important. If not done correctly, diversity policies can infringe on that basic right and evoke unnecessary fear.

9.2.1.2 *Fear of Losing Resources*

Quota is a common strategy in diversity management. Its main purpose is to create an equal playing field. Imagine a race where runner number 1 starts with the full strength of physical and mental power. For example, she was born into a white and affluent family with good connections, enjoyed good education at a private school, and grew up in safe neighborhoods. Through the connections of her parents, she now works as an intern for a famous company. In comparison, runner number 2 starts at the same time, but is confronted by a number of obstacles on the track. She was raised by a single parent who has to work two jobs to support the family. She grew up in a troublesome neighborhood and attended poorly funded public schools. She was constantly bullied for her religious practice and subjected to racial profiling, micro-aggressions, and subconscious bias. It has taken tremendous effort for her to find an internship in an ordinary company. Who do you think would make it first to the finishing line when applying for a job? This is where quota comes in, bringing the second runner more to the same line with the first one.

However, a major disadvantage of "quota" is that if it exists for too long and without a safety net for other demographics, such a policy on *diversity enlargement* can create threats and resentment among sensitive or high-status individuals. Poor diversity management can lead to the perception that benefits received by underrepresented people come at the cost of the others. In Figure 9.1, this means that the box on which the tall person stood is removed and given to the shorter person, technically *taking away the resource* and *reducing her/his status* and potentially causing resentment (we will come back to this later on with the last stage on "liberation"). In fact, this is backed up by research. In a study where half of the job seekers were informed about the company's diversity policies and the other half not, white candidates in the informed

Figure 9.1 Equality—equity—and liberation (Center for Story-Based Strategy)

group expressed concerns about being treated unfairly. In comparison with those who were not informed about the company's prodiversity policies, they also made a poorer impression during the interview and their cardiovascular responses indicated they endured more stress.[48] This suggests that diversity messages can be very sensitive for high-status individuals because they trigger identity threats and resentment.

This issue specifically involves the traditional dominant group at work: *Native-born white men*. Diversity efforts at work often *exclude* them because they are perceived as a privileged and powerful group. While there is some truth in that notion, an exclusion of native white men not only goes against the core idea of diversity and inclusion but also jeopardizes the process. This group may feel threatened as they find themselves targets of anger and frustration, watching women and minorities rise seemingly at their expense—a reason many have argued for the rise of Donald Trump. This uneasy feeling is heightened because native white men still hold a majority of leadership positions, yet they fear being labeled "sexist" or "racist" if they challenge the policies. The end result is, according to a trainer on this issue, they "shut up, sit back, and walk on eggshells," which leads to both resentment and a minimal amount of learning.[49] It is suggested that we should address these men as a group culture, giving them forums to reflect and change, to see and question their default culture. These employees must take an active role in the process for diversity efforts to stand a chance.

In the end, it's the power of self-criticism and the perceived right we have toward our own ingroups. We may complain about our own weakness, our own parents, our own religion and nation. But we can get extremely offended if an *outsider* says exactly the same thing. Telling a person that (s)he *should* change does not work exactly the same way as giving this individual an opportunity to see the mutual positive result of the change (s)he can potentially make.

9.2.1.3 Fear of Finger Pointing

Fear will nullify any diversity effort. That is why well-meaning programs that are compulsory and meant to avoid legal actions often backfire.[50] It elicits rebellion on the part of managers, triggering self-defense and a false sense of understanding.[51-52-53] This is also the reason why some tools used to prevent managers from biases, such as grievance systems, certainly have impact, but run the risk of making managers feel they are the *source of the problems*, being policed and put in the spotlight.[54] This consequently prompts them to rebel and resist the system, leading to a deep desire to punish those who complain, evidenced by a high number of retaliation charge.[55] In fact, men's involvement in diversity efforts worldwide fell from 49% in 2014 to 38% in 2015.[56]

9.2.1.4 Fear of Tokenism

A "token" is someone who is employed or placed in a certain setting as a symbolic representation of the entire minority group. The emotional stage of tokens is often detrimental and hence, needs some elaboration.

In essence, tokens feel very visible and suffer from stereotype threat because they stand out from the rest of the group.[57] In addition, others view them not as unique individuals, but rather in terms of the collective culture they represent, as *the* transgender or *the* millennial, which allows stereotypes to easily be formed or connected. Tokens, therefore, are under great pressure to behave in an expected, stereotypical way. Yet, at the same time, they have to perform and any mistakes they make will be more likely to catch attention. This leads to more frequent reprimands and more severe punishments. And because tokens are perceived as representatives of a collective minority group, they are stripped of their individual identities and their failures will be perceived as inherent weaknesses or characteristics of the whole collective culture.[58]

Tokenism is a dangerous trap in diversity policies. Companies may employ token as a quick-and-dirty trick to show a half-hearted effort of diversifying the workforce. This does harm to both sides. Employees may look at tokens and assume that they are not chosen for their competence. Tokens who are competent have to keep proving that they are chosen for quality, making their fight against biases much more challenging.

9.2.1.5 Diversity without Inclusion

Thus, diversity without the psychological safety and inclusive policies can lead to the perception that benefits received by underrepresented people come at the cost of the others. That's why diversity without inclusion is exclusion.

Diversity and inclusion are often lumped together to be the same thing. However, diversity is the representation of different cultural backgrounds, and inclusion is to let these representatives contribute to the success. It is about creating an *open and safe environment* for people to propose novel ideas, for every team member to have a voice in the decisions and share the team success. As noted diversity advocate Verna Myers put it: "Diversity is being invited to the party. Inclusion is being asked to dance." Here is an example that illustrates the complex feeling of alienation:

> We worked with a Chile-based firm that would seem to have no problems with diversity. After all, one of their most valued employees is an indigenous Peruvian, a man who is respected, well-paid, and included in the leadership team's decision-making discussions. Yet in a one-on-one interview he confided that he saw no future for his ambitions at that firm. "I know they value me," he said, "but I am an indigenous person, and they are white, legacy, and Spanish. They will never make me a partner, because of my color and background." Conventional measures would never flag this talented man for a flight risk; it's up to the narrative to tell the tale.[59]

"Being asked to dance," or "taking an initiative to join the dance," can be a challenging process. A study[60] found that women and nonwhite executives are often *penalized* for supporting the promotion of diversity in the workplace. Female and nonwhite managers are rated as *less* effective when they hire a nonwhite and female candidate instead of a white male candidate. It is risky for low-status group members to help others like them. This leads to women and minorities choosing not to advocate for other women and minorities because they don't want to be seen as incompetent and subjective, choosing their "own people." Thus, while it is a common tendency for people to advocate for their own ingroups, women and minorities must do that at their own expense. As a consequence, minorities continue to be undersponsored. In the United States, only 8% of people of color, 9% of Africans, 8% of Asians, and 5% of Hispanics have a sponsor, compared to 13% of Caucasians.[61] Having no sponsor means having no mentors who can help to navigate the complex corporate culture and map out what a career ladder looks like.

This section has listed a number of safety issues in diversity process. To conclude, both minorities and high-status individuals can feel excluded. The former for being there but not having a voice, the latter for being seen as privileged and, hence, not part of the dialogue. We will come back to the topic of inclusion with more strategic solutions in the section "Be"—Behavior later in the chapter.

9.2.2 The "T" of STREAP-Be: Trigger

9.2.2.1 Strategize the Language

The language we use every day is a rich source of subconscious triggers for biases. Businesses should weed out subconscious biases from the very first step of hiring process. A study reported that male-dominated fields tended to use more masculine words in job listings, while female-dominated fields were more neutral.[62] This emerges from a systemic bias against women, as evidenced by the fact that the language of job listings for female-dominated professions weren't similarly biased in favor of women.

If you want to hire diversity, explicitly state a phrase such as "we welcome people from different regions" in the job listing. Language is a powerful driver for thought and behavior. Even small differences in wording can send very different messages to prospective applicants. A job listing that reads "work hard play hard," "fresh," and "up-and-coming" appeals more to young candidates, but less to other demographics. "Leader," "competitive," "dominant," "best of the best," "fast-paced," "ambition," and "challenging" appeal more to men and steer women to self-select out, partly because these words have been masculinized and became positive traits for men but negative attributes for women. Similarly, "loyalty," passion," and "collaboration" have been shown to appeal more to women than men. Here is a small test. Which phrase would attract more men and which would appeal more to women?: The company is looking for candidates who can (1) "analyze markets to determine appropriate selling prices" or (2) "understand markets to establish appropriate selling prices."

Wording sends a strong signal about the existing state of the business. In a study, masculine-worded listings made people *think* there were more men at the companies, and became less appealing to women, and vice versa.[63] The indication of this study is promising because hiring teams can write job ads that are welcoming to the target group they want to attract. In short, it's not which words to use, but how and how often we use them. If in doubt, we can always lean on the safe side with inclusive terms: "Adaptable," "creative," "excellent," "imaginative," "curious," "up-to-date," "trustworthy," "thoughtful," "planning," "responsible," and "resilient." Technology has evolved to give a helping hand with *software to check subconscious biases* such as gender-decoder.katmatfield.com/.

Last but not least, the language of inclusion should be seen in overall communication and not just in job listings and interviews. In multinationals, this is often a source of disturbance and a strong feeling of exclusion when nonnative employees have to put up with native colleagues constantly using their mother tongue at work. Once a shared language is respected, the next step is to make the vocabulary inclusive, positive, and free of micro-aggression. Table 9.1 gives a detailed guideline, which is adapted and further developed from the study of the University of Wollongong[64] and another study of Derald W. Sue and her colleagues.[65]

9.2.3 The "R" of STREAP-Be: Reward

9.2.3.1 Make the Benefit of Diversity Tangible

What gets measured gets done, and what gets rewarded gets repeated. A number of organizations are doing a great job of translating diversity benefit into numbers. This includes: Diversity report, ROI, customers' feedback, reduced staff turnover among a certain cultural group, employee's satisfaction, increased diversity of partners and customers, and so forth. These kinds of measurement and acknowledgment give credibility by providing data that show results, and it also uncovers information that can serve as feedback for continuous improvement.

9.2.3.2 Not "Fit" but "Expand"

A critical reward of diversity is what it enriches the company. Once a company's culture has been established, it sounds logical to hire those who fit this culture, especially when it is a winning culture, one that makes the company grow. However, managers can go one step further and replace "fit" with "expand." New hires should enrich, not just fit the existing culture and capacity, with the ultimate aim to reach a specific business goal. Hiring teams need to consider how each candidate can add to the overall diversity, change the status quo, and reshape the current culture. At LG for example, once among the most traditional of Korean *chaebols*, LG has diversified its top management and become a truly global organization.[66] We are reminded here of an example in Chapter 5 that informed us how Japan has recently embraced foreigners in the C-suite. The new governance

Table 9.1 Guidelines for inclusive language and elimination of micro-aggressions (adapted and further developed from University of Wollongong [2012] and Sue et al. [2007])

Avoid	Alternative
"We want to hire employees with diverse/immigrant backgrounds"	"We want to attract multicultural talents"
Chairman/Chairwoman	Chairperson
Policeman/Mailman/Spokesman/Fireman/Housemaid/Waitress/Cameraman/Cleaning lady	Police officer/Postal worker/Spokesperson/Firefighter/House helper/Server/Camera operator/Cleaner
Businessman/Businesswoman	Businesspeople/Businessperson
Manpower	Workforce
Manmade	Constructed/Artificial
Ladies	Women
Colloquialism such as darling, doll, chick, ma'am (madam), love	Use person's name, refrain from generic condescending and patronizing terms
"We need someone to man the desk"	"We need someone to staff the desk"
Sportsmanship	Fair play
Housewife	Caregiver/Homemaker
Mothering/Fathering	Parenting
Wife/Husband	Partner/Spouse/Families
Use "he" as a standard pronoun: "The employee may exercise his right"	"The employees may exercise their right"/Her or his/(S)he
Dyke/Fag/Fairy/Poofta	Gay, lesbian, bisexual, transgender, intersex
Straight	Heterosexual
Transsexual	Transgender/Intersex
Non-(English/Arabic, etc.) speaking background	Culturally and linguistically diverse Or "Mexicans whose first language is Arabic"
Kiwi, Yank, or Pom	Person from New Zealand, United States of America, or Poland
Use traits as identity: Full-blood/half-cast/the handicapped worker/the disabled person/the retarded man/the deaf employee/the cripple woman	Use traits as extra information: People who identify as…/People with … backgrounds/Person with physical disability/Person with intellectual disability/Person with hearing disability/Person with mobility impairment
Confined to a wheelchair/Wheelchair bound	Wheelchair user/Wheelchair enabled
"Rachida, despite being confined to a wheelchair, will lead our project"	Focus on ability and not disability: "Rachida will lead our project"
Merry Christmas/Happy Chinese New Year	Happy Holiday/Happy Lunar New Year/Or use specific season greetings for each group
Guest worker/Immigrant worker	Expat/International mobility
Indication that others are foreigners no matter what: "Where are you *really* from?"/"Ok, where were your *ancestors* from?"/"What are you?"/"You speak good Arabic (English/Hindi) …"/"You sound so White"/"You people…"/"Your kind…"	Avoid micro-aggressions and assumption: "Where are you based?"/"Which cultures contribute to your cultural identity?"/"Please tell me a little bit about yourself"/"Do you happen to know anyone who can help with this question?"

Table 9.1 (Cont.)

Avoid	Alternative
Assumption of inferiority and ascription of capacity: "You are a credit to your race"/"Your achievement is amazing, given your origin and background"/"Oh wow, you *actually* can write so well"/"You go beyond those typical girly stuff"/"We welcome an Asian wizard to help us with all the math problem"/"Finally there is a man here to fix the electricity"/"We are grateful that the only woman in the office can take care of organizing party"/"Women are excellent with emotional intelligence"	"You have done brilliantly"/"Your achievement is amazing, given all the obstacles"/"You write excellently"/"You surprised me and I apology that I was biased" /"We welcome an expert who will help us with math problems"/"Finally there is someone to fix the electricity"/"We have realized that women have been subconsciously expected to do office's housework. We will be sharing this from now on"/"Women have been *raised* to develop emotional intelligence. Men can practice and become equally good"
Color/religion … blindness: "I never see you as a black man"/"There is only one race, the human race"/"Not black lives matter but all lives matter"/"We are all children of God"/"We absolutely have a culture of equality and transparency here, sexism and racism don't exist in our office"	"We all have biases and it's hard to rid of them. I may have implicit bias against you and I hope you can point it out for me"/"There is only one race but many levels of inequalities"/"We are all children of God and some have more privileges than others"/"We want to build a culture of equality and transparency here. Sexism and racism may still exist in our office at the subconscious level and we want to work on it"
Denial of individual bias or the impact of bias: ""I'm not racist (homophobic), I have black (Muslim/Jewish/gay) friends"/"Anyone can succeed as long as they work hard enough"/"May the best man win"/"You have only yourself to blame"	"I don't want to be racist but I'm aware that I can have subconscious biases"/"Marginalized people have to try many times harder to achieve the same level of success"/"Ability is of little account without opportunity"—Napoléon Bonaparte

code requires at least two outsiders as independent directors.[67] This is a fundamental breakaway from one of the strongest and most basic axes in Japanese social life: The separation between *uchi* (ingroup) and *soto* (outgroup). However, to boost the economy, even this deeply entrenched "us versus them" mentality can be put aside, and Japanese companies have started welcoming outsiders in their home (*uchi* = home = ingroup) to enrich themselves and expand the horizon.

The notion of "expand" or "enrich" is best illustrated by a metaphor used in Wal-Mart's training: New employees and promoted managers are seen as a "carrot," an "egg," and a "coffee bean." Put a carrot in the pan and it turns soft. It has adapted and survived; maybe it has become a team player, but it has also been weakened. Cook an egg in the pan, its outer protection remains hard, but its liquid at the center becomes hard as well. It has survived, but at a price. Drop a coffee bean into water, not only will it change the water but also add value, turning water into coffee—a *pricier commodity*. The moral is that any new employee can choose who to be. But only those who can bring positive change will help improve the company.[68]

9.2.4 *The "E" of STREAP-Be: Emotion*

9.2.4.1 *Emotional Management*

Needless to say, diversity process easily evokes emotions and it is understandable that it can sometimes get out of hand. Bottled up feelings are dangerous and can harbor deep resentment. As discussed in Chapter 7, practices such as mindfulness, focus groups, share forums, and an open, empathetic environment are critical to channel emotions. The bottom line is, emotions should be a critical input and not a destructive power.

9.2.4.2 Empathy

In Chapter 7, we learned that empathy enables us to *feel what others feel*. It is a powerful mechanism that connects humans together. We also considered in that chapter the notion that too much empathy can make you confuse others' feelings with your own feelings, and thus, may distort clear thinking.[69] However, diversity is an area of management where this risk is less of a burden because a main purpose of diversity is to understand our own colleagues at their deep emotional level. In many cases, we can move past the stage of "*think* about what others feel" and achieve the stage of "*feel* about what others feel."

Here is an example the author of this book learned from her training for PwC in Amsterdam. During the Ramadan, a number of PwC employees practice fasting with no drink and food for the whole day at work. A perspective-taking approach is to understand this ritual, knowing the "whats" and "whys." However, a manager went one step further and suggested that her department would fast for one day with their Muslim colleagues. That experience not only allowed the team to have empathy, to *feel* what others feel, but it also led to a series of change in the organizational structure such as working lunch and office hours. Muslim colleagues can choose to come to work earlier (so they can benefit the most from early breakfast) and leave the office earlier (so they can rest and enjoy the break of the fast in the evening with families—an important tradition of Ramadan).

9.2.5 The "A" of STREAP-Be: Alignment

9.2.5.1 Group Affinity

Affinity or employee resource networks are voluntary groups organized around shared interests within or across organizations. They help recruitment and retention,[70] provide built-in comfort zones for diverse new hires, create a learning environment for employees to develop and seek advice,[71] offer insights for management,[72] help companies to explore new markets,[73] and empower employees.[74] Affinity networks perform best when they support one another in the promotion of diversity and do not compete for funds and managerial priorities, or create social tensions among groups.

However, organizations with affinity networks are still in the minority, and those with such networks may not realize their full potential and optimize their capacity. In many cases, immature networks serve as little more than safe gathering places to exchange experiences among like-minded people, and the network has limited influence on the decision-making process.

Affinity networks, if not organized in balance with inclusiveness, can be counterproductive. Deloitte, for example, decided in 2017 to phase out its women's network and other affinity groups and to focus on inclusion, particularly of men. Organizations should find ways to make all employees feel included and engaged, unless they want to face the burden of "reverse discrimination," polarization in the workplace, reduced morale, and bitterness among those who perceive themselves as being excluded or even victims of the policies.

9.2.6 The "P" of STREAP-Be: People

9.2.6.1 Diversify the Hiring Team

It's difficult, if not impossible, to hire diversity effectively if the hiring team is not diverse. Women, minorities, and other nonmainstream candidates are much more likely to join a company when they can interact with those who are already there and can testify to a company's commitment to diversity. In a 2014 study, researchers found out that symposia organized by all-male teams contained only 25% female speakers, but for those with at least one woman, the number of female speakers increased to 43%.[75] Due to ingroup and confirmation bias, 30%

of all-male teams produced an all-male lineup of speakers. In other words, we need to *have a minority to get a minority*. Further, women experience greater cortisol responses when being evaluated by all-men panels as a result of stereotype threats, and vice versa.[76] It clearly matters who is on the other side of the table and making decisions on behalf of an organization. For this reason, many big companies, such as Intel, Procter & Gamble, and Verizon have made diverse hiring team a requirement in recruitment process.

9.2.6.2 Evaluate the Short List

Statistically, this stage is a good indicator of how the final recruits will look like. Studies have proven that when the final candidate pool has only one minority candidate, this person has virtually *no chances* of being hired.[77] However, the odds of hiring a minority were 79 times greater if there were at least two of them in the finalist pool. Hence, the "two in the pool effect."

Among multinationals such as Microsoft, the candidate pool has a rule of equal number: 50% male and 50% female, all *qualified* candidates. This requires hiring managers to be more active in engaging with various networks to supply for the pipeline. The approach is fairer in the long run because the equal playing field is created at the very beginning of the one's career.

9.2.6.3 Size Does Matter

Seeing is believing—that is how availability bias works. If we don't see women in tech and science, men in HR and training, people of color in leadership and management, LGBTQ in law enforcement and nonartistic fields, and so forth, we don't naturally associate these people with those jobs. Consequently, we apply confirmation bias by looking for evidence that fits our belief when hiring. To deal with availability bias, we can accentuate availability by applying enlargement diversity, which makes the elements we want to promote more obvious. That is where quota comes in. It is a radical and also controversial method to break up the pattern and galvanize new momentum of change—a strategy that most major companies and governments adopt at the initial stage of the change process.

Diversity attracts diversity, and that's why 67% of job seekers use diversity as an important factor when considering companies and job offers.[78] Experts suggest that we should have at least *three* minority individuals in the team to make availability take effect. Why three? Because one minority will be isolated, two is not enough to move the needle, and the magic number of three can disrupt the status quo and make a real impact.[79] In many cases, just one trailblazer can pave the way for others.

9.2.6.4 Expand the Networks

Diversity hiring can take advantage of ingroup bias by asking minority employees to make *referrals*. In general, we all belong to social and professional networks of like-minded and demographically similar people. Hiring teams can leverage this network, while minimizing the nepotism effect by offering extra referral bonuses to employees who make referrals that help the organization achieve its goals. Intel, for example, pays up to $4,000 in bonuses to employees who referred a woman, minority, or veteran to its workforce.[80]

Hiring diversity means going out of the comfort zone to connect with new networks. This includes placing job ads in new places; hiring from different schools; partnering with multicultural associations and student groups; building brand awareness in diverse communities through strategic sponsorship, leadership, and event; using social media, such as LinkedIn, Facebook, and Twitter to source and market to diverse talent; attending or hosting a virtual career fair to cast a broader net, and so forth. Verizon, for example, had great success in recruiting veterans through virtual fairs, and KPMG attracted more than 10,000 candidates all over the world with the same method. Other businesses deeply engage with potential pools of candidates by organizing events for underrepresented student groups. PwC, for example, boosts their diverse campus hires through their "Explore" (one-day early-identification) program and Start programs (internship experience for top-performing diverse college students).

A very engaged and strategic step of expanding the network means creating a formal program with the ultimate goal for recruitment. Walgreens has been a star in this aspect as the company built a disability-friendly warehouse in which roughly half of the staff has a disability and it is now the company's safest, most productive warehouse.[81]

9.2.6.5 Hold Managers Accountable

No diversity effort can be successful if managers don't have the ownership and become the advocates of diversity. Instead of being policed by different tools, managers have to believe in diversity and are being held accountable for what they do. Many businesses, such as Microsoft, are using a different approach by paying executive bonuses based on the diversity efforts.[82]

A statistical analysis of 829 firms in the United States over 31 years shows us that the three strategies that have brought the most significant impact on diversity are (1) appointing a Chief Diversity Officer (CDO), (2) implementing a mentoring program, and (3) creating a task force.[83] CEOs should also act as CDO by heading the executive diversity council themselves,[84] mentoring programs give mentors the opportunities to walk the talk and exercise transformational leadership, while a taskforce holds managers accountable. Collecting data—a crucial process in managing diversity and combating stereotypes—is also more likely to be prioritized with a task force. A good example comes from Google. When they noticed that women engineers were nominating themselves for promotion at lower rates than men, a senior manager sent an e-mail describing the data and nudging women to apply. Immediately, the application rate for women soared and the rate of women who received promotions rose higher than that for male engineers. This phenomenon kept occurring until, at one point, he forgot to send the e-mail and the number of female applicants dropped sharply.[85] In sum, it is a very powerful case of how effective diversity policies can be when leaders directly engage and take responsibility for the outcomes.

To conclude, the "P" for people-factor in the STREAP-Be framework means diversity has to be presented with at least two candidates in the hiring short list and three members in the working team. Diversity recruitment can take advantage of the referral system, social media, or specific programs to reach out to candidates who are in the nontraditional pipelines. Finally, the people-factor also means managers are held accountable for diversity targets.

9.2.7 The "Be" of STREAP-Be: Behavior

9.2.7.1 Focus on Criteria

Focus on criteria helps to reduce biases. It's crucial to prioritize target skills before the interview and having a *consensus* in advance about what success looks like. To unveil subconscious biases, each interview question needs a clear justification for *why* it should be asked. The next step is to *standardize* this scheme so all candidates will have the same questions and the hiring team can score responses with a grid. The selection panel can also *record* the interview and justify the decision by *matching* each job requirement with the candidate's ability to avoid a decision based on gut feeling.

Blind hiring has also become popular lately among big and small businesses alike because it can significantly reduce subconscious biases and help recruiters focus on criteria. In 2016, the Australia Bureau of Statistic doubled its proportion of female bosses by this technique.[86] Typically,

Table 9.2 Job candidates' test results (Diaz-Uda, Medina, and Schill [2013])

	Q1	Q2	Q3	Q4	Q5	Q6	Q7	Q8	Q9	Q10
Spencer			X	X	X			X	X	
Jeff	X	X			X	X	X		X	X
Rose	X	X				X	X		X	X

name, gender, age, college's name, address, graduation year, and income level are removed from a resume in blind hiring. Prehire, or sample test, is a common practice in some professions, such as software development. A classic example is how the top five symphony orchestras in the United States increased female musicians from 5% to 25% using blind auditioning behind a screen.[87] If an interview is required, an anonymous process is recommended with a take-home Q&A or a chat in real time. While hotly debated,[88] a Canadian study reported that personality assessment could also significantly increase a diverse workforce.[89]

Going beyond the diversity of gender, ethnicity, ability, religion, economic background, and sexual orientation, the latest strategy in diversity hiring is striving for *diversity of thought*. This new dimension can significantly change the way we view competence. A scenario[90] illustrates this point clearly. In Table 9.2 you will find the hiring performance test result of three candidates. Naturally, we would be inclined to pick top scorers Jeff and Rose. But we should also notice that Spencer answered correctly all the questions that the other two candidates missed, suggesting that hiring Spencer would bring different thinking to the table.

9.2.7.2 *Use Technology*

Currently, businesses have started using software in job selection. Many managers naively believe they can make the best decision by looking into an applicant's eyes. No algorithm, they would argue, can substitute for accumulated experience. However, an analysis of 17 studies showed that a simple equation outperforms human decisions by at least 25%.[91] Creators of software, such as GapJumpers, claimed that blind auditions increase recruitment opportunities for women and community college students up to 15%.[92]

However, machines are made and trained on human data. And humans are biased. In a study, researchers showed that software used to predict who is most likely to end up in jail rated black people at a higher risk than whites.[93] When Caliskan—a researcher from Turkey—used Google Translate, the gender-neutral pronoun in her language ended up as a "*he*'s a doctor." The machine assumed that when she was talking about a doctor, that person must had been a man. Caliskan then went on to let a software learn 840 billion words on the Internet and how each word is often connected with another (e.g., "bottle" often goes with "water"). Once the computer amassed its vocabulary, Caliskan and her colleagues ran it through a bias test. The result: They had created sexist and racist artificial intelligence (AI) that discriminates against black people and women.[94] The indication of these studies reminds us that AI learns about the world as it has been. It doesn't know how the world *ought* to be. Hence, technology in diversity hiring needs to be safeguarded against the very reality that we want to change.

9.2.7.3 *Practice What You Preach*

It's easy to spot businesses that use diversity as a bait rather than a policy. Job candidates can read diversity reports and check the company websites and products carefully to see if words and action go together. A company's statement of commitment on diversity is not enough, but there should be charters, images, stats, testimonials, videos, awards, events, case studies, current situations, and so forth. Many companies with diversity claim show pictures of the management board of all-white or all-native men. It's a conflict that those with subconscious biases can't easily figure out. Here is a case in point. In 2015, BBC created a recruitment film that emphasized the network's international reach of reflecting what's happing around the world. However, it was quickly pointed out that the film had an all-white cast.[95]

9.2.7.4 Change the Structure

Many of us have heard the phrase "The whole is *greater* than the sum of its parts." However, the original words of Gestalt psychologist Kurt Koffka are "The whole is *other* than the sum of the parts." Differences do not automatically bring benefits. A truly diverse and multicultural organization requires much more than increasing the number of people from nondominant culture. It is about a *critical change* in organizational philosophy and the willingness to build a new working system that values differences so everyone can eventually maximize reward from a culture of inclusion. At the larger scale, effective diversity management goes hand in hand with *significant changes* in the organizational philosophy and vision with regard to the role of diversity. This is the ultimate test of an organization's commitment. It requires the (re)construction of a comprehensive framework for leadership and management, one that can systematically bring down the deep-seated institutional barriers and drive the changes from inside. In short, effective management requires a cultural change.

Businesses can't hire some minority and assume that it will fix the culture. These new hires can't make a difference on their own without a thoughtful structure and comprehensive system to support it in the long run. In his classic book *Building a House for Diversity*, Roosevelt Thomas Jr. used the fable about a giraffe and an elephant to illustrate strategies in diversity management. The giraffe had a wonderful shop and wanted to invite the elephant to work with her. But the door was too small, and as the elephants walked around, things started to crack and collapse. Very soon they both understood that the shop had been built specifically for the giraffe, and the elephant would not be able to work there unless there were *major changes in the structure* of the shop.

The lesson is that simply raising the number of multicultural talents alone runs the risk of resembling the giraffe's workshop after inviting in the elephant. New hires can't fit in and may bear the brunt of any disorder and system failures. Surface diversity or any catch-all strategies that treat diversity as a checkbox can damage organizational structure and lead to decreased productivity. PR "window dressing" diversity programs will not bring in the expected benefit and can be harmful for workplace morale.

To make matter worse, multicultural talents will leave the organization after realizing that job advertisements and promises do *not* match the reality. Companies can advertise for diversity, but employees will soon testify that promise. Minorities vote with their feet. This is also the case of female in tech. While 40% of young talents in science and technology are female, a short way down the road, 52% of them drop out and never return.[96] In short, they choose to leave the field when experiencing (1) a *masculine culture* where 63% of women in science suffer from sexual harassment; (2) *isolation* when a woman is alone among all men who don't appreciate her, with no role models, no buddies, and no mentor; (3) a *mysterious career path* because 45% of women lack mentors and 83% lack sponsors; and (4) a *risk-rewarding culture*, in which 35% of women have difficulty, especially when they have no buddies to support them.

In Figure 9.1, the existence of the fence creates categories such as "minority," "the marginalized," and "the privileged." It represents the inherent discrimination that is deeply embedded in the institutional structure and the mindset of the people, such as subconscious bias, subtle and microprejudices, or privileges that have long been taken for granted. *Changing the structure means bringing down the fence and not asking the shorter persons to "grow up."* A good case in point can be found in the United States' PRWeek Hall of Femme in 2017. Instead of negotiating a bidirectional solution, an all-male panel choose to blame women and told females they should "speak up more loudly" because PR is a "macho" culture.[97] It is a classic case of blaming people versus blaming the system, demanding people to fit in (product of a culture) versus changing the social environment (producer of a culture).

Giving support (the boxes) is not the answer either, but dismantling the fence, which is the root of the problem, is the ultimate solution. When the fence is down, the boundary that defines dominant and marginalized groups is also dismantled. Being tall is valued as much as being short because "tall" and "short" are no longer limitations, but rather uniqueness that can contribute to the organization. Each individual can stand on her/his own, supporting costs are no longer needed, and the view as well as the fun (read: benefits) are much greater. In other words, true diversity and inclusion effort is about identifying the root causes instead of fixing the symptoms, changing the structure and mindset instead of fixing the people.

The merger of Japan Tobacco International and Gallaher is a good case in point. To achieve a solid foundation of shared values and similarities, they strived to build a corporate culture that (1) hires for attitude and trains for skills; and (2) rewards for thinking business, maximizing contribution, emerging others, and driving results. This change in mindset helped them deal with diversity in the next level, that is they did not have to think about it: "Once you get such a company culture, … you don't have to push diversity. It's irrelevant … because it just becomes *the way of life.*"[98]

Summary

1. The benefits of diversity are manifold:
   * A boost in creativity, productivity, and reduction of group-think;
   * Increased in financial gain;
   * Access to new markets;
   * Creation of new markets;
   * Development of social responsibility; and
   * Driving positive change in the society, being a producer of culture.
2. Diversity policies can be based on STREAP-Be framework of cultural change.
3. The "S" of STREAP-Be: Safety
   * Eliminate and avoid causing the fear of losing autonomy: People should feel they have a *free choice* in opting for diversity behavior.
   * Eliminate and avoid causing the fear of losing resource: High-status individuals such as native-born white men can feel threatened because they may perceive that women and minorities advance at their expense.
   * Eliminate and avoid causing the fear of finger pointing: Managers may feel they are the source of the problems.
   * Eliminate and avoid causing the fear of tokenism: Employees may look at tokens and assume that they are not chosen for their competence. Tokens who are competent have to keep proving that they are chosen for quality, making their fight against biases much more challenging.
   * Diversity is the representation of different cultural backgrounds, and inclusion is to let these representatives contribute to the success.
   * Both minorities and high-status individuals can feel excluded. The former for being there but not having a voice, the latter for being seen as privileged and hence, not part of the dialogue.

4. The "T" of STREAP-Be: Trigger
   - Language is a rich source of subconscious triggers for biases.
   - Language should be neural, inclusive, and contain minimum micro-aggression.
5. The "R" of STREAP-Be: Reward
   - Make the benefits of diversity tangible.
   - New hires should not just fit, but *enrich* the corporate culture.
6. The "E" of STREAP-Be: Emotion
   - Practices such as mindfulness, focus groups, share forums, and an open, empathetic environment are critical to channel emotions.
   - Empathy—*feel* about what others feel—is critical in cultivating understanding in diversity process.
7. The "A" of STREAP-Be: Alignment
   - Group affinity creates a great source of alignment where employees can form ingroups for support and advice.
   - However, group affinity should not be at the expense of inclusion.
8. The "P" of STREAP-Be: People
   - Diversify the hiring team.
   - Increase minority in the short list to at least two candidates.
   - Increase minority in the team to at least three members.
   - Expand the networks for recruitment with bonuses, referral systems, virtual events, and specific programs.
   - Hold managers accountable for diversity targets.
9. The "Be" of STREAP-Be: Behavior
   - Focus on criteria with standardized process, blind hiring, and aim for diversity in thinking.
   - Use technology with critical evaluation.
   - Business products and representation should show diversity. Practice what you preach.
   - Diversity management means a significant change in the organizational philosophy and vision. It is a reconstruction of organization to bring down deep-seated institutional barriers.

Notes

Don't forget to go to the end of the book for case studies.

1 Hofstede G. 2001. *Culture's Consequences: Comparing Values, Behaviours, Institutions and Organizations across Nations.* 2nd ed. Thousand Oaks, CA: Sage.

2 Rivera, Lauren A. 2012. "Hiring as Cultural Matching: The Case of Elite Professional Service Firms." *American Sociological Review* 77(6): 999–1022. doi:10.1177/0003122412463213.

3 Huasheng, Gao., and Wei Zhang. 2015. "Does Workforce Diversity Pay Evidence from Corporate Innovation." *SSRN Electronic Journal.* http://images.transcontinentalmedia.com/LAF/lacom/workforce_diversity.pdf.

4 Petrovic, Karli. 2016. "Neuroscience Helps Foster Diversity in the Workplace." *IQ by Intel.* March 18. https://iq.intel.com/neuroscience-helps-foster-diversity-in-the-workplace/.

5 Chang, Mitchell J., Kenji Hakuta, David A. Kenny, Shana Levin, Anthony Lising Antonio, and Jeffrey F. Milem. 2004. "Effects of Racial Diversity on Complex Thinking in College Students." *Psychological Science* 15(8): 507–510. doi:10.1111/j.0956-7976.2004.00710.x.

6 Loyd, D. Lewin., Cynthia S. Wang, Katherine W. Phillips, and Robert B. Lount. 2013. "Social Category Diversity Promotes Premeeting Elaboration: The Role of Relationship Focus." *Organization Science* 24(3):757–772. doi:10.1287/orsc.1120.0761.

7 Phillips, Katherine W. 2014. "How Diversity Makes Us Smarter." *Scientific American.* October 1. www.scientificamerican.com/article/how-diversity-makes-us-smarter/.

8 Rock, David., Heidi Grant Halvorson, and Jacqui Grey. 2016. "Diverse Teams Feel Less Comfortable and That Is Why They Perform Better." *Harvard Business Review*. September 22. https://hbr.org/2016/09/diverse-teams-feel-less-comfortable-and-thats-why-they-perform. better?utm_content=bufferc285e&utm_medium=social&utm_source=facebook.com&utm_campaign=buffer.

9 Page, Scott. 2007. *The Difference: How the Power of Diversity Creates Better Groups, Firms, Schools and Societies*. Princeton, NJ: Princeton University Press.

10 Smith, Zack. 2011. "Half of Silicon Valley Has Something You'd Call Asperger's: Interview with Temple Grandin." *Indy Week*. February 21. www.indyweek.com/arts/archives/2011/02/21/half-of-silicon-valley-has-something-youd-call-aspergers-interview-with-temple-grandin.

11 SAP. 2019. "Diversity and Inclusion." www.sap.com/corporate/en/company/diversity.html.

12 "Microsoft Announces Pilot Program to Hire People with Autism: Microsoft on the Issues." 2015. Microsoft Green Blog. April 3. http://blogs.microsoft.com/on-the-issues/2015/04/03/microsoft-announces-pilot-program-to-hire-people-with-autism/#sm.00003fsdce10axdt1sq6uyyiwp77p.

13 Dezsö, Cristian L., and David Gaddis Ross. 2012. "Does Female Representation in Top Management Improve Firm Performance? A Panel Data Investigation." *Strategic Management Journal* 33(9): 1072–1089. doi:10.1002/smj.1955.

14 Curtis, Mary., Christine Schmid, and Marion Struber. 2012. *Gender Diversity and Corporate Performance*. Credit Suisse, Research Institute.

15 Noland, Marcus., Tyler Moran, and Barbara Kotschwar. 2016. "Is Gender Diversity Pro Table? Evidence from a Global Survey." *Working Paper Series* 16(3): 1–35. https://piie.com/publications/wp/wp16-3.pdf.

16 Abdullah, Shamsul., Ku Nor Izah Ku Ismail, and Lilach Nachum. 2012. "Women on Boards of Malaysian Firms: Impact on Market and Accounting Performance." *Social Science Research Network*. Working Paper Series. September 10.

17 Rawani, Anand. 2009. "Women Promoters Beat Big Daddies." *The Economic Times*. March 8. http://articles.economictimes.indiatimes.com/2009-03-08/news/28488646_1_growth-rate-biocon-promoters.

18 Covert, Bryce. 2014. "Vietnamese Companies Led by Women Gained Twice as Much as Others Over 5 Years." *ThinkProgress*. March 31. https://thinkprogress.org/vietnamese-companies-led-by-women-gained-twice-as-much-as-others-over-5-years-83168956de9#.ukqu33glm.

19 Hunt, Vivian., Dennis Layton, and Sara Prince. 2015. *Diversity Matters*. McKinsey & Company. www.mckinsey.com/business-functions/organization/our-insights/why-diversity-matters?reload.

20 Nielsen, Bo Bernhard., and Sabina Nielsen. 2013. "Top Management Team Nationality Diversity and Firm Performance: A Multilevel Study." *Strategic Management Journal* 34: 373–382. doi:10.1002/smj.2021.

21 Herring, Cedric. 2009. "Does Diversity Pay? Race, Gender, and the Business Case for Diversity." *American Sociological Review* 74(2): 208–224. doi:10.1177/000312240907400203.

22 Deloitte. 2010. *The Road to Inclusion*. www.employmentaction.org/employers/links-and-resources/diversity,-inclusion-and-employment-equity/The%20Road%20to%20Inclusion.pdf.

23 Hernandez, Brigida., K. McDonald, M. Divilbiss, E. Horin, J. Velcoff, and O. Donoso. 2007. *Exploring the Bottom Line: A Study of the Costs and Benefits of Workers with Disabilities*. De Paul University. http://bbi.syr.edu/_assets/staff_bio_publications/McDonald_Exploring_the_Bottom_Line_2007.pdf.

24 Schultz, E. J. 2015. "PepsiCo Exec Has Tough Words for Agencies." *Advertising Age*. October 15. http://adage.com/article/special-report-ana-annual-meeting-2015/agencies-fire-ana-convention/300942/.

25 Hewlett, Silvia Ann., Melinda Marshall, and Laura Sherbin. 2013. "How Diversity Can Drive Innovation." *Harvard Business Review*. December. https://hbr.org/2013/12/how-diversity-can-drive-innovation.

26 Hays. 2014. *The Balance Act Creating a Diverse Workforce*. www.hays.com.au/cs/groups/hays_common/@au/@content/documents/digitalasset/hays_154080.pdf.

27 Brennan, Bridget. 2011. *Why She Buys*. New York: Crown Business.

28   Bennett, Jessica., and Jesse Ellison. 2010. "Women Will Rule the World." *Newsweek*. July 5.

29   Marketing to Moms Coalition. 2009. "The State of the American Mom."

30   Miley, Marissa., and Ann Mack. 2009. "The New Female Consumer: The Rise of Real Moms." *Advertising Age*. https://adage.com/images/random/1109/aa-newfemale-whitepaper.pdf.

31   Cunningham, Jane. 2012. *Inside Her Pretty Little Head: A New Theory of Female Motivation and What It Means for Marketing*. London: Marshall Cavendish International.

32   Deloitte. 2011. *The Gender Dividend*. www2.deloitte.com/content/dam/Deloitte/ru/Documents/public-sector/gender-dividend-en.pdf.

33   Return on Disability. 2013. "Sustainable Value Creation through Disability." http://returnondisability.com/wp-content/uploads/2012/09/The Global Economics of Disability - 2013 Annual Report.pdf.

34   Quinn, Jane B. 1995. "Able to Buy." *Incentive* 169(9): 80.

35   Haller, Beth., and Sue Ralph. 2001. "Profitability, Diversity, and Disability Images in Advertising in the United States and Great Britain." *Disability Studies Quarterly* 21(2). http://dsq-sds.org/article/view/276/301.

36   Siperstein, Gary N., Neil Romano, Amanda Mohle, and Robin Parker. 2006. "A National Survey of Consumer Attitudes towards Companies That Hire People with Disabilities." *Journal of Vocational Rehabilitation* 24(1): 3–9 https://pdfs.semanticscholar.org/0f1d/169e890fda093a 335ba57a534188f76d573f.pdf.

37   LGBT Capital. 2015. "Estimated LGBT Purchasing Power: LGBT-GDP." August. www.lgbt-capital.com/docs/Estimated_LGBT-GDP_%28table%29_-_July_2015.pdf.

38   Daniels, Chris. 2016. "Marketing to the T: Brands Get Inclusive of Transgender Consumers in LGBT Marketing." *PRWeek*. February 24. www.prweek.com/article/1384780/marketing-t-brands-inclusive-transgender-consumers-lgbt-marketing.

39   Wrench, John. 2007. *Diversity Management and Discrimination: Immigrants and Ethnic Minorities in the EU*. Hampshire, UK: Ashgate Publishing Company.

40   Australian Government. 2013. "Australia in the Asian Century." www.defence.gov.au/whitepaper/2013/docs/australia_in_the_asian_century_white_paper.pdf.

41   Asia Literacy Teacher Education Roundtable. 2013. "Asia Education Foundation." www.asiaeducation.edu.au/docs/defaultsource/Researchreports/asia_literacy_teacher_education_roundtable.pdf?sfvrsn=2.

42   PWC. 2015. "Australia's Jobs Future." ANZ PWC Asialink Business Service Report. www.pwc.com.au/asia-practice/assets/anz-pwc-asialink-apr15.pdf.

43   Stoller, Jonathan. 2013. "Workplace Diversity: 'To Win in Your Market, You Need to Hire the Market.'" *The Globe and Mail*. October 24. www.theglobeandmail.com/reportonbusiness/careers/business-education/workplace-diversity-to-win-in-your-market-you-need-to-hire-the-market/article15039793/.

44   Schwartz, Jeff., Josh Bersin, and Bill Pelster. 2014. "Introduction, Global Human Capital Trends." *Deloitte University Press*. March 7. https://dupress.deloitte.com/dup-us-en/focus/human-capital-trends/2014/hc-trends-2014-introduction.html.

45   Dice. 2014. "Dice Tech Salary Survey Results—2014." http://insights.dice.com/report/dice-tech-salary-survey-results-2014/.

46   Wheeler, Mary E., and Susan T. Fiske. 2005. "Controlling Racial Prejudice: Social-Cognitive Goals Affect Amygdala and Stereotype Activation." *Psychological Science* 16(1): 56–63. doi:10.1111/j.0956-7976.2005.00780.x.

47   Legault, Lisa., Jennifer N. Gutsell, and Michael Inzlicht. 2011. "Ironic Effects of Antiprejudice Messages: How Motivational Interventions Can Reduce (but also Increase) Prejudice." *Psychological Science* 22(12): 1472–1477. doi:10.1177/0956797611427918.

48   Tessa L. Dover., Brenda Major, and Cheryl Kaiser. 2016. "Members of High-Status Groups Are Threatened by Pro-Diversity Organizational Messages." *Journal of Experimental Social Psychology* 62: 58–67. doi:10.1016/j.jesp.2015.10.006.

49   Zurer, Rachel. 2018. "Diversity Is for White Men Too: Here's How—and Why It Matters." Conscious Company Media. January 29. https://consciouscompanymedia.com/workplace-culture/diversity-inclusion/diversity-is-for-white-men-too/.

50 Hansen, Fay. 2003. "Diversity's Business Case Doesn't Add Up—Workforce Magazine." *Workforce Magazine*. April 2. www.workforce.com/2003/04/02/diversitys-business-case-doesnt-add-up.

51 Dobbin, Frank., Alexandra Kalev, and Erin Kelly. 2007. "Diversity Management in Corporate America." *Contexts* 6(4): 21–27. doi:10.1525/ctx.2007.6.4.21.

52 Kalev, Alexandra., and Frank Dobbin. 2016. "Why Diversity Programs Fail." *Harvard Business Review*. July–August. https://hbr.org/2016/07/why-diversity-programs-fail.

53 Legault, Lisa., Jennifer N. Gutsell, and Michael Inzlicht. 2011. "Ironic Effects of Anti-Prejudice Messages: How Motivational Interventions Can Reduce (but also Increase) Prejudice." *Psychological Science* 22(12): 1472–1477. doi:10.1177/0956797611427918.

54 Dobbin, Frank., Daniel Schrage, and Alexandra Kalev. 2015. "Rage against the Iron Cage: The Varied Effects of Bureaucratic Personnel Reforms on Diversity." *American Sociological Review* 80(5): 1014–1044. doi:10.1177/0003122415596416.

55 EEOC. "Charge Statistics." US Equal Employment Opportunity Commission. www.eeoc.gov/eeoc/statistics/enforcement/charges.cfm.

56 Foresight. 2016. "When Women Thrive, Businesses Thrive," 28. https://foresight.ubs.com/media/7073/mercer-wwt-global-report-2016.pdf.

57 Roberson, Loriann., Elizabeth A. Deitch, Arthur P. Brief, and Caryn J. Block. 2003. "Stereotype Threat and Feedback Seeking in the Workplace." *Journal of Vocational Behavior* 62(1): 176–188. doi:10.1016/S0001-8791(02)00056-8.

58 Kanter, Rosabeth Moss. 1977. *Men and Women of the Corporation*. New York: Basic Books.

59 Sherbin, Laura., and Ripa Rashid. 2017. "Diversity Doesn't Stick without Inclusion." *Harvard Business Review*. February. https://hbr.org/2017/02/diversity-doesnt-stick-without-inclusion.

60 Hekman, David R., Stefanie K. Johnson, Maw-Der Foo, and Wei Yang. 2017. "Does Diversity-Valuing Behavior Result in Diminished Performance Ratings for Non-White and Female Leaders?" *Academy of Management Journal* 60(2): 771–797. doi:10.5465/amj.2014.0538.

61 Hewlett, Sylvia Ann., Maggie Jackson, Ellis Cose, and Courtney Emerson. 2012. *Vaulting the Color Bar: How Sponsorship Levers Multicultural Professionals into Leadership*. New York: Center for Talent Innovation.

62 Gaucher, Danielle., Justin Friesen, and Aaron C. Kay. 2011. "Evidence That Gendered Wording in Job Advertisements Exists and Sustains Gender Inequality." *Journal of Personality and Social Psychology*. Advance online publication: 1–20. www.fortefoundation.org/site/DocServer/gendered_wording_JPSP.pdf?docID=16121.

63 Ibid.

64 University of Wollongong Australia. 2012. "Inclusive Language Guidelines." *Inclusive Language Guidelines: Policy Directory @ UOW*. www.uow.edu.au/about/policy/UOW140611.html.

65 Sue, Derald Wing., Christina M. Capodilupo, Gina C. Torino, Jennifer M. Bucceri, Aisha Holder, Kevin L. Nadal, and Marta Esquilin. 2007. "Racial Microaggressions in Everyday Life—Implications for Clinical Practice." *American Psychological Association* 62 (4): 271–286. doi:10.1037/0003-066X.62.4.271.

66 Moon, Ihlwan. 2008. "The Foreigners at the Top of LG," 35. *Business Week*. December 11.

67 Hiura, Toshihiko, and Junya Ishikawa. 2016. "Corporate Governance in Japan: Board Membership and Beyond." www.bain.com/insights/corporate-governance-in-japan-board-membership-and-beyond/.

68 DeKrey, Steven J., David M. Messick, and Charles A. Anderson, eds. 2007. *Leadership Experiences in Asia: Insights and Inspirations from 20 Innovators*, 42–43. Singapore: John Wiley & Sons (Asia) Pte. Ltd.

69 Galinsky, Adam D., William W. Maddux, Debra Gilin, and Judith B. White. 2008. "Why It Pays to Get Inside the Head of Your Opponent: The Differential Effects of Perspective Taking and Empathy in Negotiations." *Psychological Science* 19(4): 378–384. doi:10.1111/j.1467-9280.2008.02096.x.

70 Friedman, Raymond A., and Brooks Holtom. 2002. "The Effects of Network Groups on Minority Employee Turnover Intentions." *Human Resource Management* 41(40): 405–421. doi:10.1002/hrm.10051.

71 Scully, Maureen A. 2009. "A Rainbow Coalition or Separate Wavelengths? Negotiations among Employee Network Groups." *Negotiation and Conflict Management Research* 2(1): 74–91. doi:10.1111/j.1750-4716.2008.00029.x.

72 Douglas, Priscilla H. 2008. "Affinity Groups: Catalyst for Inclusive Organizations." *Employment Relations Today* 34(4): 11–18. doi:10.1002/ert.20171.

73 Joseph, Carole. 2013. "Leveraging a Women's Network to Attract, Develop and Retain High Potential Female Talent." *Strategic HR Review* 12(3): 132–137. doi:10.1108/14754391311324480.

74 Cisco. 2010. "Employees Resource Groups That Drive Business." www.cisco.com/c/dam/en_us/about/ac49/ac55/docs/ERGreportEXTERNAL.pdf.

75 Casadevall Arturo., and Jo Handelsman. 2014. "The Presence of Female Conveners Correlates with a Higher Proportion of Female Speakers at Scientific Symposia." *mBio* 5(1): e00846-13. doi:10.1128/mBio.00846-13.

76 Duchesne, A., E. Tessera, K. Dedovic, V. Engert, and J. C. Pruessner. 2012. "Effects of Panel Sex Composition on the Physiological Stress Responses to Psychosocial Stress in Healthy Young Men and Women." *Biological Psychology* 89(1): 99–106. doi:10.1016/j.biopsycho.2011.09.009.

77 Johnson, Stefanie., David Hekman, and Elsa Chan. 2016. "If There's Only One Woman in Your Candidate Pool, There's Statistically No Chance She'll Be Hired." *Harvard Business Review*. www.researchgate.net/publication/303003812_If_There's_Only_One_Woman_in_Your_Candidate_Pool_There's_Statistically_No_Chance_She'll_Be_Hired.

78 Glassdoor Team. 2014. "What Job Seekers Really Think of Your Diversity Stats." *Glassdoor for Employers*. November 17. www.glassdoor.com/employers/blog/diversity.

79 Gallop, Cindy. 2014. "Hire 3 Women to Disrupt White-Male Hegemony." *Adweek*. January 6. www.adweek.com/brand-marketing/hire-3-women-disrupt-white-male-hegemony-154715.

80 Reisinger, Don. 2015. "Intel Ups Referral Bonus to Achieve More Diversity in Its Workforce." *CNET*. August 4. www.cnet.com/news/intel-ups-referral-bonus-to-achieve-more-diversity-in-its-workforce.

81 Cann, Sara. 2013. "The Debate behind Disability Hiring." *Fast Company*. May 8. www.fastcompany.com/3002957/disabled-employee-amendment.

82 Bass, Dina. 2016. "Microsoft to Tie Executive Bonuses to Company Diversity Goals." *Bloomberg*. November 17. www.bloomberg.com/news/articles/2016-11-17/microsoft-to-tie-executive-bonuses-to-company-diversity-goals.

83 Dobbin, Frank., Alexandra Kalev, and Erin Kelly. 2007. "Diversity Management in Corporate America." *Contexts* 6(4): 21–27. doi:10.1525/ctx.2007.6.4.21.

84 Rosenbaum, Eric. 2015. "The 10 Global Companies That Get Diversity: Study." *CNBC*. April 24. www.cnbc.com/2015/04/24/the-10-global-companies-trying-to-lead-on-diversity:-study.html.

85 Kang, Cecilia. 2014. "Google Data-Mines Its Approach to Promoting Women." *The Washington Post*. April 2. www.washingtonpost.com/news/the-switch/wp/2014/04/02/google-data-mines-its-women-problem.

86 Maguire, John. 2016. "ABS Doubles Women Bosses Thanks to Blind Recruitment." *HRD Australia*. June 6. www.hcamag.com/hr-news/abs-doubles-women-bosses-thanks-to-blind-recruitment-217161.aspx.

87 Goldin, Claudia., and Cecilia Rouse. 2000. "Orchestrating Impartiality: The Impact of 'Blind' Auditions on Female Musicians." *American Economic Review* 90(4): 715–741. doi:10.1257/aer.90.4.715.

88 Weber, Lauren., and Elizabeth Dwoskin. 2014. "Are Workplace Personality Tests Fair?" *The Wall Street Journal*. September 30. www.wsj.com/articles/are-workplace-personality-tests-fair-1412044257.

89 Ng, Eddy S. W., and Sears, Greg J. 2010. "The Effect of Adverse Impact in Selection Practices on Organizational Diversity: A Field Study." *The International Journal of Human Resource Management* 21(9): 1454–1471. doi:10.1080/09585192.2010.488448.

90 Diaz-Uda, Anesa Nes. Carmen Medina., and Beth Schill. 2013. "Diversity's New Frontier: Diversity of Thought and the Future of the Workforce." *Deloitte University Press*. www2.deloitte.com/content/dam/insights/us/articles/diversitys-new-frontier/DUP426_Cognitive-diversity_vFINAL1.pdf.

91 Kuncel, Nathan R., David M. Klieger, Brian S. Connelly, and Deniz S. Ones. 2013. "Mechanical versus Clinical Data Combination in Selection and Admissions Decisions: A Meta-Analysis." *Journal of Applied Psychology* 98(6): 1060–1072. doi:10.1037/a0034156.

92 Smith, Jacquelyn. 2015. "Why Companies Are Using Blind Auditions to Hire Top Talent." *Business Insider Australia*. June 1. www.businessinsider.com.au/companies-are-using-blind-auditions-to-hire-top-talent-2015-5?r=US&IR=T.

93 Angwin, Julia., Jeff Larson, Lauren Kirchner, and Surya Mattu. 2016. "Machine Bias." *ProPublica*. May 23. www.propublica.org/article/machine-bias-risk-assessments-in-criminal-sentencing.

94 Caliskan, Aylin., Joanna J. Bryson, and Arvind Narayanan. 2017. "Semantics Derived Automatically from Language Corpora Contain Human-like Biases." *Science* 356(6334): 183–186. doi:10.1126/science.aal4230.

95 Burrell, Ian. 2015. "No Non-White Youth in Recruitment Film about BBC." *The Independent*. October 9. www.independent.co.uk/news/uk/home-news/behind-the-scenes-newsnight-new-show-blows-the-lid-on-the-lack-of-racial-diversity-on-the-bbc-a6688291.html.

96 Sylvia, Ann Hewlett., Carolyn Buck Luce, and Lisa J. Servon. 2008. "The Athena Factor: Reversing the Brain Drain in Science, Engineering, and Technology." *Harvard Business Review*. Research Report 10094: 1–100.

97 Bonazzo, John. 2017. "All-Male PR Panel Tells Women They Can Fix Sexism by Speaking Up More Loudly." *Observer*. June 11. http://observer.com/2017/06/sexism-at-work-mansplaining-public-relations/.

98 Barmeyer, Christoph., and Peter Franklin, eds. 2016. *Intercultural Management: A Case-Based Approach to Achieving Complementarity and Synergy*, 247–248. New York: Palgrave Macmillan.

10 Cross-Cultural Motivation

Motivation is a psychological process through which individuals are driven to satisfy a need. It is also a dilemma because what motivates one individual or group may not motivate another, let alone that each individual can dynamically prioritize different motivators depending on particular contexts. However, successful international business means being able to attract and retain highly qualified personnel across many cultural groups. Much of this is tied to the motivational packages and strategies. In this chapter, we will learn the neurobiology of motivation and address the most fundamental strategies in business environment. More importantly, we will discuss the extent to which these motivational strategies are universal, cultural, and context-dependent.

10.1 The Neuroscience of Motivation

From neuroscience's point of view, motivation has a great deal to do with one's genetic makeup and a neurotransmitter called *dopamine*. In this section, we will briefly touch on the way dopamine works with reward, the extent to which genes influence motivation, and discuss how culture and behavior play a role in this complex interaction.

10.1.1 Dopamine

In our brains, motivation works according to a cost-benefit process. The brain constantly and (sub)consciously calculates and encodes costs (e.g., physical and mental effort, time, discomfort, danger, loss of potential opportunities) against benefits (physiological and psychological needs such as food or relationship).[1] Based on its coding and calculation, the brain makes decisions. The dopamine neurotransmitter regulates motivation, encouraging us to act, either to achieve something good or to avoid something evil.[2] Contrary to the common belief that dopamine controls the brain's pleasure centers, it's a motivation chemical, reacting to both reward and fear.

In the brain's language, a lack of motivation means a lack of dopamine. During periods of low motivation, a brain region that regulates sleep called Hebenula inhibits the voluntary movements, and that's why we would feel sleepy when motivation is low. Dopamine helps electrical impulses move across synapse, "convincing" other neurons to fire by graded potentials (see Chapters 2 and 4). The lack of dopamine reduces intensity of the electrical impulses and weakens graded potentials, making voluntary movements harder. Plus, to invoke the same voluntary movements, higher intensity is needed, which explains why we find the very same task much more difficult when motivation (read: dopamine) is low.

10.1.2 Reward Pathways

The reward system in the brain is complicated, but in an oversimplified way, it comes down to a few structures that are activated when we anticipate or experience pleasure. Reward stimuli, such as drug, praises, novelty, sex, interesting knowledge, the joy of getting things done, and so forth will activate the *ventral tegmental area* (VTA), where dopamine will be released. The arousal dopamine gets us ready for action because we anticipate something important is about to happen, both positive (e.g., happiness) and negative (e.g., anger). From the VTA, dopamine is sent to different parts of the brain. For example, when you receive compliments, reward pathway 1 goes to the amygdala—the emotion detector—and it may say: "The praise feels good." Reward pathway 2 goes to the hippocampus—where long-term memories are stored—and it may say: "Let me remember everything, who gave the praise, the surrounding, the voice, etc." Reward pathway 3 goes to the nucleus accumbens that involves motor functions, and it may say: "Let's do that again, so we can get another praise soon." Reward pathway 4 goes to the prefrontal cortex that helps us to consciously plan on what to do to receive another praise.

Because the brain makes value-based decision between difficulty level and reward, one logical way to keep the motivational level up is to reduce the former and increase the latter. As we already mentioned in Chapter 7 on change management, the strategy is breaking the task into small segments that ensure success, helping us to achieve "small wins." This spiral of steadily increased dopamine habituates the brain with reward pathways, pushing us to go one small step further (GCEB-Be: Brain—Behavior pathway). And of course, "one small step further" is essentially what motivation is all about.

10.1.3 Genetic Impact

Nature and nurture work together, and thus, genes should never be placed out of the picture. Our reward system motivates us to respond positively to a certain stimuli, such as study, praises, money, and even exercise. Researchers have extensively experimented the link between motivational genetics and physical activities. In a study,[3] scientists put rats in cages with running wheels—a subtle suggestion for them to start exercising—and recorded how much time each spent running during a six-day period. They then bred the top 26 runners with each other and compared them with the 26 *laziest* rats. This selective breeding process was repeated through ten generations, and researchers found that rats in the more active line would run 75% more than rats in the couch potato line, and after 16 generations, high-runners would cover double the miles as compared to those from the control group. Genetic impacts in physical motivation have been found in humans as well due to several polymorphism in MAO-A gene.[4] While still limited to the realm of physical motivation, these studies inform us of the impact of genes and the extent to which our lifestyle (read: culture and behavior) can slowly change the genetic makeup of our future generations (GCEB-Be: Behavior—Genes pathway).

Going beyond the focus on physical motivation, in 2015, scientists analyzed two groups of twins, fraternal and identical, from six different countries. It turned out that identical twins were motivated to learn and enjoyed the school subjects, while fraternal twins were motivated to learn, but didn't necessarily enjoy it. The lack of pleasure, in turn, may result in reduced motivation. Hence, this study concluded that up to 50% of the differences in a child's level of motivation to learn could be explained by their genetic inheritance.[5]

It's important to emphasize that the previously mentioned studies don't imply that there is a gene for motivation. As always, it is the result of a dynamic interaction with culture, environment, brain, and behavior (GCEB-Be). In Chapter 2, we mentioned the 7-repeat allele of the dopamine receptor D4 (DRD4-7R)—a mutation created when our ancestors migrated farther away from Africa—which probably enhanced critical cultural values of risk-taking. The 7R allele influences intrinsic motivation as well, but that doesn't imply that native South American and other nomadic groups are genetically more motivated than other cultural groups. A 2016 study[6] suggested that people with the 7R allele from higher family socioeconomic status tend to change jobs *voluntarily* (e.g., better jobs). On the contrary, those with the 7R allele in *poor* neighborhoods changed jobs *involuntarily* (e.g., getting fired). This means cultural backgrounds can interact with the very same gene and influence the course of a person's career in exactly two opposite ways (Behavior—Gene pathway).

10.1.4 Cross-Cultural Findings

Strong/weak group attachment is the cultural value that consistently involves with the neuro-biology of motivation. In Chapter 3, we learned that a combination of geographic impact, genes, and cultural strategies plays a role in creating collectivistic or individualistic tendency among certain groups of humans. A collectivistic tendency motivates people to make decision based on the broader and relational context with others. In an experiment, US and Korean participants were asked to choose one of three available IQ tests. One group chose the test in a completely private condition, the other group made their choice in front of a poster depicting watching eyes. Researchers found that US participants performed best in the private condition and Koreans performed best in the public condition. This means the Korean subjects were more motivated when they felt they were being watched by others. This result is similar to another study, in which white US children were more motivated to perform a task they have chosen, and those with an Asian background were more motivated by a choice made by their mother.[7]

Neural studies weigh in, confirming that when embracing individualism, people work harder if the task is their own personal choice. In contrast, when embracing collectivism, people are more motivated when their choice has social implication. Using feedback related negativity (FRN), a study[8] reported that Chinese participants made no significant difference between the choices they made for *themselves* and their *mother*, between themselves and their *friend*s.[9] Similarly, compared to Caucasian US subjects, Latinos showed greater activity in neural reward regions during costly donation to *family* rather than reward to themselves.[10] Another study[11] assessed electro-cortical responses of US participants from white and Asian background, as they tried to earn as many reward points as possible, either for the self or for the same-sex friend. The results showed that self-centric effects such as cognitive control to reduce errors was observed among the Western subjects in the "self" condition but not in the "friend" condition. On the contrary, such a self-centric effect was not observed among Asians, indicating "your" reward is the same as "my" reward.

10.1.5 Context Dependence

In Chapters 2 and 6, we have discussed the power of priming, brain's plasticity and multicultural mind. Cultural values influence how the brain works, but it is not set in stone. When individuals are primed with different values, their brains *contextually adapt and react accordingly*. For example, a 2014 study[12] reported that when priming individualism, the ventral striatum was activated more strongly in Chinese subjects when they won money. However, after priming collectivism, the structure was active for both the self and for a friend.

But to make people feel more attached and motivated to work with each other, beside the method of priming them with collectivistic values, a much simpler solution is to put them in a group on the basis of similarity. In an experiment,[13] people were asked to rate how similar they were to the contestants of a game show (on social, ethical, and personal preferences like favorite films or music). Results of brain scanning showed that participants felt rewarded when they *observed the similar contestant winning money*.[14] Similarity and relatedness kindle likeability and motivation—a conclusion we reached in Chapter 6. More importantly, this study indicates that reward bias can be cultivated based on ingroup association. If trivial similarities such a as a hobby can modulate support, businesses can establish common grounds and shared identities along many cultural categories to encourage collective motivation.

10.2 Motivation Approach

In Chapter 6, the Inverted Pyramid Model suggested three levels of analysis: Universal, cultural, and individual, all with particular context taken into account. Most theories attempt to satisfy the universal level, aiming to explain reality regardless of contexts. Most fail to do so because culture plays a significant role in influencing behaviors, individual diversity is too large to ignore, and contexts are too dynamic to generalize.

In this section, we will focus on the most cited motivational theory—the pyramid of needs by Maslow—and review its application through different approaches. We will discuss the claim that this theory is universal. With the assumption that national values are stable, the static paradigm posits that national values drive motivation,[15-16] for example, people from Malaysia will be motivated by collectivistic values because the national culture of Malaysia is collectivistic. However, the dynamic paradigm may dispute this assumption, and argues that particular contexts with a complex interaction of values and situations shape motivation. In this section, we will discuss all three approaches: Universal, cultural, and context based.

10.2.1 Universal Assumption Revisited

The classic study of Maslow states that humans are motivated first and foremost by basic needs (food and shelter), *then* safety needs, *then* social needs (relationship and affection), *then* egocentric needs (achievement, responsibility, reputation), and finally self-actualization needs (personal growth, fulfillment, creativity). Studies have insisted that this hierarchical model, despite being a dominant theory in management, is oversimplified, is static, lacks scientific evidence, fails to consider cultural influence, and suffers from the author's ethnocentric point of view.[17-18]

The most critical shortcoming of this motivational theory is that Maslow missed the ultimate role of social connection. None of these needs, even the most basic ones, is possible without collaboration. Humans are social and cooperative animals, using culture (i.e., accumulated knowledge shared by ingroups) as strategies to survive—a topic we discussed in Chapter 2. In many cases, we are willing to face life-threatening dangers (tier 1 and 2 of Maslow's pyramid) to become soldiers and protect others (tier 3), to keep honor and gain status (tier 4), or to prove our potential such as the case of starving artists (tier 5). All this, in turn, might ease the path to acquire a sexual partner (tier 3). This leads to the second shortcoming of Maslow because he never gave much thought to reproduction and parental desire. Evolutionarily speaking, we are motivated to reproduce; we can even die for our children to live, and thus, it has been argued to be the top motivator. From an evolutionary psychology point of view, self-actualization is also an advertising tool to communicate one's values in the social and mating markets. A successful person who has fully achieved self-potential and personal growth is more likely a good life partner for reproduction.

To conclude, needs are not hierarchical but interactive, depending on our ability to connect with others. Relationship is not a third-tier need as Maslow proposed, but one of the most fundamental drivers of motivation, be it the ancient hunter-gatherer groups or today's Facebook and Twitter. Based on this argument, Maslow's model has been rewired with a set of multiple paths (Figure 10.1). It comes with a critical management suggestion: Getting work done by employees cooperating with each other in self-organizing teams.[19]

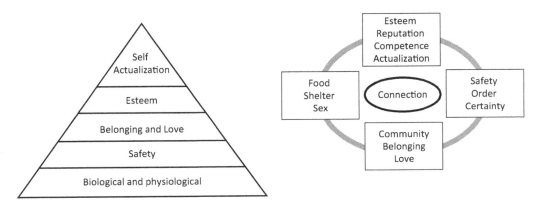

Figure 10.1 Maslow's hierarchy of needs and Maslow "rewired" (Pamela Rutledge)

10.2.2 Cross-Cultural Findings

The third shortcoming of Maslow's model is ethnocentrism. Coming from a culture where low level of group attachment (individualism) prevails, he conceived self-fulfillment—the highest motivator—as completely personal striving, unconnected from others, totally divorced from biological needs, a be-all and end-all goal of life. However, it has been argued that in societies where a high level of group attachment (collectivism) is prioritized, the needs of acceptance and community will outweigh the needs for freedom and autonomy.[20]

When other values are taken into account, we encounter a matrix of diverse motivators based on the social norms regarded as important in each country. For example, stereotypically, a US person could explain the extra effort made by the money received (masculinity), a Frenchman by personal pride (individualism), a Chinese by mutual obligations (collectivism), and a Dane by fellowship (femininity).[21] There is a large body of literature focusing on cross-cultural/cross-national spectrum, with both consistent and contradictory findings. Table 10.1 gives a summary. It doesn't include other cultural groups, such as age, occupation, economical background, religion, or gender. Studies that discuss these groups are rare, but findings are significant. For example, a study reported that children have higher physical needs and desire to be loved, esteem needs are highest among adolescents, young adults strive for self-actualization, and elderly people prioritize safety.[22]

Table 10.1 Value-based motivation strategies

Cultural Values	Motivation Strategies
Strong Group Attachment (Collectivism)	• Rewards that benefit significant others: Contribution to housing funds; care for aging parents; family allowance; child care. • Rewards that tie to commitment and loyalty: Life-long employment; job security; benefits based on seniority and membership; group recognition. • Reward that motivates team effort. For example, reward is based on the *least* productive or the *most* productive person of the team, hence galvanizing support from others to boost performance of this target person. • Emphasize group dignity, identity, and honor. Emphasize the need to fight for and live up to these collective expectations. • Job designs that enable employees to support, socialize, and empower each other: Team reward; job sharing; team autonomy; team outing; trust building; close work proximity. • Reward for self-sacrifice, team effort, and collective purpose. • Recognition from team.
Weak Group Attachment (Individualism)	• Rewards that highlight personal achievement: Employee of the month; individual-based incentives. • Job designs that enable individual autonomy and opportunities for personal advancement. • Reward for personal effort. • Recognition from peers.
Strong Hierarchy Acceptance	• Emphasize reward differences: Pay, privileges, and perks that distinguish between low and high rankings. • Emphasize ranking differences: Establish titles to reflect authority; create new titles if necessary; emphasize promotion opportunities and job status. • Reward subordinates for compliance and managers for directives. • Recognition from managers and subordinates.

Table 10.1 (Cont.)

Cultural Values	Motivation Strategies
Weak Hierarchy Acceptance (Egalitarian)	• Emphasize equality: Minimal pay gap; nondiscriminative treatments; transparent policies. • Encourage employee engagement: Collect opinions; decision-making based on consensus; strong labor unions. • Job designs that enable autonomy, flexibility, and practicality. • Reward subordinates for engagement and managers for democracy. • Informal recognition from others.
Masculine Gender Association	• Emphasize achievement: Commission-based salary; project-based pay; performance-based reward; job status; promotion. • Emphasize reward differences: Pay, privileges, and perks that distinguish between low and high performance. • Stimulate competitive environment internally and externally. • Reward for ambition, assertiveness, extraordinary individual and team performance against all odds. • Recognition from influential and powerful figures.
Feminine Gender Association	• Emphasize fringe and need-based benefits: Company car; health care; wellness program; citizen program; personal development; leaves. • Emphasize work-life balance (WLB): Flexibility; humanized workload. • Job designs that enable meaningful work: Higher purpose and greater good; job content matches individual identity and values; jobs with positive impact on others. • Reward for initiatives, cooperation, social impact, sustainability, constructive feedback, and consensus. • Recognition from broader community.
Strong Uncertainty Avoidance	• Emphasize rules, regulations, and policies of rewards and promotion. Make them simple, public, and clear. • Emphasize job security, clear career pathways, stepwise growth of salary and benefits. • Reward rule compliance, objectivity, transparency, instructive feedback. • Formal recognition from system.
Weak Uncertainty Avoidance	• Emphasize diverse alternatives of career pathways, job opportunities, and promotion. • Reward creativity, initiatives, autonomy, practicality, flexibility, and inspired feedback. • Spontaneous recognition.
Future Orientation	• Emphasize long-term benefits: Job security; pension packet; health insurance; seniority-based incentives; profit-sharing; WLB. • Reward for sustainability, long-term planning, relationship building, trust building, and corporate social responsibility (CSR) effort. • Recognition as future's reward.
Present/Short-time Orientation	• Emphasize quick benefits: Project-based incentives; productivity-based pay; instant rewards. • Reward for quick problem-solving, crisis resolution, and instant feedback. • Timely and frequent recognition when jobs are complete.

10.2.3 Context Dependence

The fourth shortcoming of Maslow's model is that it disregards changes to the hierarchy by circumstance. In a landmark study that critically reevaluates Maslow's model from evolutionary biology's perspective, the authors strongly emphasized that motivational priorities vary with the trade-offs inherent in the immediate ecological context. In their words:

> If you are having lunch with your boss, and you discover a scorpion crawling up your leg, self-protection goals are likely to trump whatever food- or status-related goals were salient a moment earlier. But if it is merely an ant on your leg, and your boss has just asked you to consider a promotion, the self-protection goal is not likely to be foremost in mind. In general, cues in the current situation are expected to dynamically interact with a person's developmental phase and recent deprivation or satisfaction of different needs, as well as the individual's cognitive, affective, or morphological traits that might make any particular threat or opportunity more threatening or potentially beneficial.[23]

Thus, the particular dynamics of different values, genetics, biological needs, job types, corporate cultures, individual preferences, and so forth can interactively change the ranking of motivators significantly. This is the reason why research findings on motivation across different categories have been inconsistent. For example, despite stereotypically described as a culture of individualism and masculinity, a study[24] among US employees in 2016 revealed that the top job satisfaction aspect was not pay but "respectful treatment of employees"—a demand that more reflects collectivism and femininity. Further, motivation strategies are extremely diverse and reflect the specific context of the workplace. For example, according a review from *HR People*,[25] Indian firms pay for aging parents, Hong Kong workers get coverage for traditional medicine, Filipinos receive bags of rice as a benefit, Chinese and Russian multinationals help to reduce the burden of mortgage and housing, Japanese employees receive incentives to have kids, Mexican firms offer "pollution-escape" trips so employees can escape from the polluted cities, executives in Brazil and Papua New Guinea are often given chauffeur-driven cars with bulletproof windows to protect them against kidnapping, and so forth.

To understand the complexity of context, let's consider a case study. Back in the mid-1970s, the traditional car assembly line was where workers stood along a moving conveyor and performed individual tasks when cars moved along the belt. Volvo was the first to change this system by creating separate platforms where a group of workers completed a list of tasks together at their own pace with no direct supervision. With this increased autonomy, rewards and recognitions are provided based on team performance rather than individual accomplishment. One would think such a collectivistic approach should be adopted in Japan, but in fact, Japanese workers keep the traditional assembly line, although they are able to move around and help each other. A hallmark of the Japanese system is that any individual worker usually has the power to stop the whole assembly line if a problem is detected. This is the case in which we see a dynamics of values, job types, and motivational strategies combining to create success. Despite the tendency to embrace individualism, Swedish workers were able to perform in a collectivistic way because the structure of reward and the nature of their job enabled them to do so. For the Japanese, their tendency to embrace collectivism does not necessarily translate into a *structure* of work group, but a *spirit* of helping each other while on individual talks. In this specific job content, collectivism gives way to (1) the effectiveness of the individual task and (2) the importance of strong uncertainty avoidance with an emphasis on quality control.

Here is another case in point. Lincoln Electric is famous for its incentive system of paying workers per unit. There is no salary, no paid vacation, and no paid sick leave, but there are generous bonuses based on their individual job performance and company benefits. The company has the lowest absenteeism and turnover rates in the industry and their employees are among the highest paid blue-collar workers in the world. While this system has been praised as a great fit for an individualistic, masculine, and weak hierarchy accepting US society, it failed in Germany—a country with a stereotypically similar value profile. In a somewhat feminine argument, German workers believed that the system was exploitative and inhumane. They refused to work excessively long hours (a change from 35 hours to 43–58 hours per week) at the expense of life quality. Lincoln Electronics perceived this as a "poor work attitude," and closed the plant.[26]

Lincoln Electric's strategy failed mainly due to a lack of knowledge of local culture. First of all, German masculinity is not the same as US masculinity. German workers excel in efficiency at work, not achievement above all else. They work hard and focus on making the best out of the time at work. In other words, Germans work fewer hours, deliver more, and earn double[27] that of their US counterparts. Second of all, German individualism and hierarchy acceptance are not the same as US individualism and hierarchy acceptance. Germany is famous for a business model called "corporatism," in which the state, labor unions, and employers form a solid economic triangle as they co-determine mutual goals. Consensus and negotiation play a central role in German business life where strong unions have a powerful voice in all levels of decision making.[28] For Lincoln Electric, a lack of communication worsened the situation, widening the difference between the way Lincoln Electric perceived the privilege of the manager (to decide the rule) and the way German unions perceived consensual decision making as fundamental between managers and workers.

When Lincoln Electric decided to open a plant in Mexico, they changed the approach. Instead of imposing the rule, the management slowly introduced their incentive system by letting two volunteers try it out with a guarantee that they would not lose the money. Soon the two employees started making more than their colleagues and the rest of the workers gradually asked to join. Despite the tendency to embrace collectivism, Mexican workers chose to work according to an extremely individualistic design—one that also contradicts the incorrect stereotype of the Mexican laid back attitude (in fact, Mexicans work the longest hours of all OECD countries).[29] This approach succeeded because Mexican workers were probably more concerned about incomes, and their individualistic way at work was meant to support a collectivistic goal at home, that is providing for (extended) families. Last but not least, the excellent communication strategy that Lincoln Electric adopted to allow volunteers and slowly navigate the water in a new market helped to create trust—a fundamental element of success.

The two case studies presented in this section suggest that value-based business strategies alone are not sufficient. A context-specific approach is more appropriate for the following reasons: (1) Value indexes from the static paradigm are limited, simplified, with different meanings confined in the same terminology; (2) effective motivation strategies are based on not only values but on the dynamics of many other factors such as job types, incomes, economic situation, business goals, and reward structure; and (3) a reminder of GCEB-Be that the Culture—Behavior pathway is dynamic, that is culture does not always dictate behavior, and that collectivistic people may voluntarily choose to work in individualistic ways. In the tree of culture, values and outward expressions are not always congruent. What one does and what one believes can appear to be the opposite (Chapter 4).

10.3 Extrinsic Reward

Extrinsic reward is tangible and visible, often offered in terms of salary, bonus, award, or public recognition. Extrinsic rewards are fundamental to all employees. In this section, we will look at the extent to which salary plays a significant role in different group cultures and contexts. Because extrinsic reward is a double-edged sword, we will also address the disadvantages of money in the reward system.

10.3.1 Cross-Cultural Findings

The static paradigm of culture posits that *values guide behaviors*, hence, people from societies with high-level masculinity tend to emphasize materialistic achievement, and thus, will prioritize money as a major motivator. While this assumption acts as a good start for understanding, it also risks stereotypes and false beliefs (see Chapter 4). For example, regardless of their gender association index on masculine versus feminine, data from diverse Asian countries suggested that one of the *most* important tools in talent recruitment and retention remains salary.[30-31-32-33-34] In fact, Chinese job market is characteristically volatile because talented employees hop jobs frequently to get better salaries. A foreign company called Rockwell Automation had to set up a new rule that required new recruits to have a resignation letter from their previous employer, just to make sure that they are not pretending to apply for a new job, and then work at it for a few days to pressure the former employer for a pay rise.[35] Further, employees in many non-Western countries are more likely to discuss their compensation package with friends and colleagues, making it possible to compare and know who earns the most.

On the contrary, a large-scale research of 7,000 workers in OECD-Western countries reported that with the exception of Hungary, pay is ranked as one of the *least* important aspects of a job.[36] However, we can't jump on a conclusion that Eastern cultures prefer money and Western cultures do not. Two surveys on work values showed that salary is the *most* important criteria in job seeking for all subgroups: (1) The feminine such as Vietnamese, Danish, Finnish; (2) the average such as the United States, the United Kingdom, and Germany; and (3) the masculine Japanese.[37-38] Another global survey among more than 200,000 job seekers from 189 countries revealed that salary ranked *low* (8th) in importance for job seekers around the world,[39] regardless of the big differences in the masculine-feminine index. We can conclude that while masculinity may lead to a stronger emphasis on monetary reward, the national index in masculinity as proposed by Hofstede can only be seen as a starting point for a thorough study with specific context taken into account.

10.3.2 Context Dependence

The inconsistence of findings in salary indicates that when acquisition of money is used as a motivator, country is clearly an unreliable variable for comparison. Hence, despite being a strong advocate for country level of analysis, Hofstede suggested that when it comes to financial compensation, *job categories* are a more effective way of examining motivation—a finding supported by a study that concluded that occupation is a good indicator of homogeneous culture rather than nationality.[40] It makes sense because salary can be a top motivator for blue-collar workers and not so for professionals and executives. Many jobs have low starting salaries but a fast growth rate, while it is the opposite for others.

Aspects such as *different phases of a career*, *positions*, or *generation* should be taken into account as well. For example, in Singapore, salary is the top motivator when individuals hunt for a job, but work-life balance (WLB) is the key that makes them stay.[41] Across Asia, securing a high salary is the top priority, but mostly for those who look to change their positions,[42] or those who lack a security net that makes family members rely on each other.[43] Similarly, fresh graduates would consider salary as one of the biggest factors due to their heavy student debt load[44]—an averaged amount of $37,000 in 2016 for the United States. But just a little further down the career, millennials are willing to give up $7,600 per year for better WLB.[45]

Socially shaped gender differences play a role too. Due to some advantages in nurturing (see Chapter 8), men are often more confident about their competence and up to nine times more willing to initiate payment negotiation than women.[46-47] Having learned to doubt their quality, when women do negotiate, they ask for 30% less money, which could add up to $1 million over the course of their career.[48] Further, when women actively ask for salary compensation, they are *penalized* by male evaluators.[49] This probably explains why when asked to pick metaphors for the process of salary negotiating, men picked "winning a ball game" and a "wrestling match," and women picked "going to the dentist."[50] Men see salary negotiation as an exciting game they may win, women see it as a painful experience. In short, these studies suggest that gender biases influence statistics on pay. Women could be motivated as strongly as men by good salary and pay rise—a possibility that is likely hidden due to the misleading data that is skewed by stereotype threats and socially expected behaviors.

10.3.3 *The Side Effect of Money*

However, no matter how critical monetary reward is, it should not be the only motivator to work. The first disadvantage is a risk of replacing intrinsic with extrinsic motivation. Here, a classic story comes to mind: An old man was bothered by kids playing ball and yelling every day outside his house. So, he offered each one of them 25 cents to play and yell real loud. The kids loved it. On the fourth day, however, the old man told them he was sorry but he could only pay them 15 cents. They grumbled but did it anyhow. The fifth day, he told them he could only pay 5 cents. The kids left and never came back! The old man had successfully changed the kids' thinking from an intrinsic motivation of "I love to play ball here" to an extrinsic motivation of "I'm just playing here for the money."

The second disadvantage of monetary reward is reduced ethics. Once basic needs are met, additional income does not affect job or life satisfaction and even starts to be destructive. A collection of 165 studies from 18 countries to date has shown that the hunger for material gains makes us *more attuned to business mode* but also *less humane*.[51] Mere subconscious cues of money can influence our behaviors. For example, after a word game that prompted people to create sentences such as "She spends money liberally," they would tend to make unethical decisions in their subsequent activities, even when there is no direct financial reward.[52] In another experiment, simply waiting in a room with some Monopoly bills on the table can decrease empathy. With money at the back of the mind, money-primed people were less likely to help others, they would give less time to colleagues in need of assistance and less money to charity. They would sit farther away from the others and tend to choose individual prizes rather than group-related ones.[53]

Indeed, wealth can influence our behaviors and morality in detrimental ways. Studies have shown that rich people are less capable at reading others' facial expressions—a marker of empathy.[54] Heart-rate monitors showed that their heart rate did not change in response to the suffering of others.[55] Rich people are less likely to stop for pedestrians, more likely to cut off other vehicles, exhibit unethical decision-making tendency, take valued goods from others, lie in a negotiation, cheat if that can increase their chances of winning, and endorse unethical behavior at work.[56] Being rich also risks self-serving bias because people with money tend to attribute luck (e.g., born into an affluent high-status family or in a developed country) with inherent quality (I got in so I must be good).[57] Subsequently, they will tend to exhibit overconfident, dominant, unfriendly, and greedy behaviors. In a rigged Monopoly game, half of the players were *secretly* given *twice* the resource.[58] They boasted about their "strategies," without knowing that it all began with luck. On the contrary, those who were randomly assigned to low-status groups with fewer resources experienced *decreased* feeling of pride and power.[59]

Money-primed people also become less emotional and oblivious to physical pain. In an experiment, researchers asked one group of participants to count money and another group to count blank paper. In the subsequent temperature test, those who had counted money could keep their hand under burning-hot water longer and felt less distress when excluded from a group game.[60] The indication is that the thought of money not only makes us less empathetic, but money can also act as a substitute for social acceptance and love. When we are with loved ones, we can endure the pain better, but when we have money, it acts as a resource and we assume we can endure the pain equally well. However, this compensation comes with a price: The reduced capacity for interpersonal relationship and compassion.

Neuroscience gives us more insight into the impact of monetary reward on thoughts and behaviors. To make it simple, *the brain on money looks a great deal like the brain on drugs.* The brain scans of addicts who were high on cocaine and game players who were about to make money were almost indistinguishable, both displayed heightened brain activation in the nucleus accumbens.[61] When we are "high" on money, the more money we have, the hungrier we become. The pursuit of wealth becomes a compulsive behavior, very much like the effect of drug. Money is no longer a goal, but the *more* of it, in other words, greed. This explains why money doesn't equate to happiness. Too much money even brings harm, as affluent people and their families suffer higher rates of depression due to ceaseless striving for material possessions.[62-63-64] The magnitude of depression is no less than poor people striving to make ends meet. The only difference is that for the poor, more money is a struggle, but for the rich, more money is an addiction. Taken together, HR practices that emphasize the goal of *maximizing profits* can cause workers to subconsciously make unethical decisions at the expense of the company and their own well-being.

Fortunately, another critical finding of neuroscience on reward shows us some positive insight. In term of functionality, money and social status activate the very *same* region of the brain.[65] Receiving compliments and gaining reputation give us similar satisfaction just like the way we work for salary. Our brains constantly perform a balancing act to decide if social benefits may outweigh monetary costs. This explains why although salary is a crucial motivator, it is not always the most important, and rarely the only criteria that motivates people to work.

Thankfully, it also explains why wealth is not necessarily tied with the psychological curse of greed, selfishness, and immorality. As discussed in Chapter 8 on how to fight biases, people in powerful and financially comfortable position can perfectly exercise empathy and compassion. For example, they can approach the less fortunate at the top level of the Inverted Pyramid Model (Chapter 6) as *unique individuals* with personal stories and not as a number;[66] they can practice *perspective taking* by imagining themselves in the position of the poor;[67] and their attitude will change if they and the poor are in the *same ingroup*. The same counts for companies that need to balance between the urge to maximize profits and the necessity of doing good. Not only will this balance bring well-being to the employees, an ethical business that does not prioritize money above all else is also what job seekers and customers nowadays demand.

10.4 Intrinsic Reward

Intrinsic reward is identified by the nature of our work. In the modern era, our work is more and more driven by a sense of purpose. Fundamentally, it revolves around *committing* to meaningful purpose, *choosing* the best way to fulfill that purpose, having the *competence* to perform, and making *progress* to achieving the purpose. In this section, we will briefly address the universal advantages of meaningful work, the extent to which it is influenced by culture and context, and strategies to cultivate meaningful work among employees.

10.4.1 The Benefits of Intrinsic Meaningful Work

Universally, meaningful work is a fundamental component of well-being[68] and hence, a key motivator to work. It is the subjective experience that what we are doing is interesting, challenging, and significant, that it facilitates personal growth and contributes to the greater good.[69] It's a kind of work that would make a person get up early, stay up late, and invest extra time and effort to get things done because they want to, not because they have to. Professor Michael Pratt at Boston College had an illustrative way to explain it by using the old tale of three bricklayers. When asked what they're doing, the first bricklayer responds: "I'm putting one brick on top of another." The second replies: "I'm making six pence an hour." And the third says: "I'm building a cathedral—the house of God." A sense of purpose, challenge, and accomplishment is what makes one's job meaningful. This has an incredible influence on performance, empowerment,[70] well-being,[71] job satisfaction,[72] and work value.[73]

Creating meaningful work is the biggest challenge for contemporary HR on motivation policies due to an epidemic phenomenon of disengagement at work. The statistics are alarming: 87% of employees worldwide are not fully engaged at work.[74] In the United States, 75% of the workforce negatively influence their colleagues, miss workdays, and drive customers away. This costs the United States 550 billion US dollars each year in lost productivity,[75] the United Kingdom 340 billion pounds,[76] and Australia 54.8 billion Australian dollars.[77]

So, what makes one's work meaningful? The "Need for Achievement" theory states that people are motivated to (1) seek a sense of accomplishment; (2) fulfill the need to lead and influence others; and (3) satisfy the need for social interaction. Meaningful work often combines all three factors. Another influential theory focuses on "identity" or "authenticity."[78] It suggests that meaningful work is what fits the way we view ourselves, for this alignment promotes feelings of internal consistency and self-congruence.[79] In other words, it's a person-job fit in which work matches own values.

10.4.2 Cross-Cultural Findings

There is a great diversity in the level of importance each cultural group would place on meaningful work. Some studies suggest that being involved in significant jobs is more critical for professionals, executives,[80] those with a higher education,[81] and those of more secured economic backgrounds. This doesn't mean people from lower-class background do not have the same desire for meaningful work. They simply face more constraints and barriers to do so.[82]

Two cultural groups with consistent emphasis on meaningful work are employees with *disability* and *millennials*. With regard to the former group, work is meaningful because it is a source of identity and feelings of normality.[83] More than anyone, people with disability want to be seen as valuable employees. They want to contribute in a meaningful way with a job that is tailored to their strength and interest, not just have a job for a job's sake, or a simple work assigned on the basis of their disabilities.[84]

The requirement of meaningful work is especially high among millennials who tend to be more educated and less likely to bear the brunt of poverty. A study of 7,700 millennials from 29 countries in 2016 showed that 56% of the participants said they had ruled out working for an organization because of its values, and 49% of them would *not* undertake a task at work if that goes against their personal values.[85] Globally, values guide who millennials work for and what they do. This is the generation who uses the word "fun" to describe their dream job, indicating that a job is to enjoy with intrinsic motivation.[86] In another study, meaningful work (30%) is on par with salary (30%) to be the top criteria for millennials during their job search.[87]

In term of cultural values, meaningful work evokes high level of both masculinity and femininity. Challenges, personal accomplishment, and leadership are associated with masculinity, while a sense of community, doing good to others, and significant and intrinsic interest are associated with femininity. As a matter of fact, individuals can score high on both values (androgynous).[88] Further, due to the dynamics of cultural groups, cross-national studies often contradict each other because they only focus on nationality and ignore other collective cultures such as management level, occupation, generation, economic background, educational level, and so forth. For example, French and Italian employees ranked work "challenge" as the top motivator out of 18 factors in this study,[89] but according to European Value Survey,[90] a sense of "achievement" only ranked 8th out of 17 factors. Hence, meaningful work is fundamentally context dependent because each individual or group is intrinsically motivated by different things at work.

10.4.3 Strategies for Intrinsic Meaningful Work

A well-cited theory that aims to increase intrinsic motivation is *employee engagement/participation*. Workers become personally and meaningfully involved with the organization beyond their tasks.[91] Another influential theory is the *job characteristics model*.[92] It posits that these five job designs can empower workers and make them intrinsically involve with their job: (1) Skill variety: Make a job more meaningful by employing different skills and talents; (2) Task identity: Well-defined jobs that contribute to a larger meaningful project; (3) Task significance: How a job affects others; (4) Autonomy: Independence and discretion in carrying out the job; and (5) Task feedback: Clear, specific, constructive, action-oriented information about the performance, and recognition for progress.

To decide which characteristic is the most influential, policy makers have to consider a wide range of culture at the collective level: Ethnicity,[93] age,[94] job type,[95] gender,[96] religion,[97] and so forth. For example, when a weak level of hierarchy acceptance prevails, such as in a stereotypical Western tech company, programmers may rank "autonomy" as the most important motivator. Autonomy also appeals to younger generation, professionals, virtual employees, and creative industries. However, the moment an employee starts a family, (s)he may swap "autonomy" for "task significance" because it allows her/him to provide for the loved ones. Similarly, the same employee would rank "task feedback" more important if (s)he is embarking a new mission. As described in the book *Purpose and Meaning in the Workplace*,[98] the dynamics of these cultural categories is immense and thus, there is no single magic solution. Following the identity theory in motivation, the best approach is: (1) First run a *cultural audit*, using measurements such as Work as Meaning Inventory,[99] and then (2) conduct a thorough analysis to build specific and contextual *identity profile* of different cultural groups in the organization. Managing meaningfulness begins with appealing to the elements found in these profiles and (re)shaping the context within which the work is performed.

At the organizational level, businesses that engage in corporate social responsibility (CSR) stand a better chance in cultivating meaningful work. The reason for this connection is because morality and prosocial attitude are inherently part of meaningfulness. This is related to point 3 (task significance) in the aforementioned job characteristics model. "Mission-driven" companies have 30% higher levels of innovation and 40% higher levels of retention, and they tend to be first or second in their market segment.[100] The cultural group that demands CSR the most is millennials. Across 30 countries, 76% of millennials expect businesses to be a force for positive social impact while frequently providing employees opportunities to engage with good causes.[101] This indicates that CSR is no longer a nice thing to do but a business strategy aimed at intrinsically motivating people.

10.5 Work-Life Balance

WLB is defined as a satisfactory level of involvement between the multiple roles in a person's life. It's a sense of harmony and fulfillment when one has opportunities to *experience many aspects of life to the fullest*. With women and millennials now making the majority of the workforce, long gone is the myth of an ideal employee: Male, full-time, works hard, fully committed to the company without any responsibility outside work.[102] WLB has become critical on management agenda because it is not only a powerful motivator for employees (they want a fulfilled life) but also an important business imperative (it brings profits).[103]

10.5.1 The Benefits of Work-Life Balance

All cultural groups face difficulties maintaining this harmony: Baby boomers who have to care for their aging parents just as they are in the prime time for leadership; women who enter the peak of their career at the same time as when their children need the most attention—entering teenage; young professionals with newly established families who struggle within a society that sees extreme long hours as a sign of work commitment, team spirit, loyalty and respect to the managers, and so forth. In today's fast-paced global environment, we are easily drawn toward an escalation of excessive working hours and workload. But it is detrimental and not necessarily effective. Those who experience work-life conflict were nearly 30 times more likely to suffer from depression and 11 times more likely to have a substance-dependence disorder (e.g., heavy drinking).[104] A one standard deviation increase in work-life conflict increases the retirement probability of males in part-time work by 5.9%, that of females in full-time work by 2.2%, and that of females in part-time work by 4.6%.[105] In cultures with long hour tradition such as Japan and Korea, women are forced to become stay-at-home mothers due to time conflict between office and home.

In contrast, employees with lower level of work-life conflict report higher job satisfaction.[106] For JetBlue, working from homes and trading shifts engendered a 30% boost in agent productivity and 38% jump in customer-service levels compared to industry averages.[107] A similar strategy saved Ctrip $2,000 per year per employee.[108] Positive experience of WLB contributes to higher retention rates, attendance, and lower turnover intentions.[109-110]

The term WLB, however, can be misleading. It signals a trade-off between work and life, that one can't possibly have a life if (s)he works long hours. The right question to measure WLB is not "how many hours do you work?" but "does your work *prevent* you from enjoying other aspects of life?" So one can have passion at work, yet not missing the joy outside her/his office. "Remember, Mondays are fine. It's your life that sucks."[111]

10.5.2 Cross-Cultural Findings

WLB signals a *contextual* evaluation. That's why the field still struggles to agree on a common definition of WLB.[112] Across cultures and individuals, WLB means different things, as "balance" for one can be interpreted as "stressful" for another.

In terms of gender and generation, WLB used to be a top requirement for women who are socially expected to be both caregivers and breadwinners. However, it turns out men and younger generations also want to "have it all," that is working at the level they are capable of and still have time for things critical to human flourishing such as spouses, kids, friends, hobbies, prayer, sleep, reflection time, volunteering, and charity work. Work-life conflict is not gender specific, as 90% of working mothers and 95% of working fathers in the United States reported the problem,[113] while 63% of the working fathers said they spent too little time with their kids.[114] In a Fortune 500 survey among male executives, 64% of the managers stated that at this stage

Table 10.2 Work motivators among millennials in 2016, excluding salary (Deloitte [2016])

Good work/life balance	16.8
Opportunities to progress/be leaders	13.4
Flexibilities, that is remote working, flexible hours	11.0
Sense of meaning from my work	9.3
Professional development training programs	8.3
The impact it has on society	6.8
The quality of its products/services	6.4
Strong sense of purpose	6.2
Opportunities for international travel	5.9
Fast growing/dynamic	4.4
A leading company that people admire	4.3
Invests in and uses the latest technology	4.1
The reputation of its leaders	3.1

of life, they would choose more time over money, and 87% agreed that WLB is a competitive advantage in attracting talent.[115] For millennials, a global survey reported that if salary is not factored in, WLB is the top motivator when they search for a job (Table 10.2).[116]

In term of values, two fundamental concerns associated with a stronger emphasis on WLB are group attachment and gender association. Those who embrace a high level of individualism and femininity are more likely to prioritize the motivational impact of WLB.[117-118] The rationale is that individualists tend to subjectively evaluate their overall quality of work and life experiences and take responsibility for achieving what they themselves perceive as a "balance," that is, less pressure to take into account opinions of their ingroups. For cultures that embrace femininity, there is higher social approval and more tolerance toward men and women pursuing their life preferences without the pressure to adhere to a traditional gender role. A feminine attitude toward life also means a preference for quality of life. The most well-known example comes from Scandinavian countries where a 34-hour work week and a part-time job are the norm, even for executives.

10.5.3 *Context Dependence*

Individualism and femininity are surely not enough to predict the importance of WLB, let alone the practice of WLB. For example, despite the stereotypical national value of a masculine culture, other values of German culture such as efficiency, privacy, and individualism have made the country a leader of WLB when it comes to working hours. Germany has the world's lowest amount of work hours per week[119] and the union is fighting for 28-hour work week.[120] In contrast, Japan has a different mixture of masculinity (work hard to rebuild their devastated country after World War II), extraordinary respect for hierarchy (employees would not leave the office if managers still stay), and intense collectivism (companies used to guarantee lifetime employment, thus deserve absolute loyalty). This context is a recipe for overwork as it's not uncommon that workers leave their office just before midnight.[121] This has caused thousands of people to drop dead or commit suicide.[122] Comparing Germany and Japan, we can conclude that, in this case, not one value but a dynamics of cultural values, historical development, and economic imperatives influence the attitude and practices of WLB.

Here is another case of engineers in India, China, and Hungary. In India, the engineers, mostly specialists, reached out directly to other team specialists when they had problems. Their sense of mutual commitment led to very long hours, finishing between 7–10 PM because everyone felt they had to be available to their colleagues. In China, the engineers never spoke to one another, all requests for help went through the project leader, and their time was rigidly controlled. That made everyone highly dependent on this person and locked them to her/his hours. In Hungary, when one engineer had a problem, (s)he'd go to whoever happened to be free. It is common for them to do errands during the day, and to work later if necessary. As a result, many people were able to help each other and it was less important for everyone to be at the office all the time. All three teams deliver similar levels of productivity. Yet the Indian team's approach was a formula for burnout, the Chinese team was at the whim of its boss, and only the Hungarian team's approach allowed a life.[123-124-125]

Thus, despite being ranked by the static framework as individualistic (80), masculine (88), and strong uncertainty avoiding (82), Hungarian engineers have the best approach to WLB with their teamwork, a possibility for quality of life, and a good level of flexibility. In fact, a Hungarian project leader in this case study left in the midst of an extremely busy time because of a planned vacation with the family and left no way for the group to get in contact because time with family is sacred. What we learn from this case is that particular context can defy any stereotypes.

Another interesting case in point is Pakistan, where WLB means *more* work while keeping the same personal life for women. Women doctors are highly sought after as brides because they are considered to have the qualities of both a professional and a housewife, plus "doctor" means "high status." But as soon as they are married, social pressure forces half of them to drop out and stay at home. A doctor bride is a trophy. That is why despite a staggering 70% of female medical students, Pakistan has a shortage of female doctors. WLB for these women comes in the form of telemedicine where they can give service from home to remote regions, to female patients who can't travel easily, and to the poor who can't afford access to big hospitals in the cities.[126] This is the case in which gender *inequality* drives WLB practices, contradicting the study cited in the previous section. Again, it reconfirms the importance of the context-based approach instead of the national value approach.

10.5.4 Strategies for Work-Life Balance

Because WLB is contextual, again, the best approach starts with running a cultural audit to find out who values what and how to synchronize the preferences. Employees need to have the freedom to define what success looks like to them and translate that into work structures. There is no one-size-fits-all solution.

The most important hallmark of WLB is *flexibility*, which encompasses a wide range of strategies that require us to *rethink* and *restructure work design* at all levels: Job stability, work security, future growth pathway, promotion pathway, phased retirement, virtual working environment, working from home and flexible locations, job sharing, part-time work, sabbatical leave, flexible business routine and travel planning, compressed work weeks, shorter work hour for parents, on-site and near-site childcare, and so forth. Latest in the trend is a fertility program, in which top tech and news companies offer female workers the chance to freeze their eggs to have children later in life and dedicate their younger years to a career.[127] A cultural audit will reveal that masculine high earners may consider trading money for time, but feminine high earners may want to trade money for long-term insurance and work security. Similarly, instead of overworking to follow a promotion path of making "director" in five years, professionals will be able to choose their own speed and design an alternative for eight or ten years, giving more time to their family when the children are still too young.

For those at the top management level who are hardest hit by extreme workload, flexibility is embedded in a job design approach that embraces two most unexpected values: Femininity and collectivism. As Xerox CEO Anne Mulcahy famously said: "Businesses need to be 24/7, but individuals don't." In an article titled "Get a Life," author Jody Miller gave three excellent examples.[128] The 20th Century Fox Television company used to have a legendary duo of long-serving presidents: Gary Newman and Dana Walden. It was not a job share, but a company with two presidents. They spent the first year doing everything together. Only when trust was firmly established did work become a dynamic flow. For everyone else, it didn't matter who was in the office because they were incredibly in sync with each other and both were up to speed on everything. Whoever got to an issue first would make a decision, and they would worry about any mismatch between them the next day. In fact, Dana called Gary her "day spouse." This arrangement was a blessing for both their personal lives and the company. *Cloning top position* is such a success that it has been adopted by a number of organizations such as the *Los Angeles Times* with three managing editors who, thanks to this job design, could go home earlier and expose themselves to other aspects of life that can, in turn, enrich their work at the office. Similarly, at JetBlue, there were three executive vice presidents; one of them worked four days per week because of his responsibilities in the Mormon church and his daily routine of Scripture readings at 8 PM in a family of nine children. These examples demonstrate that, despite the stereotypical values of the US national culture (i.e., masculine and individualistic), group cultures and individual preference can create very dynamic strategies that fit a particular context.

Another important characteristic of WLB is *humanization of workload*, or a differentiation between "passion" and "overwork." Strategies are diverse: Interpersonal relationship at work, educational programs, mentor program, life skill program, bereavement leave, paid sick leave and holiday, parental leave, relocation assistance, wellness and sport programs, health care at work, and so forth. Let's get back to Germany for an example of balanced workload. In 2014, the German labor ministry prohibited managers from calling or e-mailing staff after work.[129] Since 2012, Volkswagen has blocked e-mails sent to employees after 6:15 PM.[130] At Daimler, if you e-mail the people while they are on holiday, you will get a message like this: "I am on vacation. I cannot read your email. Your email is being deleted. Please contact Hans or Monika if it's really important or resend the email after I'm back in the office. Danke Schön."[131]

In Japan, where long hours have become a national trauma, the Japanese government in 2017 called for "Premium Friday" asking companies to allow their workers to leave at 3 PM in the last Friday of the month. This is a move with good intention but lacks practicality because the last Friday is usually the busiest day for many businesses such as finance, retail, and manufacture. As a result, half of the companies have no immediate plans to follow the call.[132] Despite "no overtime days," few workers can take advantage of such a policy and opt to stay at work with the lights off or simply take their work home. This indicates that WLB doesn't tolerate half-hearted policies. The management has to see it as legitimate, that WLB doesn't mean laziness, and to make it work, there must be significant *changes in mentality* and *company structure*.

A *context-based approach* also helps us to truly understand the dynamics of WLB practices. Let's look at IBM—a company that pioneered in remote working back in the eighties with 40% of its global staff working from home, saving $100 million annually. However, in 2017, IBM started to call employees *back* to the office because it realized that the benefit of innovation trumps the benefit of production.[133] Remote working may increase the outcomes, but not ideas—something blossoms when people work together in proximity.[134] In fact, Facebook offers workers a $10,000 bonus if they live near headquarters. Similarly, a central theme in contemporary office designs has been how to optimize interaction,[135] or the so-called watercooler effect that creates opportunities for informal meetings when employees gather around and exchange ideas casually. Working together is also an effective solution for WLB because high levels of teamwork can support employees in coping with work demands. We can conclude that two opposite strategies (remote working vs. working together in proximity) may be used to achieve the same goal of WLB. Obviously, job types and business goals play a significant role in WLB policies. Each strategy brings different dynamics of success across different working cultures and particular contexts.

Last but not least, WLB policies need to take an *inclusive approach*. For example, being inclusive is crucial in cultures where gender roles at work have changed but gender roles at home have not. In Australia, women suffer from contradictory norms that support them to work, yet insist that their primary responsibilities are to the family.[136] Ironically, in Vietnam, it is even glorified. A motto of the national women's association expects women to "excel *both* at work and at home." This doubles the burden for women while keeping men away from the benefit of involving themselves in family life. In other words, women can't "have it all" if men "can't have it all." Iceland is a good example. In this country, parents have nine months off with 80% of their salary. New moms get three months, new dads get three months, and then it's up to the couple to decide how they'll split the remaining three months. Neither parent can transfer any portion of their three-month chunk because the government wants to ensure both parents can work and that kids get to spend time with both. Thus, for WLB policies to be truly effective, they have to be inclusive for all workers.

In this chapter, we have demonstrated that motivation is influenced by a dynamic interaction of genetic makeup, cultural background, environment, neural pathway, and everyday behavior (GCEB-Be). We have critically reevaluated Maslow's framework and pointed out that social connection and reproduction are major universal motivators. While cultural values can help us with prediction, context plays a much more dynamic role in influencing motivation: Economic circumstance, job type, work structure, generation, phases of a career, gender, and so forth. That is why across three categories of motivation (extrinsic, intrinsic, and WLB), the shared point is that businesses should run a cultural audit and construct identity profiles of different cultural groups to have the optimal strategies.

Summary

1. The neuroscience of motivation:
    *   The brain constantly weighs between cost and benefit.
    *   Dopamine motivates us to act in both directions: Away from danger and toward reward.
    *   Dopamine is sent to different paths, activating different parts of the brain, helping it to remember the pleasure and wanting to repeat the experience.
    *   Motivation is influenced by a dynamic interaction of geography, genetic makeup, cultural background, and everyday habit.
    *   Collectivism and individualism rewire the brain, showing different neural activation when individuals are motivated by their own interest or the interest of their significant others.
    *   But immediate context can prime and influence motivational behaviors, regardless of the deep-rooted values.
2. Motivation theories are not universal.
    *   The pyramid of need by Maslow ignores fundamental motivators such as social connection and reproduction.
    *   Maslow's model is subjected to both ethnocentrism and a lack of emphasis on context. For example, collectivistic society emphasizes rewards that have social impacts. However, because culture is not static, contexts will drive collectivists to embrace individualistic rewards and vice versa.
3. Extrinsic rewards such as salary are universally crucial for employees.
    *   Masculinity tends to explain the preference for monetary reward.
    *   However, context plays a much more dynamic role in influencing extrinsic motivation: Economic circumstance, job type, work structure, generation, phases of a career, gender, and so forth.
    *   Monetary reward runs the risk of (1) replacing intrinsic motivation, (2) damaging one's own well-being, and (3) prompting selfish behavior and unethical decisions. Hence, business practices that emphasize maximizing profits should be cautious of the negative consequences.

4. Intrinsic motivation is driven by a sense of purpose, that what we do is meaningful.
    - Meaningful work can (1) be a sense of accomplishment, (2) lead and influence others, (3) be socially interactive, or (4) be a job that fits one's values.
    - Universally, meaningful work is a fundamental part of well-being and a key motivator. Low engagement in the modern workforce implies its increasingly important role.
    - At the cultural level, meaningful work is more critical for professionals, those with higher education and more secured economic backgrounds, millennials, and workers with disabilities. Both masculinity and femininity can explain this motivator, depending on the nature of the work. However, meaningful work is fundamentally context dependent.
    - To cultivate meaningful work, businesses should run a cultural audit and construct identity profiles of different cultural groups. Based on these profiles, management can use job designs to tap on the intrinsic side of motivation.
    - Businesses can use CSR as a strategy aimed at intrinsically motivating employees.
5. WLB occurs when one has opportunities to experience many aspects of life.
    - Universally, WLB is both a powerful motivator and an important business imperative. Employees are more productive with a decent time off. Less is more.
    - At the cultural level, WLB is traditionally important for women, but it is increasingly a demand among men. Millennials see WLB as a top motivator when pay is not factored in. Individualism and femininity tend to explain the preference of WLB.
    - However, context is too dynamic for us to draw a rule based on values. For example, masculine Germany has the lowest working hours in the world.
    - To cultivate WLB, businesses should focus on *flexibility* and *humanization of workload*.
    - The *context-based* approach requires businesses to calculate the trade-offs because WLB is contextual. For example, opposing strategies can bring the same benefit.
    - The *inclusive* approach requires WLB policies to cover all workers, to be free from subconscious biases in gender, ethnicity, generation, religion, and so forth.

Notes

Don't forget to go to the end of the book for case studies.

1 Simpson, Eleanor H., and Peter D. Balsam. 2016. "The Behavioral Neuroscience of Motivation: An Overview of Concepts, Measures, and Translational Applications." *Current Topics in Behavioral Neurosciences* 27: 1–12. doi:10.1007/7854_2015_402.

2 Salamone, John D., and Mercè Correa. 2012. "The Mysterious Motivational Functions of Mesolimbic Dopamine." *Neuron* 76(3): 470–485. doi:10.1016/j.neuron.2012.10.021.

3 Rhodes, Justin S., Stephen C. Gammie, and Theodore Garland. 2005. "Neurobiology of Mice Selected for High Voluntary Wheel-Running Activity." *Integrative and Comparative Biology* 45(3): 438–455. doi:10.1093/icb/45.3.438.

4 Good, J. Deborah., Mengjiao Li, and Kirby Deater-Deckard. 2015. "A Genetic Basis for Motivated Exercise." *Exercise and Sport Sciences Reviews* 43(4): 231–237. doi:10.1249/JES.0000000000000057.

5 Kovas, Yulia., Gabrielle Garon-Carrier, Michel Boivin, Stephen A. Petrill, Robert Plomin, Sergey B. Malykh, and Frank Spinath et al. 2015. "Why Children Differ in Motivation to Learn: Insights from over 13,000 Twins from 6 Countries." *Personality and Individual Differences* 80: 51–63. doi:10.1016/j.paid.2015.02.006.

6 Chi, Wei., Wen-Dong Li, Nan Wang, and Zhaoli Chen Song. 2016. "Can Genes Play a Role in Explaining Frequent Job Changes? An Examination of Gene-Environment Interaction from Human Capital Theory." *Journal of Applied Psychology* 101(7): 1030–1044. doi:10.1037/apl0000093.

7 Iyengar, Sheena S., and Mark R. Lepper. 1999. "Rethinking the Role of Choice: A Cultural Perspective on Intrinsic Motivation." *Journal of Personality and Social Psychology* 76(3): 349–366. doi:10.1037/0022-3514.76.3.349.

8 Zhu, X., Y. Zhang, S. Yang, H. Wu, L. Wang, and R. Gu. 2015. "The Motivational Hierarchy between Self and Mother: Evidence from the Feedback-Related Negativity." *Acta Psychologica. Sinica* 47: 807–813.

9 Varnum, Michael E. W., Zhenhao Shi, Antao Chen, Jiang Qiu, and Shihui Han. 2014. "When Your Reward Is the Same as My Reward: Self-Construal Priming Shifts Neural Responses to Own vs. Friends' Rewards." *NeuroImage* 87: 164–169. doi:10.1016/j.neuroimage.2013.10.042.

10 Telzer, Eva H., Carrie L. Masten, Elliot T. Berkman, Matthew D. Lieberman, and Andrew J. Fuligni. 2010. "Gaining While Giving: An fMRI Study of the Rewards of Family Assistance among White and Latino Youth." *Social Neuroscience* 5(5–6): 508–518. doi:10.1080/17470911003687913.

11 Kitayama, Shinobu., and Jiyoung Gauthier Park. 2014. "Error-Related Brain Activity Reveals Self-Centric Motivation: Culture Matters." *Journal of Experimental Psychology: General* 143(1): 62–70. doi:10.1037/a0031696.

12 Varnum, Michael E. W., Zhenhao Shi, Antao Chen, Jiang Qiu, and Shihui Han. 2014. "When 'Your' Reward Is the Same as 'My' Reward: Self-Construal Priming Shifts Neutral Responses to Own vs. Friends' Rewards." *Neuroimage* 87: 164–169. doi:10.1016/j.neuroimage.2013.10.042.

13 Mobbs, Dean., Rongjun Yu, Marcel Meyer, Luca Passamonti, Ben Seymour, Andrew J. Calder, and Susanne Schweizer. 2009. "A Key Role for Similarity in Vicarious Reward." *Science* 324 (5929): 900. www.ncbi.nlm.nih.gov/pmc/articles/PMC2839480.

14 Ibid.

15 Marinaș, C. V. 2010. *Managementul comparat al resurselor umane.* Bucharest: Economica Publishing.

16 van Emmerik, Hetty., William L. Gardner, Hein Wendt, and Dawn Fischer. 2010. "Associations of Culture and Personality with McClelland's Motives: A Cross-Cultural Study of Managers in 24 Countries." *Group and Organization Management* 35(3): 329–367. doi:10.1177/1059601110370782.

17 Hofstede, Geert. 1984. "The Cultural Relativity of the Quality of Life Concept." *Academy of Management Review* 9(3): 389–398. doi:10.5465/amr.1984.4279653.

18 Kenrick, Douglas T., Vladas Griskevicius, Steven L. Neuberg, and Mark Schaller. 2010. "Renovating the Pyramid of Needs: Contemporary Extensions Built upon Ancient Foundations." *Perspectives on Psychological Science* 5(3): 292–314. doi:10.1177/1745691610369469.

19 Denning, Steve. 2012. "What Maslow Missed." *Forbes.* August 10. www.forbes.com/sites/stevedenning/2012/03/29/what-maslow-missed/#2620438d661b.

20 Gambrel, Patrick A., and Rebecca Cianci. 2003. "Maslow's Hierarchy of Needs: Does It Apply in a Collectivist Culture." *Journal of Applied Management and Entrepreneurship* 8(2): 143–161.

21 Hofstede, Geert., Gert Jan Hofstede, and Michael Minkov. 2010. *Cultures and Organizations: Software of the Mind.* 3rd ed. McGraw-Hill.

22 Goebel, Barbara L., and Delores R. Brown. 1981. "Age Differences in Motivation Related to Maslow's Need Hierarchy." *Developmental Psychology* 17(6): 809–815. doi:10.1037/0012-1649.17.6.809.

23 Kenrick, Douglass T., Vladas Griskevicius, Steven L. Neuberg, and Mark Schaller. 2010. "Renovating the Pyramid of Needs: Contemporary Extensions Built upon Ancient Foundations." *Perspectives on Psychological Science* 5(3): 292–314. doi:10.1177/1745691610369469.

24 SHRM. 2016. "Employee Job Satisfaction and Engagement Report." Executive summary. www.shrm.org/hr-today/trends-and-forecasting/research-and-surveys/Documents/2016-Employee-Job-Satisfaction-and-Engagement-Report-Executive-Summary.pdf.

25 McGregor, Jena. 2008. "The Global Politics of Hiring Trends." *HRPeople.* June 11. http://hrpeople.monster.com/benefits/articles/666-the-global-politics-of-hiring-trends?print=true.

26 Steers, Richard M., Carlos J. Sanchez-Runde, and Luciara Nardon. 2010. *Management across Cultures: Challenges and Strategies.* Cambridge: Cambridge University Press.

27 Allen, Frederick E. 2013. "How Germany Builds Twice as Many Cars as the U.S. While Paying Its Workers Twice as Much." *Forbes.* November 4. www.forbes.com/sites/frederickallen/2011/12/21/germany-builds-twice-as-many-cars-as-the-u-s-while-paying-its-auto-workers-twice-as-much/#6f0592c36b78.

28 Wever, Kirsten S., and Christopher S. Allen. 2014. "Is Germany a Model for Managers?" *Harvard Business Review*. August 1. https://hbr.org/1992/09/is-germany-a-model-for-managers.

29 Smith, Oliver. 2017. "Which Nationalities Work the Longest Hours?" *The Telegraph*. February 24. www.telegraph.co.uk/travel/maps-and-graphics/nationalities-that-work-the-longest-hours/.

30 Anell, Karin., and Danielle Hartmann. 2007. "Flexible Work Arrangements in Asia: What Companies Are Doing, Why They Are Doing It and What Lies Ahead." www.bc.edu/content/dam/bc1/schools/carroll/Centers/work-family/Home/research/publications/researchreports/Flexible Work Arrangements in Asia.

31 Korm, Ribaun. 2011. "The Relationship between Pay and Performance in the Cambodian Civil Service." Thesis. University of Canberra, Canberra, Australia. www.canberra.edu.au/researchrepository/file/5aea8cba-27ff-e2e7-d368-62bedc4f79bb/1/full_text.pdf.

32 PWC. 2017. "Workforce of the Future: The Views of 10,000 Workers." www.pwc.com/gx/en/services/people-organisation/workforce-of-the-future/workforce-of-future-appendix.pdf.

33 Fisher, Cynthia D., and Xue Ya Yuan. 1998. "What Motivates Employees? A Comparison of US and Chinese Responses." *The International Journal of Human Resource Management* 9(3): 516–528. doi:10.1080/095851998341053.

34 Yang, Fang. 2011. "Work, Motivation and Personal Characteristics: An In-Depth Study of Six Organizations in Ningbo." *Chinese Management Studies* 5(3): 272–297. doi:10.1108/17506141111163363.

35 DeKrey, Steven J., and David M. Messick, eds. 2007. *Leadership Experiences in Asia: Insight and Inspiration from 20 Innovators*, 51–60. Singapore: John Wiley & Sons (Asia).

36 Clark, A. 1998. "Measures of Job Satisfaction: What Makes a Good Job? Evidence from OECD Countries." *OECD Labour Market and Social Policy Occasional Papers* 34. Paris: OECD Publishing. doi:10.1787/670570634774.

37 Qin, Li. 2010. "Employee Motivation in a Cross-Cultural Organisation." Thesis. Nylands svenska yrkeshögskola. Helsinki, Finland. www.theseus.fi/handle/10024/7228.

38 Q&Me. 2014. "Work Value Survey in Vietnam and Japan." https://qandme.net/en/report/Work-Value-Survey-in-Vietnam-and-Japan.html#links.

39 Strack, Rainer., Carsten von der Linden, Mike Booker, and Andrea Strohmayr. 2014. "Decoding Global Talent: 200,000 Survey Responses on Global Mobility and Employment Preferences." www.handelsblatt.com/downloads/13816620/2/global_talent.pdf.

40 Taras, Vas., Piers Steel, and Bradley Kirkman. 2016. "Does Country Equate with Culture? Beyond Geography in the Search for Cultural Boundaries." *Management International Review* 56(4): 455–487. doi:10.1007/s11575-016-0283-x.

41 Hays. 2016. "The 2016 Hays Asia Salary Guide." www.channelnewsasia.com/news/singapore/salary-benefits-most-important-to-job-seekers-in-singapore-surve-8188364.

42 Hays. 2018. "The 2018 Hays Asia Salary Guide." www.hays.com.sg/cs/groups/hays_common/@sg/@content/documents/digitalasset/hays_1808041.pdf .

43 Flisak, Daniel., and Thomas Bjerkhage. 2015. "How Culture Affects the Motivation of Employees." Thesis. University of Gothenburg, Gothenburg, Sweden. https://gupea.ub.gu.se/bitstream/2077/39667/1/gupea_2077_39667_1.pdf.

44 Rubin, Danny., Jenna Goudreau, and Skye Gould. 2014. "Exclusive Survey Shows How Hard It Is for Millennials to Find Good Jobs." *Business Insider Australia*. June 18. www.businessinsider.com.au/survey-on-millennials-and-first-jobs-2014-6?r=US&IR=T.

45 Business Wire. 2016. "Better Quality of Work Life Is Worth a $7,600 Pay Cut for Millennials." *Business Wire*. April 7. www.businesswire.com/news/home/20160407005736/en/Quality-Work-Life-Worth-7600-Pay-Cut.

46 Babcock, Linda., Michele Gelfand, Deborah Small, and Heidi Stayn. 2006. "Propensity to Initiate Negotiations: A New Look at Gender Variation in Negotiation Behavior." In *Social Psychology and Economics*, ed. D. De Cremer, M. Zeelenberg, and J. K. Murnighan, 239–262. Mahwah, NJ: Lawrence Erlbaum Associates.

47 Bowles, Hannah Riley., Linda Babcock, and Kathleen L. McGinn. 2005. "Constraints and Triggers: Situational Mechanics of Gender in Negotiation." *Journal of Personality and Social Psychology* 89(6): 951–965. doi:10.1037/0022-3514.89.6.951.

48 Babcock, Linda., and Sara Laschever. 2007. *Women Don't Ask: The High Cost of Avoiding Negotiation—and Positive Strategies for Change.* New York: Bantam.

49 Bowles, Hannah Riley., Linda Babcock, and Lei Lai. 2007. "Social Incentives for Gender Differences in the Propensity to Initiate Negotiations: Sometimes It Does Hurt to Ask." *Organizational Behavior and Human Decision Processes* 103(1): 84–103. doi:10.1016/j.obhdp.2006.09.001.

50 Babcock, Linda., and Sara Laschever. 2007. *Women Don't Ask: The High Cost of Avoiding Negotiation–and Positive Strategies for Change.* New York: Bantam.

51 Vohs, Kathleen D. 2015. "Money Priming Can Change People's Thoughts, Feelings, Motivations, and Behaviors: An Update on 10 Years of Experiments." *Journal of Experimental Psychology: General* 144(4): 86–93. doi:10.1037/xge0000091.

52 Kouchaki, Maryam., Kristin Smith-Crowe, Arthur P. Brief, and Carlos Sousa. 2013. "Seeing Green: Mere Exposure to Money Triggers a Business Decision Frame and Unethical Outcomes." *Organizational Behavior and Human Decision Processes* 121(1): 53–61. doi:10.1016/j.obhdp.2012.12.002.

53 Vohs, Kathleen D., Nicole L. Mead, and Miranda R. Goode. 2006. "The Psychological Consequences of Money." *Science* 314(5802): 1154–1156. doi:10.1126/science.1132491.

54 Kraus, Michael W., Stéphane Côté, and Dacher Keltner. 2010. "Social Class, Contextualism, and Empathic Accuracy." *Psychological Science* 21(11): 1716–1723. doi:10.1177/0956797610387613.

55 Stellar, Jennifer E., Vida M. Manzo, Michael W. Kraus, and Dacher Desteno Keltner. 2012. "Class and Compassion: Socioeconomic Factors Predict Responses to Suffering." *Emotion* 12(3): 449–459. doi:10.1037/a0026508.

56 Piff, Paul K., Daniel M. Stancato, Stéphane Côté, Rodolfo Mendoza-Denton, and Dacher Keltner. 2012. "Higher Social Class Predicts Increased Unethical Behavior." *Proceedings of the National Academy of Sciences* 109(11): 4086–4091. doi:10.1073/pnas.1118373109.

57 Frank, Robert H. 2016. *Success and Luck Good Fortune and the Myth of Meritocracy.* Princeton, NJ: Princeton University Press.

58 Piff, Paul. 2018. "Does Money Make You Mean?" *TED: Ideas Worth Spreading.* www.ted.com/talks/paul_piff_does_money_make_you_mean.

59 Cardel, M. I., S. L. Johnson, J. Beck, E. Dhurandhar, A. D. Keita, A. C. Tomczik, G. Pavela et al. 2016. "The Effects of Experimentally Manipulated Social Status on Acute Eating Behavior: A Randomized, Crossover Pilot Study." *Physiological Behavior* 162: 93–101. doi:10.1016/j.physbeh.2016.04.024.

60 Zhou, Xinyue., Kathleen D. Vohs, and Roy F. Baumeister. 2009. "The Symbolic Power of Money Reminders of Money Alter Social Distress and Physical Pain." *Psychological Science* 20(6): 700–706. http://assets.csom.umn.edu/assets/127771.pdf.

61 Breiter, Hans C., Randy L. Gollub, Robert M. Weisskoff, David N. Kennedy, Nikos Makris, Joshua D. Berke, and Julie M. Goodman et al. 1997. "Acute Effects of Cocaine on Human Brain Activity and Emotion." *Neuron* 19(3): 591–611. doi:10.1016/s0896-6273(00)80374-8.

62 Luthar, Suniya S., and Shawn J. Latendresse. 2005. "Children of the Affluent: Challenges to Well-Being." *Current Directions in Psychological Science* 14(1): 49–53. doi:10.1111/j.0963-7214.2005.00333.x.

63 Carroll, Jason S., Lukas R. Dean, Lindsey L. Call, and Dean M. Busby. 2011. "Materialism and Marriage: Couple Profiles of Congruent and Incongruent Spouses." *Journal of Couple and Relationship Therapy* 10(4): 287–308. doi:10.1080/15332691.2011.613306.

64 Kessler, Ronald C., and Evelyn J. Bromet. 2013. "The Epidemiology of Depression across Cultures." *Annual Review of Public Health* 34: 119–138. doi:10.1146/annurev-publhealth-031912-114409.

65 Saxe, Rebecca., and Johannes Haushofer. 2008. "For Love or Money: A Common Neural Currency for Social and Monetary Reward." *Neuron* 58(2): 164–165. doi:10.1016/j.neuron.2008.04.005.

66 Piff, Paul. 2013. "Transcript of 'Does Money Make You Mean?'" *TED: Ideas Worth Spreading.* www.ted.com/talks/paul_piff_does_money_make_you_mean/transcript?quote=1139.

67 Kraus, Michael W., Stéphane Côté, and Dacher Keltner. 2010. "Social Class, Contextualism, and Empathic Accuracy." *Psychological Science* 21(11): 1716–1723. doi:10.1177/0956797610387613.

68 Rosso, Brent D., Kathryn H. Dekas, and Amy Wrzesniewski. 2010. "On the Meaning of Work: A Theoretical Integration and Review." *Research in Organizational Behavior* 30: 91–127. doi:10.1016/j.riob.2010.09.001.

69 Steger, Michael F., Bryan J. Dik, and Ryan D. Duffy. 2012. "Measuring Meaningful Work: The Work and Meaning Inventory (WAMI)." *Journal of Career Assessment* 20(3): 322–337. doi:10.1177/1069072711436160.

70 Rosso, Brent D., Kathryn H. Dekas, and Amy Wrzesniewski. 2010. "On the Meaning of Work: A Theoretical Integration and Review." *Research in Organizational Behavior* 30: 91–127. doi:10.1016/j.riob.2010.09.001.

71 Arnold, Kara A., Nick Turner, Julian Barling, Kevin E. Kelloway, and Margaret C. McKee. 2007. "Transformational Leadership and Psychological Well-Being: The Mediating Role of Meaningful Work." *Journal of Occupational Health Psychology* 12(3): 193–203. doi:10.1037/1076-8998.12.3.193.

72 Kamdron, Tiiu. 2005. "Work Motivation and Job Satisfaction of Estonian Higher Officials." *International Journal of Public Administration* 28(13–14): 1211–1240. doi:10.1080/01900690500241085.

73 Harpaz, Itzhak., and Xuanning Fu. 2002. "The Structure of the Meaning of Work: A Relative Stability Amidst Change." *Human Relations* 55(6): 639–667. doi:10.1177/0018726702556002.

74 Crabtree, Steve. 2013. "Worldwide, 13% of Employees Are Engaged at Work." October 8. www.gallup.com/poll/165269/worldwide-employees-engaged-work.aspx.

75 Sorenson, Susan., and Keri Garman. 2013. "How to Tackle U.S. Employees' Stagnating Engagement." June 11. www.gallup.com/businessjournal/162953/tackle-employees-stagnating-engagement.aspx.

76 Hay Group. 2016. "Employee Disengagement Costs UK £340bn Every Year." *Hay Group RSS.* January. www.haygroup.com/uk/press/details.aspx?id=7184.

77 AAP. 2013. "Australians Disengaged at Work: Report." *The Australian.* October 9. www.theaustralian.com.au/national-affairs/australians-disengaged-at-work-report/news-story/8d770ce43166d06750f58ae78751f309.

78 Pratt, Michael G. 2000. "The Good, the Bad, and the Ambivalent: Managing Identification among Amway Distributors." *Administrative Science Quarterly* 45(3): 456–493. doi:10.2307/2667106.

79 Baumeister, R. F., and K. D. Vohs. 2002. "The Pursuit of Meaningfulness in Life." In *The Handbook of Positive Psychology,* ed. C. R. Snyder and S. J. Lopez, 606–618. New York: Oxford University Press.

80 Hofstede, Geert. 1972. "The Colors of Collars." *Columbia Journal of World Business* (September): 78.

81 Yang, Fang. 2011. "Work, Motivation and Personal Characteristics: An In-depth Study of Six Organizations in Ningbo." *Chinese Management Studies* 5(3): 272–297. doi:10.1108/17506141111163363.

82 Allan, Blake A., Kelsey L. Autin, and Ryan D. Duffy. 2014. "Examining Social Class and Work Meaning within the Psychology of Working Framework." *Journal of Career Assessment* 22(4): 543–561. doi:10.1177/1069072713514811.

83 Saunders, S., and B. Nedelec. 2014. "What Work Means to People with Work Disability: A Scoping Review." *Journal of Occupational Rehabilitation* 24(1): 100–110. doi:10.1007/s10926-013-9436-y.

84 Australian Human Rights Commission. 2014. "National Disability Forum 2014 Summary of Survey Results." www.humanrights.gov.au/sites/default/files/document/publication/Disability2014_Survey_Results.pdf

85 Deloitte. 2016. "The 2016 Deloitte Millennial Survey Winning over the Next Generation of Leaders." www2.deloitte.com/content/dam/Deloitte/global/Documents/About-Deloitte/gx-millenial-survey-2016-exec-summary.pdf.

86 KPMG. 2017. "Meet the Millennials." https://home.kpmg.com/content/dam/kpmg/uk/pdf/2017/04/Meet-the-Millennials-Secured.pdf.

87 Schawbel, Dan. 2014. "The Multi-Generational Job Search Study 2014." *Millennia Branding.* May 20. http://millennialbranding.com/2014/multi-generational-job-search-study-2014.

88 Bem, Sandra L. 1974. "The Measurement of Psychological Androgyny." *Journal of Consulting and Clinical Psychology* 42(2): 155–162. doi:10.1037/h0036215.

89 Iguisi, Osarumwense. 2009. "Motivation-Related Values across Cultures." *African Journal of Business Management* 3(4): 141–150. www.academicjournals.org/article/article1380533419_Iguisi.pdf.

90 GESIS Data Archive. 2010. "EVS: European Values Study 2008." http://zacat.gesis.org/webview/.

91 Aggarwal, Raj., and Betty J. Simskins. 2001. "Open-Boon Management: Optimizing Human Capital." *Business Horizons* 44(5): 5–13. doi:10.1016/S0007-6813(01)80055-0.

92 Hackman, J. R., and G. R. Oldham. 1980. *Work Redesign*, 78–80. Upper Saddle River, NJ: Pearson Education.

93 Andreassi, Jeanine., Leanna Lawter, Martin Brockerhoff, and Peter Rutigliano. 2012. "Job Satisfaction Determinants: A Study Across 48 Nations." In *Proceedings of 2012 Annual Meeting of the Academy of International Business-US North East Chapter: Business without Borders*, ed. Jing'an Tang, 193–215. Fairfield, CT: Sacred Heart University. http://digitalcommons.sacredheart.edu/cgi/viewcontent.cgi?article=1239&context=wcob_fac.

94 Hernaus, Tomislav., and Nina Pološki Vokic. 2014. "Work Design for Different Generational Cohorts: Determining Common and Idiosyncratic Job Characteristics." *Journal of Organizational Change Management* 27(4): 615–641. doi:10.1108/JOCM-05-2014-0104.

95 Oliveira, Justina. 2015. "Effects of Job Type and Culture on Relationships between Job Characteristics and Worker Outcomes: A Multilevel Analysis." *CUNY Academic Works.* Thesis. University of New York. http://academicworks.cuny.edu/gc_etds/1078.

96 Traymbak, S., P. Kumar, and A. N. Jha. 2017. "Moderating Role of Gender between Job Characteristics and Job Satisfaction: An Empirical Study of Software Industry Using Structural Equation Modeling." *International Journal of Human Capital and Information Technology Professionals* 8(2): 59–71.

97 Jelstad, Beate. 2005. "Job Characteristics and Its Outcomes: A Comparative Work Design Study of Non-Profit and Profit Organizations." www.polis.no/Paper/Aarhus05/PJELSTAD.PDF.

98 Dik, Bryan J., Zinta S. Byrne, and Michael F. Steger. 2013. *Purpose and Meaning in the Workplace*. Washington, DC: American Psychological Association.

99 Steger, Michael F., Bryan J. Dik, and Ryan D. Duffy. 2012. "Measuring Meaningful Work: The Work and Meaning Inventory (WAMI)." *Journal of Career Assessment* 20(3): 322–337. doi:10.1177/1069072711436160.

100 Bersin, Josh. 2015. "Becoming Irresistible: A New Model for Employee Engagement." *Deloitte Insights.* January 26. www2.deloitte.com/insights/us/en/deloitte-review/issue-16/employee-engagement-strategies.html.

101 Deloitte. 2017. "The 2017 Deloitte Millennial Survey. Apprehensive Millennials: Seeking Stability and Opportunities in an Uncertain World." www2.deloitte.com/content/dam/Deloitte/global/Documents/About-Deloitte/gx-deloitte-millennial-survey-2017-executive-summary.pdf.

102 Bailyn, Lotte, and Mona Harrington. 2004. "Redesigning Work for Work-Family Integration." *Community Work Family* 7(2): 197–208. doi:10.1080/1366880042000245470.

103 Miller, Jody. 2005. "Get a Life!" *Fortune.* November 28. http://archive.fortune.com/magazines/fortune/fortune_archive/2005/11/28/8361955/index.htm.

104 Frone, Michael R. 2000. "Work–Family Conflict and Employee Psychiatric Disorders: The National Comorbidity Survey." *Journal of Applied Psychology* 85(6): 888–895. doi:10.1037/0021-9010.85.6.888.

105 Angrisani, Marco., Maria Casanova, and Erik Meijer. 2017. *"Work-Life Balance and Labor Force Attachment at Older Ages."* Washington, DC: Michigan Retirement Research Center. http://crr.bc.edu/wp-content/uploads/2017/08/7c.-Full-paper_Angrisani.pdf.

106 Arif, Bushra., and Yasir Aftab Farooqi. 2014. "Impact of Work Life Balance on Job Satisfaction and Organizational Commitment among University Teachers: A Case Study of University of

Gujrat, Pakistan." *International Journal of Multidisciplinary Sciences and Engineering* 5(9): 24–29. www.ijmse.org/Volume5/Issue9/paper5.pdf.

107 Erickson, Tamara J., and Lynda Gratton. 2014. "What It Means to Work Here." *Harvard Business Review*. August 1. https://hbr.org/2007/03/what-it-means-to-work-here.

108 Bloom, Nicholas., James Liang, John Roberts, and Zhichun Jenny Ying. 2014. "Does Working from Home Work? Evidence from a Chinese Experiment." *The Quarterly Journal of Economics* 130(1): 165–218. www.povertyactionlab.org/sites/default/files/publications/649 Working from Home Nov2014.pdf.

109 Beauregard, Alexandra T., and Lesley C. Henry. 2009. "Making the Link between Work-Life Balance Practices and Organizational Performance." *Human Resource Management Review* 19(1): 9–22. doi:10.1016/j.hrmr.2008.09.001.

110 Haar, J. M., and E. A. Bardoel. 2008. "Positive Spillover from the Work–Family Interface: A Study of Australian Employees." *Asia Pacific Journal of Human Resources* 46(3): 275–287. doi:10.1177/1038411108095759.

111 Gervais, Ricky. 2013. "Remember, Mondays Are Fine: It's Your Life That Sucks." May 20. https://twitter.com/rickygervais/status/336405746239553536?lang=en.

112 Greenhaus, J., and T. Alleen. 2011. "Work–Family Balance: A Review and Extension of the Literature." In *Handbook of Occupational Health Psychology*, ed. J. C. Quick and L. E. Tetrick. 2nd ed, 165–183. Washington, DC: American Psychological Association.

113 Williams, J., and H. Boushey. 2010. "The Three Faces of Work-Family Conflict the Poor, the Professionals, and the Missing Middle Center." Center for American Progress, Hastings College of the Law. https://cdn.americanprogress.org/wp-content/uploads/issues/2010/01/pdf/threefaces.pdf

114 Livingston, Gretchen. 2018. "Most Dads Say They Spend Too Little Time with Their Children; about a Quarter Live Apart from Them." *Pew Research Center*. January 8. www.pewresearch.org/fact-tank/2018/01/08/most-dads-say-they-spend-too-little-time-with-their-children-about-a-quarter-live-apart-from-them.

115 Miller, Jody. 2005. "Get a Life!" November 28. http://archive.fortune.com/magazines/fortune/fortune_archive/2005/11/28/8361955/index.htm.

116 Deloitte. 2016. "The 2016 Deloitte Millennial Survey Winning over the Next Generation of Leaders." www2.deloitte.com/content/dam/Deloitte/global/Documents/About-Deloitte/gx-millenial-survey-2016-exec-summary.pdf.

117 Haar, Jarrod M., Marcello Russo, Albert Suñe, and Ariane Ollier-Malaterre. 2014. "Outcomes of Work–Life Balance on Job Satisfaction, Life Satisfaction and Mental Health: A Study across Seven Cultures." *Journal of Vocational Behavior* 85(3): 361–373. doi:10.1016/j.jvb.2014.08.010.

118 Ollier-Malaterre, A. 2016. "Cross-National Work–Life Research: A Review at the Individual Level." In *Oxford Handbook of Work and Family*, ed. T. D. Allen and L. E. Eby, 315–330. Oxford: Oxford University Press.

119 Smith, Oliver. 2017. "Which Nationalities Work the Longest Hours?" *The Telegraph*. February 24. www.telegraph.co.uk/travel/maps-and-graphics/nationalities-that-work-the-longest-hours/.

120 Nienaber, Michael. 2017. "Germany's Largest Trade Union Pushes for Shorter Working Hours for 3.9 Million Workers." *The Independent*. October 10. www.independent.co.uk/news/business/news/germany-working-hours-trade-unions-push-better-pay-workers-a7992906.html.

121 Weller, Chris. 2017. "Japan Is Facing a 'Death by Overwork' Problem—Here's What It's All About." *Business Insider Australia*. October 19. www.businessinsider.com.au/what-is-karoshi-japanese-word-for-death-by-overwork-2017-10?r=US&IR=T.

122 The Japan Times. 2016. "The Government's 'Karoshi' Report." *The Japan Times*. October 12. www.japantimes.co.jp/opinion/2016/10/12/editorials/governments-karoshi-report/#.WlQWflWWbIU.

123 Perlow, Leslie., and Ron Fortgang. 1989. "Commitment, Versatility and Balance: Determinants of Work Time Standards and Norms in a Multi-Country Study of Software Engineers." Working paper. https://deepblue.lib.umich.edu/bitstream/handle/2027.42/39538/wp149.pdf?sequence=3.

124 Perlow, Leslie A., Jody Hoffer Gittell, and Nancy Katz. 2004. "Contextualizing Patterns of Work Group Interaction: Toward a Nested Theory of Structuration." *Organizational Science* 15(5): 520–536. doi:10.1287/orsc.1040.0097.

125 Miller, Jody. 2005. "Get a Life!" November 28. http://archive.fortune.com/magazines/fortune/fortune_archive/2005/11/28/8361955/index.htm.

126 Zafar, Ziad. 2017. "How to Stop Female Doctors from Dropping out in Pakistan." *BBC News*. August 21. www.bbc.com/news/av/magazine-41003627/how-to-stop-female-doctors-from-dropping-out-in-pakistan.

127 Daily Telegraph. 2017. "Australian Companies in Discussions about Paying for Egg Freezing for Employees." *Daily Telegraph Australia*. November 21. www.dailytelegraph.com.au/lifestyle/health/australian-companies-in-discussions-about-paying-for-egg-freezing-for-employees/news-story/2fbde1d410bc7acf84a2e3ec9c4917b8.

128 Miller, Jody. 2005. "Get a Life!" November 28. http://archive.fortune.com/magazines/fortune/fortune_archive/2005/11/28/8361955/index.htm.

129 News18. 2014. "Germany Bans Managers from Calling or Emailing Staff after Work Hours." *News18*. March 29. www.news18.com/news/buzz/germany-bans-managers-from-calling-or-emailing-staff-after-work-hours-677249.html.

130 BBC News. 2012. "Volkswagen Turns off Blackberry Email after Work Hours." *BBC News*. March 8. www.bbc.com/news/technology-16314901.

131 BBC News. 2014. "Should Holiday Email Be Deleted?" *BBC News*. August 14. www.bbc.com/news/magazine-28786117.

132 McCurry, Justin. 2017. "Premium Fridays: Japan Gives Its Workers a Break—to Go Shopping." *The Guardian*. February 24. www.theguardian.com/world/2017/feb/24/premium-fridays-japan-gives-workers-break-go-shopping.

133 Kessler, Sarah. 2017. "IBM, Remote-Work Pioneer, Is Calling Thousands of Employees Back to the Office." *Quartz*. March 23. https://qz.com/924167/ibm-remote-work-pioneer-is-calling-thousands-of-employees-back-to-the-office.

134 Lee, Kyungjoon., John S. Brownstein, Richard G. Mills, and Isaac S. Kohane. 2010. "Does Collocation Inform the Impact of Collaboration?" *PLOS ONE* 5(12): e14279. doi:10.1371/journal.pone.0014279.

135 Waber, Ben., Jennifer Magnolfi, and Greg Lindsay. 2014. "Workspaces That Move People." *Harvard Business Review*. October 31. https://hbr.org/2014/10/workspaces-that-move-people.

136 Skinner, Natalie., and Janine Chapman. 2013. "Work-Life Balance and Family Friendly Policies." *Evidence Base*, no. 4. http://melbourneinstitute.unimelb.edu.au/assets/documents/hilda-bibliography/other-publications/2014/Skinner_etal_work_life_balance.pdf.

11 Cross-Cultural Leadership

All human societies are organized based on hierarchy. Leadership emerges spontaneously and quickly, serving to reap the benefit of being in a highly coordinated and cohesive group.[1] That is why hierarchy is a universal dimension of human relationships[2] and a major concept in intercultural communication. It was named "relation to authority" by Inkeles and Levinson,[3] "lineal" versus "collateral" by Kluckhohn and Strodtbeck,[4] "power distance" by Hofstede,[5] and "achievement" versus "ascription" by Trompenaars and Hampden-Turner.[6]

In our metaphorical tree of culture (Chapter 3), hierarchy acceptance is a universal *concern* (i.e., the trunk of tree). As a *value*, it indicates the extent to which subordinates accept an unequal distribution of prestige, status, power, and resources between them and their superiors (i.e., the branches of the tree). Note that contradicting values of strong and weak hierarchy acceptance may coexist in one culture, emerging when a specific context demands. Paradox is the norm of most multicultural societies. Finally, the *outward expressions* of hierarchy acceptance include a myriad of symbols, objects, languages, policies, rituals, behaviors, and so forth (i.e., the leaves of the tree) that can either reflect or contradict the dominant values of an individual or a culture. For a reminder of this dynamic aspect of culture, see Chapter 4.

In this chapter, we will follow the pathways of GCEB-Be (Chapter 2) and explore different aspects of leadership. Pathway Genes—Culture—Environment guides us to touch on questions such as: "Are there leadership genes?" "Are these genes distributed equally across cultures?" "Which environmental element prompted the evolution of these genes?" Pathway Culture—Brain suggests we explore: "How does the brain react to hierarchy across cultures?" Pathway Culture—Behavior brings about: "To what extent do we behave similarly and differently toward leadership across cultures?" The enveloping circle of context reminds us to explore the role of specific circumstances in which situational leadership emerges. Finally, the last section of the chapter discusses essential traits of global leadership in a working environment characterized by cultural diversity.

11.1 The Neuroscience of Leadership

In Chapter 3, we learned that the evolutionary root of hierarchy is the reduced cost of connection.[7] Hierarchy has become a cultural survival strategy because having leaders helps hierarchical groups to outlive egalitarian groups. It evolves as an effective way to coordinate group activities. It enables labor division as one needs not to make and maintain connections with everyone else. Humans are natural born followers, and this capacity begins early as babies naturally follow the eyes of parents. We can also recognize social status from facial cues within 170ms.[8] However, most of us are both leaders and followers, albeit with different proportion depending on the context. Following diverse pathways of GCEB-Be, in this section, we will explore the interplay of these drivers (genes, culture, environment, brain, and behavior) in the way leadership and followership are constructed.

11.1.1 Leadership Genes

The question whether leaders are born or bred has inspired much discussion. However, nature versus nurture is a false dichotomy. Much like the case of cultural values (see Chapter 4), the answer is "both/and" instead of "either/or." The ability to lead depends on a combination of genetic predispositions and upbringing.[9] Humans can't become leaders in a social vacuum. Hence, the point of discussion should be: To which extent do genes and culture exert different impact on the construction of leadership? Tackling this dynamic relationship is the focus of a scientific discipline called *behavioral genetics*.

So, what about the evidence? First, there *are* genes that have been associated with leadership. For a long time, we knew that about a third of the variance in leadership role occupancy can be explained by genetic factors, but researchers couldn't identify specific genes.[10,11,12] Only in 2013, a breakthrough study reported that a genotype called rs4950 appears to pass leadership ability with the heritability at 24%.[13] In 2015, another study followed up, reporting that the 10-repeat allele version of the dopamine transporter gene DAT1 (DAT1-10R) is associated with moderate rule-breaking behavior, which in turn is a characteristic associated with leadership.[14] Breaking boundaries positively correlates with assuming leadership positions in later career because it means exploration, knowledge development, and risk-taking.

Of course, this doesn't mean that if you skipped class in school, then you will get a corner office. Having the DAT1-10R allele is a mixed blessing. The pendulum swings both ways. While it positively correlates with leadership potentials, it *negatively* correlates with traits such as being deliberate, planning, and risk calculation—which are also essential for good leadership.

In the same vein, the 7-repeat variation of the dopamine receptor gene (DRD4-7R) has been tied to *both* positive and negative qualities of leadership. Following pathway Gene—Culture, as a mutation emerged during the ancient migration out of Africa, it is associated with attentional difficulties but also exploration and risk-taking (Chapter 2). But this doesn't mean those communities at the end of our migration pathways such as the Native American have more potential in taking charge. Culture makes it much more complex and dynamic. Chapter 10 cited a study in which rich people with the DRD4-7R tend to change jobs *voluntarily* by moving upward to better positions, while poor people with the DRD4-7R tend to change jobs *involuntarily* because they are fired.[15] Similarly, the tendency in financial risk-taking associated with the 7R can be deconstructive with gambling, but attractive with entrepreneurship. Thus, cultural background can activate the same gene in exactly opposite behavioral ways.

Clearly, a gene is not magically going to make us become a leader. Other factors in the cultural environment are crucial. A culmination of more than half a century of research collected on 14.5 million pairs of twins has concluded that it's always a combination of both nature and nurture, genes and culture.[16] On top of that, we should never forget the incredible influence of epigenetics. It means genes are not fixed, and behaviors can turn on, turn off, enhance, or dim the activity of genes. Having the DAT1-10R, DRD4-7R, and rs4950 doesn't mean they are always activated the way we want. One's culture can regulate the degree to which these genes become "stronger" or "weaker," and with *different social results*. The sum of who we are is, and has to be, far greater than those genes. That's the reason why genetic testing for screening potential employees offers very little credibility, let alone that it can be an ethical issue.

11.1.2 Cross-Cultural Finding

Chapter 3 briefly discussed the driving forces of diversity in hierarchy acceptance among different cultures. Following the Environment—Gene—Culture pathway, our ancestors have developed a culture of group-mindset *and* hierarchical dominance to cope with external threats such as the prevalence of pathogens and demanding climate. Those who followed the cultural rules of group conformity and hierarchical dominance had a higher chance of survival. These individuals also tend to carry a higher rate of the shorter variant of the gene that encodes serotonin transporters (s5-HTTLPR). This variant has been associated with more sensitivity and vigilance to environmental threats (an important survival skill when living in areas with high pathogen loads) and facial expressions (an important social skill to detect each other's feelings and behaviors and avoid causing damage to social harmony). Thus, strong group attachment and hierarchical acceptance favor this gene variant and make it widespread, especially among the Southeast Asian population. It's important to remember that while this variant has been associated with depression, despite having *higher* rate of the gene, this population enjoys *lower* level of depression. Among several hypotheses, one argument is that their collectivistic and hierarchical culture acts as a buffer, offering them the much-needed certainty and social support. While the candidate gene for depression has been challenged, the co-evolution between gene and culture still holds true. It shows us that culture is not only *socially learned* but also *genetically inherited*.

Following the Culture—Brain pathway, studies have shown that those with strong and those with weak levels of hierarchy acceptance tend to have different neural activities when being exposed to leadership stimuli. For example, the brain's reward circuitry was activated when Japanese participants looked at the *subordinate* figures. But for the US participants, it was the *dominant* figures that correlated with their strong response in the medial prefrontal cortex and the caudate—a key player in the mesolimbic reward system (Figure 11.1).[17] This is because in Japanese culture, exemplary employees are strong, but also maintain a profound humility, modesty, readiness for consensus and self-sacrifice for the greater good of the whole group. We see this clearly in the way Japanese employees speak humbly about their boss by referring to the boss's surname name as, for example, "Suzuki" in front of the customers, and not as "Suzuki-san." Thus

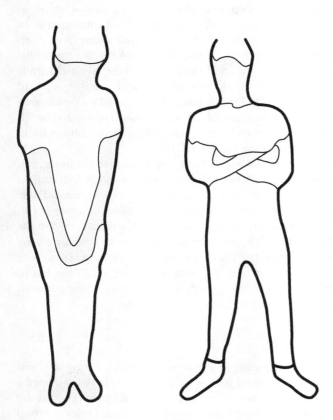

Figure 11.1 Examples of subordinate and dominant displays

they respect customers by *lowering* their manager's position.[18] This mindset of modesty explains why stimuli signaling humbleness are more rewarding. Another interesting study called "The Boss Effect" also illustrates this point.[19] While human adults typically respond faster to their own face than to the faces of others, the "boss effect" suggests that those who embrace strong hierarchy acceptance respond *faster* to their supervisor's face than to their own. To compare, confidence, independence, competitiveness, and masculinity are more reinforced in the United States, which explains the strong neural reward circuitry when participants looked at dominance figures. This is backed up by an interesting study in which researchers concluded that, in case the CEO is a white male, his company's net profits can be predicted by his facial features of dominance, competence, and maturity.[20] The more powerful he looks, the higher his company's actual net profits.

11.1.3 Context Dependence

The evidence of cross-cultural differences in the neuroscience of hierarchy doesn't mean this diversity is static. As it has been emphasized throughout the book, the deciding factor in predicting change and behavior is not a stereotypical value, but a specific context. Because *context is the software of the mind*, how an individual, an organization, a group, or a society acts upon a cultural stimuli depends on particular circumstances. To be clear about this point, let's continue with the previously mentioned study on the predictive power of CEOs' facial features.

In this study, Japanese and US participants rated a series of photos featuring faces of white male CEOs. These Japanese participants are familiar with US culture, and hence, their brain might have operated in a sort of "US mode" while giving the rating to US CEOs. That partly explains why both groups of participants produced similar results. For them, *Western* leaders' facial characteristics of power, competence, and dominance predicted business success. However, the same Japanese participants, when rating Japanese CEOs, did *not* come up with the same result. One possibility is that their brains have switched to operate in accordance with the Japanese business context in which leaders are not competitively selected based on individual achievements but from a small internal group. Japanese managers often rise to senior positions through connection, relationship with others, duration of serving time, and the ability to lead through consensus.

Studies in cognitive neuroscience support similar conclusion. For example, when Hong Kong participants were primed with US culture, they became more likely to see a fish swimming ahead of a group of other fish as "leading" instead of "being chased by other fish."[21] Another study got closer to the point.[22] Canadian participants were primed with two conditions. In the *interdependence* priming, they read a text that contains 19 plural pronouns such as "we" or "us." In the *independence* priming, the text contained singular pronouns such as "I" or "me." By subconsciously activating different levels of strong and weak group attachment, researchers found out that the 19 plural pronouns of "we" and "us" (interdependence) led to a preference of *transformational* leadership—a leadership style that prioritizes close relationship, trust, commitment, and acceptance. To compare, the 19 pronouns of "I" and "me" (independence) led to a preference of *transactional* leadership—a leadership style that is more associated with self-identity, setting goals, personal performance, and rewards, keeping followers on task.[23] Overall, this study indicates that priming followers with different cultural values can influence their preferable leadership styles.

To conclude, culture is not only socially learned but also *genetically inherited* and neurally enabled. Both genetic and social influences are dynamic, which makes culture dynamic. At the neuronal level, our mind is potentially multicultural. To a certain extent, this allows us to switch the frames and respond accordingly to a given context, choosing *which* culture to be applied in which situation.

11.2 Glocal Leadership and Local Cultures

Following pathway Culture—Behavior, in this section, we will look at major findings across cultures, and delve deep into basic aspects of leadership that diversify the most, that is, what makes a good leader according to different cultures? However, we need to repeatedly emphasize that these findings risk stereotypes. Therefore, we will also discuss *situational leadership*. It reflects the complex reality of leading in a specific context, not adhering to a rigid static cultural framework.

11.2.1 *Cross-Cultural Finding*

Countless studies have tried to identify the impact of values on leadership styles. Because culture is complex and evolving constantly, studies can be inconsistent. However, to give us an overview, Table 11.1 summarizes some of the most stereotypical and generic aspects of leadership across cultures. Note that, in reality, leadership strategies never occur so neatly. Values are just ingredients; reality is a cocktail. Different values influence each other in a dynamic interplay and create an extremely different mix. For example, when weak hierarchy acceptance is combined

Table 11.1 Leadership characteristics under the impact of cultural values

Cultural Values	Leadership Characteristics
Strong Group Attachment (Collectivism)	• Leaders are caring and protective, lead with the heart. • Emphasize harmony, trust, pride, face, and relationship. • Well-connected with multiple internal and external parties. • Consultative and consensus-decision making. • Lead change slowly from inside.
Weak Group Attachment (Individualism)	• Leaders take charge. • Emphasize vision, independence, and uniqueness. • Lead change with purposeful action and heroic decisions.
Strong Hierarchy Acceptance	• Leaders are benevolent and firm motherly/fatherly figures. • Top-down, patriarchal management. Centralized decision making. • Emphasize status, power, and rank. • Supervisory roles focus on direction and control.
Weak Hierarchy Acceptance (Egalitarian)	• Leaders are first among equals. • Emphasize equality, consensus, and participating decision making.
Masculine Gender Association	• Leaders are pathfinders. • Emphasize being tough, decisive, hard-working, status/power-conscious. • Business strategies focus on growth and profit.
Feminine Gender Association	• Leaders build and foster consensus and team spirit. • Emphasize modesty, tolerance, flexibility, compromise, and well-being. • Consultative and consensus decision making. • Business strategies balance between profit and sustainability.
Strong Uncertainty Avoidance	• Leaders are experts, giving instruction, knowing all the answers. • Give clear task-directed goals, specific deadlines, close supervision. • Emphasize rules, integrity, and competence.
Weak Uncertainty Avoidance	• Leaders are facilitators, giving support and suggestions. • Emphasize flexibility, improvisation, and innovation.
Future Orientation	• Visionary leadership: Leaders inspire and transform. • Emphasize sustainability, intrinsic motivation, and lifelong learning.
Present/Short-Time Orientation	• Leaders are problem solvers, dealing effectively with crisis. • Emphasize efficiency, speed, outcomes, and flexibility. • Top-down decision making.

Table 11.2 GLOBE leadership universal and cultural attributes (adapted from House et al. [2004])

Universal Leadership Attributes		Cultural Contingent Leadership Attributes	
Trustworthy	Excellence oriented	Anticipatory	Intragroup conflict
Just	Dependable	Ambitious	avoider
Honest	Intelligent	Autonomous	Intuitive
Foresight	Effective bargainer	Cautious	Logical
Plans ahead	Win-win problem solver	Class conscious	Micro-manager
Encouraging	Administrative skill	Compassionate	Orderly
Positive	Communicative	Cunning	Procedure
Dynamic	Informed	Domineering	Provocateur
Motive arouser	Coordinative	Elitist	Risk-taking
Confidence builder	Team builder	Enthusiastic	Ruler
Motivational		Evasive	Self-effacing
Decisive		Formal	Self-sacrificial
		Habitual	Sensitive
		Independent	Sincere
		Indirect	Status conscious
		Individualistic	Subdued
		Intragroup	Unique
		competitor	Willful
			Worldly

Table 11.3 GLOBE leadership dimensions and regional endorsement. E = Eastern; L = Latin; SE = Southeast; Confucian = Confucian Asia; S = strongly endorsed; A = average; W = weakly endorsed (adapted from House et al. [2004])

Leadership Dimensions	Characteristics of Dimensions	Endorsed by Cultures
Autonomous	Independence, self-centeredness, uniqueness	S: Germanic, E European, Confucian, Nordic, SE Asian, Anglo, African, Middle Eastern, L European, L American
Charismatic/ Value based	Vision, decisiveness, inspiration, high standard, innovation	S: Anglo, Germanic, Nordic, SE Asian, L European, L American A: Confucian, African, E European W: Middle Eastern
Humane	Compassion, generosity, support, well-being	S: SE Asian, Anglo, African, Confucian A: Germanic, Middle Eastern, L American, E European W: L European, Nordic
Participative	Engagement, equality, delegation, consensus	S: Germanic, Anglo, Nordic A: L European, L American, African W: E European, SE Asian, Confucian, Middle Eastern
Self/group protective	Status, face, procedure, safety	S: Middle Eastern, Confucian, SE Asian, L American, E European A: African, L European W: Anglo, Germanic, Nordic
Team oriented	Pride, loyalty, teamwork, common goals	S: SE Asia, Confucian, L America, E European, African, L European, Nordic, Anglo, Middle Eastern, Germanic

E = Eastern; L = Latin; SE = Southeast; Confucian = Confucian Asia; S = strongly endorsed; A = average; W = weakly endorsed (adapted from House et al. [2004])

with femininity, leaders tend to be caring, democratic, and participative. But when weak hierarchy acceptance is paired with masculinity, leaders may look like lone heroes who constantly have to prove their competence and reinforce their power.

Chapter 6 introduced the Inverted Pyramid Model with three layers: Universal, cultural, and individual. In terms of leadership, we are curious of the extent to which all great leaders have in common (i.e., universal), how their leadership is influenced by locality (i.e., cultural), and in what way their personal particularity plays a role (i.e., individual). GLOBE is a major study that addressed this issue.[24] Researchers examined 17,300 managers from 62 countries, identifying 22 leadership attributes that are universal, 35 attributes that are valued differently across cultures, and 6 leadership styles. Tables 11.2 and 11.3 summarize their findings.

11.2.2 How Much Power?

Power signifies leaders. But how much power a leader has in decision making depends largely on specific cultures and contexts. Stereotypically, when strong hierarchy acceptance prevails, so does the top-down approach. Vice versa, weak hierarchy acceptance is often associated with the consensus approach. This assumption is typically based on static indexes such as the one proposed by Hofstede. He measured the extent to which subordinates were afraid to express disagreement and how they preferred a certain decision-making style from managers. Based on a questionnaire, he placed countries along a binary spectrum of high versus low power distance,[25] which is often broadly interpreted as a tendency toward top-down versus consensus decision making. While this static ranking is helpful in imagining a big picture with a strong focus on comparison, the dynamic paradigm of culture reminds us that they are only suggestions and not the rules. They serve as "sophisticated stereotypes"[26] at the very start of our journey in understanding the complexity of cross-cultural management. As we delve deeper, the simplicity of the static ranking can both align with and contradict the dynamic of the reality.

11.2.2.1 More Power: Top-Down Approach

Let's first have a look at the power distance scores of Anglo countries such as the United States (40), Canada (39), the United Kingdom (35), and Australia (36). Despite scoring on the *low* side of the spectrum, decision making in these cultures have been characterized by a top-down approach with one person in charge. Managers are responsible of identifying, analyzing, and solving the problems, often with some help of external specialists and consultants. A similar, but less rigid approach is common in countries with *high* scores, such as many from Asia, Middle East, Latin America, and Africa. Thus, top-down approach can be employed by both low- and high-power distance countries. To conclude, national static ranking is only the first-best-guess in predicting decision-making style across cultures. A better way to understand power distribution is to focus on the prevailing value of a specific country, an occupation, an organization, or a particular context, as proposed in Table 11.1.

The top-down approach puts power in the hand of a few at the top, and it has several characteristics. Firstly, *rank-and-file employees don't usually understand the vision behind a change of policy*. When the top-down approach is paired with weak hierarchy acceptance, such as in some Western culture, staff may execute the change, motivated by extrinsic rewards, but it can take them a long time to be convinced. However, when the top-down approach is paired with strong hierarchy acceptance, such as in Asia, the Middle East, Latin America, and Africa, despite the same approach, the implementation is often rapid due to the employees' loyalty and respect. Subordinates tend to let managers decide. Leaders can be secretive and vague, keeping the strategies for themselves, with the expectation that subordinates will carry out their orders to achieve the final result. To illustrate the point, an executive in China cited the following folklore:

A king plans to abdicate and put his son in the throne. He calls in his most trusted general and orders him to be relocated to a very remote province. The general is very disappointed, but as a loyal subordinate, he follows the wish of his king. One year later, the son becomes king. He soon recalls the general back to the capital. The general is extremely grateful and becomes immediately loyal to his new king. Leaders don't always need to explain their decision, because too much explanation can defeat the purpose.[27]

Secondly, the top-down approach needs *clear instruction*. Without a detailed pathway of implementation, lower managers or staff are perfectly aware of the issues but don't feel they have the authority to speak up, challenge the bosses, or carry out the task. They may blame higher managers for an unclear order and lack of instruction, while managers may blame their staff for lack of responsibility and initiatives. This situation happens even between cultures that stereotypically share many similar values such as Australia and the United States. In an account, US managers found a reluctance to take on leadership roles in Westpac—one of Australia's oldest and largest banking corporations. Bob Joss—former CEO of Westpac recalled:

> We used to have these relief managers who would go from branch to branch and fill in for managers who were away on vacation or leave even though they didn't know anything about the customers.... When I asked why the assistant managers in each of the branches didn't fill in, why they didn't jump at the chance to show us what they were made of, I was told that that would be taking advantage of them.[28]

Thirdly, top-down approach works beautifully when decision makers from both sides work *directly* with each other. That's why an ideal leader of top-down approach is someone who is well connected, has a large amount of social capital to do others a favor and to ask for favor, and maintains close ties with VIPs such as corporate heads and government officials. However, if levels of power don't match, decision making can get stuck in the mud. In negotiation, a simple statement of "I need to check with my manager" can indicate that you are *not* high on the hierarchy, you are not the authority, and you are probably not worth the effort.

11.2.2.2 Less Power: Consensus Approach

Let's have a look at Germany, the Netherlands, Japan, and Scandinavian countries such as Sweden, Norway, and Finland. Their scores on Hofstede's power distance index are on the low side (35, 38, 54, 31, 31, and 33, respectively), not too much different from the cluster of Anglo countries we mentioned previously with the top-down approach. However, their typical decision-making style is more consensus oriented. In other words, countries with similar scores taken from the static paradigm can have two opposite styles of decision making.

Germany, for example, has federal laws that mandate employee participation in virtually all key decisions of an organization. Representatives directly join management boards, forming councils and unions. Here is a case in point. When Volkswagen AG faced a serious financial setback, its managers couldn't just lay off employees. Instead, they had to enter a long process of negotiation with the union who fervently protected workers' right. Discussion, focus groups, consultation, and so forth took place until both sides agreed on a compromised four-day workweek, leaves without pay, and leaves for educational opportunities. This win-win solution allowed workers to keep their jobs (although with reduced income) and the company to cut its costs effectively.

Japan offers another variation of this consultative style, *nemawashi*, which literally means preparing the roots of a tree for planting. When there is a problem, lower-level workers gather to gain consensus around a possible solution. The issue then moves up the hierarchy scale, gaining consensus on the way until it reaches the final stage of agreement at the top management. It takes a long time, but once implemented, things go rapidly because it has gained widespread consensus. In some Japanese companies, the lack of unions gives way for employee suggestion system. In 1986, 95% of Toyota's employees submitted 2,648,710 ideas and 96% of them were implemented.[29] In such a culture, an ideal manager is someone who encourages employees to speak up for the sake of improvement, who fosters consensus and moves the team forward. This strong relationship is built over a long period. That's why in combination with the seniority system, Japanese managers who move to another company don't usually get similar position but have to start all over again from a lower rank. *Leadership is earned.*

In short, leadership styles vary across different cultures depending on how much power they are given, which broadly results in top-down and consensus approaches in decision making. When managers and staff from two approaches come to work together, the mismatch can be problematic. Imagine a consensus-oriented manager coming to the meeting and expecting her/ his top-down-oriented staff to share their opinions. Receiving limited feedback, the manager may assume a lack of knowledge and responsibility from the staff: "It's shameful. They are asking me to be a parent. You don't get paid for being a yes-robot." Having to invest extra time, the staff may assume exactly the same thing about the manager: "It is unfair. She is asking me to do her job. You don't get twice the salary and just pick ideas from others."

The top-down and consensus approaches described in this section are oversimplified ways of categorizing the decision-making process under the impact of culture. In reality, each country, organization, profession, and group can dynamically evolve and (re)shape their own style, which more often than not, is a *complex mix* of both approaches. For example, the French offer a case of such a combination. They are known for a passion in discussion, debate, and argument, which can lengthen the time to reach final decisions, especially with the power of trade unions. At the same time, French managers can be overtly conscious about status and can act authoritatively. An executive from Jordan once commented on this style and compared it with the Islamic way of *shura* (consultation). The traditional way Arab societies use to reach and legitimize decisions is through discussion with all members. It is based on the belief that God would never permit a consensus of the Muslim community to be in error. The final decision, however, rests with the leader. (S)he is expected to solicit input from others and use her/his best judgment to make the final call.

11.2.3 How Much Knowledge?

Knowledge also signifies leaders. The question is, how knowledgeable should a leader be? In a classic study,[30] managers from a variety of countries were asked to rank this statement: "Managers must have the answers to most questions asked by subordinates." The result is summarized in Table 11.4.

While for some managers, being a leader means good motivational strategies and arguing their case well, others rely more on competence and know-how. Japanese managers top the list. They often lead by examples, allowing subordinates to silently observe and learn. That's why Japanese offices are usually open spaces where everyone can easily communicate with each other and manager can coach and teach their subordinates. For the German, their tendency to regard managers as experts comes from the fact that this country is historically known for excellent engineering. Most German managers are technically trained and accomplished some form of craft apprenticeship. This results in a corporate system of fewer admin staff, a more hands-on management style with larger floor management. In their book *The World's Business Cultures*, the authors cited a story of a British manager in a German meeting. When he opened in classic British self-undermining and egalitarian style: "I'm not in production, but speaking as…" he was cut off in mid-flight by his German colleagues: "So you are *now* a production expert?" Indeed, "Get back in your box" was the real message.[31] For these Germans, one leads by one's specialist competence.

Table 11.4 Percentage of managers who agreed with the statement (Laurent [1983])

Countries	Managers Must Have the Answers
Japan	78
Spain	77
China	74
Indonesia	73
Italy	66
France	53
Germany	46
Belgium	44
Switzerland	38
Denmark	23
UK	27
US	18
Netherlands	17
Sweden	10

When managers-as-experts is combined with a top-down decision-making approach, this mix may result in some distinctive work dynamics: (1) An imbalance of both influence and workload and (2) an increased need for supervision.

Firstly, because knowledge is power, managers are reluctant to delegate autonomy. They may not keep their staff well informed because information is privilege. By controlling information and transmitting it piecemeal to subordinates, managers (sub)consciously ensure that their staff can't outperform them and have to rely on them for instruction. The bright side is increased power. The downside is overwork. This is exaggerated in slow-trust societies such as China where it takes much longer to build trust between leaders and followers. Historical cultural and political atmosphere can also lead people to be suspicious of others.

Secondly, due to the knowledge dependence on managers, when combined with top-down decision-making approach, subordinates tend to expect supervision and see it as a condition for productivity. In Thailand, for example, the amount of supervisory support strongly correlates with the amount of success.[32] Similarly, up to 85% of Indian subordinates believed they worked better under supervision.[33] In Saudi Arabia, a local manager stopped the flow of losing money in his Aramco franchise by imposing a series of rigid controls; drivers are even penalized for every valve cap that went missing. Such a measure of supervision helped the company save two-thirds of the cost per ton-mile, compared to what it had been under US management.[34] Authors David Thomas and Kerr Inkson illustrated this point with a case study in which a manager asked her Chinese subordinate: "Do you know what you did wrong?" Using a facilitating leadership approach, she expected a learning opportunity and self-reflection. Instead, the subordinated replied: "Whatever you say I did wrong, I did wrong"—which made her even angrier.[35] This is a clear example of a clash between two kinds of expectation: Managers as *experts* and managers as *facilitators*.

11.2.4 How Much Respect?

Trompenaars and Hampden-Turner[36] proposed two kinds of status. *Achieved status* is based on performance and merit, and *ascribed status* is based on seniority, background, or sex. The former is more associated with competence. Respect has to be earned again because a manager is only as good as her/his last job. For the latter, respect is more associated with experience and social status.

Let's say a young and talented IT specialist in her twenties with stellar achievement in disruptive technology is sent to work with a senior and experienced partner. She wants people to respect her for competence and up-to-date knowledge (achieved status). She will need to be strategic to convince her client, a senior baby boomer who grew up in a culture of large industrial companies, because this person wants to be respected for experience and stability (ascribed status).

Respect manifests itself in a wide range behaviors. When ascribed status prevails, a hierarchical *chain of command* signals status. In her book *The Culture Map*, author Erin Meyer described how a Mexican manager was taken by surprise when his Dutch subordinates jumped ranks and set up a lunch meeting with the CEO, without informing anyone. In the same "blatant" autonomous style, another subordinate also e-mailed the top manager—who was five levels above him—with criticism and initiatives, without telling him a word in advance.[37] With ascribed status in mind, the Mexican manager was extremely concerned how the CEO would judge him because, in his view, the subordinate disrespected him as a boss.

Author Erin Meyer continued to give another case in which level hopping became more complicated in virtual and global working environment. This is the story of two cooperating teams from Canada and India. When Sarah—the Canadian manager—needed some information, she sent an e-mail to the staff of the Indian team, and got no response. While Sarah was fed up, the Indian manager—Rishi—struggled asking himself what he had done to break trust with Sarah, because she had chosen to *circumnavigate* him and disrespect him in front of his staff. Meanwhile, the Indian staff were paralyzed because they sensed a serious problem going on between the bosses. The last thing they wanted to do was get entangled in that fight. Hence, no response.

Respect manifests itself in a wide range of *policies and privilege*. For example, a manager can lose his/her face in a scenario in which the foreign negotiator enters the meeting room and greets her/his subordinate first, simply because that lower-rank member is standing closest to the door.[38] A first-name-basis gesture of friendliness such as "call me Marie" can drain a leader of some rank and status among those who embrace strong hierarchy acceptance. When the chairman of Hyundai dropped by a car show, because every subordinate is expected to follow her/his manager, he led a trail of 20 people, forming a long, black eel that left onlookers stunned.[39]

In his book *Business Leadership in China*, author Frank Gallo recalled his experience working for a successful US laboratory founded by a Chinese immigrant. Then, facing competition from IBM, the company had a new CEO. He immediately eliminated the hierarchical rank, closed up the executive dining room, and stopped the executive parking lot, forcing managers to eat with the rest of the employees and come to work early if they wanted a prized spot near the office. Introducing a new culture so abruptly was not the only reason why the company went bankrupt soon after, but it definitely caused major turmoil and hastened the departure of many top talents.[40]

Learning from this lesson, later in his career, author Frank Gallo could understand the horror of his Chinese staff when he asked for a smaller office and a smaller car than they thought he should have. In their eyes, by seeking smaller spaces and an average car, the manager belittled the firm's image and made them lose face.[41] With this in mind, we may understand why, in Korea, an attempt to abandon the traditional five-tier system and employ a flat hierarchy backfired. Executives felt inferior. Having been used to ascribed status, they wanted bureaucracy back.[42]

In negotiation and trust building, giving sufficient signals of status is critical. An expert working in the Gulf, let's call her Sofia, made many mistakes by honestly answering the locals' questions: "I'm an atheist," "I'm single," or "I'm staying at the local hotel just down the road." Little did she know that these questions were to measure the status she had. For many in the Middle East, religion is not a personal choice but a compass of morality, having a family is not a personal choice but a path of a responsible person, staying in a luxurious hotel is not a personal choice but a sign of a powerful decision maker. It takes extra effort for the locals to establish a strong working relationship with someone who has no compelling driver for morality (atheist), who seems to care about herself only (single), and who is clearly not on top of the decision-making hierarchy (budget or mid-range hotel). As time went by, Sofia learned to address these questions with jokes (I'll take the religion of my future husband), with a request for sympathy (I'm still waiting for the right person), and with a subtle signal of powerful connections (The minister's advisor, Mrs. Fatimah, is asking me to stay with her family). She has also developed a habit of carrying two different versions of business card, one with plain information, the other with all the titles, prefixes, degrees, and positions she holds.

The importance of respect indicates that titles and promotion are essential for those with strong hierarchy acceptance mindset. In such an organization, employees expect to climb the ladder quickly, with bigger tittles. "Manager" as a label can be used liberally, sometimes just for the sake of giving face, impressing clients, avoiding a pay rise, or retaining talents in competitive markets where employers jump ship to have a fancy title in smaller companies. For example, J.P. Morgan created an executive director rank for senior vice presidents, and Standard Chartered in China assigned executive director titles to mid-level managers across the front, mid-, and back office, as a tool to retain staff and localize the job rankings.[43] Title inflation is especially rampant in banking and tech cultures where it is not uncommon to find companies where up to 40% of the employees are vice presidents and managers. There is also a trend in how employees are given creative titles such as chief listening officer, chief Twitter officer, digital overlord (i.e., website manager), change magician, accounting ninja, retail Jedi, and so forth.[44-45] Similarly, a sense of status is what drives companies to upgrade garbage collectors to fancy titles such as "sanitation engineers" or "recycling technicians."[46]

11.2.5 How Much Care?

Respect is given in exchange for care, especially when problems arise. The notion of care varies. When weak hierarchy acceptance prevails in combination with weak group attachment, care possibly means autonomy and freedom given at work. Facing an issue, managers may want to give suggestions, guidelines, and pathways to help their staff navigating the solutions.

When strong hierarchy acceptance prevails, in combination with strong group attachment, a benevolent autocrat manager would stereotypically act like a family member with a paternalistic/maternalistic leadership style. Facing a problem, managers tend to show personal support and have direct involvement with the solutions without worrying that such a behavior may be seen as an invasion of privacy.

Interestingly, just like parents who chastise children for their own sake, strong feedback and negative reinforcement can be seen as a sign of care and consideration. Thus, subordinates in Japan reacted more positively to strict and tough managers who reprimanded employees harshly,[47] and some Albanians even viewed positive feedback as having little value.[48] Similarly, author Nancy Adler cited in her book an interesting case between the Canadian staff and their Filipino manager. The manager was seen as a control freak who constantly checked employees' work and showed distrust. It turned out he was simply showing his way of care and involvement, otherwise, the staff would have felt neglected and unimportant because they didn't get enough attention from the boss.[49]

A good indicator of care factor is what managers do when facing financial crisis. Legend has it that, in 2001, Daewoo had to lay off 7,000 employees, and the chairman took extraordinary effort to make amends. He held a job fair, sent personal letters to his counterparts at 26,000 companies begging them to hire one of the fired employees, and bowed to the employees to apology.[50] In many parts of the world where suicide is seen as a noble form of protest and redemption, managers may even commit suicide if they have to lay off employees. For example, Nobuo Shibata, the president of a Japanese metal sheet company, and his brother took their own lives and left a note: "We apologize to all our employees for the slump in our business."[51]

Such a level of care may be hard to find in organizational cultures where executives traditionally enjoy disproportional benefit, for example, in the United States. Many US CEOs slashed thousands of jobs, yet took home even larger bonuses than usual because these layoffs can boost short-term profits.[52] From a shareholder's point of view, nothing is more important than higher profit margins and higher stock prices. Here lies the difference between a corporate culture that sees employees as *variable costs*—to be replaced and disposed, in comparison with a corporate culture that regards employees as a *fixed asset*—to be nurtured, protected, and developed based on trust and mutual commitments.

11.2.6 Context Dependence

In the previous sections, it has been argued that leadership styles vary across cultures based on the amount of power, knowledge, respect, and care a leader has or is given. However, it is hard to overemphasize that the examples provided in these sections are somewhat stereotypical. More often than not, specific contexts lead to a much more dynamic and complex reality. Let's continue with the topic of layoffs to see the point. The CEO of Honeywell—an US multinational conglomerate—made headlines during the 2008 recession when he chose furloughs instead of typical mass layoffs. This femininity-oriented decision is so *unconventional* in a stereotypically masculine corporate culture that many questioned his sanity.[53] While a bonus pool remained for employees, he received zero bonus, and the management board voluntarily followed suit—an equivalent of a six-month furlough. And it paid off. Three years later, Honeywell almost doubled the pace of the Standard & Poor's 500 and outpaced its nearest competitor by almost 23 points.

Glocal leadership, therefore, does not follow any static frameworks. In fact, it follows the concept of *situational leadership*—an approach that underlines two major leadership frameworks: The Contingency Model and the Path-Goal Theory. Both frameworks bear a dynamic view, regarding a leader's effectiveness as being contingent upon her/his behavior and how it interacts with aspects of the situation. It also aligns with the way humans have evolved to make decision on leadership. If we are physically threatened, we will follow physically strong leaders. If we are uncertain, we will follow experienced leaders. Different situations call for different leadership styles. Likewise, each leadership style has the power to reshape the situation, for better or worse. A famous Israeli author, David Grossman, once said: "Time and again we choose warriors to lead us, but maybe by always choosing warriors, we doom ourselves to always be in wars."

Following the principle of situational leadership, a leader can break the local rules, as long as (s)he is successful. Honeywell is not an exception. The business world is full of such stories. We are reminded of Carlos Ghosn who helped Nissan recover in the most un-Japanese way: Mass layoffs, cutting ties with long-term suppliers, confronting the seniority system and replacing it with pay-for-performance, making English the official language, and so forth. Despite the fact that many of his changes were at odds with the local culture, he succeeded, became a much-admired leader, and his story is now a classic case study of situational leadership, of successful combination of opposing approaches (top-down and consensus).

When facing a new dynamic of culture, a leader generally has three kinds of reaction: *Freeze*, *please*, or *tease*.[54] The first reaction is a consequence of being overwhelmed with complexity and cultural shock. The second approach is what a majority of literature on cross-cultural management advocates, which is adapting to fit in with the existing culture. Leaders are bombarded with warnings and consequences if they fail to adjust, or bow down to local practices. However, going native risks losing identities, adopting even unethical and ineffective values, and missing the very opportunities that turn a manager into a leader: *Change leadership*. Successful leaders conform enough, to an extent that allows them to engage and gain leverage, to eventually change a corporate culture. In short, they *tease*. They understand what can be changed and what cannot, then operate within those constraints. They challenge the norms, but not all of them, all at once.[55]

Such a balancing act of teasing is delicate, complex, and situational. Once a leader has identified the key aspects of the cultural context that should be respected, what (s)he proceeds to promote change can be dramatic. Zhang Ruimin—CEO of Haier Group—is known for changing his company's culture in the most un-Chinese way. He would smash every single defective appliance with a sledgehammer, making the manager responsible, and putting young people in charge. He also introduced an extremely individualistic and face-sensitive 10/10 reward system: Every year, 10% of the employees are publicly praised as role models, and 10% are identified as needing improvement who would risk losing their contract if fail to advance.[56] By combining Chinese and un-Chinese policies, a right mixture of opposing values and practices helped Haier Group one of the top companies in its industry.

Another case in point is a story recalled by a Western manager in Asia. For one important meeting with clients, he decided that the team would serve customers like waiters in a restaurant to understand the service-oriented approach, and to learn about the need of their clients. The team perceived this as a face-losing tactic. Asking senior executives from a strong hierarchy accepting culture to dress up as waiters and perform the duty was unthinkable. The manager decided not to back down. He emphasized his willingness to adapt to local culture, and invited his team to do the same by adapting to his culture, once, for a change. In the end, it was a huge success. Even years later all the teams would speak fondly of it. The manager concluded that it was fine to go against stereotypical cultural norms.[57]

Situational leaders know that they can and should break the mold if that helps to promote positive change. Here is an example. When presenting his idea, the Vietnamese CEO of FPT—a multinational IT corporation—received an unprecedented comment from his technical chief: "You guys are so bloody stupid." The consequence of this exchange, if we follow the rigid static cultural framework of strong hierarchy acceptance, would be disastrous. However, in this particular situation, the CEO went on and calmly asked: "So, *can you do it?*"[58] This shift of behavior opened up a new chapter for the company. To this day, FPT is famous for having an extremely casual and satirical way of communication. Employees confront managers directly and openly in staff meetings. This shows how leadership can create a corporate culture that is very different from the stereotypical national culture where the company is located.

To conclude, situational leadership allows context to drive strategies. It is the enveloping circle around both GCEB-Be and the Inverted Pyramid Model that pins down how a specific situation is made of universal concerns, cultural values, particular behaviors, individual personality and willingness to change, the pull and push factors of genes and brain plasticity toward that change, and so forth. Situational leadership, therefore, is the leadership style that embraces dynamics, flexibility, and agility—pretty much the characteristics of business in the modern era.

11.3 Global Leadership of Diversity

When it comes to "global leadership," we often mistakenly assume the meaning of "global" as "generic." In fact, global should mean "diversity." Global leadership operates in a dynamic context of nationalities, ethnicities, social and educational backgrounds, occupations, religions, genders, sexual orientations, and so forth. A global leader deals with many cultural patterns at the same time, for example, a multicultural team. Here is a case in point. When three electronic giants—IBM, Siemens, and Toshiba—tried to form a strategic alliance, scientists from all three companies gathered and pooled their knowledge. But cultural clashes occurred quickly. Siemen experts didn't appreciate how Toshiba colleagues appeared to sleep during the meeting, failing to understand that closing their eyes was a common way to focus. Toshiba experts found it difficult to work individually and speak English all day. And from IBM, experts complained about too much planning from Siemen and indecisiveness from Toshiba.[59] The failure to understand each other contributed significantly to the meltdown of the alliance. Such a situation is the reality of international business with which a global leader needs to deal.

Therefore, in this section, instead of focusing on what makes a good global leader in general, we will focus on this question: What makes a good diversity leader?

11.3.1 *Seek Synergy*

A global manager of diversity must create a new culture in which people cooperate effectively. A traditional and often counterproductive approach is immediately focusing on differences, identifying potential problems, and using stereotypes to simplify the world. For example, because women are emotional, men are assertive, the Dutch are direct, and alcohol offends the Muslims, we need to be aware of wrong interpretation in our team. Such an approach in the mainstream intercultural training unwittingly stigmatizes cultural gaps and prepares our mindset for caution, reaction, and defensiveness (see Chapter 5). Global leaders will spend energy worrying about future problems, seeing differences as obstacles, while in fact, their main task is to *seek synergy and turn those differences into assets*, making a magic combination of opposing values and practices. For this reason, some multinationals now refuse to label their training as an intercultural or diversity workshop to avoid deepening stereotypes.

So how to achieve synergy from differences? As we discussed in Chapter 6, the Inverted Pyramid Model suggests that to turn differences into advantages, we need to start with similarities. This means building a foundation in common goals, shared interests, mutual backgrounds, similar concerns, and so forth. From an evolutionary perspective, a similarity-first approach fits well with how our brain has evolved after a long period living as small groups on the savannah, where sameness is the signal of trust and differences mean threats. We no longer live in isolated small groups, but our trust system of the ancient time still lingers.

Once a foundation of trust has been established, similarities act as a powerful springboard to approach differences, be open about misunderstanding, and work toward a joint solution. Diversity leaders rely on this synergetic approach to encourage their staff to talk openly about their differences as both weaknesses and strengths. Embracing a synergetic approach, they will step up and propose how their differences may hinder or contribute to the mutual success. When problems occur, such a synergetic approach will prompt cultural contingency—that the best solution depends on the particular cultures of those involved and the context of the event.

A good example of the synergetic approach comes from an educational project that the author of this book coordinated. Working virtually across four continents, the team of 12 experts capitalized on diversity, especially during the analysis, development, and planning stages. What we discovered was that many of the so-called issues team members had in their everyday working life turned out to be our *competitive edge*. For example, two millennials who often procrastinated on Facebook during work hours became the best marketing agents when they recruited hundreds of followers per day. When Indonesian participants had difficulties understanding the native English accent, we replaced the training positions by a Qatari and a Dutch expert whose speaking pattern was somewhat slow with a simple use of vocabulary and sentence structure— something they had considered their weakness back in their own company, but turned out to be exactly what our client needed. "Good" or "bad" qualities have *relative* meanings with such a synergy approach. Either "good" or "bad" can be understood as similarities and differences because they have the potential to contribute equally when the context is right.

11.3.2 *Cultivate Multicultural Mind*

The synergy approach also means that whenever there is a hiccup, the number one thing to avoid was a witch hunt (i.e., who to blame), but rather describing the problem without pointing fingers to anyone. Here is a simple method to identify the problems based on the three layers of the Inverted Pyramid Model: Is it an issue of *process* or *culture*, and what can an *individual* do?

First of all, at the universal level, we ask whether the problem is due to *process*—something all of us can potentially make, break, and recreate? We should avoid "culturalizing" problems[60] because not every issue originates from cultural differences. Secondly, at the cultural level, we ask whether the problem is rooted in the *different* levels of importance we place on the *same* values and outward expressions. For example, we all want a clear plan, but some people think it should be fixed, while others want to leave room for change.

Thirdly, at the individual level, team members then are invited to share, as *unique and creative problem solvers,* what they can do to improve the situation. Separating a person from her/his culture is crucial in this strategy because we don't want to fall prey to stereotypes and the assumption that we are the prisoners of our own cultures. The problem may be due to a mismatch of group attachment levels (at the cultural level), but a person from traditionally individualistic society can break away from this mold and transform into a collectivistic persona (at the individual level) to the address the problem effectively. Again, context is the software of the mind. Leadership of diversity means a belief in such an individual transformation, the potential of a multicultural mind, and endless effort in cultivating such a capacity.

11.3.3 *Be Inclusive*

In Britain, the reigning monarch is head of the Church of England, holding the title Defender of the (Anglican) Faith. As Britain is changing toward a multicultural society, it has long been reported that Prince Charles wishes to omit "the," rendering it as "Defender of Faith" to embrace other religions. This triggered a national debate.[61] The enormous concern with a tiny change in wording of the coronation oath shows us that inclusion is a critical element of diversity leadership. For more discussion on inclusive language, see Chapter 9.

Inclusion manifests itself in every aspect of leadership, not only in language. It means hiring diversity, ensuring a diverse management board, taking diversity into account in business strategies, using diversity as a framework to tailor motivation and reward system, and so forth. The Danish pharmaceutical company Novo Nordisk A/S provides a successful case of knowledge transfer through a multicultural and diversity team. In the late 1990s, facing crisis, the company developed a set of documents that clearly spelled out how the corporate culture should change. They then established a group of 14 facilitators, selected from seven nationalities with experience in different business areas. These facilitators went to all departments and acted as meditators of the company's new philosophy and (ad hoc) consultants. The inclusiveness of the team was a fundamental element in helping these change agents to translate the new philosophy into the "language" of the recipient units.[62] Table 11.5 summarizes the background of the first group, selected from 120 candidates around the world.

Table 11.5 Multicultural team of facilitators in Novo Nordisk A/S

Gender	Nationality	Age	Education	Experience	Language
Female ×3 Male ×11	Danish ×6 South African ×1 Malaysian ×1 Spanish ×1 US ×2 British ×2 Japanese ×1	38–62	Pharmacy Agricultural chemistry Engineering Pharmacology Biochemistry Anthropology Law Marketing Microbiology Business Economic Psychology	3–19 years Collectively 200 years	Chinese Danish English French German Japanese Malay Spanish Swedish

11.3.4 Make Teamwork Challenging

Diversity is primarily challenged by our biological tendency to prefer similar attributes. But we now know that when differences don't trigger the continuous fear response that pushes the energy consumption past the tipping point of eustress, diversity can be an asset. To compare, a homogeneous culture creates the perception of easiness and comfort, but "comfortable" in the long term can decrease performance. In Chapter 9, we concluded that familiarity can make us blindsided, underprepared, underestimating the complexity of the problem.[63] Hence, adding an outsider doubles the chances of better solution.[64] Because diversity prompts us to work harder to overcome the differences,[65] the outcomes are better. However, this is a *fine balance*. Choosing when to add new elements in the team and when to promote sameness is the art of diversity leadership. Leaders should feel and weigh the situation, making sure it is challenging but not overwhelming, different but not threatening, hard to achieve but possible to get done.

11.3.5 Promote Positive Change

To be a global leader, developing an awareness of cultural diversity and adapting leadership styles to match local conditions may not always be the best option. Often, leaders have to promote change and introduce new cultures instead of "going native." As with the case of situational leadership, the key to leadership success lies in the ability to *tease*, conforming just enough to the existing environment so as not to be rejected but, at the same time, harnessing power to confront the current norms, break the mold, move forward and change the local culture.

Leadership of change is not only a critical requirement of a successful business but also an expectation of employees. The new generation of workers increasingly regards businesses and managers to be ethical change agents in the wider society. Seventy-six percent of millennials see companies as a force of positive social impact, and 62% regard business leaders as drivers to help improving society.[66] Interestingly, the view of leaders as change agents is much higher in emerging markets (73%), probably because these are also countries where social improvement is much more in demand.

Some researchers suggest that *ethical/servant leadership* is the goal of evolution. Contrary to the traditional view that sees leaders as selfish and egoistic exploiters, lab experiments showed that leaders don't emerge as they compete for the right to dominate and exploit others.[67] In fact, most leaders choose to lead because they initially want to be helpful. This study paints a much more positive view than the one held by traditional evolutionary biologists. Although power does corrupt, and many leaders do abuse their power once they are in charge, for every Hitler there is a Mother Teresa. And the latter is much closer to the way we want our leaders to be: Inspiring, changing for the better, and servant.

Because leaders are increasingly expected to be ethical and to be a driver in positive social change, a company can no longer just focus on generating profit. It can no longer blindly adapt to the local norms and practices, even when they are considered harmful for a sustainable future. Consider issues such as bribe, and the choice to conform to the local way or fight against it. A multinational called RIGA (not the company's real name), opted the hard way when it expanded the market to Southeast Asia. The management board rejected advice from local partners and staff, refusing to pay any bribes to government officials—crucial figures in entering new market. They upheld business codes and explained to clients the consequences of such a practice. At the same time, they eased their way through by offering other "gifts" such as training opportunities, awards of contribution, honorary positions, and so forth, giving status instead of money. Slowly but steadily, their local staff and partners changed their view. The company gained a reputation in the industry as honest and transparent businesses—a prize that created a higher standard for newcomers and encouraged local companies to change in the same direction.

More than anyone else, leaders have the power to influence, shape, and reshape a culture. Following pathway Behavior—Brain—Culture, leaders are the most powerful agents to exercise the "magic" of the dynamic paradigm: Humans are not only products but also *producers* of culture. Repeated behaviors rewire the brain and change even deep-seated values. Leaders don't just adapt, leaders lead.

Summary

1. At the universal level, leadership emerges evolutionarily as a survival strategy to coordinate group activities.
   - A number of genes have been associated with rulebreaking and risk-taking. Depending on cultural background and upbringing, these genes can be regulated differently, fostering either positive or negative aspects of leadership.
   - At the collective level, the origin of hierarchy acceptance is rooted in the external threats in early environmental habitats that prompted humans to accept hierarchy and orders. This culture of strong hierarchy acceptance favored certain genes, and these genes became more dominant to support the culture of strong hierarchy acceptance.
   - At the individual level, holding weak or strong hierarchy acceptance can influence the wiring of the brain and, consequently, influence the behavior. However, individuals' values are not static. Priming, changes of environment, and repeated behaviors can change the attitudes and even deep-seated values. Our mind is potentially multicultural.
2. At the universal level, GLOBE established 22 leadership attributes that all good leaders commonly share. At the cultural level, GLOBE established 35 attributes that are valued differently across cultures. The combination of these attributes results in six leadership styles.
3. At the collective level, leadership varies across cultures depending on how much (1) power, (2) knowledge, (3) respect, and (4) care a leader is given or expected to give.
4. At the individual level, leadership closely ties with the personal way one interacts with a specific context. Situational leadership is dynamic. A leader can even break local norms and still achieve success.
5. Global leadership essentially means leadership of diversity. It requires the ability to:
   - Seek synergy: Build a foundation of trust based on similarities, then use this foundation as a springboard to approach differences as potential assets instead of obstacles.
   - Cultivate multicultural mind: When problems occur, apply the Inverted Pyramid Model by asking: (1) Is it in the process? (2) Is it cultural? (3) What can each individual do to improve? The last question is based on the potential of multicultural mind and individual transformation.
   - Make teamwork challenging: Find a balance between adding diversity and promoting sameness, making multicultural teamwork challenging but not overwhelming.
   - Be inclusive: Create a culture in which everyone feels included, across all organizational aspects: Language, benefit, management, hiring, reward, and so forth.
   - Promote positive change of the culture in which a leader operates: Leaders don't go native and adopt even harmful local ways. Leaders are change agents, drivers of betterment in wider society.

Notes

Don't forget to go to the end of the book for case studies.

1 Gillet, Joris., Edward Cartwright, and Mark Van Vugt. 2011. "Selfish or Servant Leadership? Evolutionary Predictions on Leadership Personalities in Coordination Games." *Personality and Individual Differences* 51(3): 231–236. doi:10.1016/j.paid.2010.06.003.

2 Fiske, Alan P. 1992. "The Four Elementary Forms of Sociality: Framework for a Unified Theory of Social Relations." *Psychological Review* 99(4): 689–723. doi:10.1037/0033-295X.99.4.689.

3 Inkeles, Alex., and Daniel J. Levinson. 1969. "National Characters: The Study of Modal Personality and Sociocultural Systems." In *The Handbook of Social Psychology*, ed. G. Lindzey and E. Aronson. 2nd ed. Vol. 4, 418–506. Reading, MA: Addison-Wesley.

4 Kluckhohn, Florence., and Fred Strodtbeck. 1961. *Variations in Value Orientations.* Evanston, IL: Row, Peterson.

5 Hofstede, Geert., Gert-Jan Hofstede, and Michael Minkov. 2005. *Cultures and Organizations: Software of the Mind.* New York: McGraw-Hill.

6 Trompenaars, Fons., and Charles Hampden-Turner. 1997. *Riding The Waves of Culture: Understanding Diversity in Global Business.* 3rd ed. London: Nicholas Brealey.

7 Mengistu, Henok., Joost Huizinga, Jean-Baptiste Mouret, and Jeff Clune. 2016. "The Evolutionary Origins of Hierarchy." *PLoS Computational Biology* 12(6): e1004829. doi:10.1371/journal.pcbi.1004829.

8 Chiao, Joan Y., Reginald B. Adams, Peter U. Tse, William T. Lowenthal, Jennifer A. Richeson, and Nalini Ambady. 2008. "Knowing Who Is Boss: fMRI and ERP Investigations of Social Dominance Perception." *Group Processes and Intergroup Relations* Special issue 11(2): 201–214. doi:10.1177/1368430207088038.

9 Birnbaum, Robert. 2012. "Genes, Memes, and the Evolution of Human Leadership." In *The Oxford Handbook of Leadership*, ed. Michael G. Rumsey, 243–266. Oxford: Oxford University Press. doi:10.1093/oxfordhb/9780195398793.013.0015.

10 Arvey, Richard D., Maria Rotundo, Wendy Johnson, Zhen Zhang, and Matt Mcgue. 2006. "The Determinants of Leadership Role Occupancy: Genetic and Personality Factors." *The Leadership Quarterly* 17(1): 1–20. doi:10.1016/j.leaqua.2005.10.009.

11 Arvey, Richard D., Zhen Zhang, Bruce J. Avolio, and Robert F. Krueger. 2007. "Developmental and Genetic Determinants of Leadership Role Occupancy among Women." *Journal of Applied Psychology* 92(3): 693–706. doi:10.1037/0021-9010.92.3.693.

12 Li, Wen-Dong., Richard D. Arvey, Zhen Zhang, and Zhaoli Song. 2012. "Do Leadership Role Occupancy and Transformational Leadership Share the Same Genetic and Environmental Influences?" *The Leadership Quarterly* 23(2): 233–243. doi:10.1016/j.leaqua.2011.08.007.

13 De Neve, Jan-Emmanuel., Slava Mikhaylov, Christopher T. Dawes, Nicholas A. Christakis, and James H. Fowler. 2013. "Born to Lead? A Twin Design and Genetic Association Study of Leadership Role Occupancy." *The Leadership Quarterly* 24(1): 45–60. doi:10.1016/j.leaqua.2012.08.001.

14 Li, Wen-Dong., Nan Wang, Richard Arvey, Richie Soong, Seang Mei Saw, and Zhaoli Song. 2015. "A Mixed Blessing? Dual Mediating Mechanisms in the Relationship between Dopamine Transporter Gene DAT1 and Leadership Role Occupancy." *The Leadership Quarterly* 26(5): 671–686. doi:10.1016/j.leaqua.2014.12.005.

15 Chi, Wei., Wen-Dong Li, Nan Wang, and Zhaoli Song. 2016. "Can Genes Play a Role in Explaining Frequent Job Changes? An Examination of Gene-Environment Interaction from Human Capital Theory." *Journal of Applied Psychology.* 101(7): 1030–1044. doi:10.1037/apl0000093.

16 Polderman, Tinca J. C., Beben Benyamin, Christiaan A. de Leeuw, Patrick F. Sullivan, Arjen van Bochoven, Peter M. Visscher, and Danielle Posthuma. 2015. "Meta-Analysis of the Heritability of Human Traits Based on Fifty Years of Twin Studies." *Nature Genetics* 47: 702–709. doi:10.1038/ng.3285.

17 Freeman, Jonathan B., Nicholas O. Rule, Reginald B. Adams, and Nalini Ambady. 2009. "Culture Shapes a Mesolimbic Response to Signals of Dominance and Subordination That Associates with Behavior." *NeuroImage* 47(1): 353–359. doi:10.1016/j.neuroimage.2009.04.038.

18 Nakata, Yumi. 2014. "Uchi Soto and Japanese Group Culture." September 25. https://blog. gaijinpot.com/uchi-soto-japanese-culture.

19 Liew, Sook-Lei., Yina Ma, Shihui Han, and Lisa Aziz-Zadeh. 2011. "Who's Afraid of the Boss: Cultural Differences in Social Hierarchies Modulate Self-Face Recognition in Chinese and Americans." *PLOS* 6(2): e16901. doi:10.1371/journal.pone.0016901.

20 Rule, Nicholas O., Keiko Ishii, and Nalini Ambady. 2011. "Cross-Cultural Impressions of Leaders' Faces: Consensus and Predictive Validity." *International Journal of Intercultural Relations* 35(6): 833–841. doi:10.1016/j.ijintrel.2011.06.001.

21 Hong, Ying-yi., Michael W. Morris, Chie-Yue Chiu, Veronica Benet-Martinez et al. 2000. "Multicultural Minds: A Dynamic Constructivist Approach to Culture and Cognition." *American Psychologist* 55(7): 709–720. doi:10.1037//0003-066x.55.7.709.

22 MacDonald, Heather A., Lorne M. Sulsky, and Douglas J. Brown. 2008. "Leadership and Perceiver Cognition: Examining the Role of Self-Identity in Implicit Leadership Theories." *Human Performance* 21(4): 333–353. doi:10.1080/08959280802347031.

23 Jung, Dong I., and Bruce J. Avolio. 1999. "Effects of Leadership Style and Followers' Cultural Orientation on Performance in Groups and Individual Task Conditions." *Academy of Management Journal* 42(2): 208–218. doi:10.5465/257093.

24 House, Robert J., ed., et al. 2004. *Culture, Leadership, and Organizations: The GLOBE Study of 62 Societies*. Thousand Oaks, CA: Sage Publications.

25 Hofstede, Geert., Gert-Jan Hofstede, and Michael Minkov. 2005. *Cultures and Organizations: Software of the Mind*, 43–44. New York: McGraw-Hill.

26 Osland, Joyce S., and Allan Bird. 2000. "Beyond Sophisticated Stereotyping: Cultural Sensemaking in Context." *Academy of Management Executive* 14(1): 65–79. doi:10.5465/ AME.2000.2909840.

27 Gallo, Frank T. 2008. *Business Leadership in China—How to Blend Best Western Practices with Chinese Wisdom*, 33. Singapore: John Wiley & Sons (Asia).

28 Blount, Frank., Bob Joss, and David Mair. 1999. *Managing in Australia* 162–163. Sydney, NSW: Landsdowne Publishing.

29 Yasuda, Yuzo. 1990. *40 Years, 20 Million Ideas: The Toyota Suggestion System*. Cambridge, MA: Productivity Press.

30 Laurent, André. 1983. "The Cultural Diversity of Western Conceptions of Management." *International Studies of Management and Organization* 13(1/2): 75–96. doi:10.1080/ 00208825.1983.11656359.

31 Tomalin, Barry., and Mike Nicks. 2010. *The World's Business Cultures: And How to Unlock Them*, 121. 2nd ed. London: Thorogood.

32 Bhanthumnavin, Duchduen. 2001. *Supervisory Social Support and the Multi-level Performance in the Thai Health Centers*. Thesis. University of Minnesota. www.hsevi.ir/RI_Thesis/View/54.

33 Kakar, Sudhir. 1971. "Authority Patterns and Subordinate Behavior in Indian Organizations." *Administrative Science Quarterly* 16(3): 298–307. doi:10.2307/2391902.

34 Weaver, Gary R. 1998. *Culture, Communication, and Conflict: Readings in Intercultural Relations*, 14. Boston: Pearson Custom Publishing.

35 Inkson, Kerr., and David Thomas. 2009. *Cultural Intelligence: Living and Working Globally*, 206. San Francisco: Berret-Koehler.

36 Trompenaars, Fons., and Charles Hampden-Turner. 1997. *Riding The Waves of Culture: Understanding Diversity in Global Business*. 3rd ed. London: Nicholas Brealey.

37 Meyer, Erin. 2014. *The Culture Map: Breaking through the Invisible Boundaries of Global Business*. New York: Ingram Publisher Service US.

38 Sebenius, James K., and Cheng Jason Qian. 2008. *Cultural Notes on Chinese Negotiating Behavior*. Boston: Harvard Business School. www.hbs.edu/faculty/Publication Files/09-076. pdf.

39 Getlen, Larry. 2016. "The Boozy, Narcissistic Culture Shock of Working in South Korea." *New York Post*. September 3. https://nypost.com/2016/09/03/the-boozy-narcissistic-culture-shock-of-working-in-south-korea/.

40 Gallo, Frank T. 2008. *Business Leadership in China—How to Blend Best Western Practices with Chinese Wisdom*, 8. Singapore: John Wiley & Sons (Asia).

41 Ibid.

42 Nam, In-Soo. 2014. "Staff Hierarchies Make a Comeback at KT Corp." *The Wall Street Journal*. June 23. https://blogs.wsj.com/corporate-intelligence/2014/06/23/staff-hierarchies-make-a-comeback-at-kt-corp.

43 Mortlock, Simon. 2016. "Job Title Inflation Sees Asian Bankers Make MD before 30." *EFinancialCareers*. November 8. https://news.efinancialcareers.com/au-en/176511/job-title-inflation-sees-asian-bankers-make-md-before-30.

44 IntaPeople. 2012. "The Ten Strangest Job Titles on LinkedIn." May 2. www.journalism.co.uk/press-releases/the-ten-strangest-job-titles-on-linkedin/s66/a549049.

45 Cenedella, Marc. 2017. "Title Inflation in the C-Suite." *ERE Media*. August 9. www.ere.net/title-inflation-in-the-c-suite/.

46 Steers, Richard M., Carlos J. Sanchez-Runde, and Luciara Nardon. 2010. *Management across Cultures: Challenges and Strategies*, 81. Cambridge: Cambridge University Press.

47 Bond, Michael H., Kwok-Choi Wan, Kwok Leung, and Robert A. Giacalone. 1985. "How Are Responses to Verbal Insults Related to Cultural Collectivism and Power Distance?" *Journal of Cross-Cultural Psychology* 16(1): 111–127. doi:10.1177/0022002185016001009.

48 Gausden, J. 2003. "The Giving and Receiving of Feedback in Central European Cultures." Unpublished master's dissertation, University of Salford, UK.

49 Adler, Nancy J., and Allison Gundersen. 2008. *International Dimensions of Organizational Behavior*, 46. 5th ed. Mason, OH: Thomson South-Western.

50 Gannon, Martin J. 2008. *Paradoxes of Culture and Globalization*, 69. Thousand Oaks, CA: SAGE Publications.

51 Sugawara, S. 1998. "From Debt to Desperation in Japan." *The Washington Post*. August 21. www.washingtonpost.com/archive/business/1998/08/21/from-debt-to-desperation-in-japan/d81f74e6-17e0-4bb2-a356-933f24705980/?utm_term=.e3a8136ef9bb.

52 Jones, Roland. 2010. "CEOs Lay off Thousands, Rake in Millions." September 1. www.nbcnews.com/id/38935053/ns/business-us_business/t/ceos-lay-thousands-rake-millions/#.Wp4f1a6WbIU.

53 Sucher, Sandra., and Susan Winterberg. 2015. "Leadership Lessons of the Great Recession: Options for Economic Downturns." *HBS Working Knowledge*. September 9. https://hbswk.hbs.edu/item/leadership-lessons-of-the-great-recession-options-for-economic-downturns.

54 Steers, Richard M., Carlos J. Sanchez-Runde, and Luciara Nardon. 2010. *Management across Cultures: Challenges and Strategies*, 259. Cambridge: Cambridge University Press.

55 Goffee, Rob., and Gareth Jones. 2006. *Why Should Anyone Be Led by You? What It Take to Be an Authentic Leader*, 109–133. Cambridge, MA: Harvard Business School Press.

56 DeKrey, Steven J., and David M. Messick, eds. 2007. *Leadership Experiences in Asia: Insight and Inspiration from 20 Innovators*, 66. Singapore: John Wiley & Sons (Asia).

57 Ibid.

58 Tùng, Thanh. 2017. "Chủ Tịch FPT Software Tiết Lộ Thực Hư Câu 'Các Anh Ngu Bỏ Mẹ'." *Chungta*. November 29. http://chungta.vn/tin-tuc/su-fpt/chu-tich-fpt-software-tiet-lo-thuc-hu-cau-cac-anh-ngu-bo-me-62465.html.

59 Browning, E. S. 1994. "Computer Chip Project Brings Rivals Together, but the Cultures Clash." *The Wall Street Journal*. May 3, A1.

60 Trompenaars, Fons., and Charles Hamden-Turner. 1997. *Riding the Waves of Culture: Understanding Cultural Diversity in Business*. London: Nicholas Brealey.

61 Sherwood, Harriet. 2017. "Prince Charles Accession 'Could Trigger Debate on Disestablishment.'" *The Guardian*. December 10. www.theguardian.com/world/2017/dec/10/prince-charles-ascension-time-for-debate-on-disestablishment-says-report.

62 Sohm, Stefanie. 2017. "Living Corporate Culture: A Case Study on Novo Facilitations and Their Applicability in Other Companies." https://blog.creating-corporate-cultures.org/wp-content/uploads/sites/2/2017/11/A-Case-Study-on-Novo-Facilitations-and-their-Applicability-in-other-Companies.pdf.

63 Phillips, Katherine W. 2014. "How Diversity Makes Us Smarter." *Scientific American.* October 1. www.scientificamerican.com/article/how-diversity-makes-us-smarter/.

64 Rock, David., Heidi Grant Halvorson, and Jacqui Grey. 2016. "Diverse Teams Feel Less Comfortable and That Is Why They Perform Better." *Harvard Business Review.* September 22. https://hbr.org/2016/09/diverse-teams-feel-less-comfortable-and-thats-why-they-perform-better?utm_content=bufferc285e&utm_medium=social&utm_source=facebook.com&utm_campaign=buffer.

65 Loyd, Denise., Cynthia Wang, Katherine Phillips, and Robert Lount. 2013. "Social Category Diversity Promotes Premeeting Elaboration: The Role of Relationship Focus." *Organization Science* 24(3): 757–772. doi:10.1287/orsc.1120.0761.

66 Deloitte. 2017. "The 2017 Deloitte Millennial Survey Apprehensive Millennials: Seeking Stability and Opportunities in an Uncertain World." www2.deloitte.com/content/dam/Deloitte/global/Documents/About-Deloitte/gx-deloitte-millennial-survey-2017-executive-summary.pdf.

67 Gillet, Joris., Edward Cartwright, and Mark van Vugt. 2011. "Selfish or Servant Leadership? Evolutionary Predictions on Leadership Personalities in Coordination Games." *Personality and Individual Differences* 51(3): 231–236. doi:10.1016/j.paid.2010.06.003.

12 Cross-Cultural Business Communication

Effective communication is vital for all organizations. A classic study estimated that up to 80% of our workday is spent in communicating, two-thirds of that in talking.[1] This chapter gives us more insight into its dynamics, introducing major communication patterns, discussing the role of body language and language, and touching on the communication aspects of business meetings and building relationship.

We will continue to use the Diagram of Diversity Pathways GCEB-Be (Chapter 2) to see how interdisciplinary studies can help us explore different angles of communication. Following pathway Culture—Brain, we will discuss how communication patterns such as direct–indirect can change the neural responses and focus our attention on different details of exchanging data, depending on our dominant culture at that moment. Pathway Culture—Behavior—Brain suggests that we explore how body language and language shape our thinking, change our decisions, and exert a significant impact on how we behave. And consistently, the enveloping circle of context reminds us to avoid the risk of stereotypes and discuss the dynamics of specific circumstances in which communication occurs.

12.1 Patterns of Communication

In the metaphorical tree of culture (Chapter 3), the canopy represents outward expressions such as external behaviors and words, either in alignment or in conflict with a dominant value—a dynamic interaction we discussed in Chapter 4. Theorists have been trying to categorize outward expressions in terms of communication styles. In this section, we will discuss three communication patterns that are most frequently mentioned in the literature: (1) direct–indirect; (2) monochronic–polychromic; and (3) affective–neutral.

12.1.1 Direct and Indirect

12.1.1.1 Cross-Cultural Findings

A prominent interculturalist, Edward Hall, identified two major approaches of communication: *Low context* relies less (low) on the surrounding cues such as body language, tones of voice, history of the relationship, and so forth. When embracing low context, people tend to be direct, take words for their literal meaning ("yes" means "yes"), and prefer specific and abundant details. On the contrary, *high context* relies more (high) on the surrounding cues to detect the true meaning of the communication. In situations in which high context prevails, people act like a sensitive radar that goes back and forth across time and space, picking up every tiny signal. There are layers of meanings behind each smile, each comment, and each promise. The ability to "feel the air" and "read between lines" decides the accuracy of interpretation.

Table 12.1 Typical outward expressions in direct and indirect communication pattern

Direct	Indirect
Rely less on nonverbal cues	Rely more on nonverbal cues
Communication is explicit, direct, and rational	Communication is implicit, indirect, and intuitive
Rely more on words	Rely on both words and nonverbal elements
Start with main points, end with details	Full of details, main points are implied
More content oriented	More context oriented (body language and surrounding)
Information should be abundant, detailed, and specific	Information is embedded in the surrounding
Concerned with patterns of events, details of the picture	Concerned with the "shape" of events, holistic picture

Stereotypically, the Dutch and German are known for their directness (read: low context), while the British and the Asian may think and say differently (read: high context). There are countless of cautious and hilarious stories that seem to confirm this stereotype. For example, when a Brit says "that's interesting," low-context dependent people read "awesome," while the actual meaning could be "weird" or "useless." Similarly, for an Asian, a smile is an effective mechanism to show happiness, shield embarrassment, hide sadness, cope with anxiety, and so forth. Table 12.1 summarizes the characteristics of these two communication patterns.

Following pathway Culture—Brain—Behavior, cognitive neuroscience weighs in, reporting that when observing an image, Westerners tend to focus on *objects in the center*,[2] their brains show activation in areas associated with structural and perceptual analysis. In comparison, East Asians tend to focus more on *contexts, relationship between objects*, and *backgrounds*.[3] Their brains show more activation in the ventral visual cortex.[4] Thus, when embracing indirect communication style, people tend to recall the background of a situation better than when direct communication prevails. In another study, participants saw a picture with a central person and a group of people in the background. When rating the emotion of the central figure, Japanese participants tended to be influenced by the emotion of the group in the background, more so than North American participants.[5] This indicates their tendency to take social cues, group relationship, hidden message, incongruity, and indirect information in to account—a conclusion drawn by many other neural studies.[6-7-8-9-10] Hence, they communicate by "feeling the air." Interestingly, as US participants are more likely to infer a trait of a person based on the behaviors *without* much consideration of the context, a study concluded that they are *more prone to biases* than their US Asian counterparts.[11]

Attentional biases lead to the way we give more weight to emotion portrayed by the eyes or the mouth.[12-13] For indirect communication, people tend to focus on the eyes—features that are more difficult to manipulate and, thus, show true feeling. For direct communication, people tend to focus on the whole face, but especially the mouth—the most expressive part of the face. As a result, a study concluded that emoticons in Japan are quite different from those used in Western cultures,[14] as we see in Table 12.2.

Table 12.2 Emoticons in Eastern and Western cultures (Pogosyan and Engelmann [2017])

Eastern	Emotion	Western
(^_^)/	Happy	:-)
(>_<)	Angry	>:(
{{(>_<)}}	Fearful	=:-0
(_ ;)	Embarrassed	:$

12.1.1.2 Context Dependence

However, as being emphasized throughout the book, these are sophisticated stereotypes and can only act as a first-best-guess. Culture is dynamic with paradoxes and constant changes of circumstances. For example, under the impact of globalization, indirect Finland is shifting toward being direct, and India is much more direct than what the stereotype tells us.[15] Within a society, both direct and indirect communication patterns can simultaneously coexist: Anyone who holds the static and stereotypical view that the Chinese are indirect can be surprised that they may turn out to have quite a blunt and testy negotiation style.[16] They are perfectly fine in ignoring nonverbal cues, challenging everything, and questioning every clause.[17] Another counterstereotype example coming from China is the very direct and progressive sex education. There are explicit illustrations of the penis, vagina, a naked couple making love in bed, as well as direct talk about homosexuality.[18] If we do not bear in mind the dynamic nature of culture, we will tend to *look for stories and incidents that fit the stereotypes.*

Back to neuroscience, we know that simply priming the participants with either group-oriented words (e.g., "we," "our," "us") or self-oriented words (e.g., "I," "me," "my") can switch their brain's activity and redirect their behavior into different value patterns. This is demonstrated by a study in which individualistic and collectivistic priming altered neural responses during visual perception, exposing a preference to holistic (indirect) and analytic (direct) thinking style.[19] Thus, a simple change in context can lead to a change in communication approach. This indicates that we are the *product* of culture by adapting to the context, but we can also choose to be the *producer* of culture by actively changing the context and our own behaviors.

12.1.2 M-Time and P-Time

12.1.2.1 Cross-Cultural Findings

Edward Hall also came up with a generic categorization of working and living rhythms—a spectrum ranging between *Monochronic* (M-time) and *Polychronic* (P-time). The former indicates a *sequential approach*, viewing time as a resource, emphasizing punctuality, rigid, stepwise organization, detailed schedules, and doing one thing at a time.[20] Time can be spent, saved, wasted, and lost.[21] An appointment needs to be set up even weeks or months in advance, meetings start more or less on time, and a daily agenda tells people what tasks are important. Time is a framework that controls people's lives.

The latter (P-time) indicates a *cyclical approach*. When embracing P-time, people tend to do many things at the same time, constantly weighing what should be done *in the moment*, constantly adjusting to the circumstances, being spontaneous to the current situation, the people, and the big picture. Time is not a framework that controls people's lives, but an instrument to serve relationships. As the Nigerian proverb goes: "A watch did not invent the man." Things get done when time is right, not when the clock strikes a number.

As a result, punctuality is not as strongly emphasized as it is at the M-time level. An employee may be late for a meeting because an important talk with the new intern who struggles with her/his first day is the priority in that moment. Deadlines can be flexible because their purpose is to support people. Therefore, forcing a deadline when P-time prevails can be offensive. The same counts for forcing a project to go exactly as planned. For example, many businesspeople have come to a broad conclusion that in Southeast Asia, rarely was an event organized in a linier way. Things change in the last minute, but it all works out in the end.

Table 12.3 Typical outward expressions in M-time and P-time

M-time	P-time
Time is money	Time is the servant of people
Time is a commodity and can be gained or lost	There is always more time
Structure and order are central	Relationship and people are central
Strict schedules and plans	Flexible schedules and plans
One task at a time, linear order, no interruptions	Multitasking, cyclical, priority adjustable
Emphasis on punctuality, task orientation	Emphasis on a harmonious relationship

P-time also allows an intertwined mixture of work and life. Hence, M-time executives from headquarters who manage their P-time staff can be perceived in a disadvantageous way. For example, they are sometimes regarded as "corporate seagulls because they fly in, shit on you from above, and fly out again." This is an observation in *Bridging the Cultural Gap*, illustrated by a Swiss manager who "parachuted" in his subsidiaries in Ireland and didn't like how the employees spent frequent long coffee breaks of 20 minutes. He decided to close the canteen, except for lunch time, without knowing that for the Irish, coffee breaks were essential for networking and seeking advices—a P-time pattern of working.[22] Table 12.3 summarizes the characteristics of these two communication patterns.

12.1.2.2 Context Dependence

The static paradigm of culture tends to see North America and northwestern Europe as M-time cultures; Africa, Asia, and the Middle East as P-time cultures; while Southern European countries lie somewhere in between. However, the dynamic paradigm allows us to see that paradox is the norm rather than exception. In France, for example, meetings can commence 15 minute late, but meal time and restaurants reservations are sacred, so much so that the French are said to be "born with a clock in their stomach."[23] In Japan, people are more M-time with foreigners but P-time with their compatriots.[24] In business, Japanese people are extremely M-time with regard to appointments, but quite P-time in the way they spend a lengthy period gaining trust and building relationships before a partnership commitment.

Within a dominant culture, cocultures have their own habits. When we step inside the doctor's waiting room, we also switch our perception and turn on our P-time system, one that emphasizes the well-being of other people, because it's normal to wait. Some patients may need more time than others. While neuroscience has not yet properly studied the dynamic interaction between the brain and M-P time communication pattern, one indication we can be sure is that the brain's plasticity enables us to accommodate different cultural systems, *adapt to a certain culture*, as well as *actively change a culture*. Specific situations and occasions can prompt us to act in an M-time or P-time way. This explains why we can live with paradoxes and accept that superstars can arrive late, but the warm-up bands should not; a CEO and very important managers may arrive late, but not the staffs; technical people, event and project managers can gain a competitive edge from M-time, but not necessarily other professions, and so forth.

12.1.3 Affective and Neutral

12.1.3.1 Cross-Cultural Findings

Trompenaars and Hampden-Turner coined the terms *affective* and *neutral*[25] to describe the third pattern of communication. When embracing the affective style, people tend to find an outlet for their feelings, and their body language is also more animated. When embracing the neutral style, people tend to hold their emotions and control their body movements.

The static paradigm tends to place Asia in the neutral box, Latin America, Southern Europe, and the Middle East in the affective box, and the rest lies somewhere in between. As the stereotypes go, the Vietnamese would avoid too much direct eye contact when talking to senior people (read: neutral), the Arab like to maintain intensive gaze, the Italian talk with their whole body in a way that looks like they are having a fight, and the Mexican touch, hug, kiss, and express their emotion passionately (read: affective), and so forth. In a classic study, US and Japanese participants watched a stressful movie under two conditions: Alone and with an experimenter in the room. They produced similar facial expression when watching alone, but with the presence of the experimenter, the Japanese *masked their negative emotions with smiles*.[26] This is also an example of how two patterns of communications, "neutral" and "indirect," interact with each other and result in a potentially confusing outward expression: Smiling when being upset.

The cultural emphasis on suppressing emotion may alter biological processes during emotion regulation. A neural study reported that for Asians, their amygdala feedback showed *reduced* response during emotion suppression, but the same did not happen among white US participants.[27] This means for Asians, suppressing emotion is a cultural and communicative norm, and *their brain has changed to support that norm* (Culture—Brain pathway).

12.1.3.2 Context Dependence

Let's have a look at a study on cross-cultural communication with a dynamic role of genes. The oxytocin receptor polymorphism (OXTR rs53576) has two variants, the G allele and the A allele. Those who carry the G allele are more socially sensitive. However, "socially sensitive" behaviors mean different things in different cultures, either expressing emotion freely or hiding emotion when needed. In a study, the same allele helps US participants to express emotion, but helps Korean participants to suppress emotion—both behaviors are considered more culturally appropriate in the United States and Korea, respectively. Thus, in communication, US G allele people tend to show *less* emotional suppression while Korean G allele people tend to show *more* emotional suppression.[28] Further, US G allele people seek emotional support when being distressed, whereas Korean G allele people don't.[29] Following the Gene—Culture—Behavior pathway, we can conclude that depending on the values and practices of the dominant culture at that moment, people with the *same genes adopt different behaviors* to display social sensitivity in a culturally appropriate manner.

Once again, the plasticity and adaptation of the brain, genes, and behaviors indicate that affective-neutral communication pattern as described by many stereotypes is not set in stone. They are generalizations and can only act as first-best-guesses. More often than not, we will encounter paradoxes and shifting values in every culture. For instance, despite being described as neutral cultures, in Vietnam, Japan, Korea, and Malaysia, karaoke bars serve as an emotional outlet where people go wild with drinking, singing, dancing, and making brutal conversations. In many Asian countries, it's not uncommon to be neutral with outsiders and affective with ingroups. In the Middle East, men are affective toward each other as they embrace and kiss each other frequently and publicly, but that usually happens among men and not so much between men and women. In the United States, people tend to be affective with words and but less so with body language. This list goes on.

Such dynamics not only exists within a culture but also within an individual. We may communicate passionately on this subject and not the other, with this person and not the other, during a certain period of our life and not the other. People *change themselves* and, at times, *change the culture* around them. We are reminded here of leaders who not only fit in to gain trust but also reshape the norms and values of their own organization.

12.1.4 Communication Style Is Not Value Indicator

Some theorists tend to connect the communication patterns we mention here with group attachment. For example, the tendency is to link "collectivism" with "indirect," "M-time" and "neutral" communication, and to link "individualism" with "direct," "P-time," and "affective" style. This is problematic—an issue of neoracism and binary reductionism that neuroscientists have been warned.[30] Thus, studies tend to put people in boxes of "collectivistic" and "individualistic."

Communication styles and values do not match so neatly. For example, collectivistic Asians tend to be neutral, but collectivistic Latin Europeans tend to be affective. Collectivistic Middle Eastern both suppress emotion to preserve harmony, but can be very affective with extensive use of verbal and animated body language. Finland is a culture that has individualistic values cloaked in an indirect communication style[31] and an M-time way of organizing everyday activities. Finns use silence as a component of communication and employ ultrataciturnity; yet, despite these trademarks of high context dependence, Finland is stereotypically seen as an individualistic culture.

We are reminded of the dynamics of culture in terms of how values and behaviors contradict each other (Chapter 4). Using outward expressions to predict values is even more unreliable than using values to predict behaviors. More than any aspects of our field, communication styles are extremely context dependent.

12.2 Body Language

In this section, we will explore the role of body language and how it speaks volumes about us without us uttering a word. We will also discuss body language strategies that can go beyond the overgeneralization along the line of ethnicity and nationality.

12.2.1 The Universal Role of Body Language

Thanks to the evolution of language, the body is no longer the main instrument to communicate. Hopping up and down is not the only way to show joy anymore. However, nonverbal channels such as facial expressions and gestures retain their values today as an *external evidence of our internal state*. Thus, jumping around is an extra proof of joy.

Because body language was the primary means before language even existed, it can have an impact *eight times* more powerful than verbal messages.[32] When body language and actual words *contradict* each other, people are more likely to believe the nonverbal cues than the words.[33] These "gut feeling" and "first impressions" influence the flow of the interaction *before* verbal messages even have a chance to arrive. As we discussed in Chapter 8, the amygdala immediately and subconsciously categorizes individuals into ingroup and outgroup. A minimal exposure of as little as 100 milliseconds is sufficient to draw a judgment about a stranger's face.[34] We know that this is rooted in our evolutionary past, when the ingroup was the primary source of survival and outgroups were often the enemy. It helped our ancestors to quickly and subconsciously decide whether they should fight or flight when meeting a stranger.

12.2.2 Cross-Cultural Strategies for Body Language

While different body languages acted as signs of outgroup in the past, in the modern era, where strangers are potential partners, diversity in body languages becomes a source of misunderstanding. Body language is an indicator for judgment. But our judgment is heavily influenced by the *cultural patterns that dominate our brain at that specific moment*. Hence, the same gesture may signify different meanings. Here is a contrast: "They looked down when talking to senior people, they must be *respectful* employees" versus "They look down when talking to me, they must be *hiding* something."

It is, however, pointless to list here or categorize how culture shapes perception of body language. There are as many as 700,000 distinct physical signs, of which 1,000 are different bodily postures, 5,000 are hand gestures, and 250,000 are facial expression.[35] Part of these body movements are universal, and the rest is shaped by the dominant culture of the moment, or by individual preferences. Because we are both the product and producer of cultures, it makes more sense to leave this extensive list aside, and talk about how we can (1) *tune in* with others, and thus become the product of a desired culture to gain trust; and (2) *actively reshape* or reproduce our perception, values, and cultures by purposefully changing the body language of ourselves and others.

12.2.2.1 Tune In: Be the Product of Culture with Mirror Neurons

To blend in with a culture, the best method is to follow what evolution has taught us to do: *Imitate*. In Chapter 7, we discussed the mirror neurons. As early as infancy, the mirror neurons[36] in our brain trigger an instant mirroring reaction that helps us to automatically copy the behaviors that we see.[37] When we communicate, they subconsciously pick up *thought*, *emotion*, and *movement* from others, putting us in the *same* state of mind, so that we can understand others and have empathy with them without even sharing it verbally. Combine this with the principle that "similarities signal ingroup," we can understand why mirroring each other's body language will boost trust, create bond, and establish empathy.[38]

This indication is crucial in working internationally. *Instead of trying to learn endless stereotypes* that the Arab maintain intensive eye contact, the Asian give soft handshakes, the Latin American love to embrace each other, and so forth, it may be more fruitful to *mirror* the body language of the specific person with whom we are communicating. There are many reasons for it: Each society is full of paradoxes, culture changes, individuals are unique, and each one of us can (sub) consciously transform from moment to moment, depending on the context. Thus, as long as we understand the meaning of the gesture, mirroring is the safest and quickest way to sync with the most dominant cultural pattern that "runs" the brain of a person *at that very moment*. In fact, job candidates who mirrored the friendly body language of the interviewers fared better because they built a better rapport.[39] Even more promising, the best predictor of creativity is linked to body synchronization, that is, the more you and your colleague mirror each other, they more ideas you collectively create.[40] Here is a small activity you can do: Next time when giving a handshake, instead of imposing your idea of what a good handshake should be, try to quickly feel the other and adjust the firmness to the same level. Regardless of the cultural background of this person, if you are successful in mirroring her/his handshake, you are culturally in tune and off to a good start.

12.2.2.2 Actively Reshape: Be the Producer of Personal Value with Intended Body Language

The second strategy is to actively reshape our perception, values, and cultures by purposefully changing the body language of ourselves and others. This is based on the notion that *our body postures influence our mind* (Behavior—Bain pathway). For example, the high-power posers (hands on hips or clasped behind the head, chin tilted upward, feet planted wide apart) showed a 19% increase in testosterone and a 25% decrease in cortisol. The low-power posers (hands rested closer to the body, legs closed together, heads held downward) showed the opposite pattern.[41] Thus, if you expand your body when you feel powerful, then you also naturally feel powerful when you expand your body.[42] By adopting a certain body language and ritual, our mind will react accordingly, and we will eventually *feel* accordingly.

In a classic study, researchers asked participants either to nod or shake their head while listening to a story over headphones. They believed they were evaluating the headphone's quality by giving different body movements that resemble jogging and cycling. The results showed that nodders did agree with the story over the headphones more than shakers.[43] By the act of nodding, these people subconsciously *switch their mind to the mode of agreement.* Another interesting study reported that people rated cartoons as funnier when they gripped a pen between their teeth (stimulate smiling) versus between their lips (stimulate frowning).[44] Similarly, people have more positive evaluation during their arm flexion (stimulate grasping desirable things toward) than during arm extension (stimulate pushing unwanted things away).[45] In sum, *bodily actions can influence how we think.*

The indication from these studies is crucial. Because action and attitude feed one another, we can venture beyond the static and unidirectional idea that culture shapes and fixes our body language. For a thought experiment, imagine how we can shift the attitude of ourselves and others by adopting a different body language. For instance, knowing that your prevalent cultural patterns are humility and strong hierarchy acceptance, you can purposefully adopt a power pose or put your legs on the table to boost confidence before attending an important meeting. Similarly, you can lower your head or bow to trigger the respect pattern in your inner self. You can nod so that other may nod back; you can have standing meetings and take chairs away from offices to increase group cooperation, decrease territorial behaviors,[46] and save 34% of the working time;[47] you can choose to have a conversation while playing golf or walking so that these relaxing activities can make the mind more creative;[48] you can make sure your partners are welcome with a warm drink because it makes them friendlier,[49] and so forth. As long as these body gestures don't cause misunderstanding and people are not coerced into doing it, we can expect a change in the state of mind. Because *your body shapes who you are.*[50]

12.2.2.3 Actively Reshape: Be the Producer of Collective Value with Intended Body Language

Can body language influence culture at the *collective level* of the Inverted Pyramid Model, that is on a mass scale? As discussed in Chapter 2, the answer is "yes" (Behavior—Culture pathway). For many Germans during the Nazi era, executing the public greeting "Heil Hitler" was a powerful conditioning device. Because they have done it as an outward expression of conformity, their inner feelings changed, and they started to believe in what they did.[51] Repeated body language not only changes a person's values but also collective values when such a behavior is reinforced at the collective level.

Recognizing the collective impact of body language, a council in Australia even considered banning negative gestures at work such as eye rolls, deep sighs, and shoulder shrugs.[52] From the United Kingdom, employees of an engineering company start their day by hugging their colleagues—part of a caring atmosphere that led to 200% increase of profit in three years.[53] Going one step further, another British company organized Naked Friday to boost their team spirit, displaying the ultimate expression of trust: Having no clothes while working together in the office. Despite some initial hesitation, the result was positive as this extraordinary experiment did build courage, create honesty, and bring down barriers among team members.[54] The mentality is: I can trust you this much, there is nothing that we can't conquer together. In short, if the body leads, the mind will follow.

12.3 Language

Language is undoubtedly one of the most exquisitely sophisticated and powerful products of the human mind. In this section, we will explore the role of language from evolution's point of view. We will discuss how we create language but also how language creates us. With regard to international context, we will go through a number of language strategies and evaluate the extent to which they are useful at the universal level and the extent to which they should be adapted at the cultural level.

12.3.1 *Language as Resource Regulator*

Human is one species physically, but language seems to tell us that we are not. We are probably the only animal that can find itself in a situation in which two individuals might not be able to communicate with each other. The reason lies deep in how language has evolved to become a mechanism of survival within and between groups.

Because culture in its evolutionary sense is a survival strategy (see Chapter 2), the capacity of having a culture (i.e., learning from others) also means ideas, knowledge, and resources can be stolen by one group at the expense of the other. If you see that my tool is catching more fish than yours, you can steal my innovation just by studying my tool carefully, and then making the same one, even better. So what can I do to protect my cultural ideas? Thus, language evolved as a crucial mechanism for dealing with the possibilities of ideas being stolen.[55] It helps us to negotiate cultural resources, convincing the other to exchange their tools for our tools and starting a relationship based on mutual benefit.[56]

Language facilitates deal making, negotiation, and agreement. And because its purpose is also to safeguard knowledge and information in competition with other groups, many languages were formed. When we don't know each other and I am not sure of your intentions, my distinctive language helps to keep any innovations within my own group and my own culture. It would be very difficult for you to steal my ideas if you don't know my language and the complex code of behavior that it governs. But once you have shown your intentions to be good and fair, we will somehow overcome the language barrier to cooperate. Trading across the globe has operated in more or less this way, with linguistic and cultural diversity as an inherent *regulator*, used by one group to *safeguard and negotiate cultural resources* with another. In fact, you don't need to look far to see the similarity of language evolution with what we still do every day: Kids creating a secret language to write their diary or communicate with friends, codes and cyphers used by military and diplomatic forces to exchange confidential information, and businesses who send data that has been encoded to protect trade secrets.

12.3.2 *Language Shapes Our Reality?*

A cognitive scientist once did a simple experiment. She asked a room full of experts and professors to close their eyes and point southeast. These talented people pointed in every possible direction. But a five-year-old Australian girl from Kuuk Thaayorre tribe always got it right. The secret of her built-in compass lies in her language. It doesn't have directional words such as "left" or "right." It uses cardinal-direction terms, for example: "There is a spider southeast of your legs." Such a language requires/forces its users to always stay oriented, or else they cannot communicate at all. It also enables them to see the world differently, to function and organize life differently as well. For example, they would organize a series of sequential cards depending on the cardinal directions. When they face north, the card order goes from right to left. When they face south, the cards go from left to right.[57]

The Sapir-Whorf hypothesis has been one of the most influential theories in communication. It posits that language is not only a tool to *express* our thoughts but also language *shapes* our thoughts. Similar to the case of the aboriginals in Australia, Chinese-speaking people often make sequential arrangement vertically rather than horizontally[58] due to their traditional writing system; Swedish speakers talk in terms of length (e.g., "That's a *short* time") while Spanish speakers talk in terms of amount ("That's a *small* time");[59] Russian language distinguishes two shades of blue (dark and light), and thus, Russian speakers are *quicker* to identify the difference in shades of blue;[60] Germans refer to bridges as "elegant" because the word for bridge in German is feminine, but Spanish speakers refer to bridges as "sturdy" because the Spanish word for bridge is masculine,[61] and so forth. This theory also explains why novelist Vladimir Nabokov wrote three *different* versions of his memoir because each language evoked different memories in his brain. In the same vein, many long-term expats in the Netherlands have learned to consciously switch to Dutch—a very direct language—when they want to be straightforward, so that they can say "no" without feeling too much guilt. We are slightly different persons in the languages we speak.

Taking one step further, languages also change our evaluation and morality. Facing a dilemma, we tend to be more *rational in foreign language*, while our judgment is more of a *quick, gut-feeling in native language*.[62] Here is the reason: When we use a foreign language, we unconsciously set our brain in a mode called "ready for challenges." This readiness makes us more careful, deliberate, and calculative, thus having an impact on the decision we make. In contrast, our native languages are much more laden with emotional intensity than those leaned in the classroom. As a result, judgment made in our native languages are filled with emotional reactions, gut feelings, and visceral responses. In a study that measured emotional arousal using skin's electrical conductivity, participants who heard the words in their native language gave a powerful reaction compared to a mild response in a foreign language.[63] According to an experienced trainer, her training in Dutch, English, and Vietnamese have different evaluation scores despite having exactly the same structure. Participants judge her harsher when the training is conducted in their foreign language. Thinking in foreign languages tend to motivate people to place more emphasis on outcomes than intentions.[64] This may lead to clearer, more conscientious decision making, which is a vital skill in doing business. In contrast, communicating in a native language evokes more emotional responses, creating more powerful impact, making memories last longer, and building relationship quicker—also vital skills in business.

Neurolinguistic studies give us extra evidence,[65] showing that collectivistic linguistic cues such as "we" and "us" trigger collectivistic behaviors, while individualistic cues such as "I" and "myself" trigger individualistic responses in the same person. When tested in English, Hong Kong students switched to a more individualistic mode and showed more self-enhancing bias (I score high because I'm good, not because I'm lucky) than when tested in Chinese.[66] Speaking Chinese or English also changes the way their brain's network functions.[67] In 2016, the movie *Arrival* grossed more than $200 million worldwide with exactly the same idea. By leaning the aliens' language, a scientist could foresee the future, thus changed her worldview and the whole mechanism of time and the universe. These examples indicate that we see the world, think, and behave differently depending on the language we speak.[68] In the words of the famous English writer George Orwell: "If thought corrupts language, language can also corrupt thought."[69]

12.3.3 Multilingual Capital

Thus, when you learn a new language, you don't simply learn a new way of talking but also a new way of thinking. Neuroscience has repeatedly proved that bilingual people have superior brain functions to monolinguals with more gray matter.[70] The ability to process different languages simultaneously allows bilinguals to fare better in their careers[71] and to excel at communication[72] and cognitive control,[73-74] such as approaching problems from different perspectives,[75] reducing decision biases,[76] task-switching, attention, flexibility, planning, and understanding the complexity of context. These advantages are obviously essential in multicultural organizations and an international living environment. In fact, those who assimilated to the extent that they lost their original language skills suffered an annual earnings penalty of up to $3,200.[77]

Due to this multilingual capital, employers prefer polyglot applicants,[78] knowing that they enrich the organization with different thinking, provide better customer service, and are less likely to miss out on global business opportunities. Many countries have exploited multilingualism in the globalized economy. Take Switzerland for example, the economy value of language is estimated to be 10% of its GDP.[79] In the case of Facebook founder Mark Zuckerberg, learning Chinese is not only personally motivated (his wife's family is from China) but a market-driven incentive as his company has long been trying to penetrate China. For Canada's Prime Minister Justin Trudeau, his fluency in French definitely helped in winning the vote.[80]

Meanwhile, lacking this economic power of language,[81] the United Kingdom for example, loses about 3.5% of its GDP every year because its workforce is too monolingual.[82] Despite having a multicultural background, one in six US businesses is losing out due to a lack of language skills and cultural awareness.[83] Many English-only speakers miss out the emotional side of personal interactions because they could not extend solidarity to other colleagues. It is not just a general disadvantage but a professional one.

In multinationals that use of a common language, while uniting voices, such a lingua franca may undermine the benefit of multilingual capital. The differences in ability to speak the language of choice create an *unequal playing field*. Foreign-language speakers may feel threatened as native speakers use their mother tongue to exert influence and exclude others. Because foreign-language users are anxious about admitting they don't understand, native speakers can simply break into and dominate a conversation by speaking louder than those who speak "broken" language. With richer vocabulary and perfect fluency, such an attitude is usually mistaken for competence and confidence.

However, does that mean if we *lack the vocabulary*, then we don't have the *tool to think* in a certain way? If we think in words, does that mean the more words we know, the more thoughts we have? If a job candidate's language does not have a word for "evidence-based decisions," does that mean (s)he can't understand and execute such a mental task? That hypothesis is a step too far, argued other studies.[84-85] The fact that there is no word for "democracy" in Arabic doesn't mean Arabic-speaking people don't understand what "democracy" means and never try to achieve it. In the classic case of knowledge facilitation in Novo Nordisk, the team who is responsible for transferring new company visions found it difficult to straightforwardly translate essential ideas into languages such as Japanese, Chinese, and Korean. The concept always needed careful diplomatic explanation. A unit in Hong Kong was convinced that facilitation was a waste of time. However, it all changed when they experienced it.[86] Thus, practice can compensate the lack of vocabulary. In another study, cognitive neuroscientists conducted an experiment among the Pirahã, whose language has no number words at all, only "around one," "some," and "many." The result was that they failed in a counting task only when they had to *rely on memory*.[87] Thus, words are handy mnemonics and acronyms that help us to remember, but they don't necessarily constrain our cognitive ability.

To conclude, while more words do not mean more thoughts, a richer vocabulary does make it *easier* to remember those thoughts[88] and formulate new ones. We are definitely not a hopeless product of our own language. The United Kingdom and the United States share the same language, but their cultures are both strikingly similar and different. Language is a tool, even a driver of cognition, but not a master of our cognition.

12.3.4 *Use Language to Shape New Reality*

In the previous section, we discussed how language shapes us. In this section, we look further at how we can *proactively* aim for a language that will shape us in the way we want. That means we can change the language, and let that language subsequently change us.

There is a strong line of research that advocates the use of language to reshape our mindset and change our behavior. In *Words Can Change Your Brain*,[89] the authors—a neuroscientist and a communication expert—wrote: "A single word has the power to influence the expression of genes that regulate physical and emotional stress." Negative words trigger the amygdala and cause stress hormones, shutting down the logic and reasoning process in the frontal lobes. On the contrary, positive words such as "cooperation," "sustainable," or "mutual interest" stimulate the frontal lobe. This is where the language centers are located and connected to the motor cortex—part of the brain that moves us into action. As functions in the brain start to change, the way we view ourselves and others will change as well because the positively primed brain will bias us toward seeing certain things and leave out others. A filter has formed and the information flow into the thalamus—the data center—has changed. In a sort of self-fulfilling prophecy, *we move toward what we keep telling ourselves* (see Chapter 5). This explains why gratitude journal (e.g., for three months, writing down each day three things that went well and explaining why) increases degrees of overall well-being.[90-91]

To conclude, we can be both the product and the producer of language. We can let the language shape us so we may fit in with a new culture, but we can also craft the language in a way that it will eventually move us to a desirable state of mind and behavior.

12.3.5 Universal Assumptions of Using Foreign Language

In a *Financial Times* article on how to sell cars to the German, the reporter claimed that the breakdown in communication between the British government and BMW over the future Rover car group was partly the phrase used by the British ministers: "It's five minutes to midnight." It meant there was little time left to reach an agreement. However, it confused and irritated the German, who were too proud to ask what it meant.[92] Lesson: Using idioms across cultures is a risky business.

The community of internationally working people has accumulated many generic lessons, advices, and assumptions, similar to the case of using idioms. While suffering from some overgeneralization and stereotypes, Table 12.4 summarizes suggestions that are most frequently mentioned in literature and practice.

12.3.6 Cross-Cultural Findings

Because language shapes thinking, and thinking also shapes language, this intertwined relationship dynamically influences how we communicate. German, for example, is a grammatically rigid language. It's elaborated, like a Mercedes car, splendidly overengineered, a precise instrument of great robustness, not economical, but less susceptible of misunderstanding.[93] German language, to a certain extent, shapes and reflects the German management behavior that prioritizes direct communication pattern and strong uncertainty avoidance. This language is characterized by extensive hierarchy, rules, structures, and logics. As a result, when communicating with the German, some useful stereotypes to consider are the use of titles, formality, well-thought arguments, sharp rationale, and appropriate methodology in giving solution.

In contrast with German, Japanese and Vietnamese languages are both products and producers of cultures that emphasize indirectness, high context, strong group attachment, and hierarchy acceptance. For example, in Japanese, the word you use to talk *about* your mother is not the same one when talking *to* her. It changes again when you talk about another person's mother, and yet many times more depending on age and situation.[94] In Vietnamese, it is common to ask for each other's age because it defines how people put each other on different ranks of hierarchy with different pronouns. These extremely rich languages enable a culture of reading between lines, hidden messages, and implicit suggestions. Talking to a Japanese, one should understand that the constant affirmation "Hai" does not mean "Yes" at all, but "Yes, I hear you." Reading an e-mail from a Vietnamese who ended the writing with "By the way..." it is very likely that this sentence is the main point of the whole e-mail.

Table 12.4 Foreign-language strategies based on tasks

Tasks	Language Strategies
Communicating in foreign languages	• Keep it short and simple (KISS). • Speak slowly, leave a beat, a short pause between sentences and phrases. • Slightly pronounce the consonant at the end of each word to make it clear and create a mini-pause: "I would <u>like</u> to emphasi<u>ze</u> this." • Repeat each important idea using different words to explain the same concept. • Avoid colloquial language, slang, idioms, and jokes. • Avoid too many phrasal verbs: "Calculate" and not "add up," "cancel" and not "call off," "see" and not "make out." • Listen more, speak less. Don't jump in just to fill the silence. The other person is probably thinking slower in foreign languages. • Don't equate poor grammar and mispronunciation with lack of intelligence. Such misjudgment can make you underestimate the opponent and have poorer preparation. • Never embarrass nonnative speakers. Restrain from correcting others on their grammar and pronunciation. • Praise and encourage others on how they speak their nonnative languages. • Don't judge, ask "why": "*Why* did they write the report this way?" • Don't assume, ask "how": "*How* can I address this issue properly?" • Don't impose, ask "can": "My apology for not being able to speak your language. *Can I/ Do you mind* if I speak Portuguese with you?" • Don't ask "Do you understand?" because many will say "yes" to save face. Instead, let them paraphrase their understanding back to you. Let them explain what they understood.
E-mails	• Keep it short and simple (KISS). • Using short sentences (15–30 words), with a space line between the greeting and paragraphs. • Avoid colloquial language, slang, idioms, and jokes. • Use lists or bullet points instead of dense text. • Be clear about what you want. • Keep sentences active: "The executives *will* sign the contract" and not "The contract *will be signed* by the executives."
Presentation	• Prepare both slides and handouts, so that the audience won't get anxious about missing information. • Use visual restatements such as pictures, graphs, and tables. • Give overview and summary.

Table 12.5 gives us some stereotypical suggestions of language strategies based on (1) cultural values and (2) patterns of communication mentioned at the beginning of this chapter, that is direct–indirect, M–P time, and affective–neutral. Of course, reality is much more complex because different values and patterns interact with one another, let alone the dynamics of specific contexts. However, this should give us some ideas, a *first-best-guess*, especially when we still know very little about the culture and the people we are going to communicate with.

12.3.7 *Context Dependence*

With context taken into account, the interaction of language and culture reveals a much more dynamic aspect. Within one culture, characteristics of a language may contradict with the

Table 12.5 Foreign-language strategies based on values and communication patterns

Cultural Values Patterns of Communication	Language Strategies
Strong Group Attachment (Collectivism)	<ul><li>Use collective language such as "us," "we," "they," "our."</li><li>Consider using face to face or calling before e-mail.</li><li>Apology for what you are going to say to save face, not *after* you have said it (by then, face has been lost).</li><li>Use positive and collective language to keep group harmony and everyone happy.</li><li>The amygdala doesn't see race, gender, or religion, but only ingroup or outgroup. Thus, create new ingroups to facilitate solidarity, to be on the same side.</li><li>Consider adopting a new name in the language of the collective. It shows your commitment and willingness to be part of the ingroup.</li></ul>
Weak Group Attachment (Individualism)	<ul><li>Use language that signals personal direct involvement (e.g., "You will achieve this degree if you work for 500 hours").</li><li>Emphasize individual uniqueness.</li></ul>
Strong Hierarchy Acceptance	<ul><li>Carefully consider when to use surnames or first names, how to address people with degrees and honorary titles.</li><li>Note that the order of first name and surname is reversed in many cultures.</li><li>Give prime time, sitting position, service, and introduction to figures of authorities and influences.</li><li>Repeatedly refer to figures of authorities and influences during talks and presentations.</li><li>Speak humbly to the senior, and show confidence to the junior.</li></ul>
Weak Hierarchy Acceptance (Egalitarian)	<ul><li>Emphasize equality, but always check to avoid moving to first-name basis too early. Ask how a person prefers to be addressed.</li><li>Repeatedly refer to the rule of democracy and consensus.</li></ul>
Masculine Gender Association	<ul><li>Emphasize will, performance, status, and achievement.</li><li>Speak with confidence, optimism and "can-do" attitude, for example, "We are going to nail it."</li></ul>
Feminine Gender Association	<ul><li>Emphasize equality, consensus, and collective welfare.</li><li>Speak modestly and humbly, for example, "We will try our best."</li></ul>
Strong Uncertainty Avoidance	<ul><li>Begin with a fact, statement, principle, or opinion. Later, add concepts to back up and explain the conclusion.</li><li>Begin with an executive summary or bullet points.</li><li>Theory first, application second: "This is why we should do it" and then "Here is how."</li></ul>
Weak Uncertainty Avoidance	<ul><li>The structure of discussion and presentation can be more flexible.</li><li>Application (e.g., examples, case studies, illustrations) can come first to get attention and build up argument. Theory or principle can finish as conclusion: "This is how we should do" and then "Here is why."</li></ul>
Future Orientation	<ul><li>Emphasize long-term visions, future benefits, for example "Eye on prize."</li><li>Use the language of preparation and planning, for example, "Practice makes perfect."</li></ul>
Present/Short Time Orientation	<ul><li>Emphasize quick and immediate benefits, for example, "I can taste the victory."</li><li>Use the language of action and implementation, for example, "Go for it."</li></ul>

(*continued*)

Table 12.5 (Cont.)

Cultural Values Patterns of Communication	Language Strategies
Indirect	• Many may use jokes, understatement, and smiles as a defense mechanism to shield embarrassment, awkwardness, or to relieve frustration. • Many may begin an e-mail with warm, personal notes such as comments about the weather, congratulations on others' success, and requests for forgiveness or understanding. • Many may use *downgraders* such as "soft of," "kind of," "slightly," and "partially." • The most important message may be at the end of the conversation. • People may communicate the weaknesses or negative points by purposely *not* mentioning them, instead, they emphasize the opposite and the positive. They give you a hidden message. • Be attentive to hidden and implicit messages. Each word may have different meanings. • Every single story, picture, gift can carry a deep meaning. • Deductive: "These are the reasons, and hence, here is the proposal." • Employ wishful requests: "We hope you will response."
Direct	• Use clear and direct language. • Many may use upgraders such as "absolutely," "totally," and "completely." • The most important message is at the beginning of the conversation. • Don't mistake directness for rudeness, transparency for a lack of empathy. Consider straightforward conversation as a sign of care and honesty. • Inductive: "This is the proposal, and here are the reasons." • Employ specification requests: "We expect and appreciate your response."
M-Time (Linier)	• Have a clear agenda of issues to discuss. • Conduct discussions in a practical, point-by-point manner. • Use ordering adverbs such as "firstly," "secondly," "next," "finally."
P-Time (Cyclic)	• Allow spontaneous conversation. • Allow different voices, opinions interacting at the same time. • Allow arguments and conclusions to go back and forth in a nonlinear manner.
Affective	• Use extensive amount of body language. • Many may have fast, loud, animated, passionate, emotional pattern of speaking. • Many may use an extensive amount of proverbs, sayings, idioms, songs, historical stories to enrich the meaning and persuade the audience. For example, Muslims may quote verses from the Quran to justify their arguments. • Emphasize eloquence and "flowery" prose.
Neutral	• Pay attention to formality and rituals. • Count to three before giving an answer. • Restrain from raising voice, speaking fast, showing too much emotion, smiling too often, and interrupting others.

stereotypical values of the people who live in it. For example, the English language is built on extremes, such as "far" and "near," "old" and "young," and so forth. While the lack of vocabulary to describe the middle area may force users to adopt one of the polar ends,[95] English people are known for being indirect and subtle. Similarly, English literature is no less sophisticated just because its language is dominated by extremes. This paradox reminds us that contrasts and opposites coexist in our everyday life, and that no aspect of culture is a simple binary.

12.4 Meeting

Naturally, meeting is a "stage" for communication. Depending on specific cultures and circumstances, meeting has different styles. In this section, we will discuss three major ones: Linear, cyclic, and ritual meeting.

12.4.1 Cross-Cultural Findings

The first type of meeting, *linear meeting*, is meant for decision making and problem solving. Values and communication styles such as strong uncertainty avoidance, present orientation, direct, and M-time generally produce this kind of meeting. Full details are circulated well beforehand for preparation. There is often a set agenda, a tight timetable, a point-by-point way of solving issue by issue, and a decision to act upon with a chain of defined responsibility.

The second type of meeting, *cyclic meeting*, is meant to exchange ideas and debate, which makes agenda look like a wish list of things to cover rather than a detailed order of a discussion. Weak hierarchy acceptance, weak uncertainty avoidance, femininity, future time orientation, P-time, and especially affective communication often contribute to this variation of meeting. In many ways, it is a battle of opinions. A decision is not an absolute must-have outcome, but essentially a forum to express thought, voice concern, weigh the impact, and test each idea. More often than not, an agenda is only formality because people may discuss several topics at the same time (P-time). It is common that the minutes of such a meeting do not reflect the content of the discussion. Stereotypically, the French are famous for this kind of debate. For many, the meeting is simply an outlet for personal feelings. Once their voice has been heard, a final decision that goes against their opinion doesn't sting too badly anymore.

Third, *ritual meeting* is a procedure to ratify decisions that have already been finalized. Strong hierarchy acceptance and group attachment tend to support this variation. Authorities either follow a top-down approach by imposing their decision, or they have gathered contribution in a less formal channel.

Imagine a corporate culture where employees don't confront the boss, don't want to lose face in front of others by saying the wrong thing, and don't want to disturb the harmony by standing out as opinionated individuals. For the same reason, in contexts where harmony is more important than contribution, a Q&A session after a presentation can turn into a complete silence when the presenter asks for feedback. A manager who wants a *participatory* decision-making process shouldn't change this culture abruptly by forcing ideas on the spot. A buffer process works better, for example, talking to employees individually in informal settings, gathering ideas on paper, letting the group discuss in private and come back with collective suggestions, and so forth. This also gives rise to the practice of meeting in cafes, restaurants, and bars. The author of this book, while working as a managing editor in Asia, observed that each team leader had her/his favorite café or restaurant near the office where most of their meetings occurred. They would make decisions in small groups of two to five people; any meetings with more than five are for information sharing or to put a formal stamp on what have been collectively agreed. Thus, if one hears about change in a meeting, it's probably too late to influence it.

12.4.2 Context Dependence

In reality, each organization maintains a complex and evolving mixture of *all three meeting variations*, depending on the context. There is no fixed meeting style for any organizations, and a global worker should read the context effectively to *fit in*, adjust, or *change* the existing culture if needed. Stereotypes often mislead. In the US series *Friends* for example, main character Rachel felt left out and tried to develop a new habit of smoking cigarettes because all the decision making took place during smoking breaks outside her office.

Flexibility is essential to optimize contribution. Here are some examples of both failure and success in dealing with diversity in meeting. An engineer from Belgium, let's call her Karin, attended a meeting with her colleagues in the Netherlands. She suggested that they would discuss the new hiring policy. To her shock, the coordinator bluntly refused because it was *not on the agenda*. Karin should have added this on the list when the meeting agenda was sent to everyone. Losing face and demotivated, Karin regarded this rigid attitude as noncooperative. The coordinator, however, regarded Karin as unorganized.

However, when differences are optimized, synergy emerges as a blessing. In a German-Japanese joint venture, instead of choosing between a Japanese style (lengthy and multiple meetings, involve people from all departments, absolute consensus) and a German style (short, only experts, logic based), the teams invented a new decision-making process. Meetings would involve fewer people with a maximum of two meetings for all decisions, and codirectors can make decisions without having to go through the group discussion phase.[96]

12.5 Relationship Building

We tend to believe that our business decisions are calculative and objective. We want to think that a tight or loose relationship does not significantly influence our rationality. The fact is, relationship often tips the scale in all decision-making processes. In this section, we will first briefly explore why relationship building is essential. Next, we will touch on a number of strategies for building relationships across cultures.

12.5.1 The Neuroscience of Emotion in Relationship Building

In Chapter 7, we discussed the indispensable role of emotion. Humans are not at all rational beings. Emotion helps us to make ethical, good decisions. It's when the amygdala can communicate thoroughly with the frontal cortex for a good balance of "feeling" and "logic." In fact, we don't have time or capacity to only use the frontal cortex and calculate the statistical probabilities that come with every choice. So we rely on heuristics—a mental shortcut that produces good-enough solutions given a limited time frame. This mental shortcut is often triggered by emotion, from the familiarity that drives us to buy the same old product, to the feeling of comfort that makes us sign a business deal with a partner we know. We can spend a long period weighing up the pros and cons, but to come down on one side, *emotion is often the ultimate end of our decisions*.

Because emotion tips the scales, who you know is often more important than what you know. Competence is essential, but relationship reigns supreme. Ingroup and availability biases are strong, and it's pointless to deny it (see Chapter 8). Hence, relationship building is an essential part of working internationally. Because relationship allows fast decision, we try to give every signal that can help to send a message of connection: We hint that our company belongs to the first lady, we flash the alumni ring, we print on the business card names of organizations and clubs of which we are members, and so forth.

When business doesn't even need a contract to bear fruitful outcomes, then relationship *is* the contract. We hate to accept it, but biases do kick in. Whoever is more emotionally available, collectively relatable, and personally attached to us will attract our attention, and thus, get closer to our approval. Advances in neuroscience have shown that the hormone oxytocin produced naturally in the brain is associated with increased trust and collaborative behavior.[97] We achieved more oxytocin by shaking hands, hugging, swapping names, discussing common interests, and so forth—things we do when we build relationships. Business is hardly ever just business. *Business is personal*, albeit with different levels.

12.5.2 Start with Similarities

At the universal level, the safest way to build a relationship is to follow the generic rule of "similarities signal ingroup," that is starting with the bottom layer of the Inverted Pyramid Model. Common interest and mutual goals can transcend cultural boundaries. We are reminded here of how an Italian manager used music to create a bond with his team members in India (Chapter 6). Because occupation is the best indicator of cultural homogeneity,[98] using professional background as a transnational culture is a good strategy. Further, a relationship starts off better with a mutual contact, to the point that unsolicited e-mails and introduction will be ignored—a practice that is common even in stereotypically individualistic cultures such as the United States, Australia, and many others.

At the collective level and individual level, the beginning point to build relationship varies. For instance, when weak group attachment prevails, a contract tends to take priority. Once this legal trust has been established, social interaction will enhance and slowly replace the need to rely on a lawful document (we started off as business partners, and now we are like friends). When strong group attachment prevails, it may take a long time to build up trust and to test the commitment (we need to know each other well to do business).

12.5.3 Self-Disclosure

Unfortunately, cultural biases have become such a destructive source of injustice and many international businesspeople are now confused how to ask others about their cultural background without offending them or giving a signal of ethnocentrism. Here is a very common example. We may think it's a compliment to tell someone who appears to be a new immigrant: "You speak the language well." But if the person has been born and raised in the country for many years or several generations, (s)he could feel quite insulted. For this person, it means (s)he is an outsider, no matter how long (s)he has been living in a culture.

So how do you ask about culture and show our genuine interest without accidently offending others? The easiest way is *self-disclosure*. By casually bringing up our own ethnic or professional background, we show our trust in others. People like those who share their stories with them. And they give back. Reciprocity is the rule. This is proven in a famous study in which the authors concluded that any two strangers would eventually fall in love with each other after asking each other 36 questions.[99] The idea is that mutual *self-disclosure fosters closeness*.

12.5.4 Social Activities

The social activities with which one builds a relationship are shaped by collective cultures, personal choice, and unique circumstances. In many Asian cultures, eating and drinking together play a crucial role in business bonding. The Japanese spend approximately 2% of their GNP on entertaining clients—an amount larger than their national defense budget.[100] Bars, cafes, restaurants, and karaoke lounges are indirectly part of the working environment. To a certain extent, there is a pressure for new employees and potential partners to join these gatherings. The Japanese even have a name for it: "Nomunication," stemming from the Japanese word "nomu" = "to drink" combining with the English word "communication." Formal, quiet, and reserved colleagues (read: neutral) can become very animated, talkative, and easy to communicate with (read: affective) after a long evening of well-lubricated socializing. It's an affective, direct, and rather weak hierarchy accepting culture that exists *outside* the office, in parallel with a neutral, indirect, and strong hierarchy accepting culture *inside* the office. It allows people to express what they feel, showing other parts of their real inner character. If you decide to blend in, it's not a bad advice to go with the flow and get drunk. To a certain extent, it shows your trust. You have left your guard down, and hence, you consider others as friends.

Fortunately, social activities include more than drinking, eating, and singing parties. Sport and entertainment provide good opportunities for relationship building. For example, it's not for no reason that golf is popular among businesspeople. It's ideal to create a bond by spending hours with just a few partners, have long walks and talks without distraction, or judge their characters in a game of unique regulations and mannerism. For many Fins, going (half)naked together with their potential business partners in the sauna is a perfect way to build relationship. The sauna provides a mechanism of social leverage that fits the Finns egalitarian mentality, that when you dress down in the sauna, you also reduce the level of hierarchy acceptance as everyone becomes more equal. Being indirect, neutral, low-key, and rather formal, saunas also give the Finns a natural setting in which to relax, to open up and strengthen their relationships. So when a Fin wants to talk business with you after many beers in a sauna, (s)he doesn't trick you into agreeing to a bad deal, it's negotiation in good faith.

Next to sport and entertainment, cultural events offer perfect opportunities to show respect to someone's background, let them show their pride, and ask questions without feeling out of place. Most importantly, this kind of event allows people to blend in without being accused of *cultural appreciation*—an act of donning a cultural practice without respect, proper acknowledgment, or deep understanding.

12.5.5 Gift Giving

Relationship building hardly goes without gift exchange. The purposes are (1) to create a positive first impression; (2) show appreciation for relationships and favor in the past; and (3) return a favor or expect a favor in return.[101] Gifts have a profound effect. Even small trinkets, such as pens and mugs from pharmaceutical companies have been found to subconsciously influence doctors' attitudes,[102] so much so that the drug industry in the United States has banned them from marketing campaigns.[103]

Gift giving is strongly determined by cultural and personal preferences. For example, expensive gifts or brands may be in favor when strong hierarchy acceptance (thus "status"), strong group attachment (thus "face"), and masculinity (thus "achievement") prevail. In China for example, some premium mooncakes are considered a status gift because those who buy them won't eat them, and those who eat them didn't pay.

Gifts are meant to obtain favors. The German call it *schmiergeld* (grease money), the French *pot-de-vin* (jug of wine), in the Middle East it is a *baksheesh* (tip), in Italy a *bastarella* (little envelope), and in Mexico a *mordida* (a bite). However, gifts can be seen as bribes. Anticorruption laws can prevent people from accepting gifts, causing a cultural tension among societies where gift giving is traditionally a common practice.[104] If refusing a gift can offend the giver, consider accepting it on behalf of the company and then forward it to HR department.

In cultures where superstition, cultural belief, and religious practices are significant to the locals, do research on what is taboo (e.g., alcohol to Muslims, leather made from cowhide to Hindus) and what brings good luck. Check with the local and experts other gift etiquettes, such as when to give a gift (before or after a project), how to give a gift (during personal exchange or during a ceremony such as in Japan, Vietnam, and China), and when to open a gift (right away as in Europe or afterward to avoid losing face as in Asia). Be mindful of the current political and cultural situation so to avoid what German Chancellor Angela Merkel gave to Chinese President Xi Jinping: A 1735 map which shows China's territory without Hainan, Taiwan, Xinjiang, Tibet, and other areas in Mongolia and Manchuria. The present was regarded as a "slap in the face" because, regardless of actual events, most Chinese people learned that these territories have been parts of China for a long, long time: "The map tells a different story. What is Merkel's hidden message? Is she challenging China's international policies?"[105]

12.5.6 *Maintain Relationship*

Frequency, *spontaneity*, and *genuineness* are the three main principles of maintaining a good relationship. People can quickly see if someone calls only when a favor is needed. Keeping a calendar with festive dates and birthdays is a good idea. It allows you to send greetings in the most significant moments. In many countries where strong group attachment prevails, social media is not only reserved for families and friends, and thus, offers a good instrument with opportunities to interact spontaneously and to become part of a close circle. Lucilla Martinez—a software developer from Argentina—shared her experience:

> If a client or a business partner accepts my Facebook friend request, I consider it a win because I can interact with this person naturally, quickly, frequently, and effortlessly. To catch up with someone or to keep them update without a good reason is hard. It's too formal with an email, too abrupt with a call, and too business-like via LinkedIn. I have become an expert with privacy setting on Facebook. I tailor setting for each post, so it can be seen by friends and/or families, and/or colleagues. Likes, and comments on Facebook are a casual mode of communication that can shift the relationship dynamics immensely, to the extent that many times, I drop them a message with an offer and they replied at midnight with a "yes."

Relationship thrives on long-term time orientation, so don't wait until a favor is given to give it back. Helping genuinely not only leaves a long-lasting impact but stocks up the social capital that will benefit the giver in the long run. Simple acts of kindness go a long way. In the end, what we want to build is the kind of relationship that would allow us to call people at short notice, even out of office hour. That can only be done when trust is created beforehand. Think of constructing a road, one has to build it *before* the vehicle runs and reaps the benefit of a smooth journey.

Summary

1. Three most common dimensions of communication are:
   - Direct–indirect: The extent to which one relies on implicit or explicit social cues.
   - M–P time: The extent to which one organizes communication in a linier or cyclic pattern.
   - Affective–neutral: The extent to which one expresses or holds her/his emotion and controls body movements.
2. While each culture has a stereotype of its dominant communicative pattern (e.g., the Italian are affective), the reality is more dynamic as each situation and individual may (sub)consciously choose to communicate in a specific way.
3. Before the birth of language, body language was the primary way for us to communicate. With the aid of language, body language still remains an *external evidence of our internal state.*

4. Instead of trying to learn cultural stereotypes that can be wrong, it's more effective to have a mixed approach:
   - Tune in, be the product of culture by imitating others' body language to build trust.
   - Actively reshape, be the producer of personal values by intended body language. Be mindful that repeated body language done by a collective can influence the value of that collective.
5. Language evolved as a mechanism to deal with the possibilities of ideas being stolen, to recognize who we can trust.
6. Language is both the product and the producer of human beings. This means, language shapes us, and we also shape the language.
7. There are three main types of meetings:
   - Linier: Decision making and problem solving
   - Cyclic: Debate and exchange ideas
   - Ritual: Ratify decisions
   - In reality, meetings are often a mixture of all three.
8. Relationship tips the scale of all decision-making processes.
9. Strategies for building relationship are:
   - Start with similarities
   - Self-disclosure
   - Gift giving
   - Social activities
   - Maintain relationship with frequency, spontaneity and genuineness

Notes

Don't forget to go to the end of the book for case studies.

1 Klemmer, E. T., and F. W. Snyder. 1972. "Measurement of Time Spent Communicating." *Journal of Communication* 22(2): 142–158. doi:10.1111/j.1460–2466.1972.tb00141.x.
2 Chua, Hannah Faye., Julie E. Boland, and Richard E. Nisbett. 2005. "Cultural Variation in Eye Movements during Scene Perception." *Proceedings of the National Academy of Sciences* 102(35): 12629–12633. doi:10.1073/pnas.0506162102.
3 Nisbett, Richard E., and Yuri Miyamoto. 2005. "The Influence of Culture: Holistic versus Analytic Perception." *Trends in Cognitive Sciences* 9(10): 467–473. doi:10.1016/j.tics.2005.08.004.
4 Gutchess, Angela H., Robert C. Welsh, Aysecan Boduroglu, and Denise C. Park. 2006. "Cultural Differences in Neural Function Associated with Object Processing." *Cognitive, Affective, and Behavioral Neuroscience* 6(2): 102–109. doi:10.3758/cabn.6.2.102.
5 Masuda, Takahiko., Phoebe C. Ellsworth, Batja Mesquita, Janxin Leu, Shigehito Tanida, and Ellen Van De Veerdonk. 2008. "Placing the Face in Context: Cultural Differences in the Perception of Facial Emotion." *Journal of Personality and Social Psychology* 94(3): 365–381. doi:10.1037/0022-3514.94.3.365.
6 Jenkins, Lucas J., Yung-Jui Yang, Joshua Goh, Ying-Yi Hong, and Denise C. Park. 2010. "Cultural Differences in the Lateral Occipital Complex While Viewing Incongruent Scenes." *Social Cognitive and Affective Neuroscience* 5(2–3): 236–241. doi:10.1093/scan/nsp056.
7 Lewis, Richard S., Sharon G. Goto, and Lauren L. Kong. 2008. "Culture and Context: East Asian American and European American Differences in P3 Event-Related Potentials and Self-Construal." *Personality and Social Psychology Bulletin* 34(5): 623–634. doi:10.1177/0146167207313731.
8 Lao, Junpeng., Luca Vizioli, and Roberto Caldara. 2013. "Culture Modulates the Temporal Dynamics of Global/local Processing." *Culture and Brain* 1(2–4): 158–174. doi:10.1007/s40167-013-0012-2.
9 Hedden, Trey., Sarah Ketay, Arthur Aron, Hazel Rose Markus, and John D. E. Gabrieli. 2008. "Cultural Influences on Neural Substrates of Attentional Control." *Psychological Science* 19(1): 12–17. doi:10.1111/j.1467-9280.2008.02038.x.

10 Goh, Joshua O., Michael W. Chee, Jiat Chow Tan, Vinod Venkatraman, and Andrew Hebrank, Eric D. Leshikar, Lucas Jenkins, Bradley P. Sutton, Angela H. Gutchess, and Denise C. Park. 2007. "Age and Culture Modulate Object Processing and Object-Scene Binding in the Ventral Visual Area." *Cognitive, Affective, and Behavioral Neuroscience* 7(1): 44–52. doi:10.3758/cabn.7.1.44.

11 Na, Jinkyung., and Shinobu Kitayama. 2011. "Spontaneous Trait Inference Is Culture-Specific." *Psychological Science* 22(8): 1025–1032. doi:10.1177/0956797611414727.

12 Yuki, Masaki., William W. Maddux, and Takahiko Masuda. 2007. "Are the Windows to the Soul the Same in the East and West? Cultural Differences in Using the Eyes and Mouth as Cues to Recognize Emotions in Japan and the United States." *Journal of Experimental Social Psychology* 43(2): 303–311. doi:10.1016/j.jesp.2006.02.004.

13 Jack, Rachael E., Caroline Blais, Christoph Scheepers, Philippe G. Schyns, and Roberto Caldara. 2009. "Cultural Confusions Show That Facial Expressions Are Not Universal." *Current Biology* 19(18): 1543–1548. doi:10.1016/j.cub.2009.07.051.

14 Pogosyan, Marianna., and Jan Benjamin Engelmann. 2017. "How We Read Emotions from Faces." *Frontiers for Young Minds* 5. doi:10.3389/frym.2017.00011.

15 Nishimura, Shoji., Anne Nevgi, and Seppo Tella. 2008. "Communication Style and Cultural Features in High/Low Context Communication Cultures: A Case Study of Finland, Japan and India." Proceedings of a subject-didactic symposium in Helsinki. www.helsinki.fi/~tella/nishimuranevgitella299.pdf.

16 Kynge, James. 2000. "EU Trade Deal Clears China's Way into WTO." *Financial Times*. May 20–21.

17 Blackman, Carolyn. 2000. "An Inside Guide to Negotiating." *The China Business Review*. May–June, 44–46.

18 Tan, Kenneth. 2017. "China Introduces Surprisingly Progressive Sex Education Curriculum for Kids, Some Parents Freak Out." *Shanghaiist*. March 6. http://shanghaiist.com/2017/03/06/comprehensive-sexuality-education.php.

19 Lin, Zhicheng., Yan Lin, and Shihui Han. 2007. "Self-Construal Priming Modulates Visual Activity Underlying Global/local Perception." *Biological Psychology* 77(1): 93–97. doi:10.1016/j.biopsycho.2007.08.002.

20 Smith, Peter B., and Michael Harris Bond. 1994. *Social Psychology across Culture: Analysis and Perspective*, 149. Boston: Allyn and Bacon.

21 Hall, Edward T., and Mildred Reed Hall. 1990. *Understanding Cultural Differences*. Yarmouth, ME: Intercultural Press.

22 Carté, Penny., and Chris Fox. 2008. *Bridging the Culture Gap: A Practical Guide to International Business Communication*, 14. London: Kogan Page.

23 Engle, Jane. 2005. "Punctuality: Some Cultures Are Wound Tighter Than Others." *Los Angeles Times*. December 11. http://articles.latimes.com/2005/dec/11/travel/tr-insider11.

24 Hall, Edward T. 1983. *The Dance of Life*, 53–54. Garden City, NJ: Anchor Press.

25 Trompenaars, Fons., and Charles Hampden-Turner. 2012. *Riding the Waves of Culture: Understanding Diversity in Global Business*. 3rd ed. New York: The McGraw Hill Companies.

26 Ekman, Paul. 1971. *Universals and Cultural Differences in Facial Expressions of Emotion*, 207–282. Lincoln: University of Nebraska Press.

27 Murata, Asuka., Jason S. Moser, and Shinobu Kitayama. 2013. "Culture Shapes Electrocortical Responses during Emotion Suppression." *Social Cognitive and Affective Neuroscience* 8(5): 595–601. doi:10.1093/scan/nss036.

28 Kim, Heejung S., David K. Sherman, Taraneh Mojaverian, Joni Y. Sasaki, and Jinyoung Park, Eunkook M. Suh, and Shelley E. Taylor. 2011. "Gene-Culture Interaction: Oxytocin Receptor Polymorphism (OXTR) and Emotion Regulation." *Social Psychological and Personality Science* 2(6): 665–672. doi:10.1177/1948550611405854.

29 Kim, Heejung S., David K. Sherman, Joni Y. Sasaki, Jun Xu, Thai Q. Chu, Chorong Ryu, Eunkook M. Suh, Kelsey Graham, and Shelley E. Taylor. 2010. "Culture, Distress, and Oxytocin Receptor Polymorphism (OXTR) Interact to Influence Emotional Support Seeking." *Proceedings of the National Academy of Sciences* 107(36): 15717–15721. doi:10.1073/pnas.1010830107.

30 Mateo, M. Martínez., M. Cabanis, J. Stenmanns, and S. Krach. 2013. "Essentializing the Binary Self: Individualism and Collectivism in Cultural Neuroscience." *Frontiers in Human Neuroscience* 7. doi:10.3389/fnhum.2013.00289.

31 Lewis, Richard D. 2005. *Finland: Cultural Lone Wolf.* Boston: Intercultural Press.

32 Mehrabian, Albert. 1971. *Silent Messages.* Belmont, CA: Wadsworth.

33 Burgoon, Judee K., David B. Buller, and W. G. Woodall. 1989. *Nonverbal Communication: The Unspoken Dialogue*, 9–10. New York: Harper and Row.

34 Willis, Janine., and Alexander Todorov. 2006. "First Impressions: Making Up Your Mind after a 100-Ms Exposure to a Face." *Psychological Science* 17(7): 592–598. doi:10.1111/j.1467-9280.2006.01750.x.

35 Collett, Peter., Peter Marsh, and Marie O'Shaughnessy. 1979. *Gestures: Their Origins and Distribution.* London: Cape.

36 Keysers, Christian., and Valeria Gazzola. 2010. "Social Neuroscience: Mirror Neurons Recorded in Humans." *Current Biology* 20(8): 353–354. doi:10.1016/j.cub.2010.03.013.

37 Pineda, Jaime A. 2007. *Mirror Neuron Systems: The Role of Mirroring Processes in Social Cognition*, 191–212. Atlanta: Emory University.

38 Iacoboni, Marco. 2008. *Mirroring People: The New Science of How We Connect With Others.* New York: Picador.

39 Word, Carl O., Mark P. Zanna, and Joel Cooper. 1974. "The Nonverbal Mediation of Self-Fulfilling Prophecies in Interracial Interaction." *Journal of Experimental Social Psychology* 10(2): 109–120. doi:10.1016/0022-1031(74)90059-6.

40 Won, Andrea S., Jeremy N. Bailenson, and Joris H. Janssen. 2014. "Automatic Detection of Nonverbal Behavior Predicts Learning in Dyadic Interactions." *IEEE Transactions on Affective Computing* 5(2): 112–125. doi:10.1109/TAFFC.2014.2329304.

41 Cuddy, Amy J. C., Caroline A. Wilmuth, and Dana R. Carney. 2012. "The Benefit of Power Posing before a High-Stakes Social Evaluation." *Harvard Business School Working Paper* 13-027. September. https://dash.harvard.edu/bitstream/handle/1/9547823/13-027.pdf?sequence=1.

42 Cuddy, Amy. 2015. *Presence: Bringing Your Boldest Self to Your Biggest Challenges.* New York: Little, Brown and Company.

43 Wells, Gary L., and Richard E. Petty. 1980. "The Effects of Over Head Movements on Persuasion: Compatibility and Incompatibility of Responses." *Basic and Applied Social Psychology* 1(3): 219–230. doi:10.1207/s15324834basp0103_2.

44 Strack, Fritz., Leonard L. Martin, and Sabine Stepper. 1988. "Inhibiting and Facilitating Conditions of the Human Smile: A Nonobtrusive Test of the Facial Feedback Hypothesis." *Journal of Personality and Social Psychology* 54(5): 768–777. doi:10.1037/0022-3514.54.5.768.

45 Cacioppo, John T., Joseph R. Priester, and Gary G. Berntson. 1993. "Rudimentary Determinants of Attitudes: II. Arm Flexion and Extension Have Differential Effects on Attitudes." *Journal of Personality and Social Psychology* 65(1): 5–17. doi:10.1037/0022-3514.65.1.5.

46 Knight, Andrew P., and Markus Baer. 2014. "Get Up, Stand Up: The Effects of a Non-Sedentary Workspace on Information Elaboration and Group Performance." *Social Psychological and Personality Science* 5(8): 910–917. doi:10.1177/1948550614538463.

47 Bluedorn, Allen C., Daniel B. Turban, and Mary Sue Love. 1999. "The Effects of Stand-Up and Sit-Down Meeting Formats on Meeting Outcomes." *Journal of Applied Psychology* 84(2): 277–285. doi:10.1037//0021-9010.84.2.277.

48 Oppezzo, Marily., and Daniel L. Schwartz. 2014. "Give Your Ideas Some Legs: The Positive Effect of Walking on Creative Thinking." *Journal of Experimental Psychology: Learning, Memory, and Cognition* 40(4): 1142–1152. doi:10.1037/a0036577.

49 Williams, Lawrence E., and John A. Bargh. 2008. "Experiencing Physical Warmth Promotes Interpersonal Warmth." *Science* 322(5901): 606–607. doi:10.1126/science.1162548.

50 Cuddy, Amy. 2012. "Amy Cuddy: Your Body Language Shapes Who You Are." TED video, filmed in June. www.ted.com/talks/amy_cuddy_your_body_language_shapes_who_you_are?language=en.

51 Grunberger, R. 1971. *A Social History of the Third Reich*, 27. London: Penguin Books.

52 Buckley, Tammy. 2014. "No Deep Sighing Allowed Here: Council Bans Bad Body Language." *HRD.* March 3. www.hrmonline.co.nz/news/no-deep-sighing-allowed-here-council-bans-bad-body-language-184797.aspx.

53 Britten, Nick. 2002. "How a Hug in the Office Can Help to Triple Profits." *The Telegraph*. April 5. www.telegraph.co.uk/news/uknews/1389863/How-a-hug-in-the-office-can-help-to-triple-profits.html.

54 Leach, Ben. 2009. "Staff Strip Naked to Improve Morale." *The Telegraph*. July 2. www.telegraph.co.uk/news/newstopics/howaboutthat/5718984/Staff-strip-naked-to-improve-morale.html.

55 Pagel, Mark. 2012. *Wired for Culture: Origins of the Human Social Mind*. New York: W. W. Norton & Company.

56 Pagel, Mark. 2011. "Mark Pagel: How Language Transformed Humanity." TED Talks, filmed in July. www.ted.com/talks/mark_pagel_how_language_transformed_humanity.

57 Boroditsky, Lera., and Alice Gaby. 2010. "Remembrances of Times East: Absolute Spatial Representations of Time in an Australian Aboriginal Community." *Psychological Science* 21(11): 1635–1639. doi:10.1177/0956797610386621.

58 Boroditsky, Lera., Orly Fuhrman, and Kelly McCormick. 2011. "Do English and Mandarin Speakers Think Differently About Time?" *Cognition* 118(1): 123–129.

59 Bylund, Emanuel., and Panos Athanasopoulos. 2017. "The Whorfian Time Warp: Representing Duration through the Language Hourglass." *Journal of Experimental Psychology: General* 146(7): 911–916. doi:10.1037/xge0000314.

60 Winawer, Jonathan., Nathan Witthoft, Michael C. Frank, Lisa Wu, Alex R. Wade, and Lera Boroditsky. 2007. "Russian Blues Reveal Effects of Language on Color Discrimination." *Proceedings of the National Academy of Sciences* 104(19): 7780–7785. doi:10.1073/pnas.0701644104.

61 Boroditsky, Lera., Lauren A. Schmidt, and Webb Phillips. 2003. "Sex, Syntax, and Semantics." In *Language in Mind: Advances in the Study of Language and Cognition*, ed. Gentner Dedre and Susan Goldin-Meadow. Cambridge, MA: MIT Press.

62 Costa, Albert., Alice Foucart, Sayuri Hayakawa, Melina Aparici, Jose Apesteguia, Joy Heafner, and Boaz Keysar. 2014. "Your Morals Depend on Language." *PLoS ONE* 9(4): e94842. doi:10.1371/journal.pone.0094842.

63 Harris, Catherine L., Ayse Ayçiçegi, and Jean Berko Gleason. 2003. "Taboo Words and Reprimands Elicit Greater Autonomic Reactivity in a First Language Than in a Second Language." *Applied Psycholinguistics* 24(4): 561–579. doi:10.1017/s0142716403000286.

64 Geipel, Janet., Constantinos Hadjichristidis, and Luca Surian. 2016. "Foreign Language Affects the Contribution of Intentions and Outcomes to Moral Judgment." *Cognition* 154: 34–39. doi:10.1016/j.cognition.2016.05.010.

65 Thierry, Guillaume. 2016. "Neurolinguistic Relativity: How Language Flexes Human Perception and Cognition." *Language Learning* 66(3): 690–713. doi:10.1111/lang.12186.

66 Lee, Spike W. S., Daphna Oyserman, and Michael Harris Bond. 2010. "Am I Doing Better Than You? That Depends on Whether You Ask Me in English or Chinese: Self-Enhancement Effects of Language as a Cultural Mindset Prime." *Journal of Experimental Social Psychology* 46(5): 785–791. doi:10.1016/j.jesp.2010.04.005.

67 Ge, Jianqiao., Gang Peng, Bingjiang Lyu, Yi Wang, Yan Zhuo, Zhendong Niu, Li Hai Tan, Alexander P. Leff, and Jia-Hong Gao. 2015. "Cross-Language Differences in the Brain Network Subserving Intelligible Speech." *Proceedings of the National Academy of Sciences* 112(10): 2972–2977. doi:10.1073/pnas.1416000112.

68 Zlatev, Jordan., and Johan Blomberg. 2015. "Language May Indeed Influence Thought." *Frontiers in Psychology* 6. doi:10.3389/fpsyg.2015.01631.

69 Orwell, G. 1946. *Politics and the English Language*, 167. London: Horizon.

70 Georgetown University Medical Center. 2015. "Bilinguals of Two Spoken Languages Have More Gray Matter Than Monolinguals." *ScienceDaily*. July 16. www.sciencedaily.com/releases/2015/07/150716135054.htm.

71 Rumbaut, R. G. 2014. "English Plus: Exploring the Socioeconomic Benefits of Bilingualism in Southern California." In *The Bilingual Advantage: Language, Literacy, and the Labor Market*, ed. R. M. Callahan and P. C. Gándara, 182–205. Bristol, UK: Multilingual Matters.

72 Fan, Samantha P., Zoe Liberman, Boaz Keysar, and Katherine D. Kinzler. 2015. "The Exposure Advantage." *Psychological Science* 26(7): 1090–1097. doi:10.1177/0956797615574699.

73 Kovács, Ágnes Melinda., and Jacques Mehler. 2009. "Cognitive Gains in 7-Month-Old Bilingual Infants." *PNAS* 106(16): 6556–6560. doi:10.1073/pnas.0811323106.

74 Adesope, Olusola O., Tracy Lavin, Terri Thompson, and Charles Ungerleider. 2010. "A Systematic Review and Meta-Analysis of the Cognitive Correlates of Bilingualism." *Review of Educational Research* 80(2): 207–245. doi:10.3102/0034654310368803.

75 Goetz, Peggy J. 2003. "The Effects of Bilingualism on Theory of Mind Development." *Bilingualism: Language and Cognition* 6(1): 1–15. doi:10.1017/s1366728903001007.

76 Keysar, Boaz., Sayuri L. Hayakawa, and Sun Gyu An. 2012. "The Foreign-Language Effect." *Psychological Science* 23(6): 661–668. doi:10.1177/0956797611432178.

77 Agirdag, Orhan. 2014. "The Literal Cost of Language Assimilation for the Children of Immigration: The Effects of Bilingualism on Labor Market Outcomes." In *The Bilingual Advantage, Language, Literacy, and the U.S. Labor Market*, ed. R. M. Callahan and P. C. Gándara, 160–181. Bristol, UK: Multilingual Matters.

78 Porras, D., J. Ee, and P. Gándara. 2014. "Surveying the Linguistic Landscape: Bilingualism and Employment Opportunities." In *The Bilingual Advantage: Language, Literacy, and the Labor Market*, ed. R. Callahan and P. Gándara, 234–257. Bristol, UK: Multilingual Matters.

79 Bradley, Simon. 2008. "Languages Generate One Tenth of Swiss GDP." November 20. www.swissinfo.ch/eng/languages-generate-one-tenth-of-swiss-gdp/7050488.

80 "Did Justin Trudeau's French Skills Help Him to Win Canada's Election for Prime Minister?" 2015. Pantera Language Studio. October 23. http://panteralanguage.weebly.com/blog/did-justin-trudeaus-french-skills-help-him-to-win-canadas-election-for-prime-minister.

81 Hogan-Brun, Gabrielle. 2017. *Linguanomics: What Is the Market Potential of Multilingualism?* London: Bloomsbury Academic.

82 Richardson, Hannah. 2014. "Modern Languages 'Recovery Programme' Urged by MPs." *BBC News*. July 14. www.bbc.com/news/education-28269496.

83 Conversis. 2015. "Importance of Global Talent within International Businesses." www.conversis.com/ConversisGlobal/media/ConversisMedical-Images/Conversis-Global-Talent-Report-Download.pdf.

84 Pinker, Steven. 2010. *The Language Instinct: How the Mind Creates Language*. London: Penguin Books.

85 Li, Peggy., Linda Abarbanell, Lila Gleitman, and Anna Papafragou. 2011. "Spatial Reasoning in Tenejapan Mayans." *Cognition* 120(1): 33–53. doi:10.1016/j.cognition.2011.02.012.

86 Holden, Nigel J. 2002. *Cross-cultural Management: A Knowledge Management Perspective*, 208–209. Harlow, UK: Financial Times Prentice Hall.

87 Frank, Michael C., Daniel L. Everett, Evelina Fedorenko, and Edward Gibson. 2008. "Number as a Cognitive Technology: Evidence from Pirahã Language and Cognition." *Cognition* 108(3): 819–824. doi:10.1016/j.cognition.2008.04.007.

88 Hartshorne, Joshua. 2009. "Does Language Shape What We Think?" *Scientific American*. August 18. www.scientificamerican.com/article/does-language-shape-what.

89 Newberg, Andrew B., and Mark Robert Waldman. 2013. *Words Can Change Your Brain: 12 Conversation Strategies to Build Trust, Resolve Conflict, and Increase Intimacy*. New York: Plume.

90 Nezlek, John B., David B. Newman, and Todd M. Thrash. 2017. "A Daily Diary Study of Relationships between Feelings of Gratitude and Well-Being." *The Journal of Positive Psychology* 12(4): 323–332. doi:10.1080/17439760.2016.1198923.

91 Emmons, Robert A., and Michael E. Mccullough. 2003. "Counting Blessings versus Burdens: An Experimental Investigation of Gratitude and Subjective Well-Being in Daily Life." *Journal of Personality and Social Psychology* 84(2): 377–389. doi:10.1037/0022-3514.84.2.377.

92 "When in Germany, It's All Right to Mention the War." *Financial Times*. www.ft.com/content/746104f8-d481-11da-a357-0000779e2340.

93 Holden, Nigel J. 2002. *Cross-Cultural Management: A Knowledge Management Perspective*, 232. Harlow, UK: Financial Times Prentice Hall.

94 "How Do You Say Mom in Japanese? It Can Change Based on This." Japanese Tactics. https://japanesetactics.com/how-do-you-say-mom-in-japanese-it-can-change-based-on-this.

95 Chaney, Lillian H., and Jeanette S. Martin. 2005. *Intercultural Business Communication*, 88. 4th ed. Upper Saddle River, NJ: Pearson/Prentice Hall..

96 Salk, J. 1996. "De la créativité interculturalelle: un exemple germano-japonais." *Les Annales de l'École de Paris deu Management* 3: 337–345.

 97 Zak, Paul J., Robert Kurzban, and William T. Matzner. 2005. "Oxytocin Is Associated with Human Trustworthiness." *Hormones and Behavior* 48(5): 522–527. doi:10.1016/j.yhbeh.2005.07.009.

 98 Taras, Vas., Piers Steel, and Bradley L. Kirkman. 2016. "Does Country Equate with Culture? Beyond Geography in the Search for Cultural Boundaries." *Management International Review* 56(4): 455–487. doi:10.1007/s11575-016-0283-x.

 99 Aron, Arthur., Edward Melinat, Elaine N. Aron, Robert Darrin Vallone, and Renee J. Bator. 1997. "The Experimental Generation of Interpersonal Closeness: A Procedure and Some Preliminary Findings." *Personality and Social Psychology Bulletin* 23(4): 363–377. doi:10.1177/0146167297234003.

100 Adler, Nancy J. 2002. *International Dimensions of Organizational Behavior*, 218–219. 4th ed. Cincinnati, OH: South-Western.

101 Arunthanes, Wiboon., Patriya Tansuhaj, and David J. Lemak. 1994. "Cross-Cultural Business Gift Giving." *International Marketing Review* 11(4): 44–55. doi:10.1108/02651339410069245.

102 Grande, David., Dominick L. Frosch, Andrew W. Perkins, and Barbara E. Kahn. 2009. "Effect of Exposure to Small Pharmaceutical Promotional Items on Treatment Preferences." *Archives of Internal Medicine* 169(9): 887–893. doi:10.1001/archinternmed.2009.64.

103 Harris, Gardiner. 2008. "Drug Industry to Announce Revised Code on Marketing." *The New York Times*. July 10. www.nytimes.com/2008/07/10/business/10code.html?ref=health.

104 O'Shannassy, Timothy F. 2017. "Gift Giving, Guanxi, Bribery and Corruption Challenges in Australia-China Business: An Ethical Tension between the Global South and the East." In *Research in Ethical Issues in Organizations Ethics in the Global South*, ed. Michael Schwartz and Howard Harris, 131–151. Bingley, UK: Emerald Publishing Limited. doi:10.1108/s1529-209620170000018006.

105 Lu, Rachel. 2014. "A Merkel, a Map, a Message to China?" *Foreign Policy*. April 1. http://foreignpolicy.com/2014/04/01/a-merkel-a-map-a-message-to-china/.

13 Cross-Cultural Negotiation

Negotiation is a fundamental part of human communication. In fact, we negotiate all the time without realizing it, with everyone from our partners to children, friends, and colleagues. While negotiation has become somewhat a subconscious process with those who share similar values and behaviors, negotiating with those who come from different cultures, generations, professions, or nationalities requires us to be more aware and adaptive. In business, negotiation is an integral part. We don't get what we deserve, we get what we negotiate.[1]

In this chapter, we will discuss critical aspects of negotiation. We begin with the preparation work such as the importance of learning about others, the role of relationship building, how to select team members, the impact of time, the power of place, and the significance of priming tactics. We then discuss how negotiation strategies vary along the line of cultural values and national profiles. To keep a balance, we emphasize the decisive factor of specific context, which more often than not overrides the stereotypes. With regard to GCEB-Be (Chapter 2), namely pathway Brain—Behavior, we will have a look at how our brain is biased when making decisions, and how these biases are employed as negotiation tactics to persuade and influence others.

13.1 Preparation

The Roman philosopher Seneca once said: "Luck is when preparation meets opportunity." This is absolutely true with negotiation—a situation in which the immense dynamics of similarities and differences is condensed in a rather short period of intensive interaction. In this section, we will discuss the most critical aspects of the preparation work that businesspeople need to do before negotiations begin.

13.1.1 Learning about Others

In October 1962, the United States and the former Soviet Union came to the brink of nuclear war in the Cuban Missile Crisis. In the middle of this harrowing conflict, President Kennedy offered that if all Russian nuclear weapons were removed from Cuba, he would pledge not to invade Cuba in the future. Soviet Premier Nikita Khrushchev accepted. In that specific context, this deal allowed him to declare that he had saved Cuba from attack, and therefore satisfied his core motives of *saving face* and *retaining power*. Kennedy's proposal was suggested by an advisor, Tommy Thompson, who had lived with Khrushchev and had intimate knowledge of his fundamental interests.[2]

This example illustrates the powerful advantage of having a deep understanding of one's opponent. Knowing the motives behind the position of the other party can illuminate strategies to secure a better deal. On the contrary, assuming that the other party has the same priorities (i.e., the fixed-pie bias) prevents us from understanding them deeply.[3] For the same product, a buyer from a large country may show more interests in market share due to the big local market, a buyer from a developed country may think more about future revenue and profits due to the competition back in her/his home, a buyer from a developing country may want to know if the product is labor intensive so (s)he can take advantage of the low wage rates, a buyer who follows Islamic faith may care deeply about the question of whether the product is *halal*, and so forth.

Learning about the others also means having an *open mind* to understand the counterpart's motives. If we enter the negotiation and pursue one particular figure, we will follow a single narrow path through the woods. When we hold a fixed outcome in our memory, a great amount of the brain's mental processing power is needed, leading to an "ego-depletion state."[4] This state limits the capacity to take the perspectives of others, blocking a creative win-win solution. Becoming too charmed by our own arguments can blind us to a better deal.[5] A great anecdote comes to mind here: Two children argue over the last orange left in the house. The father intervenes and asks for their purposes. One child wants to make fresh orange juice and the other wants to add orange zest to the cake. The father then gives the orange peel to the second child and the rest to the first. By focusing on the motives (why) and not a fixed result (what), both parties are happy. Learning about the other leads to better payoffs.[6] Thus, a critical lesson in negotiation: *Think of interests, not outcomes.*

In business context, learning about others includes, but is not limited to, tasks such as researching the other party's past negotiations, their competitors, the kind of agreements they reached, and their negotiation styles; speaking with those who are working for them; considering hiring those who used to work with them; figuring out their goals, strengths, and weaknesses; learning their culture and history, and so forth. The more the better. In negotiation with multiple parties, the chance of idea conflict is significantly higher and negotiators may forget about their company's need. In this situation, if one negotiator makes sure (s)he is sympathetic with other parties' viewpoints, individually, (s)he stands a greater chance to win the deal while others are busy arguing.

To illustrate this point, *Financial Times* once gave an advice to British sellers in (Western) Germany:

> If you sit down to dinner after the meeting, do not believe the old adage about "not mentioning the war." The Second World War retains a fascination for many Germans. Sometimes it is hard to get them off the subject. Expect your German hosts to tell you how much poorer the country has become since reunification. If you pre-empt them by telling them that 3 to 4% of West German gross domestic product flows to the east each year, they will think you are hugely knowledgeable. Your chances of winning that sale will rise.[7]

Such a process of getting to know the other requires *perspective taking*—an ability to step outside the constraints of our own ego and look at the issue from other points of view (i.e., in the preceding case, understanding how Germans from the West think about the East). It is fundamentally different from *empathy*, which is the ability to feel what others feel and show them compassion (i.e., feeling the frustration of Germans from the West with the same emotional wavelength). We touched on this difference between "think about what others feel" and "feel what others feel" in Chapter 7. These two processes activate different brain regions and prompt differences in behaviors.[8] In a study, those who were told to "imagine what the other person was thinking" produced the highest level of long-term negotiation value than those who were told to "imagine what the other person was feeling."[9] In sum, learning about the other involves the ability to be in their shoes, with the heart, but even more importantly, with the *head*.

13.1.2 Building Relationship

While perspective taking tends to be more beneficial than empathy during *direct negotiation*, it's impossible to make a clear-cut line between the two during the whole process. In the end, the commitment we make, more often than not, is to honor people, not the contract. People do business with whom they trust. And "trust" is essentially a matter of feeling. Emotion tips the scale, as we discussed in Chapter 12. For this reason, at the *universal level*, building relationship is vital for a successful negotiation, regardless of cultural backgrounds. It doesn't mean we need to make a plan to become lifelong friends with our partners. Rather, it is about the degree of trust that enables each party to understand and stick with the agreement and solve any potential problems in a dignified manner.

When it comes to the *collective* and *individual level*, some cultures, people, or contexts emphasize the aspect of relationship more than others. In a negotiation where weak group attachment prevails, people may get down to business quickly, using contracts as an important milestone. Relationship will be built slowly afterward and, at one point, may replace the contract because the trust level is high. In comparison, when strong group attachment prevails, people may see relationship as a condition before signing the contract. This process of trust building takes days, weeks, months, or years. While some consider this a waste of time, others see it as a testing period and a good investment in a relationship, so that future business won't even need a contract to bear fruitful outcomes. In short, relationship can either come first as a *requirement* for a deal or come afterward as a *consequence* of a deal. Across the world, from the Asia to the America, there are many business leaders who rely on relationship to facilitate global deals without the rigid procedure of legal contracts. They are successful negotiators who have reached an ideal point where they can make deals seamlessly because, at that point, the relationship *is* the contract.

One of the most obvious ways to build relationship is to start with seeking similarity. Evolutionarily speaking, we tend to have trust toward those who are similar to us (see Chapter 6). Successful negotiation benefits immensely from a foundation of shared values and common goals.[10] More often than not, a small but significant similarity can overcome big differences. For example, in a joint venture between a Brazilian and a Chinese company, the similar level of importance both cultures put on relationship immensely facilitated the negotiation. This shared value trumped big differences between the two cultures, acting as a common ground for the joint venture to be built upon. In the words of one Brazilian director: "The Chinese are the Brazilians of Asia."[11]

However, outward expressions and values of a culture don't always synchronize with each other, that is, the same outward expression does not signal the same value (see Chapter 4). In negotiation, misunderstanding can rise from a perception of similarity that is not shared by both parties. For example, many Arab and African businesspeople have a good command of either French or English because these are often their first languages. Together with a modernized lifestyle, such outward similarity can prompt negotiators from the West to have a misleading perception of cultural sharing. They quickly see their counterparts as similar, hence, giving more trust to the other party and falsely expecting the same to be given back.[12] At the same time, the reverse does not occur with the Arabs and Africans. Despite speaking the same language and having similar lifestyle, they still perceive their Western counterparts as different. Thus, they may feel no obligation to return the same amount of trust—a situation that may allow them to exploit this mismatch for their own advantages.

13.1.3 Team Selection

13.1.3.1 Negotiator Profile and Team Selection Strategies

Successful negotiation teams choose players carefully because they are those who make or break a deal. Skilled negotiators consider twice as wide a range of action, options, and outcomes; thrice as much attention on similarities and common ground; and twice as much time focusing on long-term issues.[13]

Table 13.1 Team-selection strategies

Cultural Values	Team-Selection Strategies
Strong Group Attachment (Collectivism)	• Trust is initially built on similarity and relationship. To give a signal of trust, select team members who share a coculture or who are related with the other party. • Explore the network to find team members who are related to the other party in terms of nationality, ethnicity, gender, religion, profession, hobby, kinship, hometown, ex-members of a network or school, political affiliation. • A lawyer present at the beginning of the negotiation may signal distrust (i.e., I don't trust you, so my lawyer has to be here from the very start). • Negotiation team may not be fixed. New people may join negotiation sessions to be in the loop. Team size tends to be big. • Negotiation may involve an intermediary (i.e., middle person) due to the power of personal connection.
Weak Group Attachment (Individualism)	• Teams tend to be smaller in size. • Inquire in advance to make sure that team sizes are balanced. The physical presence of more people signals power and solidarity. Even if not everyone contributes, they can observe and detect important nonverbal cues and hidden messages.
Strong Hierarchy Acceptance	• Top managers should be at the opening talk. • During the negotiation, positions from both side should match, especially in terms of social reputation, seniority, authority, and age. "Match eagles with eagles"—Malaysian saying. The North and South Korea talks collapsed because North Korea was insulted when the lead negotiator from the South wasn't of equal status.[a] • Many team members attend just to be in the loop. They may sit to listen rather than contribute.
Weak Hierarchy Acceptance (Egalitarian)	• The presence of top managers at the opening talk is not a must but highly recommended. During the negotiation, position matching can lean more toward practicability. • Many team members can attend to give input.
Masculine Gender Association	• Tend to select assertive negotiators. Both men and women value competition, achievement, and performance.
Feminine Gender Association	• Tend to select collaborative negotiators. Both men and women value cooperation, consensus, equality, and sustainability.
Strong Uncertainty Avoidance	• Keep the same team throughout the negotiation process. • Select top experts in the team. Professional and technical aspects are essential. • Select negotiators with good reputation, who have work or personal relationship with the other party or those who are related. • Be attentive to rituals, procedures, formality, deadline, and structure.
Weak Uncertainty Avoidance	• Dealing with weak uncertainty avoidance may bring anxiety because of the unknown. Select experienced negotiators who can be extremely patient. • Other traits that help in dealing with weak uncertainty avoidance: Open-mindedness, big-picture thinking, flexibility, more *outcome*, and less *process*-oriented.
Future Orientation	• Select team members who are patient, flexible, and relationship oriented. • In combination with strong uncertainty avoidance and strong group attachment, a change of negotiators can have a significant impact. Collectivists negotiate with people they trust, not companies.
Present/Short-Time Orientation	• Select team members who are competitive and goal oriented. • Get ready for backup, changing team components to suit the demand.

Note

a "International Negotiations: North and South Korea Talks Collapse." 2016. *PON—Program on Negotiation at Harvard Law School*, December 16. www.pon.harvard.edu/daily/international-negotiation-daily/top-10-international-negotiations-of-2013-north-and-south-korea-talks-collapse/.

Across cultures, the requirements of a good negotiator may vary. For example, a study suggested that the most important characteristic to negotiate successfully is "planning/ preparation skill" in the United States and Brazil, "dedication to job" in Japan, and "persistence/ determination" in Taiwan.[14] However, the dynamic paradigm of culture reminds us that there is no fixed profile of a national negotiator. On the negotiation table, people don't just negotiate a business deal but also *negotiate their own cultural elements*. They may change, embracing a new value or communication pattern in response to a specific context. When a certain value prevails, negotiation style may consequently shift. Table 13.1 summarizes some of the most important aspects to consider along the line of cultural values.

13.1.3.2 Gender and Negotiation

Gender plays a role in negotiation as well. In general, women suffer from the competence-likability tradeoff (see Chapter 8), that is the social pressure to appear as a nice person may stop a woman from having a real fight. Assertive behaviors that would be considered normal if employed by men may be characterized as offensive and threatening when employed by women. Biases are at the root of this issue because societies expect women to be caring and men to be competitive. In their book *Women Don't Ask*, the authors remark that while 57% of male business studies graduates negotiate their starting salaries, only 7% of women do so, resulting in male starting salaries 7.6% higher than those attained by women, contributing significantly to the gender pay gap.

However, according to a meta-analysis on gender differences in negotiation outcomes,[15] women negotiate better than men under one of these three conditions: (1) When they have experience; (2) when they know about the bargaining range, for example upper and lower limit of a salary range; and (3) when they negotiate for *other individuals*, such as their employees. With regard to the last condition, fighting for others is a collaborative behavior consistent with the stereotypical gender role, and women may feel more comfortable pushing harder for others than they do for themselves. Experts give women a mental trick: "Change your perspective and think beyond yourself. Imagine you are negotiating for your family."[16]

Further, many male negotiators find it difficult to act competitively toward women because they can't overcome the stereotype that women are soft. Hence, they allow women to influence their behaviors with a bargaining advantage. Men often make a mistake of assuming that women will behave collaboratively and nicely, that women won't employ "games" and manipulative tactics. On the opposite end, other male negotiators are aware of the gender bias, and may try to gain a psychological advantage by purposely being aggressive. They would try to embarrass their female opponents, exposing the women's tactics, reminding them of their "traditional female roles," and sending a clear signal of willingness to fight. Female negotiators should not back down. They have the right to use nonstereotypical strategies. They can be upfront and state that they want to be seen first and foremost as negotiators, everything else is irrelevant.

13.1.4 Interpreter

Interpreters bring words to life. They are essentially multicultural people who *translate the meaning* and not just words. We simply can't translate the language properly without understanding the context properly because language without context can be meaningless.[17] Misinterpreting context can lead to serious consequences. For example, World War II and the use of atomic bomb may well have been the result of such translation error. In response to the ultimatum in the Potsdam Declaration, the Japanese responded: "The government does not see much value in it. All we have to do is *mokusatsu* it." The word was intended to mean "no comment," but the Western translator chose one of the word's other meanings, which is to "ignore or to treat with silent contempt."[18]

Thus, using interpreters can affect the negotiation process in both positive and negative ways. On the positive side, here are the advantages: (1) You have more time to think carefully about your next point while your previous statement is being translated; (2) a multicultural interpreter can be a strategic advisor who helps with revealing hidden message, decoding the context, reading inner thought, evaluating the level of honesty, and predicting the decision; (3) a skillful interpreter can also convey passion, giving the audience not just the meaning of the words but also the *personality* of the speaker and the *atmosphere* of the talk; (4) and, finally, interpreters can actively help in building relationship. For example, Athanasios Tsifis—a professor of interpretation—advised her students that they should keep up to date with sports because match results are an excellent common ground in meetings.[19]

On the negative side, the biggest danger is, of course, a failure in conveying the intended message due to the nuances of the language involved. When an interpreter is not multicultural, her/his thoughts and feelings are formulated according to the native language, hence, resulting in a mismatch between what is intended and what is translated. Language can act as a frame that morphs thoughts and behaviors into a certain pathway (see Chapter 12). Further, it is wise to hire your own interpreter. When the interpreter is provided by one party, her/his loyalty is, of course, with the employer.

13.1.5 *Time*

Time is an important aspect of negotiation. Time orientation exerts significant impact on how each party perceives their planning. When embracing a present/short-term orientation, negotiators tend to expect quick reward. They are more likely to make early concessions and find it easier to walk out. When embracing a future/long-term orientation, negotiators plan for slow reward. They may wait to make concessions in the last minute, and they tend to be more persistent with their demand. Here is a classic case from history:

> During the Paris Peace Talks, designed to negotiate an end to the Vietnam War, the American team arrived in Paris and made hotel reservations for a week. Their Vietnamese counterparts leased a chateau for a year. As the negotiations proceeded, the frustrated Americans were forced to continually renew their weekly reservations to accommodate the more measured pace of the Vietnamese.[20]

Valuing the present/short-term creates a sense of urgency. Because time is money, negotiators who embrace this value and the value of masculinity (i.e., achievement oriented) tend to become impatient and make more concessions when their deadline is near to get a signed contract. The other party has the power of time on their side because they can "outwait" the impatient opponent.[21] Recognizing this time and achievement consciousness, a Brazilian company invited their US counterparts to negotiate in the week before Christmas. Wanting to return to the United States with a deal done before the year ends, they quickly reached the final agreement with favorable clauses for the Brazilian.[22]

When future/long-term time orientation and strong group attachment prevail, *patience* is the best planning strategy. It's wrong to assume that the West is stuck with its stereotypical shot-term orientation. It took Volkswagen seven years to do business in China, and it took McDonald's nearly a decade to start selling hamburgers in Moscow, but they adjusted and succeeded. Building relationship and establishing trust take time for those who embrace the value of the long term and collectivism. A businessperson may have to make "frequent courtesy calls" throughout the year, engage in long discussions on random topics such as "office furniture," and "drink enough coffee to float a small ship" to close the deal.[23] This seems like a challenge. But we should never forget our brain's incredible ability to adapt.

In another business case,[24] time is used to test commitment. A banker was invited by a Middle Eastern sheikh for a meeting in London. After two days of waiting, he was told to fly to Saudi Arabia. After three days of waiting in Riyadh, he finally met the sheikh who eventually became an invaluable business partner. His patience and willingness to adapt finally paid off. Thus, depending on specific contexts, adjusting to the other party's value (i.e., become the product of a new culture) can lead to immense success.

13.1.6 Place

A location is never just a location. The place where negotiation occurs can significantly affect the nature and outcome of the talk.

When meetings are held in the office of one party, then that party has more control. As we know, *the brain is built to resist change* (Chapter 7). Having the home court advantage means one party can spare their brain energy to focus on important issues rather than having to get used to a new environment. The host can enjoy *eustress*—a combination of security and the right amount of excitement that encourages people to venture into new territory. Meanwhile, the guest may move past eustress quickly and move closer to *distress*—a point where excitement turns into tiredness due to new and complex situations. This is the result of (1) having to travel to a new location, getting to know new people, language, culture, food, pace of life, and different styles of working; (2) having limited control over time, setting, order, ritual, and office arrangement; (3) suffering from travel cost, jetlag, stress, homesickness, lack of support from personnel, and limited social life; losing access to immediate resources, for example, getting an urgent document or a second opinion from colleagues, and so forth. On top of that, we are *taught to be polite as guests.* This psychological force allows the host to be more assertive, while it prevents the guest from exercising control.

The biggest advantage of negotiating on your counterpart's territory is that it gives you opportunities to learn about them, understand the conditions under which business will operate, build a long-term relationship, and show serious intent to make a deal, especially when you are the seller. When embracing the values of strong group attachment and hierarchy acceptance, one party may expect the other to take the initiative and go to their place first, thus, showing respect and a willingness to commit. Once goodwill has been shown, it is easier for collectivistic and authoritative businesspeople to do it in return and go to the place of their counterpart as guests.

Because both "my place" and "your place" show clear pros and cons, a neutral site is often the best pick. It's common for businesses to negotiate in a resort geographically located between their headquarters. In December 1989, the summit meeting between George Bush and Mikhail Gorbachev did not take place in any specific country. Rather, the two leaders choose to meet on two ships, one from each country, both in the Mediterranean off the coast of Malta.[25] A division of Caterpillar of California moved one step further. They took their clients out on the company's yacht, thus creating a neutral site. At the same time, they still kept control while removing their clients from distraction.

13.1.7 Priming the Culture and Environment

13.1.7.1 The Power of Priming

We know that priming has the power to sway our brain and prompt out thought in the direction of available and anchoring data. Here is a simple example of priming: When given a word with a missing letter S O _ P, we tend to make it SOUP if the word we saw before was EAT, and we tend to make it SOAP if the word we saw before was WASH. Thus, EAT primes SOUP and WASH primes SOAP.

This priming effect occurs in all aspects of life. In a study, two groups viewed Chinese and US pictures before evaluating a conflict situation. Those who had viewed the Chinese pictures interpreted the conflict according to Chinese values, and those who had viewed the US pictures used US values.[26] The environment around us is full of stimuli that can change our behaviors dramatically. In another classic study, when the polling station was set up in a school, voters were more likely to favor extra funding for education.[27] The setup of the school environment (sub) consciously influenced their response to the policies they deemed important. In fact, embodied cognition is so powerful that we would favorably review a job candidate if we're holding something warm in our hands and respond less favorably to the candidate if someone hands us a bottle of cold drink just before we pick up the resume.[28]

There are two main reasons to explain the power of priming: (1) The autopilot System 1 in our brain constantly looks for the most available data, the best shortcut, and the easiest way to operate *quickly*, thus, saving as much *energy* as possible—a discussion we had in Chapter 4; and (2) the incredible adaptability of our brain, which can *switch* value systems, thinking patterns, and behaviors to fit a specific situation. Context is the software of the mind. These two characteristics of the brain make it very susceptible to stimuli from the surrounding environment. Hence, the setting of the negotiation can help push the other party into thinking or feeling in a certain manner.

13.1.7.2 *Priming Strategies in Negotiation*

The old school of negotiation techniques often focuses on the win-lose paradigm, and thus, its priming strategies include ideas such as seating the opponent to look into the sun, on a lower chair, with their back facing the door, keeping them waiting, not offering drinks, negotiating in a room too hot or too cold, making no place for available for private talk, commenting on the appearance (e.g., "Were you up all night? You look *tired*), and so forth. These environmental cues trigger subconscious fear responses, which may work in short term.

On the contrary, the contemporary approach emphasizes the win-win paradigm, and thus, its priming techniques are more collaborative. Priming a negotiation with the language of fairness, equity, and mutual benefit triggers the bargaining partner to forgo monetary payoffs, to behave in a cooperative manner,[29] influencing the strategies they choose and the outcome of the negotiation.[30] Similarly, researchers have suggested that lawyers should be careful not to stress the kind of written demands they often start with in legal negotiation because the text can provoke behaviors (e.g., competitiveness or defensiveness) that would undermine the discussion that follows.[31]

Putting the indication in practice, we can prime the other party by sending in advance information that *triggers the feelings we want them to experience*. A phone call prior to submitting a written proposal may set up the recipient's expectation. At the early stage of the negotiation, breaking the ice or small talks should not be wasted with conversation about bad weather, traffic, business troubles, or market crisis. We can put thoughts of collaboration in other people's head by showing a notice board in the reception with stories of working together, generosity, and kindness. In the office setting, we can sit side by side with our counterparts rather than across the table,[32] posting all information related to the negotiation on the wall,[33] just structuring the setting so that all parties "face a shared problem" instead of "facing a competitor." If we want to raise the price, getting words like "increase" and "higher" in some posters displaying in the hallway before the discussion might help. If we want the deal to be concluded quickly, we can show evidence of previous contracts that successfully reached final agreements in a certain amount of time—a strategy proved while working in research lab.[34] If we want our clients to spend more money, a luxurious setting may help to do the job. Knowing that a business setting with conference room can ignite competitive behaviors,[35] we can move the negotiation to more casual places such as a golf course, a coffee shop, or a restaurant. We can prime our counterparts with movies, performances, presentations, activities, and so forth that *trigger the values we want them to portray*. An Omani company, for example, invited their clients to visit a mosque where they joined the Omani negotiation team in a prayer. Such an activity can powerfully influence people's mindsets, priming for an Omani way of working. It gears thinking and behaviors toward a pattern of paying more attention to respect, relationship, and hierarchy, while letting go of control, assertiveness, and time pressure.

13.2 Biases as Strategies in Negotiation

Negotiation is among the situations in which we really want to act rationally. However, decision making is often affected by cognitive biases, which rarely make our thoughts rational. Our brain is not a calculator but a survival mechanism operated under the impact of experiences, emotion, and priorities. Therefore, many cognitive biases involve in the process of negotiation, influencing how we bend our judgment and change selection criteria based on relationship, expectation, gender, level of likability, availability of information, or personal attachment to the object. In this section, we will look at some of the most critical biases employed by negotiators as strategies to persuade and sway others.

13.2.1 Framing

Generally speaking, there are two basic strategies for negotiation: *Competitive/distributive win-lose* and *problem-solving/integrative win-win*. The win-lose approach begins with unrealistically high demands, making concessions slowly and grudgingly, threatening, withholding information, and using manipulation and dirty tricks with little thought given to long-term relationship. It is like a tug-of-war game in which opponents outmaneuver, outsmart, and overpower each other. The objective of the win-lose approach is victory, not agreement.

By contrast, the win-win approach begins by seeking a mutually satisfactory ground, proposing reasonable demands, sharing information, and showing sincere effort to reach a *creative new way* that benefits both parties. The objective of the win-win approach is agreement, not victory.

In negotiation, the competitive win-lose approach suggests that you should threaten and force the other side to accept your deal: "If you don't accept this price, we will terminate our delivery in the previous contract." This strategy may make them reconsider your proposal and make your current offer more attractive. But neuroscience says otherwise.

In Chapter 7, we learned that the brain is highly motivated to avoid loss. The impact of losing food stock—the result is starvation—is greater than gaining more food stock—the result is just some extra free time. This psychology of loss aversion shapes the brain's function (Figure 13.1). The impact of losing $5 is much *more powerful* than the impact of gaining $5. Our brain has greater sensitivity to losses than gains. Gains activate the reward circuitry, losses reduce it,[36] and increase the activation of the amygdala.[37]

This result indicates a huge disadvantage of competitive win-lose negotiation approach, that is threatening tactic might, in fact, diminish your counterpart's ability to appreciate the value of your offer. Their brain spends more energy focusing on the negative consequences of the loss rather than analyzing the great advantages of the gain. Take this example of framing: A company offers its employees (1) a $20,000 *increase* over their current salary of $100,000 versus (2) a $20,000 *decrease* from their demand of $140,000. If presented with the latter proposal, the employees are more likely to focus on the impact of "decrease" and does not fully appreciate the advantages of the $20,000 gain. Because the impact of losing $20,000 is greater, they are less likely to accept the deal and more likely to resist compromises or declare impasses. When loss is emphasized, both parties also become more risk-taking and competitive.

On the contrary, when gain is emphasized, both parties tend to take less risk, cooperate better, and achieve greater joint benefits.[38] However, the gain framing is also not perfect. If the other party presents the situation as half-full glass, negotiators will be more interested, biased, and oblivious to risks. It's important to be aware of risks (gain framing) and not attract risks unnecessarily (loss framing). Negotiators should base their evaluation on the quality of the deal and not the quality of the *presentation.*

Gain/loss framing is a typical bias application of the competitive negotiation approach. However, it restricts negotiators' perspectives. For those who prefer the win-win problem-solving approach, neuroscience has some indication. In Chapter 5, 7 and 10, we learned about the power of short-term rewards and small wins. Each time we achieve something, even if it is small, the brain releases dopamine and this neurotransmitter motivates us to move one step further, so that we can have that experience again. Moving just one step further creates the power of progress,[39] and these small steps make success beget success.

In negotiation, the application is "aim for low-hanging fruit." If both parties agree on some small points early on, the history of agreeing will motivate bargaining parties to move further. This means major issues can wait, and both parties probably *discuss minor issues first*, creating a comfortable and positive atmosphere. Loss aversion will discourage both sides to jeopardize the progress made. By "chopping" a big negotiation issue into a series of small gains to achieve, we can take advantage of the way our brain works, that is away from loss, closer to reward.

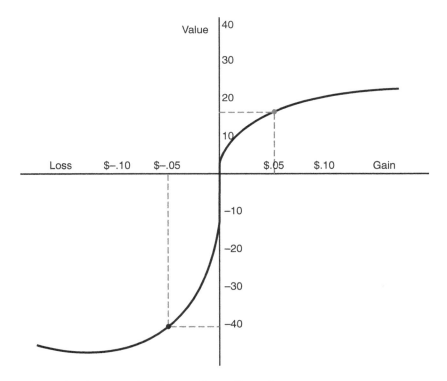

Figure 13.1 Loss aversion (Lauren Rosen Berger)

13.2.2 Cognitive Shortcuts

In Chapter 8, we learned that snap judgment has been a survival skill for humans. It allows us to use the most immediate and available information from the past and the present to make a quick decision (e.g., darkness, strange noise → run away). On the savannah, for our ancestors, it was better safe than sorry. However, lacking a big picture, this decision is always biased. Such a cognitive shortcut may spare us mental power, but it also means that in the modern era, we constantly face the risk of misinformed decisions.

In negotiation, *anchoring* is one of the most common cognitive shortcuts. It is the tendency to rely on the first piece of information such as first offer or first impression. Novice negotiators often wait for their counterpart's opening offer and make counteroffers based on this, allowing this reference point to dictate the entire negotiation. On the contrary, experienced negotiators open the bargaining and anchor the range rather than wait for the first offer, such as in the case of salary negotiation.[40] Many competitive sellers also tend to set an extremely high opening price, but low enough so customers won't walk away immediately. In nonvaluation negotiation, it has been suggested that the most critical conditions should be clear from the very beginning. For example, a job candidate may want to manage the expectation early on by saying that (s) he wants free child care and a mentor who will help with the promotion pathway. If these critical conditions are proposed later in the negotiation, it is more difficult to achieve because the employer will perceive them as concessions they have to make and will ask for something else in return.

13.2.3 Fairness

The brash business figures of the twentieth century were infamous for the aggressive win-lose negotiation practices. A big disadvantage of this competitive approach is that it is *unfair*. This is supported by decades of lab experiments. In the classic ultimatum economic game with two players, one can propose to split $10 and the other can decide whether to accept or reject the offer. If the brain is rational, the second player should accept any deal because it means (s)he walks away with some free money. However, because humans are essentially emotional beings, half of the players will reject the offer outright if it is less than 25% of the money.[41] People are ready to sacrifice their own rewards so they can punish the unfair party.[42] When they reject unfair offers, there is an increase of activity in the *anterior insula*—a critical part of the brain for emotional awareness.[43] This indicates the role of emotion (i.e., revenge) in their decision to punish the unfair counterpart rather than make a buck themselves. This psychology plays a critical role in all negotiations, including large-scale international deals. For example, reflecting on the nuclear tug of war with Iran, a neuroscientist argued that:

> The impulse to reject perceived unfairness is what motivated Iran's nuclear ambition. It would cost Iran at least 10 times less to import enriched uranium. But, defying economic logic, the country is willing to suffer well over $100 billion in lost foreign investment and oil revenue to defend a nuclear program that can only meet 2 per cent of the energy needs. The nuclear program for Iran is not nuclear but defending their integrity and independent identity against the pressure of the rest. Rejecting perceived unfairness, even at substantial cost, is a powerful motivation unto itself.[44]

The globalized economy has made us more interconnected and interdependent. We don't make a deal and run but create a network of sustainable business. Therefore, the integrative win-win approach is getting more mainstream. In the end, negotiation sets the tone for the future of working together. Screwing over the other party creates distrust and insecurity—a shaky ground for cooperation and a fertile ground for losers to seek revenge. Sharklike negotiators might get what they want, but at the cost of reputation and long-term profit. They won a battle but might lose the war. Thinking beyond number will pay off in the long run. *At the end of a negotiation is the start of a relationship.* The potential values are much greater than the extra spread one might gain from being aggressive.

13.3 Negotiation Strategies across Cultures

The process of intercultural encounter in negotiation has been described as a dance in which one party dances a waltz and the other dances a tango.[45] Culture plays an important—although certainly not exclusive—role in setting the limits and creating the opportunities. In this section, we will look at the dynamics of negotiation strategies under the influence of cultural values. We also recognize the role of national stereotypes, especially when one has no prior knowledge of the opponent. However, we strongly emphasize the decisive power of context in which specific circumstances trigger negotiators to stand their grounds or dynamically adapt to each other.

13.3.1 Stereotypical National Negotiation Styles

Negotiation patterns across cultures have been the focus of many studies that follow the static paradigm of culture.[46-47] The assumption is that national culture is fixed, and all negotiations are consistently influenced by this fixed culture in more or less the same way. Of course, this is not entirely correct. However, when one has absolute no prior knowledge of a certain culture, this approach has some advantages because it provides some simplified guesswork and a first-best-guess based on at least some kind of research.

Among cross-national studies, a classic experiment with managers from Japan, Brazil, and the United States is frequently cited.[48] Managers were put in 30-minute negotiation sessions for observation. Brazilian negotiators, for example, said "no" nine times more frequently than did US negotiators, and almost 15 times more frequently than did the Japanese. They also commanded more often, made more initial concessions than the other two groups. Their affective communication style reflects on how they interrupted each other more often while maintaining a higher frequency of physical and eye contact with the counterparts. Table 13.2 summarizes results of other tactics.

To follow are some other national stereotypes in negotiations.

China

For the Chinese, trust is often the beginning of a business deal. A friend coming to introduce and explain is always better than an outsider. Negotiators with the best network of relationship win because relationship (*guanxi*) means favors are given and will be returned.

The Chinese frequently use an extreme initial offer to prolong the process, gain more information, and create more room for concession. They often imply that there is no room for compromise, but in reality it is quite possible.[49] The Chinese are known for ruthless bargaining skills and they don't mind haggling over price. The other party may want to have flexible bargaining limits or margins because a concession given without reciprocation will make the Chinese lose face.[50-51] Renegotiation is not uncommon among the Chinese because the contract should be seen in the context of changing circumstances.

France

The French often consider themselves world leaders in fashion, art, literature, and cuisine—a stereotype of which negotiators in these fields should be aware. Due to a strong sense of pride in language, it is quite important to have a good interpreter. A relatively strong degree of hierarchy

Table 13.2 Negotiation behaviors between pairs of Japanese–Japanese, US-US, and Brazilian-Brazilian in half an hour (Graham [1985])

Negotiation Tactics and Communication Patterns	Japan	Brazil	US
Self-Disclose (We need to reduce the price 50% to cover the cost)	34	39	36
Question (Can you describe your pricing policies?)	20	22	20
Commitment (I will keep this price for five years)	15	8	13
Command (Lower your price)	8	14	6
Promise (I will keep this price for five years if you stay with us)	7	3	8
Threat (I will go to your competitor)	4	2	4
Recommendation (Your new price will attract new customers)	7	5	4
Normative appeal (We always get this from all suppliers)	4	1	2
Warning (If we can't agree, some giant companies will benefit	2	1	1
Reward (I will come to your office next time to save you the travel)	1	2	2
Punishment (I will review the clauses if you don't keep this promise)	1	3	3
Say "No"	5.7	83.4	9.0
Silent periods of at least ten seconds	5.5	0	3.5
Number of interruptions	12.6	28.6	10.3
Touching (not including handshakes)	0	4.7	0
Number of minutes looking at other's face (per ten minutes)	1.3	5.2	3.3
Initial concessions	6.5	9.4	7.1

acceptance means that team members should be selected with an eye on matching educational degree, social background, debate skill, authority level, and quality orientation. Mealtimes and food are sacred and, hence, can be used as a great opportunity to build trust.

Germany

Protocol, formality, and manner are critical. Stereotypically, Germans often prefer strong uncertainty avoidance of institutional rules, that is explicit contract, regulations, and the use of power in negotiation.[52] They scrutinize every detail and conceivable negative point before the final decision. This approach leads to a high regard of technical instead of marketing experts in the negotiation team.

Despite a score that reflects individualism according to the static paradigm, Germans tend to be group oriented in negotiation and decision making. Thorough input from the team contributes to the final consensus. Toward the other party, they may initially keep a distance because they believe that a close relationship can complicate negotiation.

To persuade German negotiators, extensive assessment of data has to be ready at hand. Arguments should focus on the "why" and "how." According to the author of *The Cultural Map*, Germans follow a *principle-first* style of reasoning: You need to learn the method, be convinced that the method is good, then you will accept the recommendation or application.[53] If German negotiators want to justify the need to open a new branch for example, they will stereotypically have questions such as: "How was the need analysis carried on?" "What is the data collection method?" "How reliable is the method of evaluation?" "Is the conclusion justified?"

India

Paradoxes are part of the normality in Indian business culture. For example, the belief that fate is predetermined in Hinduism has ingrained a deep sense of fatalism into its followers, which may lead to business behaviors that are somewhat risky. However, Indian negotiators can be extremely cautious due to their value of strong group attachment, that is whatever they do will have an impact on their larger ingroups such as families and companies. That's why it is not uncommon to see third parties at the negotiation who silently sit there to observe and give advice.[54] Trust must be earned, and the green light may come during a social gathering such as over dinner.

The hierarchical society in India emphasizes acceptance of power and privileged. Authority impact is stronger than gender impact. This explains why female managers are not rare in India. For women, high position will override the disadvantages of gender inequality and strong group attachment.

Compared to other Asian counterparts, Indians are somewhat more direct, more affective, and more hierarchy accepting. Negotiators from this country may surprise others with their competitive masculine mindset. In *What's This India Business*, it was noted that Indians would act with shock and horror when they hear the price. But one should disregard it and repeat the position. Indian negotiators are also very patient, which will wear their counterparts down. It is acceptable to leave the table because the Indian will wait for you to come back, and negotiation can start again. Patience is a virtue, and it is wise to allow the Indian to take the lead in the negotiation such as when and how to proceed.[55]

Japan

Negotiators should be aware of the *keiretsu* system—a group of companies that supply parts, equipment, service, and finance to each other, ensuring the lowest price with an acceptable return on investment. This long-term commitment among a closed circle of partners is a challenge for outsiders to step in and negotiate contracts.

Informal negotiation usually happens with a long period of discussion and consensus building among many individuals in various places inside and outside working environment. Once an agreement has been reached, formal meeting is rather a ritual than a place to make decision or change one's mind.[56] Matching authority, consensus, and long-term commitment characterize Japanese negotiators. They are excellent at learning about others, and they demand an extensive amount of information to be persuaded.

Netherlands

The Dutch have been traditionally excellent traders and negotiators due to their country's small size and the need to trade internationally. Their business culture is a mixture of strong uncertainty avoidance when it comes to rules, regulation, and contracts, but weak uncertainty avoidance when it comes to cultural values. They are known for being tolerant of different viewpoints and ways of life. Femininity plays a central role in the decision-making process with plenty of lengthy discussion. Their negotiation style is based on consensus. To persuade the Dutch, these factors are critical: Facts, logics, pragmatism, directness, honesty, and modesty.

Russia

Despite a feminine score on the static index of Hofstede (36), Russia is stereotypically masculine. They use extreme initial offers and expect every concession to be returned. The Cold War has made many believe that Russian negotiators often tough things out, regarding concession as a sign of weakness and not a gesture of goodwill, flexibility, or trust. In the postwar negotiation, the United States made 82% of its concessions in the first round, considerably more than did the Russians.[57]

The author of *The World's Business Cultures and How to Unlock Them* suggested that because "Russians combine hard-nosed negotiation skills with the personal touch," one should show the "human side" by understanding their many layers of hierarchy,[58] the need of status, the strong sense of pride, and the emphasis on social bonding. Russian culture is stereotypically a "coconut" culture in which people tend to be "hard" on the outside. They rarely smile, don't easily engage in conversation, look tough and even aggressive. However, if you manage to break through the hard outer shell, they can become your most loyal, truthful, and collaborative business partners.

United Kingdom

Negotiators from the United Kingdom are stereotypically analytical. They tend to regard emotional displays as improper. For those who are not used to indirect communication and reading between lines, negotiating with the partners from the United Kingdom can be confusing. However, despite the stereotypes of being indirect and polite, "the English can be tough and ruthless. They excel at intelligence gathering and political blackmail. Because they sometimes appear quaint and eccentric, negotiators may underestimate their skills."[59]

United States

Stereotypically, negotiators from the United States tend to embrace a masculine approach, that is goal, profit, and deal oriented. Their short-term orientation often quickly moves the negotiation past the phase of learning about each other and relationship building quickly. Their negotiation is typically a factual approach with logical appeals.[60] They make concessions early in the negotiation to establish relationship and continue to make many small ones throughout the process until they can finalize the list of concessions into an overall agreement.

A very stereotypical US negotiator, as described by the authors of *Smart Bargaining*, is someone who may appear to overembrace her/his self-confidence and masculinity with somewhat demanding tactics: "Get to the point, don't waste my time," "put your card on the table," "a deal is a deal," and so forth.[61] The advantages of this approach are that negotiators tend to make their priority message clear, showing trust willingly and spontaneously with a problem-solving mindset. The disadvantages of this approach are that it makes negotiators appear aggressive with a minimal interest in relationship and long-term commitment.

It is extremely important that the previously mentioned stereotypes are understood as truly stereotypes. They should be used as first-best-guesses only when we have little or absolute no prior knowledge of the counterparts. Culture is dynamic, and if we rely on stereotypes, we will send ourselves down a very problematic path.

13.3.2 Cross-Cultural Findings

If we go one step beyond the static mindset of national profiles, a value-based framework of negotiation strategies offers further advantages. As national borders are removed, we can start to see how negotiators can be both the product of their cultural values and the producer of a new culture as they may adjust to the values of their counterparts. Table 13.3 gives an overview of negotiation strategies along the line of values that prevail in various situations of negotiation.

13.3.3 Context Dependence

A major weakness of the current literature on negotiation is that the focus is limited within a "national style." Let's go back to the classic study on negotiation behaviors of managers from Japan, Brazil, and the United States (Table 13.2). What we learn from this study is that when negotiators from these countries negotiate with *their own compatriots*, they tend to have

Table 13.3 Negotiation strategies across cultural values and communication patterns

Cultural Values Patterns of Communication	Negotiation Strategies
Strong Group Attachment (Collectivism)	• Trust comes before business. Strategy: Arrange ample time for relationship building. For example, hosting an introduction-week trip where one party is invited to the host country prior to the negotiation. • Tend to have long and detailed discussion. Strategy: Translate clauses into their language and send these in advance. • Tend to use attachment to an ingroup as excuses (e.g., I'm with you, but my partner does not agree"). Strategy: Get it in writing and/or negotiate directly with the partner. • Tend to be conscious about face. Strategy: Avoid direct criticism; create a face-saving way for them to come back to the negotiation, or to make concessions without appearing to give in; giving face whenever possible. • Tend to prioritize connection. Strategy: Show them your network, for example, former clients; get ready to negotiate through third parties and mediation. • May regard verbal agreement or a handshake as binding. Strategy: Informally put it in written form such as a "thank you" letter. • Legality such as citing what would happen if one side acted fraudulently may be interpreted as distrust. Strategy: Say that it is more a matter of formality than trust. You have no doubt that the agreement is mutually respected. • May see the contract as a signal of trust and relationship, or a generic guide for future negotiation rather than a binding agreement. Partners should go deeper than mere simple and literal written words and be flexible when circumstances change. Strategy: Prepare in advance which clauses/ conditions can be reopened and renegotiated; think of the contract as a single step in a chess game rather than a game that is finished. • The goal of negotiation is not a signed contract, but the creation of a relationship.
Weak Group Attachment (Individualism)	• Tend to have fixed-pie bias, failing to realize that the counterparts may have opposite priorities.[a] Strategy: Plan carefully on what to show as your real interests. • Tend to have self-serving bias, that is, attributing positive events to one's own character (e.g., We are being fair, so we will give you free service), and negative events to external factors (e.g., We can't deliver on that date because of the custom policies). Strategy: Bring it to their attention. Say: "You have the power to change the situation." • Tend to have a strong sense of fairness for one's self, rejecting offers if they are perceived as unfair,[b] or if offers are put in the loss frame.[c]
Strong Hierarchy Acceptance	• Tend to have more loss aversion.[d] • Tend to have top-down decision approach. • In combination with indirect communication, hard to identify the decision maker. Strategy: Pay attention to canteen rituals and seating arrangement, to those who get the greeting, who team members quietly look at, who are served tea first, and so forth. Ask questions and observe to whom people turn their eyes. • Tend to have power vested in person than position. Influential people can be a mother whose name is not even on the organizational chart but wields decisive power. • Decision maker is often busy with multiple projects. Strategy: Organize the negotiation in a foreign country to create extended access to the chief negotiator. • Match authorities of similar level to speed up decision making and avoid face loss. • When the chief negotiator is not present, make all commitment tentative and conditional.[c] • Practice patience and accept prolonged periods of no progress, especially before final approval.

(continued)

Table 13.3 (Cont.)

Cultural Values Patterns of Communication	Negotiation Strategies
Weak Hierarchy Acceptance (Egalitarian)	• May employ both consensus (e.g., the Netherlands) and top-down (e.g., the United States) approach decision-making process. • May have similar titles but different functions. Strategy: Invest in identifying decision makers.
Masculine Gender Association	• Tend to have more loss aversion.[f] • Tend to view concessions as a sign of weakness. • Tend to dominate with power tactics/win-lose approach. • Tend to start with extreme positions such as a high price. Strategy: Bring it to their attention. Ask: "Why is it a reasonable demand? What is your principle?"; give a warning and explain the consequence: "If that is the price, this will happen."
Feminine Gender Association	• May have less extreme positions or may regard extreme positions as a discouragement for cooperation. • Tend to go for win-win/problem-solving approach
Strong Uncertainty Avoidance	• Tend to have logical appeals based on objective facts and numbers. Strategy: To persuade, give great importance to documentation and formal sources as proof. • Tend to legitimize position with reference to law, procedures, and moral codes.[g] Strategy: Use authority of law and regulation to persuade, for example, "I'm sorry, but I have to adjust to regular procedures." • Tend to use formal language.[h]
Weak Uncertainty Avoidance	• Tend to be more flexible with structure, rituals, deadlines, and procedures. Strategy: Gain sympathy from them; share with them the serious consequence you have to endure.
Future Orientation	• A successful deal means more than a deal; it also means a long-term interpersonal relationship. Strategy: Highlight long-term benefit and mutual interest in the future. • Tend to prioritize sustainability and quality.
Present/ Short-Time Orientation	• Tend to aim for rapid deals. Tend to negotiate quickly with substantial concessions. Tend to prefer quick, short-term reward. The goal is to get the deal. Strategy: Outwait them, let them win over small issues; leave major concessions until the final stage. However, note that if you don't make concessions on time, they will break off easily and try their luck with other parties. • Tend to be opportunistic, analyzing the deal in terms of payoff, grabbing the chance for an easy profit. • Tend to take risk.
Direct	• Tend to rely on verbal, explicit messages. Tend to rely on facts. • May appear to be aggressive, pushy, claiming values. Strategy: Separate people from problem.
Indirect	• Tend to avoid writing things down, prefer verbal agreement, especially when combined with weak uncertainty avoidance. This open-endedness can lead to renegotiation, that is what has been agreed upon will be brought back and reconsidered. • Tend to imply with implicit messages. For example, "We have a difficult situation" indicates an impasse. Strategy: Read between lines; be attentive; be proactive in asking questions; employ native interpreters or mediators. • May not provide many facts and detail for the other party to work with, hence, creating a feeling of confusion/operation in the dark.

Table 13.3 (Cont.)

Cultural Values Patterns of Communication	Negotiation Strategies
M-time	• Tend to outline alternatives, contingencies, backup positions, bluffs, guarantees, and tests of compliance ahead of time. • Tend to make many small concessions during the whole process and expect the counterparts to reciprocate. It's a task-oriented linear form of relationship building (i.e., relationship is built gradually by gives and takes). • Deadlines are important guidelines to progress.
P-Time	• Tend to formulate positions gradually during the process with strong personal investment. Therefore, rejecting this position may be taken personally. • Tend to discuss all issues prior to making concessions. Major concessions are made near the final agreement. It's a holistic approach to relationship building (i.e., relationship has been established before the negotiation, tested during, and fostered after the negotiation). • Deadlines are to be changed according to specific contexts. Motivation is more important than momentum. Future is uncertain, and there should be provisions for a respectable withdrawal if promises can't be kept.
Affective	• May use somewhat insulting tactics to test the commitment of the opponent. If you really want the deal, wait patiently, and separate the people from the problem. • When the counterpart is silent, affective negotiators tend to interpret this lack of response as rejection. They then argue or, worse, make unnecessary concessions (i.e., lower the price) or disclose more information than needed.
Neutral	• Manners are as important as scoring points, that is how one negotiates versus what one negotiates. • Balance and restrain are essential. Affective emotional expression is seen as a lack of experience and self-control. Strategy: Show comfort with silence, practice active listening and observation of nonverbal cues.

Notes

a Gelfand, Michele J., and Sophia Christakopoulou. 1999. "Culture and Negotiator Cognition: Judgment Accuracy and Negotiation Processes in Individualistic and Collectivistic Cultures." *Organizational Behavior and Human Decision Processes* 79(3): 248–269. doi:10.1006/obhd.1999.2845.
b Gelfand, Michele J., Marianne Higgins, Lisa H. Nishii, Jana L. Raver, Alexandria Dominguez, Fumio Murakami, Susumu Yamaguchi, and Midori Toyama. 2002. "Culture and Egocentric Perceptions of Fairness in Conflict and Negotiation." *Journal of Applied Psychology* 87(5): 833–845. doi:10.1037//0021-9010.87.5.833.
c Wang, Mei., Marc Oliver Rieger, and Thorsten Hens. 2016. "The Impact of Culture on Loss Aversion." *Journal of Behavioral Decision Making* 30(2): 270–281. doi:10.1002/bdm.1941.
d ibid.
e Glenn, E. S., D. Witmeyer, and K. A. Stevenson. 1977. "Cultural Styles of Persuasion." *International Journal of Intercultural Relations* 1(3): 52–66. doi:10.1016/0147-1767(77)90019-0.
f Wang, Mei., Marc Oliver Rieger, and Thorsten Hens. 2016. "The Impact of Culture on Loss Aversion." *Journal of Behavioral Decision Making* 30(2): 270–281. doi:10.1002/bdm.1941.
g Giebels, Ellen., Miriam S. D. Oostinga, Paul J. Taylor, and Joanna L. Curtis. 2017. "The Cultural Dimension of Uncertainty Avoidance Impacts Police–Civilian Interaction." *Law and Human Behavior* 41(1): 93–102. doi:10.1037/lhb0000227.
h Merkin, Rebecca S. 2006. "Uncertainty Avoidance and Facework: A Test of the Hofstede Model." *International Journal of Intercultural Relations* 30(2): 213–228. doi:10.1016/j.ijintrel.2005.08.001.

certain behaviors and follow certain strategies. However, international business means negotiating with foreigners. Depending on specific contexts, they might have the same or completely different behaviors. If we take within-group data for the truth, we will be taken by surprise to see that at between-group level, people deviate significantly from what would be the stereotypical attitude in their native culture.[62] For example, Japanese may not "act Japanese"[63] because they tend to adjust with more direct communication style when doing business with non-Japanese.[64] Similarly, due to self-adjustment, Chinese negotiators may appear to be both very deceptive and very sincere.[65] Despite being stereotypically indirect, the Chinese can have quite a blunt and testy negotiation style[66] in which they ignore nonverbal cues and challenge everything and question every clause.[67] In another study, French-speaking Canadians choose a more win-win approach when negotiating with English-speaking Canadians than they normally do among themselves.[68]

The dynamics of context also manifests itself in the way individuals from each culture perceive their counterparts. For example, a study found that Portuguese managers prefer to do business with Scandinavians—who are more culturally different, and not with Brazilians and Spaniards with whom they are culturally more similar. For them, cultural similarities are for social relationships, and cultural differences—in this case—bring advantages for business.[69] Factors such as history and politics play a critical role. Vietnamese negotiators, for example, will behave differently toward business counterparts from the United States, Korea, Japan, France, and China. While all these countries were addressed as "invaders" in their history textbook, in the mind of many Vietnamese people, Korea's role in the war is forgotten, the United States is forgiven, Japan is respected, France is loved, and China is a frenemy with deep shared interests and deep mutual distrust.[70] Thus, *inter*cultural negotiation is a whole world different than *intra*cultural negotiation. And simple international comparisons are, in fact, fallacies.

It is critical to note that negotiation contains elements different from those in usual communication. In negotiation, people exchange masses of information *not* because they want to intellectually understand each other. When negotiators communicate, their ultimate goal is not about gaining a thorough insight of the counterpart's belief, values, and attitude. Rather, their goal is to have mutual adjustments in view of maximizing outcomes. Their main job is to *negotiate*, that is give and take, exchange and switch, adapt and lead, discard and replace, and so forth until an agreement is reached. Thus, negotiation, by definition, is a process of shaping and reshaping ideas, values, assumptions, and behaviors. Negotiators tend to adapt to a certain extent that they deem useful. That's why during negotiation, *national culture is a relatively poor predictor of process and outcomes.*[71] Instead, there is no simple formula for success. Each situation must be assessed within its own unique set of circumstances.

Summary

1. Learning about others:
   - Have an open mind to understand that the counterparts may have different motives than we do. Think of interest, not outcomes.
   - Think about what others feel (perspective taking), not only feel what others feel (empathy).
2. Building relationships:
   - Relationship can be either a *requirement* for a deal to happen, or comes afterward as a *consequence* of a deal among trusted partners. Regardless of the process, negotiators strive for the point where contract is no longer necessary because, by then, relationship *is* the contract.
   - Building a relationship starts with seeking similarities. Small similarities can overcome big differences.
3. Team selection:
   - A good negotiator is someone who can match the cultural value that prevails at a specific moment of negotiation.
   - Due to gender biases, women face both advantages and disadvantages in negotiation.

4. Interpreter: The best interpreters are multicultural people who can reveal hidden messages and act as a bridge in building a relationship.
5. Time: Negotiators with future orientation and flexibility often outwait those with short-term orientation and gain advantage.
6. Place: Home court is a critical advantage in negotiation.
7. Priming: Negotiators can prime the environments to trigger the feelings and behaviors they want the counterparts to have.
8. Biases are commonly used as negotiation strategies:
    - Loss framing gets more attention but also makes us ignore the benefit of gain.
    - Anchoring makes us stick to the first price. Negotiators should open the bargaining instead of waiting for the first offer.
    - Consider fair play because negotiators may choose to sacrifice their own benefit to punish unfair counterparts.
9. National negotiation styles are often stereotypes, but can act as first-best-guesses when one has no prior knowledge about the counterparts. A value-based framework of negotiation strategies offers further advantages.
10. Negotiation is a process of *shaping* and *reshaping* ideas, cultural values, assumption, and behaviors. Negotiators tend to adapt to a certain extent that they deem useful. They negotiate with different partners in different ways. National profiles are often unreliable in predicting negotiation outcomes.

Notes

Don't forget to go to the end of the book for case studies.

1 Karrass, Chester Louis. 1996. *In Business as in Life: You Don't Get What You Deserve You Get What You Negotiate.* Los Angeles: Stanford Street Press.
2 Galinsky, Adam D., William W. Maddux, Debra Gilin, and Judith B. White. 2008. "Why It Pays to Get Inside the Head of Your Opponent." *Psychological Science* 19(4): 378–384. doi:10.1111/j.1467-9280.2008.02096.x.
3 Mumpower, Jeryl L., Jim Sheffield, Thomas A. Darling, and Richard G. Miller. 2004. "The Accuracy of Post-Negotiation Estimates of the Other Negotiator's Payoff." *Group Decision and Negotiation* 13(3): 259–290. doi:10.1023/b:grup.0000031089.91654.26.
4 Baumeister, Roy F., Mark Muraven, and Dianne M. Tice. 2000. "Ego Depletion: A Resource Model of Volition, Self-Regulation, and Controlled Processing." *Social Cognition* 18(2): 130–150. doi:10.1521/soco.2000.18.2.130.
5 Bendersky, Corinne., and Jared R. Curhan. 2009. "Cognitive Dissonance in Negotiation: Free Choice or Justification?" *Social Cognition* 27(3): 455–474. doi:10.1521/soco.2009.27.3.455.
6 Traavik, Laura E. M. 2011. "Is Bigger Better? Dyadic and Multiparty Integrative Negotiations." *International Journal of Conflict Management* 22(2): 190–210. doi:10.1108/10444061111126701.
7 Marsh, David. 2006. "When in Germany, It's All Right to Mention the War." *Financial Times.* April 25. www.ft.com/content/746104f8-d481-11da-a357-0000779e2340.
8 Tusche, A., A. Bockler, P. Kanske, F.-M. Trautwein, and T. Singer. 2016. "Decoding the Charitable Brain: Empathy, Perspective Taking, and Attention Shifts Differentially Predict Altruistic Giving." *Journal of Neuroscience* 36(17): 4719–4732. doi:10.1523/jneurosci.3392-15.2016.
9 Galinsky, Adam D., William W. Maddux, Debra Gilin, and Judith B. White. 2008. "Why It Pays to Get Inside the Head of Your Opponent." *Psychological Science* 19(4): 378–384. doi:10.1111/j.1467-9280.2008.02096.x.
10 Raider, Ellen. 1982. *International Negotiations: A Training Program for Corporate Executives and Diplomats.* Brooklyn, NY: Ellen Raider International, and Plymouth, MA: Situation Management System.

11 Azevedo, Guilherme. 2008. "Brazilian Management in China and a Theory of the Formation of Hybrid Organizational Cultures." Paper presented at the European Group of Organizations Studies (EGOS) conference, Amsterdam, the Netherlands.

12 Davel, Eduardo., Jean-Pierre Dupuis, and Chanlat Jean-François. 2013. *Cross-Cultural Management Culture and Management across the World*, 46–147. London: Routledge.

13 Adler, Nancy J. 2002. *International Dimensions of Organizational Behavior*, 223. 4th ed. Cincinnati, OH: South-Western.

14 Graham, John L. 1983. "Brazilian, Japanese, and American Business Negotiations." *Journal of International Business Studies* 14(1): 47–61. doi:10.1057/palgrave.jibs.8490506.

15 Mazei, Jens., Joachim Hüffmeier, Philipp Alexander Freund, Alice F. Stuhlmacher, Lena Bilke, and Guido Hertel. 2015. "A Meta-Analysis on Gender Differences in Negotiation Outcomes and Their Moderators." *Psychological Bulletin* 141(1): 85–104. doi:10.1037/a0038184.

16 "Women and Negotiation: Are There Really Gender Differences?" 2015. Knowledge@Wharton. October 26. http://knowledge.wharton.upenn.edu/article/women-and-negotiation-are-there-really-gender-differences/.

17 Halliday, M. A. K. 1991. "The Notion of 'Context' in Language Education." In *Language Development: Interaction and Development*, ed. T. Le. and M. McCausland, 269–290. Launceston: University of Tasmania.

18 Jandt, Fred E. 2005. *An Introduction to Intercultural Communication: Identities in a Global Community*. 4th ed. Thousand Oaks, CA: Sage Publications.

19 Fotiadi, Ioanna. 2015. "Interpreters: The Invisible Force behind the Negotiation." *Altar of the Twelve Gods Sees the Light*. August 19. www.ekathimerini.com/200704/article/ekathimerini/community/interpreters-the-invisible-force-behind-the-negotiation.

20 Adler, Nancy J. 2002. *International Dimensions of Organizational Behavior*, 219. 4th ed. Cincinnati, OH: South-Western.

21 Engholm, Christopher. 1991. *When Business East Meets Business West: The Guide to Practice and Protocol in the Pacific Rim*. New York: Wiley.

22 Adler, Nancy J. 2002. *International Dimensions of Organizational Behavior*, 219. 4th ed. Cincinnati, OH: South-Western.

23 Ferraro, Gary P. 2002. *The Cultural Dimension of International Business*, 123. 4th ed. Upper Saddle River, NJ: Prentice Hall.

24 Harris, Philip R., and Robert T. Moran. 1987. *Managing Cultural Differences*. 2nd ed. Houston, TX: Gulf Publishers.

25 Salacuse, Jeswald W., and Jeffrey Z. Rubin. 1990. "Your Place or Mine? Site Location and Negotiation." *Negotiation Journal* 6(1): 5–10. doi:10.1111/j.1571–9979.1990.tb00548.x.

26 Morris, Michael W. 2005. "When Culture Counts-and When It Doesn't." *Negotiation* June: 3–5.

27 Berger, Jonah., Marc Meredith, and S. Christian Wheeler. 2008. "Contextual Priming: Where People Vote Affects How They Vote." *Proceedings of the National Academy of Sciences* 105(26): 8846–8849. doi:10.1073/pnas.0711988105.

28 Williams, Lawrence E., and John A. Bargh. 2008. "Experiencing Physical Warmth Promotes Interpersonal Warmth." *Science* 322(5901): 606–607. doi:10.1126/science.1162548.

29 Maxwell, Sarah., Pete Nye, and Nicholas Maxwell. 1999. "Less Pain, Same Gain: The Effects of Priming Fairness in Price Negotiations." *Psychology and Marketing* 16(7): 545–562. doi:10.1002/(sici)1520–6793(199910)16:7<545::aid-mar1>3.0.co;2-i.

30 McGinn, Kathleen L., and Markus Nöth. 2012. *Communicating Frames in Negotiations*, 1–16. Working paper. Harvard Business School.

31 Sperling, Carrie. 2010. "Priming Legal Negotiations through Written Demands." *Catholic University Law Review* 60(1): 107–143. https://scholarship.law.edu/cgi/viewcontent.cgi?article=3228&context=lawreview.

32 Fisher, Roger., and William Ury. 1981. *Getting to Yes*. Boston: Houghton Mifflin, and New York: Penguin.

33 Adler, Nancy J. 2002. *International Dimensions of Organizational Behavior*, 218–219. Cincinnati, OH: South-Western.

34 Zhou, Jing., Zhang-Ran Zhang, and Tian Xie. 2014. "Making Collaborators Happy: The Outcome Priming Effect in Integrative Negotiation." *Public Personnel Management* 43(3): 290–300. doi:10.1177/0091026014533876.

35 Kay, Aaron C., S. Christian Wheeler, John A. Bargh, and Lee Ross. 2004. "Material Priming: The Influence of Mundane Physical Objects on Situational Construal and Competitive Behavioral Choice." *Organizational Behavior and Human Decision Processes* 95(1): 83–96. doi:10.1016/j.obhdp.2004.06.003.

36 Tom, Sabrina M., Craig R. Fox, Christopher Trepel, and Russell A. Poldrack. 2007. "The Neural Basis of Loss Aversion in Decision-Making under Risk." *Science* 315(5811): 515–518. doi:10.1126/science.1134239.

37 Yacubian, Juliana., Jan Gläscher, Katrin Schroeder, Tobias Sommer, Dieter F. Braus, and Christian Büchel. 2006. "Dissociable Systems for Gain- and Loss-Related Value Predictions and Errors of Prediction in the Human Brain." *Journal of Neuroscience* 26(37): 9530–9537. doi:10.1523/jneurosci.2915-06.2006.

38 Neale, Margaret A., and Max H. Bazerman. 1985. "The Effects of Framing and Negotiator Overconfidence on Bargaining Behaviors and Outcomes." *Academy of Management Journal* 28(1): 34–49. doi:10.2307/256060.

39 Amabile, Teresa., and Steven J. Kramer. 2016. "The Power of Small Wins." *Harvard Business Review*. https://hbr.org/2011/05/the-power-of-small-wins.

40 Thorsteinson, Todd J. 2011. "Initiating Salary Discussions with an Extreme Request: Anchoring Effects on Initial Salary Offers." *Journal of Applied Social Psychology* 41(7): 1774–1792. doi:10.1111/j.1559-1816.2011.00779.x.

41 Camerer, Colin F. 2011. *Behavioral Game Theory: Experiments in Strategic Interaction*. Princeton, NJ: Princeton University Press.

42 Sanfey, Alan G., James K. Rilling, Jessica A. Aronson, Leigh E. Nystrom, and Jonathan D. Cohen. 2003. "The Neural Basis of Economic Decision-Making in the Ultimatum Game." *Science* 300(5626): 1755–1758. doi:10.1126/science.1082976.

43 Gu, Xiaosi., Patrick R. Hof, Karl J. Friston, and Jin Fan. 2013. "Anterior Insular Cortex and Emotional Awareness." *Journal of Comparative Neurology* 521(15): 3371–3388. doi:10.1002/cne.23368.

44 Wright, Nicholas., and Karim Sadjadpour. 2014. "The Neuroscience Guide to Negotiations with Iran." *The Atlantic*. January 14. www.theatlantic.com/international/archive/2014/01/the-neuroscience-guide-to-negotiations-with-iran/282963/.

45 Tinsley, C., J. Curhan, and R. S. Kwak. 1999. "Adopting a Dual Lens Approach for Examining the Dilemma of Differences in International Business Negotiations." *International Negotiation* 4(1): 5–22. doi:10.1163/15718069920848345.

46 Tenbrunsel, Anne E., and Max H. Bazerman. 2000. "Working Women." In *Teaching Materials for Negotiation and Decision Making*, ed. Jeanne M. Brett. Evanston, IL: Northwestern University, Dispute Resolution Research Center.

47 Wade-Benzoni, Kimberly A., Tetsushi Okumura, Jeanne M. Brett, Don A. Moore, Ann E. Tenbrunsel, and Max H. Bazerman. 2002. "Cognitions and Behavior in Asymmetric Social Dilemmas: A Comparison of Two Cultures." *Journal of Applied Psychology* 87(1): 87–95. doi:10.1037//0021-9010.87.1.87.

48 Graham, John L. 1985. "The Influence of Culture on the Process of Business Negotiations: An Exploratory Study." *Journal of International Business Studies* 16(1): 81–96. doi:10.1057/palgrave.jibs.8490443.

49 De Lozier, M. W., and Chi, Y. 2000. Rules to Follow for Successful Chinese Business Relationships. In *International business practices: Contemporary readings*, ed. D. L. Moore, and S. Fullerton, 179–184. Ypsilanti, MI: Academy of Business Administration.

50 Ghauri, Pervez., and Tony Fang. 2001. "Negotiating with the Chinese: A Socio-Cultural Analysis." *Journal of World Business* 36(3): 303–325. doi:10.1016/s1090-9516(01)00057-8.

51 Ma, Zhenzhong. 2006. "Negotiating into China: the Impact of Individual Perception on Chinese Negotiation Styles." *International Journal of Emerging Markets* 1(1): 64–83. doi:10.1108/17468800610645013.

52 Tinsley, Catherine H. 2001. "How Negotiators Get to Yes: Predicting the Constellation of Strategies Used across Cultures to Negotiate Conflict." *Journal of Applied Psychology* 86(4): 583–593. doi:10.1037/0021-9010.86.4.583.

53 Meyer, Erin. 2014. *The Culture Map: Breaking through the Invisible Boundaries of Global Business.* New York: Public Affairs.

54 Foster, Dean Allen. 1992. *Bargaining across Borders: How to Negotiate Business Successfully Anywhere in the World*, 254. 2nd ed. New York: McGraw-Hill.

55 Moran, Robert T., and William G. Stripp. 1991. *Dynamics of Successful International Business Negotiations.* Houston, TX: Gulf.

56 Sebenius, James K. 2002. "The Hidden Challenge of Cross-Border Negotiations." *Harvard Business Review* 80(3): 76–85.

57 Jensen, Lloyd. 1976. "Soviet-American Behavior in Disarmament Negotiations." In *The 50 % Solution*, ed. I. W. Zartman, 288–321. New York: Anchor.

58 Tomalin, Barry., and Mike Nicks. 2014. *The World's Business Cultures and How to Unlock Them*, 125. Thorogood Publishing Ltd.

59 Chaney, Lillian H., and Jeanette S. Martin. 2007. *Intercultural Business Communication*, 212. 4th ed. Upper Saddle River, NJ: Pearson/Prentice Hall.

60 Glenn, E. S., D. Witmeyer, and K. A. Stevenson. 1977. "Cultural Styles of Persuasion." *International Journal of Intercultural Relations* 1(3): 52–66. doi:10.1016/0147-1767(77)90019-0.

61 Graham, John L., and Yoshihiro Sano. 1989. *Smart Bargaining: Doing Business with the Japanese.* New York: Harper & Row.

62 Bazerman, Max H., Jared R. Curhan, Don A. Moore, and Kathleen L. Valley. 2000. "Negotiation." *Annual Review of Psychology* 51(1): 279–314. doi:10.1146/annurev.psych.51.1.279.

63 Bird, Allan., and Michael J. Stevens. 2003. "Toward an Emergent Global Culture and the Effects of Globalization on Obsolescing National Cultures." *Journal of International Management* 9(4): 395–407. doi:10.1016/j.intman.2003.08.003.

64 Adair, Wendi L., Tetsushi Okumura, and Jeanne M. Brett. 2001. "Negotiation Behavior When Cultures Collide: The United States and Japan." *Journal of Applied Psychology* 86(3): 371–385. doi:10.1037//0021-9010.86.3.371.

65 Fang, Tony. 1999. *Chinese Business Negotiating Style.* Thousand Oaks, CA.: SAGE.

66 Kynge, James. 2000. "EU Trade Deal Clears China's Way into WTO." *Financial Times.* May 20–21, 1.

67 Blackman, Carolyn. 2000. "An Inside Guide to Negotiating," *The China Business Review*, 44–46. May–June.

68 Adler, Nancy., and John L. Graham. 1989. "Cross-Cultural Comparison: The International Comparison Fallacy?" *Journal of International Business Studies* 30(3): 515–537.

69 Costa e Silva, Susana., and Luciara Nardon. 2007. "An Exploratory Study of Cultural Differences and Perceptions of Relational Risk." Paper presented at the European International Business Academy Conference, Catania, Italy.

70 Jennings, Ralph. 2017. "China and Vietnam, Best 'Frenemies' Forever." *Forbes.* November 3. www.forbes.com/sites/ralphjennings/2017/11/03/china-and-vietnam-best-frenemies-forever/#1e19daf0901c.

71 Tinsley, Catherine H., and Jeanne M. Brett. 1997. "Managing Work Place Conflict: A Comparison of Conflict Frames and Resolutions in the U.S. and Hong Kong." *Academy of Management Proceedings* 1997(1): 87–91. doi:10.5465/ambpp.1997.4980926.

14 Cross-Cultural Marketing

An interesting paradox of globalization is that, on the one hand, the world is looking more homogenous, making marketing a world-encompassing discipline. On the other hand, cultural differences are also becoming more obvious due to many factors such as the unequal development between different regions of the world, the clashes of values, the need to reserve cultural identities, and the role of local culture as resources (see Chapter 1). Marketers need to navigate through this complexity and find a balance between standardization and localization, bearing in mind the absolute need to take particular contexts into account.

In this chapter, we begin with some basic understanding of neuroscience in marketing such as the role of subconscious buying, how this may differ across different cultures, and in what way the insight from neuroscience can help marketers to conduct market research and decide on pricing policies. We then discuss how marketing strategies vary in terms of cultural values and communication styles. We also touch on the value paradox, that is, the difference between thinking and doing, between what we want for ourselves and the society. Finally, we will look at the role of advertising as the product and/or the producer of culture by analyzing how brands adapt and/or shape consumers' behaviors in the way they think about gender roles, racial stereotypes, and cultural borrowing.

14.1 The Neuroscience of Marketing

Consumer research is a well-established discipline, but it has always been limited to the impact of external conditions such as how packaging influences buyers' behaviors. With the integration of neuroscience, it is possible for marketers to discover the neural explanation for those behavioral changes. This provides interesting insight, revealing not only the true reasons for changes but also the mechanism that governs those changes.

14.1.1 Sensory Marketing

As far back as 1949, researchers already reported that most people couldn't tell the difference between Coke and Pepsi.[1] Yet, it is Coke that has been winning the branding war. The power of branding was confirmed in a 2004 study[2] in which participants gave similar neural response to Pepsi and Coke in the blind test. However, when the drinks were labeled, the region of the brain associated with reward activated strongly with a preference for Coke. The taste is similar, but customers still prefer the *idea* of drinking Coke.

A major reason for this phenomenon is that people don't simply buy a product. Instead, they make a decision based on all the memories and emotions associated with the product. Because memories and emotions are personal and cultural, the decision is also personal and cultural. When exposed to an image of Coke or Pepsi, our brain will subconsciously scan and process years of memories and emotions in which the drink is involved. They are parties (joyful with friends or cozy with families?); a talk with colleagues in the canteen (pleasant or uncomfortable?); a gathering in the local café's terrace (in the warm sunlight as in Northern Europe or in the burning sun as in Asia?); the last time of cola consumption (during Ramadan or Thanksgiving?), and so forth. Our conscious brain was probably not aware of the drinks in these events. We would not even remember what we consumed, let alone other information such as the weather or who was wearing what. However, the subconscious brain recorded them all. Like a *secret army of secretaries who silently work for us*, the subconscious brain "tags" every detail of the surrounding world (e.g., the shop's interior design, other people, music, voices, smell, light levels, clothes) with emotional "labels" (e.g., joyful, lonely, satisfied, surprised). Note that emotions can be unconscious, while feelings are usually the physical interpretation of emotions. Billions of these "detail-emotion matches" are then stored in the vast memory "bank" of the subconscious mind, without us ever knowing about it.

This is where marketers apply the principle of "conditioning." Tobacco companies are leaders in this field because they are often banned from explicit advertising. The solution is to create a stimulus that replaces the product, then tag this stimulus with positive emotions. Customers will be reminded of the product whenever they come across the stimulus. It works. In *Buyology*, Martin Lindstrom and colleagues found out that the brain's craving region of smokers were activated strongly in both conditions: (1) Looking at the Marlboro cigarette logos and (2) looking at subliminal images such as a red Ferrari—famously sponsored by Marlboro in Formula 1. It is very likely that whenever smokers watch the race, the excitement and the red Ferrari cars trigger their craving for cigarettes as much as an explicit cigarette advertisement. Similarly, Silk Cut had positioned its logo against a background of purple silk before the cigarette advertising ban, so customers could recognize the product later on with only the purple silk.[3] In the case of Coke, the company has successfully transferred the positive emotions of Christmas to another variable: Santa Claus. For many people, seeing a big jolly man in the red suit (sub)consciously reminds them of drinking Coca-Cola.

The aforementioned examples illustrate a concept called "sensory marketing." It is based on the notion that *our bodily sensations influence conscious decision making.* Firstly, marketers make sure that the stimuli they use through five senses (sight, taste, sound, touch, and smell) are paired with their own product and trigger the right emotion. In the second stage, whenever customers encounter stimuli (e.g., the red Ferrari), these elements will immediately trigger the intended emotions, making the product more attractive, even when the product is not visible. In the last stage, an established emotional relationship between customers and the brand automatically makes the product the first choice, without the need to think. Customers also recognize the associated stimuli much quicker in their everyday life. This relationship is illustrated by Figure 14.1.

The bottom line of sensory marketing is that not only *seeing* (sight is just one sense) but also *feeling is believing* (all five senses). (Sub)conscious emotions from the past do not ultimately put the product in the shopping basket, but they give the judgment first, they weigh in early, and they

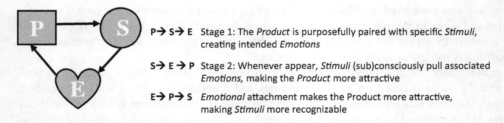

P→ S→ E   Stage 1: The *Product* is purposefully paired with specific *Stimuli*, creating intended *Emotions*

S→ E → P   Stage 2: Whenever appear, *Stimuli* (sub)consciously pull associated *Emotions*, making the *Product* more attractive

E→ P→ S   *Emotional* attachment makes the Product more attractive, making *Stimuli* more recognizable

Figure 14.1 The PSE model of sensory and emotional marketing

tip the scale. Humans feel first and think second. That's why the pioneer neuroscientist Damasio once said: "We are not necessarily thinking machines. We are feeling machines that think."[4]

14.1.2 Sensory Marketing and Cross-Cultural Findings

While a red Ferrari can trigger a strong emotion and subconsciously link it with smoking, it surely does not have the same meaning for everyone. Stimuli that trigger the right emotion for customers of this culture may not be effective for those from another culture.[5] For example, English speakers judge a brand name more *vocally*, such as whether the name or the jingle sounds appealing.[6] However, customers from a cultural background with pictographic language such as China and Japan tend to judge a brand name based on its *visual* appeal using logos, web design, or packaging. They are more likely to recall a brand if they can write it down. Generally in Asia, visual branding is the key aspect of a firm's corporate identity.[7] This may explain why advertisements from Japanese and Korean companies display corporate identity logos more frequently than US and German companies.[8]

In another study, the English were reported to be more sensitive than the French on "sound" and "sight," and less sensitive on "smell."[9] With regard to the last sense, smell is extremely effective in provoking vivid memories. While almost all sensory stimuli have to go through an information center called the *thalamus* before being sent to different regions of the brain for processing (see Chapter 4), smell stimuli go directly to the emotional center, connecting directly with memories in the past, unleashing a powerful flood of emotion. This insight from neuroscience has triggered interests in scent/olfactory marketing—a field that is historically undervalued in Western markets, making it an interesting case of cross-cultural sensory marketing.[10] Here is a summary of the comparison from a study:

> Smell has relatively low status in Western cultures in comparison with Eastern cultures. Colloquial terms for "nose" are somewhat derogatory (schnozzle, conk, hooter, snoot, snout, etc.). "Something smells" often indicates "bad smell." A large nose is considered ugly. In contrast, the Ongee of the Andaman Islands have a calendar based on the scent of flowers that bloom throughout the year. To refer to oneself, a person touches her/his nose, gesturing "me and my odor." Smell represents identity because it is the only sense that is personally different. When greeting someone, the Ongee ask: "How is your nose?" In India, greetings may include smelling someone's head. Body odor for the Bororo of Brazil and many Arabs is associated with the life-force of a person and is not something to be ashamed of. Stepping away from someone with body odor may send a negative signal of non-communication.[11]

The situated meanings of smell, as well as other senses, mean that marketers need to anchor culturally positive emotions with the sensory stimuli they use. For example, which scent is more effective to evoke good memories in the home decor department, the smell of freshly baked bread or the agarwood incense? The former is connected to an indispensable staple many people in the West traditionally rely on as a primary source of calories, the latter is linked to a daily practice in many Asian and Middle Eastern cultures. Both scents signal peace, love, family, and connectedness, but do they work at the same level for everyone?

14.1.3 Subconscious Buying

Excellent sensory marketing leads to a strong emotional attachment between a brand and its customers. In Chapter 4, we learned that the autopilot System 1 often controls our activities to prevent the consciousness from being overloaded with information and simple routine tasks. We don't want to, and we cannot rationally compare many different kinds of a product every time

Figure 14.2 Framing of a product

we want to make a purchase. The only way we can avoid spending the whole day analyzing pros and cons of each product is to *use emotions as guidance*. When we reach out to take a drink from the shop's shelves, our subconscious brain runs through all the "emotion tags" that the drink and its stimuli evoke. This happens automatically without involvement of our consciousness. In that split second, the subconscious brain performs a gigantic number of matches. Based on life events accumulated over time, the subconscious brain decides to choose Coke or Pepsi. The best emotional fit wins. *A primary decision is made in the brain without us knowing about it.* After a decision has been made, the conscious brain receives the signal and we recognize the intention to act (see Chapter 8), that is, a clear, recognizable thought "Let's choose Coke." Coke wins the branding war not necessarily because it tastes better than Pepsi, but because its marketing strategies are more successful in connecting the product with positive emotional experiences. In other words, *brands are emotions they create*. As illustrated in the stage 3 of the PSE model (Figure 14.1), these emotions act like a hidden force, giving us the nudge to pick the product without the need to think. And even if we try to think, we would not even know why we simply fall for this specific product.

Thus, the conscious brain does not completely control which brands to buy. Instead, the decision maker is our emotional history with all the life's data recorded in the subconscious brain, hidden from view. The emotions guide our thoughts and behaviors. That's why we often make the choice first, then rationalize it, make up evidence, and find logical reasons to *justify* the choice: "I prefer Coke because it tastes better"; "I picked this dish because it is healthy." In fact, better taste and healthiness are very unlikely the real reasons for purchase. Instead, underlying memories and emotions in the past trigger a deep desire to relive a certain personal experience or feeling. This is why market research usually fails. A survey or sample test asking people what they think of a product can only record a conscious relationship customers have with a brand at that very moment, not a subconscious and intuitive connection they form over a lifetime. In his book *Unconscious Branding*, Douglas van Praet succinctly concluded that brands are expectations based on memories.[12]

Daniel Kahnemans—Nobel laureate and author of *Thinking, Fast and Slow*—stated that a brand is a frame for the product the company sells. In Figure 14.2, the inner squares (read: product) have the same color (read: quality), but the frames (read: brand) have a great impact on perception. A dark frame makes the inner square lighter, and vice versa. In other words, the subconscious mind provides the frame that influences how the conscious mind perceives the picture. This explains why comparable products have different market values. Customers may want to pay a significant price premium for the frame—the intangible asset that marketers call "brand equity."

14.1.4 Reward, Pain, Goal, and Decision Making

A purchase process involves four elements. The brain needs to weigh between (1) the *reward* of owning the product and (2) the *pain* of paying for it. Base on how well the purchase can meet (3) their *goals*, customers will make (4) a *decision*.

In Chapter 10, we discussed how reward is operated in the brain. When we see images of the product we like, different reward pathways activate. The intensity of this activation is based on (sub)conscious associated memories and emotions accumulated over time. But when we see the price, a different area of the brain—the insula, often associated with pain—is activated. In other words, when looking at price, the brain experiences pain. Facing a dilemma, the brain will calculate the "trade-off" we have to make. For this reason, in a critical study on reward-pain calculation, neuroscientists suggested that we have two levers to influence the decision making: Increase the reward (e.g., emphasize benefits such as after-sale service) and reduce the pain (e.g., focus on the difference between the original and the discount price).[13]

The driving force to decide a touching point between maximum reward and minimum pain is our goal. Based on personal experience and expectations, our brain calculates the extent to which a product helps to achieve our goal. There are (1) *explicit* goals that are specific, such as drinks to quench thirst, and (2) *implicit* goals or values we want to achieve, such as status, fun, courage, or caring. If the drink is associated with the right value, it stands a much better chance of purchase.

However, because many of the goals are implicit, customers would be unlikely to declare that they buy a drink because they want to be seen as "successful people." In fact, they would reject such an irrelevant connection. A drink is a drink. Yet, the fact is, customers subconsciously connect a product with a value. For example, in an experiment,[14] two groups of participants solved a matching test on the screen. While showing the pictures, neuroscientists quickly inserted the IBM logo for the first group, and the Apple logo for the second group. The logo display was only for an extremely short period, so that participants could not consciously see it. However, their subconscious brain could still capture the image. Immediately afterward, participants performed a creativity test. Those who had "seen" the Apple logo came up with significantly more ideas than those who had "seen" the IBM logo. The value that Apple represents (i.e., creativity with the motto "Think Different") triggered behavioral changes at an implicit level. This means Apple customers may not specifically declare that they buy an Apple product because it helps them to look and/or become creative, but subconsciously they are drawn toward this brand because it matches a goal desired by themselves, but also *hidden* from their own knowing: Creativity.

The aforementioned study is critical because it shows that understanding implicit goals are crucial to attract customers. Steve Jobs once said: "People don't know what they want until you show it to them." While this is a bold statement that is not necessarily true (customers *do* know their explicit goals), it is much more useful to interpret his words with regard to customers' implicit goals—goals they don't know that they have, or even deny that they have. This requires marketers to work like psychologists. They need to do the kind of market research that not only reveals the obvious but also allows them to understand the hidden layer of desire, wish, yearning, aspiration, craving, and so forth that a target group holds dear in their subconscious mind. This is especially true from cultural perspectives because cultural values are like "water" to "fish" and "air" to "humans," that is, they are often taken for granted. We are not aware they exist. Here is an example: Many customers from societies with strong group attachment (collectivistic) and strong hierarchy acceptance are more willing to buy luxurious goods. An expensive bag signals high social status and sends out an indirect message that the owner belongs to a privileged community. In *Cult of the Luxury Brand,* the authors stated that 94% of Tokyo women in their 20's own a Louis Vuitton bag.[15] Their implicit goals are to achieve social acceptance and to show achievement, wealth, and prestige. However, if we ask the customers, many of them would honestly give different reasons why they bought a product that is out of line with their income. In contrast, typical lux consumers in Western countries are over 40. They are not easily swayed by peers and social pressure. The implicit goals behind a purchase of an expensive item are likely style and self-enhancement rather than status.

So how do customers decide? We know that when we look at a product in the supermarket, the subconscious mind processes a vast amount of information of which we are consciously not aware: Attached emotions, associated memories, and everything in the surrounding. Imagine that we type a word in Google search engine, and the subconscious mind immediately pulls out millions of search results, but we (or the conscious mind) can only see the results listed on the first page. The subconscious mind has a huge capacity of processing 11 million bits per second, while we can only consciously process 40 bits,[16] which is the upper limit of our working memory, roughly seven chunks of information such as numbers, words, or faces. The limited capacity of the conscious mind means that even if we want to make a decision rationally, we can't, because it would take forever to regard every bit of information available. We could only rely on the results listed on the first search page because it is impossible to go through thousands of others. However, what appear on the first page are usually those that have the best match, the strongest connection with our experience in the past, the most powerful emotional and cultural fit, and the nearest to reach our implicit goals. The subconscious mind has filtered a sea of information and provided us a short-list.

When we click on a result, that's when the conscious mind makes a deliberate decision. This decision, in turn, will influence how we continue to make further decisions in the future. Just like the search engine, the more we search on a certain topic, the more we get them back in the future. A search engine uses an algorithm to predict our interest, bringing us what it assumes we will like (that's why a Google search of the same keyword has different results for different people). Similarly, a deliberate decision we make today with our conscious mind will nudge and reinforce an automatic decision we make with the subconscious mind in the future. Repeatedly using the conscious pilot System 2 will bring us to the autopilot System 1. Repeated behaviors will transform into habits. That's when we stroll down the supermarket aisle, talking on the phone, and reach out to pick up a product without even thinking about it.

14.1.5 *The Benefits of Consumer Neuroscience*

David Ogilvy, an advertising tycoon, once said: "The trouble with market research is that people don't think how they feel, they don't say what they think and they don't do what they say." His words get into the heart of what has been one of the biggest challenges in business and marketing: How can we identify the gap between what people say they feel and how they feel, and further, between what they say and what they do?

Because the subconscious mind chooses a product for one reason, and the conscious mind justifies it by another, what *customers feel, say, and do are not consistent*. Hence, more businesses are replacing traditional methods with new ways of conducting market research such as MRI scanning, cap electrode EEG, biometrics, facial decoding software, eye-tracking, and implicit association tests. The benefit is manifold.

Firstly, outputs from new methods are more reliable than conscious self-reported statements from customers. There are many barriers that prevent people from giving an *honest response*, especially looking from cultural perspectives. When entering a new market, marketers are confronted by values and behaviors that not only difficult to understand but also challenging to talk about. Consumer neuroscience uses nontraditional methods to read the mind, predicting the likely acceptability of new products, brand extensions, packaging designs, advertising effectiveness, and so forth. For example, in a study carried out in Malaysia, a global supplier of personal care products could identify which of several designs communicated the concept of the modern Muslim woman. Talking about this issue can be confronting in a society that has many different perceptions of what "modern" is meant to be. For some, "modern" may even overlap "immoral." By using implicit association test, respondents were required to give immediate reaction, obtained in less than a second, to different illustrations. With no time to think, and thus, no time for the conscious mind to reshape and influence the gut instinct, the method produced a clear statistically significant result of which design elicited the most desirable emotional attributes.[17]

Secondly, outputs such as brain activities or facial expressions can reveal the subconscious mind, and thus we can capture the real thoughts and emotions that customers might *not* even be aware. For instance, Gemma Calvert—a world's leading neuromarketing expert—was taken by surprise when she discovered an unexpected twist in her finding: While 66% of the smokers declared that threatening labels effectively put them off from smoking, on a subconscious level, the labels stimulated the nucleus accumbens—the craving spot that lights up when there is intense desire for something.[18] It is a lie detector, revealing the difference between what one claims and what one feels. Thus, the antismoking campaigns were counterproductive because warning labels can trigger smokers to purchase more cigarettes.

Thirdly, consumer neuroscience helps *pricing policies* by identifying the point at which the expected pleasure of having the product exceeds the pain of paying. For example, by analyzing customers' brain reactions to a "tall" Starbucks coffee, a neuroscientist concluded that people would be willing to pay 33% more for a coffee before this product reaches the point of becoming too pricey.[19] In other words, Starbucks is missing out on millions in profits because it is not fully exploiting customer's willingness to pay. The indication of neuropricing is critical from cross-cultural perspective. Marketers know that culture influences pricing, for example, the differences range from 37% to 100% for comparable products between mainstream US and Chinese supermarkets.[20] Neuropricing helps to identify the ideal price point for diverse cultural groups, especially among those who are price and status conscious.

To conclude, the neuroscience of marketing can be associated with sensory marketing (bodily sensations influence conscious decision making) and subconscious buying (emotions guide our conscious purchase decisions). The reward of owning a product and the pain of paying for it trigger two different regions of the brain, forcing it to make a calculation. This calculation is driven by explicit goals (known to consumers) and implicit goals (unknown to consumers). With regard to the implicit goals, neuroscience helps marketers to get more reliable data, including thoughts of which consumers are not aware.

14.2 Cross-Cultural Findings

In this section, we will discuss the impact of cultural values in marketing. More specifically, we will look at appeals that are more likely to match with (sub)conscious emotional tags when a certain value prevails.

14.2.1 Group Attachment

14.2.1.1 Independent Self and Ingroup Appeal

The difference between the independent and dependent belief has a crucial impact on marketing appeals. When weak group attachment (individualistic) prevails, stimuli involved personal choice and individual success are more likely to match with positive emotions stored in the subconscious mind. When strong group attachment (collectivistic) prevails, stimuli involved group benefit, harmony, family, face, and relationship are more capable to trigger the right emotional match. For example, there are words that resonate with collectivistic values (e.g., consensus, children, bonds, wisdom, together, sharing) and individualistic values (e.g., special, discover, choice, one of a kind, first time).[21] The tagline that Hermesetas used in Portugal "It is so good you want to share it with others" matches the collective emotional tags in the mind of the customers, while the tagline that Magnum used in Germany, "I share many things, but not everything," does the opposite.

Ingroup appeal is universal because we survive and thrive by learning from our ingroup, and thus, we have evolved to favor our own culture. However, ingroup appeal can be more powerful in cultures and contexts where strong group attachment prevails. A good case in point is the creation of Mecca Cola. During the US-led invasion of Iraq, some products were boycotted, including Coke. Riding on anti-Western anger over other issues such as Palestine, Iran, Afghanistan, and the Danish Muhammad cartoons, a Tunisian-born entrepreneur in France launched Mecca Cola with a slogan: "No more drinking stupid—drink with commitment!" and "Don't shake me, shake your conscience!" The company claims on its website that 20% of its net profits goes to charities[22]—aligning with an important tenet of Islam.

14.2.1.2 Categorization versus Relationship

Group attachment influences how people categorize things. Individualistic value nudges people to look at objects according to their traits, while collectivistic value leads to a grouping strategy based on relationship.[23] For example, a collectivistic African is more likely to put a knife with a potato because one needs a knife to slice a potato.[24] In Dutch supermarkets, pasta is next to rice (category), while in Belgian supermarkets, pasta is more likely next to sauce or wine (relationship).[25] A local store in Lebanon brilliantly put a picture of a tasty traditional Lebanese *mezze* next to the nuts. It triggered all sorts of (sub)conscious emotions, from family gathering to the joyful time with friends, prompting customers to buy not just nuts but also other ingredients to make the *mezze* (relationship); many of them were placed at the other end of the store.

In her seminal book *Global Marketing and Advertising*, Marieke de Mooij argued that differing levels of emphasis on group attachment can also influence brand strategy.[26] Customers who embrace individualistic values tend to categorize based on traits, which leads to a separation between the product and its company. This tendency may make it more challenging for a brand to extend its product range. A new product must "fit" the existing categories. For example, it would take more effort to make customers accept a new food line from a traditional cosmetic company (mismatch in categorization). A better strategy is to create a new label. In comparison, collectivistic values can influence customers by blending all products that belong to a company into their zone of trust. For example, the Spanish brand Chupa Chups has gone far beyond its original product of the lollipop and covered a large product range from candy to toys and seasonal gifts. Loyal customers with collectivistic values will be more likely to accept a variety of products under the brand name Chupa Chups because the image alone provides sufficient justification to give new products a try. This may also explain why, in South Africa, packages tend to exhibit brand/producer name in a prominent way.[27]

14.2.1.3 Social Opinion

Before a purchase decision, social opinions such as those from parents may exert impact on buyers. However, this impact is stronger under the influence of collectivistic values, as shown in a study comparing Thailand, Singapore, the United States, and Australia.[28] Not only opinions from families matter but those who embrace collectivistic values also rely strongly on peer recommendation, word of mouth,[29] online forums, consumer websites, and social networks.[30] They also search more frequently and visit more shops for comparison.[31] This means marketers should pay attention to discussion platforms to encourage sharing of opinions. In contrast, customers who embrace individualistic values may rely less on social opinions and search information more on their own, which means marketers should emphasize information features, website navigation, keyword search, and virtual product display.[32]

Collective purchase behaviors support group buying—a business model that offers products at a significantly reduced price on the condition that a minimum number of buyers would make the purchase. Originally from China, group buying has become a major feature of the modern e-commerce. Due to the impact of peer review, the *popularity* of a website significantly influenced the Chinese consumers' intention to buy, while for the US consumers, not the popularity but the *perceived trust* they have toward a group-buying website leads to purchase intention.[33]

14.2.1.4 Social Interaction

When Citibank launched its credit card in some emerging Asian countries, it adopted a door-to-door sale approach rather than direct mail and advertisement on print and TV. This method was not only cheaper but also allowed personal interaction that is more appreciated in collectivistic societies, which led to high conversion rates.[34]

Such a preference for social interaction is a major reason why live-stream shopping has taken a hit in Asia. Viewers watch from home a blogger visiting a store in a faraway country, trying different products, talking to the owner, and discussing the features. Customers can enjoy the thrill of shopping with others while their identities remain hidden. They can post comments and get answers immediately. This lifelike interaction is what makes consumers with collectivistic values connect more easily with live-stream influencers. In essence, *e-commerce mixes with social platform, shopping and socializing become one activity*. It's interesting to link with China where the government bans Facebook. This partly makes social media apps like WeChat emerge as a prominent platform for all kinds of activities, a super all-in-one app that combines Facebook, banking, gaming, Uber, and so forth where people can order food delivery, book a doctor appointment, and buy movie tickets, all within a single app. It works because it's as interactive and interconnected as life is.

14.2.2 Hierarchy Acceptance

14.2.2.1 Status Appeal

The belief and acceptance that we are to a certain extent unequal have a profound impact on marketing. One's social standing is often associated with what one purchases. Aldi provides a good case in point. The brand originated in Germany and is widely known by its discounts and strong focus on basic goods for customers with low incomes. However, with the tagline "Don't change your lifestyle, change your supermarket," Aldi transformed itself into a highly tailored supermarket to fit the UK market—a hierarchical society where social class matters greatly.[35]

In the first section of this chapter, we learned that luxury goods are more associated with social status. Let's continue to look at this example to understand the complexity of status appeal. When strong hierarchy acceptance prevails, customers have a need to enhance their social standing through purchases of expensive, exclusive, and beautiful items.[36] If we look at the world's top countries for personal luxury goods, many of them are stereotypically perceived as status-conscious societies (e.g., Hong Kong, Japan, South Korea, China, and the Middle East).[37] Included in the list are the United States, Germany, and France, but culture places different meanings on luxury,[38] so customers in these country are drawn toward luxury goods for different reasons. According to a study,[39] in the United States, it's about hedonism and self-fulfillment (read: individualism). In Germany, quality trumps prestige as the motivation for luxury purchase (read: strong uncertainty avoidance). To compare, French customers have a strong sense of pride and heritage, and luxury goods are attractive because they are exclusive, reserved only for a specific group of people (read: status/hierarchy acceptance). This is the same reason many customers in Asia buy lux products. It explains why Louis Vuitton risked losing the market in Asia because the brand expanded too quickly, becoming a symbol of "accessible luxury" instead of "exclusive luxury,"[40] an item that even a domestic helper can afford.

Status appeal is also a major reason behind the market of counterfeits with the value of $461 billion worldwide.[41] People buy counterfeit to meet status need. A study went deeper and investigated customers' concern after buying counterfeit. The authors reported that while status was the first concern for German buyers, their next concern was about quality (read: strong uncertainty avoidance). However, for South Korean buyers, strong group attachment made social perception their next concern, as they worried that others would find out about the fake products.[42]

14.2.2.2 *Influencers*

The differing levels of hierarchy acceptance indicate the extent to which a person can influence the behavior of others. This means marketers should be able to separate the "product user" from the "decision maker" and the "payer." For example, who should be the target group in a marketing campaign advertising for studying abroad, just the students or also their parents and grandparents? In societies in which strong hierarchy acceptance is combined with strong group attachment, those who have money are not necessarily those who have the final say. Working parents pay for the tuition fees, but grandparents or housewives can be extremely influential in the decisions of what career to follow and in which country to study.

The use of an influencer is essential in marketing, but their characteristics may vary across cultures, for example, in terms of "expertise" and "sociability."[43] When weak hierarchy acceptance prevails, influencers are famous actors, singers, sport stars, or comedians. When strong hierarchy acceptance and group attachment combine, new aspects emerge. In Japan for example, there are "stars" and there are "talents"—the latter are chosen based on their cute look, just above average, enough to create a bond with the followers, giving them the sense that they too can become idols if they try hard enough.[44] To a somewhat similar extent, influencers in China are mostly "wanghong"—internet celebrities who have doll-like faces, that is pointed chin, large eyes, and small mouth. This restricted concept of beauty is linked with firms that produce wanghong-like "factories." Their power is so attractive that 54% of college-aged respondents in a study identified "online celebrity" as their number one career choice,[45] making the retailer industry heavily dependent on the magnet of these key opinion leaders next to famous celebrities.

14.2.3 *Gender Association*

14.2.3.1 *Achievement Appeal*

Universally a hot button, achievement appeal is deeply rooted in our psych. As observed by William Feather, the philosophy behind much of advertising is based on the notion that every individual is really two persons, the person (s)he is and the person (s)he wants to become. However, for those who embrace masculinity, this appeal matches quicker with their (sub)conscious emotional tags. Bold, assertive, competitive, and larger-than-life advertisements trigger purchase intention with taglines such as "The King of Beers" (Budweiser), "The Breakfast of Champions" (Wheaties), and "The Ultimate Driving Machine" (BMW).

When femininity prevails, Carlsberg provides a good case in point. Its famous tagline triggers the achievement appeal in a rather modest way: "*Probably* the best beer in the world." In 2016, as part of the experimental marketing around the theme "If Carlsberg did," the company revealed a pop-up bar in London, measuring five meters wide, made up of nearly half a ton of chocolate, serving half-pints of Carlsberg in branded chocolate glasses. It is a proud, impressive, but also very feminine way to show off the product's high quality in a playful and memorable way.

14.2.3.2 *Comparative Advertising*

To convince consumers that their products are better, it's tempting for marketers to make comparisons. In cultures and situations in which femininity and/or strong group attachment prevail, comparison is less favorable because its competitive nature can cause confrontation and face loss. A study reported that comparative advertising is viewed as informative in the United States, while Taiwanese consumers think it is distasteful.[46] Thus, weak group attachment and masculinity make it more likely for comparison to happen, at least in a playful way. For example, the slogan of Virgin Atlantic "Keep Discovering—Until You Find the Best" is in fact a sneaky way to play on Emirates Airlines whose slogan is "Keep Discovering." Another good example is 7UP's famous nick name: The Uncola.

14.2.3.3 Aesthetic Appeal

Based on the stereotypical perception of how men and women's bodies look like, products' shape and color can be gendered.[47] Vertical, bold, solid, straight, edgy, angular, and sharp characteristics of brand logos and products enhance brand masculinity, while airy, delicate, curved, soft, round, and smooth brand logos enhance brand femininity.[48] In terms of color, women generally have lighter skin than men, which leads to the assumption that lighter colors are perceived as feminine while darker colors are perceived as masculine. There is also a tendency of using greater number of colors with preference for warm shades for feminine products, and a fewer amount of colors with a preference for cooler shades for masculine products.[49] In cultures in which both values prevail (e.g., men are expected to be masculine and women feminine), women's products tend to come in packaging that displays softer and more harmonious colors.[50] Each culture develops its own nuances as well. For example, in many Asian markets, both male and female consumers consider glitter and faux diamond-studded accessories trendy, however, such as taste is considered kitschy in Western markets. Understanding the aesthetic perception in terms of gender is critical for marketing, as pointed out in *Why She Buys*. The author cited the case of Snugli—a high-quality baby carrier but generated little sale. After her bold evaluation "It's *ugly*, that's why it's not selling," the product was redesigned and transformed into a hit among mothers, include celebrities.[51]

14.2.3.4 Gender Appeal

In societies in which both masculinity and femininity prevail, but separately for men and women, advertisements tend to have gender role stereotypes. Men dominate in working scenarios with typically male occupational roles, sports, or relaxing activities.[52] Their body images are often alert, conscious of surroundings, open eyes, controlled bodies, serious, muscular, physically active, hands in pockets, and standing upright.[53] The associated traits with men are bravery, rationality, effectiveness, adventurousness, and technology competence. In contrast, women usually advertise for beauty, cooking, nurturing, and home products. They are often portrayed as not alert, confused, eyes closed, vulnerable, touching self, caressing an object, sexy or sexually available, dressed like a child, and lying or sitting. In Hong Kong and Taiwan, where women appear in working roles as frequently as men,[54] men are more likely to be portrayed as product authorities and women as product users.[55] Despite the rise of feminism together with the dramatic shift in the labor force and family structure, gender stereotypes persist,[56] albeit less in societies where femininity values prevail such as Scandinavian countries.

14.2.4 Uncertainty Avoidance

14.2.4.1 Safety/Fear Appeal

Universally a hot button due to its root in survival instinct, however, safety appeal triggers more emotional matches in cultures and situations in which strong uncertainty avoidance prevails. This is a critical indication for insurance, food, hygiene, and health care industry.[57]

When communicating with consumers who embrace strong uncertainty avoidance, marketers can choose to highlight the safety aspect of the product/service, or to trigger the fear appeal by making people feel that they are taking a risk if they don't make the purchase. Fear appeal is used more frequently in Japan than in the United States.[58]

Strong uncertainty avoidance also means customers are more likely to pay for high-end products because luxury indicates quality. They prefer rich, detailed, clear, and accessible information about the product, guarantee, and service policies. For example, knowing that Japanese tourists stereotypically want to overprepare, Club Med sent them brochures with airport maps showing toilets, custom booths, and other facilities.[59] Similarly, the use of influencers with expertise work everywhere. However, using professionals (e.g., doctors, technicians, teachers) to demonstrate and explain the product matches more with strong uncertainty avoidance.

14.2.4.2 Luck Appeal

Nothing is more unpredictable than the business world, and people seek ways to gain control, including superstitious practices. Fengshui, for example, is a widely popular practice in Asia, aiming to use architecture design, among others, to attract good and deflect bad energy. Hong Kong Disneyland and the Hyatt Hotel in Singapore are among many cases in which fengshui was used to boost business, from shifting the front gate by 12 degrees[60] to moving the angle of the glass door.[61]

Let's take a look at the case of "number." To adapt to the local culture, marketers often steer clear of those that are associated with bad luck. For example, Renault sold its R17 model as R117 because number 17 is considered bad luck in Italy. Cars and telephone services in Afghanistan are aware that number 39 is considered unlucky. In the United States and Europe, many airlines don't have row thirteen in their planes and many buildings skip the thirteenth floor, make it a public space, or give it an alternative designation such as "12A." For Western markets, Canon skipped number 13 in its Powershot series, and for the Asian market, it skipped number 14 because number 4 is not favored in China and Japan.

By contrast, marketers can choose to capitalize on superstition. For example, some shops played off the superstition and got people to come out with special deals on Friday the thirteenth. Icelandair ran a successful promotion allowing customers to add on excursions for $7 each, provided they booked by July 7, 2007. Similarly, Wal-Mart granted seven couples a free wedding ceremony for 77 guests on the lucky date. In China, Ericson consciously labeled some of its models with the digit 8 because it is a lucky number. Continental Airlines did the same with its simple ad: "$888 to Beijing. Lucky You." It is no surprise that the 2008 Olympics in China began at 8 PM, on the eighth day of the eighth month (August). In Vietnam, phone numbers containing or ending with 68 or 86 are fervently sought out and bought with handsome amounts of money. In Taiwan, superstitious customers are willing to spend 50% more on 25% *fewer* goods (NT$343 for a pack of eight tennis balls rather than NT$227 for a pack of ten).[62] Thus, understanding local superstitious belief is critical in pricing policies.[63]

14.2.4.3 Humor Appeal

Universally, humor is frequently used to trigger emotional matches. Jokes modulate the mesolimbic reward centers, activating the same brain region as drug, giving us the hedonistic high with a boost of dopamine.[64] However, humor is culturally specific. For example, a comparative study between Belgium and Dutch commercials showed that strong uncertainty avoiding in Belgium matches easier with explicit and straightforward jokes. But for the Netherlands, weaker uncertainty avoidance is more in sync with subtle types of humor, puns, words games, irony, satire, and parody, especially those that don't take experts seriously.[65] Another study of

12,351 ads in the United Kingdom and Greece[66] reported that British advertisements provide a great deal of pure entertainment for the low uncertainty avoiding UK consumers. On the contrary, Greek print ads emphasize cognitive humorous appeals, in an attempt to provide credible information to the strong uncertainty avoiding Greek audience. The authors concluded that "in individualistic countries with low uncertainty avoidance, consumers prefer humor-dominant messages, but in collectivistic countries with high uncertainty-aversion attitudes, humor can be used as a Trojan horse to convey the required information to the target group."

14.2.5 Time Orientation

14.2.5.1 Attitude toward Advertisement

Several studies among Macao, Georgian, British, and Chili subjects reported that consumers with past orientation are more likely to avoid advertisement, while those with present orientation enjoy advertisement for hedonistic reasons, and those with future orientation evaluate advertisements in terms of future benefit.[67-68]

14.2.5.2 Saving, Loan, and Pay Back

Among Czech samples,[69] the *future*-oriented consumers save and often pay back their loans significantly more than other people. They are also more likely to make furnishing purchases. Meanwhile, people who embrace *present fatalism* (i.e., fate decides, what will be will be) pay back their loans for purchases, but don't save much. They also show a negative tendency toward vacations abroad. Next, people with a tendency toward *present hedonism* (i.e., live in the moment, seeking instant reward) do not score high with saving and loan payment. Yet, they plan to buy. Their plan is not realistic, which makes them "appear more like dreamers who only imagine what they might buy." This study gives important indications for market research. Marketers need to know who plans to buy and who has the capacity to buy and pay back the loan.

14.2.5.3 Impulse Purchase

Impulsive buying is a sudden, compelling, hedonistic complex purchasing behavior without planning. Advertisements that trigger impulsive buying activate a sense of urgency with time limit (Sale only today), with must-haves (A perfect house cannot be without…), discounts on multiples (Buy one, get the second 50% off), rebates (Spend $50 now, get 50% off your next purchase), and images of love, sex, and food. It's estimated that $4 billion is spent annually in an impulsive manner,[70] 63% of sales in supermarkets and 80% of sales in luxury goods.[71] A tendency toward present time orientation,[72-73] individualism,[74] and masculinity[75] contribute significantly to this purchase behavior. In a study among Turkish and Iranian subjects, those with present time orientation scored higher on customer innovativeness—a tendency toward purchasing new products.[76] In contrast, future time orientation reduces the influence of impulsive buying.[77] In cultures and situations in which strong group attachment prevails, impulsive buying is considered irresponsible and socially discouraged.[78-79]

14.2.5.4 Nostalgia Appeal

Because the past will always have more emotional appeal than the present, nostalgia is an extremely important emotional driver in marketing. Nostalgic stimuli open a well of memories in the past, putting people in an emotional mood, and creating a stronger sense of connection with the brand. However, while nostalgia is a universal emotion, what triggers nostalgia is strictly culture and person specific, as reported by a study that investigated the phenomenon across 18 different countries.[80] For example, among the French, personal and cultural nostalgia are influential,[81] reflecting a past orientation of those whose pride is deeply rooted in their cultural heritage, history, time-honored traditions, and nationalism. In contrast, cultural nostalgia is less likely to be part of the experience among US subjects,[82] reflecting the young nature of the country.

Nostalgia is received differently across generations. Boomers and Gen X consumers respond to nostalgia because it takes them back to their youth and childhood. Millennials and Gen Y/Z consumers purchase retro brands because the products enable them to mix the "cool" things of their parent's generation with the technology of today[83] because "old" can be marketed as "classic" and "classic" as "cool." For example, in Vietnam, the successful coffee shop chain Cộng—meaning "communism"—has a retro style that is a glaring and shameless copy of the war time. The waiters often dress in camouflage clothing, drinks are served in kettles and military cups, and the decoration is completed with old furniture and communist propaganda posters. However, the majority of customers are young people, most of them have no direct experience of the war that occurred half a century ago. Nostalgia is *fashionable* and has little to do with personal life.

In contrast, the nostalgia wave that recently swept China involves those who were born after 1980. According to an analysis,[84] this cohort is the nation's first generation of the one-child-only policy in 1979. They are more predisposed to loneliness, confusion, and instability. They grew up in the dramatic transition to the market economy, carrying on their shoulder the mission of defining what it means to be both modern and Chinese, coping with financial challenge, fighting in the volatile job market, and taking care of senile parents. The uncertainty and anxiety are most unbearable to the posteighties, urging them to seek confirmation in the past. Nostalgia is an *emotional buffer*, helping people fight the future with a supportive hand from the past.[85] And this is an example of how marketers don't miss the chance: A restaurant in Beijing where

> diners sit at old-style wooden desks rather than tables. The menu is a multiple-choice test. Instead of waiters, there are class monitors, who respond to raised hands. The restaurant is designed exclusively for people born between 1980 and 1989; I.D.s are checked at the door.[86]

14.2.6 Direct-Indirect Communication

14.2.6.1 Implicit and Explicit Message

Communication style in terms of directness has a profound impact on marketing. In a study, Dutch and Belgium subjects judged the complexity level of 12 advertisements. Being more indirect than the Dutch, the Belgians were able to understand the ads at a *deeper* level, and thus, they perceived the ads as less complex, and more favorable.[87] For those who embrace low context and direct communication style, marketers need to consider straightforward messages; easy to understand, explicit images; strong call to action; and clear information. This also applies to situations in which customers have little or no prior experience with the product. Regardless of their cultural/personal communication style, an implicit message is difficult to catch if the context behind it is not understood.

14.2.6.2 Visual Appeal

Animation and images are more effective than text for consumers who embrace indirect style. Texts convey the message directly but graphics tend to imply. A study comparing product design between South Africa and Canada reported that indirect South African style of communication results in smaller amount of text and less product information on packages.[88] While Asian visitors like online game-animated intros, European visitors don't see their usability.[89] In South Korea, advertisements utilize much more multimedia presentation than the United Kingdom and the United States, providing a wholesome, lifelike communication style with customers.[90] Adjusting to the local ways, global brands create more *literal* visuals in the United Kingdom, the United States, and Germany, but more *symbolic* visuals in Japan, South Korea, and China.[91]

14.2.7 An Important Reminder

In this section, we have discussed a wide range of marketing strategies based on a framework of universal concerns and cultural values. It is important to keep in mind that a country does not have a fixed and static value system. Within and across countries, we also have many group and organizational cultures that the scope of this chapter can't possibly cover. Further, many of the research outcomes in this section seem to conform to the stereotypes, for example, Asian cultures are more associated with strong group attachment. This is the result of how the static paradigm of culture has dominated the field for a long time. By assuming that (1) cultural values are rather fixed, (2) opposing values can't possibly coexist, and (3) culture equates to country, research on cross-cultural marketing tends to confirm stereotypes, downplays nuances, and puts consumer behavior in separate national boxes. Marketers should be aware that indexes such as those from Hofstede's study that give a number to each country can only be seen as a *first-best-guess*. The reality is much more dynamic. It's not a number, but each particular context that determines how consumers are likely to think and behave. We will discuss this in the next section.

14.3 Context Dependence

International marketing as a study has been developed along the debate of to which degree marketers should *standardize* and *localize* their strategies in a new market. The latest approach is *contingency perspective*, which is based on the notion that effective strategies depend on particular context.[92]

14.3.1 Standardization and Universal Appeal

In 1971, L'Oréal launched its hair-color business in the United States with the famous slogan "Because I'm worth it"—written by a female copywriter, featured by a woman proudly announcing her reason of purchase as to satisfy her own need, at a time when most ads were narrated by men, selling (feminine) products that women can use to satisfy a man's needs. It came at the right time, in tandem with the gender equality movement. But when consumers in Asia read it as "Because *you* are worth it" to reduce the egocentric message of the "I" in the slogan, the company changed it accordingly.[93] In late 2009, the slogan was changed again to "Because *we're* worth it" to create stronger consumer involvement from all its markets.

L'Oréal and its legendary slogan provide an interesting case of how a brand dynamically navigates itself through the complexity of universal appeal and cultural nuances. It went from adapting to a local market (the United States) to a regional market (Asia), and then ended up with a global result. Many other brands travel the other way around, that is, start with a standardized global strategy and localize later down the way, or commit to both strategies. Regardless of the direction, standardization can work successfully if it triggers universal values such as love, family, safety, autonomy, relationship, success, and so forth. Think about Lipton's "Enjoy together" and McDonald's "I'm lovin' it." Both slogans are rooted in the universal concern of group attachment, albeit at different levels of values. "Enjoy together" triggers collectivistic emotional tags while "I'm lovin' it" triggers individualistic emotional tags. Would these two brands one day, like L'Oréal, change their slogans to "*We*'re loving it" and "*I* enjoy Lipton"? We don't know, but one thing we know for sure, the power of a truly universal appeal is not a myth.

Understanding the potential of universal appeals helps us to avoid confusion when coming across contradicting research outcomes. For example, a meta-analytic review reported that *culturally adapted* ads are only slightly more persuasive and better liked than *unadapted* ads, applied mainly to US participants and Asians along the values of individualism and collectivism.[94] This is probably a case of adapting within the boundary of universal appeal. In another example, participants came from Belgium, the United Kingdom, Germany, the Netherlands, and Spain—countries with stereotypical different values in gender association. However, these participants showed similar appeal to modesty (femininity) and adventure (masculinity), regardless of their nationalities.[95] The authors raised a question of whether it is "necessary to adapt advertising appeals for national audiences in Western Europe?" to which the answer is potentially both "yes" and "no." "Yes," if a company wants to localize with a specific effect, for a specific product, within a specific context. "No," if the company is certain that a more global appeal is good enough, especially when it wants to take advantage of economies of scale and reduced costs.

14.3.2 Localization

Nowadays, few companies question the need to adapt. Multinationals like Coca-Cola have gone beyond the classic adage of "Think Global. Act Local" to a new level of "Think Local. Act Local." Procter & Gamble even went inside the homes of 80 families around the world, filming their life's daily routines, gathering insight into consumer behaviors so that the company can improve their products.[96]

For most brands, localization is more a question of the *degree of adaptation*. Here is an example. In Asia and the Middle East, McDonald's extended its central theme of happiness to cover family life. But KFC localized one step further by not only depicting a harmonious family relationship but also adopting specific traditional themes such as Peking Opera in China.[97] In another case, Marks and Spencer did not adapt enough when it opened a shop in Shanghai. The Chinese considered it too British, and the expats thought that it was too Chinese.[98] Localization to the right amount is an art of international marketing.

14.3.3 Contingency Perspective

14.3.3.1 Value Paradox

In Chapter 4, we discussed the paradoxical nature of culture. Opposing values exist, within a society and each individual person. This is down to the neural level, as our brain can "host" many contradictory thinking patterns. A specific circumstance triggers a specific appeal, which may be the opposite of an appeal that attracted *the same person in a different context*. Because of this situational dynamics, a great part of cross-cultural marketing should be examined on a case-by-case basis.

Let's look at a study of Generation X in China for an example.[99] A paper reported that highly educated Gen Xers are *equally* persuaded by both individualistic and collectivistic ad appeals. When it comes to personal-use products, they are even more attracted by individualistic ad stimuli. The author concluded that there is a rising *biculturalism* in China where young consumers adapt to both new and old values. According to another analysis,[100] the young generations in China are experiencing a profound cultural dislocation and transformation. They walk a thin line between traditional ideas and freedom to explore new ways of life. Online social commerce functions like an alternative world where they can build their emerging identities and live a different life that may not be compatible with reality. The result is, they hold dear to both value systems that are contradictory in nature but perfectly possible to coexist.

In Chapter 4, GLOBE—a large-scale cross-cultural study—made a critical point when it reported that people may want one thing for themselves (desired) and the opposite for the society (desirable). What we do and what we believe can totally contradict each other. For example, we want to be powerful, but we dislike bossy colleagues. Consequently, market research that asks consumers about "what they want" and "how others should behave" will produce different results. With the same reasoning, an advertisement that triggers what people prefer for themselves will look very different from the one that triggers what people think their society should look like. And *both* advertisements can be very successful, to the *same* audience. This explains why Honda used "I'm independent" in Japan, and in general, Japanese ads make *less* use of group appeals and more use of individualistic appeals than the United States.[101] Similarly, while impulsive buying is associated with individualism, yet, when it comes to smartphone, Vietnamese consumers are more involved with impulsive buying than Finnish customers.[102]

14.3.3.2 *Trade-Off of Value Interaction*

Such a contextual approach also helps us to understand the trade-offs that marketers can make in each particular market. In her book, Marieke de Mooij provided some excellent cases to illustrate this perspective. For example, consumers from both Japan and China may embrace a holistic thinking style and strong hierarchy acceptance. Holistic thinking emphasizes relationship among different products, which makes IKEA's total concept of having all furniture displayed in a real-life setting very attractive. Strong hierarchy acceptance emphasizes the power of customers over sellers, and the quality of service. In Japan, IKEA failed partly because Japanese consumers marked down the do-it-yourself model, as they value quality service more than the benefit of real-life setting. In China, IKEA did better partly because for Chinese customers, the benefit of do-it-yourself outweighs a lack of service. The trade-off works in China, but not in Japan.[103] Here is a case in which the trade-off does work in Japan: While the Wal-Mart's model of low price may contradict with how the Japanese tend to associate cheap price with bad quality, the economic recession has made this model successful.[104] The lesson here is, values do not stand alone but constantly interact with each other, promoting and cancelling each other, creating a wide range of particular contexts. As we have repeatedly emphasized in this book, values are ingredients, reality is always a cocktail.

14.3.3.3 *Multicultural Marketing*

The contingency approach is critical in *multicultural marketing*. In essence, it is about creating a message that appeals to a society of many different cultures. An example comes from one of the most important moments of marketing each year: Lunar New Year. It is a catch-all phrase that is appropriate in a multicultural society where the Chinese celebrate Chun Jie or "Spring Festival," the Vietnamese celebrate Tet, the Korean celebrate Seollal and many other Asian communities still welcome the new year according to a different calendar. Asian customers of non-Chinese background will be more likely to walk in shops that show an inclusive greeting. For many, the use of "Happy Chinese New Year" seems like a "hijack" of their own cultural experience. The moment of Lunar New Year is influenced by the Chinese calendar in origin, in the same way that the Gregorian calendar is influenced by the Roman. Yet, billions of people nowadays don't celebrate the new season saying, "Happy Roman New Year," which may explain why Asian customers of non-Chinese backgrounds don't favor a monopoly of name or an attempt on "copyright," especially when that name is not even used by the Chinese. More than anyone,

Mark Zuckerberg was aware of his customer base in Asia, and he carefully used the phrase "Lunar New Year" in most of his communication.

However, let's consider a case that may give us more insight into the complexity of multicultural marketing. In 2018, Liu Wen—a model of Victoria's Secret—tweeted "Happy Lunar New Year" and received backlash from some of her Chinese fans. They insisted that, because Liu Wen is Chinese, she should say "Chinese New Year," even when such a phrase does not exist in Chinese but is only a sign of national pride. She backed down, changed it to "Happy Chinese New Year," upsetting other Asian customers and missing a chance to be an influencer instead of an adapter. The solution in her case, as mentioned in Chapter 9, is to be specific and authentic to each community. Using the correct name for each fan base takes more time ("Spring Festival," "Tet," "Seollal," etc.), but when inclusiveness is sensitive, it is the best option in multicultural marketing.

Multicultural marketing is also about not overrelying on stereotypes. No magic formula works here. Let's have a look at a 2018 ad of SunRice in Australia for an example. An Asian family is having white guests for dinner. They nervously look at the Asian food on the table (stereotype). A woman is serving (stereotype again). But when she brings out bowls of rice, the guests are happy because they could recognize a familiar food. Both the Asian boy and the white guest proceed to eat rice with … ketchup—a brilliant detail that reflects the authentic of multicultural life in Australia where cultural practices mix and evolve in surprising twists.

To conclude, culture is dynamic. Only by analyzing each particular context, marketers can come up with the ultimate combination of universal and cultural appeal for a specific product.

14.4 Advertising: Product or Producer of Culture?

Throughout this book, we have repeatedly emphasized the two-way interaction between the role of human beings as both the product and the producer of our own culture. The notion of plasticity is not only applied to our brain but also to our behaviors and values. This gives us the capacity to fit in a new culture (being the product) or to change our own culture if needed (being the producer). In advertising, this interaction is linked to a long-lasting debate between the role of advertisements as the "mirror" versus the "mold." As the "mirror," ads *reflect* the existing values and behaviors that are dominant in the society. In contrast, as the "mold," ads *shape* the society by changing existing values and behaviors, creating new patterns of thinking and doing. In this section, we will look at some of the current issues in contemporary advertising and the ways brands choose their battle: To reflect, or to create a cultural pattern.

14.4.1 Sexism

14.4.1.1 Gender and Sex Appeal

As briefly touched in the previous section, gender appeal is crucial in advertising. Up until the fifties, ads told women they need to serve the men and their place was at home (Kellogg: "So the harder a wife works, the cuter she looks"). Nowadays, woman have joined the workforce and, in many countries, outnumber men,[105] but ads still tell them they should be sexy. At one point, on the American Apparel website, male models posed in normal positions but female models posed in sexually suggestive postures.[106] This is an objectification of women, that is, women are presented not as consumers but *part of the product*, being there just to make the product look good—a regular case in car advertising. Of course, men are objectified too, but the consequence is different. A study showed that when looking at men and women in underwear, the brain perceives sexy men as "people" and sexy women as "objects."[107]

Sex appeal is a complex phenomenon. In the nineties, women found the way they were portrayed in ads offensive. During this period, it was argued that men continued to objectify women because they subconsciously want to regain power.[108] However, the third wave of feminism embraces sexuality and sees sex as power.[109] Here lies the difference between men and women. Men are generally attracted to sex appeal, but they are less likely to remember the brands being advertised in sexy ads.[110] For women, sex appeal works only when the products are expensive,[111] and when the nature of sex stimuli is commitment, such as in relationship, parenting, or romance.[112] Further, sex stimuli don't necessarily result in purchase intention, especially among women.[113] This is probably because sex has been desensitized in a society saturated with sex stimuli. Note that sex was originally used in marketing to attract heterosexual men during the time they were still the major source of buyers. Now that women control up to 80% of purchases,[114] it's time to reconsider the role of sex appeal. For example, Carl's Jr. decided in 2016 to end its famously sexualized ads, most of which featured women eating burgers while in various stages of undress.

Indeed, the field of marketing is expecting to see a powerful shift. There are two major trends that marketers need to pay attention to: "Gender fluidity" and "fem-vertising."

14.4.1.2 Gender Fluidity

Gender is fundamentally different from sex. To make it simple, sex is between one's legs, and gender is between one's ears. It means, gender is a self-perception. Gender fluidity indicates that gender identity can change between masculine and feminine, across all time scales, every few years, or even every few hours. People announce their gender identity through the way they dress, express, describe, or choose to identify themselves. As of 2018, there were nine countries with a gender-neutral option on the passport, among them India, Nepal, Pakistan, Australia, Germany, Malta, New Zealand, Denmark, and Canada. Around half of millennials in the United States believe gender does not come in two labels (male/female) but is a *spectrum*,[115] and 12% of them identify as transgender or gender nonconforming,[116] meaning they don't identify with the sex they were assigned at birth.

As consumers increasingly reject labels and stereotypes, brands are trying to align with this cultural movement. Because gender stereotypes start in childhood, toy companies are taking note, both voluntarily and under the pressure of consumers. Facing protest from a campaign group, Toys R Us and Target removed gender labels and organized toys by theme instead of gender. In 2015, for the first time, Barbie included a little boy in its ads, showing that boys, too, can play with the doll. In the fashion industry, transgender models grace the catwalk, including the boy child of actor Will Smith who appeared in a Louis Vuitton campaign, androgynously, in a skirt. In 2016, CoverGirl featured a boy on its cover.[117] The cultural zeitgeist is reaching beyond toys and fashion industries. Coca-Cola, for example, came out in 2016 with the campaign "Dude or Diva," offering teens the chance to share both sides of their personalities: "Sometimes they feel more like a dude, and other times more like a diva."[118]

Are these brands *reflecting* or *shaping* a new cultural pattern? On the one hand, they are reflecting a cultural movement and responding to consumers' demand. On the other hand, what they do is not mainstream (yet), and they are pioneers, leading the pack. Further, part of the reason why they do it is ethical. These brands consciously acknowledge the impact they make on the society, and that their ads influence how people think and behave. In that sense, these brands lean more toward the "producer" of culture than merely the "product" of a trend.

14.4.1.3 Fem-vertising

When Starbucks opened its coffee shops in Saudi Arabia, it removed the mermaid from the logo, keeping only her crown. This story did not gain a great deal of traction. But when IKEA erased all images of women, including its female designer from the 2012 Saudi catalogue in an attempt to align with the local practice of sex segregation, there was a strong backlash. IKEA apologized, yet continued to do the same thing in its 2017 catalogue for the ultra-Orthodox Jewish community in Israel. It apologized again.[119]

As a multinational, IKEA knows very well that localization is the key to success. For example, because kitchens in China are usually small, it cropped the photograph to make it cozier; or knowing that conservative Jewish families are usually big, it highlighted bunk beds and bookshelves that can handle extensive collections on Jewish law, and so forth. However, these adjustments are very different from creating women-free catalogues. Local women harshly criticized the Swedish brand for not upholding to its femininity values.[120] Its attempt to conform to the local norms sabotaged the long-term struggle of many who have been fighting for gender equality and women's right. In a case of advertising being the "product" of culture, IKEA went a step too far, not only becoming a product but also a product that many of its customers considered outdated and harmful for the social progress.

A brand can choose to be safe by releasing ads that align with the mainstream ideas. But a brand can also support ideas that *will be* the norms in the future. In 2004, when Dove found out that only 2% of adult women would consider themselves beautiful, it decided to flip the traditional script: Instead of telling women who they should be, Dove encouraged women to celebrate who they are. Its images of six ordinary-looking women of all shapes and size became one of the first advertising campaigns that went viral on social media. Dove's share of the firming location market in the United Kingdom soared from 1% to 6%, with a 700% increase in sales.[121] Dove has pioneered a powerful shift in advertising, one that *sells empowerment* to consumers,[122] disrupting the habitual thinking and calling for a change.

And so, fem-vertising was born, coupling feminism with capitalism. Since Dove's campaign, many brands have followed suit. EDF encouraged young girls to explore jobs in science, Pantene

Figure 14.3 Dove's "Real Beauty" campaign

exposed the blatant double standard that women suffer every day at work, Always and Verizon shook the conscience of millions of viewers when they showed how strong and confident little girls turned into incompetent and uninterested adults as a result of gender stereotypes, and so forth. In short, these brands tell their consumers that they can go shopping and, at the same time, challenge the norms, rewrite the rules, being the change that they want to see in the society. It's not an easy commitment for the brand. To profit from fem-vertising,[123] brands have to practice what they preach. These include donating to social cause, gender-diversifying the management board, choosing socially responsible partners, and so forth. For brands, being the "producer" of culture goes far beyond creating a good commercial, but rather becoming active agents and practitioners of what they advocate.

14.4.2 Racial Issues

14.4.2.1 Whitewash

"Whitewash" refers to the assumption that white is more beautiful. For example, L'Oréal Paris made Beyoncé's skin and hair color significantly lighter—a common case with many other celebrities such as Halle Berry, Mariah Carey, Rihanna, Tyra Banks, and so forth. Similarly, Nivea's ad boasted the slogan "White is Purity." In a Chinese ad that went viral in 2016, a woman pushes a black man she is about to kiss in a washing machine, and when the wash cycle is over, the man comes out with lighter skin.

Whitewashing occurs beyond the realm of cosmetic industry. In 2006, Sony put giant billboards all over the Netherlands, featuring a tough-looking white woman aggressively gripping a black woman by her jaw with the slogan: "PlayStation Portable White is coming." In 2013, the Italian sweet producer Ferrero made a parody of Obama's campaign with "Yes White Can" and "Germany Chooses White." In 2016, Snapchat attracted public criticism for having whitewashing filters.

Another infamous incident happened with a Coca-Cola's ad, in which white young people arrived at an indigenous town to cheer up the locals with presents. The ad accidently reinforces the stereotype that the indigenous are inferior, as they need to be saved and rescued by white people. In most cases, the companies apologized. But that does not stop some people from wondering if they brought out the ads on purpose to gain media attention, because sometimes bad advertising is good advertising. Racism can be less subtle, as in 2018, when the Swedish fashion company H&M released an ad with a dark-skinned boy wearing a green-hooded sweatshirt that said: "Coolest Monkey in the Jungle." It caused intense outrage, forcing the company to close its stores in South Africa.[124] Such accidental racist advertising happens occasionally with a great deal of media attention and damage to the company's reputation in the long term.

14.4.2.2 Racial Stereotypes

Stereotype marketing is based on common perceptions and not necessarily fact. It takes on many forms, such as portraying black people in sport, Latin Americans in outdoor activities or at leisure, and Asians at work.[125] For example, in an ad for a hotel chain, an Asian male is pictured alongside a text suggesting that, for Asians, working and living is the same thing. The hotel has "space to work, to sleep, to lounge and to live." Ads like this perpetuate the harmful side effects of the Model Minority (i.e., Asians are hard-working and successful). Despite the fact that Asian minorities have also been marginalized and face racism like other collective cultures, this positive stereotype creates an illusion that Asians do not suffer from social inequality. It dismisses problems and denies chances that the disadvantaged deserve. Worse still, this positive stereotype has been used to justify the exclusion of those in need in the distribution of government support.[126] In the 1980s, several Ivy League schools admitted that they chose other minority groups over Asian applicants in an attempt to promote a national agenda of racial diversity.[127] Holding Asians to a much higher standard also presses them to live up to unrealistic expectations, resulting in tremendous stress and mental illness, even suicide attempts among young people who are unable to deal with pressure from parents and society to be exceptionally high achievers.[128]

To conclude, brands rely on stereotypes to align with the values of consumers. However, a sense of social responsibility can influence their choice of the battle, either to (1) reinforce the stereotypes or (2) challenge the existing perceptions.

14.4.3 Cultural Appropriation

14.4.3.1 When Borrowing Becomes Exploitation

During the years of 2013–2017, the United States was shocked with a number of deaths as a result of police brutality. It sparked the creation of Black Lives Matter, and this movement spread with many poignant protests. In 2017, Pepsi released a commercial using a protesting crowd as the background. In the ad, the main character, Kendall Jenner, dropped her photoshoot, joined the protest, and finally gave the police at the front line a Pepsi. The tone-deaf ad caused public outcry on social media, condemning Pepsi for using the painful struggle of black communities for financial gain.[129] In a case somewhat similar to Pepsi, Topshop's 2017 collection caused outrage as it sold a Chinese-made jumpsuit using the *keffiyeh* pattern.[130] By turning a Palestinian symbol of struggle for independence into a festival playsuits, Topshop was accused of not only failing to acknowledge the culture that inspired its designs but also profiting off the hardship and bloodshed that typify the Palestinian nationalism.

The Pepsi and Topshop cases are classic for cultural appropriation. In essence, this means stealing, borrowing, and making profit off the cultural heritage of an already at risk and underprivileged community without proper acknowledgment or compensation. It should not be confused with cultural exchange or cultural sharing. The two main points that distinguish the difference are (1) *a power imbalance* between the party who borrows and the party who maintains the cultural heritage,[131] and (2) the more powerful party makes *profit* from the cultural heritage that they borrow without an effort to *honor* the heritage or solve the imbalance of power.

The marketing world has been stirred up with many cases of cultural appropriation. For example, Nike had to pull the legging that used the Samoan tattoo pattern.[132] The brand was accused of capitalizing on the cultural heritage of the Pacific community without paying them due acknowledgment and compensation. Similarly, Channel was lambasted by Aboriginal groups for selling thousands of Channel-branded boomerangs, each with a tag price of almost $2,000— of which none goes to the underprivileged communities.[133] In a lesser-known case, "The Lion Sleeps Tonight" is an extremely well-known song recorded by some 150 artists worldwide and played in more than 13 movies. Yet, the author of the song, a musician in South Africa, received only less than one dollar by the time he recorded it in 1952. He lived a life stricken by poverty, and when he died, his widow had no money for a gravestone.[134]

14.4.3.2 Strategies

The first and most important strategy to avoid cultural appropriation is to have a *diverse staff*. Having people with knowledge of different cultures is a sure-fire way to stay away from potential pitfalls. Companies should check the diversity level of marketing, design, and management teams on all aspects of culture: Ethnicity, age, gender, religion, sexual orientation, and educational and economic backgrounds.

The second strategy is *authentic*. In 2016, Valentino came under fire as it hardly hired any black models in a fashion show that was inspired by African culture.[135] According to critics, Valentino did not just borrow some cultural heritage but it also ignored the inequality that black models suffer in the fashion industry, and refused to give them the opportunity to be the authentic presenters of their own culture. The solution is to engage with the target culture and make it real. A good example is the 2015 Costume Institute Exhibition on the theme of China. The organizer chose to work directly with Chinese designers and promoted their products instead of imposing their own perception of China without the involvement of authentic cultural actors.

The third strategy is *respect*. In 2012, a model of Victoria Secret appeared on the catwalk wearing a colorful headdress. For the Native American community, such a war bonnet is a spiritual garb with a deep meaning. Each feather symbolizes a brave act of the warrior. It has to be earned, and it is reserved for revered elders. Facing the outrage, the brand tweeted an apology and removed the outfit from the broadcast.[136]

The fourth strategy is *giving back*, don't "crop and prop." The article 31 of the UN Declaration of the Rights of Indigenous Peoples states clearly that they "have the right to maintain, control, protect and develop their cultural heritage [as well as] their intellectual property over such cultural heritage." Here is a good example. In return for a permission to adapt their tattoos and fabric, designer Osklen paid the Ashaninka tribe in the Peruvian forest and helped them build a school.[137]

It is a good reminder for brands that the new generation of consumers increasingly regards businesses to be ethical change agents in the wider society. Seventy-six percent of millennials see companies as a force of positive social impact, and 62% regard business leaders as drivers to help improve society.[138] Brands can't be neutral anymore. They may have to take side. In the midst of our hyper-interconnected world, brands must fight for what they believe in to maintain a place in consumers' hearts.

Summary

1. Sensory marketing is based on the notion that our bodily sensations influence conscious decision making. A product is purposely paired with specific stimuli (across five senses), creating intended emotions. From then, whenever they appear, stimuli pull associated emotions, making the product more attractive even when the product is not visible.
2. The impact of stimuli varies across cultures. For example, visual appeal is very important to consumers from Asian backgrounds.
3. Subconscious buying refers to the notion that emotions guide our purchase decisions. We are not aware of these emotions, and they significantly influence which product to buy *before* we consciously know about it.
4. The reward of owning a product and the pain of paying for it trigger two different regions of the brain, forcing it to make a calculation. This calculation is driven by explicit goals (known to consumers) and implicit goals (unknown to consumers themselves).
5. Neuroscience helps marketers to get more reliable data, including thoughts of which consumers are not aware. It is also helpful in pricing policies.
6. Major appeals with regard to *group attachment* are ingroup, social opinion, and social interaction; with regard to *hierarchy acceptance* are status and opinion from influencers; with regard to *gender association* are achievement, comparison, aesthetics, and gender; with regard to *uncertainty avoidance* are safety/fear, luck, and humor; with regard to *time orientation* are saving, loan and pay back, impulse purchase, and nostalgia.
7. Marketers need to navigate through this complexity and find a balance between standardization and localization, bearing in mind the absolute need to take particular context into account.

8. Advertisements both reflect and reshape a culture. A brand can choose to be a product of culture by adapting to the local norms and stereotypes, or challenging the practices and ways of thinking, thus becoming a producer of culture. This choice is reflected most clearly in how brands deal with current issues such as sexism, racism, and cultural appropriation in a multicultural society.

Notes

Don't forget to go to the end of the book for case studies.

1 Pronko, N. H., and J. W. Bowles. 1949. "A Progress Report on Some Experiments with Cola Beverages." *Transactions of the Kansas Academy of Science (1903–)* 52(1): 82–85. doi:10.2307/3626128.

2 McClure, Samuel M., Jian Li, Damon Tomlin, Kim S. Cypert, Latané M. Montague, and P. Read Montague. 2004. "Neural Correlates of Behavioral Preference for Culturally Familiar Drinks." *Neuron* 44(2): 379–387. doi:10.1016/j.neuron.2004.09.019.

3 Lindstrom, Martin. 2010. *Buyology: Truth and Lies about Why We Buy*. New York: Broadway Books.

4 Damasio, Antonio R. 2005. *Descartes Error: Emotion, Reason, and the Human Brain*. New York: Penguin Books.

5 Althagafi, Abdulelah., and Mahmood Ali. "Understanding the Relationship between Culture and Sensory Marketing in Developing Strategies and Opportunities in Emerging Economies." *Advances in Marketing, Customer Relationship Management, and E-Services: Promotional Strategies and New Service Opportunities in Emerging Economies*, ed. Vipin Nadda, Sumesh Dadwal, and Royal Rahimi, 236–262. Hershey, PA: IGI Global. doi:10.4018/978-1-5225-2206-5.ch011.

6 Schmitt, Bernd H. 1995. "Language and Visual Imagery: Issues of Corporate Identity in East Asia." *Columbia Journal of World Business* 30(4): 28–36. doi:10.1016/0022-5428(95)90003-90009.

7 Tavassoli, Nader T., and Jin K. Han. 2002. "Auditory and Visual Brand Identifiers in Chinese and English." *Journal of International Marketing* 10(2): 13–28. doi:10.1509/jimk.10.2.13.19531.

8 Souiden, Nizar., Norizan M. Kassim, and Heung-Ja Hong. 2006. "The Effect of Corporate Branding Dimensions on Consumers Product Evaluation." *European Journal of Marketing* 40(7/8): 825–845. doi:10.1108/03090560610670016.

9 Flambard, Véronique., and Adnane Alaoui. 2017. *Sensorial Marketing: A Cross-Cultural Comparison between UK and France*, 1–37. Proceedings of 26th Annual CIMaR Conference. Consortium for International Marketing Research, Florence, Italy.

10 Moeran, Brian. 2007. "Marketing Scents and the Anthropology of Smell." *Social Anthropology* 15(2): 153–168. doi:10.1111/j.0964-0282.2007.00014.x.

11 Fox, Kate. 2009. *The Smell Report: An Overview of Facts and Findings*, 1–33. Social Issues Research Centre. www.sirc.org/publik/smell.pdf.

12 Praet, Douglas Van. 2014. *Unconscious Branding: How Neuroscience Can Empower (and Inspire) Marketing*. Basingstoke, UK: Palgrave Macmillan.

13 Knutson, Brian., Scott Rick, G. Elliott Wimmer, Drazen Prelec, and George Loewenstein. 2007. "Neural Predictors of Purchases." *Neuron* 53(1): 147–156. doi:10.1016/j.neuron.2006.11.010.

14 Fitzsimons, Gráinne M., Tanya L. Chartrand, and Gavan J. Fitzsimons. 2008. "Automatic Effects of Brand Exposure on Motivated Behavior: How Apple Makes You 'Think Different.'" *Journal of Consumer Research* 35(1): 21–35. doi:10.1086/527269.

15 Chadha, Radha., and Paul Husband. 2006. *The Cult of the Luxury Brand: Inside Asia's Love Affair with Luxury*. London: Brealey.

16 Zimmermann, M. 1986. "Neurophysiology of Sensory Systems." *Fundamentals of Sensory Physiology*, ed. R. F. Schmidt, 68–116. Berlin: Springer. doi:10.1007/978-3-642-82598-9_3.

17 Calvert, Gemma. 2014. "How Neuromarketing Can Unlock Cross-cultural Understanding." Futures Centre. December 12. https://thefuturescentre.org/articles/1901/how-neuro marketing-can-unlock-cross-cultural-understanding.

18 Calvert, Gemma., Karine Gallopel-Morvan, Sarah Sauneron, and Olivier Oullier. 2010. "In the Smoker's Head: Neuroscience and Smoking Prevention." In *Improving Public Health Prevention*

with Behavioural, Cognitive and Neuroscience, ed. Oliver Oullier and Sarah Sauneron, 74–93. Paris: Centre d'analyse Stratégique.

19 Müller, Kai-Markus. 2012. *NeuroPricing: Wie Kunden Über Preise Denken*. Freiburg, Germany: Haufe-Gruppe.

20 Ackerman, David., and Gerard Tellis. 2001. "Can Culture Affect Prices? A Cross-Cultural Study of Shopping and Retail Prices." *Journal of Retailing* 77(1): 57–82. doi:10.1016/s0022-4359(00)00046-4.

21 McCall, J. B., and M. B. Warrington. 1984. *Marketing by Agreement: A Cross-Cultural Approach to Business Negotiations*, 170. Chichester, UK: John Wiley.

22 "Homepage." Mecca Cola. www.mecca-cola.com/homepage/.

23 Ji, Li-Jun., Zhiyong Zhang, and Richard E. Nisbett. 2004. "Is It Culture or Is It Language? Examination of Language Effects in Cross-Cultural Research on Categorization." *Journal of Personality and Social Psychology* 87(1): 57–65. doi:10.1037/0022-3514.87.1.57.

24 Ramdas, A. 2008. "Geef mij maar onzin kennis." NRC/Handelsblad. March 10, 7.

25 These are examples of findings by students of the master of retail design at the Willem de Kooning Academy at Rotterdam, 2006, 2007, and 2008. They compared the Dutch supermarket Albert Heijn with the Belgian supermarket Delhaize, using stores of the same size in similar neighborhoods. Cited in Mooij (2014).

26 Mooij, Marieke K. De. 2014. *Global Marketing and Advertising: Understanding Cultural Paradoxes*, 135. 4th ed. Thousand Oaks, CA: Sage.

27 Appadu, Kavitanjali Razmee. 2004. *Branding, a Blend of Senses: The Cross-Cultural Role of Aesthetics in Package Design*. Master's thesis, Simon Fraser University, Burnaby, BC.

28 Kongsompong, Kritika., Robert T. Green, and Paul G. Patterson. 2009. "Collectivism and Social Influence in the Buying Decision: A Four-country Study of Inter- and Intra-National Differences." *Australasian Marketing Journal* 17(3): 142–149. doi:10.1016/j.ausmj.2009.05.013.

29 Schultz, D. E., and M. P. Block. 2009. "Understanding Chinese Media Audiences: An Exploratory Study of Chinese Consumers Media Consumption and a Comparison with the U.S.A." In *Proceedings of the 2009 American Academy of Advertising Asia-Pacific Conference*, ed. H. Li, S. Huang, and D. Jin, 27–30. American Academy of Advertising, in conjunction with China Association of Advertising of Commerce, and Communication University of China.

30 Vuylsteke, Alexander., Zhong Wen, Bart Baesens, and Jonas Poelmans. 2010. "Consumers Search for Information on the Internet: How and Why China Differs from Western Europe." *Journal of Interactive Marketing* 24(4): 309–331. doi:10.1016/j.intmar.2010.02.010.

31 Consumer Empowerment. 2011. Special Eurobarometer Report (EBS 342). April.

32 Ko, Hanjun., Marilyn S. Roberts, and Chang-Hoan Cho. 2006. "Cross-Cultural Differences in Motivations and Perceived Interactivity: A Comparative Study of American and Korean Internet Users." *Journal of Current Issues and Research in Advertising* 28(2): 93–104. doi:10.1080/10641734.2006.10505201.

33 Tsai, Wan-Hsiu Sunny., and Jie Zhang. 2016. "Understanding the Global Phenomenon of Online Group Buying: Perspective from China and the United States." *Journal of Global Marketing* 29(4): 188–202. doi:10.1080/08911762.2016.1138565.

34 Kotler, Philip., Swee Hong Ang, Siew Meng Leong, and Chin Tiong Tan. 2003. *Marketing Management an Asian Perspective*, 396. Singapore: Pearson/Prentice Hall.

35 Rudolph, Thomas., Bodo B. Schlegelmilch, András Bauer, Josep Franch, and Jan Niklas Meise. 2012. *Diversity in European Marketing Text and Cases*, 148. Wiesbaden, Germany: Gabler Verlag.

36 Kim, Youngseon., and Yinlong Zhang. 2014. "The Impact of Power-Distance Belief on Consumers' Preference for Status Brands." *Journal of Global Marketing* 27(1): 13–29. doi:10.1080/08911762.2013.844290.

37 Deloitte. 2018. "Global Powers of Luxury Goods 2018; Shaping the Future of the Luxury Industry." www2.deloitte.com/content/dam/Deloitte/at/Documents/consumer-business/deloitte-global-powers-of-luxury-goods-2018.pdf.

38 Wiedmann, Klaus-Peter., Nadine Hennigs, and Astrid Siebels. 2007. "Measuring Consumers' Luxury Value Perception: A Cross-Cultural Framework," *Academy of Marketing Science Review* 7(7): 1–21.

39 Hennigs, Nadine., Klaus-Peter Wiedmann, Christiane Klarmann, Suzane Strehlau, Bruno Godey, Daniele Pederzoli, and Agnes Neulinger et al. 2012. "What Is the Value of Luxury? A Cross-Cultural Consumer Perspective." *Psychology and Marketing* 29(12): 1018–1034. doi:10.1002/mar.20583.

40 Bae, In Young. 2017. "Louis Vuitton Losing Past Luster in Korean Market." Retail in Asia. November 16. http://retailinasia.com/in-markets/japan-korea/korea/louis-vuitton-losing-past-luster-in-korean-market/.

41 OECD. 2016. "Global Trade in Fake Goods Worth Nearly Half a Trillion Dollars a Year—OECD & EUIPO." OECD Better Policies for Better Lives. www.oecd.org/industry/global-trade-in-fake-goods-worth-nearly-half-a-trillion-dollars-a-year.htm.

42 Hennigs, Nadine., Klaus-Peter Wiedmann, Christiane Klarmann, and Stefan Behrens. 2015. "When the Original Is Beyond Reach: Consumer Perception and Demand for Counterfeit Luxury Goods in Germany and South Korea." *Luxury Research Journal* 1(1): 58–75.

43 Marshall, Roger., and Indriyo Gitosudarmo. 1995. "Variation in the Characteristics of Opinion Leaders across Cultural Borders." *Journal of International Consumer Marketing* 8(1): 5–22. doi:10.1300/j046v08n01_02.

44 Praet, Carolus L. C. 2001. "Japanese Advertising, the World's Number One Celebrity Showcase? A Cross-Cultural Comparison of the Frequency of Celebrity Appearances in TV Advertising," In *Proceedings of the 2001 Special Asia-Pacific Conference of the American Academy of Advertising*, ed. M. Roberts and R. L. King, 6–13. Chiba, Japan: Kisarazu.

45 Hall, Casey. 2018. "Welcome to China's KOL Clone Factories." The Business of Fashion. June 6. www.businessoffashion.com/articles/global-currents/welcome-to-chinas-kol-clone-factories.

46 Chang, Chingching. 2006. "Cultural Masculinity/Femininity Influences on Advertising Appeals." *Journal of Advertising Research* 46(3): 315–323. doi:10.2501/s0021849906060296.

47 Tilburg, Miriam Van., Theo Lieven, Andreas Herrmann, and Claudia Townsend. 2015. "Beyond 'Pink It and Shrink It' Perceived Product Gender, Aesthetics, and Product Evaluation." *Psychology and Marketing* 32(4): 422–437. doi:10.1002/mar.20789.

48 Lieven, Theo., Bianca Grohmann, Andreas Herrmann, Jan R. Landwehr, and Miriam Van Tilburg. 2015. "The Effect of Brand Design on Brand Gender Perceptions and Brand Preference." *European Journal of Marketing* 49(1/2): 146–169. doi:10.1108/ejm-08-2012-0456.

49 Moss, Gloria., Rod Gunn, and Jonathan Heller. 2006. "Some Men Like It Black, Some Women Like It Pink: Consumer Implications of Differences in Male and Female Website Design." *Journal of Consumer Behaviour* 5(4): 328–341. doi:10.1002/cb.184.

50 Berg-Weitzel, Lianne Van Den., and Gaston Van De Laar. 2001. "Relation between Culture and Communication in Packaging Design." *Journal of Brand Management* 8(3): 171–184. doi:10.1057/palgrave.bm.2540018.

51 Brennan, Bridget. 2011. *Why She Buys.* New York: Crown Business.

52 Tan, Thomas Tsu Wee., Lee Boon Ling, and Eleanor Phua Cheay Theng. 2002. "Gender-Role Portrayals in Malaysian and Singaporean Television Commercials: An International Advertising Perspective." *Journal of Business Research* 55(10): 853–861. doi:10.1016/s0148-2963(00)00225-3.

53 "The Codes of Gender." Media Education Foundation Online Store. https://shop.mediaed.org/the-codes-of-gender-p177.aspx.

54 Yeung, Kevin., and K. F. Lau. 1993. "Gender Role Stereotyping in Print Advertisements: A Comparison of Hong Kong, Taiwan and Japan." *Proceedings of the 4th Symposium on Cross-Cultural Consumer and Business Studies,* ed. Gerald Albaum et al., 225–231. Honolulu: University of Hawaii.

55 Siu, Wai-Sum. 1996. "Gender Portrayal in Hong Kong and Singapore Television Advertisements." *Journal of Asian Business* 12(3): 47–61.

56 Eisend, Martin. 2010. "A Meta-Analysis of Gender Roles in Advertising." *Journal of the Academy of Marketing Science* 38(4): 418–440. doi:10.1007/s11747-009-0181-x.

57 Reardon, James., Chip Miller, Bram Foubert, Irena Vida, and Liza Rybina. 2006. "Antismoking Messages for the International Teenage Segment: The Effectiveness of Message Valence and Intensity across Different Cultures." *Journal of International Marketing* 14(3): 115–138. doi:10.1509/jimk.14.3.115.

58 Zhao, Dan. 2017. "The Effects of Culture on International Advertising Appeals: A Cross-Cultural Content Analysis of U.S. and Japanese Global Brands," 1–36. Thesis, University of Nebraska–Lincoln.

59 Toy, S. 1995. "Storm, Terrorists, Nuke Tests: Why Is Club Med Smiling?," 20. *Business Week*. October 16.

60 Holson, Laura M. 2005. "Disney Bows to Feng Shui." *The New York Times*. April 25. www.nytimes.com/2005/04/25/business/worldbusiness/disney-bows-to-feng-shui.html.

61 Sacred Fengshui Design. "Fengshui Tour of Singapore." www.sacredfengshuidesign.com.au/feng-shui-tour-of-singapore.html.

62 Block, Lauren., and Thomas Kramer. 2008. "The Effect of Superstitious Beliefs on Performance Expectations." *Journal of the Academy of Marketing Science* 37(2): 161–169. doi:10.1007/s11747-008-0116-y.

63 Simmons, Lee C., and Robert M. Schindler. 2003. "Cultural Superstitions and the Price Endings Used in Chinese Advertising." *Journal of International Marketing* 11(2): 101–111. doi:10.1509/jimk.11.2.101.20161.

64 Mobbs, Dean., Michael D. Greicius, Eiman Abdel-Azim, Vinod Menon, and Allan L. Reiss. 2003. "Humor Modulates the Mesolimbic Reward Centers." *Neuron* 40(5): 1041–1048. doi:10.1016/s0896-6273(03)00751-7.

65 Scheijgrond, L., and Volker, J. 1995. Zo dichtbij, maar toch ver weg [So close yet so far away]. Unpublished study for the Hogeschool Einghoven, studierichting Communicatie.

66 Hatzithomas, Leonidas., Yorgos Zotos, and Christina Boutsouki. 2011. "Humor and Cultural Values in Print Advertising: A Cross-Cultural Study." *International Marketing Review* 28(1): 57–80. doi:10.1108/02651331111107107.

67 Rojas-Méndez, José I., and Gary Davies. 2005. "Avoiding Television Advertising: Some Explanations from Time Allocation Theory." *Journal of Advertising Research* 45(1): 34–48. doi:10.1017/s0021849905050154.

68 Kaynak, Erdener., Ali Kara, Clement S. F. Chow, and Ali Riza Apil. 2013. "Pattern of Similarities/Differences in Time Orientation and Advertising Attitudes." *Asia Pacific Journal of Marketing and Logistics* 25(4): 631–654. doi:10.1108/apjml-09-2012-0087.

69 Klicperová-Baker, Martina., Jaroslav Košťál, and Jiří Vinopal. 2015. "Time Perspective in Consumer Behavior." In *Time Perspective Theory; Review, Research and Application*, ed. M. Stolarski, N. Fieulaine, and W. van Beek, 353–369. Cham, Switzerland: Springer. doi:10.1007/978-3-319-07368-2_23.

70 Liao, Jiangqun., and Lei Wang. 2009. "Face as a Mediator of the Relationship between Material Value and Brand Consciousness." *Psychology and Marketing* 26(11): 987–1001. doi:10.1002/mar.20309.

71 Ruvio, Ayalla A., and Russell W. Belk. 2013. *The Routledge Companion to Identity and Consumption*. London: Routledge.

72 Norum, Pamela S. 2008. "The Role of Time Preference and Credit Card Usage in Compulsive Buying Behaviour." *International Journal of Consumer Studies* 32(3): 269–275. doi:10.1111/j.1470-6431.2008.00678.x.

73 Roberts, James A., Chris Manolis, and John F. (Jeff) Tanner. 2003. "Family Structure, Materialism, and Compulsive Buying: A Reinquiry and Extension." *Journal of the Academy of Marketing Science* 31(3): 300–311. doi:10.1177/0092070303031003007.

74 Kacen, Jacqueline J., and Julie Anne Lee. 2002. "The Influence of Culture on Consumer Impulsive Buying Behavior." *Journal of Consumer Psychology* 12(2): 163–176. doi:10.1207/s15327663jcp1202_08.

75 Ali, Saiyed Wajid., and Swati Sudan. 2018. "Influence of Cultural Factors on Impulse Buying Tendency: A Study of Indian Consumers." *Vision* 22(1): 68–77. doi:10.1177/0972262917750247.

76 Ünalan, Musa., Tevfik Şükrü Yaprakli, and Ali Absalan. 2017. "The Relationship between Time Orientation and Consumer Innovativeness: The Case of Turkey and Iran." *International Journal of Economic and Administrative Studies* 22: 209–222. doi:10.18092/ulikidince.348341.

77 Bearden, William O., Bruce R. Money, and Jennifer L. Nevins. 2006. "A Measure of Long-Term Orientation: Development and Validation." *Journal of the Academy of Marketing Science* 34(3): 456–467. doi:10.1177/0092070306286706.

78 Mai, Nguyen Thi Tuyet., Kwon Jung, Garold Lantz, and Sandra G. Loeb. 2003. "An Exploratory Investigation into Impulse Buying Behavior in a Transitional Economy: A Study of Urban Consumers in Vietnam." *Journal of International Marketing* 11(2): 13–35. doi:10.1509/jimk.11.2.13.20162.

79 Kacen, Jacqueline J., and Julie Anne Lee. 2002. "The Influence of Culture on Consumer Impulsive Buying Behavior." *Journal of Consumer Psychology* 12(2): 163–176. doi:10.1207/s15327663jcp1202_08.

80 Hepper, Erica G., Tim Wildschut, Constantine Sedikides, Timothy D. Ritchie, Yiu-Fai Yung, Nina Hansen, and Georgios Abakoumkin et al. 2014. "Pancultural Nostalgia: Prototypical Conceptions across Cultures," *Emotion* 14(4): 733–747.

81 Merchant, Altaf., John B. Ford, Christian Dianoux, and Jean-Luc Herrmann. 2015. "Development and Validation of an Emic Scale to Measure Ad-Evoked Nostalgia in France." *International Journal of Advertising* 35(4): 706–729. doi:10.1080/02650487.2015.1090049.

82 Merchant, Altaf., Kathryn Latour, John B. Ford, and Michael S. Latour. 2013. "How Strong Is the Pull of the Past?" *Journal of Advertising Research* 53(2): 150–165. doi:10.2501/jar-53-2-150-16

83 Nurko, Christopher. 2003. "Nostalgia Branding: Out with the Old and in with the Old." *Brand Strategy* 175: 6.

84 Martinez, Amanda R. 2013. "Why a Great Wave of Nostalgia Is Sweeping through China." *The New Yorker.* May 30. www.newyorker.com/tech/elements/why-a-great-wave-of-nostalgia-is-sweeping-through-china.

85 Juhl, Jacob., Clay Routledge, Jamie Arndt, Constantine Sedikides, and Tim Wildschut. 2010. "Fighting the Future with the Past: Nostalgia Buffers Existential Threat." *Journal of Research in Personality* 44(3): 309–314. doi:10.1016/j.jrp.2010.02.006.

86 Martinez, Amanda R. 2013. "Why a Great Wave of Nostalgia Is Sweeping through China." *The New Yorker.* May 30. www.newyorker.com/tech/elements/why-a-great-wave-of-nostalgia-is-sweeping-through-china.

87 Hornikx, Jos., and Rob Le Pair. 2017. "The Influence of High-/Low-Context Culture on Perceived Ad Complexity and Liking." *Journal of Global Marketing* 30(4): 228–237. doi:10.1080/08911762.2017.1296985.

88 Appadu, Kavitanjali Razmee. 2004. "Branding, a Blend of Senses: The Cross-Cultural Role of Aesthetics in Package Design." Master's thesis, Simon Fraser University, Burnaby, BC.

89 Pollach, I. 2011. "The Readership of Corporate Websites: A Cross-Cultural Study." *Journal of Business Communication* 48(1): 27–53. doi:10.1177/0021943610385657.

90 Hermeking, Marc. 2005. "Culture and Internet Consumption: Contributions from Cross-Cultural Marketing and Advertising Research." *Journal of Computer-Mediated Communication* 11(1): 192–216. doi:10.1111/j.1083–6101.2006.tb00310.x.

91 An, Daechun. 2007. "Advertising Visuals in Global Brands' Local Websites: A Six-Country Comparison." *International Journal of Advertising* 26(3): 303–332. doi:10.1080/02650487.2007.11073016.

92 Agrawal, Madhu. 1995. "Review of a 40-year Debate in International Advertising." *International Marketing Review* 12(1): 26–48. doi:10.1108/02651339510080089.

93 Sulaini, K. E. 2006. "Blink: Tackling the Communication Flux within the Asia-Pacific Region." A research project submitted in fulfillment of the requirement for the degree of bachelor of communication, RMIT University, Melbourne, Australia and MARA University of Technology, Malaysia.

94 Hornikx, Jos., and Daniel J. O'Keefe. 2009. *Adapting Consumer Advertising Appeals to Cultural Values: A Meta-Analytic Review of Effects on Persuasiveness and Ad Liking*, ed. C. S. Beck, 38–71. New York: Lawrence Erlbaum.

95 Hoeken, Hans., Marianne Starren, Catherine Nickerson, Rogier Crijns, and Corine Van Den Brandt. 2007. "Is It Necessary to Adapt Advertising Appeals for National Audiences in Western Europe?" *Journal of Marketing Communications* 13(1): 19–38. doi:10.1080/13527260600950999.

96 "Procter & Gamble to Film Reality in 80 Homes." May 22, 2001. www.deseretnews.com/article/844068/Procter–Gamble-to-film-reality-in-80-homes.html.

97 Lu, Jia. 2010. "Multiple Modernities and Multiple Proximities: McDonald's and Kentucky Fried Chicken in Chinese Television Commercials." *International Communication Gazette* 72(7): 619–633. doi:10.1177/1748048510378146.

98 Parry, Simon. 2009. "Shoppers Shun Flagship M&S Store in China for Being 'Too British and Expensive.'" *Daily Mail Online*. January 5. www.dailymail.co.uk/news/article-1104775/Shoppers-shun-flagship-M-S-China-British-expensive.html.

99 Zhang, Jing. 2010. "The Persuasiveness of Individualistic and Collectivistic Advertising Appeals among Chinese Generation-X Consumers." *Journal of Advertising* 39(3): 69–80. doi:10.2753/joa0091-3367390305.

100 Shirata, Tim. 2017. "Social Commerce, Live Streaming, and Virtual Goods: Chinese E-Commerce Innovation Pulls Ahead." Guild Investment Management. June 2. https://guildinvestment.com/asia/social-commerce-live-streaming-virtual-goods-chinese-e-commerce-innovation-pulls-ahead/.

101 Okazaki, Shintaro., and Barbara Mueller. 2008. "Evolution in the Usage of Localized Appeals in Japanese and American Print Advertising." *International Journal of Advertising* 27(5): 771–798. doi:10.2501/s0265048708080323.

102 Minh, Hoang. 2015. "The Impacts of Individualism/collectivism on Consumer Decision-Making Styles: The Case of Finnish and Vietnamese Mobile Phone Buyers," 6–58. Thesis, Turku University of Applied Sciences.

103 Mooij, Marieke K. De. 2014. *Global Marketing and Advertising: Understanding Cultural Paradoxes*, 343. 4th ed. Thousand Oaks, CA: Sage..

104 Banjo, Shelly. 2012. "Wal-Mart Says Time Is Right for Japan." *The Wall Street Journal*. September 27. www.wsj.com/articles/SB10000872396390044358930457763568349033443 6.html.

105 Ortiz-Ospina, Esteban., and Sandra Tzvetkova. 2017. "Working Women: Key Facts and Trends in Female Labor Force Participation." *Our World in Data*. October 16. https://ourworldindata.org/female-labor-force-participation-key-facts.

106 Wade, Lisa. 2013. "Men Need Clothes; Women Need to Look Sexy—Sociological Images." The Society Pages. August 7. https://thesocietypages.org/socimages/2013/08/07/men-need-clothes-women-need-to-look-sexy-in-clothes/.

107 Bernard, Philippe., Sarah J. Gervais, Jill Allen, Sophie Campomizzi, and Olivier Klein. 2012. "Integrating Sexual Objectification with Object Versus Person Recognition." *Psychological Science* 23(5): 469–471. doi:10.1177/0956797611434748.

108 Booth, Alison. 1999. "The Mother of All Cultures: Camille Paglia and Feminist Mythologies." *The Kenyon Review* 21(1): 27–45. www.jstor.org/stable/4337811.

109 Choi, Hojoon., Kyunga Yoo, Tom Reichert, and Michael S. Latour. 2016. "Do Feminists Still Respond Negatively to Female Nudity in Advertising? Investigating the Influence of Feminist Attitudes on Reactions to Sexual Appeals." *International Journal of Advertising* 35(5): 823–845. doi:10.1080/02650487.2016.1151851.

110 Lull, Robert B., and Brad J. Bushman. 2015. "Do Sex and Violence Sell? A Meta-Analytic Review of the Effects of Sexual and Violent Media and Ad Content on Memory, Attitudes, and Buying Intentions." *Psychological Bulletin* 141(5): 1022–1048. doi:10.1037/bul0000018.

111 Vohs, Kathleen D., Jaideep Sengupta, and Darren W. Dahl. 2014. "The Price Had Better Be Right: Women's Reactions to Sexual Stimuli Vary with Market Factors." *Psychological Science* 25(1): 278–283. doi:10.1177/0956797613502732.

112 Lanseng, Even J. 2016. "Relevant Sex Appeals in Advertising: Gender and Commitment Context Differences." *Frontiers in Psychology* 7: 1456. doi:10.3389/fpsyg.2016.01456.

113 Wirtz, John G., Johnny V. Sparks, and Thais M. Zimbres. 2017. "The Effect of Exposure to Sexual Appeals in Advertisements on Memory, Attitude, and Purchase Intention: A Meta-Analytic Review." *International Journal of Advertising* 37(2): 168–198. doi:10.1080/02650487.2017.1334996.

114 Brennan, Bridget. 2011. *Why She Buys: The New Strategy for Reaching the World's Most Powerful Consumers*. New York: Crown Business.

115 Wong, Curtis M. 2016. "50 Percent of Millennials Believe Gender Is a Spectrum, Fusion's Massive Millennial Poll Finds." *The Huffington Post*. February 2. www.huffingtonpost.com/2015/02/05/fusion-millennial-poll-gender_n_6624200.html.

116 Goodman, Matt. 2017. "Accelerating Acceptance: GLAAD Study Reveals Twenty Percent of Millennials Identify as LGBTQ." GLAAD. March 30. www.glaad.org/releases/new-glaad-study-reveals-twenty-percent-millennials-identify-lgbtq.

117 Safronova, Valeriya. 2016. "Meet CoverGirl's New Cover Boy." *The New York Times*. October 12. www.nytimes.com/2016/10/16/fashion/meet-covergirls-new-cover-boy.html.

118 Dua, Tanya. 2016. "From Coca-Cola to Barbie: The Fierce Rise of Gender-neutral Advertising." Digiday. March 29. https://digiday.com/marketing/theyre-just-fierce-rise-gender-fluid-advertising/.

119 "Ikea Israel Apologizes for Female-Free Catalog.". *The Times of Israel*. February 17. www.timesofisrael.com/ikea-israel-apologizes-for-female-free-catalog/.

120 Idan, Naama. February 20, 2017. "Ikea Owes Ultra-Orthodox Women More Than an Apology." Haaretz. www.haaretz.com/opinion/.premium-ikea-is-behind-the-times-1.5438662.

121 CIM—Chartered Institute of Marketing. 2009. "Less Smoke, More Fire: The Benefits and Impacts of Social Marketing," . *Shape the Agenda* 15. www.australiancollegeofmarketing.com.au/marketing/agenda/social-marketing.pdf.

122 Hunt, Alexandra Rae. 2017. "Selling Empowerment: A Critical Analysis of Femvertising," 1–73. Thesis, Boston College.

123 Castillo, Michelle. 2014. "These Stats Prove Femvertising Works." *Adweek*. October 10. www.adweek.com/digital/these-stats-prove-femvertising-works-160704/.

124 Mwakideu, Chrispin. 2018. "South Africa: EFF Supporters Attack H&M Stores over 'Racist Jumper Advert.'" DW Made for Minds. January 13. www.dw.com/en/south-africa-eff-supporters-attack-hm-stores-over-racist-jumper-advert/a-42136978.

125 Paek, Hye Jin., and Hemant Shah. 2003. "Racial Ideology, Model Minorities, and the 'Not-So-Silent Partner': Stereotyping of Asian Americans in U.S. Magazine Advertising." *Howard Journal of Communications* 14(4): 225–243. doi:10.1080/716100430.

126 Taylor Saito, Natsu. 1997. "Model Minority, Yellow Peril: Functions of Foreignness in the Construction of Asian American Legal Identity." *Asian American Law Journal* 4(6): 71–95. https://scholarship.law.berkeley.edu/cgi/viewcontent.cgi?article=1034&context=aalj.

127 Mathews, Jay. 2005. "Learning to Stand Out among the Standouts: Some Asian Americans Say Colleges Expect More from Them." *The Washington Post*. March 21. www.washingtonpost.com/wp-dyn/articles/A55160-2005Mar21.html.

128 "Asian American Student Suicide Rate at MIT Is Quadruple the National Average." Reappropriate. May 20, 2015. http://reappropriate.co/2015/05/asian-american-student-suicide-rate-at-mit-is-quadruple-the-national-average/.

129 Victor, Daniel. 2017. "Pepsi Pulls Ad Accused of Trivializing Black Lives Matter." *The New York Times*. April 5. www.nytimes.com/2017/04/05/business/kendall-jenner-pepsi-ad.html.

130 Dahan, Nadine. 2017. "Topshop Pulls 'Keffiyeh Playsuit' after Row over Cultural Theft." Middle East Eye. April 6. www.middleeasteye.net/news/topshop-removes-product-after-twitter-backlash-over-palestinian-struggle-1853057347.

131 Scafidi, Susan. 2005. *Who Owns Culture? Appropriation and Authenticity in American Law*. New Brunswick, NJ: Rutgers University Press.

132 "Nike Tattoo Leggings Pulled after Deemed Exploitative of Samoan Culture (PHOTOS)." *The Huffington Post*. December 6, 2017. www.huffingtonpost.com/2013/08/15/nike-tattoo-leggings_n_3763591.html.

133 "Chanel's $2,000 Boomerang Sparks Complaints and Confusion from Indigenous Australians." ABC News. May 17, 2017. www.abc.net.au/news/2017-05-16/chanels-$2000-boomerang-sparks-aboriginal-appropriation-claim/8531496.

134 Lafraniere, Sharon. 2006. "In the Jungle, the Unjust Jungle, a Small Victory." *The New York Times*. March 22. www.nytimes.com/2006/03/22/world/africa/in-the-jungle-the-unjust-jungle-a-small-victory.html.

135 "PFW: Valentino under Fire for Show of 'Cultural Appropriation.'" October 6, 2015. The Fashion Law. www.thefashionlaw.com/home/pfw-valentino-under-fire-for-cultural-appropriation.

136 THR Staff. 2012. "Victoria's Secret Yanks Native American Costume From Broadcast." *The Hollywood Reporter*. December 11. www.hollywoodreporter.com/news/victorias-secret-native-american-costume-yanked-broadcast-389580.

137 Varagur, Krithika. 2017. "Is This the Right Way for Fashion to Do Cultural Appropriation?" *The Huffington Post*. January 17. www.huffingtonpost.com/entry/fashion-cultural-appropriation_us_5632295ce4b00aa54a4ce639.

138 Deloitte. 2017. "The 2017 Deloitte Millennial Survey Apprehensive Millennials: Seeking Stability and Opportunities in an Uncertain World." www2.deloitte.com/content/dam/Deloitte/global/Documents/About-Deloitte/gx-deloitte-millennial-survey-2017-executive-summary.pdf.

Discussion Cases

Usually, case studies are often introduced with the chapter. This makes it easy for instructors and learners to apply specific knowledge from the text. For examples, cases presented in the leadership chapter would focus on leadership issues.

However, that's not how it works in reality. Our international working environment is a holistic context where *any incident represents itself with many layers of cross-cultural aspects*. A challenge or an opportunity does not come to our desk with a label on it that says: "This is a leadership case. Please apply leadership knowledge."

Hence, we list case studies at the end so readers can be proactive in looking at any issue from a broad viewpoint, considering all possible layers of meaning, and be creative in combining different areas of knowledge for an optimal solution.

Here is a simple guideline for working with the cases. For each incident, please answer the following generic questions:

- What are the aspects of cross-cultural managements that you can recognize in this case? Scan all the chapters to make sure you don't miss any potential aspects.
- Analyze the dominant fundamental concerns and cultural values in the incident (Chapter 3) then compare these values with the stereotypical values in the wider culture to explore the dynamics of cultures (Chapter 4). Note that we have four units of analysis: Global, national, organizational, and group culture (Chapter 6).
- If an incident looks like a cultural misunderstanding, try to use the Inverted Pyramid model (Chapter 6) to figure out if the issue is in the process (universal layer), or it is truly a cultural mismatch (collective level), of just a personal/specific circumstance (individual level).
- Are the parties in the case acting as a product or a producer of culture?
- Do you agree with the solution in the case? What would you do if you were in that situation? Try to look for similarities and the way to create synergy from the differences. Search for more information on the internet to back up your solutions.
- If you want to advocate a change, what would be your activities, using STREAP-Be framework? STREAP-Be is applied for bias, change, and diversity management.

1 No Makeup on the Train

Tokyu Corporation, a private railway company in Japan, has produced an ad suggesting it is not proper etiquette to apply makeup on the train. In the ad, two young women are applying lipstick and mascara in a relatively empty train car. Then a barefaced actress, Sawa Nimura, mutters: "Women in the big city are all beautiful. But they can be ugly sometimes."

While Japan has all sorts of guidelines dictating considerate train behavior, from not wearing your backpack on your back to not talking on your cellphone or eating on the train, this latest directive is a bridge too far.

The ad frowning on women—many of whom are presumably on their way to work—comes at a time when the Abe government is trying to break down gender barriers to encourage more women into the workplace. Despite the government campaign to "let women shine," Japan is going backward in the rankings. The latest *Global Gender Gap Report* from the World Economic Forum put Japan at 111th of 144 countries, ten places lower than the previous year (adapted from *Washington Post*, October 28, 2016: "Women Doing Their Makeup on the Train Are 'Ugly,' Says Japanese Commercial").

2 A Symbol of Religion or Oppression?

In 2017, Nike launched a hijab custom designed so that a Muslim woman who wants to cover her head can still work out. This created a wave of publicity but also plenty of backlash. There were those who praised Nike for taking into account their specific need. But there were also many people who accused them of being complicit in the subjection of women. They argued that the Pro Hijab "normalizes the oppression of women." There were musings online as to whether sport burqas (full veil with a split for eyes) would be next and if Nike would have served women better by point blank refusing to make a garment that covers their heads.

While hijab is common, not all Muslim women wear it. Before the Arab Spring, the majority of women in Tunisia, Egypt, Syria, and Lebanon did not wear hijab at all. The young generation has gone more conservative. Next to those who voluntarily or habitually adopt the hijab, there are also girls and women who feel the pressure of the families and society to cover their head, especially in Iran and Saudi Arabia where hijab is enforced by law (adapted from News.com.au, March 17, 2017: "Backlash as Nike Launches Sports Hijab").

3 The Heartless Boss

I have been working in this company for more than one year, and I do my job with joy. The only thing that I still need to figure out is what to think about my boss. She is extremely competent, but I'm not sure she is the kind of boss I would give my loyalty.

Everyone in the department knows that my mother has been diagnosed with cancer, and people ask about her once in a while. Not-my-boss. Not-a-word. She knows of course. She approved my day-off to bring my mother to the hospital. But the next day when she saw me, it was business as usual. What a heartless boss! (personal communication).

4 Sexism in the House of Common

In 2018, the UK Foreign Secretary Boris Johnson made headlines as he called the shadow foreign secretary Emily Thornberry "Baroness whatever-it-is," then referred to her as "Lady Nugee" in the House of Common. Ms. Thornberry is married to a top judge named Sir Christopher Nugee, meaning she has the right to the title "Lady." But she never uses it and does not adopt her husband's surname.

Boris was blasted by Speaker John Bercow, who said Mr. Johnson was being "inappropriate and frankly sexist." He said: Firstly, we don't name-call in this chamber. Secondly, we do not address people by the titles of their spouses. The shadow foreign secretary has a name and it's not 'Lady Something', we know what her name is, and it is inappropriate and frankly sexist to speak in those terms. That parlance is not legitimate, it will not be allowed and it will be called out. I've said what the position is and believe me that is the end of the matter. Labor MPs started clapping in response to the Speaker's comments. And Boris replied with a groveling apology (adapted from *The Guardian*, March 27, 2018: "Johnson Apologises for 'Sexist' Reference to Emily Thornberry").

5 Why Good Leaders Make You Feel Safe

One of the most viewed TED talks was given by Simon Sinek in 2014. Here are some of the main points he made:

- Leadership is rooted in the notion that people are protected by strong ones at the top. This definition still holds true in the military. We give medals to people who are willing to sacrifice themselves so that others may gain. In business, we give bonuses to people who are willing to sacrifice others so that they may gain. We have it backward.
- At the airport, when a passenger attempted to board before his number was called, he was treated like a criminal. The agent said the reason she treated him that way was because if she didn't follow the rules, she could lose her job. In fact, all she was saying was that she didn't feel safe, she didn't trust her leaders. When the corporate culture is not safe, we are forced to expend our own time and energy to protect ourselves from each other, and that inherently weakens the organization. When we feel safe inside the organization, we will naturally combine our talents and our strengths and work tirelessly to face the dangers outside and seize the opportunities.
- At Next Jump, CEO Charlie Kim implemented a policy of lifetime employment. Employees cannot get fired for performance issues. They will get support if that happens. In another case, Barry-Wehmiller lost 30% of their orders overnight during the recession. Instead of layoffs, CEO Bob Chapman came up with a furlough program. Every employee, from secretary to CEO, was required to take four weeks of unpaid vacation. He said, it's better that we should all suffer a little than any of us should have to suffer a lot, and the morale went up. They saved 20 million dollars, and most importantly, as would be expected, when the people feel safe and protected by the leadership in the organization, the natural reaction is to trust and cooperate. And quite spontaneously, nobody expected, people started trading with each other. Those who could afford it more would trade with those who could afford it less. People would take five weeks so that somebody else only had to take three.
- Leaders are like parents. Great parents and great leaders want the same thing. They want to provide their children/people opportunity and education, discipline when necessary, build their self-confidence, give them the opportunity to try and fail; all so that they could achieve more than we could ever imagine for ourselves (adapted from *TED2014*, "Why Good Leaders Make You Feel Safe").

6 Did the World Get Aung San Suu Kyi Wrong?

Aung San Suu Kyi is a world-famous activist because of her nonviolent struggle against the brutal dictatorship in Myanmar. She won the 1991 Nobel Prize for Peace while under house arrest. She later became the de factor head of the country in the role of state counsellor.

However, in 2017, she became the target of worldwide criticism for standing by as her country's military waged a campaign of murder, rape, and torture against the Rohingya minority group. Hundreds of thousands of Rohingya Muslims had to risk death to flee persecution to the neighboring Bangladesh. Ms. Suu Kyi was accused of not doing enough to prevent the crisis.

One of the reasons why Ms. Suu Kyi has very little influence over events is that the military retains control of three vital ministries: Home affairs, defense, and border affairs. Speaking out in support of the Rohingya would almost certainly prompt an angry reaction from Buddhist nationalists and military officials. Not to mention the general public who have very little sympathy for the Rohingya.

Observing the situation, in *The New York Times* (October 31, 2017), the writer wrote:

> Western leaders champion individuals, often activists who have made heroic sacrifices, as the one-stop-shopping solution to the problems of dictatorship or shaky new democracy. In their zeal to find a simple solution to the complex problem of political change, they overlook their heroes' flaws, fail to see the challenges they will face in power, and assume that countries are the products of their leaders, when it is almost always the other way around.

7 Jew and Arab Cofounders Are Good for Business

Forsan Hussein and Ami Dror are close friends of each other. When people see them together, many could not believe that a Jew and an Arab could be so close. According to them, Israel is one of the most diverse countries in the world, yet the diversity has not been converted into a competitive business advantage—if anything it has been a source of suspicion and division.

So, the two founded Zaitoun Ventures—a hybrid investment firm that upholds the value of diversity. With every company they invest in, they require the CEO to lead a diversification process. Within three years from the moment of investing, they set the goal of 30% diversification in human capital. This means hiring Arabs, Haredim (ultra-Orthodox Jews), Ethiopian immigrants, and women.

The cultural and religious backgrounds of the cofounders attract media and investors. Many of the investors have been making a great deal of money, but that's not enough anymore. They also want to do good. Zaitoun Ventures fits that purpose because the firm does not merely create business, it also creates hope (adapted from *The Times of Israel*, January 31, 2016: "Why Jewish and Arab Cofounders Are Good for Business").

8 Diversity Means I Have a Place Too

Any accountant working in a Big 4 firm knows that becoming a partner is a big achievement. Part of the partnership admission process is to make an incredible presentation of one's business case. It's a nerve-wracking event.

It was one of those presentations and we had a young colleague who was extremely nervous. He could not even make the first part of presentation clear. I thought he had some signs of slight autism. At one point, I asked for a permission to talk with him quickly in private. I encouraged him, and told him to come back to the room when he was ready.

Although he was still nervous, he made it through. Here was what he said at the end: 'I know what you are thinking. I know I speak slowly. I know I don't have the self-confident and assertive attitude that partnership candidates usually have. But I work hard, I know the job, and I am extremely committed. Our firm is advocating diversity. And that means people like me have a place too.'

We were taken away by his honesty and argument. He is now a partner (personal communication).

9 A Company with Grand Purpose

The year 1946 was very bleak for Japan. The country faced ignominious defeat and national humiliation as the result of World War II. In that context, a Japanese businessman called Konosuke Matsushita developed a corporate philosophy based on the conviction that the ultimate aim of manufacturing was to eliminate poverty and foster prosperity. He announced a 250-year plan for the completion of the company mission: Eradicating poverty from the planet. The business principles are (a) service to the public; (2) fairness and honesty; (3) teamwork for the common cause; (4) untiring effort for improvement; and (5) courtesy and humility.

With human at the center of business, his prices were set at an appropriate level, from three important perspectives: Good for the customer, good for the company, and good for society. Matsushita believed that any other kind of price would be an insult to the precious people who were so important to the company and society.

To many Japanese, Matsushita is "the god of management." His spirit lives on in Panasonic employees in the form of the company's management philosophy (adapted from *Matsushita Leadership*, by John Kotter, 1997).

10 Face Job

Face, or public dignity, is universally important. However, the degree of importance and the way we achieve face are very different. In China, working with or hiring Westerners means the company has prestige, money, and the increasingly crucial connections to businesses abroad. It gives the company face.

The needs of face have led to a practice of hiring a Westerner for a day, a weekend, a week, up to even a month or two. Some Chinese companies are willing to pay high prices for fair-faced foreigners to join them as fake employees or business partners. There are many names for this: "White Guy Window Dressing," "White Guy in a Tie" events, "The Token White Guy Gig," or, simply, a "Face Job."

To a lesser extent, some companies in the Middle East have the same practice of inviting noble and important people to business events. "Rent-a-sheikh" sends a signal of prestige and relationship.

11 Convenient Diversity

An expert on diversity management, let's call her Layla, often received positive feedbacks from clients after her training in a diversity program. With her immigrant background, she also added significant insight to the training. She loved the program because she could bring out her personal stories and make people change their mind. However, after running for one year, she was taken out of the project because the coordinator thought that running a small program with two trainers takes too much administrative work.

After what happened, the coordinator e-mailed her, asking Layla to give a guest talk *for the very training program she had been taken out, on diversity*. This prompted Layla to conclude that her coordinator valued diversity when it was useful for her (with the guest talk, and Layla being an immigrant lecturing on diversity issues). At the same time, the coordinator conveniently refused to take some extra effort to change the program structure (admins work) to let Layla remain a part of the project. Layla saw the invitation as an insensitive move, for it reflected window dressing and an opportunistic way to exploit the benefit of diversity without having to change anything to support diversity in a sustainable way (personal communication).

12 What Makes a "True" Woman?

An Argentinian food manufacturer decided to launch a new product in Uruguay—cake and desert mixes. There was only one competitor in the market, and the company thought that it would be very easy to bring this product to the market because the country's culture is similar to their own, so nothing could go wrong, as they thought.

They introduced the product together with a TV commercial, which was the Argentinian version with a Uruguayan voice-over. Three months later, the product was still on the shelves—no one was buying it. So the company ran a focus group to find out why.

Consumers, who were 20–45-year-old middle-class mothers, explained that it was a disgrace to buy a prepackaged cake or desert. The true identity of a mother or a wife was only proven when she could cook something delicious for her loved ones herself, so they would make every single ingredient by themselves (adapted from Marie-Joëlle Browaeys and Fons Trompenaars. 2000. *Case Studies on Cultural Dilemmas: How to Use Transcultural Competence for Reconciling Cultural Dilemmas.* Nyenrode, the Netherlands: Nyenrode University Press).

13 The Danone Group in Mexico

R1esearcher d'Iribarne studied the French multination food-product corporation—the Danone group—in Mexico to find an answer for their remarkable success. He observed a clever mix of modern management and traditional Mexican culture.

In terms of modern management, the organization has shortened its chain of command, removing echelons and bringing the directors closer to each other. It has an open-door policy, encouraging dialogues between managers and staff—something that did not frequently happen before. The company advocates the use of the familiar form of "you" to narrow the hierarchy. The executive dining room is replaced by a common dining room for all.

According to d'Iribarne, these modern measures have been successful because they are combined with the core idea of Mexican culture. It integrates the notion of family in the way all employees treat each other. Friendship, brotherhood, and mutual aid reign supreme in the company's environment. This feeling of trust, security, and the climate of personal and collective growth create a very strong emotional bond with the organization. A notable example of this spirit is the "Let's Build Their Dream" program for the community's children in difficulties.

d'Iribarne concluded that a successful approach involves the creation of hybrid and innovative management practices that borrow from many participating cultures. These hybrid practices also optimize two seemingly opposing value systems and sets of behaviors (adapted from Jean-Pierre Dupuis. 2013. "Intercultural Analysis in Management." In *Cross-Cultural Management—Culture and Management across the World*, 40–70, ed. Jean-François Chanlat, Eduador Davel, and Jean-Pierre Dupuis. New York: Routledge, 2013).

14 Not So Japanese?

- While Japanese companies often have a rigid hierarchical structure, Shiseido has banned the addressing of colleagues in the traditional fashion indicating their relative rank.
- NEC's researchers have flexible working hours, can wear whatever they please, and even need not to report to work at all if they do not want to. Outstanding researchers have their pictures displayed in the research center's Hall of Fame.

Problem-Solving Cases

A holistic and integrated approach in teaching and coaching cross-cultural management is using a portfolio. Here are some suggestions for teachers and coaches:

- At the beginning of the course, each student brainstorms or searches for a specific issue (s) he wants to address. Here are some examples: "How to deal with gender pay gap in the country"; "How to make diversity work in my company"; "If I were elected as head of the department, how can I change the current corporate culture to a happy workplace,"; "Suppose I were going to work in Egypt for three years, what can I do to prepare?"; "My company is going to expand to a new market, what can I contribute to make this successful?" Students are encouraged to take real-world issues as their assignments. If students want to tackle an issue in the company they are working for, teachers can cooperate with a supervisor in that company to co-grade the final paper and measure the practicability it may bring in the business context.
- Teachers should approve the proposal to make sure that the issue is broad enough to apply as much as possible the knowledge from the book. In case the topic is too narrow, students can choose two or more topics.
- As the course continues, students gradually apply and shape their plan of action in their portfolio. Each week, they can discuss with other students and the teacher to collect comments and suggestions on their own topics. They can organize their working progress in a topic-structure that follows the order of the book or the topics discussed in the class.
- At the end of the course, students submit a portfolio in the form of a research paper with (1) executive summary; (2) overview of the issue; (3) research gap and research questions; (4) literature review or what has been done; (5) student's solutions/ plan of action based on knowledge from the course; and (6) conclusion.
- Grades will be based on (1) how well the paper has applied knowledge from the course; (2) justification of solutions; and (3) market value, or how helpful this paper can be for other parties.

The following are several cases that can be used in the class for discussion, small projects for teamwork, or mini-exams.

1 Support for Expats

Your company has recently established a collaborative partnership with a Moroccan business counterpart. There is going to be a team of 15 Moroccan colleagues coming to your city for one year, 7 of them are male and 8 are female, 10 are married. All of them have never lived abroad before.

Please develop a plan to deal with this work-life transition with concrete and specific practices and policies. Think of diverse aspects of HR tasks such as leadership, motivation strategies, working styles, decision-making process, meeting styles, teamwork, new consensus, ethnic and cultural sensitivity, training, orientation, accommodation, social and religious practice, work structure, language, stereotypes, and so forth. Please apply as many cultural theories, models, and concepts from the book as possible. Your grade is based on the accurate concepts/models/values you apply.

Generic ideas such as "consider the Moroccan values and leadership style" or "be sensitive with religious issues" are not valid. Note that every policy, practice, and strategy has to start with a *concept* or a *theory* taken directly from the reading material. Start a suggestion with the title of the chapter, the section or concept, and then follow by a specific *action*. For example:

> Diversity management—Hold managers accountable: Conduct a cultural audit to see the similarities and differences of working styles among both teams.

2 Diversity for New Markets

In your company, 72% of the employees are native, male, and white individuals who are above the age of 45. The rate of this demographic is 100% in the management board. However, 64% of your product is consumed by women, 75% by millennials, and 42% by nonnative in the current market. In five years, the company wants to expand to other markets in the Middle East and Asia.

Propose a plan of *specific actions* to increase diversity and reap more benefit from diversity in your company. Think beyond the topic of diversity and explore how the current structure may support or hinder the company's goal in terms of leadership, bias, motivation, and marketing. Think about cultural change and not just some tactics. Please apply as many cultural theories, models, and concepts from the book as possible. Your grade is based on the accurate concepts/models/values you apply.

Generic ideas such as "hire more women" are not valid. Note that every policy, practice, and strategy has to start with a *concept* or a *theory* taken directly from the reading material, then follow by a specific *action*. For example:

> Training the brain for goal: Practice name-blind recruitment process.

3 Dealing with Bias

Your company has acknowledged that there is a bias against employees with a Middle Eastern background. The management wants to tackle this bias and create a positive change of attitude toward employees with a nonnative background in the working environment.

Please detail a plan with *specific actions* aiming at changing the current corporate culture. Think beyond the topic of bias management and explore other cultural patterns such as communication, current issues in media, diverse motives for work, the role of leadership, and so forth. Please apply as many cultural theories, models, and concepts from the course as possible. Your grade is based on the accurate concepts/models/values you apply.

Generic ideas such as "try to think before giving judgement," "organize a bias training, "who is biased will be punished and held accountable," "create a safe workplace where people can speak out," and so forth are not valid. Note that every policy, practice, and strategy has to start with a *concept* or a *theory* taken directly from the reading material. Start a suggestion with the title of the chapter, then the theory or concept, then follow by a specific *action*. For example:

Bias management—Highlight the capacity to override biases: "Make a poster of reminder in the hallway that reads STRONGWILL TRUMPS BIASES."

Change management—The A of STREAP-B, Alignment: Create work projects that native employees have to rely on their colleagues of Middle Eastern background to accomplish the task.

4 Prepare for Negotiation

You are about to lead a negotiation team to work with a Saudis company on a potential project of exporting high-quality cheese product from your country to Saudi Arabia. You have been talking to and e-mailing the head of the department in Saudi—a woman with strong opinions and who is extremely busy.

Read Chapter 13 on negotiation, and for each section, detail any possible plan you could think of to proceed. This goes down to details such as whether your team should travel to Saudi first or you should invite the Saudis team to your country.

Read Chapter 12 on communication and note down strategies and plans you may use to create trust, seek similarities, develop synergy, and avoid pitfalls. This goes down to details such as how are you going to greet, what are the topics for small talks, what are the activities, and so forth. Don't forget a critical approach from Chapter 6: Think global, plan local, act individual.

Read Chapter 14 on marketing and note down any ideas you may want to propose or discuss with the Saudis team.

Read Chapter 9 on diversity and note down any creative and hybrid ideas coming from a synergy of cultural differences between two teams/companies.

Conduct a search on the Internet to get updated on the fast-changing cultural environment in Saudi Arabia under the new leadership.

Generic ideas such as "respect the Islamic customs" are not valid. Note that every policy, practice, and strategy has to start with a *concept* or a *theory* taken directly from the reading material. Start a suggestion with the title of the chapter, then the theory or concept, then follow by a specific *action*. For example:

> Business Communication—Language: Learn some basic Arabic greetings such as "Assalama Aleykum" (Peace be upon you).

5 Product Malfunction

Your company has been working with an Indonesian supplier for roughly a year. The latest chips they ordered from Indonesia arrived with malfunction.

The coordinator of the project sent a lengthy and detailed e-mail copying three related executives of the Indonesian supplier to let them know about the problem:

> *The last order was not up to standard. There is a malfunction. Two out of five samples we took out did not work properly. We are certain that it is your responsibility to have a check on the quality of the product. We kindly ask for a replacement before the end of this month in order to keep up with our distribution planning.*

There was a silence from the other side for three days. An e-mail was sent later, apologizing for the incident, stating that they "will look at it carefully." In another e-mail a few days later, the Indonesian suggested that because the contract has come near the end, both sides should revise it. They suggested a price term that would push the product cost for your company up to 25%.

You are the product manager and you see a crisis coming. You sense that there are more reasons behind the reaction of the supplier. Some insiders suggested a direct approach to the CEO of the Indonesian company—Ms. Kemala Nasution—a woman who had several top-management meetings with your CEO last year when the contract was signed, but whom you have never met.

- Explain *briefly* why there is such clash with bullet points. Use cultural theories and models for each bullet point.
- Because your company has to reply, you (or someone in the company) need to write an e-mail to Ms. Nasution. The e-mail should not exceed 400 words. While writing this e-mail, keep in mind cultural theories and models.
- At the end of the e-mail, explain briefly with bullet points why and how the e-mail text has applied cultural concepts and theories, taken from the book. Underline the chapter and section where that knowledge comes from.

6 A Joint-Management Team

Recently, a Japanese multinational made an acquisition of a Dutch company in Rotterdam. The new Japanese-Dutch company in Rotterdam will receive 20 Japanese managers (both middle and senior) from Japan on a three-year's assignment. They are going to form a joint-management team with 20 Dutch managers in the company. Half of the Japanese have never been posted abroad for a long period. None of them will bring their families to the Netherlands.

The corporate culture where they come from is typical of Japan: Decision is made with group consensus. Individuals are inspired by broad company's vision. They first discuss with the team among the low level, and then slowly move up to the top hierarchy. Teamwork is extremely important; everyone knows a little bit of everything so (s)he can contribute. Working hard is a criteria for success and acceptance. Rules, process, deadlines, and routines are sacred and cannot be violated for any reasons. Conflict is avoided and is not openly discussed. They get down to business immediately, but trust and relationship are developed and reinforced during the process.

- What are the challenges of this joint management team?
  Please be specific about the challenges and avoid a generic answer, such as "cultural/value differences/bias will affect the corporation of the team." A good example looks like this:

  Stereotypically, the Japanese are indirect/high context. They may not express feeling and opinion directly in the meeting forwardly such as the Dutch.

- What are the opportunities/advantages of this join management team?
  See the previous question for how to answer in a specific and concrete manner. Generic statements such as creativity or innovation as a result of diversity will not be qualified.
- You are CDO (Chief Diversity Officer) of the company. You will create a plan of actions/list of advice for the management team.

Note that every policy, practice, and strategy has to start with a *concept* or a *theory* taken directly from the reading material. Generic statements such as "align the leadership style," "organize a cultural training," and so forth will not be counted as a qualified activity. Start a suggestion with the title of the chapter, then a theory or concept, and then follow by a specific *action*. Your grade is based on how well you use these concepts, terminology, and theories in an applied manner. For example:

- Global/Glocal Leadership—Context Dependence: Create a framework of cooperation in which there are suggestive steps that the joint team will keep in mind when working together. These are (1) asking each other: "*How do you usually tackle this issue?*"; (2) *What are the good things we can take from that?*; and (3) *How can we combine and create something better?*

7 Critical Review of a Current Ad

In Chapter 14, we concluded that advertisements both reflect and reshape a culture. A brand can choose to be a product of culture by adapting to the local norms and stereotypes, or challenging the practices and ways of thinking, thus becoming a producer of culture. This choice is reflected most clearly in how brands deal with current issues such as sexism, racism, and cultural appropriation in a multicultural society.

Take any advertisement that is currently on the media and critically analyze it from the all possible aspects of cross-cultural managements that you have learned, for example:

- Globalization: Is the company a local going global, or global going local, or local transforming local?
- Cultural values: What are the dominant values presented in the ad? Do they align or contradict the stereotypical values and practices in the target group that the ad wants to approach? How about other collective cultures?
- Does the ad support or divert from diversity? Are there any issues of racial, gender, or other cultural stereotypes?
- Is the ad a product or a producer of culture?
- Do you support the ad? Would you do anything differently? Why? If you don't agree with the ad, what is your plan of actions? Don't forget the power of customers to force brands to change.

8 We're Shaping the Evolution

As more mothers now need surgery to deliver babies due to their narrow pelvis size, scientists say that we are shaping the evolution.

In the past, 30 out of 1,000 babies cannot fit down the birth canal. The current rate is 36/1,000. Women with a narrow pelvis would not have survived birth 100 years ago. They do now and pass on their genes encoding for a narrow pelvis to their daughters.

Humans have a major effect on our own biological makeup and the environment. Think about the way we increasingly use technology, travel, sit at the desk, eat genetically modified food, use pesticides, and so forth. Please use the Diversity Pathway GCEB-Be (Chapter 2) and conduct a search on the Internet to explore many other ways we have been shaping the evolution of ourselves and other species. A way to do it is to give each arrow of interaction a number. For each number, do some quick research and find an example to illustrate the dynamic relationship between these factors. You can use search phrases such as "influence of X on Y" or "interaction between X and Y. "

In the second part of this task, search on the latest advancement of genetic selection in humans. Discuss with your teammates the possibilities in various aspects of business such as leadership, entrepreneurship, emotional intelligence, technical competence, and so forth. Are these possibilities ethical? Should we ignore the (dis)advantage that genes present?

Index